RACE AND RACISM
IN THE UNITED STATES

RACE AND RACISM IN THE UNITED STATES

An Encyclopedia of the American Mosaic

VOLUME 1: A–E

Charles A. Gallagher and Cameron D. Lippard,
Editors

AN IMPRINT OF ABC-CLIO, LLC
Santa Barbara, California • Denver, Colorado • Oxford, England

Library of Congress Cataloging-in-Publication Data

Race and racism in the United States : an encyclopedia of the American mosaic / Charles A. Gallagher and Cameron D. Lippard, editors.
pages cm
ISBN 978-1-4408-0345-1 (hardback) — ISBN 978-1-4408-0346-8 (ebook) 1. United States—Race relations—Encyclopedias. 2. United States—Ethnic relations—Encyclopedias. 3. Racism—United States—Encyclopedias. I. Gallagher, Charles A. (Charles Andrew), 1962– editor. II. Lippard, Cameron D., editor.
E184.A1R254 2014
305.800973—dc23 2013024041

ISBN: 978-1-4408-0345-1
EISBN: 978-1-4408-0346-8

18 17 16 15 14 1 2 3 4 5

This book is also available on the World Wide Web as an eBook.
Visit www.abc-clio.com for details.

Greenwood
An Imprint of ABC-CLIO, LLC

ABC-CLIO, LLC
130 Cremona Drive, P.O. Box 1911
Santa Barbara, California 93116-1911

This book is printed on acid-free paper ♾
Manufactured in the United States of America

Contents

Alphabetical List of Entries

Topical List of Entries

Civil Rights

Criminal Justice

Economics

Education

Extremist Groups and Hate Crimes

Government and Politics

Health and Science

Housing

Ideas and Concepts

Identity

Immigration and Migrations

Movements and Activism

Popular Culture

Television and Racial Stereotypes
Television Drama and Racism
Toomer, Jean
Valdez, Luis
White Savior Films
Williams, Bert

Race Riots

Ashbury Park (NJ) Riot of 1970
Atlanta (Georgia) Riot of 1906
Atlanta (Georgia) Riot of 1967
Bellingham Riots (1907)
Bensonhurst (New York) Incident 1989
Biloxi Beach (Mississippi) Riot of 1960
Black Church Arsons
Bloody Sunday
Boston (Massachusetts) Riots of 1975 and 1976
Brownsville Incident
Charleston (South Carolina) Riot of 1919
Chattanooga (Tennessee) Riot of 1906
Chester and Philadelphia (Pennsylvania) Riots of 1918
Chicago Commission on Race Relations
Chicago (Illinois) Riot of 1919
Cincinnati (Ohio) Riot of 2001
Cincinnati (Ohio) Riots of 1967 and 1968
Cleveland (Ohio) Riot of 1966
Detroit (Michigan) Riot of 1943
Detroit (Michigan) Riot of 1967
East St. Louis (Illinois) Riot of 1917
Election Riots of the 1880s and 1890s
Greensburg (Indiana) Riot of 1906
Greenwood Community
Harlem (New York) Riot of 1935
Houston (Texas) Mutiny of 1917
Howard Beach (New York) Incident (1986)
Johnson-Jeffries Fight of 1910, Riots Following
Knoxville (Tennessee) Riot of 1919
Long Hot Summer Riots (1965–1967)
Longview (Texas) Riot of 1919
Los Angeles (California) Riot of 1965
Los Angeles (California) Riots of 1992
Miami (Florida) Riot of 1982
New Bedford (Massachusetts) Riot of 1970
New Orleans Riot of 1866
New York City Draft Riot of 1863
New York City Riot of 1943
Newark (New Jersey) Riot of 1967
Orangeburg Massacre of 1968
Philadelphia (Pennsylvania) Riot of 1964
Prison Riots
Red Scare and Race Riots
Red Summer Race Riots of 1919
Rosewood (Florida) Riot of 1923
Sainte Genevieve (Missouri) Riot of 1930
San Francisco (California) Riot of 1966
Sleepy Lagoon Case (1942)
Springfield (Ohio) Riot of 1904
Tampa (Florida) Riots of 1987
Texas Southern University Riot of 1967
Tulsa (Oklahoma) Riot of 1921
Vietnam War and Race Riots
Washington (D.C.) Riot of 1919
Washington (D.C.) Riots of 1968
Wilmington (North Carolina) Riot of 1898
Zoot Suit Riots

Slavery

Abolitionist Movement
Abraham Lincoln and the Emancipation of Slaves
African American Humor and Comic Traditions
Black Churches
Carver, George Washington
Castration
Coolie
Cosmetics
Fifteenth Amendment (1870)
Fourteenth Amendment (1868)
Fugitive Slave Act (1793)
Jim Crow Laws
Juneteenth Celebration
Labor Unions
Nadir of the Negro
Paine, Thomas
Plantation System
Reconstruction Era
Reparations
Runaway Slave Advertisements
Scott v. Sandford (1857)

Violence

War and Terrorism

Work and Labor

List of Primary Documents

Preface

According to a 2011 *USA Today*/Gallup poll, a majority of Americans believe the goals of the civil rights movement such as equality of opportunity, socioeconomic mobility, and the eradication of racism and discrimination have been achieved. The same poll found that 86 percent of Americans approve of marriage between blacks and whites. Realize that as recently as 1967 it was illegal in most states for blacks and whites to marry until the Supreme Court struck down these prohibitions in its landmark *Virginia v. Loving* case that made marriage across the color line legal. According to a 2012 Gallup poll, First Lady Michelle Obama is the second most-admired woman in the United States. Her husband, President Barack Obama, was voted the number one most-respected man in the nation. According to Americans in this poll, five of the women and three of the men ranked in the top ten most-admired individuals were racial minorities. These trends in interracial respect, harmony, and acceptance are historically unprecedented.

What this polling data suggests is that the United States is more tolerant, less racist, and has moved to the point where equal opportunity is afforded to all regardless of creed or color. It would appear that the United States has finally transcended the racial divisions that have divided our nation since its inception. Given the perception of race relations currently held by a majority in the United States, the need for publication of *Race and Racism in the United States: An Encyclopedia of the American Mosaic* sounds a bit like going to an electronics store and asking to purchase a typewriter or a VHS recorder. The idea and practice of racism, that is, treating individuals differently because of something as superficial as their skin color, is now perceived to be thoroughly outdated, an anachronistic belief and behavior that have more in common with the Jim Crow racism of the 1950s than the supposed era of colorblindness that elected the same black man as president of the United States twice in the twenty-first century.

Occurring alongside this rather optimistic narrative of race relations, however, is a more sobering and problematic story. In 2012 the FBI reported that race-based hate crimes had increased, with the steepest rise in the reported number of anti-Islamic crimes (FBI 2012). In the last five years we have seen new racially loaded words enter the public discourse, words that have quickly become part of the common vernacular of popular culture. The media now speaks of anchor babies, a post-race society, the Dream Act, the Jena Six, Pimps and Hoes Parties, and the New Jim Crow (or often the New Juan Crow). What these words and phrases suggest is that racism, discrimination, and xenophobia are not static categories nor are manifestations of racism like smallpox, an age-old disease that through scientific, government, and public efforts was eradicated. The racial hierarchies that remain in place in the United States are dynamic socioeconomic systems that evolve, mutate, and are constantly being reconstituted to maintain and reorder race-based privilege. It is because race is a fluid category in a constant state of flux and redefinition and the reality that race and racism continue to shape the life chances of all Americans, that an encyclopedia of race, written by race and ethnicity scholars, is still very much needed.

It is with this need in mind that *Race and Racism in the United States* was produced. We have assembled race scholars from around the country to examine race and racism from almost every conceivable perspective. From a historical viewpoint we detail how the concept of race emerges in the 1600s as a cultural or geographic designation and slowly morphs into a wholly fabricated scientific category only to be reframed, defined, and understood in the twentieth and twenty-first centuries as a grouping that is socially and politically constructed.

Hundreds of entries throughout the *Race and Racism* describe the myriad ways racism and discrimination are articulated and expressed by individuals and institutions. For example, both racism and discrimination can be found in entries as wide ranging as housing, government policy, the military, the media, and the criminal justice system. From a social, psychological, and theoretical perspective, race and racism are addressed in entries like modern racism, laissez-faire racism, institutional discrimination, and racist ideologies like eugenics and white supremacy. Just as every facet of how race and racism are described through hundreds of entries, so too are the people and institutions that fought, and continue to fight, to eradicate racism, prejudice, and discrimination. This includes entries on abolitionists from the Civil War era to modern-day civil rights leaders.

What makes *Race and Racism in the United States* particularly user-friendly is a number of important features. Many of the 700+ entries include sidebars with useful information. Most of the entries feature *See also* cross references that list other related entries and conclude with a "Further Reading" section that lists references the reader can turn to for more detailed information on the entry subject. A detailed person and subject index offers greater access to terms and concepts within entries. *Race and Racism in the United States* also includes an introduction that traces the history of American racism, a brief chronology of racism in the United States, and a selection of the full text or excerpts of important primary documents relating to U.S. racism.

We undertook the extremely difficult task of editing *Race and Racism* mainly because of its practical value for contributing to the understanding of racism in the United States. We hope the encyclopedia will be helpful to high school and college students who are conducting research on race-related and minority issues. In addition, we believe *Race and Racism* will serve as a valuable resource for graduate students and faculty members who teach and conduct research on race relations and racial inequality.

Charles Gallagher
Cameron D. Lippard

Introduction

Social scientists are fond of pointing out that the concept of race is a social construction. What this term implies is that the characteristics, traits, or features thought to be a relevant and essential part of a definition, in this case race, in reality reflects social and cultural values, not any type of unchanging, universal scientific law. The clearest example of how race is indeed a social construction is the simple fact that the definition of race and racial categories changes over time and from one country to the next. In the United States the racial categories used by the Census Bureau have changed in almost every decennial census since the first census was conducted in 1790. Individuals widely regarded as white in Puerto Rico may be considered black in the United States or South Africa because the definition of racial categories varies from one country to the next. Who is placed in each racial category is as variable as the country doing the defining.

Below are the U.S. Bureau of Census (2012) definitions of racial categories that appear in government forms. A new census category, SOR (Some Other Race) was included in the 2010 decennial census. This category allowed respondents to select out of the established categories if they felt the existing categories did not reflect their social identity, for example those who self-define as mixed race. However, if respondents did mark one of the existing categories and went on to mark SOR as well, they were counted in the established race categories. Individuals could also mark more than one race. The Hispanic category is defined by the Census as an ethnic group, not a racial category. A large percent of Hispanics choose the SOR classification. What these overlapping and often mutually exclusive categories of racial and ethnic classification point to is that this type of human taxonomy based mostly on skin color is a social construction and as such is in a constant state of flux.

Population estimates use the race categories mandated by the Office of Management and Budget's (OMB) 1997 standards: White; Black or African American; American Indian and Alaska Native; Asian; Native Hawaiian and Other Pacific Islander. These race categories differ from those used in Census 2010 in one important respect. Census 2010 also allowed respondents to select the category referred to as Some Other Race. When Census 2010 data were edited to produce the estimates base, respondents who selected the Some Other Race category alone were assigned to one of the OMB-mandated categories. For those respondents who selected the Some Other Race category and one or more of the other race categories, the edits ignored the Some Other Race selection. This editing process produced tabulations from our estimates that show fewer people reporting two or more races than similar tabulations from Census 2010, because respondents who selected Some Other Race and one of the

OMB mandated races in Census 2010 appear in the single OMB race category in the estimates base.

White. A person having origins in any of the original peoples of Europe, the Middle East, or North Africa. It includes people who indicate their race as "White" or report entries such as Irish, German, Italian, Lebanese, Arab, Moroccan, or Caucasian.

Black or African American. A person having origins in any of the Black racial groups of Africa. It includes people who indicate their race as "Black, African Am., or Negro" or report entries such as African American, Kenyan, Nigerian, or Haitian.

American Indian and Alaska Native. A person having origins in any of the original peoples of North and South America (including Central America) and who maintains tribal affiliation or community attachment. This category includes people who indicate their race as "American Indian or Alaska Native" or report entries such as Navajo, Blackfeet, Inupiat, Yup'ik, or Central American Indian groups or South American Indian groups.

Asian. A person having origins in any of the original peoples of the Far East, Southeast Asia, or the Indian subcontinent including, for example, Cambodia, China, India, Japan, Korea, Malaysia, Pakistan, the Philippine Islands, Thailand, and Vietnam. It includes people who indicate their race as "Asian Indian," "Chinese," "Filipino," "Korean," "Japanese," "Vietnamese," and "Other Asian" or provide other detailed Asian responses.

Native Hawaiian and Other Pacific Islander. A person having origins in any of the original peoples of Hawaii, Guam, Samoa, or other Pacific Islands. It includes people who indicate their race as "Native Hawaiian," "Guamanian or Chamorro," "Samoan," and "Other Pacific Islander" or provide other detailed Pacific Islander responses.

Two or more races. People may have chosen to provide two or more races either by selecting two or more race response check boxes, by providing multiple responses, or by some combination of check boxes and other responses.

The concept of race is separate from the concept of Hispanic origin. Percentages for the various race categories add to 100 percent, and should not be combined with the percent Hispanic.

Non-Hispanic White alone persons. Individuals who responded "No, not Spanish/Hispanic/Latino" and who reported "White" as their only entry in the race question. Tallies that show race categories for Hispanics and non-Hispanics separately are also available (U.S. Bureau of the Census).

Each of these categories were created, altered, or expanded as part of a socio-historical process that reflects an ever changing racial hierarchy. This racial hierarchy is the central focus of *Race and Racism in the United States*: how did race become both a social category and the basis for racism, that is, prejudice or discriminatory behavior directed at individuals or groups because of certain phenotypes (skin color, hair texture, or facial features)? Over the last 500 years and as a direct result of colonialism, a global racial hierarchy emerged where "whites" from Western Europe dominated much of the world's political and economic resources. This is how the idea of race emerged and how the ideology of racism came to define every facet of social interaction in the United States. We have assembled hundreds of reference entries on various manifestations of racism and scores of original documents that define the various ways racism is articulated through popular culture, law, religion, economics, and gender. Key concepts, such as symbolic racism, racial gerrymandering, and post-racialism, inform readers about how these ideas relate to the understanding of racism in U.S. society.

The Prevalence of Racism in Early U.S. History

African Americans

In its classic form, racism refers to the belief that on the basis of their genetic difference some racial groups are innately superior to other racial groups in intelligence, temperament, and attitudes. Racist ideology began to develop during the 15th century, the European Age of Discovery, when white Europeans began encountering large numbers of nonwhite peoples in the Americas, Asia, Africa, and Oceania. In North America, South America, the Caribbean Islands, and South Africa, European colonial rulers established slavery as an effective way to control and exploit African workers on plantations. White racial supremacy was institutionalized with the establishment of the racial slavery system. To justify this system, European Christian settlers emphasized their cultural and moral superiority to African blacks. To perpetuate the system, Europeans tightly supervised and controlled the behaviors and movements of African slaves.

By far, the most rigid form of racial slavery developed in the American South. It has been noted that the absence of a substantial intermediate group of free people of color set the stage for a sharp dichotomy between whites and blacks in the antebellum South. Meanwhile, less restrictive manumission requirements enabled more sizable and socially significant free colored groups to develop in the slave societies of South America, the Caribbean, and South Africa. The racial caste system characterized the form of slavery in the American South, but it did not fit the other three slave societies, where many free blacks married white settlers and thereby gained higher status.

Black slaves in the American South were liberated from slavery after the Civil War, in 1865. But the white violence and physical intimidation—especially with the rise of the Ku Klux Klan during Reconstruction (1865–1877)—effectively prevented black men from competing with white workers in the labor market. Thus, African Americans endured worse economic conditions during Reconstruction than they had under slavery. Moreover, the failure of Reconstruction in 1877 led to the establishment by Southern states of Jim Crow segregation laws to control the black threat to the economic and social advantages of white Americans. Jim Crow segregation laws and other statutes that disenfranchised blacks helped maintain the de facto racial caste system in the South until the early 1960s. In 1903, when Black Nationalist W. E. B. Du Bois wrote that "the problem of the twentieth century is the problem of the color line," he was mainly concerned about racial separation and inequality as it existed at the time in the United States. The United States preserved a very rigid racial caste system for more than three centuries, from the time of the agrarian economy of the 18th and 19th centuries into the industrial economy of the 20th. Only the apartheid system established in South Africa in 1948 was more rigid than the racial caste system in the United States.

Race riots of the Jim Crow era were almost always white-on-black riots, that is, the attempts of "white mobs . . . to maintain the status quo of Jim Crow." Most of these riots occurred when white workers attacked black workers, who were often used by white business owners or managers as strikebreakers. Approximately 250 race riots occurred between 1898 (Wilmington, Delaware) and 1943 (Detroit), claiming the lives of approximately 4,300 blacks. Also, numerous minorities, mostly blacks, were victimized by lynching, another common form of white-on-minority violence. More than 3,500 instances of lynching occurred in the United States between 1885 and 1914 (Knopf, 1975).

Native Americans

Other racial minority groups in the United States, while spared slavery, were subjected to other forms of racial prejudice and discrimination. Ethnocentrism, conquest, and racial domination-subordination strongly characterized the relationship between European whites and Native Americans. From the beginning of their encounters, European white Protestant settlers perceived Native Americans as uncivilized and intellectually and morally inferior. Plantation owners in the South used some American Indians as slaves but preferred blacks to Natives because in the case of Indian servitude, white physical security and control could not be guaranteed: Indian slaves could obtain help and support from their own, nearby peoples and territories. White settlers initially tried to solve the "Indian problem" by killing them all. When this failed, the U.S. government tried by force to remove tribes from their native lands in the East and relocate them to unfamiliar and barren lands west of the Mississippi. In the process, many American Indians died and most tribes lost all or a portion of their lands.

In the late 19th century, a change in government Indian policy from separation to assimilation only ended up taking more lands from American Indians, who were also left culturally uprooted. For example, the policy of sending young Natives to boarding schools was meant to destroy ties to traditional Native culture and "civilize" these youths. By the mid-20th century, the federal policy of termination, which dissolved tribal governments, proved to be disruptive to life in Native America by further uprooting individuals. This contributed to the migration of many Natives to urban areas, who established new communities in Los Angeles and the San Francisco Bay Area in California, and Anchorage, Alaska, among other places. The resultant loss of autonomy and cultural identity was not addressed by the federal government until the 1970s when many of these communities were restructured. Despite the restoration of reservation autonomy, the continued marginalization of these communities has led to such social issues as substance abuse and domestic violence, endemic poverty, and economic isolation. By the early 20th century, the issue of Native representations, particularly in sports mascotry, continues to be controversial.

Latinos

The initial settlement of the Spanish in Florida, California, and other parts of the Southwest represented the first Hispanic incursion into what later became the United States. Mexican Americans, who account for approximately 60 percent of the Latino population in the United States, also were initially absorbed into American society as a conquered group, a fact that set the stage for the colonial pattern of their race relations with American Anglos. Texas, which won its independence from Mexico in 1836, was annexed, over Mexican objections, by the United States in 1845. About half of the remaining Mexican territory, including California and New Mexico, came to the United States at the end of the Mexican-American War (1846–1848). Under the terms of the Treaty of Guadalupe Hidalgo, which ended the war, the U.S. government guaranteed the Mexican residents of these territories political and property rights and promised to safeguard their culture, especially by guaranteeing the right to use the Spanish language and to practice the Catholic religion. However, English gradually replaced Spanish as the standard language, and Anglos in the Mexican states began to develop and exhibit prejudice against Mexican Catholics. Moreover, Anglos gradually took the property of Mexicans through official and unofficial means and through fraud, thus transforming the Mexicans into a colonial work force.

In the early 20th century, United States also colonized Puerto Rico, after annexing the island as a spoil of war from Spain following the Spanish-American War. It also established inroads into Cuba, creating economic and political links with that country. Puerto Rican migration, particularly to New York City, led to the development of a vibrant transnational community. Cuban migration, much of it in the form of exiles fleeing the Fidel Castro regime, led to the formation of a Cuban American diaspora in Florida. From the 1960s and into the 1980s, U.S. foreign policy in Central America, which led to civil wars and social chaos, shaped the influx of migration from Guatemala, El Salvador, and Nicaragua. These newer migrants into the United States drastically changed the character of "Latino" identity by adding to its already diverse tapestry. Moreover, the experience of these migrants, while similar in many regards to that of Mexican Americans, differed in others. Cuban Americans, in particular those of white complexion, were typically not prone to the same type of xenophobic discrimination endured by Mexican Americans or migrants from Central America. This was a sharp contrast to those of Afro-Latino origins, who have been marginalized for being both black and Latino.

By virtue of their in-between racial status, Latinos have been treated better than African Americans in terms of selection of residential areas, public accommodation, and access to social-club membership. Yet, their physical and cultural differences and generally low economic status have also subjected them to prejudice, discrimination, police harassment, and racial violence.

Asian Americans and Pacific Islanders

The migration of Asians to the United States started after the California Gold Rush of 1848–1849, when Chinese farmers were recruited to California to work in mining and railroad construction. Initially, Californians praised Chinese immigrants as "hard-working" and "compliant." Yet, white workers came to believe that industrious Chinese immigrants were a threat to their employment; thus, prejudice against and stereotypes of Chinese immigrants quickly developed among whites. Lobbying by white workers, and the overall anti-Chinese sentiment on the West Coast, led to passage of the Chinese Exclusion Act in 1882, which prohibited the immigration of Chinese for more than 60 years. The Chinese Exclusion Act is the only U.S. government measure to ban the immigration of a particular national-origin group.

Enforcement of the Chinese Exclusion Act led to the recruitment of Japanese and other Asian workers in Hawaii and California. Moreover, after the Spanish-American War, and the subsequent U.S. annexation of the Philippines, Filipino immigration to the United States occurred primarily in to meet increasing labor needs in ever-expanding California agribusiness. But these groups also encountered a series of immigration restrictions by the U.S. government, which culminated in the National Origins Act of 1924. Moreover, Asian immigrants were not allowed to be American citizens until 1952. In 1913, California passed the Alien Land Law to prohibit Japanese immigrants from owning farmland, and other West Coast states passed similar laws targeting Japanese and other immigrants. California and other states later used the law to prevent Asian immigrants from purchasing real estate. As noncitizen residents, Asian immigrants before World War II did not receive legal protection even if they were victimized by racial violence. Finally, all Japanese

Americans living on the West Coast (excluding Hawaii), including native-born citizens, were incarcerated in internment camps during World War II for "security" reasons. Because of their incarceration, innocent Japanese Americans in relocation camps incurred not only monetary and property losses but also psychological damage. Later, the Immigration Act of 1965 and the influx of refugees from Southeast Asia on account of the Vietnam War drastically changed the character of Asian immigration. In addition to Chinese migrants, growing numbers of refugees from Vietnam, Laos, and Cambodia entered the United States, establishing significant enclaves in such California cities as Sacramento, Stockton, and Westminster. In addition, by the late 20th century, with the technological development of the personal computer and associated software systems, highly skilled Indian professionals also entered the United States, mostly on H-1B visas.

Ethnic White Immigrant Groups

Catholic, Jewish, and Eastern Orthodox Americans of heavily Eastern and Southern European ancestry have today been incorporated into mainstream white American society. But, when large numbers of these non-Protestant European immigrants arrived in the United States at the end of the 19th and beginning of the 20th century, they were considered physically different from native-born Anglos and thus were subjected to prejudice, discrimination, and racial violence. Southern Italians suffered not only antagonism directed against Catholics in general but also severe anti-Italian sentiments because of their peasant background. Italians suffered physical violence as well as negative images and stereotypes. Killings and lynchings of Italian immigrants occurred in the United States, especially in the South, between 1890 and 1910 (Gambino, 1977). Nicola Sacco and Bartolomeo Vanzetti, two Italian immigrants, were charged with and found guilty of murder and armed robbery and executed in 1927, even though numerous witnesses testified that they were not involved in the crime.

For many centuries, Jews suffered negative stereotypes, prejudice, and discrimination, including legal discrimination, in European Christian countries. Although American Jews fared better than European Jews in terms of legal discrimination, they also encountered anti-Semitism in different forms. Anti-Semitism in the United States increased in the 1880s with the influx of Eastern European Jewish immigrants and reached its high point in the 1920s and the 1930s. The Ku Klux Klan and some white industrialists, such as Henry Ford, filled the media with anti-Semitic propaganda, spreading the idea of a "world Jewish conspiracy" (Marger, 2000). Jews were often denied accommodation at hotels and admission to social clubs. As the number of Jewish students in prestigious universities and professional schools increased, the latter took measures to restrict Jewish admissions. Jewish Americans were also subjected to discrimination in professional occupations, especially in law, medicine, and academia.

Nativist reactions to and prejudice against Jewish, Catholic, and Asian immigrants in the United States in the first decade of the 20th century contributed to the development of "biological racism," a racist ideology that sees so-called Nordic races as genetically—and therefore also intellectually and morally—superior to other races, including Eastern and Southern Europeans, African Americans, Mexicans, and Asians (Grant, 1916). Such well-known psychologists as Lewis Terman and C. W. Gould argued that based on scores of IQ (intelligence quotient) tests, Eastern and Southern European immigrants and African Americans had lower levels of intellectual ability but tended to "outbreed" people of "Nordic" races. Their arguments supported the eugenics movement, which emerged after World War I. These ideas also contributed to the passage of discriminatory immigration laws in the early 1920s, which severely reduced immigration from Eastern and Southern European countries and entirely banned Asian immigration. Moreover, anti-Semitism influenced the federal government's reluctance to allow Jewish refugees from Nazi Germany to enter the United States in the 1930s. After World War II, de jure segregation of Jews from certain neighborhoods, through the use of restrictive housing covenants (known by the euphemistic term "gentlemen's agreement") showed the persistence of anti-Semitism in the United States.

The Persistence of Racism in the Post–Civil Rights Era

The passage of civil rights laws, including affirmative action programs, in the 1960s may lead many people to believe that racism is no longer an important factor for the adjustment of minorities in the 21st century. The ethnic and racial diversities created by the influx of immigrants from the developing world, the increasing emphasis on multiculturalism by government and schools, and the increase in intermarriages since the early 1970s may further enhance the belief about the insignificance of racism in contemporary American life. Jews, Italians, and other turn-of-the-century white immigrant groups have been incorporated into mainstream America (Foner, 2001). However, the social-science literature accumulated since the 1980s reveals that African Americans still suffer high levels of racial prejudice and discrimination in all aspects of their lives, and other nonwhite minority groups also experience different forms of unequal treatment because of their nonwhite status. Based on their findings, the authors of these studies have suggested that the color line continues to divide American society in the 21st century, just as it did in the 20th.

Although legal discrimination against African Americans ended with the civil rights legislation of the early 1960s, enough evidence exists to support the view that African Americans still have to deal with racism—both individual and institutional—on a daily basis. Many people tend to believe that racial prejudice and discrimination are problems confronted only by poor blacks concentrated in inner-city neighborhoods and that well-educated, middle-class blacks do not have to deal with it. However, based on personal interviews with middle-class blacks, two social scientists, Joe Feagin and Melvin Sikes, have challenged this view. They conclude that "racism is the everyday experience" for middle-class blacks as well and that experiences with serious racial discrimination "have a cumulative impact on particular individuals, their families, and their communities" (Feagin and Sikes, 1994) Summing up his view of white-black separation in contemporary America, political scientist Andrew Hacker similarly commented that "America's version of apartheid, while lacking overt legal sanction, comes closest to the system even now being overturned in the land of its invention" (South Africa) (Hacker, 1995).

Sociological studies show that the high level of segregation for African Americans has not been moderated since the 1970s (Farley, Steeh, Krysan, Jackson, and Reeves, 1994). Housing discrimination by real estate agents, commercial banks, and local white community leaders, and the racial gap in socioeconomic status, are partly responsible for what has been called "American apartheid" (Massey and Denton, 1993). But racial prejudice against blacks on the part of white Americans is mainly responsible for racial segregation. Residential isolation, in turn, further enhances antiblack racial prejudice and creates further socioeconomic disadvantages for African Americans (Massey and Denton, 1993). Segregated black neighborhoods are characterized by all kinds of social ills, such as high poverty and unemployment rates, high mortality and crime rates, and poor educational and health-care facilities.

Since the 1978 publication of his controversial book, *Declining Significance of Race*, William Wilson has paid keen attention to the class division within the African American community and focused on poverty among residents in inner-city black neighborhoods. He has argued that the disappearance of blue-collar jobs from black neighborhoods, which is a result of deindustrialization rather than racism, is the main cause of poverty among inner-city black residents. However, various studies reveal that regardless of their class background, blacks experience racial discrimination in the labor market.

No doubt, deindustrialization, along with the poor school performance overall of black children, is an important contributing factor to the exceptionally high unemployment and poverty rates among young blacks. But the preference of employers for Latino legal and illegal workers over black workers is also responsible for the difficulty young blacks have finding employment. Studies by Roger Waldinger and Michael Richter have found that regardless of industry, employers and managers prefer Latino immigrants to blacks because they perceive the former to be more "subservient" and "docile." Moreover, Feagin and Sikes have shown that black professionals also encounter discrimination in finding employment and in salaries, evaluations, and promotions. According to an analysis of census data by Hacker, black men with a bachelor's degree earned $764 for every $1,000 earned by their white counterparts. It can be argued that the racial gap in earnings is caused mainly by racial discrimination.

The influx of immigrants from the Caribbean Islands since the 1970s has contributed to a phenomenal increase in the black immigrant population. Unlike African Americans whose ancestors were brought to the United States by force for economic exploitation, Caribbean immigrants are voluntary migrants who came here for better economic and educational opportunities. An interesting question is: will the adaptation of Caribbean black immigrants and their descendants follow the pattern taken by voluntary minority groups or by colonial minority groups? Mary Waters's 1999 study of Caribbean immigrants in New York City reveals that the children of lower-class immigrants assimilate quickly, becoming African American children. This finding indicates the importance of race as well as class for the racialization of Caribbean immigrants.

Although Latinos in the United States are currently better accepted than African Americans, they are also subjected to prejudice, stereotypes, and discrimination. Their in-between physical characteristics and their generally lower economic class and immigrant backgrounds enhance the negative image of Latinos. The influx of legal and illegal Mexican immigrants during recent years has led to stereotypes of native-born Mexican Americans as undocumented residents and manual laborers. Because of a long history of Anglo-Mexican racial stratification, Mexicans in Texas, in particular, still experience semi-involuntary segregation in using public facilities and racial harassment by the police similar to that experienced by African Americans. Probably because of their darker skin, Puerto Ricans experience residential segregation from white Americans that is more similar to that of African Americans than to other Latino groups. Moreover, Puerto Ricans, regardless of generational status, exhibit low educational and occupational levels and a high poverty rate comparable to African Americans.

Most Asian-American groups currently have a higher socioeconomic status than whites. Moreover, approximately 40 percent of U.S.-born Asian Americans engage in intermarriages, in most cases with white partners (Lee and Fernandez, 1998). These facts have led some social scientists to predict that Asian Americans are likely to be incorporated into white society in the near future. However, contemporary Asian immigrants are socioeconomically polarized, with one group representing professional and business classes and the other group consisting of poor refugees from Indochina and working-class migrants. Moreover, the social-science literature on Asian Americans indicates that not only Asian immigrants but also U.S.-born Asian Americans encounter racial violence, racial discrimination, and rejection because of their nonwhite racial characteristics. In the past two decades, dozens of incidents of racial violence against Asian Americans have occurred in many U.S. cities, killing a dozen people. Studies based on personal interviews with or personal narratives by second-generation Asian Americans reveal that most informants experienced rejection, with such taunts as "Go back to your country" or "What country are you from?" Third- and fourth-generation white Americans have an option to choose their ethnic identity or not, because they are accepted as full American citizens. However, one ethnographic study showed that society forces most third- or fourth-generation Japanese and Chinese Americans to accept their ethnic and racial identities, even though they, like multigeneration white Americans, are thoroughly acculturated to American society.

The influx of large numbers of Latino, Caribbean, and Asian immigrants into a predominantly white society since the 1970s has increased anti-immigrant prejudice and actions, including a resurgence of white supremacist groups. In particular, Mexican immigrants, accounting for about one-fifth of total immigrants, have been subjected to nativist attacks for serving the interest of their homeland, not being assimilable, and taking welfare monies (Lamm and Imhoff, 1985). In the late 1980s and early 1990s, California, Florida, and other states passed referenda making English the standard language, which partly reflects anti-immigrant attitudes toward Latino immigrants. In 1994, Californians also passed Proposition 187, which was intended to make the children of illegal residents ineligible for free medical treatment and education. Although the proposition was invalidated, it targeted mainly Mexican illegal residents.

Although the separation of church and state and the emphasis on religious pluralism have helped many ethnic groups preserve their ethnic traditions through the practice of religious faith and rituals, white racism and Protestantism, as the foundational elements of American culture, have served each other since the colonial era. At the end of the 19th and beginning of the 20th century, Jewish and Catholic immigrants from Eastern and Southern Europe suffered prejudice and racial discrimination by native Protestants. At the beginning of the 21st century, Muslim, Sikh, and Hindu immigrants from South Asia and the Middle East are experiencing prejudice and discrimination by white Christians, especially by white evangelical Protestants. Many Middle Eastern and South Asian Muslims and Sikhs have been subjected to two types of discrimination and physical violence in the post–September 11 era. First, they have become targets of hate crimes and bias incidents, such as arson, assaults, and shootings perpetrated by ordinary American citizens. Second, they have been subjected to supervision, detentions, and other forms of civil rights violations carried out by the U.S. government at the federal and local levels. Although Jewish Americans have successfully assimilated into white society, they are not safe from hate crimes either. Several white supremacist organizations, such as the Ku Klux Klan, the Christian Identity Movement, and skinheads, target Jews as well as other racial minority groups.

Contemporary Forms of Racism

To better understand the contemporary forms of racism in the United States, we need to make a series of distinctions among different types of racism. Until the 1960s, social scientists focused on individual racism, the belief that some racial groups are morally, intellectually, or culturally superior to other races. However, following the path-breaking book *Black Power* (1967) by Stokely Carmichael and Charles Hamilton, two Black Nationalism leaders, social scientists now usually distinguish between individual racism and institutional racism. Institutional racism means that social institutions are arranged in such a way that they are disadvantageous to minority racial groups. According to one source, "Institutional racism, unlike individual racism, is not an immediate action but the legacy of a past racist behavioral pattern." Specifically, institutional racism refers to "the discriminatory racial practices built into such prominent structures as the political, economic, and educational system" (Doob, 1998).

Racial minority groups in the United States, especially African Americans in the post–civil rights era, suffer more from institutional racism than from individual racism. As shown by Francois Pierre-Louis in his essay on this topic (Institutional Racism) in this encyclopedia, there are many examples of institutional racism, such as cultural biases in intelligence tests and the low quality of schools in inner-city black neighborhoods that keep children of lower-income black families at a disadvantage. The 1973 Rockefeller Drug Laws in New York State are another salient example of institutional racism. The laws have imposed severe penalties on those who have sold or possessed narcotic drugs and crack cocaine, and as a result of these laws, the state's prison population has increased rapidly. Most of the prisoners are African American men because users of crack cocaine are heavily concentrated in this population.

Social scientists also tend to divide individual racism into two types: biological racism and symbolic racism. As previously noted, biological racism, which emphasizes the intellectual superiority of northwestern Europeans, was popular in the first decade of the 20th century. By contrast, symbolic racism focuses on a racial minority group's purported behavioral deficiencies, such as being welfare dependent, lazy, and criminally oriented, which conflict with traditional American values such as hard work and self-reliance. Individual racism against minority groups in the post–civil rights period usually takes the form of symbolic racism. That is, white Americans generally attribute the lower socioeconomic status and poverty of African Americans and other minority groups to the latter's lack of motivation and work ethic, and to their unstable families. Most white Americans seem to accept the culture-of-poverty thesis endorsed by conservative scholars and policymakers.

Given the contemporary knowledge of human development, few people could persuasively argue for the genetic basis of the intellectual superiority of particular racial groups. Nevertheless, biological racism has reemerged among academics in contemporary America. In his controversial 1969 article, Arthur Jensen, an educational psychologist, argued that Asians have the highest level of cognitive abilities, blacks have the lowest, and whites are in the middle, and that these differences were largely determined by biology. Based on his findings, Jensen suggested that the Head Start program that was created at that time to boost the IQ of minority children would have a limited impact. About 25 years later, Richard Herrnstein and Charles Murray made a similar argument for biologically determined differences in cognitive abilities among Asians, whites, and blacks. They further claimed that the differences in the cognitive abilities account for some of the social stratification among the three groups.

Joel Kovel made a distinction between dominative racism and aversive racism. This distinction is also of great use for understanding the nature of racial separation in contemporary America. While dominative racism involves unfair treatment of minority members, "aversive racism" refers to the tendency to try to avoid contact with blacks and other minority members. This form of racism is the main cause of the high level of residential segregation of African Americans from white Americans and the lack of white-black social interactions at the personal level. Since the unwillingness of white Americans to contact minority members at the personal and neighborhood levels does not involve civil rights violations, the government cannot use any short-term measures to facilitate interracial friendship and dating.

Finally, most contemporary Americans can be said to commit color-blind racism, which is a form of racism that serves to maintain the racial dominance of whites by ignoring the continuing effects of historical prejudice on the life chances of minority members. Many whites believe that because minority members have enjoyed equal opportunity since the enforcement of the civil rights laws, the racial category should no longer be considered as a factor in college admission or employment. They claim that the United States should be a color-blind society that gives rewards only based on individual merits. Those who embrace color-blind racism argue that race-based affirmative action programs are not only unfair to white Americans, they are also demeaning to minority members of society because they imply that minorities are not equal to white Americans. The main problem with their argument is that they ignore how minorities' opportunities for socioeconomic attainment have been affected by past and current racial discrimination.

Color-blind racism can be said to be "unintentional racism" in that some white Americans do not pay attention to the current status of racial inequality and the special needs of American society's minority members mainly because they are ignorant of the lingering effects of past racial discrimination and of different forms of current racial discrimination. But many other white conservatives intentionally avoid discussion of racial issues and vaguely emphasize meritocracy to protect their racial privileges.

Since the end of the civil rights movement, debates around affirmative action and institutional racism illustrate how racism, particularly against communities of color, has continued to shape U.S. society. From the acquittal of Los Angeles police officers responsible for beating Rodney King in 1992, which led to the city-wide riots of that year, to that of Trayvon Martin's shooter, George Zimmermann, in 2013, race relations have continued to be significantly strained in the contemporary United States. The lingering public debates over affirmative action in education, most notably in the recent 2003 *Fisher v. University of Texas* Supreme Court decision, show how such policies continue to garner national attention given their relationship to problems around race and ethnicity.

After the 2008 election of President Barack Obama, the first African American president, many public commentators heralded the beginning of the "postracial" era in U.S. history. They argued that Americans had moved beyond the social stigma of race. However, the overt and covert instances of racism, sometimes directed at the president himself, have illustrated that such notions of a postracial era were premature and inaccurate. If anything, institutionalized racism and discrimination, often shaped by classism, continues to be a prominent problem in U.S. society.

Pyong Gap Min, with contributions from
Charles Gallagher and Cameron D. Lippard

References

American Sociological Association. "The ASA Statement on the Importance of Collecting Data and Doing Social Science Research on Race." February 2002.

Blauner, Robert. *Racial Oppression in America.* New York: Harper and Row, 1972.

Bonilla-Silva, Eduardo. *Racism without Racists: Color-Blind Racism and the Persistence of Racial Inequality in the United States.* New York: Rowman & Littlefield, 2003.

Bowser, Benjamin P., and Raymond G. Hunt. *Impacts of Racism on White Americans*, 2nd ed. Thousand Oaks, CA: Sage Publications, 1996.

Cople Jaher, Frederic. *A Scapegoat in the New Wilderness: The Origins and Rise of Anti-Semitism in America.* Cambridge, MA: Harvard University Press, 1994.

Doob, Christopher Bates. *Racism: An American Cauldron*, 3rd ed. New York: Longman, 1998.

Farley, Reynolds, Charlotte Steeh, Maria Krysan, Tara Jackson, and Keith Reeves. "Stereotypes and Segregation: Neighborhoods in the Detroit Area." *American Journal of Sociology* 100 (1994): 750–80.

Feagin, Joe. *Discrimination, American Style.* Englewood, NJ: Prentice Hall, 1978.

Feagin, Joe. "The Continuing Significance of Race: Anti-Black Discrimination in Public Places." *American Sociological Review* 56 (1991): 101–16.

Feagin, Joe R., and Karyn D. McKinney. *The Many Costs of Racism.* Lanham, MD: Rowman & Littlefield, 2003.

Feagin, Joe, and Melvin P. Sikes. *Living with Racism: The Black Middle-Class Experience.* Boston: Beacon Press, 1994.

Ferber, Amy. *White Man Falling: Race, Gender, and White Supremacy.* New York: Rowman & Littlefield, 1998.

Foner, Nancy. *From Ellis Island to J.F.K. Airport: Immigrants to New York City*. New Haven, CT: Yale University Press, 2001.

Frederickson, George. *White Supremacy: A Comparative Study of American and South African History*. New York: Oxford University Press, 1981.

Gambino, Richard. *Vendetta*. Garden City, NY: Doubleday, 1977.

Gans, Herbert. "The Possibility of a New Racial Hierarchy in the Twentieth-First Century United States." In *The Cultural Territories of Race: Black and White Boundaries*, edited by Mechele Lamont. Chicago: University of Chicago Press, 1999.

Gap Min, Pyong. "An Overview of Asian Americans." In *Asian American: Contemporary Trends and Issues*. Thousand Oaks, CA: Sage Publications, 1995.

Gap Min, Pyong. *The Second Generation: Ethnic Identity among Asian Americans*. Walnut Creek, CA: AltaMira Press, 2002.

Gap Min, Pyong, and Rose Kim, eds. *Struggle for Ethnic Identity: Narratives by Asian American Professionals*. Walnut Creek, CA: AltaMira Press, 1999.

Grant, Madison. *The Passing of the Great Race*. New York: Charles Scribner's Sons, 1916.

Grebler, Leo, Joan W. Moor, and Ralph C. Guzman. *The Mexican-American People: The Nation's Second Largest Minority*. New York: Free Press, 1970.

Hacker, Andrew. *Two Nations: Black and White, Separate, Hostile, Unequal*, 2nd ed. New York: Random House, 1995.

Herrnstein, Richard J., and Charles Murray. *The Bell Curve: Intelligence and Class Structure in American Life*. New York: Free Press, 1994.

Higham, John. *Strangers in the Land*. New York: Atheneum, 1955.

Ignatiev, Noel. *How the Irish Became White*. New York: Routledge, 1995.

Jaret, Charles. "Troubled by Newcomers: Anti-immigrant Attitudes and Action During Two Eras of Mass Immigration to the United States." *Journal of American Ethnic History* 18 (1999): 9–39.

Kasinitz, Philip. *Caribbean New York: Black Immigrants and the Politics of Race*. Ithaca, NY: Cornell University Press, 1992.

Knopf, Terry Ann. *Rumors, Race and Riots*. New Brunswick, NJ: Transaction Books, 1975.

Kovel, Joel. *White Racism: A Psychohistory*. New York: Pantheon, 1970.

Lamm, Richard D., and Gary Imhoff. *The Immigration Time Bomb: The Fragmenting of America*. New York: Truman Talley, Dutton, 1985.

Lee, Sharon, and Marilyn Fernandez. "Trends in Asian American Racial/Ethnic Inter-Marriage: A Comparison of 1980 and 1990 Census Data." *Sociological Perspectives* 41 (1998): 323–42.

Marger, Martin. *Race and Ethnic Relations: American and Global Perspectives*, 5th ed. Belmont, CA: Wadsworth, 2000.

Massey, Douglas S., and Nancy Denton. *American Apartheid: Segregation and the Making of the Underclass*. Cambridge, MA: Harvard University Press, 1993.

Mayo, Louise A. *The Ambivalent Image: Nineteenth-Century America's Perception of the Jew*. Rutherford, NJ: Fairleigh Dickenson University Press, 1988.

McWilliams, Carey. *North from Mexico: The Spanish-Speaking People of the United States*. New York: Greenwood Press, 1968.

Newport, Frank. Gallup Poll, "Hillary Clinton, Barack Obama Most Admired in 2012." December 31, 2012.

Ogbu, John. "Immigrant and Involuntary Minorities in Comparative Perspective." In *Minority Status and Schooling: A Comparative Study of Immigrant and Involuntary Minorities*, edited by Margaret Gibson and John Ogbu. New York: Garland Publishing, 1991.

Ong Hing, Bill. *Making and Remaking of Asian America through Immigration Policy*. Stanford, CA: Stanford University Press, 1993.

Page, Susan, and Carly Mallenbaum. *USA Today*, 8/17/2011.

Pettigrew, Thomas, ed., *Racial Discrimination in the United States*. New York: Harper and Row, 1975.

Rotenberg, Paula S. *White Privilege: Essential Readings on the Other Side of Racism*. New York: Worth Publishers, 2002.

Sakamoto, Arthur, and Chomghwan Kim. "The Increasing Significance of Class, the Declining Significance of Race, and Wilson's Hypothesis." *Asian American Policy Issue* 12 (2003): 19–41.

Sakamoto, Arthur, Jeng Liu, and Jessie Tzeng. "The Declining Significance of Race among Chinese and Japanese American Men." *Research in Social Stratification and Mobility* 16 (1998): 225–46.

Saxton, Alexander. *The Indispensable Enemy: The Labor and the Anti-Chinese Movement in California*. Berkeley: University of California Press, 1971.

Schuman, Howard, Charlotte Steeh, Lawrence Bobo, and Maria Krysan. *Racial Attitudes in America: Trends and Interpretations*, rev. ed. Cambridge, MA: Harvard University Press, 1997.

Sears, David. "Symbolic Racism." In *Eliminating Racism: Profiles in Controversy*, ed. Phyllis Katz and Dalmas Taylor. New York: Plenum, 1988.

Simmons, Ozie G. "The Mutual Image and Expectations of Anglo-Americans and Mexican-Americans." In *Chicanos: Social and Psychological Perspectives*, edited by Nathaniel N. Wagner and Marsha J. Haug. St. Louis, MO: Mosby, 1971.

Slavin, Stephen L., and Mary A. Pratt. *The Einstein Syndrome: Corporate Anti-Semitism in America Today*. New York: World Publishers, 1982.

Steinberg, Stephen. *The Ethnic Myth: Race, Ethnicity, and Class in America*, 2nd ed.. Boston: Beacon Press, 1988.

Takaki, Ronald. *Strangers from a Different Shore: A History of Asian Americans*. Boston: Little, Brown, 1989.

Thornton, Russell. *American Indian Holocaust Survival: A Population History since 1492*. Norman: University of Oklahoma Press, 1987.

Tuan, Mia. *Forever Foreigners or Honorary Whites? The Asian Ethnic Experience Today*. New Brunswick, NJ: Rutgers University Press, 1999.

U.S. Bureau of the Census, Population Estimates Program. http://quickfacts.census.gov/qfd/meta/long_RHI525211.htm

Van den Berghe, Pierre. *The Ethnic Phenomenon*. New York: Elsevier, 1981.

Waldinger, Roger. *Still the Promised City? African Americans and New Immigrants in Postindustrial New York*. Cambridge, MA: Harvard University Press, 1996.

Waldinger, Roger, and Michael I. Richter. *How the Other Half Works: Immigration and the Social Organization of Race*. Berkeley: University of California Press, 2003.

Waters, Mary. *Ethnic Options: Choosing Identities in America*. Berkeley: University of California Press, 1990.

Waters, Mary. *Black Identities: West Indian Immigrant Dreams and American Realities*. New York: Russell Sage Foundation, 1999.

Webster, Yehudi. "Racial Classification: A Wrong Turn." *Footnotes*, January 31, 2003.

West, Cornel. *Race Matters*. New York: Vintage Books, 1994.

Wilson, Aaron. "Rockefeller Drug Laws Information Sheet." Partnership for Responsible Drug Information, 2000.

Wilson, William. *The Declining Significance of Race*. Chicago: University of Chicago Press, 1978.

Wilson, William. *The Truly Disadvantaged: The Inner City, the Underclass, and Public Policy*. Chicago: University of Chicago Press, 1987.

Wilson, William. *When Work Disappears: The World of the New Urban Poor*. New York: Knopf, 1996.

Zhou, Min. "The Changing Face of America: Immigration, Race/Ethnicity, and Social Mobility." In *Mass Migration to the United States: Classical and Contemporary Periods*, edited by Pyong Gap Min. Walnut Creek, CA: AltaMira Press, 2002.

Chronology

1790 Congress passes the Naturalization Act establishing the first rules and procedures to be used in granting citizenship to immigrants.

1800 Gabriel Prosser leads slave uprising in Virginia.

1820 Congress enacts the Missouri Compromise (1820) by admitting Missouri as a slave state but prohibiting slavery in Louisiana Purchase territories north of Missouri's southern boundary.

1822 Denmark Vesey leads a slave insurrection in Charleston, South Carolina.

1824 The Bureau of Indian Affairs (BIA) is created as part of the U.S. War Department to manage encounters and interactions with Native Americans.

1830 President Andrew Jackson signs the Indian Removal Act, which sets the stage for the negotiation of treaties that would relocate Native Americans from their lands east of the Mississippi River to federal territory in the west.

1831 In *Cherokee Nation v. Georgia*, the U.S. Supreme Court declares Georgia laws confiscating Cherokee lands unconstitutional.

Nat Turner leads a slavery uprising in Virginia.

1832 In *Worcester v. Georgia*, the U.S. Supreme Court rules that the Cherokee Nation holds distinct sovereign powers.

1833 American Anti-Slavery Society is formed in Philadelphia.

1835 Publication of Alexis de Tocqueville's *Democracy in America*, an analysis of the nature of American democracy in the early 19th century.

1836 New Philadelphia, the earliest known black town, is established in Pike County, Illinois.

1838–1839 U.S. government forcibly removes the Cherokee from their lands in Georgia to Oklahoma.

1845 Publication of the *Narrative of the Life of Frederick Douglass*, the autobiography of ex-slave abolitionist Frederick Douglass.

The term *Manifest Destiny* is coined by journalist John L. O'Sullivan in the July–August edition of the *United States Magazine and Democratic Review.*

The United States annexes Texas.

1848 Signing of the Treaty of Guadalupe Hidalgo, which ends the Mexican-American War and results in the U.S. acquisition of Mexican territory that today makes up Arizona, California, and New Mexico, and parts of Colorado, Nevada, and Utah.

1849 The Bureau of Indian Affairs (BIA) is transferred to the U.S. Department of the Interior.

1850 Congress passes a new Fugitive Slave Act (1850) as part of the Compromise of 1850, which mandates the return of runaway slaves who escape to Northern states.

The Know-Nothing Party, a nativist, anti-immigrant political party, is founded.

California enacts the Foreign Miners License Tax to protect white miners from foreign competition, especially from Chinese immigrants.

1852 Publication of Harriet Beecher Stowe's novel *Uncle Tom's Cabin.*

1854 The Kansas-Nebraska Act effectively repeals the Missouri Compromise (1820) and opens the new territories of Kansas and Nebraska to the possibility of slavery.

In *The People v. Hall*, the California Supreme Court rules that the testimony of Chinese immigrants is inadmissible in court, effectively setting free a white man convicted for the murder of a Chinese laborer. The ruling is based on the judges' opinion that the Chinese are "a race of people whom nature has marked as inferior."

1857 In the *Dred Scott v. Sanford* decision, the U.S. Supreme Court strikes down the Missouri Compromise (1820), declaring that Congress has no power to prohibit slavery.

1859 Abolitionist John Brown raids the federal arsenal at Harpers Ferry, Virginia, in an effort to initiate a slave uprising.

1863 President Abraham Lincoln issues the Emancipation Proclamation (1863), which frees slaves only in territories not under Union control.

Believing they are being forced to fight and die for African Americans, with whom they are in competition for jobs, Irish immigrants riot against the Civil War draft in New York City.

1865 The Thirteenth Amendment is ratified, abolishing slavery in the United States.

The Freedmen's Bureau is established by Congress to oversee all matters relating to war refugees and freed slaves.

The Ku Klux Klan is founded in Pulaski, Tennessee.

1866 Race riots erupt in Memphis, Tennessee, when white mobs attack African American soldiers and residents.

1868 The Fourteenth Amendment is ratified, requiring equal protection under the law for all citizens.

1871 An anti-Chinese race riot erupts in Los Angeles after a white man is accidentally killed while trying to stop a dispute between two Chinese men.

1877 In the Compromise of 1877, to settle the disputed presidential election of 1876, Democrats concede victory to Republican Rutherford B. Hayes, who in turn withdraws federal troops from the South, thereby allowing "Redeemer" governments to overturn the political and social advances made by African Americans during Reconstruction.

1877–1950s Southern states and municipalities pass and enforce a series of enactments known as Jim Crow laws, which are designed to create and maintain racial segregation and to discriminate against African Americans.

1882 Congress passes the Chinese Exclusion Act, which prohibits Chinese laborers from entering the United States and denies naturalized citizenship to Chinese already in the country.

1884 Publication of Mark Twain's novel *The Adventures of Huckleberry Finn.*

1887 Congress passes the General Allotment Act, known as the Dawes Act, to distribute parcels of tribal land to each tribal member or family on the reservation.

1890 U.S. troops massacre Lakota Sioux Indians at Wounded Knee, South Dakota.

1894 Immigration Restriction League is founded in Boston to protect the "American way of life" from an influx of "undesirable immigrants," mainly Jews and Catholics from southern and eastern Europe.

1896 In *Plessy v. Ferguson*, the U.S. Supreme Court declares the separate-but-equal doctrine constitutional.

1898 The United States annexes Hawaii.

White Democrats in Wilmington, North Carolina, stage a violent coup d'état based on a campaign of white supremacy that results in the removal of a democratically elected local government consisting of both black and white Republicans. Hundreds of Wilmington's black residents are killed or forced to flee during this upheaval, part of larger efforts in the South to reverse the socioeconomic and political progress African Americans had made since Reconstruction.

1903 Publication of W.E.B. Du Bois's classic work, *The Souls of Black Folk.*

1905 The Asiatic Exclusion League, originally called the Japanese and Korean Exclusion League, is formed by white nativist labor unions.

Niagara Movement is founded by W.E.B. Du Bois to advocate civil rights and manhood suffrage for African Americans.

1906 The San Francisco school board orders the segregation of Japanese and Korean children in the city's public schools.

1907 The Bellingham Riots begin when a mob of white men, who fear the loss of their jobs to immigrants, attacks a Hindu community in Bellingham, Washington.

1908 Japan accepts the so-called Gentlemen's Agreement, agreeing to issue no passports for immigration to the United States except to relatives of Japanese workers already in the country.

1909 The National Association for the Advancement of Colored People (NAACP) is founded by an interracial group of citizens in Springfield, Illinois.

1910 In a boxing match billed as "The Fight of the Century," James J. Jeffries fails in his attempt to reclaim the heavyweight title from Jack Johnson, who became the first African American heavyweight champion in 1908.

1911 The Dillingham Report on immigration to the United States is issued by the U.S. Commission on Immigration, a congressional commission chaired by Senator William P. Dillingham.

1913 The Alien Land Law is enacted in California to prevent immigrants from owning or leasing land for more than three years.

The Anti-Defamation League of B'nai Brith is founded to combat prejudice, discrimination, and violence against Jews.

1915 Release of D. W. Griffith's film *The Birth of a Nation*, a racist view of U.S. history that is instrumental in the revival of the Ku Klux Klan.

Leo Frank, a Jewish man convicted of murdering a girl in Georgia in 1913, is abducted from prison and lynched, despite the existence of evidence that casts doubt on his guilt.

The Ku Klux Klan is refounded in Georgia by William J. Simmons.

1916 The New York chapter of the Universal Negro Improvement Association (UNIA) is established by organization founder Marcus Garvey.

Publication of Madison Grant's widely read *The Passing of the Great Race*, which argues that race is a primary factor in differences in intelligence, work ethic, and social and psychological characteristics.

1917 Congress prohibits all immigration from the "Asiatic Barred Zone," which includes various parts of Asia and the Middle East.

Competition for jobs leads to a deadly white-on-black race riot in St. Louis, Missouri.

1919 In the summer and fall, bloody race riots, instigated by whites against African Americans, occur in many cities across the United States. Some of the deadliest events of these "Red Summer" riots take place in Chicago; Elaine, Arkansas; and Washington, D.C.

1920 American Civil Liberties Union (ACLU) is established.

1921 Tulsa, Oklahoma, becomes the scene of one of the worst race riots in U.S. history. By the end of the conflict, hundreds of people are injured or killed, and Greenwood, the city's African American district, is destroyed by white mobs.

1922 In *Ozawa v. United States*, the U.S. Supreme Court declares that a Japanese person is not eligible for citizenship in the United States.

President Warren G. Harding signs into law the Cable Act, which permits a woman to maintain her U.S. citizenship following marriage to a foreign national.

1923 The African American community of Rosewood, Florida, is completely destroyed as the result of a deadly race riot, which erupts after a white woman claims she had been attacked by a black man.

In *United States v. Thind*, the U.S. Supreme Court denies citizenship to Indian immigrants.

1924 President Calvin Coolidge signs into law the Immigration Act of 1924, or the Johnson-Reed Act, severely restricting the flow of immigrants to the United States.

President Coolidge signs the Indian Citizenship Act, granting U.S. citizenship to all Native Americans who are not already citizens under some other law or treaty.

1927 Execution of Nicola Sacco and Bartolomeo Vanzetti, two Italian American anarchists convicted, on largely circumstantial evidence, of two murders committed during a robbery in 1920.

In *Buck v. Bell*, the U.S. Supreme Court upholds a Virginia law allowing for the forced sterilization of mentally retarded individuals.

1928 The Meriam Report, which assesses the condition of American Indian reservations, is issued to the Secretary of the Interior.

1929 League of United Latin American Citizens (LULAC) is founded to advocate for Latino civil rights.

1930s Rising anti-immigrant sentiment as a result of the Great Depression leads to the repatriation of tens of thousands of Mexicans and Mexican Americans.

1930 The Japanese American Citizens League (JACL) is founded to protect the civil rights of Japanese Americans and other Asian Americans.

The Nation of Islam (also known as Black Muslims) is founded in Detroit by Wallace D. Fard.

1931 A group of black teenagers known as the Scottsboro Boys are falsely accused and convicted of raping two white women aboard a train. The case results in several important U.S. Supreme Court rulings that address racial inequalities within the criminal justice system, such as the use of all-white juries and inadequate legal counsel.

1932–1972 The U.S. Public Health Service conducts and funds the "Tuskegee Study of Untreated Syphilis in the Negro Male," which exploits and misleads hundreds of African American men in the name of science.

1934 The Federal Housing Administration (FHA) is created.

President Franklin D. Roosevelt signs into law the Indian Reorganization Act, also known as the Wheeler-Howard Act, to increase Native American self-governance and to foster tribal economic independence.

U.S. senators Edward P. Costigan and Robert F. Wagner sponsor an anti-lynching bill in response to the racially motivated murders of African Americans, but the proposed legislation is defeated the following year.

1935 President Franklin D. Roosevelt signs the Wagner Act, also known as the National Labor Relations Act (1935), giving workers the right to independent, union representation for purposes of collective bargaining with their employers.

1941 President Franklin D. Roosevelt signs Executive Order 8802, which prohibits racial discrimination in the federal government and defense industries. The order also creates the Fair Employment Practices Committee to ensure compliance with the new policy.

1942 The Emergency Labor Program, popularly called the Bracero Program, is established to allow Mexican workers into the United States to meet the labor needs of Southwestern agriculture growers during World War II.

The Congress of Racial Equality (CORE) is founded as a pacifist group seeking to fight racism, integrate public facilities, and work for civil rights for African Americans.

President Franklin D. Roosevelt signs Executive Order 9066, clearing the way for internment of Japanese Americans.

The War Relocation Authority (WRA) is established by executive order of President Roosevelt as the government agency responsible for removing persons believed to be threats to national security.

1943 The Detroit Race Riot of 1943 comprises a series of violent encounters, sparked by competition for jobs and housing, between whites and African Americans in Detroit, Michigan.

The Zoot Suit Riots, consisting of white attacks on Mexican American youths, erupt in Los Angeles.

1944 In *Korematsu v. United States*, the U.S. Supreme Court case upholds the internment of Japanese Americans during World War II.

National Congress of American Indians (NCAI) is founded to lobby for Native American rights and causes.

1946 Congress creates the Indian Claims Commission (ICC) to hear and determine claims against the U.S. government made by any Native American tribe or group.

1947 Jackie Robinson joins the Brooklyn Dodgers, becoming the first African American player in Major League Baseball.

In the California civil rights case *Mendez v. Westminster*, the U.S. Court of Appeals for the Ninth Circuit rules that segregation of Mexican American students into separate schools is unconstitutional. The decision serves as a legal precedent for the landmark school desegregation case *Brown v. Board of Education* (1954).

1948 President Harry S. Truman issues Executive Order 9981, racially integrating the U.S. military.

In *Shelley v. Kraemer*, the U.S. Supreme Court rules that the equal protection clause of the Fourteenth Amendment prevents racially restrictive housing covenants from being enforceable.

The American G.I. Forum, an organization devoted to securing equal rights for Hispanic American veterans, is founded by Hector P. Garcia.

In *Oyama v. California*, the U.S. Supreme Court strikes down California's Alien Land Laws as unconstitutional.

1952 Congress overrides President Harry S. Truman's veto to enact the Immigration and NationalityAct of 1952, or the McCarran-Walter Act, which eases certain restrictions on immigrants of particular national origins.

1954 In *Brown v. Board of Education* (1954), the U.S. Supreme Court declares racial segregation in public schools unconstitutional.

Publication of Gordon Allport's *The Nature of Prejudice*, an influential work examining and defining the nature of racial prejudice.

The U.S. Immigration and Naturalization Service (INS) launches the controversial paramilitary repatriation program, "Operation Wetback," which targets Mexicans working "illegally" in the agricultural industry of the Southwest.

1955 Rosa Parks refuses to give up her seat on a Montgomery, Alabama, bus to a white passenger, thereby initiating the Montgomery Bus Boycott.

Publication of John Higham's *Strangers in the Land*, a classic analysis of nativism in the United States.

1956 Publication of Kenneth Stampp's *The Peculiar Institution*, which views slavery as a coercive and profit-seeking regime, a significant revision in the way historians had previously seen the institution.

1957 The Southern Christian Leadership Conference (SCLC) is created in New Orleans by a group of ministers, labor leaders, lawyers, and political activists concerned about the impact of segregation on their communities.

The U.S. Commission on Civil Rights (USCCR) is created by the Civil Rights Act of 1957 as an independent, fact-finding arm of the federal government.

President Dwight D. Eisenhower sends federal troops to protect nine black students (the Little Rock Nine) attempting to integrate Central High School from angry whites in Little Rock, Arkansas.

1958 The John Birch Society is founded by Robert Welch to advocate limited government, anti-communism, and American isolationism.

1959 The American Nazi Party is founded by George Lincoln Rockwell.

1960 The Student Nonviolent Coordinating Committee (SNCC) is founded at Shaw University in Raleigh, North Carolina, to coordinate nonviolent protest actions against racial segregation.

Publication of John Howard Griffin's *Black Like Me*, the story of the extensive loss of rights and privileges suffered by a white man who darkened his skin to pass for black.

1961 President John F. Kennedy issues Executive Order 10925, which makes first use of the term "affirmative action" in calling on government contractors to treat employees "without regard to their race, creed, color, or national origin."

Freedom Riders, blacks and whites who travel together across the South in buses, protest racial segregation.

Release of *West Side Story*, a groundbreaking film adapted from a 1957 Broadway musical about white–Puerto Rican race relations.

1962 The National Farm Workers Association (NFWA), later the United Farm Workers (UFW), is founded by César Chávez and Dolores Huerta.

1963 The 1963 March on Washington is organized to bring attention to the lack of job opportunities and civil rights for African Americans. Martin Luther King, Jr. delivers his "I Have a Dream" speech before the Lincoln Memorial in Washington, D.C.

King writes his "Letter from a Birmingham Jail" while incarcerated for his role in anti-segregation demonstrations in Birmingham, Alabama.

Reies López Tijerina founds the Alianza Federal de Pueblos Libres (Federal Alliance of Land Grant) to reclaim Spanish and Mexican land grants held by Mexicans and Native Americans before the Mexican-American War.

1964 Congress passes the Civil Rights Act of 1964 to end the deeply entrenched practices of racial segregation and other forms of racial discrimination.

The Organization of Afro-American Unity (OAAU) is founded by Malcolm X to coordinate political action and self-organization among African Americans toward the goal of racial equality.

Harlem riot begins when a white police officer shoots and kills an African American youth in Yorkville, New York.

1965 On February 21, civil rights activist Malcolm X is shot and killed in Harlem by members of the Nation of Islam.

In Selma, Alabama, hundreds of civil rights marchers on their way to the state capital of Montgomery are brutally attacked by police in an incident known as Bloody Sunday.

President Lyndon B. Johnson signs legislation that creates the federal Department of Housing and Urban Development (HUD).

Publication of Paul M. Siegel's groundbreaking article, "On the Cost of Being a Negro," which examines the true extent of the income gap between blacks and whites.

El Teatro Campensino (The Farmworkers Theater) is founded by Luis Valdez as part of the organizing effort of César Chávez's United Farm Workers (UFW) union.

President Johnson signs into law the Voting Rights Act of 1965, which requires certain state and local jurisdictions to get federal approval before altering their voting procedures.

President Johnson signs into law the Immigration and Nationality Act of 1965, or the Hart-Celler Act, phasing out national-origin quotas and emphasizing the reunification of families.

In a series of urban uprisings known as the "Long Hot Summer," hundreds of race riots erupt each summer from 1965 to 1967. Some of the most intense occur in the Watts neighborhood of South Central Los Angeles in 1965 and in Newark and Detroit in 1967.

Publication of Daniel Patrick Moynihan's *The Negro Family in America: The Case for National Action*, which blames the poverty and social problems afflicting African Americans on the breakdown of the family.

1966 The Black Panther Party for Self-Defense (BPP) is formed by Huey P. Newton, Bobby Seale, and other radical Black Power activists.

In *Miranda v. Arizona* (1966), the U.S. Supreme Court establishes suspects' right to an attorney and to be informed of their rights before questioning by police.

Maulana Karenga, professor of Black Studies at California State University at Long Beach, develops Kwanzaa as a cultural holiday to promote the African American experience.

1967 Publication of *Black Power: The Politics of Liberation in America* by Stokely Carmichael and Charles V. Hamilton.

The National Advisory Commission on Civil Disorders (the Kerner Commission) is formed by President Lyndon B. Johnson to investigate the causes and implications of the "Long Hot Summer" urban riots occurring in black sections of many major cities.

In the landmark civil rights case *Loving v. Virginia*, the U.S. Supreme Court rules that laws prohibiting interracial marriage are unconstitutional.

1968 On April 4, civil rights leader Martin Luther King, Jr., is assassinated in Memphis, Tennessee.

The American Indian Movement (AIM) is founded.

Congress passes the Civil Rights Act of 1968 to ensure fair housing practices (Title VIII, known as the Fair Housing Act) and confer various civil rights on Native Americans.

The Bilingual Education Act is passed by Congress.

The Kerner Commission (the National Advisory Commission on Civil Disorders) issues its report on the series of urban race riots that occurred in 1967.

The Mexican American Legal Defense and Education Fund (MALDEF) is founded in San Antonio, Texas, to protect the civil rights of Latinos and promote their empowerment and full participation in society.

1969 Arthur Jensen publishes a widely cited article in the *Harvard Education Review* attacking Head Start programs and claiming that African American children have a low average IQ that cannot be improved by social engineering.

MEChA (Spanish acronym for the "Chicano Student Movement of Aztlán"), a national college student organization for Chicanos, is founded.

Native American activists begin a nineteen-month occupation of Alcatraz Island in San Francisco Bay.

1970 The National Chicano Moratorium demonstration against the Vietnam War and discrimination against Latinos at home occurs in Los Angeles.

1971 The Alaska Native Claims Settlement Act is passed by Congress to resolve Native Alaskan claims to lands appropriated by the federal government.

The United Farm Workers (UFW) is created from a merger of the Agricultural Workers Organizing Committee, led by Filipino labor organizer Larry Itliong, and the National Farm Workers Association, led by Mexican American labor organizer César Chávez.

The Arab Community Center for Economic and Social Services (ACCESS), an Arab American support and advocacy organization, is established.

1972 Congress passes the Equal Employment Opportunity Act of 1972 to amend the Civil Rights Act of 1964, making it more effective in ensuring equal job opportunities.

In *Furman v. Georgia*, the U.S. Supreme Court declares the death penalty "capricious and arbitrary" and thus unconstitutional.

Publication of Robert Blauner's *Racial Oppression in America*, which challenges the traditional theoretical paradigm of racial relations in the United States, that is, the classical assimilation theory, and proposes instead the internal-colonialism paradigm.

1973 The Organization of Chinese Americans, Inc. (OCA), a national nonprofit, nonpartisan advocacy organization of concerned Chinese and Asian Americans, is founded.

American Indian Movement (AIM) members occupy Wounded Knee, South Dakota.

In *Lau v. Nichols*, the U.S. Supreme Court rules that the San Francisco public school system violated the Civil Rights Act of 1964 by denying non-English-speaking students of Chinese ancestry a meaningful opportunity to participate in public education.

1974 Publication of Nathan Glazer's *Affirmative Discrimination: Ethnic Inequality and Public Policy*, which argues that affirmative action is actually "affirmative discrimination" against individuals.

The Asian American Legal Defense and Education Fund (AALDEF) is founded to protect the legal rights of Asian Americans.

1975 Congress amends the Voting Rights Act of 1965 to protect the voting rights of citizens of certain ethnic groups whose first language is not English.

President Gerald Ford signs into law the Indian Self-Determination and Education Assistance Act to implement tribal self-determination in matters relating to delivery of educational, health, and other services to Native Americans.

1976 In *Gregg v. Georgia*, the U.S. Supreme Court reinstates the death penalty.

Publication of Alex Haley's *Roots: The Saga of an American Family*, a semiautobiographical history of Haley's family and their experiences as slaves.

1977 Aryan Nations, a white-supremacist, anti-Semitic group, is founded by Richard G. Butler.

1978 In *Regents of the University of California v. Bakke*, the U.S. Supreme Court upholds the concept of affirmative action.

Publication of William J. Wilson's influential *The Declining Significance of Race*, a polemic on the relative importance of race and class for life chances of African Americans.

Publication of Joe Feagin's *Discrimination, American Style*, which argues that racial discrimination, or institutional racism, is embedded in institutions and policies designed to address the concerns of white European men.

1980 The American-Arab Anti-Discrimination Committee is established.

1981 The U.S. Department of Education formulates a clear policy that Ebonics is a form of English, not a separate language, and thus not eligible for public funding.

1982 Vincent Chin is murdered in Detroit, Michigan, by two white autoworkers who mistake him for Japanese and blame him for the loss of American jobs.

1983 Publication of Thomas Sowell's *Economics and Politics of Race*, in which a conservative social scientist argues that culture makes a difference in the success of an ethnic group and that racial strife has affected human society throughout history.

1984 Publication of Charles Murray's *Losing Ground: American Social Policy, 1950–1980*, a controversial examination of U.S. government social programs.

The National Rainbow Coalition is founded by Rev. Jesse Jackson to unite people of diverse ethnic, religious, economic, and political backgrounds in a push for social, racial, and economic justice.

1985 The Arab American Institute is established to represent the interests of Americans of Arab descent in politics and to foster their civic and political empowerment.

1986 The Howard Beach incident occurs, in which Michael Griffith, a black Trinidadian immigrant, is killed after he and two other men are attacked by a gang of white teenagers in the white Howard Beach neighborhood in Queens, New York.

Publication of Michael Omi and Howard Winant's *Racial Formation in the United States: From the 1960s to the 1980s*, a groundbreaking work on racial theory.

1987 The "Dotbuster" attacks occur, in which Latino gangs in Jersey City, New Jersey, threaten violence and vandalism against Indian residents who do not leave the city.

1988 President Ronald Reagan signs into law the Civil Liberties Act of 1988, which apologizes for internment of Japanese Americans during World War II and provides reparations for their treatment.

Osama bin Laden, the son of a Saudi billionaire, forms al-Qaeda, an organization that develops in the 1990s into a global terrorist network that promotes an extremist and militant form of Islam and attacks U.S. global interests.

The Bensonhurst incident occurs, in which black teenager Yusef Hawkins is beaten to death by white youths in the Bensonhurst neighborhood of Brooklyn, New York.

The Fair Housing Amendments Act of 1988 strengthens provisions of the Fair Housing Act of 1968 by giving the Department of Housing and Urban Development (HUD) greater power to enforce the earlier legislation.

1989 Publication of Stephen Steinberg's *Ethnic Myth: Race, Ethnicity and Class in America*, which challenges various prevailing ideas about race and ethnicity in the United States.

In *City of Richmond v. J. A. Croson Company*, the U.S. Supreme Court rules that a city affirmative action program violates the equal protection clause of the Fourteenth Amendment.

1990 President George H. W. Bush signs into law the Native American Graves Protection and Repatriation Act (NAGPRA), which gives tribes greater access to sacred objects held by educational and government institutions.

President Bush signs into law the Hate Crimes Statistics Act, which requires the Department of Justice to compile annual national data on hate crimes and publish an annual summary of findings.

1991 Yankel Rosenbaum, a Jewish yeshiva student, is murdered by a black mob in Crown Heights, New York.

Los Angeles police officers are taped beating Rodney King, an African American motorist, after King refuses to be pulled over.

Congress passes the Civil Rights Act (1991) to reverse recent court rulings that seem to weaken enforcement of earlier civil rights legislation.

1992 Riots erupt in Los Angeles after the acquittal of the police officers accused in the Rodney King case.

1994 California voters pass Proposition 187, the Save Our State Initiative, which denies publicly funded nonemergency medical care, education, and social services to illegal immigrants and their foreign-born children.

The Council on American Islamic Relations (CAIR) is established to advocate for the civil rights of Muslim Americans.

Publication of scholar Cornel West's *Race Matters*, which examines the role of race in shaping the African American experience.

Richard J. Herrnstein and Charles Murray publish *The Bell Curve: Intelligence and Class Structure in American Life*, in which they present statistical evidence that supposedly supports the notion of racial superiority based on IQ.

1995 Minister Louis Farrakhan of the Nation of Islam sponsors the Million Man March on Washington to support African American families.

Publication of *Black Wealth/White Wealth: A New Perspective on Racial Inequality*, a book by Melvin L. Oliver and Thomas M. Shapiro detailing disparities in wealth between whites and blacks.

Right-wing extremists bomb the Alfred P. Murrah Federal Building in Oklahoma City.

O. J. Simpson, an African American football legend, is acquitted of murdering his wife, Nicole Brown Simpson, and Ron Goldman, who were both white.

Publication of John Yinger's *Closed Doors, Opportunities Lost: The Continuing Costs of Housing Discrimination*, examining various housing studies to determine how closely the housing industry is adhering to the Fair Housing Act of 1968.

1996 California voters pass Proposition 209, the California Civil Rights Initiative, which repeals affirmative action in public employment, education, or contracting.

In *Shaw v. Hunt*, the U.S. Supreme Court declares that race cannot be the sole factor in redrawing congressional districts.

1998 California voters pass Proposition 227, the English Language Education for Children in Public Schools Initiative, which eliminates bilingual education in California public schools.

James Byrd Jr., a black man, is murdered in Jasper, Texas, by three white racists who slit his throat and drag his body behind a truck.

1999 Publication of Mary Waters's *Black Identities: West Indian Immigrant Dreams and American Realities*, an award-winning book that explores the experiences of West Indian immigrants in New York City.

Amadou Diallo, an African immigrant working as a street vendor in New York, is shot to death by four undercover police officers, who mistake him for a rape suspect.

Wen Ho Lee, a Chinese American engineer working at the Los Alamos Research Laboratory, is accused of spying by the government and fired from his job in violation of his civil rights. He is later cleared of all charges.

2001 Members of the militant Islamist organization al-Qaeda, acting on orders of the group's leader, Osama bin Laden, launch terrorist attacks on New York City and Washington, D.C.

The PATRIOT Act is passed in the wake of the September 11, 2001, terrorist attacks to increase the effectiveness of U.S. law enforcement in detecting and preventing further acts of terrorism.

2003 The U.S. Supreme Court renders decisions in two University of Michigan affirmation action cases—*Grutter v. Bollinger* (2003) and *Gratz v. Bollinger* (2003)—declaring that race can be considered in university admissions decisions but cannot be a "deciding factor."

California voters reject Proposition 54, the Racial Privacy Initiative (RPI), which would have banned the use and production of racially coded data by various state and municipal agencies.

2004 The Smithsonian's National Museum of the American Indian opens on the National Mall in Washington, D.C.

2005 Hurricane Katrina devastates New Orleans and much of the central Gulf Coast region. A delayed response by the George W. Bush administration and the Federal Emergency Management Agency (FEMA) lead to allegations of racism.

2006 In Jena, Louisiana, six black teenagers known as the "Jena Six" are charged with attempted murder for attacking a white student after a series of racially charged events that included the discovery of nooses hanging from a schoolyard tree. The case, which raises questions about race and justice, sparks nationwide protests and media attention.

2008 Democrat Barack Obama is elected the first African American president of the United States. The Tea Party movement emerges as a influential component of the Republican Party, advocating greater fiscal austerity and states' rights.

2010 In April, Arizona governor Jan Brewer signs into law the controversial Senate Bill (SB) 1070, otherwise known as the Support Our Law Enforcement and Safe Neighborhoods Act, allowing state law enforcement officials to detain individuals suspected of being undocumented aliens.

In May, Gov. Brewer signs into law House Bill (HB) 2281, which effectively bans ethnic studies from being taught in Arizona public schools.

2011 President Barack Obama releases his long-form birth certificate in response to allegations by the birther movement that he is not a native-born U.S. citizen.

2012 In February, African American teenager Trayvon Martin is killed by neighborhood watch volunteer George Zimmerman while unarmed and walking in a gated community in Sanford, Florida. The incident renews a nationwide discussion on race and criminal justice, including such issues as racial profiling and the manner in which law enforcement officials handle cases involving communities of color.

On November 6, President Barack Obama is reelected to a second term in the White House. Key to his victory is the support of women, racial minorities, and young people—the same coalition that propelled him to office as the first African American U.S. president four years earlier.

On November 26, the $3.4 billion settlement to *Cobell v. Salazar* is finalized. The class-action lawsuit, which spanned 13 years, was brought against the U.S. government for its mismanagement of land trust royalties intended for Native Americans.

287(g) Delegation of Immigration Authority

287(g) is one of a number of ICE ACCESS (Agreements of Cooperation in Communities to Enhance Safety and Security) programs that enables state and local law enforcement agencies to collaborate with federal immigration authorities in the enforcement of federal immigration law. Named for its section number, 287(g) was amended to the 1965 Immigration and Nationality Act (INA) through the 1996 Illegal Immigration Reform and Immigrant Responsibility Act (IIRIRA). Under section 287(g), state and local law enforcement agencies may enter into agreements with Immigration and Customs Enforcement (ICE) to receive delegated authority to enforce federal immigration law. The 287(g) program deputizes law enforcement officers to perform immigration enforcement duties, such as identifying unauthorized immigrants and processing them for removal (deportation).

The 287(g) program operates as three different models: the task force model, the jail enforcement model, and the hybrid model. In the task force model, designated officers acting in the course of their regular law enforcement duties are permitted to verify individuals' immigration status or legal presence. In the jail enforcement model, designated officers in state and local jails are authorized to verify the immigration status or legal presence of arrested individuals. The hybrid model enables local agencies to operate a combination of the task force and jail enforcement models.

State and local jurisdictions must enter into a memorandum of agreement (MOA) with ICE in order to receive delegated authority through one of these models. The MOA specifies the scope and limitations of delegation of authority and outlines the responsibilities of each party. Among other responsibilities, ICE agrees to train and supervise designated officers. The local jurisdiction assumes most other costs, including the salary of officers designated to perform immigration-related duties. To date, few agencies have implemented the 287(g) program, possibly as a result of limited local resources and the potentially high fiscal cost to local jurisdictions. As of 2012, the 287(g) program is implemented in just 57 agencies across 21 states.

The 287(g) program has received considerable criticism from both immigrant advocacy organizations and law enforcement officers, who suggest that the program and its implementation are fundamentally flawed. Some contend that the 287(g) program, like other ACCESS programs, erodes trust in local law enforcement—particularly among immigrant communities—and therefore undermines community safety. In particular, immigrant rights groups and law enforcement officers argue that unauthorized immigrants may be reluctant to report crimes and cooperate with police if local officers are tasked with enforcing immigration law.

Others claim that 287(g) encourages police officers to engage in racial profiling, a contention that has earned merit in some jurisdictions. In recent years, accusations of racial profiling in Maricopa County, Arizona, and Alamance County, North Carolina, have increased public scrutiny of the 287(g) program. In 2011, the Department of Homeland Security (DHS) terminated the 287(g) agreement between ICE and the Maricopa County Sheriff's Office, citing reasonable cause to believe that the Sheriff's Office had engaged in discriminatory practices against Latinos, including unlawful stops, detentions, and arrests of Latinos, and differential treatment of Latino inmates. The following year, DHS terminated Alamance County's 287(g) agreement, again citing a pattern of biased policing that included differential treatment for Latinos during traffic stops and checkpoints. In its multiyear investigations of both Maricopa County and Alamance County, the Department of Justice found that officers in both jurisdictions targeted Latinos for increased enforcement and disregarded constitutional policing practices.

Finally, some argue that the 287(g) program is implemented indiscriminately to identify, apprehend, and remove unauthorized immigrants who do not fit into ICE's stated priorities.

In 2010, ICE Director John Morton issued a memo that outlined enforcement priorities, emphasizing that ICE's limited resources should be used to target immigration offenders who pose a threat to public safety or national security. Yet, the 287(g) program has led to the identification and apprehension of low-priority immigration offenders, including those who have committed traffic offenses and minor misdemeanors.

In 2010, the Office of Inspector General (OIG) issued *The Performance of 287(g) Agreements*, a report on the lack of oversight and accountability in 287(g) programs. Among other conclusions, the OIG found that ICE and local law enforcement agencies did not comply with the terms of their MOAs; that those arrested and processed through 287(g) did not conform to ICE priorities; that ICE provided inadequate training, supervision, and oversight; and that local agencies did not collect sufficient data to enable monitoring of potential civil rights violations.

After the OIG conducted its investigation, but prior to the publication of its report, ICE implemented a series of changes focused on reforming the operations and impacts of the 287(g) program. ICE contends that the report does not reflect the current 287(g) program. However, analysis by the independent and nonpartisan Migration Policy Institute (MPI) finds that reforms have not substantially altered the functioning of the 287(g) program. Specifically, the MPI report finds that the 287(g) program continues to fail to prioritize criminal offenders, that it functions inconsistently across jurisdictions, and that the program contributes to mistrust and fear of police.

In 2012, ICE announced that it would phase out the 287(g) task force model, citing its lack of efficiency and cost effectiveness compared to other ACCESS initiatives such as Secure Communities. However, the jail model continues to be active in jurisdictions across the country.

Meghan Conley

See also

Anchor Baby; Anti-Immigrant Sentiment; Arizona Senate Bill 1070 (SB 1070) (2010); Immigration Acts; Immigration and Customs Enforcement (ICE); National Origins Act of 1924; Operation Wetback; Secure Communities; Unauthorized Immigration; United States Border Patrol

Further Reading:

Capps, Randy, Marc R. Rosenblum, Cristina Rodriguez, and Muzzafar Chisti. *Delegation and Divergence: A Study of 287(g) State and Local Immigration Enforcement.* Washington, DC: Migration Policy Institute, 2001.

Immigration and Customs Enforcement. *Delegation of Immigration Authority Section 287(g) Immigration and Nationality Act.* http://www.ice.gov/287g/.

Office of Inspector General. *The Performance of 287(g) Agreements.* Washington, DC: Department of Homeland Security, 2001.

Abernathy, Ralph David (1926–1990)

Considered one of the "Big Three" leaders of the Civil Rights Movement, Ralph David Abernathy joined Martin Luther King, Jr., Fred Shuttlesworth, and a long list of African American clergymen who worked to undermine segregation and racism using the doctrine of nonviolence. Born in Linden, Alabama, in 1926, Abernathy was the 10th of the 12 children born to William and Louivery (Bell) Abernathy. Abernathy's parents named him David, which family members called him throughout his youth; he registered as Ralph David Abernathy when he enlisted in the U.S. Army in 1944.

The Abernathy family was solidly middle class, in comparison to other residents of Marengo County in rural Alabama in the 1930s and 1940s. William Abernathy owned several hundred acres of fertile land, from which the family drew most of its food and resources. The family also enjoyed an elevated status in Linden as William Abernathy was a deacon at Hopewell Baptist Church and a successful farmer. At the insistence of Louivery Abernathy, all of the Abernathy children attended primary and secondary school. World War II erupted while Abernathy was still in high school, and he enlisted in the army in 1944. Abernathy was honorably discharged at the rank of sergeant in the summer of 1945.

In September 1945, Abernathy entered Alabama State College (now Alabama State University) in Montgomery. At Alabama State, Abernathy studied mathematics and the political activism of civil disobedience. As president of the Student Council, Abernathy met with the president of Alabama State to protest the living conditions of veteran students, who lived in barracks with no heating and poor plumbing. After the meeting, promises for improvements were made and kept. Abernathy later remarked that his meetings with the intimidating president of Alabama State prepared him for debates over civil rights with future presidents John F. Kennedy, Lyndon B. Johnson, and Richard M. Nixon. Abernathy graduated in 1950 with a BS in mathematics.

Abernathy also found a religious calling while he was a student at Alabama State. He gave a number of sermons at First Baptist Church in Montgomery. When he enrolled at Atlanta University to earn a master's degree in sociology in 1950, he attended the historical Ebenezer Baptist Church. There he met two influential figures in Atlanta's church community, Vernon Johns and Martin Luther King, Jr. After graduating in 1951, Abernathy returned to Alabama, where he took two positions, one as dean of men at Alabama State College, and another as the primary pastor at First Baptist Church. Three years later, King and his family moved to Montgomery, where he was named chief pastor at Dexter Avenue Baptist Church. Abernathy and King had similar political interests, including a fascination with the writings of Mahatma Gandhi and the peaceful withdrawal of the British from colonial India after World War II. The two pastors became close friends, and their relationship remained steadfast until King's death in 1968.

Baptist clergyman Ralph Abernathy was Martin Luther King, Jr.'s closest coworker during the civil rights movement and the leader of the Southern Christian Leadership Conference (SCLC) after King's death. Abernathy resigned the SCLC presidency in 1977 and devoted himself to his pastorate at the West Hunter Baptist Church, lecturing on civil rights, and writing his life story. (Library of Congress)

Abernathy and King's first organized attack to defeat segregation was the Montgomery Bus Boycott of 1955–1956. Set off by the arrest of Rosa Parks, a seamstress and secretary of the NAACP Montgomery chapter, the boycott of Montgomery's segregated city buses quickly galvanized African American support. Jo Ann Gibson Robinson, leader of the Women's Political Council of Montgomery and a professor of English at Alabama State, had expertly organized a complex network of carpools and private transportation for a one-day boycott in December 1955. Abernathy and King joined with Robinson's network to form the Montgomery Improvement Association (MIA). Arranging a system of phone banks, reduced-fare taxis, private cars, and escorts, the MIA extended the boycott over 12 months. The MIA also professed nonviolent resistance and civil disobedience. The Montgomery Bus Boycott emerged successful in December 1956, when the city surrendered to the demands of the MIA and abolished segregation on its public transportation. After the boycott, King became the charismatic scholar and pastor of the civil rights movement, and Abernathy became its chief tactician.

The success of the Montgomery Bus Boycott led to the founding of the Southern Christian Leadership Conference (SCLC) in Atlanta, Georgia. Abernathy joined King, Fred Shuttlesworth, Joseph Lowery, and other prominent clergymen to establish an organization dedicated to the eradication of Jim Crow and to nonviolence. The SCLC's mission differed from the National Association for Advancement of Colored People (NAACP) and the NAACP Legal Defense and Education Fund. The SCLC focused on gathering moral and religious objections to Jim Crow, while the NAACP Legal Defense Fund broke down the legal structures of segregation and white supremacy. Together, the two groups worked to dismantle Jim Crow and change American consciousness, which had tolerated the worst abuses in white supremacy.

Yet, Abernathy's activism in the state of Alabama drew harassment and violent backlash. In 1957, while he attended a planning session of the SCLC in Atlanta, his home and church were bombed. His pregnant wife, Juanita, and their child Juandalynn narrowly escaped injury, but the arsonists were never caught. Moreover, three other churches were bombed the same night: Bell Street Baptist, Hutchison Street Baptist, and Mount Olive Baptist. The bitter resistance to the civil rights movement in Montgomery forced Abernathy to move his family to Atlanta in 1960. In 1962, Abernathy and three other clergymen were sued for libel by the attorney general of the state of Alabama. The lawsuit claimed that Abernathy, Joseph Lowery, S. S. Seay, Fred Shuttlesworth, and the *New York Times* had slandered the city by supporting an advertisement in the newspaper to raise funds for King's legal defenses. In *Sullivan v. New York Times*, the jury initially found for the plaintiffs, but the U.S. Supreme Court overturned the ruling on appeal in 1964.

In Atlanta, King, Abernathy, and the SCLC launched their most memorable nonviolent attacks on Jim Crow. They maintained their conviction that nonviolence, primarily surrendering to inevitable suffering, would transform the hearts and minds of segregationists and white supremacists. Abernathy's faith and his adherence to nonviolence shaped the critical involvement of the SCLC in the civil rights movement of the mid-1960s. They supported the Freedom Rides of 1961 by taking the riders and their families into the West Hunter Street Baptist Church. They organized the marches against segregation in Birmingham and Selma, and were arrested several times. Abernathy saw King and the SCLC through the difficult period following the Albany marches, and the high point of the 1963 March on Washington. He also rallied for protests in St. Augustine, Charleston, and Chicago in the latter half of the decade.

Eventually, the violence following the leaders of the civil rights movement caught up with the two leaders. In April 1968, the SCLC traveled to Memphis to support a sanitation workers' strike. Standing on the balcony at the Lorraine Hotel, King was shot and killed by James Earl Ray on April 4. Abernathy was the last person to see King alive. The assassination of King left a profound void in the civil rights movement, particularly in newer, more militant incarnations. After King's death, Abernathy was vaulted into the presidency of the SCLC. His immediate task was to assess the popularity of groups that had turned to Black Power for answers. Once a close political ally, the Student Nonviolent Coordinating Committee (SNCC) had become increasingly dissatisfied with nonviolence and the goals of integration. The Black Panthers and the US movement amassed a large following of young African Americans, and college students across the country rallied for changes in university curricula to reflect African American contributions. The SCLC had a difficult time appealing to the newer recruits to the civil rights movement, and nonviolence appeared to lose its place as the nation struggled with the assassination of Robert F. Kennedy and the escalation of the Vietnam War.

Stepping into King's shoes as president of the SCLC proved exceedingly difficult for Abernathy. Not only did national events necessitate a response from the organization, but Abernathy's style and leadership were often unfavorably compared with that of King. For example, Abernathy carried on King's program for a Poor People's March on Washington, D.C., but the 1968 march attracted much less interest and the tent city, Resurrection City, was taken down by the National Guard. Though Abernathy and the doctrine of nonviolence took the moral high ground amid the violence of the late 1960s, the SCLC competed with the increasingly popular Black Power movement and its militant message. The SCLC was also under considerable pressure to raise funds to continue its work, and it needed new, dues-paying members to fund its activism. The difficulty confronting Abernathy was determining the type of activism a post-King SCLC should undertake to preserve the organization and the movement.

By the mid-1970s, the SCLC split into two distinct halves—a section of older, middle-class protestors espousing nonviolence and marches, and a section of younger students espousing direct action and self-protection from the police, especially gun ownership rights. In 1977, a vote on the future of the organization was put to the members of the SCLC. The older generation of activists won out, and the SCLC continued its program of nonviolence. Yet, the dispute took its toll on Abernathy's presidency, and he resigned later that year. He ran for a congressional seat representing Georgia in 1977, but his bid was unsuccessful. A fellow cofounder of the SCLC, Joseph Lowery, followed Abernathy as president of the SCLC.

Abernathy later returned to his position as pastor of West Hunter Baptist in Atlanta. He served there from 1977 to 1990. His church deepened its commitment to empowering black communities in Atlanta by establishing the Foundation for Economic Enterprises Development. In 1989, Abernathy published his autobiography, *And the Walls Came Tumbling Down*, a moving description of the highs and lows of the civil rights movement from 1955 to 1968 with King and the SCLC. Abernathy's autobiography also disclosed some embarrassing mistakes in King's personal life, which drew much criticism from other members of the movement. Abernathy died a year later in Atlanta.

NIKKI BROWN

See also

Civil Rights Movement; King, Martin Luther, Jr.; Southern Christian Leadership Conference (SCLC)

Further Reading:

Abernathy, Ralph David. *And the Walls Came Tumbling Down*. New York: Harper & Row, 1989.

Branch, Taylor. *Parting the Waters: America during the King Years, 1954–63*. New York: Simon and Schuster, 1988.

Fairclough, Adam. *To Redeem the Soul of America: The Southern Christian Leadership Conference and Martin Luther King, Jr.* Athens: University of Georgia Press, 1987.

Garrow, David J. *Bearing the Cross: Martin Luther King, Jr., and the Southern Christian Leadership Conference, 1955–1968*. New York: Morrow, 1986.

Abolitionist Movement

The United States in the three decades before the Civil War was flooded with various reform movements. Inspired by the religious revivals of the Second Great Awakening, these reform movements sought to improve or perfect human society by eliminating any evil the reformers believed was an affront to the moral and spiritual health of the nation. Reformers attacked such issues as failure to observe the Sabbath, poor treatment of the mentally ill, crime and punishment, temperance, women's rights, and the abolition of slavery. General antislavery sentiment had developed in both the North and the South during and immediately after the American Revolution. Ironically, by the mid-1820s, there were more antislavery societies in the South, more than 100, than in the North, where there were just 24. However, by 1830, Southern antislavery sentiment had largely disappeared. The larger antislavery movement included advocates of the colonization movement; gradualists who believed in a slow move toward emancipation through voluntary manumission; free-soil advocates who simply opposed further extension of slavery; and abolitionists who pursued an immediate compulsory end to slavery. It was not until the late 1820s and 1830s, as part of the massive push to reform society, that immediate abolition came to dominate the antislavery movement.

As late as the mid-1700s, most organized Western religions or denominations had failed to discourage their congregations from practicing slavery. Many European governments were actively engaged in the slave trade. Slaves could be found in all of the 13 British North American colonies, and throughout the American Revolution many of the Founding Fathers were slaveholders. Antislavery sentiment, prior to 1787, was largely limited to those practicing the Quaker faith. Quakers would continue to be leaders of the movement until slavery was eventually abolished. In 1787, as the nation took its first steps, Congress barred slavery in the Old Northwest territory, the area north of the Ohio River, and included in the U.S. Constitution the provision that the Atlantic slave trade would be outlawed in 1808. Most believed that the institution of slavery was destined to die out.

The first large-scale, organized emancipation movement appeared in 1817 with the creation of the American Colonization Society (ACS). A major hurdle for those who supported emancipation was the pervasive view that blacks and whites could not coexist equally within one nation. Thus, any plan for emancipation required the separation of the two. The colonization movement pushed for voluntary manumission and gradual emancipation, along with the return of blacks to Africa. Supporters of the American Colonization Society included Thomas Jefferson, James Madison, John Marshall, and James Monroe. To encourage this process, the ACS helped establish the country of Liberia in 1820. Its capital, Monrovia, was named in honor of President James Monroe. Within 10 years, the society had brought a little more than 1,400 free blacks to Liberia. American free blacks thus founded the nation of Liberia, located south of Sierra Leone. Nevertheless, most African Americans rejected the notion of colonization and saw the process as nothing more than a program for ridding the United States of its growing free black population. By the 1830s, colonization was seen as an unrealistic way to end slavery.

As stated previously, the evangelical fervor and reform-mindedness of the Second Great Awakening helped to bring about the rise of abolitionism. During the 1820s, the preaching of Lyman Beecher in New England and the revivals that began in western New York led by Charles Granderson Finney swept through much of the North, creating a powerful impulse toward social reform. Emancipation of the slaves was chief among the reform movements, and among Charles Finney's converts were leading abolitionists Theodore Dwight Weld and the brothers Arthur Tappan and Lewis Tappan. Weld became a leading antislavery lecturer and author of *American Slavery as It Is: Testimony of a Thousand Witnesses* (1839), which exhibited the horrors of slavery and became the abolitionist's handbook for more than a decade. Arthur and Lewis Tappan, two wealthy New York philanthropists, were greatly influenced by Finney's revivalism and threw themselves headlong into support of the abolitionist cause. Other leading abolitionists included New Englander William Lloyd Garrison and the former slave Frederick Douglass.

The nation's most famous abolitionist was William Lloyd Garrison of Massachusetts. In 1831, he began publication in Boston of a new antislavery newspaper, the *Liberator*, and organized the New England Anti-Slavery Society. Garrison grew up in poverty and educated himself while an apprentice to a newspaper publisher. Early in his career, Garrison edited a number of antislavery papers, but he soon became impatient with the strategies of gradualism and colonization. In the first issue of the *Liberator*, he renounced the doctrine of gradualism and vowed to be uncompromising in his assault on the institution of slavery. Throughout the 1830s, Garrison became the nation's most passionate and uncompromising opponent of slavery.

In December 1833, Garrison and the Tappan brothers were the chief organizers of the American Anti-Slavery Society. At a convention held in Philadelphia, along with 60 other delegates, they denounced slavery as a moral evil and demanded immediate abolition without compensation for slaveholders. The most radical demand emerging from the convention was the one for legal equality of the races. They hoped to use the publicity created when the British antislavery movement persuaded Parliament, also in 1833, to end slavery throughout the entire British Empire. However, they did not follow the British lead in providing compensation for slaveholders. In 1835, the society initiated an enormous propaganda campaign. It inundated the slave states with abolitionist literature, sent representatives all over the Northern states to organize state and local antislavery societies, and sent numerous petitions to Congress calling for the abolition of slavery in the nation's capital.

By 1834, 200 antislavery societies had been formed in the North. Support for these organizations came from evangelical reformers and Quakers, middle-class merchants and artisans, and most of all from women. Within two years, the number of societies had grown to over 500, and within four years, there were nearly 1,300 active antislavery societies. A petition campaign in 1838–1839 gathered more than 2 million signatures proclaiming the sinfulness of slavery.

Initially, the abolitionists were generally condemned and mistreated. Mobs attacked them in the North; Garrison was a frequent target and was physically assaulted several times after speeches in Boston, and antiabolition riots plagued Northern cities. Southerners burned antislavery pamphlets and blamed Nat Turner's Revolt in August 1831 on abolitionist agitation. There is no evidence that Turner had read any antislavery pamphlets or the *Liberator*, yet Southerners were convinced that the new, more aggressive abolitionist rhetoric was the cause. These events, and the mob attack and murder of Illinois abolitionist Elijah Lovejoy in 1837, led many abolitionists to fear that the approach taken by the more radical abolitionists such as Garrison was detrimental to the cause.

As the abolition movement grew, debates over strategy increased. At the beginning of the 1840s, two clear and disparate camps had emerged within the abolitionist movement: one, often referred to as "radical abolitionists," led by Garrison; and another, the "political abolitionists," led by New Yorkers Arthur and Lewis Tappan, wealthy New Yorker Gerrit Smith, and James G. Birney of Alabama, a former slaveholder.

Garrison and his more radical followers, often called Garrisonians, embraced nearly every important reform of the day: abolition, pacifism, temperance, and women's rights. Additionally, these radicals believed that American society was corrupted from top to bottom and should be reformed. Their primary mode of protest was that of moral persuasion, aiming to convince their adversaries of the sinfulness of slavery. As part of their protest, they removed themselves from all corrupted institutions, including religion and government. Garrison broke with the organized church and along with his followers refused to vote, hold public office, or file lawsuits. He also burned a copy of the Constitution in protest. The schism in the movement came at the 1840 meeting of the American Anti-Slavery Society in New York. Two issues tore the movement asunder: whether women should be allowed to participate in the organization as equal members, and whether the society should nominate abolitionists to run as independent political candidates.

The issue of women's rights was particularly controversial. Women had, of course, been active in the abolitionist movement from its inception, but primarily in female-only societies. In the late 1830s, however, activists Sarah and Angelina Grimké brought the issue of women's rights to the forefront. The Grimké sisters were daughters of a South Carolina slaveholder but disagreed with their parents' slaveholding practices and left for the North. Both converted to Quakerism and became abolitionists and women's rights activists. After attending numerous training conferences for abolition activists, they began publicly speaking against slavery, first to female audiences and later to those of mixed gender. Their activities brought condemnation from ministers in other denominations for taking part in unfeminine activities. At the 1840 American Anti-Slavery Society meeting, the radicals insisted on the right of women to participate equally in the organization, and eventually won this point. The Tappans' New York delegation, however, argued that women's rights and abolition should remain separate issues and broke away from the American Anti-Slavery Society to form the American and Foreign Anti-Slavery Society.

One result of this split was the growth of the women's rights movement out of the radical abolitionist cause. Another result of the split was that those favoring a political solution to end slavery formed political parties. The Tappans, Gerrit Smith, and James Birney created the Liberty Party in 1840. The party petitioned Congress to end the slave trade in Washington, D.C., repeal local and state "black codes," end the interstate slave trade, and discontinue admitting slave states to the Union. The Liberty Party nominated Birney for president in the 1840. He received just over 7,000 votes, and Garrisonians assailed the results of his candidacy as foolish. Nevertheless, the Liberty Party persisted and nominated Birney again in 1844. This time, however, he garnered over 61,000 votes and captured enough votes to deny the Whig Party candidate, Henry Clay, the presidency.

Between 1844 and 1848, political abolitionists suffered a number of setbacks. The annexation of Texas in 1844 as a slave state and the acquisition of half of Mexico's territory after the 1846 Mexican-American War threatened to further expand the institution of slavery. However, they did persuade some Northern Democrats and Whigs that there was a compelling need to end slavery. These factions, along with the Liberty Party, formed the Free Soil Party in 1848 and nominated Martin Van Buren for president. In many ways, this new party was seen as a softer version of the Liberty Party. The Free Soil Party limited its attack on slavery to abolition of the slave trade in Washington, D.C., and the prohibition of slavery from any new states. No longer was there a political call for abolition or equal rights for free blacks, as there had been with the Liberty Party. The Free Soil Party garnered over 290,000 votes for Van Buren and thus helped elect Zachary Taylor (Whig) as president. They also placed a number of Free Soil candidates in Congress. Support for the Free Soil Party waned, and their 1852 presidential candidate, John P. Hale, gained less than 160,000 votes.

Radical critics of the Free-Soil Party denounced the organization as racist because the party declined to renounce racial discrimination, and many held overtly racist views. Yet for most Free-Soilers, avoiding abolition and the rights of free blacks was wholly a political decision to gain further support. For this reason, most black abolitionists could be counted with the more radical branch of abolitionism.

Abolitionism held a specific allure for free blacks in the North. Poor living conditions and racial oppression, which at times could be as bad for them as for their slave counterparts, were facts of life for the nearly 500,000 free blacks in the antebellum period. Nonetheless, they were proud of their freedom and never forgot their brothers and sisters in bondage. Although many in the 1830s came to support Garrison and his goals, they also backed leaders from the black community.

Many black abolitionist leaders were either Baptist or Methodist ministers; however, the most famous black abolitionists were such former slaves as Sojourner Truth, Harriet Tubman, and Frederick Douglass. William Lloyd Garrison claimed that Douglass and other former slaves were the best qualified to inform the public of the horrors of slavery. Douglass's autobiography, *Narrative of the Life of Frederick Douglass*, was published in 1845. While a slave, he had learned to read and write as a servant for a kind mistress in Baltimore. After the *Narrative* was published, he feared being captured. Thus, as a fugitive slave, he spent several years in England before returning in 1847, after abolitionist friends purchased his freedom. Upon his return to the United States, he established the antislavery newspaper the *North Star*. Living in Rochester, New York, he edited the *North Star* (under various names) for nearly two decades in support of the abolitionist cause.

Early in his abolitionist career, Douglass aligned himself with Garrison and the radicals. However, after his time in England with British abolitionists, Douglass began to see the advantages of political action. He used the *North Star* to support political parties and candidates, such as James Birney and the Liberty Party. During the 1850s, Douglass backed the Republican Party, even though their platform called only for an end to the expansion of slavery. In many ways Douglass was a pragmatist, who envisioned a future where all American racial and cultural differences were blended to create a single American nationality. Through his writings and speeches, Douglass was the one of the nation's most eloquent critics of racial inequality.

During the 1850s, as Douglass, Garrison, and other abolitionists struggled to end slavery through moral suasion and protest, the political system became unable to contain the sectional disputes surrounding slavery. Possibly the most significant event to bolster the abolitionist cause was the passage of the Compromise of 1850. The most threatening provision of the Compromise was that it implemented vigorous enforcement of the Fugitive Slave Law, first passed in 1793. The new version of this law stripped runaway slaves of the right to trial and the right to testify in their own defense. Additionally, it required Northern citizens to assist in the recovery of fugitive slaves. In essence, this measure forced even antislavery Northerners into the service of the slave hunters. It brought more people into the fold of the abolitionist camp, people such as the essayist and philosopher Ralph Waldo Emerson, who previously had held antislavery sentiments but had avoided concerted action. Emerson saw the passage of the compromise as a call to arms, a call all men of conscience must answer. Using his fame as a lecturer and writer, Emerson took to the antislavery lecture circuit, calling on everyone to fight or at the very least ignore the new Fugitive Slave Law.

Mob riots against the Fugitive Slave Law broke out in a number of Northern states, including Michigan, Pennsylvania, Wisconsin, and Massachusetts. In most cases, the aim of the mob was to free a fugitive slave captured by slave catchers. After several fugitives were rescued by abolitionist mobs, the state and federal governments stepped in to help the slave catchers. In Boston, federal marshals and 22 companies of state troopers were needed to prevent a crowd, estimated at 50,000, from storming a courthouse to free Anthony Burns, a fugitive slave.

Frederick Douglass (1817–1895)

Possibly the most famous American abolitionist, Frederick Douglass was also a prolific writer, orator, and social activist. Frederick Augustus Washington Bailey was born near Easton, Maryland, to Harriet Bailey, a black slave, and an unknown white man. After a failed first attempt, Frederick escaped slavery in 1838 and took the name Douglass.

Douglass found work as a laborer and later learned to read with the help of a white woman in Baltimore. According to history, his extemporaneous speech during a meeting of the Massachusetts Anti-Slavery Society in 1841 was so eloquent that he was solicited to be one of its agents and took part in lecture tours to inform the masses about the evils of slavery. As a central figure in the abolition movement, Douglass made frequent speeches to rouse support for the cause, founded the abolitionist newspaper, *North Star*, and edited it for 17 years. In 1845, Douglass wrote his autobiography, *Narrative of the Life of Frederick Douglass*. Douglass supported political redress as the primary mechanism to both abolish slavery and deal with its aftermath. Douglass was the first black citizen to hold high political rank. His numerous posts included secretary of the Santo Domingo Commission (1871), marshall of the District of Columbia (1877–1881), and U.S. minister and consul general to Haiti (1889–1991). Douglass also served as advisor to President Abraham Lincoln during the Civil War and championed constitutional amendments to guarantee civil and voting rights for blacks. He died in Washington, D.C., in 1895.

Sandra L. Barnes

As the furor over the Fugitive Slave Law grew, the most persuasive item of abolitionist propaganda was published in 1852. *Uncle Tom's Cabin* by Harriet Beecher Stowe presented a fictionalized account of slavery, which through Stowe's eyes was an abominable sin. Within a year of publication, the book had sold over 300,000 copies and was reissued numerous times. The abolitionist message was brought to an enormous new audience, not only through those who read the book but also through those who saw dramatizations of the book in local theaters across the nation.

In response to the Kansas-Nebraska Act of 1854, some critics of slavery determined that more drastic measures should be taken, and a few began to advocate violence. Essentially, the act nullified the Missouri Compromise of 1820 that forbade slavery in the northern portions of the Louisiana Purchase. The Kansas and Nebraska territories would determine if they were slave or free through popular sovereignty. Everyone generally agreed that Nebraska would be free; however, Kansas was up for grabs. Both proslavery and abolition supporters sent "settlers" to Kansas to assure their side won the vote. In the end, two separate territorial governments, one proslavery and the other antislavery, were created. As the tension escalated, violence ensued.

Among the most fervent abolitionists in Kansas was John Brown, a 56-year-old Connecticut native. Brown's antislavery zeal had prompted him to move to Kansas with his sons in order to fight to make sure Kansas was a free state. After a proslavery mob attacked and burned the free-state town of Lawrence, Kansas, Brown and seven other men, including four of his sons, went on the offensive. In May 1856, they targeted the proslavery town of Pottawatomie and murdered five proslavery settlers. Known as the Pottawatomie Massacre, Brown's actions set off a guerrilla war in Kansas that lasted through the fall.

Up until the Kansas-Nebraska Act, most abolitionists had been averse to the use of violence. But by the late 1850s, this aversion had faded, and some began to openly court armed conflict. After returning from Kansas, John Brown began to seek northeastern support for his cause, making visits to Massachusetts and establishing there his Secret Six, who would help fund his planned invasion of the South. He gained financial support from prominent abolitionists, including Samuel Gridley Howe, Thomas Wentworth Higginson, Theodore Parker, Franklin B. Sanborn, Gerrit Smith, and George L. Stearns. Brown also discussed his plans with Frederick Douglass and asked the former slave to join him. Douglass declined, considering the plan hopeless and suicidal. On October 16, 1859, Brown and a group of 18 followers attacked and won control of a federal arsenal in Harpers Ferry, Virginia (in present-day West Virginia). The slave uprising Brown hoped to spark did not occur, and he very quickly found himself pinned down in the arsenal by citizens and the local militia. U.S. troops under the command of Robert E. Lee eventually forced Brown to surrender.

John Brown was tried in a Virginia court for treason and sentenced to death. He and six of his followers were hanged. Throughout the North on December 2, 1859, Brown's execution date, church bells rang out, flags were flown at half-mast, and buildings were draped in black. William Lloyd Garrison, a longtime advocate of nonviolent measures to end slavery, proclaimed that Brown's death had shown him that violence was needed to destroy slavery.

Even after the election of Abraham Lincoln in 1860 and the beginning of the Civil War in 1861, abolitionists continued their struggle to end slavery and to promote the civil rights of African Americans. During the Civil War, abolitionists, including Frederick Douglass, encouraged President Abraham Lincoln to make ending slavery a goal of the war and pressured him to deliver the Emancipation Proclamation. Many abolitionists joined the Union Army and personally took active roles in military operations to ensure the success of the Union cause. After the war, abolitionists were in the forefront of the fight for black suffrage and protection of freedmen's civil rights. Abolitionists in Congress advocated the creation of the Freedmen's Bureau and brought forward the constitutional amendments that abolished slavery, guaranteed citizenship, and gave suffrage to black men.

It is true that some abolitionists held racist views and adopted paternalistic attitudes toward African Americans. Additionally, abolitionism failed to change society's fundamental inequalities and injustices faced by blacks in America. Yet the movement that Garrison and others launched, and that thousands of activists kept alive for over 30 years, was instrumental in the fight to end slavery and in the eventual passage of the Thirteenth Amendment.

IRA LEE BERLET

See also

Fugitive Slave Act (1793); Slavery; Slavery in the Antebellum South

Further Reading:

Dillon, Merton L. *Slavery Attacked: Southern Slaves and Their Allies, 1619–1865*. Baton Rouge: Louisiana State University Press, 1990.

Duberman, Martin, ed. *The Antislavery Vanguard: New Essays on the Abolitionist*. Princeton, NJ: Princeton University Press, 1965.

Goodman, Paul. *Of One Blood: Abolitionism and the Origins of Racial Equality*. Berkeley: University of California Press, 1998.

McCarthy, Timothy Patrick, and John Stauffer, eds. *Prophets of Protest: Reconsidering the History of American Abolitionism*. New York: New Press, 2006.

Oubre, Claude F. *Forty Acres and a Mule: The Freedmen's Bureau and Black Land Ownership*. Baton Rouge: Louisiana State University Press, 1978.

Perry, Lewis, and Michael Fellman, eds. *Antislavery Reconsidered: New Perspectives on the Abolitionists*. Baton Rouge: Louisiana State University Press, 1979.

Stewart, James B. *Holy Warriors: The Abolitionist and American Slavery*. New York: Hill and Wang, 1976.

Abraham Lincoln and the Emancipation of Slaves

Abraham Lincoln was elected president on November 6, 1860, and even before he took office, South Carolina seceded from the Union. The Confederate States of America was born in early February 1861, and by mid-April the Civil War had begun, starting with the Confederate attack on Fort Sumter. Within another month, North Carolina had seceded, thus bring the Confederacy to its full complement. With the Union defeat at Bull Run that July, it became clear that rebellion would not be put down easily.

This quick and dramatic succession of events united the antislavery forces in Congress and the military to act on their convictions. In early August, Congress passed the First Confiscation Act, which nullified all claims to fugitive slaves involved in the South's war effort. These slaves worked in munition factories, produced needed foods, and served as teamsters and laborers in the Confederate Army. At the end of the month, General John Frémont freed the slaves of pro-Confederate owners in Missouri, but Lincoln claimed Frémont had exceeded the intention of Congress in doing so and eventually ordered him to revise his emancipation edict. Likewise, when General David Hunter began recruiting black soldiers in South Carolina in 1862,

Lincoln's War Department refused to fund his effort, and when Hunter emancipated all slaves in South Carolina, Florida, and Georgia, Lincoln proclaimed his action null and void.

Lincoln attempted to steer what he saw as a middle ground. He asked Congress to adopt a policy that employed federal funds to entice states to emancipate slaves gradually and compensate owners. Indeed, on March 16, 1862, Congress abolished slavery in Washington, D.C.; agreed to compensate owners who were loyal to the Union; and funded efforts to colonize freed slaves in places such as Liberia. Lincoln had long been enamored of these so-called colonization plans, which he saw as a legitimate answer to the solution of the race issue. His insistence on compensation to slave owners seemed to him a political imperative at the time based on the belief, imbedded in the Constitution he swore to uphold as president, that slaves were property. However, when Lincoln tried to convince congressmen from the border states that a policy of compensation, colonization, and gradual emancipation was the best way to proceed, he was roundly rejected.

Congress moved quickly on its own agenda. In July 1862, it passed the Second Confiscation Act, which provided for freeing the slaves and seizing and selling the property of anyone involved in or abetting the rebellion. Furthermore, it prohibited military personnel from making decisions on any claims to freedom by fugitive slaves or surrendering any fugitives to those who claimed them. Most significantly, however, Congress authorized Lincoln to employ African Americans to put down the rebellion. Lincoln now had to make a decision, which, he later claimed, was a decision between choosing the Constitution or preserving the Union.

Still clinging to the notion of colonization for emancipated slaves and wavering between gradual and immediate emancipation, on September 22, 1862, Lincoln proclaimed that, effective January 1, 1863, slaves in any rebellious state or part thereof would be forever free. He committed the federal government and the military to safeguard the freedom of the former slaves. This preannouncement allowed Confederate states the opportunity to rejoin the Union by sending duly elected representatives to Congress, for the Proclamation defined states or parts thereof in rebellion as those not represented in Congress. When January arrived, however, it was clear that this political gambit failed. Slaves were freed in the following rebellious states: Arkansas, Texas, Mississippi, Alabama, Florida, Georgia, North Carolina, and South Carolina. Slaves in parts of Louisiana and Virginia were also freed.

In his Proclamation, Lincoln asked the newly freed slaves to shun violence except in defense of themselves and, in the Republican Party preference for free soil and free labor, to work faithfully for reasonable wages. He also invited emancipated slaves in good condition to join the Union Army and Navy. This last provision, echoing the previous intent of Congress, proved to be quite important. Lincoln wrote in an 1864 letter that his difficult decision to emancipate the slaves had turned out quite for the good, because it added to the Union military forces 130,000 black soldiers it would not otherwise have had. Even with this additional manpower, however, Lincoln was forced to initiate a very unpopular conscription program.

The Emancipation Proclamation did not, contrary to popular belief, free all the slaves, only those living in areas and states declared to be in rebellion. Thus, for example, slaves in border states that permitted slavery but remained pro-Union, and slaves in Confederate territory already under Union domination were not freed. Although Lincoln claimed that he had found the institution of slavery to be immoral from his earliest memory, he was not a radical abolitionist, as some in his party were, nor was he ever one to miss scoring a political point. By freeing the slaves only in Confederate hands, he managed not only to raise an army but to disrupt plantation lifestyle and production, while avoiding the slavery issue altogether in those areas contributing to the Union cause. Only when the Thirteenth Amendment was ratified on December 18, 1865, was slavery completely abolished in the United States.

Benjamin F. Shearer

Further Reading:

Fredrickson, George. *The Arrogance of Race: Historical Perspectives on Slavery, Racism, and Social Inequality.* Middletown, CT: Wesleyan University Press, 1988.

Guelzo, Allen C. *Lincoln's Emancipation Proclamation: The End of Slavery in America.* New York: Simon & Schuster, 2004.

Abu-Jamal, Mumia (b. 1954)

Mumia Abu-Jamal is a famous African American prisoner who many believe is being punished more for his political convictions than for any criminal actions. Born Wesley Cook on April 24, 1954, Abu-Jamal became the Minister of Information for the Philadelphia chapter of the Black Panther Party (BPP) in 1969. Nationwide the BPP was highly critical of the role of the police in black communities. The BPP was a target of both the FBI and local police forces, including that of Philadelphia. There are over 600 pages of FBI documents detailing the surveillance of Abu-Jamal, who had no criminal record.

Early on the morning of December 9,1981, Officer Daniel Faulkner stopped William Cook, who was driving the wrong way on a one-way street, and the two fought. Cook's brother, Abu-Jamal, a licensed taxi driver, witnessed the scene from his taxi and got out. Both Abu-Jamal and Officer Faulkner were shot, the latter fatally. Abu-Jamal had a permit for a gun, a .38 that was found at the scene. He had been shot twice by Faulkner's weapon and was bleeding heavily. Police quickly arrived, and Abu-Jamal was arrested and charged with first-degree murder, his gun supposedly the murder weapon. He was also severely beaten by the police and taken to the hospital for his injuries. In 1982 a jury found Abu-Jamal guilty of murder. He was sentenced to death.

Convicted police killer Mumia Abu-Jamal is seen in this undated file photo. (AP Photo/Jennifer E. Beach)

The Philadelphia police force has a long history of corruption, brutality, and racism. Chief Frank Rizzo is on record making racist remarks and is known for overseeing a police department that brutalized African Americans. In 1979, the U.S. Justice Department (DOJ) claimed that Philadelphia's political leaders were complicit with police brutality. In support of the charges, the DOJ noted that within a four-year period 290 people, mostly people of color, had been shot by the Philadelphia police. When he became mayor, Frank Rizzo seemed especially tolerant of such incidents. Several of the officers involved in Abu-Jamal's case were later sent to prison on a variety of charges including tampering with evidence.

A guiding premise in U.S. courtrooms is that a person is presumed innocent unless shown to be guilty beyond a reasonable doubt. There are many doubts about whether this was the case in Abu-Jamal's trial. The presiding judge in 1981 was Albert Sabo. Sabo had close relations with law enforcement personnel and organizations in Philadelphia. Sabo had sentenced a record number of people to death, with 29 out of the 31 sentenced being people of color. Sabo presided over subsequent hearings in Abu-Jamal's case with commentators noting his hostility to Abu-Jamal and his favoritism toward the prosecution. Despite Abu-Jamal's objections, attorney Anthony Jackson was appointed to defend him, although the lawyer felt unprepared for this case. Jackson was not given adequate funds to investigate the evidence and to hire expert witnesses. After a challenging selection process, the jury had only two blacks, and was not statistically representative of Philadelphia's racial mix. Several of the white jury members had friends or relatives on the police force.

There were questions about the truthfulness of testimony given at Abu-Jamal's trial. A police officer and a hospital security guard testified that they had heard the badly wounded Abu-Jamal, in his hospital bed, shout that he had done the shooting and hoped Faulkner would die. Another police officer, Gary Wakshul, who was with Abu-Jamal at the same time, had written in his report that Abu-Jamal made no comments. Attending doctors also claimed they heard no such confession. In 1995, at an appeal, Wakshul testified that he had in fact heard Abu-Jamal's supposed statement. At the original trial, the defense was misled about Wakshul's whereabouts and he was not called to testify.

There were also questions about alleged eyewitness accounts. At least two witnesses seem to have been given favorable treatment by the police in exchange for testimony corroborating the police account. Witnesses favorable to Abu-Jamal, on the other hand, were treated with hostility. Unusually for a murder case, no appropriate ballistics tests were conducted. Abu-Jamal's hands were not inspected at the time of his arrest to test for gun residues. Neither gun was properly examined. There are doubts regarding whether Abu-Jamal could even have shot Faulkner given the ways in which both alleged murderer and victim were situated. In his summation speech the prosecuting attorney used political statements Abu-Jamal had made as a teenager as evidence that Abu-Jamal wished to kill a cop.

In 1989 and in 1998 Abu-Jamal's appeals to the Pennsylvania Supreme Court were denied, but in 2001 a federal appeals court overturned the death sentence on the grounds that the jurors had been improperly instructed. The U.S. Supreme Court reaffirmed this in 2011. In 2012, the Pennsylvania Supreme Court rejected Abu-Jamal's appeal for an overturning of his conviction. Abu-Jamal is now in the general prison population, sentenced to life imprisonment without parole. The Pennsylvania Fraternal Order of Police and Maureen Faulkner continue to insist Abu-Jamal is guilty. His many supporters insist that only a new and fair trial will serve justice.

Abu-Jamal is a published author, a radio commentator, and a journalist who has used these forums for advancing social justice. He has many and international supporters, including Amnesty International, the NAACP, and Nobel Peace Prize laureate Desmond Tutu. There are two streets in France named for him. His supporters agree he did not receive anything approaching a fair trial.

Barbara Chasin

Further Reading:

Abu-Jamal, Mumia. *Live from Death Row.* Boston: Addison-Wesley Publishing Company, 1995.

Amnesty International. *A Life in the Balance: The Case of Mumia Abu-Jamal.* Amnesty International. AMR 51/01/00 February 2000.

Lindorff, David. *Killing Time: An Investigation into the Death Row Case of Mumia Abu-Jamal.* Monroe, ME: Common Courage Press, 2003.

Williams, Timothy. "Execution Case Dropped against Abu-Jamal." *New York Times.* December 7, 2011. http://www.nytimes.com/2011/12/08/us/execution-case-dropped-against-convicted-cop-killer.html.

Academic Racism

Academic racism refers to academic theories and scholarly research and writing that perpetuate the notion of racial superiority. Scientists and academicians in the United States have often used their work as the basis for advocating racist theories. Academic racism can emanate from a diversity of fields, including science, social science, history, and the humanities. As these theories of academic racism become dominant within academia, racism can be perpetuated through the higher-education curriculum, as well as through popular press and media. Because these theories are endowed with what is perceived to be the scientific and intellectual integrity of academia, they are often automatically conferred legitimacy and authority by students, popular media, and government decision makers.

Throughout the twentieth century, many eminent academicians in the United States used their work to advance theories of racial superiority. The most well known early example was the eugenics movement, which was forwarded in the United States by Charles Benedict Davenport, a biologist with a PhD from Harvard University. Embraced by public-health officials, activists, and the intelligentsia, the eugenics movement resulted in as many as 20,000 forced sterilizations by the late 1930s and had a profound effect on public policy and in shaping the discourse on the emerging racial and ethnic diversity of the United States in the twentieth century.

Academic racism and its effects on public policy were most discernible during the period between the 1880s and the 1920s. Negative reaction to the changing immigrant stream in the United States led to one of the most evident applications of academic racism to national policy making. The majority of immigrants during this period were unskilled workers or farmers from eastern and southern European countries who were radically different from the Protestant, English, German, and Scandinavian immigrants of the earlier immigrant flows. In the early 1900s, eugenicists such as scientist H. H. Goddard promoted the use of the new "intelligence quotient" test, the IQ test. When the United States entered World War I in 1917, eugenicists saw the potential for testing with a large sample and convinced the army to administer the IQ test on draftees, which resulted in a sample of almost 2 million draftees. Based on these results, Henry Laughlin from the Eugenics Record Office testified before Congress that more than 75 percent of the new immigrants were feebleminded and that their presence, along with their high fertility rate, was a threat to the biological makeup of the country. Based on this testimony, Congress passed the Immigration Act of 1924 (also known as the National Origins Act). This act placed stringent restrictions on immigration by setting quotas for incoming immigrants based on the 1910 census, rather than the 1920 census. This effectively stymied the flow of "undesirable" immigrants from southern and eastern Europe.

The field of psychology and the advent of the IQ test remains a racially contested arena. In the 1960s, William Shockley, a physicist at Stanford University and a Nobel Prize winner, advocated programs of voluntary sterilization of people with an IQ score lower than 100. In 1969, educational psychologist Arthur Jensen published an article in the *Harvard Education Review* attacking Head Start programs, claiming that African American children only have an average IQ of 85 and that no amount of social engineering would improve their performance. Within a few years Jensen's article had become one of the most widely cited studies in psychology. In the 1980s, J. Phillipe Rushton, a widely published Canadian psychology professor and an elected fellow of the American Association for the Advancement of Science as well as of the American Psychological Association, argued that behavioral differences among African Americans, whites, and Asians are the result of evolutionary variations in reproductive strategies. African Americans are at one extreme, Rushton claimed, because they produce large numbers of offspring but offer them little care; at the other extreme are Asians, who have fewer children but indulge them; whites lie somewhere in between. Further, Rushton argued that African Americans have smaller brains and larger genitals than whites, making them less intelligent and more promiscuous. More recently, in their 1994 book *The Bell Curve: Intelligence and Class Structure in American Life*, Richard J. Herrnstein and Charles Murray presented an argument for racial superiority based on IQ, which, they claimed, was scientifically supported by large-scale statistical evidence.

Beyond introducing the racist ideology into public discourse, the consequences of academic racism can be observed in many areas of public policy. As evidenced by the Immigration Act of 1924, policy makers are liable to act on, and legislate based on, the racist theories that academics espouse. Present-day arguments against the welfare state often echo the theories of Social Darwinism. The eugenics movement has been reconstructed in recent decades in the form of cash incentives for the poor, who are disproportionately black, to undergo sterilization or other extreme forms of birth control. In the 1990s, legislators in Kansas backed a proposal to offer $500 to any welfare mother who agreed to have Norplant (a five-year contraceptive device) surgically implanted. Legislators in Connecticut and Florida also introduced bills that would offer cash bonuses to welfare recipients who would accept Norplant. In Florida, a bill was introduced to offer $400 to men living below the poverty line to have a vasectomy. In Colorado, legislators introduced a bill that would have offered early release to criminals who had a vasectomy. One scholar stated that "the growth of scientific ideas within society is not normally haphazard. The ideas of scientists usually do not arise in some vacuum, but can be connected with underlying political or economic trends" (Billig 1998).

Tracy Chu

See also
Racism

Further Reading:

Billig, Michael. "A Dead Idea That Will Not Lie Down." *Searchlight Magazine*, 1998.

Herrnstein, Richard J., and Charles Murray. *The Bell Curve: Intelligence and Class Structure in American Life*. New York: Free Press, 1994.

Mehler, Barry. "In Genes We Trust: When Science Bows to Racism." *The Public Eye: A Publication of Political Research Associates* 9, no. 1: 1995.

Accommodationism

Accommodationism refers to an ideology that endorses cooperation and concession to the viewpoint or actions of the opposition. Booker T. Washington and, to a disputable extent, Martin Luther King, Jr. are examples of black leaders who have embraced this concept as a strategy against racial segregation. Competing ideologies developed largely in response to the mass violence that blacks experienced at the hands of whites.

Washington, an influential black leader during the Jim Crow era, is widely recognized as a prominent accommodationist. He promoted black acquiescence to the system of discrimination and disenfranchisement of post-Reconstruction life as a tactic to bring about social and political empowerment. He frequently collaborated with white leaders. However, Washington's philosophy is believed to have "increased anti-black violence" (Reiland 2005: 3). In contrast to Washington's accommodationism, W.E.B. Du Bois and others advocated protest and black self-defense and launched public attacks against segregation and white aggression. Blacks aggressively confronted discrimination and violence in the Brownsville (Texas) Riot of 1906.

Although supporters of the quieter, more gradual process of change via participation in municipal politics believed that the civil rights movement was a radical response, the nonviolent protests of the 1950s and 1960s were fundamentally accommodationistic in their general concession to retaliatory white violence and cooperation with white-dominated institutions. Frustration with the mounting brutality, particularly during the Freedom Rides and Freedom Summer (Mississippi) of 1964, caused young blacks to break away from the philosophy of nonviolence in favor of a more militant and separatist approach. By the mid-1960s, violence was the widely employed strategy of protest in black ghettos.

Gladys L. Knight

See also

Black Panther Party (BPP); Du Bois, W.E.B.; Freedom Rides; Jim Crow Laws

Further Reading:

Booker, Christopher B. *"I Will Wear No Chain!": A Social History of African American Males.* Westport, CT: Praeger Publishers, 2000.

Reiland, Rabaka. "Accommodationism." In *Encyclopedia of Black Studies*, edited by Molefi Kete Asante and Mambo Ama Mazama, 1–3. Thousand Oaks, CA: Sage Publications, 2005.

"Acting White"

The "acting white" stage of life refers to that phase of social identity development during which children of color have internalized social messages about the inferiority of their own race and act like white people. Studies show that even before they reach young adulthood, minority children in the United States usually accept consciously or unconsciously the messages about the inferiority of their physical characteristics and their cultures. They have developed an internal ideology of racial subordination and ethnic inferiority and embraced it in a way that is manifested as a rejection of nonwhite characteristics. These negative ideations may be held simultaneously with and despite the existence of more positive ideas and feelings about their racial and ethnic groups. Among children and adolescents, feelings associated with acting white often involve embarrassment about the youth's ethnic/racial background.

There are both active and passive forms of acting white. Some people of color exhibiting passive, or "internal," forms are unaware of the degree to which their thoughts, feelings, and behaviors reflect the white mainstream ideology. They may demonstrate an unconscious identification with and rationalization of the oppressor's logic system. Typical attitudes may include "People are people," "If I just work hard, I will be judged by my merits," "The problem is that people of color who don't want to work hard enough mess things up for the rest of us," and "White people are generally smarter than people of color and they get ahead because they work hard." Among immigrants, a common ideation of acting white conflates the notion of becoming American—and thereby achieving social and financial success—with becoming more like white Americans. Indeed, among many immigrant groups the words *American* and *white* are effectively synonymous.

In the active form of acting white, a person of color may consciously identify with the dominant group and its ideology. For example, some people of color are opposed to affirmative action because they believe people of color are less successful solely due to their own laziness and pathological culture. Behaviors include accepting and conforming to white social, cultural, and institutional standards and seeking interaction with and validation from whites and white social groups. A person of color may also avoid organizations, committees, and social groups that focus on race or racism because participation in such groups emphasizes the racial identity with which she is uncomfortable. Likewise, she will often "go along with" or excuse the racist behaviors she observes.

Acting white can also be manifested as conflict with members of one's family or racial group. A person of color who is acting white will often refuse (or be unable) to recognize and acknowledge institutional racism. A person of color may also actively reject association with his or her ethnic group, such as by refusing to speak the home language with parents or peers, eschewing "ethnic" food and garb, or disassociating from ethnoreligious organizations. Alternatively, an individual may act white only in certain contexts, such as in the workplace or at school, but embrace her race and ethnic culture in other contexts.

When racism is perceived as existing only at the individual level, even negative race-based experiences can be rationalized as being external to the victim's own identity. People of color who retain this worldview successfully rationalize efforts on the part of others to change their consciousness. Even people of color who experience an urge to question their current status may find themselves seduced into remaining in place by the rewards offered from the dominant white society.

Khyati Joshi

See also

Oppositional Culture

Further Reading:

Cross, William E., Jr. *Shades of Black: Diversity in African American Identity*. Philadelphia: Temple University Press, 1991.

Jackson, Bailey, and Rita Hardiman. "Conceptual Foundations for Social Justice Courses." In *Teaching for Diversity and Social Justice*, edited by Maurianne Adams, Lee Anne Bell, and Pat Griffin, 16–29. New York: Routledge, 1997.

Tatum, Beverly D. *"Why Are All the Black Kids Sitting Together in the Cafeteria?" and Other Conversations about Race*. New York: Basic Books, 1997.

Advertising

Racism in advertising is the intentional and unintentional use of race in an attempt to sell products. In the past, racism was almost an accepted form of advertising and was often rooted in the racialized ideas associated with morality and cleanliness. In the United States, this centered largely on African Americans as inferior and used stereotypes such as the "Mammy," the "Savage," and the "Minstrel." Fortunately, attitudes about race have evolved to a point that overt racism is largely absent from advertising; nevertheless, racism hidden behind humor remains a large part of the advertising landscape.

Media, and the advertising it promotes, plays an essential role in defining the social world, including our ideas about race. As one of the most powerful institutions in American society, advertisers, in particular, provide us with definitions about who we are as individuals, groups, and larger collectives, such as nations. They support and reinforce norms and values of our society and perpetuate certain ways of seeing the world and peoples within that world. Advertisers also define what race signifies in the United States; they support and create norms and values related to race; and they tell what we can and can't say about race.

Racism has a long history in advertising largely due to the fact that advertising does not exist in isolation from the society in which it is embedded. Advertisers draw ideas, values, and norms from the same "common sense" knowledge that is part of a pool of knowledge that informs all of our lives. This means that, in terms of race, it is common, and often encouraged, to present racial stereotypes in advertising as these socially constructed ideals are part of this "common sense" knowledge. Brands, such as PopChips, Burger King, and American Apparel, have been accused of using racism in their advertising. The PopChips example is one in which a "white" actor was painted in brownface and asked to reflect stereotypes of Indians and other South Asians. The advertisement, which is captioned with the phrase "These are the Bombay," is presented as a minstrel show that has the ultimate goal of humor and the presentation of a quality product. Unfortunately the advertisement actually reflected negative and harmful stereotypes of Indians.

Every advertisement we see causes us to conjure up shared beliefs and frames that allow us to understand both the advertisement and the larger world. Although explicit

Advertising Technologies and Race

Particular technologies can also be used to support and further racial ideas in advertising. Photoshop is often used in the manipulation of advertising images and is not limited to making women "look" thinner, it is also used to make models "look" *whiter*. This process is another subtle endeavor by advertising firms to use racism to sell a product. In this case, advertisers use the long-held stereotype that whiteness is the highest form of beauty. In a controversial advertisement by L'Oreal, the model, Beyoncé, had her skin lightened in a print ad. When the original and the advertised images were compared, it was evident that the model's skin was "lightened" to make her "look" whiter. The implementation of this method is used for the same reason all forms of racism are used in advertising—to sell products. In this particular case the ad suggests that whiteness is the form of beauty that all peoples should attempt to attain.

representations of racism have largely disappeared from mainstream media, racism remains. No racial group is immune from the representations; however, minority groups are largely represented with negative and demeaning images. Aside from the clear selling point of the advertisement, they are essentially about making meaning. All advertisement, therefore, must take into account the qualities of the product they are selling, but also they must find ways to make these products meaningful.

A brand can have numerous meanings attached to it, including gender, social standing, nationality, and race. Each of these meanings can be quickly, and sometimes, unconsciously invoked in the viewer. A brand can also stand for other meanings, such as trustworthiness, purity, and family. The Marlboro Man is an example in which the use of red and white box is used to signify freedom, satisfaction, and masculinity. These advertisements are used as a way to increase the value of products, but they are also created to resonate with social and ideological values, thereby creating a particular image in the mind of the consumer, which ultimately leads to the purchasing of a particular product. In terms of race, these techniques serve to create a dichotomy of "us" versus "them." In many cultures, this dichotomy suggests that the "us" are white and modern and the "them" represent minorities who are violent, problematic, and threatening.

This separatism creates power differentials that are often expressed in racial terms. Advertisers take advantage of these socially based power differentials, stereotypes, beliefs, and norms to sell products while also influencing the definitions and understanding we have of race and racism. Nevertheless, advertisers are generally recirculating information they find in the larger society (Kitch, 2001). Advertisers can be thought of as a mirror for society, reflecting its good and bad qualities. They continue, in the present, to search for constituents who will buy their products, and they accomplish this feat through the creation and buttressing of race-based hierarchies and difference.

James W. Love

Further Reading:

Ferranti, Michelle. "An Odor of Racism: Vaginal Deodorants in African-American Beauty Culture and Advertising." *Advertising and Society Review* 11, no. 4 (2011).

Kitch, Carolyn. *The Girl on the Magazine Cover: The Origins of Visual Stereotypes in American Mass Media*. Chapel Hill: University of North Carolina Press, 2001.

McCracken, G. "The Value of the Brand: An Anthropological Perspective." In D. Aaker and A.L. Biel (eds.), *Brand Equity Is Advertising: Advertising's Role in Building Strong Brands*. Mahwah, NJ: Lawrence Erlbaum, 1993.

Van Dijk, T.A. "Discourse, Power and Access." In C.R. Caldas-Coulthard and M.Coulthard (eds.), *Texts and Practices: Readings in Critical Discourse Analysis*, pp. 84–104. London: Routledge, 1996.

Affirmative Action

Affirmative action is based on presidential directives, government guidelines and regulations, laws, and court decisions and can be defined as a government policy designed to combat discrimination and equalize opportunity for traditionally disadvantaged groups by giving preferential treatment to equally qualified minorities and women in employment, college admission, and government contracting. Literally, affirmative action means taking affirmative or positive steps to ensure equal opportunity for minorities and women. However, in the public mind, the meaning of

Affirmative Discrimination: Ethnic Inequality and Public Policy

Published in 1974 by Nathan Glazer, a distinguished Harvard sociologist, *Affirmative Discrimination: Ethnic Inequality and Public Policy* was the first systematic, vocal challenge to the government's affirmative action policy, which was designed to counter discrimination and equalize opportunity by giving preferential treatment to equally qualified women and members of minority groups historically discriminated against in employment, college admissions, and government contracting.

In this influential book, Glazer argues that as an effort to redress past discrimination against minority groups as well as women, the color- and group-conscious affirmative action policy implemented in the 1970s counters the traditional U.S. public policy that emphasizes the primacy of the individual and threatens to overturn the principle of fairness to the individual citizen. He concludes that despite its admirable intentions, affirmative action is indeed "affirmative discrimination" against individuals. He suggests a return to the simple and clear understanding of individual rights rather than group rights and an adoption of public policy that promotes fairness and equality regardless of race, color, or national origin. This book generated a huge controversy after its publication and set off an ongoing debate on affirmative action that continues today.

PHILIP YANG

affirmative action can be highly subjective and represent notions as varied as equal opportunity; proportional representation; special privilege given to minorities and women; reserved quotas of jobs, school spots, or government funding for minorities and women; or even government-mandated discrimination against white Americans.

No civil rights laws or executive orders on affirmative action authorize the use of reverse discrimination, quotas, or even preferential treatment. No laws or government regulations endorse the idea that unqualified or less qualified minorities or women can be hired, admitted, or given government contracts. In practice, however, some organizations did use quotas for minorities and women, lower standards to admit or hire less qualified minority and female applicants, or give contracts to less qualified firms owned by minorities and women. These practices violate the laws or regulations and are not what affirmative action intends to be. Court rulings, nevertheless, did sanction, either explicitly or implicitly, the use of preferential treatment of minorities and women.

For example, in the first significant case on affirmative action addressed by the U.S. Supreme Court, *Regents of the University of California v. Bakke* (1978), the Court held that while race could not be used as a quota to set aside specific positions for minority candidates, it could be considered as a factor in admission. As Supreme Court Justice Harry Blackmun put it, "In order to go beyond racism, we must first take account of race. There is no other way. And to treat some persons equally, we must treat them differently." Other rulings that allowed for a temporary use of preferential treatment for redressing past discrimination include *United Steelworkers of America v. Weber* (1979), which permitted the union to favor minorities in special training programs; *Sheet Metal Workers v. EEOC* (1986), which approved a specific quota of minority workers for the union; *International Association of Firefighters v. City of Cleveland* (1986), which gave the green light to the promotion of minorities over more senior whites; *United States v. Paradise* (1987), which endorsed favorable treatment of minority state troopers for purposes of promotion; *Johnson v. Transportation Agency, Santa Clara County* (1987), which approved preference in hiring of minorities and women over equally qualified men and whites; and *Metro Broadcasting v. FCC* (1990), which supported federal programs aimed at increasing minority ownership of broadcasting licenses.

Before the 1960s, discrimination against minorities and women was widespread. Conscious efforts were made by the federal government in the 1940s and 1950s to reduce discrimination in employment. In the early 1940s, President Franklin Roosevelt issued executive orders to halt discrimination in the federal civil service and created the Fair Employment Practices Committee. During the 1950s, President Harry S. Truman issued two executive orders to establish fair employment procedures within the federal government structure, to nullify discrimination in the armed forces, and to formulate compliance procedures for government

Hundreds of demonstrators gathered to support affirmative action and the University of Michigan's admissions policies as the U.S. Supreme Court prepared to debate the issue. On June 23, 2003, a divided Supreme Court ruled that universities can consider race in the admissions process but that race cannot be the deciding factor. (AP Photo/Teru Iwasaki)

contractors. The basic approach then was voluntary nondiscrimination. However, the voluntary good-faith approach proved to be ineffective and insufficient in combating deeply rooted patterns of discrimination.

Affirmative action policy emerged in the 1960s as an alternative to the early voluntary approach. It originated from a series of executive orders issued by presidents John F. Kennedy and Lyndon B. Johnson and related legislation enacted during their presidencies in the 1960s. In March 1961, President Kennedy issued Executive Order 10925, in which the phrase "affirmative action" first surfaced. The order required government contractors and subcontractors to take "affirmative action to ensure that applicants are employed, and that employees are treated during employment, without regard to their race, creed, color, or national origin." That order did, for the first time, "place the full prestige of the presidency behind the moral imperative of non-discrimination."

In the mid-1960s, the civil rights movement entered its climax, as black protests escalated. The outcome was the passage of the landmark Civil Rights Act of 1964. Title VII of the act forbade discrimination "against any individual because of such individual's race, color, religion, sex or national origin." Seeking to appease the opposition to preferential treatment, Section 703(j) of Title VII stated that "nothing contained in this title shall be interpreted to require any employer, employment agency, labor organization, or joint labor-management committee subject to this title to grant preferential treatment to any individual or to any group . . . on account of an imbalance which may exist with respect to the total number and percentage of persons of any race, color, religion, sex, or national origin" (Bureau of National Affairs, 1964).

However, simply making discrimination illegal by law was not enough. The government had to find an effective way to enforce the 1964 Civil Rights Act, to monitor the progress, and to ensure equal opportunity for every citizen. Under this context, President Johnson issued Executive Order 11246 on September 24, 1965, thereby laying an important ground for affirmative action policy. This order was a continuation of Executive Order 10925, but it proposed specific requirements. It mandated contracts with the government to include a nondiscrimination clause and federal contractors with 100 or more employees to take "affirmative action" to achieve the goal of nondiscrimination in "employment, upgrading, demotion and transfer; recruitment or recruitment advertising; layoff or termination; rates of pay or other forms of compensation; and selection for training, including apprenticeship." It required contractors and their subcontractors to submit compliance reports with information on the practices, policies, programs, and racial composition of their work force. It imposed penalties for noncompliance, in the form of cancellation, termination or suspension of federal funds, and ineligibility for further federal contracts. To implement the foregoing executive orders and the Civil Rights Act of 1964, the Equal Employment Opportunity Commission (EEOC) and the Office of Federal Contract Compliance (OFCC) located in the Department of Labor were founded.

In October 1967, President Johnson issued Executive Order 11375, which expanded affirmative action stipulations to include sex discrimination and required every federally funded organization with more than 50 employees and a contract in excess of $50,000 to submit a "written affirmative action compliance program" with goals and timetables. Goals consisted of expected percentages of new employees from various minority groups; specifically, the ethnic or racial makeup of an organization was expected to roughly match the makeup of the general population. The timetables were timelines for achieving the goals.

The enforcement of affirmative action policy continued even during the Nixon administration and Ford administration in the late 1960s and the 1970s. Executive Order 11478 of August 1969 issued by President Richard M. Nixon listed affirmative action steps. During the Carter administration, the Office of Federal Contract Compliance Programs (OFCCP, until 1975 was OFCC) published the *Construction Compliance Program Operations Manual* detailing the responsibilities of contractors, federal contract agencies, and the OFCCP. The regulations required contractors to include in affirmative action programs the utilization analysis of minority and women in the workforce and to increase their representation.

Although the executive orders and related regulations did not explicitly approve the use of preferential treatment, pressures to increase the representation of minorities and women resulted in the consideration of race, ethnicity, and gender in hiring, contracting, and college admissions. In various rulings, the Supreme Court ratified preferential treatment because the most important element of the 1964 act was to eliminate discrimination against minorities and women and to bring up equal opportunity. The Supreme Court called such an action of compensatory preferences for minorities and women benign race-conscious decision making.

In its most recent June 2003 rulings, the U.S. Supreme Court narrowly upheld the affirmative action policy of the University of Michigan Law School in considering race as a plus factor in the admission process. However, the Court also declared that universities cannot use rigid, quota-like point systems that use race as a decisive factor in undergraduate admissions and must adopt race-neutral policies "as soon as practical." These rulings do not draw an end to this controversy. Affirmative action will remain a highly controversial and divided issue in the years to come.

It should be noted that affirmative action was never intended to be permanent. It was considered a temporary measure for offsetting the effects of past and present discrimination. Once discrimination is no longer a major problem and everybody has an equal opportunity, affirmative action will not be needed. In his 1978 *Bakke* decision, Supreme Court Justice Blackmun speculated that race-conscious policy could be eliminated in 10 years. In her latest opinion, Justice Sandra O'Connor wrote that the Court expects that 25 years from now racial preferences "will no longer be necessary."

Since its inception, affirmative action policy has been encircled by controversies and legal challenges. Over time three major arguments for affirmative action have been developed. The compensation argument contends that affirmative action is a remedy or a compensatory measure for correcting historical and contemporary discrimination

Richmond v. Croson (1989)

In *City of Richmond v. J. A. Croson Company*, 488 U.S. 469, the U.S. Supreme Court ruled on January 23, 1989, that the City of Richmond's "Minority Business Enterprise" (MBE) program, an affirmative action program, violated the equal protection clause of the U.S. Constitution's Fourteenth Amendment. To promote minority participation in city construction contracts, the City of Richmond, Virginia, had adopted in 1983 a minority business utilization "set-aside" plan, which required successful bidders on government contracts to subcontract at least 30 percent of the dollars to minority-owned firms. The city refused the only bidder, J. A. Croson Company, on a project for the provision and installation of certain plumbing fixtures in the city jail on the grounds that the company did not meet the requirement. J. A. Croson sued the city, claiming that the MBE program violated the equal protection clause. The District Court upheld the city's ordinance in all respects. The Court of Appeal initially affirmed the ruling but later reversed it upon the Supreme Court's order of reconsideration. On appeal, the Supreme Court affirmed the reversion in a 6-to-3 vote. The Court ruled that an affirmative action program must be targeted to proven discrimination against minorities within the Richmond area. It made clear that "generalized assertions" of past racial discrimination could not justify "rigid" racial quotas for the awarding of public contracts.

Some, including Justice Thurgood Marshall, took the ruling as a setback in the affirmative action policy. Others said that the ruling did not overthrow affirmative action itself but specified the standards by which an affirmative action program could be considered legitimate. The decision, they argued, would strengthen rather than weaken affirmative action. In the decade after the ruling, local governments created more than 100 new MEB programs.

Dong-Ho Cho

against minorities and women. Since past and present discrimination put minorities and women in a disadvantageous position to compete with white males, *temporary* preferential treatment should be given to minorities and women until everybody is starting from the same point. This race/gender-conscious remedy is the prelude to color- and gender-blind competition.

Emphasized in recent debates, the diversity argument claims that affirmative action is necessary to diversify the student population and the workforce (e.g., Jackson, 1995). This new argument departs from the compensation argument in moving affirmative action from a temporary measure to an open-ended task because of the necessity and desirability of diversity.

Finally, the effective argument maintains that affirmative action is effective and beneficial to the whole society. It has significantly increased the representation of minorities and women in educational institutions and the workforce; it has benefited not only minorities but also white women and their families as a result of now having two wage earners in their households; and it has helped corporations to diversify their labor force and to reach out to consumers of different ethnic groups.

At the opposite camp, opponents have made four major arguments against affirmative action. The reverse-discrimination argument argues that affirmative action is reverse discrimination against white males. Namely, white males have become victims of affirmative action. Some white men contest that since they personally have not discriminated against minorities or women, why should they be unfairly punished for past discrimination. Some argue that reverse discrimination has heightened racial division, resentment, and disharmony and that it pits one group against another.

The nonmeritocracy argument holds that affirmative action disregards individual merit and lowers the quality of the labor force or student body by giving positions or admissions to less qualified persons since set-aside quotas must be filled by less qualified candidates.

The ineffectiveness argument asserts that affirmative action is ineffective in advancing the positions of minorities and women (e.g., Smith and Welch, 1984). Some contend that well-off minorities reap the benefits of affirmative action programs to the detriment of poor minorities, since they are more likely to be preferred over those truly disadvantaged who lack job skills, educational preparation, and resources (e.g., Wilson, 1987). Furthermore, some whites who

Tokenism

Tokenism is a modern form of racism involving a symbolic but empty gesture of support for diversity. It can be classified as racism because it helps to maintain certain stereotypes and keeps the structure of racist institutions intact. Although clothed with the language and image of egalitarianism and "political correctness," tokenism is only a superficial attempt to embrace multiculturalism; it rarely results in the outcomes it purports to advance. Tokenism can exist in virtually any social context, from the workplace to educational settings to social situations. It diminishes the persons of color involved by attaching the value of their presence to their race or ethnicity rather than to their contribution or performance, which has the effect both of isolating them and of robbing them of their individuality by placing them in the position of representative and spokesperson for their racial or ethnic group.

The quintessential example of tokenism is the practice of hiring or appointing a person from an underrepresented group to a position of visibility and, by appearances, of substantial responsibility. Such a step is often undertaken in response to past criticism or to avoid future criticism of an organization's lack of diversity. The person's differences are highlighted, and his or her role more often than not is prescribed and limited in power, with real decision-making power remaining in another person or in the organization's majority group. The situation is therefore robbed of its opportunity to foment change because the "token" is not enabled or permitted to undertake the advances in diversity that are his or her putative role in the organization.

Khyati Joshi

are rejected for college admissions or employment might be poor and disadvantaged ones who need help the most.

The counter-productivity argument contends that affirmative action hurts the very minorities and women it intends to help. On the one hand, qualified and competent minority members and women may be viewed as less qualified and as being favored by the government, and be stereotyped as people who cannot really make it on their own merit. On the other hand, it could create a feeling of inferiority or self-doubt among its beneficiaries and undermine their self-esteem. Along this line, some opponents (e.g., Sowell, 1984) argue that affirmative action may discourage hard work and acquisition of skills since it encourages minorities to think that they can still get admitted or employed, even if they do not work at it.

Opposition to the existing affirmative action policy led to some collective actions at the state and national levels. Proposition 209 (the California Civil Rights Initiative), passed by California voters in November 1996 and effective in November 1997, was the first ballot measure in the nation that scrapped affirmative action policy. However, despite some countermaneuvers, affirmative action remains a national policy today.

Both sides of the debate have their valid points. It is difficult to reconcile the conflicting interests involved. It is more fruitful to work out compromises or alternatives that could accomplish the same goals. Since affirmative action has never been intended to be permanent, the real question is, Is now the time to abolish this policy? There are currently two approaches to this question: "end it" represented by the conservative Republicans, and "mend it" represented by former president Bill Clinton. To determine whether to end it or mend it, some believe a comprehensive overhaul of affirmative action policy and programs is needed; specifically, we need to evaluate whether the goals of affirmative action policy have been accomplished and whether preferential treatment toward minorities and women (the means) is the best way to achieve the goals of affirmative action. An Associated Press poll conducted in February–March 2003 found that 59 percent of the respondents considered the country "not close" or "not too close" to eliminating discrimination against racial/ethnic minorities, while 38 percent responded with "very close" or "fairly close." Fifty-one percent of the respondents believed that affirmative action programs are needed to help minorities such as blacks and Hispanics, compared to 43 percent responding with "not needed." The Clinton administration completed a comprehensive review of all federal affirmative action programs in July 1996. Based on the review, Clinton declared that "when affirmative action is done right, it is flexible, it is fair, and it works." He set four criteria for all affirmative action programs to comply with: (1) no quotas, in theory or in practice; (2) no illegal discrimination of any kind, including reverse discrimination; (3) no preference for unqualified individuals for jobs or other opportunities; and (4) termination of programs once the goals have been achieved.

There are other alternatives to affirmative action beyond the yes/no framework. One alternative is affirmative action based on class or economic status, or giving preference to people who are at an economic disadvantage, regardless of their race or gender. This option is favored by most Americans of different races. Another alternative is to create diversity programs or use diversity approaches. Opinion polls found that most Americans favor diversity. But diversity can be achieved by programs other than affirmative action. The "top 10 percent rule" in college admissions in Texas is a telling example. Since 1997, the top 10 percent of students in each graduating class of the public high schools, including rich or poor ones and racially segregated or mixed ones, have received automatic admission to any of the public universities or colleges in Texas, including the flagship campus in Austin. This program appears to work well in maintaining the ethnic diversity in the University of Texas system. In California, ranking in the top 4 percent of the graduating class of any public high school makes students eligible for admission to at least one of the University of California campuses. Outreach programs that attempt to recruit or reach out to underrepresented minorities and women can help achieve the same goal of diversifying a student body or the workforce without using race or gender.

Philip Yang

See also

Berea College v. Kentucky (1908); College Admissions, Discrimination in; Educational Achievement Gap; Hiring Practices; UC Berkeley Bake Sale. Documents: *Regents of the University of California v. Bakke* (1978); Glass Ceiling Commission: Summary of Recommendations (1995)

Further Reading:

Bureau of National Affairs. *The Civil Rights Act of 1964.* Washington, DC: Bureau of National Affairs, 1964.

Glazer, Nathan. *Affirmative Discrimination: Ethnic Inequality and Public Policy.* New York: Basic Books, 1974.

Jackson, Jesse. "Affirming Affirmative Action." A press release to the National Press Club, March 1, 1995.

Murray, Charles. *Losing Ground: American Social Policy, 1950–1980.* New York: Basic Books, 1984.

Smith, James, and Finis Welch. "Affirmative Action and Labor Markets." *Journal of Labor Economics* (1984): 269–299.

Sowell, Thomas. "Black Progress Can't Be Legislated." *Washington Post Outlook*, August 12, 1984, sec. B, pp. 1–2.

Wilson, William Julius. *The Truly Disadvantaged: The Inner City, the Underclass, and Public Policy.* Chicago: University of Chicago Press, 1987.

African American Humor and Comic Traditions

As a characteristic element of black culture, humor has played an important role in the lives and experiences of African Americans since slaves first encountered the New World. Historically, African American comic performances have appeared in slave shanties and on plantation fields, on the minstrel stage and in vaudeville, on the radio and television, in films and literature, in nightclubs, barbershops, and salons, in kitchens and living room parlors, and on the street corner. In short, comedy has always permeated every inch of African American culture, from the spectacular to the quotidian. Humor has historically served the purposes of emotional and spiritual survival and of gaining recognition of black humanity at the same time that it was a source of the stereotypes of black people that would impede this process. Indeed, the blurred line between black humor and black people as a source of humor generates a complex relationship of African Americans to comedy.

African American comic sensibilities originate with traditions of humor carried with slaves from Africa. Clever, ironic speech, signifying, tall tales or "lies," and animal stories featuring the trickster in various guises, for example, maintained a prominent role in the rich oral cultures of the Western and Central African countries from where the majority of black slaves were taken. While the humor of African comic traditions was reserved primarily for joyous occasions, the humor of black slaves took on a tragicomic tone that reflected the misfortune of chattel slavery. Thus, African American comedy in its earliest form developed in direct response to conditions on the plantation.

The comedy of slaves manifested as both a form of redress and a form of resistance. In 1851, Samuel A. Cartwright wrote in *Diseases and Peculiarities of the Negro Race* of a particular ailment which he called "dysaethesia aethiopica," referring to the tendency of some slaves toward "rascality." Cartwright was observing, albeit through the distorted lens of white racist culture, the comic act of "playin' the fool" or "puttin on ole massa." In other words, slaves employed a misleading naïveté and subversively engaged in Sambo-like behavior, completed work at an agonizingly slow place, stole from the plantation, and were generally duplicitous in order to sabotage the enterprise of forced servitude. Cartwright was not able to understand how this behavior, which he took to be a pathological condition, actually exhibited politically tinged irony, subterfuge, distortion, and contradiction. The comic mask of the slave would continue to resurface in black culture as mode of resistance and as a strategy for negotiating the limits of popular representation.

A staple of the black comic tradition, folktales featuring the trickster slave and powerful but ignorant master recorded in oral literature the comic resistance of those that would be considered nonhuman objects. "John and Ole Massa" tales overtly criticized the culprits of the peculiar institution, and thus were performed in slave quarters for the purposes of entertainment and redress. However, these same tales appeared in disguise as adaptations of traditional African animal tales. Brer Rabbit and Brer Fox stood in for the trickster and the slave master respectively, the camouflage of which enabled these tales to eventually become well known among white Southerners who had constant contact with black slaves and their culture. One such white Southerner, Joel Chandler Harris, famously attempted to transcribe this impressive body of folklore in his collections of "Uncle Remus stories." Harris's collections, which feature the happy-go-lucky slave Uncle Remus, brings up the problem of when African American humor comes up against what Ralph Ellison called "comedies of the grotesque," or those white performances of black culture that served to ridicule black people through crude, racist impersonations and stereotypes. The parallel legacy of black comic traditions that feature blacks as humorous individuals finds its origins on the plantation as well. The laughter of slaves was originally taken as a threat by whites who, perhaps rightly at times, assumed they were the source of amusement. Additionally, whites publicly expressed undue anxiety at the sound of black laughter, which they found to be unusually raucous and mysterious, so much so that on plantations one might find a "laughing barrel" into which slaves were required to channel their amusement. On the other hand, the sight of the happy-go-lucky, grinning and laughing slave became the source of endless amusement for the planter class. Slaves who evinced such a disposition were often prized highly as commodities. The black clown became the target of impersonation within blackface minstrelsy, America's first form of popular entertainment.

Minstrelsy, a burlesque of impersonated black performance and caricature performed originally by white actors in blackface makeup, began appearing as early as the 1820s. The humor of the minstrel stage consisted primarily of one-liners, riddles, quips, gibes, malapropisms, parodic and nonsensical stump speeches, as well as slapstick comedy and antic humor, centered on the popular myth of the happy slave and a romanticization of the plantation. The minstrel show generally had an established format featuring the interlocutor, a straight man, and the comic "endmen," Mr. Bones and Mr. Tambo, so named for the instruments they played. The form consisted of a "walkaround" and opening song, followed by the "circle" or comic exchange between the interlocutor and endmen, the olio, and finally a plantation skit or farce of well-known play; Harriet Beecher Stowe's abolitionist novel *Uncle Tom's Cabin*, for example, was frequently parodied.

With the popularity of the stage performances of Edwin Forrest and British actor Charles James Matthews (known, strangely enough, as the father of American humor), two of the first known blackface entertainers, "Negro impersonation" began to gain prevalence. Around 1828, Thomas Dartmouth (T. D.) Rice invented a caricature that would leave a lasting mark not only on the minstrel imaginary, but also on the entire conception of U.S. race relations for over a century to come. Rice relates the story of having seen a disabled, black stable groom singing to himself and dancing a peculiar dance. Impressed by the spectacle, Rice alleges to have copied the song and dance, and even to have bought the clothes off of the stable groom's back, bringing song, dance, and character to the stage. Performing the song and impersonation between acts of *The Rifle*, "Jim Crow" Rice became one of America's best known comedians. Likewise, the popular representation of "Jim Crow" soon came to stand in for all black people.

The conspicuous link between popular entertainment and legal apartheid reflects the impact of precarious representations of blackness on the conditions of unfreedom for blacks in the United States. Remarkably, many of the official institutions of apartheid culture find their influence in the minstrel tradition. For example, the Confederate rallying song "Dixie" was written by one of the Virginia Minstrels, Dan Emmett. As well, "Carry Me Back to Old Virginny" by James Bland became Virginia's state song in 1940.

Between the 1840s and 1850s, minstrelsy sprang up from coast to coast with professional troupes such as the African Melodists, the Congo Minstrels, the Buckley Serenaders, the Ethiopian Mountain Singers, and Bryant's Minstrels generating extreme popularity for this form of entertainment. While minstrelsy in its original form began to disappear as early as the 1880s, with the closing down of the Al D. Field Minstrels in 1928 possibly signifying the official end, a few troupes continued to tour into the first couple of decades of the 20th century. As well, the minstrel show appeared in vaudeville, on the radio, in film, and eventually on television after World War II. While minstrelsy is properly remembered for its lasting impact on the misrepresentation of black people, the form is simultaneously responsible for the emergence and popularity of black entertainers and the comic tradition they would instantiate. While the early minstrel stage was racially restricted to white actors, the early white minstrels report being highly influenced by the black performers Signor Cornmeali (or "Old Corn Meal") and John "Picayune" Butler of New Orleans. Occasionally, black performers found their way into white troupes—for example, when William Henry "Juba" Lane, known as the father of tap dancing, performed with minstrel troupes in the 1840s. Thomas Dilward, or "Japanese Tommy," a dwarf, also performed with white minstrels from the 1850s to the 1860s.

Black minstrel troupes, which were less successful than their white counterparts, began to appear around 1855. These troupes catered to both black and white audiences, and in either case to the lower levels of society. The small number of black bourgeoisie strongly protested these performances, while the white gentry expressed distaste in the minstrel show's lack of refinement. One of the best known black troupes, Brooker and Clayton's Georgia Minstrels, which eventually became Sam Hague's Slave Troupe of Georgia Minstrels, featured the talented Charles "Barrey" Hicks, Bob Height, and Billy Kersands at different points in time. The Georgia Minstrels were very popular in the 1870s and, over the course of the next few decades, were eventually joined by several other black troupes. F. S. Wolcott's Rabbit Foot Minstrels would continue to tour through the middle of the 19th century, and featured famous black blues singers such as Bessie Smith, Gertrude "Ma" Rainey, Big Joe Williams, Ida Cox, and Rufus Thomas, as well as the comic duo Butterbeans and Susie.

Billy Kersands of the Georgia Minstrels, who had started his own black minstrel troupe in 1885, represents one of the first black comic stars. He was well known for his comic singing, dancing, acrobatics, and drumming, but most of all for his comic facial contortions and unusually large mouth. He was known to put objects, such as billiard balls, in his mouth while dancing, for a thunderous reaction. Other well-known black minstrels include Tom Fletcher, Sam Lucas, Tom McIntosh, A. D. Sawyer, Charles Hicks, the self-proclaimed inventor of the cakewalk Billy McClain, and the prolific songwriter and cerebral comedian James Bland. Starting with these actors, the dilemma of black comedians could be characterized by the fine line between satirizing white stereotypes and contributing to those very stereotypes. What remains true of minstrelsy in the black comic tradition is that it became the arena for black performers to create and test out comic tropes and antics that would remain into the present day.

Into the first part of the 20th century, servile examples of black comedy continued to fuel performances on the mainstream stage, in vaudeville, in print, on the radio and in the new medium of silent film. Comic shorts such as *Laughing Ben*, *A Nigger in a Woodpile*, and *Who Said Chicken?* that played in nickelodeon theaters around the turn of the century would establish film as a prominent medium for such examples. While popular black comedians and film stars employed the stereotypes and comic devices of minstrelsy, including the use of blackface, they often did so with hints of subversion. Such has been said of the celebrated comedian and film actor Stepin Fetchit (born Lincoln Theodore Monroe Andrew Perry) and his comic offshoot Mantan Moreland, as well as Hattie McDaniel, Willie Best, and others. As well, the comic duos of Bert Williams (America's first black comic superstar) and George Walker and of Flournoy Miller and Aubrey Lyles perpetuated these "comedies of the grotesque" in the musical theater, even as they were able to experiment and expand their comic repertoire.

At the same time, however, black comedy directed primarily toward black audiences began to reflect pent-up resentment and a more irreverent critique of white racist society. Bombastic performances of mythic "Bad Nigger" ballads and toasts like "Shine and the Titanic," "The Signifying Monkey," "Dolemite," "Stackolee," and those featuring actual African American cultural heroes like the racially controversial boxing champion Jack Johnson began surfacing at black, predominantly male venues. As well, the "John and Ole Massa" stories reappeared in the oral literature of this period and replaced animal representations and childish portrayals of the trickster. For obvious reasons, these more overtly critical folktales did not get printed by the mainstream white press in the way that the Brer Rabbit tales did. However, Zora Neale Hurston, Arthur Huff Faucet, and other black ethnologists began accumulating in print such folklore in the context of people's everyday lives.

Some of the best achievements in black comedy during the early decades of the 20th century occurred through the literature of the New Negro Movement, starting with the breakthroughs of Paul Lawrence Dunbar's dialect poetry and Charles W. Chesnutt's recasting of Harris's Uncle Remus tales in *The Conjure Woman*. Rudolph Fisher, George Schuyler, and Wallace Thurman presented the culture with satirical novels that leveled the absurdity, on both sides of the equation, of American race relations. The prolific writer Langston Hughes eventually gained recognition as a notable humorist with the publication of his novel *Not without Laughter* in 1930, followed later on by the creation of his wartime serialization of "Simple" stories in the *Chicago Defender*. Zora Neale Hurston's literary renderings of the folklore she amassed as an anthropologist, such as those recalled in her celebrated collection *Mules and Men* (1935), brilliantly and hilariously capture the comic sensibilities of traditional African American humor—sensibilities that would continue to shape the acts of black comedians to this day.

African American comedy took a notable turn in the 1950s when the mounting frustration over racial injustice finally came to a head with the mass organization of the civil rights struggle in the South and across the nation. Tolerance for popular representations of black people as coons and buffoons finally met its limit. Protests against these portrayals became more regular and more successful due in part to the backdrop of televised atrocities streaming out of the Jim Crow South into the living rooms of white Northerners. Protests against the *Amos 'n' Andy* television program organized by the National Association for the Advancement of Colored People (NAACP), for example, generated enough pressure to force the show's cancellation after just two seasons in 1953. Continuing pressure would eventually prompt the CBS Corporation to cease all reruns in 1966.

In literature, Ralph Ellison's *Invisible Man* paved the way for a new kind of satirical novel that employed African American comic sensibilities to deeply explore the absurdity of American racism and critique the problems of black protest without restraint or fear of censorship. Over the course of the tumultuous decades of the civil rights and Black Power movements, comedic novels of this sort would be produced by Chester Himes, Ishmael Reed, Charles Wright, Cecil Brown, and others. Similarly during this era, black stand-up comedians with politically charged humor begin to dominate the popular scene. Slappy White, the "father of the integrated joke"; Moms Mabley, "the funniest woman in the world"; Redd Foxx, with his raunchy nightclub acts; and others unleashed their unrestrained wit on stages along the "chitlin' circuit." In the 1960s, Dick Gregory reached comic superstar status with his cerebral and overtly political humor. Gregory, as well as the collective contributions of comedians of the civil rights era, had a great influence on the comic genius Richard Pryor. Pryor, who channeled the entire African American comic tradition in his sharply political stand-up act, set the tone for the comic greats of the last part of the century, including Whoopi Goldberg, Bill Cosby, Eddie Murphy, Chris Rock, and Dave Chappelle.

Danielle C. Heard

See also

Amos 'n' Andy

Further Reading:

Beatty, Paul. *Hokum: An Anthology of African-American Humor.* New York: Bloomsbury, 2006.

Boskin, Joseph. *Sambo: The Rise & Demise of an American Jester.* New York: Oxford University Press, 1986.

Dance, Daryl Cumber. *Honey, Hush! An Anthology of African American Women's Humor.* New York: W. W. Norton, 1998.

Levine, Lawrence W. *Black Culture and Black Consciousness: Afro-American Folk Thought from Slavery to Freedom.* New York: Oxford University Press, 2007.

Schechter, William. *The History of Negro Humor in America.* New York: Fleet Press Corp., 1970.

Watkins, Mel. *On the Real Side: A History of African American Comedy.* Chicago: Lawrence Hill Books, 1999.

Watkins, Mel, ed. *African American Humor: The Best Black Comedy from Slavery.* Chicago: Lawrence Hill Books, 2002.

African Blood Brotherhood

The African Blood Brotherhood for African Liberation and Redemption (ABB) was a secret paramilitary organization established by Cyril V. Briggs in New York City in 1919. It became the first black auxiliary of the Communist Party in the United States in 1923. Briggs and many in the New Negro Movement found frustrating the failed promises of self-determination and "Africa for the Africans" made in President Woodrow Wilson's Fourteen Points, particularly during the rampant racial violence of the 1919 Red Summer.

After World War I ended, many African American war veterans and members of the Northern black intelligentsia turned to alternative and radical organizations to find solutions for racial inequality. Although many turned to A. Philip Randolph and the Socialist Party, Briggs was dissatisfied with the organization's unwillingness to address the unique position of the black worker in the United States. Inspired by the Sinn Fein's revolutionary nationalism in Ireland and the postwar Zionist movement, Briggs founded the ABB on an ideology that fused black nationalism, anticolonialism, anticapitalism, class consciousness, race consciousness, and Pan-Africanism. As a response to numerous race riots, lynchings, and a renewed Ku Klux Klan, the organization promoted armed self-defense against racist attacks, an element that gained significant attention after the *New York Times* linked the ABB to the Tulsa Riot of 1921. The ABB also denounced issues that divided the black community, such as skin complexion and regional discrimination caused by the Great Migration. Furthermore, they pledged to support a race-first stance, referred to by Briggs as "race patriotism," an encompassing term for patronizing black businesses, teaching black history, supporting black political candidates, and working toward international black liberation. The most radical aspect of their program called for an independent state for people of African descent somewhere in the western United States, although the exact location varied.

The group drew its core membership from New York's West Indian population, World War I veterans, the black working class, and readers of Briggs's newspaper *The Crusader*. The only qualifications for membership were to be of African descent and to pay the dues. Formation of a local post required seven interested members. Beyond its headquarters in Harlem, the secret organization had posts in Chicago, Tulsa, and West Virginia's coal mining region. In cities where the Ku Klux Klan dominated, the ABB announced in local newspapers future plans to organize local chapters, but no evidence exists that these chapters were established. According to Briggs, the ABB never had more than 3,000 active members, but had nearly 5,000 paying dues; and his newspaper *The Crusader*, the ABB's official organ, had over 30,000 subscribers. Most historians believe these estimates are exaggerated, since the newspaper stopped production in 1922 due to financial concerns. The ABB opened membership to women, and their Supreme Council included activist Grace Campbell, although her role remained confined to secretarial duties.

In 1920, the ABB had its first convention, in which it promoted a political program of traditional self-reliance, black labor issues, black cooperatives, a "race first" program, the creation of a black organizational united front, and organized resistance to the Ku Klux Klan. Eventually, they lessened their initial demand for an independent state in America to promote Marcus Garvey's Back to Africa movement; however, they dropped their support after Garvey met with Klan officials in 1921. With many socialist and communist members, they also encouraged the black working class to assume leadership roles in the larger movement for equality, positions traditionally held by the black middle class. They also cooperated with other groups to create a united black front that included labor's perspectives, an effort that largely failed. After the Comintern—formed in 1919 as a propaganda organ that disseminated communist principles to foreign governments and, in the 1930s, became a fierce political weapon for Josef Stalin—encouraged the Communist Party in the United States to pay attention to racial oppression, the ABB joined as an auxiliary. In doing so, it quickly lost its own identity. The organization declined throughout 1924 and 1925.

KATHERINE KUEHLER WALTERS

See also

Garvey, Marcus; Ku Klux Klan (KKK); Randolph, A. Philip

Further Reading:

Hill, Robert D., and Cyril V. Briggs. *The Crusader* 1, no. 6. New York: Garland Publishing, 1987.

Makalani, Minkah. "For the Liberation of Black People Everywhere: The African Blood Brotherhood, Black Radicalism, and Pan-African Liberation in the New Negro Movement, 1917–1936." PhD diss., University of Illinois, 2004.

Solomon, Mark. *The Cry Was Unity: Communists and African Americans, 1917–36.* Jackson: University Press of Mississippi, 1998.

Alabama Council on Human Relations (1954–1961)

The Alabama Council on Human Relations originated as a state affiliate of the Commission on Interracial Cooperation (CIC), a biracial federation organized in 1919 in response to 26 post–World War I race riots that shook the nation. While its board was composed of blacks and whites and offered a forum for interracial dialogue, the CIC was not a radical organization. The leadership, whose primary goal was to prevent violence, maintained that segregation and reform could coexist.

Although the CIC created the Southern Commission on the Study of Lynching in 1930 and placed black advisors in several New Deal agencies, it was increasingly criticized for its efforts to "improve segregation." In February 1944, the CIC merged with the Southern Regional Council (SRC), an early think tank whose founders believed that racial animosity could be alleviated by improving economic conditions for *all* Southerners. From its Atlanta headquarters, it reorganized the CIC state affiliates and put volunteers to work gathering economic data and monitoring race relations. Detailed reports and research papers were published several times a year. Alabama's CIC affiliate became the Alabama Division of the Southern Regional Council in 1944, and the Alabama Council on Human Relations in 1954.

Like the CIC, the SRC was slow to attack segregation because it hoped to attract white moderate support, and the SRC did not publicly declare its opposition to segregation until 1949. Regarded as the preeminent Southern race relations organization, after the U.S. Supreme Court's 1954 *Brown v. Board of Education* decision declaring segregated public education unconstitutional, the Ford Foundation's Fund for the Republic granted the SRC $240,000 to support race relations education. These funds were used to hire 13 full-time regional directors to organize and support local biracial committees, which would in turn assist local communities in achieving school desegregation without violence. The SRC's leadership, perhaps naively, maintained that the Deep South would voluntarily desegregate if the alternative was submitting to federal intervention.

On February 8, 1955, 26-year-old Methodist minister Robert Hughes, a graduate of both the University of Alabama and Emory University, was appointed executive director of the Alabama Council on Human Relations, headquartered in Montgomery. Thomas Thrasher, rector of the city's largest Episcopal church, served on his board, as did white activists Clifford and Virginia Durr and Aubrey Williams, and Martin Luther King, Jr. The membership was composed almost exclusively of middle-class black and white businessmen, ministers, teachers, and housewives. Hughes marketed the council's role as "bridge building," and meetings were held on the campus of the black Alabama State University or in the basements of black churches, since integrated public meetings violated the capital city's municipal code. When King established his Montgomery Improvement Association later that year, he recruited Hughes.

The Montgomery Bus Boycott began on Monday, December 5, 1955, and initially the city commissioners refused to meet with the protest leaders. Hughes offered his services as a mediator and he and Thrasher brought the Montgomery

Improvement Association, the city commissioners, and representatives from the bus company together on December 8. Their attempts to broker a settlement were not only unsuccessful, but interpreted by the white community as a betrayal of white interests.

Montgomery's chapter of the White Citizens Council (WCC) was organized in October 1955, shortly after the implementation order for the *Brown* decision was delivered and two months prior to the bus boycott. Its purpose was to resist any attempt to desegregate schools, public transportation, or public facilities. The leadership charged that "human relations" was merely a euphemism for integration, and that Hughes and his council members were communists.

On February 10, 1956, state senator Sam Engelhardt Jr., executive secretary of the Alabama Association of Citizens' Councils, hosted a recruitment rally in Montgomery to celebrate the successful defense of segregation at the University of Alabama that month when black graduate student Autherine Lucy was prevented from attending classes, and to encourage continued opposition to the bus boycott. The audience of 12,000 included farmers, mill hands, businessmen, municipal workers, teachers, attorneys, and students.

The following evening, the Alabama Council on Human Relations celebrated its first anniversary on the campus of Alabama State College. The contrast was stark. Of the 300 who attended, fewer than half were black. Unlike the mix of middle-class, working-class, and poor whites at the WCC rally, most of the HR Council delegates were white, middle class, and lived outside Montgomery. In July, when the ACHR's lease for its headquarters on South Court Street expired, the WCC pressured the landlord not to renew. Hughes subsequently relocated to Birmingham, where the ACHR was once again compelled to hold meetings in the basements of black churches. It was the only biracial organization in the city at that time.

In October 1957, the Birmingham city police broke up an ACHR meeting and wrote down the names and addresses of all present. Their employers subsequently received anonymous letters reporting their attendance at a "communist front" meeting, which violated the municipal ordinance against integrated gatherings. The ACHR lost most of its members and half its officers that evening, and it did not meet again for several months. The Methodist Laymen's Association, organized to oppose the Council of Methodist Bishops' support of the *Brown* decision in 1954, also viciously attacked Hughes. The group sent letters to every Methodist congregation in Birmingham accusing him and the HR Council of supporting racial integration of the congregations. Hughes received death threats, and the Ku Klux Klan burned a cross on his front lawn.

It was evident that the ACHR was too small and too weak to effect any meaningful change. Hughes grew frustrated as he presided over meaningless sessions with a few middle-class blacks and whites who politely discussed issues of little consequence, then fled when segregationists called them communists. It angered him too because he knew that several members of the affluent Young Men's Business Club, who had spoken with him privately, supported the SRC's mission, but were reluctant to declare themselves. Hughes was aware that negative publicity about the Magic City made them nervous since it discouraged new business investment. In a last-ditch effort to force these business progressives into the open, Hughes began to copy the national press on his monthly reports to the SRC. These reports documented the violence and fear that ruled in Birmingham. On December 15, 1958, *Time* magazine carried an article describing Birmingham's ugly racial climate, based almost entirely on information provided by Hughes. In April 1960, Harrison Salisbury of the *New York Times* met secretly with the minister and subsequently produced a scathing exposé charging that in Birmingham, "Every channel of communication, every medium of mutual interest, every reasoned approach, every inch of middle ground has been fragmented by the emotional dynamite of racism." When the Birmingham and Bessemer City commissions sued Salisbury for criminal libel, Hughes was subpoenaed by a Jefferson County Grand Jury and directed to submit the ACHR's membership and correspondence files. He refused, knowing that they would be published, and was cited for contempt and jailed for four days. While prominent Birmingham attorney Charles Morgan successfully defended him, Hughes had destroyed his career with the Methodist church. When the North Alabama Conference convened its 1960 Annual Meeting in Birmingham that year, the angry Methodist Laymen's Association prevailed on the conclave to demand that Hughes resign from the ACHR. When he refused, they voted to defrock him, a decision supported by Bishop Bachman Hodge, on September 5, 1960. After Hughes was released from jail, he personally appealed to Hodge, who agreed to rescind the decision on the condition that Hughes accept a missionary assignment to Salisbury, Rhodesia. He and his family left for Africa before the end of 1960 and remained there for four years until the Rhodesian government expelled him for supporting a national liberation movement.

Years of frustration and failure had radicalized Hughes. He believed that he and the council had accomplished little through their local efforts at mediation and bridge building. By engaging the national press, however, he had made Americans outside of Alabama aware of what blacks and white progressives were coping with. The articles captured the nation's attention and gave Americans some sense of the seething resentments that were brewing in Birmingham just one year before the beatings of the Freedom Riders, and two years before the brutalization of the demonstrators, and the bombing of the Sixteenth Street Baptist Church. Although Hughes was not in Birmingham to see it, his actions also spurred the progressive white business community to action. Men like Charles Morgan, David Vann, and Sid Smyer became involved in negotiating the desegregation of downtown Birmingham in 1963. By that time, it was too late. Two years after Hughes was banished from the Magic City, Birmingham imploded.

MARY STANTON

See also

King, Martin Luther, Jr.; Montgomery Bus Boycott; New Deal; White Citizens' Council

Further Reading:

McWhorter, Diane. *Carry Me Home: Birmingham, Alabama, the Climactic Battle of the Civil Rights Revolution*. New York: Simon & Schuster, 2001.

Sosna, Morton. *In Search of the Silent South: Southern Liberals and the Race Issue*. New York: Columbia University Press, 1977.

Stanton, Mary. *Journey Toward Justice: Juliette Hampton Morgan and the Montgomery Bus Boycott*. Athens: University of Georgia Press, 2006.

Thornton, J. Mills. *Dividing Lines: Municipal Politics and the Struggle for Civil Rights in Montgomery, Birmingham, and Selma*. Tuscaloosa: University of Alabama Press, 2002.

Albany Civil Rights Movement

A branch of the extensive Southern Civil Rights Movement took place in the city of Albany, Georgia. One of the largest cities in southern Georgia, Albany was the nexus of protest and demonstrations against the segregated practices in place throughout southwest Georgia. Black Albanians grew tired of the prejudiced practices of the city. Segregated bus stations, eateries, and even classified advertisements divided the city by race. The local newspaper, the *Albany Herald*, ran "Negro Only" classifieds for African Americans in search of a job. The Albany Movement was the first attempt to desegregate an entire city. Prior to the organization of the 1960s movement, war veteran C. W. King established Albany's branch of the National Association for the Advancement of Colored People. In the 1950s, a group of concerned black citizens formed the Lincoln Heights Groups and demanded change.

In 1961, members of the Student Nonviolent Coordinating Committee (SNCC) descended into Albany. Charles S. Sherrod, Cordell Reagon, and Charles Jones began organizing mass meetings and protests. The Albany Movement organization was established on December 17, 1961, and elected William G. Anderson as its president. To give motivation to those participating in the movement, Martin Luther King, Jr. and Ralph Abernathy were invited to participate in the events taking place. King and Abernathy arrived in December 1961. After delivering a speech at Shiloh Baptist Church and crossing the street to address the overflow of the mass meeting in Mount Zion Baptist Church, King marched with Albany protesters. He was jailed and refused to post bail. Other prominent members of the black Albany community, including attorney C. B. King and his brother Slater King, a successful real estate broker, participated in the outcry for civil rights and contributed their services to those ready to protest. C. B. King provided legal services to imprisoned protesters, including Martin Luther King, Jr. and Ralph Abernathy. Slater King served as the vice-president of the Albany Movement. After being beaten by Sheriff Cull Campbell while trying to check on a jailed protester, C. B. King's bloodied and battered body was photographed and sent across newswires throughout the country, and his picture made the *New York Times*.

Mass protests and outcries continued in Albany. Major factors in the Albany Movement continuation included

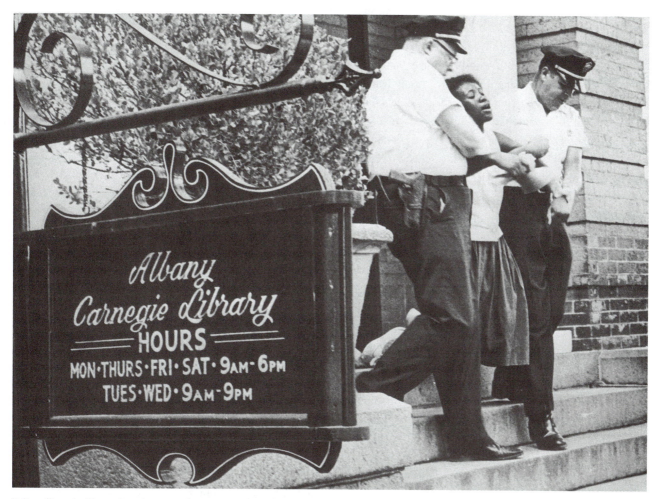

Police officers in Albany, Georgia, carry a demonstrator down the steps of the Albany Carnegie Library during a civil rights protest, July 31, 1962. (Bettmann/Corbis)

college students and youth who participated. Students from the historically black Albany State College (now Albany State University) demonstrated and protested in Albany's streets. Many students, including Dr. Janie Rambeau and Bernice Johnson Reagon, were expelled from Albany State because of their actions. Students transferred to other surrounding schools, including Fort Valley State College (now Fort Valley State University) in Fort Valley, Georgia, and Spelman College in Atlanta, Georgia. The Freedom Singers, an a capella group established by Bernice Johnson Reagon, sang spirituals to keep protestors uplifted. McCree Harris, a teacher at Monroe Comprehensive High School, also participated with the Freedom Singers. Harris encouraged her students to participate in Albany's fight for equality and rights. Many Freedom Singers were jailed because of their protest and sang songs to keep themselves and other imprisoned protesters positive and committed to their cause. Supporters of the Albany Movement who did not publicly demonstrate diligently worked behind the scenes making signs, fixing meals, and giving monetary donations.

In an effort to squelch the growing influence of equality protests and events, Albany sheriff Laurie Pritchett encouraged police officers to not use violent reproach against protesters in public spaces or in front of media. He contacted jails in the surrounding counties of Mitchell, Baker, and Lee counties to cover the overflow of protestors in Albany's jails. Over 1,000 protestors or supporters of Albany's movement were jailed. When Martin Luther King, Jr. and Abernathy returned in the summer of 1962 for sentencing on their December convictions, they chose to be jailed instead of paying

fines. Pritchett organized for King's and Abernathy's fines to be paid so that both were released from prison unwillingly. After continuing unsuccessful efforts through August and being jailed once more, King left Albany feeling defeated. Albanians, however, felt successful. Albany's black community rallied to support Thomas Chatmon, a successful black businessman and director of voter registration for the Albany Movement. Votes for Chatmon resulted in a runoff election. The following spring, all segregation laws were removed from Albany civil codes.

Using Albany as a guide, King continued his fight for civic equality by staging demonstrations in Birmingham, Alabama. Members of SNCC expanded to other areas of southwest Georgia, including Americus and Camilla, calling for the end of legal segregation. C. B. King continued the fight for social equality in legislation and other civic venues. He unsuccessfully ran for the House of Representatives in 1964, the first African American to do so since Reconstruction. He later was supported by black legislators to run for governor in 1969. In 2002, Albany's newly constructed courthouse was named after the late civil rights attorney. A scholarship for minority aspirants in law was also established in his honor. Slater King continued to advocate literacy and integration efforts in southwest Georgia. After an untimely death in 1969, an adult learning center he designed was named in his honor. Bernice Johnson Reagon continued the legacy of the Freedom Singers through establishing the popular gospel group Sweet Honey in the Rock.

As a whole, the Albany Movement has been memorialized in Albany's Civil Rights Museum, opened in 1998. The building was formerly Mount Zion Church, one of the sites of the numerous mass meetings during the movement. A memorial dedicated to participants in the Albany Movement was also erected in 1998. It is located in Charles S. Sherrod Park, named after the SNCC member who helped organize the movement in 1961.

REGINA BARNETT

See also

Abernathy, Ralph David; King, Martin Luther, Jr.

Further Reading:

Lyon, Danny. *Memories of the Southern Civil Rights Movement.* Chapel Hill: Published for the Center for Documentary Studies, Duke University, by the University of North Carolina Press, 1992.

Tuck, Steven G. N. *Beyond Atlanta: The Struggle for Racial Equality in Georgia, 1940–1980.* Athens: University of Georgia Press, 2001.

Alexander v. Sandoval (2001)

Until January 2001, many Americans believed they could use section 601 of Title VI to bring suit against the federal government in cases of discrimination. (Title VI is a part of the Civil Rights Act of 1964. Its role is to stop discrimination in federally funded programs.) During the last three to four decades, since the Civil Rights era, Title VI had been used as a way to pursue social justice. However, in April 2001, in a vote of 5 to 4, the Supreme Court justices ruled that would no longer be the case.

In *Alexander v. Sandoval*, Martha Sandoval believed the Alabama Department of Public Safety was discriminating against her. Recently, the state had adopted a constitutional amendment making English the official, state language. Following the adoption, the department of public safety made it a policy to administer driver license tests only in English. Martha Sandoval, who is a Mexican immigrant, felt this policy was unfair, because it made it difficult for her and other immigrants, who cannot speak English, to pass the test.

With the help of Alabama's Southern Poverty Law Center and two other civil rights organizations, Sandoval filed a class-action lawsuit. The lawsuit alleged the state's new policy discriminated against non-English-speaking individuals based on their national origin. The lawsuit asked the state to disengage from such procedure, and it also asked the court to find this policy unlawful under the Title VI regulations.

This lawsuit was based on two sections of Title VI which were passed as a part of the Civil Rights Act of 1964. Section 601 of the Act forbids discrimination based on race, color, or national origin in a number of programs and activities covered by the government. Section 602 of the Act gives federal agencies the authorization to implement 601 through issuing regulations. In addition, the United States Department of Justice had issued a regulation requiring organizations and agencies that receive funding from federal agencies to adhere to the same antidiscriminatory policies. (The policies do not have to be intentional to be found discriminatory. Disparate impact regulations—policies that have a face value of appearing to be neutral but can be discriminatory in its application or affect—can still be ruled to be discriminatory.)

According to the prosecutors of the *Alexander v. Sandoval* trial, Alabama's Department of Public Safety had accepted federal funds and was required to abide by Title VI. The Middle District court of Alabama agreed with the prosecutors. After the verdict the Alabama Department of Public Safety appealed to the U.S. Court of Appeals for the 11th Circuit. This court also took sides with Sandoval. However, the U.S. Supreme Court then agreed to hear the case. In 2001, a majority vote of 5 to 4 reversed the district court's decision. According to the opinion written by Justice Anthony Scalia, private individuals could not privately sue to enforce the disparate-impact regulations of the federal government. There was no support for a private cause of action found in Title VI. Only agencies receiving the funds had the right to sue.

Justice Stevens was the only one who dissented from the majority decision. He said the court had already determined there was a cause of action in Title VI. He also added that even if the topic had not already been decided, the legislative history of Title VI, and the verdicts taken by the lower courts, had already shown there was a private course of action.

This verdict was a shock to the country, because it brought Americans' recourse in discrimination lawsuits a step backwards. Before the U.S. Supreme Court ruling, 9 of the 12 U.S. Courts of Appeals had no dispute over the private actions allowed by Title VI. Also, when there was no dispute, the Supreme Court usually did not hear cases which centered around those nondisputed issues. However, Americans can no longer use Title VI as a basis for anti-discriminatory lawsuits. However, there are other avenues that can be used. One can use Section 1983 of Title 42 of the U.S. Code. This legislation, created during the Reconstruction era, says that lawsuits against the government or government officials are authorized if these officials or the government is responsible for the "deprivation of any rights, privileges, or immunities secured by the Constitution and laws." Another alternative can be to turn to Congress for help in turning Title VI's authority to its original state before the *Alexander v. Sandoval* case.

Alan Vincent Grigsby and Rasha Aly

See also

Document: Glass Ceiling Commission: Summary of Recommendations (1995)

Further Reading:

Alexander v. Sandoval, 532 U.S. 275, 2001.

Associated Press. *English-Only Challenge to Alabama Driver's License Test Knocked Down by State Supreme Court.* March 4, 2011. Retrieved December 15, 2012, from http://blog.al.com/wire/2011/03/english-only_challenge_to_alab.html.

Black, Derek. "Picking up the Pieces after *Alexander v. Sandoval*: Resurrecting a Private Cause of Action for Disparate Impact." *North Carolina Law Review* (2002): 1–40.

Labow, Benjamin. "*Alexander v. Sandoval*: Civil Rights Without Remedies." *Oklahoma Law Review* (2003): 1–24.

Miller, Tanya L. "*Alexander v. Sandoval* and the Incredible Disappearing Cause of Action." *Catholic University Law Review* (2003): 1–38.

Nielsen, Laura Beth, and Robert L. Nelson. "Scaling the Pyramid: A Sociolegal Model of Employment Discrimination Litigation." *Handbook of Employment Discrimination Research* (2008): 3–34.

U.S. Department of Justice, Civil Rights Division. *Title VI Legal Manual.* Washington, DC, 2001.

Welner, K. G. "*Alexander v. Sandoval*: A Setback for Civil Rights." *Education Policy Analysis Archives* 9, no. 24 (2001): 1–7.

al-Qaeda

In Arabic, *al-Qaeda* means "the base" or "the foundation." Around 1988, Osama Bin Laden, the son of a Saudi billionaire, formed, with the aid of other Islamist groups, an organization named al-Qaeda, which in the 1990s became a global terrorist network with cells in a number of countries. Al-Qaeda promotes an extremist and militant form of Islam and seeks to attack U.S. interests around the world.

In the 1980s, Bin Laden financed and recruited Arab/Muslim men to fight on behalf of Afghanistan (not an Arab country, though a Muslim nation) against the Soviet invasion. These recruits came to be known euphemistically as Arab Afghans. When the effort against the Soviets proved surprisingly successful, Bin Laden was emboldened to redirect his *jihad*, or holy war, beyond Afghanistan, and al-Qaeda was formed. One of al-Qaeda's goals was to overthrow the U.S.-supported Saudi government. It believed that the Kingdom of Saudi Arabia, which houses Mecca and Medina, the two holiest sites in Islam, should not harbor the "infidel" U.S. armed forces that remained after the first Gulf War in 1990. Al-Qaeda also wanted to challenge U.S. support for the

Israeli government, which it held accountable for the oppression of the Palestinians.

Al-Qaeda represents a fringe group in the Muslim world, and is based on an extremist and puritanical interpretation of the Qur'an, the holy book of Islam. Its followers distort religion to justify their global militant agenda, which includes attacking civilians and wreaking havoc on U.S. and Western interests.

Al-Qaeda was responsible for the September 11, 2001, terrorist attacks, which killed 3,021 innocent people at the World Trade Center in New York City (2,843) and the Pentagon in Washington, D.C, and, in an aborted attack, an airplane that crashed in Pennsylvania. This was by far the biggest terrorist incident on U.S. soil.

In response to 9/11, the United States launched the War on Terrorism, which included the invasion of Afghanistan to destroy al-Qaeda's bases and to overthrow the Taliban (literally, "religious students"), the country's strict fundamentalist rulers who harbored al-Qaeda. Domestically, Congress passed new legislation (the Patriot Act), and the U.S. Attorney General issued a series of initiatives meant to monitor and arrest potential terrorists. These policies were generally not effective in achieving their aim. Instead, they profiled persons of Middle Eastern and South Asian origin, leading to detentions and deportations of thousands of immigrants. They also reinforced commonly held stereotypes and suspicious beliefs about Arabs and Muslims. The United States in the post-9/11 period has been marked by a meteoric escalation of hate crimes and bias incidents. The FBI, which keeps statistics by the religious affiliation of the victim, not by ethnicity, reported "a very dramatic increase in the number of anti-Islamic crimes—28 in 2000 and 481 in 2001 (a 1,600% increase)." It is ironic that al-Qaeda's terrorism cost Middle Eastern American communities dearly, since these are the very people with whom it shared an ethnic and religious affiliation. On May 2, 2011, Navy Seal commandos assassinated Osama Bin Laden in his compound in Abbottabad, Afghanistan.

Mehdi Bozorgmehr and Anny Bakalian

See also

Islamofascism; Islamophobia; Patriot Act of 2001

Further Reading:

Gunaratna, Rohan. *Inside Al Qaeda: Global Network of Terror.* New York: Berkeley Publishing Group, 2003.

American Apartheid

American apartheid, a concept coined by sociologists Douglass Massey and Nancy Denton and set forth in their 1993 book *American Apartheid: Segregation and the Making of the Underclass*, is the racial segregation of blacks in American society brought about by actions, patterns, and the active support of most whites in the United States. American apartheid, like apartheid in South Africa, effectively perpetuates racial inequality leading to a deprivation in socioeconomic status for blacks in America. American apartheid in the form of residential segregation is a major system of racial injustice that results in the geographic isolation of blacks into American ghettos. Under this system, blacks are forced to reside in and live under harsh physical conditions, substandard infrastructures, and poor social conditions where inadequate educational systems exist, families are fragmented, and crime and violence are rampant. The basic premise of American apartheid holds that opportunities and the chances for blacks to achieve social and economic success become very limited after sustained, continuous, and lengthy exposure to a segregated environment.

Black segregation cannot be compared to the segregation experienced by other groups, such as Italians and Poles who came to America and settled into segregated neighborhoods, because the segregation those groups experienced was very limited and transient. In contrast, blacks in America have experienced unprecedented levels of residential segregation and racial isolation. This segregation has been imposed on blacks through a combination of self-conscious actions and institutional arrangements purposefully devised by some whites, including some public policies that continue into the 21st century.

One of the standard measures of racial segregation is known as the *index of dissimilarity*, which measures the degree to which blacks and whites are evenly spread among neighborhoods in a city. The index of dissimilarity refers specifically to the percentage of blacks that would have to move from one area to another in order to achieve an "even" residential pattern; in other words, every neighborhood represents the racial composition of the city. For example, during the 1860s, black-white levels of segregation were lower in Southern cities than in Northern cities, as free blacks were more likely to live among whites than other blacks. During the 1870s, levels of dissimilarity were also low for immigrant groups such as Jews, Poles, and Czechs who also experienced segregation from whites. Nevertheless, blacks still experienced higher degrees of social isolation than those immigrant groups, and by the 1930s the levels of black-white dissimilarity skyrocketed.

American apartheid holds that racial segregation and the black ghetto are the two most important factors responsible for the persistence of black poverty in the United States. In *American Apartheid*, Massey and Denton put forth the argument that residential segregation is an organizational feature of American society responsible for creating the urban underclass and the black ghetto environment. They outline several dimensions of geographic variation including unevenness, isolation, clustering, centralization, and concentration that they claim result in racial segregation, ultimately leading to the creation of the black ghetto.

Massey and Denton describe the creation of the black ghetto as a result of spatial isolation: after 1900, the black population grew in the urban north and blacks were relegated and restricted to specific areas, not only physically but socially as well. As a result of this spatial isolation, blacks had very little interaction with whites and were unable to involve themselves in social and cultural activities.

From 1930 to 1970 the level of spatial isolation of blacks doubled among northern cities. In 1930, neighborhoods dominated by whites also included black residents, but by 1970 the complete opposite was true, and the average black resident lived in a predominantly black neighborhood. The isolation levels of blacks were slightly higher (2 percent higher) in southern cities such as Atlanta, Baltimore, Dallas, Memphis, Miami, and Washington, D.C. during this time than in northern cities. By the 1980s, the degree of spatial isolation remained extreme, as it was highly unlikely for blacks and whites to reside in the same neighborhood within most metropolitan areas at this time. This unevenness in distribution of minority populations is the second aspect of racial segregation that Massey and Denton cover in their book.

Clustering is the third dimension of racial segregation discussed by the authors, and it refers to the extent to which minority neighborhoods adjoin one another in space. The authors claim that large concentrations of minorities are confined to a limited selection of neighborhoods where the incidence of poverty is significantly higher for minorities than for whites. Low-income blacks and Latinos, even in recent years, have been highly clustered in predominantly minority neighborhoods.

Centralization is the fourth dimension of racial segregation, and it describes the extent to which a group is located near the center of an urban area. Centralization is measured by the spatial distance of a group from the central business district (CBD). Nearness to the CBD is associated with high levels of crime, social disorder, and economic marginality. Massey and Denton have found that these densely populated neighborhoods located around the urban core are generally inhabited by black Americans.

A fifth aspect of racial segregation is *concentration*, and it refers to the amount of physical space a minority group occupies in the urban environment. Racial segregation causes an increase in the geographic concentration of poverty, which is confined primarily to black neighborhoods. By the late 1970s, Massey and Denton found that black families lived primarily in neighborhoods where at least a third of the families were poor. There is a strong correlation between black-white segregation and the rate of black poverty. By the 1980s, poverty concentration was highest in cities where blacks were both highly segregated and very poor. The combination of all five

Residential Segregation

Residential segregation is considered the "forgotten factor" of American race relations and is not discussed when discussing the American underclass. Policy makers and citizens of the United States must discuss and understand the plight of the urban poor and completely recognize the effects of segregation in order for the United States to truly consider itself to be colorblind.

Most Americans vaguely realize that urban America is still a residentially segregated society, but few appreciate the depth of Black segregation or the degree to which it is maintained by ongoing institutional arrangements and contemporary individual actions. They view segregation as an unfortunate holdover from a racist past, one that is fading progressively over time. If racial residential segregation persists, they reason, it is only because civil rights laws passed during the 1960s have not had enough time to work or because many Blacks still prefer to live in Black neighborhoods. (Massey and Denton, 2001: 135) of these elements of racial segregation—unevenness, isolation, clustering, centralization, and concentration—results in a pattern Massey and Denton refer to as *hypersegregation*.

Segregation is responsible for several unfortunate conditions. Black neighborhoods have experienced concentrated poverty resulting in a mutually reinforcing and self-feeding spiral of decline. Additionally, the lack of employment in black neighborhoods has caused high rates of poverty and socioeconomic deprivation to become concentrated in these neighborhoods, resulting in the social, economic, and geographic isolation of blacks from the rest of society.

Segregation combined with high poverty is also responsible for black neighborhoods being vulnerable to market-based economic fluctuations. An event that causes the black poverty rate to increase will cause a change in the concentration of poverty and in turn, change the social and economic makeup of black neighborhoods. As a result of this change, commercial development withdraws from black neighborhoods and the distribution of goods and services is decreased or in some cases, completely eliminated from black neighborhoods.

Additionally, segregation makes black neighborhoods more susceptible to decline. Specifically, high levels of racial segregation cause black poverty to increase, resulting in the abandonment of housing, increased crime, and increased social disorder. This ultimately leads to social instability in poor black neighborhoods. Once these factors become part of the residential structure of the neighborhood, blacks residing in the ghetto adapt, and conditions such as drug use, joblessness, welfare dependency, teenage pregnancy, and unwed parenting become a normal part of daily life.

Lastly, segregation has political consequences for black Americans. Segregation may make it easier to elect political representatives; however, segregation ultimately limits the political influence of blacks. Segregation can marginalize blacks within American society by preventing them from participating in the political process based on common self-interest.

Blacks and whites lived in integrated neighborhoods until the end of the 19th century. The concept of American apartheid holds that black Americans did not segregate themselves and did not voluntarily want to live in all black neighborhoods, but rather became residentially confined to ghettos within American cities. While European immigrants lived in neighborhoods where they did not predominate and became more integrated into American society as their socioeconomic status rose, this did not occur with blacks. On the contrary, blacks were forced to live in neighborhoods that were predominantly black, causing them to become socially isolated.

By the 1970s, black-white segregation had become widespread in American cities despite the Fair Housing Act enacted in 1968, and by the 1980s the situation had not significantly changed. Levels of segregation remained high at this time with many neighborhood residents moving to the suburbs. Even as late as the 1990s, racial segregation was extremely high in urban areas. The concept of American apartheid holds that the processes sustaining racial segregation remain entrenched and institutionalized even today, despite the existence of fair housing laws.

American apartheid, better known as racial segregation, is a barrier to social mobility. Therefore, segregation is a very powerful obstacle to the socioeconomic progress of black Americans, creating an institution whereby blacks are confined to relatively disadvantaged neighborhoods. Blacks are the only racial group in the United States to experience this pattern of constant and extreme segregation known as hypersegregation. Ultimately, the persistence of racial segregation in American cities results in extreme socioeconomic disadvantages for black Americans.

Sonja V. Harry

Further Reading:

Massey, Douglass S. "American Apartheid: Segregation and the Making of the Underclass." *American Journal of Sociology* 96 (1990): 329–357.

Massey, Douglass S., and Nancy A. Denton. "The Dimensions of Residential Segregation," *Social Forces* 67 (1983): 281–315.

Massey, Douglass S., and Nancy A. Denton. *Apartheid: Segregation and the Making of the Underclass*. Cambridge, MA: Harvard University Press, 1993.

Massey, Douglass S., and Nancy A. Denton. "American Apartheid," in *Crisis in American Institutions*, edited by Gary E. Skolnick. New York: Allyn & Bacon, 2001.

American Dilemma, An

An American Dilemma: The Negro Problem and Modern Democracy was the largest social, political, economic, and psychological study of African American culture ever

Dr. Frederick P. Keppel, president of the Carnegie Corporation, 1917. (Harris & Ewing/Library of Congress)

attempted in the United States. Specifically, *An American Dilemma* was a study of race relations in the United States, particularly of those obstacles, like segregation, racial discrimination, and mob violence that barred African Americans from full participation in American society and enjoyment of their constitutional rights.

An American Dilemma had its genesis in 1938, when Dr. Frederick P. Keppel, president of the Carnegie Corporation, invited Gunnar Karl Myrdal, a Swedish sociologist and economist, to conduct a two-year study of African Americans. The extent and complexity of Myrdal's study is suggested by the six years it took to complete. The final draft contained two volumes of nearly 1,550 pages. Myrdal was specifically selected to head this project because, as a citizen of a country devoid of a history of colonial domination or imperialism and aggression toward other countries, he would bring with him a fresh and invigorating perspective unblemished by particular biases in regard to racial relations. To help complete *An American Dilemma*, Myrdal assembled a distinguished coalition of social scientists, including numerous African American scholars such as Ralph Bunche, Allison Davis, St. Charles Drake, E. Franklin Frazier, Charles S. Johnson, and Kenneth Clark.

Prior to *An American Dilemma*, there was a general consensus among many social scientists that the basis of "the Negro problem" was the Negro. This line of thinking concluded that African Americans' inferior status in American society was due to an inherent or genetic inferiority complex that made them less capable of competition with whites. In other words, the Negro, or individuals of African ancestry, were naturally inferior. Interestingly enough, many of these same theories of racial superiority were applied to Southern and Eastern European immigrants who were also viewed as genetically inferior, amid concerns that if the flow of immigration from these countries was not stemmed, the United States would be committing a form of racial suicide.

Paradoxically, Booker T. Washington, founder of the Tuskegee Institute in Macon County, Alabama, and one of the most prominent African Americans of the late 19th and early 20th centuries, also subscribed to the philosophy of white superiority. Although throughout his life he continued to encourage African Americans to be industrious and self-reliant and built a monument to those endeavors, he, nevertheless, believed in the superiority of white civilization and that slavery rescued Africans from the barbarity of the wilds of Africa and brought them under the civilizing influence of white society.

This controversy over what constituted "the Negro problem" generated, in part, the subtitle of Myrdal's study: *The Negro Problem and Modern Democracy*. Myrdal concluded that the so-called Negro problem was, in reality, a white problem that stemmed to a large extent from white people's perceptions of African Americans. But perception alone did not account for the violent racial division that existed in the United States. He stated that from his investigations he discovered that African Americans were inherently not much different from other people, and their "subordinate status" in American society was the consequence of the attitudes, beliefs, and actions of white people who controlled the majority of political, economic, and social power—a consequence of slavery that continued throughout the 19th and into the 20th century.

Another problem African Americans faced in American society, according to Myrdal, was the discrepancy between white Americans' purported belief in justice, liberty, and equality and the treatment of African Americans who, because of their subordinate status, both de facto and de jure, were unable to achieve any of these noble ideals. On a daily basis, white Americans witnessed black people being denied their constitutional rights but continued to believe in, and practice, the principles outlined in the covenant of their country, which had become the binding legacy of the Founding Fathers. To negate the very ideals that they professed to believe in was another aspect of "the Negro problem" that white Americans could not overcome, ignore, or make go away. *An American Dilemma* exposed these contradictions and many others. However, Myrdal was a true optimist in the sense that he believed that one of the fundamental ways of improving race relations in the United States was to highlight these conflicts and tensions, and that through education, white Americans would learn to adjust their beliefs and actions to be more in line with the promise articulated by the Founding Fathers. Myrdal was not alone in his belief. Martin Luther King, Jr. and members of the civil rights movement articulated the same ideals in their struggle for liberty, justice, and equality.

Having discarded the genetic or inherent inferiority theory to justify African Americans' circumstances in American society, Myrdal searched for another explanation to clarify the discrepancies between blacks and whites. He employed the "vicious circle" or culture-of-poverty thesis to explain the difference between African Americans' achievement (or lack of achievement) in a society dominated by a white power structure influenced by racism, racial stereotypes, and other forms of violent discrimination. According to this thesis, white prejudice and discrimination played a significant role in the disenfranchisement of African Americans in terms of impoverished living standards, lack of adequate health care, employment, and education. These circumstances give credence to white prejudices and stereotypes about African Americans being low achievers: as a result of their inability to achieve, blacks must somehow be inferior to whites, who were capable of rising above their own difficult circumstances.

The conclusions drawn from this study influenced American social policy regarding race relations for several decades and set the standard for social science research. It is even possible that *An American Dilemma* played an important role in ending segregation when the U.S. Supreme Court cited the work as a footnote in the 1954 landmark case *Brown v. Board of Education of Topeka, Kansas.*

John G. Hall

See also

Myrdal, Gunnar

Further Reading:

Bok, Sissela. "Introduction (*An American Dilemma* Revisited)." *Daedalus* 124 (Winter 1995): 1–13.

Cherry, Robert. "The Culture-of-Poverty Thesis and African Americans: The Work of Gunnar Myrdal and Other Institutionalists." *Journal of Economic Issues* 29 (December 1995): 1119–1133.

Myrdal, Gunnar. *An American Dilemma: The Negro Problem and Modern Democracy*. New York: Harper Torchbooks, 1944.

Urquhart, Brian. *Ralph Bunche: An American Life*. New York: W. W. Norton & Company, 1993.

American Dream Ideology

The American dream ideology is the belief that any American, regardless of ethnic or racial background, can achieve economic success and social mobility through hard work and determination. The tenets of this conservative ideology stress rugged individualism, personal achievement, a strong work ethic, frugality, delayed gratification, and the accumulation of material possessions such as homes and automobiles. This ideology also stresses the importance of education in the achievement of upward mobility. The American dream ideology, often referred to as mainstream or middle-class values, is rooted in notions of a Protestant work ethic as described by Max Weber (1930) in *The Protestant Ethic and the Spirit of Capitalism*. People who hold with the American dream ideology seldom recognize the social barriers to success encountered by minority groups.

Large numbers of immigrants from Southern and Eastern European countries, predominantly non-Protestant (Catholic, Jewish, and Eastern Orthodox), arrived in the United States between 1880 and 1920. They came to the United States with the belief that through hard work they could achieve the American dream and economic success in a manner that was difficult or impossible in their native countries. In the United States, members of these "new immigrant" groups initially experienced economic difficulty, prejudice, and discrimination. But they gradually achieved socioeconomic mobility. By the 1970s third- and fourth-generation Italian, Polish, Jewish, and Irish Americans had caught up with or outperformed Protestant ethnic groups in socioeconomic status. They also achieved high levels of social assimilation, as reflected in their exceptionally high (60–75 percent) intermarriage rates.

Native white Americans who are familiar with stories of their ancestors' hardships in this new land believe that all Americans, including members of racial minority groups, can make it here through hard work and determination. Their logic is this: our immigrant ancestors started in this country from the bottom, but they made it through hard work and determination, and over generations we have achieved high social mobility. If blacks and other minority group are motivated and work hard as our ancestors did, they too can make it. Thus, they fail to understand that as whites they have privileges in the United States and that many members of racial minority groups experience disadvantages owing to racism. Not only white Americans, but also many Asian Americans and even members of other disadvantaged minority groups, accept the American dream ideology. Some conservative blacks, such as U.S. Supreme Court justice Clarence Thomas, believe that many blacks are poor mainly because they lack motivation and a strong work ethic.

Sandra L. Barnes

See also

Ethnicity; Immigration Acts

Further Reading:

Baritz, Loren. *The Good Life*. New York: Knopf, 1989.

Lewis, Oscar. "The Culture of Poverty." *Scientific American* 115 (1966): 19–25.

Quarles, Benjamin. *The Negro in the Making of America*. New York: Simon & Schuster, 1987.

Weber, Max. *The Protestant Ethic and the Spirit of Capitalism*. Los Angeles: Roxbury Publishing Company, 1930.

American Eugenics Movement

The popularity of scientific discourses on race led scientists in the late 19th and early 20th century to hypothesize the perfection of race through self-directed evolution, or eugenics. As an ideology eugenics was extraordinarily useful in

Great Britain's Francis Galton was a 19th-century mathematician and anthropologist who is best known as the founder of eugenics. Galton believed humans could transcend natural selection by shaping their own evolution through selective breeding. (Library of Congress)

maintaining structural inequality. Disparities between rich and poor could be explained by the biological superiority or inferiority of particular groups. It became not just morally but scientifically necessary to protect against interracial marriage by passing anti-miscegenation laws. Protection of the gene pool became a subject of national interest, and efforts to halt immigration from undesirable countries were enacted. Finally, as it was the case that the poorer classes of society were reproducing at a faster rate than the upper class, forced sterilization was seen as a legitimate means to curb population growth among groups deemed undesirable.

Eugenics was a popular movement in the United States from Reconstruction until World War II when it became associated with the Nazis. American eugenic programs, however, predate similar programs in Nazi Germany, and Nazi defendants cited American precedent in their defense at the Nuremberg trials. There were approximately 64,000 forced sterilizations carried out under eugenics legislation in the United States. The vast majority of these were women, lower class, and nonwhite. Some prison populations were also affected too: men were more likely to be sterilized as the result of criminal activity under so-called punitive sterilizations. By comparison the Nazis may have sterilized as many as 450,000. Forced sterilization is now considered to be a violation of human rights.

Laws prohibiting interracial marriage had existed since colonial times, but eugenics brought the patina of science to such legislation. According to the eugenicists, persons of mixed racial heritage inherited the worst qualities of both races, suffering from chronic health problems and poor morality. Their concern to limit miscegenation was codified through state laws preventing marriages between blacks and whites. A few states broadened this to include marriages between whites and Indians or Chinese, while others prevented blacks from marrying other nonwhite races. The majority of states have had some version of anti-miscegenation legislation at one point in time, as this was by no means limited to the U.S. South. Several failed attempts were made to introduce an anti-miscegenation amendment to the Constitution. The Supreme Court of the United States ruled that anti-miscegenation laws were unconstitutional in *Loving v. Virginia* (1967).

Another major component of the eugenics movement in the United States was advocating for strict immigration policies. Persons from Northern Europe were believed to be of superior racial stock, particularly if they were upper class, whereas those who hailed from Southern Europe such as the Italians, or Eastern Europe such as the Slavs, posed a biological threat. At this time the cultural definition of whiteness was exclusive of Jews and the Irish as well. After the Immigration Act of 1924 it became more difficult for anyone without Anglo-Saxon or Nordic backgrounds to enter the United States.

Perhaps the key element in eugenicist thinking was the supposed correlation between race and intelligence. The modern IQ test grew out of research conducted by Francis Galton, and through the efforts of his student James McKeen Cattell such testing became popular in the United States in the 1890s. In some cases test performance was used to determine whether or not one was fit for reproduction, and poor performance could lead to compulsory sterilization. It was further argued that good test scores by upper- and middle-class white women was an indication that they should bear more children, hence why they should be denied birth control.

At the height of its popularity between the years 1910–1930 eugenics commanded the advocacy of prominent and well-respected scientists, doctors, and politicians, receiving funding through leading corporations and philanthropic organizations. There were even feminist advocates of eugenics who called for the improvement of society's gene pool by providing access to free birth control for those living in poverty, who were disabled, suffered from mental illness, or were "feeble minded."

The Supreme Court of the United States, in *Buck v. Bell* (1927), upheld forced sterilization as in the best interest of the nation as a whole. The case concerned a Virginia law for the sterilization of the mentally retarded. An 18-year-old woman named Carrie Buck was an institutionalized resident of a state mental hospital. As evidence of her "promiscuous" behavior and "feeble mindedness," the state alleged that not only had she become pregnant out of wedlock but her mother was a prostitute as well. In the majority opinion, Chief Justice Oliver Wendell Holmes wrote "three generations of imbeciles are enough," referring to Buck, her mother, and her illegitimate offspring. Historians now consider Buck's pregnancy to be the result of rape and her institutionalization to represent her family's shame that the rapist was her cousin.

Sterilization for undesirable populations still holds an allure for some. Funded by anonymous donors, the nonprofit organization Project Prevention pays a lump sum to drug addicts and alcoholics if they agree to be sterilized or accept long-term birth control such as an IUD. Founded in 1997, the group has paid for the sterilization of more than 3,800 individuals.

Matthew D. Thompson

See also
Galton, Francis

Further Reading:

Allen, Garland E. "The Misuses of Biological Hierarchies: The American Eugenics Movement, 1900–1940." *History and Philosophy of the Life Sciences* 5 (1983): 105–28.

Allen, Garland E. . "Eugenics and American Social History." *Genome* 31 (1989): 885–89.

Begos, Kevin. *Against Their Will: North Carolina's Sterilization Program and the Campaign for Reparations*. Apalachicola, FL: Grey Oak Books, 2012.

Black, Edwin. *War Against the Weak: Eugenics and America's Campaign to Create a Master Race*. New York: Dialog Press, 2012.

Lombardo, Paul A. *Three Generations, No Imbeciles: Eugenics, the Supreme Court, and* Buck v. Bell. Baltimore: Johns Hopkins University Press, 2012.

American G.I. Forum (AGIF)

The American G.I. Forum (AGIF) is a civil rights organization that has been a key player in many legal and political struggles to secure equal rights for Latinos. One of several major civic-minded, service-oriented, and politically active groups founded by Mexican Americans during the 20th century, the AGIF is unique in that it was organized specifically to promote the interests of Mexican American veterans. A local chapter is the basic unit of the organization, where veterans must provide 75 percent of their members. Like the Veterans of Foreign Wars, there are often auxiliary (spousal) and junior organizations attached to a local unit. Beyond the local units, there are district, state, and, since 1958, national governing bodies. Today, AGIF has more than 150,000 members in some 500 chapters in 40 states and Puerto Rico.

Among the group's most influential leaders was Hector Pérez García, MD, of Corpus Christi, Texas, a former U.S. Army physician who served in Europe during World War II. García and several hundred Mexican American veterans met in Corpus Christi in early 1948, initially to discuss strategies to secure benefits promised under the 1944 GI Bill of Rights. They founded AGIF to give a single, strong voice to this effort. Ultimately, the group addressed a variety of veterans' concerns, such as the need to enhance the medical care delivered by the Veterans Administration, and even the low rate of Mexican American representation on local draft boards.

As was to be expected of an organization founded during the early years of the Cold War, and especially one composed of recent veterans, the AGIF charter emphasized the loyalty and patriotism of its membership. The charter also prohibited official endorsement of any political parties or candidates. Soon after the founding, however, García led the organization in a lobbying campaign that proved that this particular stricture did not blunt the group's potential as a political force. In 1949, AGIF members were outraged when the director of the only funeral home in Three Rivers, Texas, refused to open his chapel for the funeral of Private Felix Longoria, who had been killed in the American campaign to recapture the Philippines. García organized a protest that gained national attention and brought the intervention of newly elected U.S. senator Lyndon B. Johnson, who arranged for Longoria to be buried with honors in Arlington National Cemetery. The so-called Longoria Incident gained the young Sen. Johnson an important following among Mexican Americans in Texas, and established the new organization's reputation as an effective advocate for Hispanic rights. The AGIF grew quickly as local units were soon founded across the Southwest. In 1950, García was among those interviewed by Pulitzer Prize–winning author Edna Ferber, who was interested in accurately depicting the Mexican American experience in Texas in her novel *Giant* (1952).

The AGIF's activities soon expanded beyond lobbying and organizing solely on behalf of veterans, and it came to support a broader Mexican American civil rights agenda, such as securing fair housing, quality public education, widespread voter registration, and better employment opportunity. When necessary, AGIF also supported litigation to achieve its goals. In 1954, AGIF-affiliated lawyers collaborated with the older organization League of United Latin American Citizens (LULAC), to defend Pete Hernández against murder charges. Hernández was convicted by an all-white jury—in a county that was heavily Mexican American yet one that had not used a Hispanic juror for decades—and the legal team appealed. In the 1954 landmark decision, *Hernández v. Texas* (1954), the U.S. Supreme Court agreed with the AGIF and LULAC argument that, although legally classified as "white," Mexican Americans in Texas had suffered discrimination as a class and were entitled to protections under the Fourteenth Amendment. In 1957, one of the AGIF lawyers from the *Hernández* case, James DeAnda, convinced a federal court to declare school segregation of Mexican American children in Texas schools unconstitutional. A decade later, DeAnda sought and won the first judicial application of the due process clause of the Fourteenth Amendment with regard to de facto Mexican American school segregation in Corpus Christi. In 1979, DeAnda himself was appointed to the federal judiciary by President Jimmy Carter. Outside the courtroom, AGIF members mounted efforts to register Mexican Americans to vote, protested incidents of police brutality, raised money for scholarships, supported improving labor and living conditions of migrant farm workers, and, naturally, continued to lobby for veterans' health care and other needs.

García, and other prominent AGIF members, played a critical role in the 1960 presidential campaign, by organizing Viva Kennedy clubs (earlier "Viva Johnson") in Texas. The John F. Kennedy administration recognized their contribution, but did not reward Mexican Americans with much increased attention. President Johnson, however, appointed García to be the first Hispanic member of the U.S. Civil Rights Commission and made him a member of the U.S. delegation to the United Nations. Johnson also selected Vicente T. Ximenes, another AGIF founder and a former national chair, to serve as the first Hispanic member of the federal Equal Employment Opportunity Commission, and appointed him to chair the Committee on Mexican American Affairs, the first cabinet-level office for Hispanic issues. AGIF members, affiliates, and supporters, whether working on behalf of the organization or, increasingly, operating from important positions in government, played significant roles in extending Great Society programs into the *barrios*. AGIF continued its work even as the Civil Rights era effectively came to its end in the 1970s. In 1983, García received an award for distinguished accomplishment from President Ronald Reagan.

S. Harmon Wilson

See also
Veterans Groups

Further Reading:

Allsup, Carl. *The American GI Forum: Origins and Evolution*. Austin: Center for Mexican American Studies, 1982.

García, Ignacio M. *Hector P. García: In Relentless Pursuit of Justice*. Houston: Arte Público Press, 2002.

Ramos, Henry A. J. *The American GI Forum: In Pursuit of the Dream, 1948–1983*. Houston: Arte Público Press, 1998.

American Indian Movement (AIM)

Modeled on African American civil rights organizations, the American Indian Movement (AIM) was formed as a Native

American response to white hegemony in the United States. Exhorting American Indians to re-embrace their sacred and cultural traditions, AIM sought to advance the cause of Native American rights. During the 1970s, AIM succeeded in restoring Native Americans to the public consciousness and raising awareness of their plight.

Four Native American activists—Dennis Banks, Clyde Bellecourt, Eddie Benton-Bonai, and George Mitchell—established the first AIM chapter in Minneapolis in 1968. AIM was conceived at the height of the antiwar and black power movements; "Red Power" had begun to appear beside spray-painted black power slogans throughout the country, and the movement caught on quickly.

Other Native American rights groups had conducted such demonstrations as fish-ins and the occupation of Alcatraz Island in 1964 and 1969, respectively, but AIM members were involved in the major Native American protests of the early 1970s—including the Trail of Broken Treaties (1972), which declared their opposition to government policy toward Native Americans, and the Wounded Knee occupation (1973), which was carried out to protest the tactics of the president of the Oglala Nation. The occupation of Wounded Knee led to gunfights between protesters and government agents that left three people dead, and AIM's militancy worried the federal government.

Following the end of a siege in Custer, South Dakota, that resulted in the burning of the courthouse there, AIM released what it called its Three-Point Program. First, AIM demanded the formation of a Senate Treaty Commission to examine the 371 treaties made between Native Americans and the federal government (which had broken many of the agreements) and to enforce the conditions of those treaties. Second, AIM called for the repeal of the Indian Reorganization Act of 1934. Third, AIM stipulated the transformation of the Bureau of Indian Affairs (BIA) into an independent, Native American–run agency, as well as reparations for the BIA's corrupt dealings with Native Americans in the past.

In the last two decades, AIM activists Banks and Russell Means have remained at the forefront of the fight for Native American rights, but the organization as a whole has lost some of its high national profile. AIM members see the lack of media interest as a criticism of the group's past violent tactics and its rejection of the "American way." Nevertheless, AIM still enjoys a strong following. Most recently, AIM has been instrumental in the campaign against the use of inappropriate Native American epithets in sports teams' names. In addition, they have maintained the cause for freeing AIM member Leonard Peltier, who many maintain is innocent of the charges against him. (Peltier was arrested for allegedly shooting two Federal Bureau of Investigation agents during the Wounded Knee occupation.)

AIM also maintains a historical archive and a speakers' bureau, conducts research, compiles statistics, and offers charitable and children's services. Its activities also include educational programs for preschoolers up to adults, offered through the Heart of the Earth Survival School. Membership is open only to Native Americans.

ABC-CLIO

See also

American Indian Religious Freedom Act (1978); Means, Russell; Native American Graves Protection and Repatriation Act (1990); Native Americans, Conquest of; Native Americans, Forced Relocation of; Occupation of Alcatraz Island; Peltier, Leonard; Red Power Movement

Further Reading:

American Indian Movement: http://www.aimovement.org.

Cheatham, Kae. *Dennis Banks: Native American Activist.* Berkeley Heights, NJ: Enslow, 1997.

Johnson, Troy, Joane Nagel, and Duane Champagne, eds. *American Indian Activism: Alcatraz to the Longest Walk.* Urbana: University of Illinois, 1997.

Klein, Barry T. *Reference Encyclopedia of the American Indian.* West Nyack, NY: Todd Publications, 1995.

Matthiessen, Peter. *In the Spirit of Crazy Horse.* New York: Penguin, 1992.

American Indian Religious Freedom Act (1978)

The American Indian Religious Freedom Act (1978), also known as AIRFA, is a landmark law based on congressional findings that the Constitution has not protected indigenous religious liberty. Infringements existed on a massive scale in 1978, and legislation was necessary to protect those inherent rights. Accordingly, Section One establishes a U.S. policy to "protect and preserve for American Indians their inherent right of freedom to believe, express, and exercise the traditional religions of the American Indian, Eskimo, Aleut, and Native Hawaiians, including but not limited to access to sites, use and possession of sacred objects, and the freedom to worship through ceremonials and traditional rites."

Section Two directed the president to evaluate federal laws, policies, and procedures to identify changes necessary to preserve indigenous religious rights and report recommendations to Congress. AIRFA is remarkable in three respects, even though it only establishes a "policy" and makes no substantive rules.

First, important findings about the government's treatment of Native American religions were made in the "whereas clauses" of this legislation, which have provided the policy backdrop for all subsequent laws and legislative efforts. For the first time Congress acknowledged that freedom of religion is an "inherent right" guaranteed to Native Americans by the First Amendment and declared that their religious practices "are an integral part of" indigenous "culture, tradition and heritage, such practices forming the basis of Indian identity and value systems." Because these religions were found to be "an integral part of Indian life" and "indispensable and irreplaceable," the lawmakers were troubled that federal policy "has often resulted in the abridgement of religious freedom for traditional American Indians." In short, AIRFA formally acknowledged a dark side of U.S. history, determined that our nation must address serious human rights infringements, and inaugurated the need for social change.

Second, Native Americans seemingly held no constitutional rights prior to AIRFA. That history could no longer be ignored, however, after the declarations made in AIRFA. Those findings corroborated facts long known to historians, who have documented that separation of church and state was disregarded in the government's treatment of Native Americans. Government-sponsored religion was imposed on Native groups for more than 100 years by hiring Christian missionaries as Indian agents, placing indigenous nations under the administrative control of different religious denominations to convert and separate them from their traditions, conveying Native land to religious groups for the building of churches and religious schools on reservations, proselytizing Native American youth in federal boarding schools, and using federal funds to support those activities.

Third, AIRFA's legislative history, findings, and report to Congress also document present-day government infringements. That record reveals a shocking list of human rights violations. Problems included the outright denial of access to religious ceremonies, holy places, and burial grounds (including a complete lack of legal protection for those places), as well as the natural materials needed as sacred objects for religious observances (such as peyote, certain plants, mineral substances, eagle feathers, and marine mammal and other animal parts) when located on federal lands or protected by conservation laws. Grave looting, trafficking in human body parts and burial offerings, and massive warehousing of sacred objects and human remains by museums were also documented. Many infringements were found to stem from a "lack of knowledge or the insensitive and inflexible enforcement of federal policies and regulations premised on a variety of laws" that are "designed for such worthwhile purposes as conservation and preservation of natural species and resources but were never intended to relate to Indian religious practices." Nonetheless, Congress found that these laws and policies often denied access to sacred sites required in Native religions, prohibited the use and possession of sacred objects needed for rites and ceremonies, and permitted intrusions and interference with, and in a few instances banned, traditional ceremonies.

The findings of Congress continue to provide the foundation for legislative policy to protect Native American religious liberty and will remain in that role until each documented injustice is addressed by the American people and corrected by appropriate legislation. However, in redressing these injustices AIRFA also teaches that "policy" alone is insufficient to protect human rights. AIRFA's policy was not enforced by the courts.

On October 6, 1994, President Bill Clinton signed into law the American Indian Religious Freedom Act Amendments. After the U.S. Supreme Court ruled in *Department of Human Services of Oregon v. Smith* (1990) and *Oregon v. Black* (1988) that the First Amendment's guarantee of free exercise of religion does not protect the use of peyote in Native American traditional religious practices, Congress amended the AIRFA to extend such protection.

Walter R. Echo-Hawk

See also

American Indian Movement (AIM); Means, Russell; Native American Graves Protection and Repatriation Act (1990); Native Americans, Conquest of; Native Americans, Forced Relocation of; Occupation of Alcatraz Island; Peltier, Leonard; Red Power Movement

Further Reading:

Echo-Hawk, Roger C., and Walter R. Echo-Hawk. *Battlefields and Burial Grounds: The Indian Struggle to Protect Ancestral Graves in the United States*. Minneapolis: Lerner Pub, 1994.

Hirschfelder, Arlene, and Paulette Molin, eds. *Encyclopedia of Native American Religions*. New York: Checkmark Books, 2000.

Miller, Robert J. "Exercising Cultural Self-Determination: The Makah Indian Tribe Goes Whaling." *American Indian Law Review* 25 (2001): 165–273.

Trope, Jack. "Protecting Native American Religious Freedom: The Legal, Historical, and Constitutional Basis for the Proposed Native American Free Exercise of Religion Act." *New York University Review of Law and Social Change* 20 (1994): 373–403.

American Literature and Racism

Racism has been both present in topic and a topic of American literature for centuries. Thomas Dixon's novel *The Clansman*, for example, inspired D. W. Griffith's film *Birth of a Nation* (1915), which contains vivid scenes of a white woman jumping off a cliff for fear of being raped by a black man, and black politicians eating chicken and sitting with their feet on the desks in the legislature. The book and film were instrumental in the revival of the Ku Klux Klan. More recently, William Styron's 1960s novel *The Confessions of Nat Turner* was attacked by many black critics because of the fictionalized motivation for Turner's rebellion: Styron's Turner feels that he must kill to conquer his lust for a white woman. Hence, in his reinterpretation of the slave rebellion that took place in 1831 in Virginia (during which Nat Turner led almost 70 blacks, and which resulted in the deaths of approximately 70 whites), Styron places emphasis on Turner's desire for sex with a white woman, for which there is no factual evidence, more than on his desire for freedom. Many readers have perceived racism to be present in the works of other major American writers such as Harriet Beecher Stowe, Mark Twain, and William Faulkner.

Uncle Tom's Cabin by Harriet Beecher Stowe, published in 1852, is a central novel in the debate about racism in American literature. Though the book is clearly arguing against slavery, its argument for blacks' worth is embodied in Uncle Tom, whose name has become a derogatory phrase denoting blacks who are servile and submissive to whites. While Stowe stresses her belief in Uncle Tom's unrelenting nobility as a result of his unwavering Christianity, his almost superhuman humility has proved objectionable to many readers and critics.

President Abraham Lincoln attested to the book's power as an abolitionist text with his oft-quoted description of Stowe as the "lady who caused this great war." Nevertheless, despite Stowe's emancipatory beliefs, the sentimentality of the novel in general and the portrayal of Uncle Tom in particular are perhaps what have given rise to much of the criticism of the book. For instance, in "Everybody's Protest Novel," included in his collection *Notes of a Native Son* (1955), James Baldwin crystallized the objection to Stowe's sentimentality and rejected attempts to defend the book by critics who stated that the book's power could be found in this very quality, which was also a convention of much 19th-century literature. Baldwin stated that sentimentality is actually characterized by hatred, that is, the inability to perceive, and thus portray, blacks as fully human, complex beings. Baldwin also believed that the novel tainted whites' perceptions of blacks for generations by crystallizing the myth of the docile and servile black. Thus, the critique of the meaning of the novel's central figure has raised questions concerning what sort of black person whites find acceptable, even admirable—thus leading to a dangerous literary and societal stereotype.

Mark Twain's novel *The Adventures of Huckleberry Finn*, published in 1884, also makes slavery a prominent topic, in this case in the depiction of the relationship between Huck and the runaway slave, Jim. Long the subject of debate has been whether aspects of the text are racist. The more obvious focus of the controversy is the use of the word *nigger*, which appears in the text well over 100 times, most obviously referring to "Nigger Jim." While some may believe that Twain, as a regional writer, wanted to capture the language that would

Imperium in Imperio

Imperium in Imperio (1899) is Sutton Griggs's first novel and perhaps his most important and influential work of fiction because it introduces the reader to many of the major themes that Griggs explores in his writing. *Imperium in Imperio* is also considered one of the first militant black nationalist novels in African American literature.

Griggs wrote during the post-Reconstruction or disenfranchisement era when African Americans faced increasing violence and racial discrimination. As a result, he was concerned with the impact of lynching, mob violence, and repression of black people, and he attempts in his novels to provide solutions to these violent circumstances. In *Imperium in Imperio* (*Nation within a Nation*), he presents the story of an organization of black revolutionaries who are determined to unite all African Americans under a single cause—the elimination of racial injustice—or to create a separate black nation within the United States with its own government and disciplined military. They also intend to publicize to the world the crimes committed against black people.

Sutton Griggs (1872–1933) was a visionary writer whose sense of black pride and determination, especially as demonstrated in *Imperium in Imperio*, anticipated much of the Black Nationalism movement of Marcus Garvey during the 1920s, the black separatist movement propagated by the Nation of Islam and Black Muslims during the 1940s and 1950s, and the Black Power and Black Arts movements of the 1960s. His concept of the New Negro, which he presents in *Imperium in Imperio*, became a rallying call for the young writers and artists of the Harlem Renaissance, as well as the title of an anthology of literature, music, and art edited by Alain Locke, which is still considered to be a definitive text of the Harlem Renaissance.

John G. Hall

have been used by people in real life, others have demanded that the book be removed from elementary and secondary school reading lists because of this epithet. What is also intriguing is that as with Stowe, Twain incorporates elements that seem at odds with his criticism of racism, which is especially noteworthy, as much of the book condemns the moral corruption of society in general.

In addition to the use of the word *nigger*, the final part of the book has been the subject of intense criticism regarding the level of Twain's racial consciousness. When Tom Sawyer enters the book, the novel becomes a boy's adventure story, and Tom and Huck make sport of Jim by exploiting his superstitious nature, having him do such things as write in blood as they make a game out of his desire for freedom. The ultimate irony comes when the reader learns that Jim already is free, without his knowing it. The final part of the book undermines readers' perceptions of the bond that has developed between Huck and Jim. As African American novelist Toni Morrison points out in *Playing in the Dark: Whiteness and the Literary Imagination* (1992), "The humiliation that Huck and Tom subject Jim to is baroque, endless, foolish, mind-softening—and it comes after we have experienced Jim as a caring father and a sensitive man" (57). Yet, Morrison believes that the book is valuable in getting readers to analyze the nature of black-white interdependence as represented in Huck and Jim's relationship. In short, *Huckleberry Finn*, a classic American text, still inspires debates about Twain's view of race and about its inclusion in educational curricula.

William Faulkner is a particularly complex figure in the exploration of racism and American literature. While Faulkner has been hailed as a stylistic genius whose complex narratives make for intricately woven literature, he has also been the subject of criticism. Race and the fragmentation of Southern society after the Civil War and well into the 20th century are two of Faulkner's recurring themes, evident in such novels as *The Sound and the Fury* (1929), *Light in August* (1932), and *Absalom, Absalom!* (1936). Yet, he is certainly not simply a critic of Southern racism; instead, at times he is an example of it.

Faulkner made several disturbing statements during the civil rights movement, which make evident that however flawed he thought the Old South was, it was more comfortable to him than the idea of change in the racial hierarchy of the era. For example, in an interview in the March 1956 issue of *The Reporter*, Faulkner stated that if desegregation led to a race war in the South, he would support segregationists, "even if it meant going out into the streets and shooting negroes" (Leeming 1994: 117). In an article written for *Life* in March 1956, in the aftermath of the *Brown v. Board of Education* decision, Faulkner also declared: "I was against compulsory segregation. I am just as strongly opposed to compulsory integration" (51). He argued that the Supreme Court should not impose integration on the South, and that such court decisions could lead to violence by whites. Faulkner also made a statement that reflects his belief that Southern whites became the "underdog" in the face of court-ordered integration. Comments Faulkner made in 1957–1958 during talks at the University of Virginia, collected in *Faulkner in the University* (Gwynn and Blotner 1959), are equally troubling. He compares the integration of blacks into Southern society as letting "unbridled horses loose in the streets, or say a community of five thousand cats with five hundred unassimilated dogs" (209). Faulkner also claims that only whites could teach blacks "self-restraint, honesty, dependability, purity . . . If we don't, we will spend the rest of our lives dodging among the five hundred unbridled horses" (211).

These comments raise the question of exactly what Faulkner's stance was regarding racism and segregation as laid out in his books. His novels seem to stop at diagnosing the societal and psychological problems of the racially divided South—they do not point toward a future where the problem of race can be addressed positively. Hence James Baldwin's remarks are important to examine in a discussion of the ideology behind Faulkner's writings, both before and during the civil rights movement: "Faulkner . . . is so plaintive concerning this 'middle of the road' from which 'extremist' elements of both races are driving him that it does not seem unfair to ask just what he has been doing there until now. Where is the evidence of the struggle he has been carrying on there on behalf of the Negro?" (Leeming 1994: 117).

Perhaps Baldwin's question is the one that underlies the controversy about racism and American literature. Many authors have raised issues about race, and some of them—for example, Stowe and Twain—seem to think their works were well intentioned. But the conflicted nature of representations of race in American literature shows that to many writers, race presented a difficult challenge to their imagination and their artistry.

Jane Davis

See also
Academic Racism; Cultural Racism; Griggs, Sutton

Further Reading:

Andrews, William L., Francis Smith Foster, and Trudier Harris, eds. *The Oxford Companion to African American Literature.* New York: Oxford University Press, 1997.

Campbell, Jane. "A Necessary Ambivalence: Sutton Griggs's *Imperium in Imperio* and Charles Chesnutt's *The Marrow of Tradition.*" In *Mythic Black Fiction: The Transformation of History*, 42–63. Knoxville: University of Tennessee Press, 1986.

Faulkner, William. "A Letter to the North." *Life*, March 5, 1956, 51–52.

Griggs, Sutton E. *Imperium in Imperio.* New York: Arno Press and *New York Times*, 1969 [1899].

Gwynn, Frederick L., and Joseph L. Blotner, eds. *Faulkner in the University.* Charlottesville: University of Virginia Press, 1959.

Leeming, David. *James Baldwin: A Biography.* New York: Henry Holt, 1994.

Morrison, Toni. *Playing in the Dark: Whiteness and the Literary Imagination.* Cambridge, MA: Harvard University Press, 1992.

Americanization Movement

In the first two decades of the 20th century, a few federal, state, and local government agencies and many private groups consisting of native-born Americans (especially those of Anglo-Saxon ancestry) tried to transform the recently arrived immigrants in the United States by encouraging or coercing them to change their foreign cultural orientations, political loyalties, and social behavior to become, very rapidly, "thoroughly American." These efforts soon became known as the Americanization Movement. Its sponsors were concerned and fearful that the massive wave of immigrants arriving since 1890 were not giving up their Old World ways and adopting an American mode of living quickly and completely. Proponents of Americanization believed that the heavy influx of newcomers who appeared so different (and in their eyes seemed degraded and inferior) would harm and destabilize American society unless strong remedial measures were taken to resocialize millions of immigrants and their children. The Americanization Movement has been characterized as an attempt to strip the immigrants of their native culture and make them over into Americans along Anglo-Saxon lines. As one of this movement's leaders put it: "Our task is to break up these [immigrants'] groups or settlements, to assimilate and amalgamate these people as a part of our American race, and to implant in their children, so far as can be done, the Anglo-Saxon conception of righteousness, law and order, and popular government, and to awaken in them a reverence for our democratic institutions and for those things in our national life which we as a people hold to be of abiding worth."

The Americanization Movement's most intense activity took place during World War I (1914–1918). Out of fear that immigrants might support their home countries—some of which were U.S. enemies—in the war, possibly with espionage or sabotage, the primary focus in these years was immigrants' political allegiance and loyalty. Americanization leaders went into immigrants' work sites, schools, and gathering places, making speeches and distributing pamphlets that urged recent immigrants and their children to give up any attachment they had to political leaders or factions in their homeland and become patriotic, proud, flag-waving U.S. citizens via the naturalization process. Many business owners, such as Henry Ford, who employed large numbers of immigrants, reinforced these efforts by having their workers take classes about U.S. history, politics, and citizen education. Of course, an equally important thrust of the Americanization Movement involved attempts to make immigrants learn and use the English language. Evening classes were held in many venues, and immigrants were urged to attend and then shift to English as quickly as possible, both as a sign of their willingness to "convert" from "foreign" to "American" and to ease their passage into the social and cultural "mainstream."

Beyond adopting English, U.S. citizenship, and patriotism, the Americanization Movement also sought to change immigrants' social behaviors and perspectives in matters like style of dress, diet and food preference, selection of first or last name, and habits of work or play. Immigrant workers and their children were indoctrinated on the importance of being punctual, dependable, obedient employees. Groups of native-born women sometimes participated in the Americanization Movement by visiting immigrants' homes and making recommendations on how a mother/wife should make it less foreign and more American, via changes in diet or cooking, household cleaning, personal hygiene, or child rearing.

While President Theodore Roosevelt, with speeches condemning the "hyphenated-American" and extolling the "100 percent American," may be the most prominent figure who supported the Americanization Movement, organizationally the most central person in it was Frances A. Kellor. She helped start or led the most active groups in the Americanization Movement, including the New York branch of the North American Civic League for Immigrants (1909), the Committee for Immigrants in America (1914), the National Americanization (Day) Committee (1915), and the Division of Immigrant Education within the federal Bureau of Education (1915). Both Roosevelt and Kellor had a genuine, but conditional, respect for and appreciation of the immigrants they felt they were assisting—they welcomed them and saw them as a positive addition *only if* they took the transforming steps offered by the Americanization Movement.

The Americanization Movement faded out in the 1920s as American leaders embraced harsher and more negative beliefs about immigrants and decided to allow immigration from Northern and Western Europe but restrict immigration from Southern and Eastern Europe and from Asia. Those unwanted immigrants were alleged to be so inherently different and inferior by nature that no resocialization through English classes, civics lessons, or changes in dress or surname could turn them into suitable Americans.

Looking back, it is understandable that social scientists favorably inclined toward cultural diversity and pluralism severely criticize the Americanization Movement. One called it a "fundamentally misguided" and "semi-hysterical attempt at pressure-cooking assimilation" based on "thinly veiled contempt" and a mistrust of immigrants that did not show an understanding of the utility of immigrants' cultural retentions and slower-paced adaptations to American life (Gordon 1964: 106). Another suggests that despite the energies expended and the ethnocentric rhetoric disseminated, the Americanization Movement had only a small effect on the immigrants—most were not directly involved in its programs and in many ways adjusted to American life at their own pace and in their own manner.

Charles Jaret

See also
Assimilation; Nativism and the Anti-Immigrant Movements

Further Reading:

Gordon, Milton. *Assimilation in American Life*. New York: Oxford University Press, 1964.
Hartmann, Edward G. *The Movement to Americanize the Immigrant*. New York: Columbia University Press, 1948.
Higham, John. *Strangers in the Land: Patterns of American Nativism, 1860–1925*. 1955. Reprint, New York: Atheneum, 1975.

Amos 'n' Andy

Amos 'n' Andy was one of the most popular and longest-running radio entertainment shows in the history of American broadcasting. Despite its popularity and longevity, *Amos 'n' Andy* represented some of the worst stereotypes of African Americans during the 1930s and 1940s. In the 1950s, it became a short-lived television series.

Charles Correll and Freeman Gosden were white radio entertainers at station WGN in Chicago in 1925. They created the first nightly radio serial, which was called *Sam 'n' Henry,* and which debuted on WGN in 1926. It was based on the comic strip *The Gumps* and consisted of two blackface minstrelsy characters. In 1927, Correll and Gosden moved to radio station WMAQ and created *Amos 'n' Andy*. In a few months, the success of the show caught the attention of the NBC radio network, of which WMAQ was a part. With Pepsodent as a sponsor, *Amos 'n' Andy* went national in August 1929. An instant hit, NBC changed the show's time slot from 11:00 P.M. EST to 7:00 P.M. EST in order to capture more of the Eastern market. However, due to protests from the Midwest and West, the 15-minute show was rebroadcast at 11:00 P.M. to accommodate the rest of the nation. At its peak in the 1930s, the show was heard by 40 million people, or one-third of the country.

Correll played Amos Jones and Gosden played Andy Brown, two black men who had migrated to Chicago from Atlanta. Along with an assortment of characters such as George "Kingfish" Stevens, Sapphire Stevens, Ramona Smith (Sapphire's Mama), Madame Queen, Algonquin J. Calhoun, and Lightnin', the show chronicled Amos and Andy's misadventures. Correll and Gosden stayed with NBC from 1929 to 1938. Then they changed to CBS and had a new sponsor, Campbell's Soup. Despite its overt racism, the show was a milestone in radio broadcasting. The popularity of the show certified the triumph of the fledging radio broadcasting industry as a form of mass entertainment. Their success, despite the overt stereotyping, exemplified friendship, a never-give-up attitude, a strong work ethic, and common sense.

CBS's *Amos 'n' Andy*, (June 1951–April 1953) starring Spencer Williams (left), Tim Moore (center), and Alvin Childress (right). (AP/Wide World Photos)

February 1943 was the final episode of the original *Amos 'n' Andy*. The show returned in the fall in a half-hour weekly format. It now included a studio audience and a full cast of supporting actors who were primarily African American. The role of Kingfish became more prominent. Many of the shows were written by Joe Connelly and Bob Mosher, who would go on to produce the television shows *Leave It to Beaver* and *The Munsters*. The new weekly half-hour show lasted for 12 years as one of the most popular weekly programs on the air.

In June 1951, *Amos 'n' Andy* debuted on CBS television. Instead of Correll and Godsen, the cast was entirely black: Alvin Childress as Amos Jones, Spencer Williams as Andy, Tim Moore as George "Kingfish" Stevens. Only Ernestine Wade as Sapphire Stevens and Amanda Randolph as Ramona Smith were originally from the radio show. The show pioneered the use of filming a television series with a multicamera setup. The hit show lasted through 78 episodes but was a center of controversy. Many in the black community protested the reinforcing of racial stereotypes in the show. The National Association for the Advancement of Colored People (NAACP) protested most vigorously by citing the show's lack of respect for black people. As a result of the protests, CBS pulled the show from the air in 1953, although it continued in reruns until 1966, when again it was pulled from the air because of complaints from not only the NAACP, but also those in the civil rights movement. The *Amos 'n' Andy* radio show was inducted into the Radio Hall of Fame in 1988.

Sanjeev A. Rao, Jr.

See also
Blackface; Minstrelsy

Further Reading:

Andrews, Bart, and Ahrgus Juilliard. *Holy Mackerel! The Amos 'n' Andy Story*. Boston: E. P. Dutton, 1986.

Ely, Melvin Patrick. *The Adventures of Amos and Andy: A Social History of an American Phenomenon*. New York: Free Press. 1991.

McLeod, Elizabeth. *The Original Amos 'n' Andy: Freeman Gosden, Charles Correll and the 1928–1943 Radio Serial*. Jefferson, NC: McFarland, 2005.

Anchor Baby

An *anchor baby* is a child of unauthorized immigrant parents who is born in the United States and, therefore, given U.S. citizenship as granted by the U.S. Constitution's Fourteenth Amendment's Citizenship Clause. As a term in media and political usage, anchor baby also describes a potential migratory process for future migrants: once 21 years of age, the anchor baby can sponsor family members to come to the United States and become citizens. Anchor baby is generally regarded as a pejorative, although the term has, until recently, frequently appeared in dictionaries, media sources, and political discourse without noting its negative meaning.

Anchor baby partly originates from *anchor child*, another pejorative used to describe the children of Vietnamese immigrants coming to the United States following the Vietnam conflict, and from the idea that the children of unauthorized immigrants are dropped (like an anchor) in the United States, thus tying the child's family to the United States. The anchor metaphor further links to the term *chain migration*, in that the anchor baby could theoretically create a chain between the United States and the child's family abroad, making it easier for other family members to migrate (with or without authorization) to the United States by reducing the social and economic costs of migration in addition to nearly insurmountable legal hurdles. Anchor babies are also related to the terms *drop and leave* and *birth tourism*, which imply that unauthorized immigrant mothers (or in the case of birth tourism, mothers with travel visas) intentionally and willfully enter the United States to have babies so the child receives U.S. citizenship as granted under the Fourteenth Amendment. In modern context, anchor baby is most commonly used to describe Latino children born in the United States to unauthorized parents, and is frequently found in arguments against Latino immigration.

Immigration opponents (particularly those opposing Latino immigrants entering the United States) argue that anchor babies are a planned, willful action intended to sidestep the U.S. immigration system. Opponents to Latino immigrants commonly argue that anchor babies represent an unfair drain on community resources (such as school systems and health care) and that anchor babies and their family members eventually acquire jobs that could go to other U.S. citizens. Additionally, opponents also argue that anchor babies manipulate the immigration system by initiating a link to family members abroad so that they may receive preferential migration status down the road. In the political sphere, certain state lawmakers (such as Lindsey Graham, a senator from South Carolina) have spurred the creation of state laws looking to clarify or reinterpret the

Fourteenth Amendment and close what is described as a loophole in the amendment encouraging the proliferation of anchor babies.

Immigration scholars counter these claims by noting that using anchor babies to enter the United States is a relatively poor migration strategy. For example, an anchor baby cannot sponsor his or her parents for citizenship until the baby reaches 21 years of age. Other family members would still be subject to quotas, causing extensive delays in becoming naturalized citizens, which limits the value of anchor babies as a migration strategy. Meanwhile, parents would experience over a two-decade delay in utilizing anchor babies to obtain their own citizenship and attempting family reunification, making the idea of anchor babies as a viable migration strategy a weak argument.

Additionally, anchor babies are a relatively uncommon phenomenon. Research by the Pew Research Center finds that, in 2008, an estimated 340,000 babies were born to unauthorized immigrant parents in the United States. This accounts for approximately 8 percent of the babies born in the United States in 2008. This does not mean that every baby would be counted as an anchor baby, however. In fact, very few immigrant parents identify the intent to have babies in the United States (and thus create the purported anchor link to the United States) as a reason for migrating to the United States.

The term anchor baby is experiencing a period of revision as information regarding its negative meaning spreads. The term initially dispersed rapidly across media sources as slang used to quickly describe a purported phenomenon in immigration without explaining the details or the term's role as a pejorative. The term temporarily entered common usage as a result. Today, print and online dictionaries (such as American Heritage) have initiated the process of correcting the meaning of the term and noting it as derogatory and slang in its entry. Using a different approach to addressing the meaning of anchor baby, a handful of descendents who identify their heritage as being attached to an anchor baby have recently initiated efforts to reclaim and embrace the term. They see the term as a celebration of immigrants and their culture while noting the dramatic role of immigration in U.S. history.

James Maples

See also

Arizona Senate Bill 1070 (SB 1070) (2010); Chain Migration

Further Reading:

Campoverdi, Alejandra. "Anchor Babies: Alejandra Campoverdi Reclaims the Idea of the 'Anchor Baby' for Her Family and All Immigrants." *Kennedy School Review* 8 (2008): 111–14.

Ignatow, Gabe, and Alexander T. Williams. "New Media and the 'Anchor Baby' Boom." *Journal of Computer-Mediated Communication* 17 (2011): 60–76.

Rosenbloom, Rachel E. "Policing the Borders of Birthright Citizenship: Some Thoughts on the New (and Old) Restrictionism." *Washburn Law Journal* 51 (2012): 311–30.

Anti-Chinese Sentiments

Chinese immigrants first arrived in California in 1849 to seek their fortunes as prospectors and miners on Gold Mountain. The China they left behind suffered from drought, overpopulation, local wars, and national chaos from imperialist intrusions after the Opium Wars (1839–1842), and a devastating civil war during the Taiping Rebellion. The immigration of Chinese, mostly young men, to the United States was a continuation of a centuries-old pattern of out-migration from southern China in search of economic opportunity. Leaving their wives and families behind for what they considered a short-term employment opportunity, they bought tickets to America on credit and quickly settled into California's rapidly expanding mining industry and agricultural sector. Employers initially welcomed the Chinese immigrants, commonly referred to as "celestials," as flexible, cheap, and cooperative. In the volatile economic times of the new California, employers often turned to Chinese workers because of their willingness to work for lower wages than white immigrants. In the 1860s, Chinese laborers engaged in railroad construction projects, including the building of the western spur of the transcontinental railroad. They served not only as laborers but also as cooks and laundry men, playing the role of female domestics because there were so few women at the work sites. Chinese immigrants eventually made up 90 percent of the construction force, at enormous savings to the Central Pacific Railroad, which paid white workers $31 a month plus housing, but Chinese $31 without housing.

California's 19th-century economy fluctuated wildly from boom to bust, leaving workers anxious and uncertain. White laborers considered the Chinese to be a threat to jobs and wages, and cheap Chinese labor became a scapegoat for their economic woes. In this environment, anti-Chinese sentiments spread quickly and Chinese workers became frequent targets of violence, including riots, beatings, and lynchings. California's nativist politicians, scrambling for workers' votes in a state evenly balanced between Democrats and Republicans, played upon whites' fears of foreigners and nonwhites. Beginning with the Foreign Miners License Tax in 1852, the California government enacted a series of laws to protect "California for Americans," particularly against the Chinese. The numerous exclusionary laws that followed were designed to marginalize Chinese immigrants, exclude them from full participation in California society, and secure the political support of the white working class. In 1855, the state levied a landing tax of $50 a head on the owner or master of any ship carrying immigrants who could not become naturalized citizens. In 1862, the state passed a law "To Protect Free White Labor against Competition with Chinese Coolie Labor, and to Discourage the Immigration of the Chinese into the State of California" that established a tax of $2.50 each month on all Chinese residents of the state, with the exception of those who were licensed to work in mines, operating businesses, or engaged in certain kinds of agriculture. The 1,875-page law prohibited the entry of Chinese prostitutes, but the accompanying rigorous interrogations and cross-examinations hampered the immigration of all Chinese women. Arrivals of Chinese women declined by 68 percent between 1876–1882 compared with the previous seven-year period. In the 1854 case *People v. Hall*, the California Supreme Court ruled that Chinese, like blacks, mulattos, and American Indians, could not testify for or against whites in court, leaving Chinese Americans extremely vulnerable to discrimination and violence.

The opening of the transcontinental railroad in 1867 facilitated Chinese migration to the East Coast, where Chinese workers were drawn into labor conflicts and they quickly discovered that anti-Chinese sentiment was not limited to the American West. East Coast traders, missionaries, and diplomats who had encountered Chinese immigrants as early as 1785, before the Gold Rush, often portrayed them as immoral heathens, dishonest, and barbaric. Scientific racial classification projects expressed concerns over race mixing. In 1870, Calvin T. Sampson hired 75 Chinese workers from California to break a strike at his shoe factory in Adams, Massachusetts. The practice quickly spread, and anti-Chinese sentiments among white East Coast workers quickly escalated. The rise in anti-Chinese sentiments was initially brought to national attention by California politicians, but it found a receptive audience and culminated in the Chinese Exclusion Act of 1882, which banned the immigration of Chinese laborers into the United States. The Chinese Exclusion Act, enforced until its repeal in 1943, marked the beginning of efforts to restrict all immigration to the United States, finally codified in the National Origins Act of 1924.

Kenneth J. Guest

See also

Asian American Legal Defense and Education Fund (AALDEF); Chinese Exclusion Act of 1882; National Origins Act of 1924. Documents: The Chinese Exclusion Act (1882); The National Origins Act of 1924 (Johnson-Reed Act)

Further Reading:

Salyer, Lucy E. *Laws Harsh as Tigers: Chinese Immigrants and the Shaping of Modern Immigration Law*. Chapel Hill: University of North Carolina Press, 1995.

Takaki, Ronald. *Strangers from a Different Shore: A History of Asian Americans*. Boston: Back Bay Books, 1998.

Anti-Immigrant Movement

Groups and organizations that are opposed to the arrival of new immigrants can be traced back to the colonial period when prominent citizens expressed a fear of German immigrants who tended to congregate, share the culture of the country of origin, and use the German language rather than English. The opposition to immigrants continued and in the 1850s gained popularity in the political party known as the Know-Nothings. The original Whig party failed to address growing concerns from native-born Protestants over the arrival of new immigrants and especially Catholic immigrants. The Know-Nothing or American Party grew out of a semisecret nativist society known as the Order of United Americans (OUA) whose stated purpose was the creation of economic opportunity and a homogenous

LIBERTY
THE UNION.
MILLARD FILLMORE,
AMERICAN CANDIDATE FOR PRESIDENT OF THE UNITED STATES.

Millard Fillmore was the 1856 presidential candidate of the Know-Nothing Party (also called the American Party), a group that epitomized the growing tide of anti-Catholic and anti-immigrant feeling in the United States in the 1850s. The election was won by Democrat James Buchanan. (Corbis)

culture for the nation. While all humans were due an equal opportunity, some humans were viewed as deficient and therefore not entitled to the same benefits. Deficiency was often assigned to newly arrived immigrants and Catholics. During the 1850s, the target of opposition was mostly Germans who were viewed as radicals unfit for American democracy, and the Irish who owed their allegiance to the Roman Catholic Church. Repeatedly, the Know-Nothings conjured up visions of a foreign invasion led by German and Irish immigrants. The Know-Nothings also considered the government to be part of the plot to turn over America to foreigners by allowing parochial schools and giving funds to foreigners thus burdening the American social benefits such as public education. Attitudes such as these and the use of newspapers led to the worst anti-immigrant massacre in American history. After a series of articles in the *Journal* of Louisville, Kentucky, armed citizens who envisioned a horde invading the Middle West attacked German and Irish immigrants on August 6, 1855. "Bloody Monday" took the lives of 22 immigrants and forced hundreds to leave the area. Eventually the American Party disappeared, but other organization such as the Ku Klux Klan (KKK) and American Protective Association were active by the 1860s. The American Protective Association believed the nation

Farmingville

Farmingville, New York, provides the backdrop for intense anti-immigrant behavior and an organization determined to stop immigrants from coming to the area. Located on Long Island, the community became a center of the border war. Filmmakers Catherine Tambini and Carlos Sandoval produced a 2004 documentary chronicling the rise of the Sachem Quality of Life (SQL) group and their efforts to curtail an "immigrant invasion." The primary targets for harassment were day laborers gathered on street corners waiting for employment. However, immigrant families and supporters of immigrants were also targeted. In 2000, two day laborers were severely beaten and stabbed. The SQL hosted a "Day of Truth" forum featuring several known white supremacists and leaders of anti-immigrant groups. The SQL splintered into separate groups in 2004.

was being overrun by "alien people" and that this was especially true in the Middle West.

The KKK adopted this attitude in the early 20th century. During the last half of the 19th century, the KKK was primarily associated with racism that focused on African Americans and by the end of the century had begun to see a decline in membership. However, mass immigration related to industrialization in the early 20th century and the participation in World War I gave the organization new targets for hatred. By 1917, the KKK called for social vigilance to protect the American way of life and sought to defend the country from aliens, idlers, and organized labor. A violent approach was taken against anyone seen as a threat. Blacks, Jews, Catholics, Asians, Mexicans, immigrants, and the immoral were beaten, tarred-and-feathered, shot, and lynched. Vigilante violence became the norm of the organization, and by the 1960s, a new wave of immigrants entered the country. However, the KKK changed in appearance and exchanged robes for camouflage as paramilitary groups became outspoken on the immigration issue.

The late 20th century and early 21st century saw the rise of militias and "Patriot Support Groups" within the KKK and an expansion of anti-immigrant/vigilante organizations. Many groups in the 21st century have returned to the same dehumanizing language of the Know-Nothing Party and exploit the same fears used by earlier anti-immigrant organizations. However, the target has shifted from the earlier ethnic groups and has become focused on Hispanic people. Once again, immigrants are depicted as an invading force determined to destroy American culture by refusing to speak English and maintaining the culture of country of origin. Immigrants are portrayed as "third world invaders," carriers of disease, lazy, criminals, and a burden on society. Anti-immigrant organizations spread this ideology through print and media campaigns but in many cases, anti-immigrant behavior takes the form of violence and vigilantism.

As late as 2012, undocumented immigrants attempting to cross the Mexican-American border have been detained and in some cases killed by citizen groups dedicated to stopping the invasion. While much of the physical violence takes place in border states such as Arizona, coalitions of anti-immigrant organizations and groups have multiplied on both the West and East coast. Groups such as the Minutemen, the American Patrol, the U.S. Patriot Patrol, and many others are listed by the Anti-Defamation League and the Southern Poverty Law Center as anti- immigrant organizations operating along the U.S. border. Some of these groups act as armed vigilantes who protect America by detaining border crossers and engaging in gun battle with suspected drug smugglers. These groups also call for stricter limitations on immigration and increased enforcement of current deportation laws. Similar to the Know-Nothings, modern organizations cite the failure of the government to listen to the people as justification for their actions, and, just as the earlier anti-immigrant organizations, their actions have the potential to become violent.

R. Randall Adams

Further Reading:

Anti-Defamation League. "Border Disputes: Armed Vigilantes in Arizona." http:/www.adl.org (accessed December 2, 2012).

Anti-Defamation League. "Immigrants Targeted: Extremist Rhetoric Moves into the Mainstream." http:/www.adl.org (accessed December 2, 2012).

Biggers, Jeff. *State Out of the Union*. New York: Nation Books, 2012.

Levine, Bruce. "Conservatism, Nativism, and Slavery: Thomas R. Whitney and the Origins of the Know-Nothing Party." *Journal of American History* 88 (2001): 455–488.

Know-Nothing Party

The American, or Know-Nothing, Party was an anti-immigrant party that gained some strength in mid-19th-century America. The party grew out of a secret nativist organization, the Order of the Star-Spangled Banner, which was founded in 1850. The members of the party were often called know-nothings because of their origins as a secret organization whose members insisted, when questioned, that they "know nothing" about it. From 1852 through 1854, the nativist Know-Nothing Party gained surprising strength. In the elections of 1854, those voters who believed that immigration was the greatest threat to the American way of life cast their ballots for the Know-Nothing Party. In that election, 75 congressmen and many city, county, and state officials from the party were elected.

Their primary objective was to restrict the flow of immigration to the United States. The Know-Nothings opposed the admission of paupers, criminals, and any other "undesirable immigrants," including Catholics, into the country. They believed that the period required for naturalization should be extended from five to 21 years. The party's slogan was "America for the Americans," and its platform urged that only "native" white Americans be permitted to hold public office. Throughout the 1850s, nativist hostility against immigrants, especially Irish Catholics, intensified with the Know-Nothing Party's support. The powerless immigrants were exploited as scapegoats for the problems by the politicians to enhance their own political interests. The targeted group at that time was Irish immigrants, but the pattern has continued up to today.

Heon Cheol Lee

McGlynn, Edward. "The New Know-Nothingism and the Old." *North American Review* 145 (1887): 192–205.

Southern Poverty Law Center. "Climate of Fear: Latino Immigrants in Suffolk County, N.Y." http:/www.splcenter.org (accessed December 12, 2012).

Southern Law Poverty Center. "Ku Klux Klan: A History of Racism and Violence." 6th Edition, http:/www.splcenter.org (accessed December 2, 2012).

Anti-Immigrant Sentiment

Attitudes and concerns are often informed by geographical location and identity but in a globalized world, individuals are often forced to migrate. Migration often leads to the interaction of different cultural and ethnic groups. Negative attitudes towards immigrants are often formed when host citizens fail to have contact, perceive immigrants as a threat to their way of life, or have a strong sense of national identity. Pehrson, Viznoles, and Rupert define nationalism as "a culture, in the sense of a shared representation of ideal social relations, in which the nation is envisaged as the basic source of sovereignty and object of solidarity" (Pehrson et al., 2009: 25). In other words, a strong sense of identity with the nation can have adverse effects on the attitudes concerning newcomers who are not viewed as part of that nation or are viewed as a threat. Pehrson et al. identify two types of nationalism: *civic* and *ethnic*. Civic nationalism concerns ideas of citizenship, commitment to national institutions, and participation in national institutions. Ethnic nationalism is concerned with such things as common ancestry, sharing of a common language, cultural homogeneity, and a sense of distinctiveness from others. Late in the 19th century as theories of race became popular, ethnic nationalism provided a background for anti-immigrant sentiments and a call for immigrant exclusion. Prejudice towards immigrants is positively linked to nationalism when a common language is viewed as one of the more important criteria for being a part of the nation, when immigrants tend to be less educated and lower skilled, and when national identification is based more on cultural aspects than on ideas concerning good citizenship. Historically, a sense of nationalism informed reactions to immigrants in two periods of mass migration in the United States.

Mass migration to the United States took place from the 1880s to the 1920s and from the 1970s until the early 2000s. Reception and attitudes concerning immigrants were similar but with some striking differences. Nativism became

Understanding Immigrants

The immigrant issue has remained at the forefront of the American conversation since the founding of the nation. Numerous books have been written about the positive and negative experiences of immigrants in the United States.

Roger Daniels in *Guarding the Golden Door* explores the laws and acts that have formed immigrant policy since the Chinese Exclusion Act (To Execute Certain Treaty Stipulations Relating to Chinese) of 1882. The author establishes a pattern that remains steady throughout the 20th and 21st centuries. Steven V. Roberts gives a series of vignettes describing the life of immigrants from all around the globe in *From Every End of This Earth*. Roberts chronicles the motivations, the hardships, and the success of immigrants as they come to the United Sates for a better life. Ted Conover describes the risk and hazards of undocumented workers as they try to gain economic security in *Coyotes*. Traveling with undocumented migrants and later visiting their homes, Conover humanizes the faceless shadows shown in the media as men and women desperate to provide a good life for their families. Desperation leads to tragedy in Jorge Ramos's *Dying to Cross*. The fatal trip of undocumented immigrants smuggled in the back of an enclosed truck allows the reader to understand the motivation and cost of coming to America.

Philip Yang

increasingly prevalent during these immigration epochs. As migration shifted in the 1870s to include Southern and Eastern Europeans, nativists became concerned about the quality of new immigrants. Individuals were concerned that the immigrants were worthless and unable to assimilate to American culture. Similar expressions of concern have been expressed after the 1970s as immigration shifted to Latin America, Asia, and the Caribbean. During both periods the diversity of these immigrants were viewed as threatening the Anglo-Saxon nature of America and producing a social and economic burden on natives by allowing inferior stock into the country. Language also became an issue during both periods. The Americanization Movement of the 1910s placed an emphasis on teaching and requiring the use of English, the only "true language of the United States" (Jaret, 1999: 14). A similar reaction may be observed today in the number of "English only" ordinances presented to legislatures. Other laws designed to discriminate against immigrants have included licensing laws designed to limit immigrant occupations, forbidding the ownership of property, setting quotas, and in the 21st century the restriction of social services. Violence has accompanied both periods as well as the fear that immigrants seek to destroy American values and norms. These negative and prejudiced attitudes can be found in all geographical areas of the country.

The Southern Poverty Law Center produces many studies of anti-immigrant environments particularly in the South and Northeast. Reports published in 2009 establish the consistency of anti-immigrant sentiment present in the United States. While immigrants arrive from all parts of the globe, a focus on Latino immigrants has become the center for anti-immigrant activity. However, the focus on Latino immigrants often serves as a small-scale version of U.S. anti-immigrant sentiments and actions. In the 2000s, a consistent rise in harassment of Latino immigrants took place. Low-level harassment became commonplace and at times escalated to the point of murder. Racial profiling by state and local officials also became the norm. The results have been the creation of a subclass of individuals who live in constant fear and see no available help. Many of the victims are undocumented or H2 visa workers.

The late 20th and early 21st century have seen a fixation on the undocumented migrant. Undocumented status along with the H2 visa, which ties a worker to a certain job, creates a target that is easily exploited. Workers are threatened with deportation when they complain. This has led to underpayment of wages, unsafe working conditions, and workers who view themselves as prisoners of an unjust system. They cannot complain or seek justice without losing the poverty-ending jobs that many came in search of. State and local officials often exacerbate the problem by passing discriminatory laws or participating in federal programs such as 287(g) which allowed local law enforcement to check immigration status and start deportation proceedings.

Americans have long harbored anti-immigrant sentiments. Although the ethnic groups change, the attitudes

Dillingham Report

The Dillingham Report was a voluminous report issued in 1911 by the U.S. Commission on Immigration, a congressional commission chaired by Senator William P. Dillingham. After extensive hearings held between 1907 and 1911, the Dillingham commission issued a report that contained four major conclusions: (1) new immigrants tended to congregate residentially and were slow to assimilate; (2) they were less skilled and educated than the native born; (3) they had a greater criminal tendency; and (4) they were willing to accept low wages and a low standard of living. As a solution to these negative characteristics of new immigrants, the commission suggested that immigrants be given a mandatory literacy test and that the number of immigrants be restricted based on the racial and ethnic compositions of the population in the United States.

Prodded by this report, the U.S. Congress passed a literacy-test bill, which was vetoed by President William Howard Taft. This report provided an empirical justification for the racially biased immigration restriction laws passed in subsequent years, which culminated in the National Origins Act of 1924. Analyses of empirical findings in this report were flawed because it was based on simplistic categories, an unfair comparison of different waves of immigrant groups, little consideration of the differences in native countries of immigrant groups, the length of residence in the United States, the changing socioeconomic conditions of the United States, and other factors.

Shin Kim and Kwang Chung Kim

often remain the same. Immigrants are viewed as a threat to both economic opportunity and the social fiber of the United States. Attitudes such as these have remained fairly stable over time but at the beginning of the 21st century there have been some modest changes.

In June of 2012, the Pew Research Center reported a number of shifts in the American attitude. While most Americans supported strong limitation of the number of immigrants allowed into the country, the percentage of individuals supporting this view declined slightly. In 2007, 75 percent of individuals believed immigration should be limited, but only 69 percent held the same view in 2012. However, Americans remain evenly divided on the question of immigrants' effects on core values and customs. While 46 percent of individuals believed in a negative impact, 48 percent believed that the impact on values and customs was slight. Characteristics such as race, age, and level of education continue to inform individuals' attitudes toward immigrants. African Americans are often less accepting of immigrants while those with a higher level of education seem to be more willing to accept immigrants as part of the society. Americans remain cautious in their acceptance of immigrants.

R. Randall Adams

See also

287g Delegation of Immigration Authority; Anchor Baby; Anti-Immigrant Sentiment; Arizona Senate Bill 1070 (SB 1070); Immigration Acts; Immigration and Customs Enforcement (ICE); National Origins Act of 1924; Operation Wetback; Unauthorized Immigration; United States Border Patrol

Further Reading:

Bauman, Zygmunt. *Liquid Times: Living in an Age of Uncertainty*. Malden, MA: Polity Press, 2007.

Jaret, Charles. "Troubled by Newcomers: Anti-Immigrant Attitude and Action during two Eras of Mass Migration to the United States." *Journal of American Ethnic History* 18 (1999): 9–39.

Pehrson, Samuel, Vivian L. Viznoles, and Rupert Brown. "National Identification and Anti-Immigrant Prejudice: Individual and Contextual Effects of National Definitions." *Social Psychology Quarterly* 72 (2009): 24–38.

Southern Poverty Law Center. "Climate of Fear: Latino Immigrants in Suffolk County, N.Y." http:/www.splcenter.org (accessed December 12, 2012).

Southern Poverty Law Center. "Under Siege: Life for Low-Income Latinos in the South." http:/www.splcenter.org (accessed December 12, 2012).

U.S. Immigration Commission. *Brief Statement of the Conclusions and Recommendation of the Immigration Commission with the View of the Minority*. Washington, DC: U.S. Government Printing Office, 1910.

Anti-Lynching Campaign

The anti-lynching campaign, composed of various individuals and organizations, emerged in the late 19th century in response to the widespread growth of the lynching of African Americans by white mobs across the United States, advocating federal legislation and social activism against the phenomenon of lynching. Between 1882 and 1968, at least 4,743 people, including around 3,450 African Americans, were lynched in the United States. In the single year of 1892, which marked lynching's peak, at least 230 black people were killed. However, that year also marked the beginning of the country's first sustained anti-lynching campaign. Three of the men who died in 1892 were friends of the Memphis-based journalist Ida B. Wells-Barnett.

Wells began to investigate the lynchings of the previous decade and wrote a controversial editorial challenging the concept that the assault of white women by African American men was at the core of these acts by white mobs. She followed the editorial with a pamphlet, *Southern Horrors*, which discussed consensual interracial sex, connected lynching to slavery, and advocated black boycotts of white businesses, armed self-protection, migration, and legislative action. In another anti-lynching pamphlet, she asked readers to support the Blair Bill, a resolution coming before the U.S. House of Representatives in August 1894.

She continued her work into the 20th century, and, in 1909, she helped to found the National Association for the Advancement of Colored People (NAACP), which launched

Members of the National Association for the Advancement of Colored People (NAACP) New York City Youth Council picketing for anti-lynching legislation before the Strand Theatre in Times Square in 1937. (Library of Congress)

Anti-Lynching Bureau

The Anti-Lynching Bureau was established in 1899 in response to the increasing brutalization of African Americans during the post–Reconstruction era. A division of the National Afro-American Council, the Anti-Lynching Bureau was dedicated to the investigation of incidents of lynching and other atrocities committed against African Americans. Founded by T. Thomas Fortune in 1898, the National Afro-American Council espoused a less militant ideology of resistance than its predecessor, the National Afro-American League. Through the creation of the Anti-Lynching Bureau, the Council hoped to put an end to the most savage mode of white-on-black intimidation. In its efforts to combat disenfranchisement and to right the wrongs perpetrated against members of the African American community, the National Afro-American Council served as a precursor of future civil rights organizations such as the Niagara movement and the National Association for the Advancement of Colored People.

While serving as chair of the Anti-Lynching Bureau, Ida B. Wells-Barnett published a series of pamphlets and articles condemning the practice of lynching as a crime against humanity that threatened the nation's moral fiber. Detailing the torture, hanging, burning, and dismemberment of victims, Wells-Barnett sought to arouse public sentiment. Unfortunately, the Anti-Lynching Bureau's desperate financial situation seriously hampered its efforts. With only 300 members, the organization lacked the funds to publish the very documents intended to pressure Congress into passing federal anti-lynching legislation. In a letter dated January 1, 1902, Wells-Barnett implored the Bureau's members to renew their memberships and encourage others to join the organization so that the Bureau might continue its efforts to end mob violence and eradicate lynching. Wells-Barnett's untiring devotion to the Anti-Lynching Bureau and its cause earned her the title of the nation's foremost anti-lynching crusader.

CAROL GOODMAN

its own anti-lynching campaign. Led by Walter White, who personally investigated more than 40 lynchings, the association amassed vast amounts of lynching data. From 1916 onward its Anti-Lynching Committee developed legislative and public awareness campaigns, and in 1919 it documented the deaths of 3,224 people in a 30-year period. Throughout the early 1920s, it advertised lynching statistics in national newspapers and lobbied for the passage of the federal Dyer Bill, which proposed to punish anyone who participated in a lynching or who failed to prosecute lynchers.

Introduced in 1918 and passed by the House in January 1922, the bill was halted by a filibuster in the Senate. But one important legacy of the failed bill was the organizational model of the Anti-Lynching Crusaders. Established in 1922, this group of African American women within the NAACP raised money to promote the Dyer Anti-Lynching Bill and attempted to unite black and white women around a renewed anti-lynching effort. After the death of the bill, the Anti-Lynching Crusaders' model was taken up by Jessie Daniel Ames's Association of Southern Women for the Prevention of Lynching (ASWPL).

On November 1, 1930, Ames held a meeting in Atlanta for Southern white women who wanted to help end lynching. This was an important role, she explained, because lynching was frequently justified in their name, as a method of protecting them from rape. Women from seven of the southeastern states attended the meeting, and on November 6, another group of women—from Louisiana, Arkansas, Oklahoma, and Texas—joined with Ames's group to create a movement across the South. The newly formed association launched an informational campaign condemning lynching and disavowing the notion of "protection" for white womanhood. They followed this with outreach efforts, asking sheriffs to protect the rule of law. Within their communities, Southern white women congregated wherever a lynching was rumored to take place and tried to prevent it from unfolding. The ASWPL was deeply subversive to the Southern social and sexual hierarchy. By speaking out, its members overturned the patriarchal order that had kept white women in their place and in need of white male "protection." And although results are impossible to quantify with any precision, the ASWPL may have contributed to a 50 percent reduction in the incidence of lynching by 1938. Membership had reached 40,000 by 1939.

Other activism during the 1930s included the campaign to pass the Costigan-Wagner Anti-Lynching Bill of 1935, led by the NAACP. The bill's text was the same as the Dyer Anti-Lynching bill, proposing fines and imprisonment for any governmental body that failed to protect an individual from a mob. Some campaigners felt these proposals did not go far enough, and so a coalition of left-wing organizations, including the League of Struggle for Negro Rights, proposed its own legislation—a "Bill for Negro Rights." This made lynching punishable by death and outlawed the Ku Klux Klan. It garnered little support, and Congress also failed to pass the Costigan-Wagner Bill. The 200 other anti-lynching bills introduced between 1882 and 1968 met the same fate.

Yet while their lobbying efforts failed, anti-lynching campaigners did succeed in challenging both the gender dynamics surrounding lynching (including the stereotype of the black male as a sexual beast) and the white supremacist notion of racially redemptive violence. The legacy of anti-lynching campaigning was further evident in 2005, when the Senate finally passed a resolution related to lynching. Summarizing the long history of anti-lynching campaigns, the Senate went on to issue an apology to lynching victims for its own failure to enact anti-lynching legislation.

Zoe Trodd

See also

Anti-Lynching League; Anti-Lynching Legislation; Lynching. Documents: Ida B. Wells' Exposé on Lynching (1895); The "Anti-Lynching" Hearings (1920); *Bee Publishing Company v. State of Nebraska* (1921)

Further Reading:

Brundage, W. Fitzhugh, ed. *Under Sentence of Death: Lynching in the South.* Chapel Hill: University of North Carolina Press, 1997.

Duster, Alfreda M., ed. *Crusade for Justice: The Autobiography of Ida B. Wells.* Chicago: University of Chicago Press, 1970.

Hall, Jacquelyn Dowd. *Revolt Against Chivalry: Jessie Daniel Ames and the Women's Campaign against Lynching.* New York: Columbia University Press, 1993.

Library of Congress. "After Reconstruction: Problems of African Americans in the South." http://memory.loc.gov/learn/lessons/rec/congress.html.

Royster, Jacqueline Jones, ed. *Southern Horrors and Other Writings: The Anti-Lynching Campaign of Ida B. Wells.* Boston: Bedford Books, 1997.

Wells-Barnett, Ida B. *To the Members of the Anti-Lynching Bureau.* Library of Congress, African American Perspectives: Pamphlets from the Daniel A.P. Murray Collection, 1818–1907. Chicago: Office of Anti-Lynching Bureau, 1902. http://memory.loc.gov/ammem/aap/aaphome.html.

Anti-Lynching League

The Anti-Lynching League (also referred to as the British Anti-Lynching League) was founded in 1899 by journalist, activist, and philanthropist Ida B. Wells-Barnett, who also founded the National Association of Colored Women (NACW). Wells-Barnett became the single most influential individual in history to levy an anti-lynching campaign. The Anti-Lynching League was used as a mechanism to illuminate the systematic practice of lynching and lynch law that was practiced overwhelmingly in the Southern United States. Always outspoken, her commitment to combat lynching began after three of her friends, who were prominent Negro businessmen, were lynched in Memphis, Tennessee, in 1892.

They were targeted because their business, the People's Grocery Store, had become successful competition for the white grocery store in the community. As a result of this occurrence, Wells-Barnett began challenging the longstanding belief that lynchings were in response to white men protecting the chastity of white women, and suggested that the true motivation behind this extralegal activity was the fear that Negroes could become economic competition (see Rape as Provocation for Lynching).

Wells-Barnett traveled throughout the United States, Scotland, and Great Britain illuminating the condition of Negroes in the United States. The establishment of the Anti-Lynching League came as a result of Wells-Barnett's second tour of Great Britain, which focused on informing the English of the atrocities occurring in the United States against Negroes in the form of lynchings. She appealed to the British to assist her in the anti-lynching crusade, not only because of the sense of honor and justice of the British, but also because of the historical commitment of the English in combating other wrongs against American Negroes, such as slavery. Upon return from her second tour of speeches to

British community organizations, churches, and political figures, the British contributed £5,000 to establish the Anti-Lynching League. This funding was to be used specifically to investigate and make public the lynching activity occurring in the United States. The organization worked to promote the creation and passing of anti-lynching legislation.

NIA WOODS HAYDEL

See also

Anti-Lynching Legislation; Lynching; Wells-Barnett, Ida B.

Further Reading:

Altman, C.B. "Wells-Barnett, Ida B." http://www.learningtogive.org/papers/index.asp?bpid=134.

Lerner, Gerda. "Early Community Work of Black Club Women." *Journal of Negro History* 59, no. 2 (1974): 158–67.

Tucker, David M. "Miss Ida B. Wells and Memphis Lynching." *Phylon* 32, no. 2 (1960): 112–22.

Wells-Barnett, Ida B. *The Memphis Diary of Ida B. Wells.* Boston: Beacon Press, 1995.

Zackodnik, Teresa. "Ida B. Wells and 'American Atrocities' in Britain." *Women's Studies International Forum* 28 (2005): 259–73.

Anti-Lynching Legislation

Lynching permeated American life for almost 100 years. Lynchings often focused on African Americans and their perceived violations of Jim Crow etiquette, whether real or not. The result was mob action and the violent death of men who were usually innocent. The list of transgressions that resulted in a lynch mob was long and varied and included everything from rape and murder to indolence, unruly behavior, and acting suspiciously.

Often times, lynchings were treated like circuses with whites enjoying the spectacle of the execution as entertainment, taking pictures and saving them as souvenirs. Less than 1 percent of participants were ever convicted. Most of the almost 5,000 reported lynchings between 1882 and 1968 (3,445 were of blacks) occurred in the South, but the problem was nationwide and, by 1918, all but six states had experienced lynchings.

The lynching of a black person by a white mob was rarely investigated, even more rarely prosecuted, and almost never punished. This was despite the fact that by the 1930s most Southern states had specifically outlawed lynching. These laws were often ineffective because they were not enforced. In the rare instance where an indictment was issued, juries would not convict, even though the incidents and perpetrators were often common knowledge.

Local sheriffs tended to be apathetic toward the laws and commonly took no action to prevent mobs from taking possession of the prisoner and killing him. In addition, rarely was an attempt made to apprehend the lynchers. Finally, not only was law enforcement usually absent, but often, the very person charged with preventing the lynching took an active part.

At the federal level, all three branches of government failed miserably. Federal judicial interference was rare. In one case, the U.S. Supreme Court stepped in, because, as Justice Holmes noted in *Moore v. Dempsey* (1923), the conviction of five black men in Arkansas under the shadow of threats of mob violence amounted to judicially sanctioned lynching. If the state courts could not provide minimal procedural fairness, then the federal courts had a clear duty to "secure to the petitioners their constitutional rights" (Bennett, 1999).

Congress also failed to respond. Early on during Reconstruction, Congress passed several civil rights acts to outlaw black codes, provide for criminal sanctions against any person involved in private conspiracy to violate another's federal rights, and stifle the Ku Klux Klan. However, many of these laws were declared unconstitutional, and those that were not were later repealed by Congress. In addition, more than 200 anti-lynching bills were introduced in Congress with none becoming law. Although the House of Representatives passed anti-lynching bills three times, the legislation was blocked repeatedly by senators from the South. During the Woodrow Wilson administration, Congress not only failed to pass anti-lynching legislation but entertained at least 20 bills calling for more segregation.

Congress came closest to passing anti-lynching legislation in 1921, when the House passed the Dyer Anti-Lynching Bill, but it failed in the Senate (see Dyer, Leonidas C.). The debate in the House, although rooted in constitutional and legal arguments, revolved mostly around racist attacks that were practically a defense of lynching. The bill passed 231–119. In the Senate, the argument of unconstitutionality and a threatened filibuster, which Republicans made no real effort to block, stalled the bill without a vote.

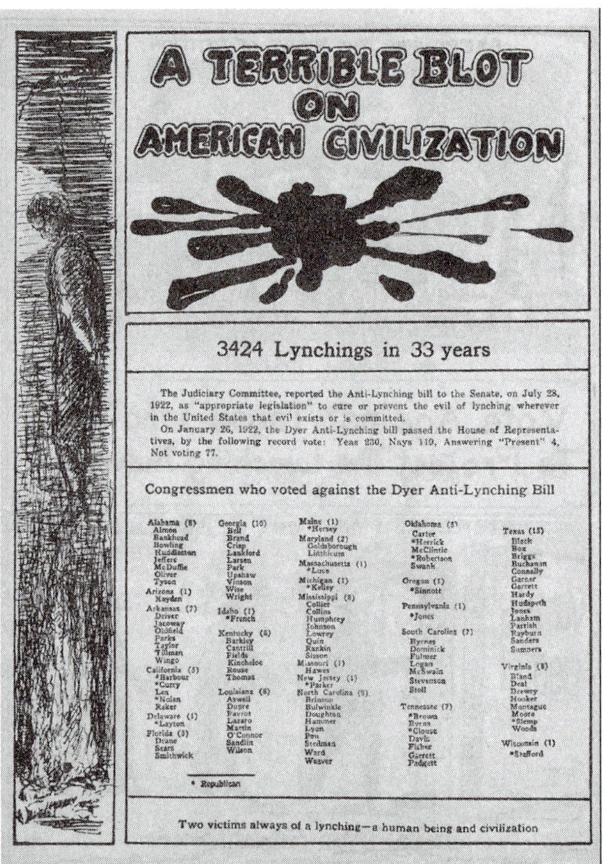

A TERRIBLE BLOT ON AMERICAN CIVILIZATION

3424 Lynchings in 33 years

The Judiciary Committee, reported the Anti-Lynching bill to the Senate, on July 28, 1922, as "appropriate legislation" to cure or prevent the evil of lynching wherever in the United States that evil exists or is committed.

On January 26, 1922, the Dyer Anti-Lynching bill passed the House of Representatives, by the following record vote: Yeas 230, Nays 119, Answering "Present" 4, Not voting 77.

Congressmen who voted against the Dyer Anti-Lynching Bill

Alabama (8)
Almon
Bankhead
Bowling
Huddleston
Jeffers
McDuffie
Oliver
Tyson

Arizona (1)
Hayden

Arkansas (7)
Driver
Jacoway
Oldfield
Parks
Taylor
Tillman
Wingo

California (5)
*Barbour
*Curry
Lea
*Nolan
Raker

Delaware (1)
*Layton

Florida (3)
Drane
Sears
Smithwick

Georgia (10)
Bell
Brand
Crisp
Lankford
Larsen
Park
Upshaw
Vinson
Wise
Wright

Idaho (1)
*French

Kentucky (6)
Barkley
Cantrill
Fields
Kincheloe
Rouse
Thomas

Louisiana (8)
Aswell
Dupre
Favrot
Lazaro
Martin
O'Connor
Sandlin
Wilson

Maine (1)
*Hersey

Maryland (2)
Goldsborough
Linthicum

Massachusetts (1)
*Luce

Michigan (1)
*Kelley

Mississippi (8)
Collier
Collins
Humphrey
Johnson
Lowrey
Quin
Rankin
Sisson

Missouri (1)
Hawes

New Jersey (1)
*Parker

North Carolina (9)
Brinson
Bulwinkle
Doughton
Hammer
Lyon
Pou
Stedman
Ward
Weaver

Oklahoma (5)
Carter
*Herrick
McClintic
*Robertson
Swank

Oregon (1)
*Sinnott

Pennsylvania (1)
*Jones

South Carolina (7)
Byrnes
Dominick
Fulmer
Logan
McSwain
Stevenson
Stoll

Tennessee (7)
*Brown
Byrns
*Clouse
Davis
Fisher
Garrett
Padgett

Texas (15)
Black
Box
Briggs
Buchanan
Connally
Garner
Garrett
Hardy
Hudspeth
Jones
Lanham
Parrish
Rayburn
Sanders
Sumners

Virginia (8)
Bland
Deal
Drewry
Hooker
Montague
Moore
*Slemp
Woods

Wisconsin (1)
*Stafford

* Republican

Two victims always of a lynching—a human being and civilization

A Terrible Blot on American Civilization. NAACP activists helped to push the Dyer Anti-Lynching Bill through Congress, though many representatives opposed its passage. (Library of Congress)

The Dyer debate exposed the fear that such a bill would give Southern blacks social equality, which was unacceptable to most Southern whites. An anti-lynching bill would ignite unruly blacks and incite demands for equality.

The election of Franklin Roosevelt in 1932 gave the National Association for the Advancement of Colored People (NAACP) hope that lynching would end. These hopes proved false. Pressure from his wife, Eleanor Roosevelt, failed to convince the president to act and, in 1935, Roosevelt did not support the Costigan-Wagner Anti-Lynching Bill that would have punished sheriffs who failed to protect their prisoners from lynch mobs. Roosevelt feared white voters in the South would reject him and cost him the election of 1936. Even the lynching of Rubin Stacy in 1935 failed to change Roosevelt's mind. Stacy was lynched while six deputies were escorting him to a jail in Miami, Florida. He was taken from police protection by a white mob and hanged. The national attention the incident drew did not sway Roosevelt.

President Harry S Truman also feared alienating the Southerners who controlled Congress. But, in the end, he supported anti-lynching laws, set up a president's commission on civil rights, and, through Executive Order 9981, ended formal segregation in the armed forces.

Thus, by the 1950s, with little help from the government, lynching had subsided. Occasional incidents still occurred that shocked the country and stirred action. In 1955, Emmett Till, a 14-year-old Chicago boy who was visiting his family in Mississippi, was beaten and thrown in the river for the alleged offense of insulting a white woman. In response to the Emmett Till incident, growing racial violence in the wake of court-ordered integration, and the growing fight for the right to vote by African Americans in the South, President Dwight Eisenhower established a Committee on Civil Rights in 1957. Although he did endorse anti-lynching laws, desegregation of the armed forces, ending poll taxes, and an end to segregation in federal employment, Eisenhower was reluctant to use federal power because he thought blacks could achieve their goals through the vote.

The last recorded lynching occurred in 1964 with the murder of three civil rights workers, James Chaney, Andrew Goodman, and Michael Schwerner, in Mississippi (see Freedom Summer [Mississippi] of 1964) with Congress never having passed an anti-lynching statute. Finally, in June 2005, the Senate passed a nonbinding resolution to apologize for its past failure to enact anti-lynching legislation. Ironically, 20 Southern senators declined to originally cosponsor the resolution, which stated that the Senate "expresses the deepest sympathies and most solemn regrets of the Senate to the descendants of victims of lynching, the ancestors of whom were deprived of life, human dignity, and the constitutional protections accorded all citizens of the United States" (U.S. Senate, 2005).

Gary Gershman

See also

Anti-Lynching League; Anti-Lynching Campaign; Costigan-Wagner Anti-Lynching Bill; Lynching. Documents: Ida B. Wells' Exposé on Lynching (1895); The NAACP Report *Thirty Years of Lynching in the United States: 1889–1918* (1919); The "Anti-Lynching" Hearings (1920); *Bee Publishing Company v. State of Nebraska* (1921)

Further Reading:

Bennett, Harrison. "The Phillips County Riot Cases." *ChickenBones: A Journal for Literary & Artistic African American Themes* (December 1999). http://www.nathanielturner.com/phillipscountyriotcases.htm.

Dray, Philip. *At the Hands of Persons Unknown: The Lynching of Black America.* New York: Random House, 2002.

Tolnay, Stewart A., and E. M. Beck. *A Festival of Violence: An Analysis of Southern Lynchings, 1882–1930.* Urbana: University of Illinois Press, 1995.

U.S. Senate. S. Res. 39. *Apologizing to the Victims of Lynching and the Descendants of Those Victims for the Failure of the Senate to Enact Anti-Lynching Legislation.* 109th Cong., 1st sess, February 7, 2005.

Wells, Ida. *On Lynchings.* Amherst, NY: Humanity Books, 2002.

Zangrando, Robert L. *The NAACP Crusade Against Lynching, 1909–1950.* Philadelphia: Temple University Press, 1980.

Anti-Miscegenation Laws

Anti-miscegenation laws in the United States are one of the longest-lasting American racial restrictions. Miscegenation, with Latin roots that mean "to mix," was an anxiety for white U.S. citizens. Anti-miscegenation laws were first implemented during the colonial era and then reinforced during the Jim Crow era, conveying white supremacy and the protection of white purity. Although some states focused on sex, marriage was the primary focus in anti-miscegenation policies due to the economic benefits and social assumptions about marriage.

From the 1660s, anti-miscegenation laws reaffirmed attitudes towards race and racial mixing. In 1661 the colonies passed an act that made mixing between the English and slaves, negroes (Spanish word for black that was commonly used prior to the 1960s to describe black Americans), and Indians punishable by banishment and fines, and any resulting children were bound to the church as wards until they reached the age of 30. After U.S. independence in 1787, the category of "mulatto" was created. A person who was a quarter or more of "negro" ancestry was considered mulatto. As categories of mixed identities were defined, so too were the bans against interracial marriage. In 1792, Virginia was the first state to enact a law that placed a ban on free whites mixing with "negroes" or mulattos. Fines and jail time were the norm for those who committed the crime of miscegenation. For those who committed bigamy, death was the punishment. The emancipation of black slaves and the persistence of the Jim Crow era in the United States led to the normalization of anti-miscegenation laws. In 1866 the term *mulatto* was deemed null and instead the quantification of blood that constituted a "person of color" was lowered from one-quarter to one-sixteenth.

By the early 20th century, Asian Americans were targeted; 14 states included anti-miscegenation laws that targeted Chinese, Japanese, and Koreans and nine states focused on Filipinos (referred to as "Malays"). U.S. anti-miscegenation laws were contradictory at times; this is best described with the 1924 Racial Integrity Act of Virginia, also known as the Pocahantas exception. As states banned interracial marriages, an exception was made for the descendants of the famous John Rolfe and Matoaka (most famously known as Pocahontas) assuring their whiteness and lineage to Rolfe.

An examination of anti-miscegenation laws illustrates that not only was whiteness constructed, but also whom it was intended to protect: white women from brown men. The Cable Act of 1922, also known as the Married Women's Independent Nationality Act, illustrates how U.S. anti-miscegenation laws not only policed interracial marriage among citizens, but also international relations. In particular, white women who married noncitizens. The consequence for a white woman who married a noncitizen was losing her U.S. citizenship. In contrast, this law did not impact men.

As states passed anti-miscegenation laws, it was not met without resistance as seen in *Pace v. Alabama* (1883). In 1881 Tony Pace and Mary J. Cox were indicted under section 4189 of Alabama state law, which stated that a conviction of interracial marriage, fornication, or adultery led to the penitentiary or a sentence of hard labor for no less than two years and no more than seven years (Section 4189 of the Code of Alabama). Pace, an African American man, and Cox, a white woman, were indicted and convicted. They attempted to charge the state with breaching Pace's Fourteenth Amendment right, however, as early as 1870, judges declared anti-miscegenation laws constitutional and that racial groups were equally punished, and equally allowed the right to marry within their own race.

Two important milestones occurred in U.S. anti-miscegenation legal history: *Perez v. Sharp* (1948) and *Loving v. Virginia* (1967). In 1948, Andrea Perez, a Mexican American woman, and Sylvester Davis, an African American man, filed a lawsuit against the Los Angeles County Clerk's Office for denying them a marriage license. Perez and Davis charged that California's ban on interracial marriage was an infringement of their religious rights since it denied them the right to receive the Sacrament of Matrimony. *Perez v. Sharp* was the first to overturn California's anti-miscegenation laws that had been in effect since 1850. Ten years later in 1958 Richard Loving, a Caucasian 24-year-old bricklayer from Caroline County, Virginia, married his childhood sweetheart, Mildred Jeter, who was African American, in Washington, D.C. After returning to their Virginia home as a married couple, law enforcement arrested them late at night. The county judge sentenced the Lovings to one year in jail unless they left the state and did not return for 25 years. The Lovings went to live with a family member in Washington, D.C. When they returned to visit family five years later, they were arrested for traveling together. The Lovings wrote to the Attorney General, Robert F. Kennedy, who forwarded their letter to the American Civil Liberties Union (ACLU). The ACLU represented their case in the Supreme Court; *Loving v. Virginia* led the courts to rule state bans on interracial marriage as unconstitutional.

In 2009, 40 years after *Loving v. Virginia*, Justice of the Peace Keith Bardwell refused to issue a marriage license to an interracial couple on the grounds that he was concerned about what would happen to their mixed race children.

Annie Isabel Fukushima

See also

Domestic Violence; Down Low; Illegitimacy Rates; Lesbian, Gay, Bisexual, Transgender, Intersex, Queer, and Queer Questioning Community (LGBTQ); Mixed Race Relationships and the Media; *Plessy v. Ferguson* (1896); Tripping Over the Color Line. Document: *Plessy v. Ferguson* (1896)

Further Reading:

Moran, Rachel F. *Interracial Intimacy: The Regulation of Race and Romance*. Chicago: University of Chicago Press, 2003.

Pascoe, Peggy. "Miscegenation Law, Court Cases, and Ideologies of 'Race' in Twentieth-Century America." *Journal of American History* 83, no. 1 (June 1996): 44–69.

Romano, Renee C. *Race Mixing: Black-White Marriage in Postwar America*. Cambridge, MA: Harvard University Press, 2003.

Wadlington, Walter. "The Loving Case: Virginia's Anti-miscegenation Statute in Historical Perspective." *Virginia Law Review* 52, no. 7 (Nov. 1966): 1189–1223.

Anti-Racism

Anti-racism refers to whites who challenge racist systems and practices in a white-dominated society. Throughout U.S. history there have been whites who have not conformed with the dominant racial ideology. Bonilla-Silva notes, "Historically, racial progress in America has always transpired because of the joint efforts of racial minorities and white progressives. No one can forget the courageous efforts of whites such as John Brown, Thaddeus Stevens, Charles Sumner, Lydia Maria Child, the Grimke sisters, and the many whites who joined the Civil Rights Movement; no one should ever ignore white militants who struggled for racial equality and who risked their lives for this goal. Therefore today, as yesterday, a portion of the white population is not singing the tune of color-blindness" (2010: 131–32). As suggested by Bonilla-Silva, ideas of anti-racism and sympathetic whites are often a key component to the success of social change when it comes to race. He further suggests that in order for there to be further progress, collaboration among vulnerable groups in the United States is key.

In order to develop antiracist beliefs, whites must become conscious and aware of the racial reality in the United States. Bonilla-Silva argues, "Being an antiracist begins with understanding the institutional nature of racial matters and accepting that all actors in a racialized society are affected *materially* (receive benefits or disadvantages) and *ideologically* by the racial structure. This stand implies taking responsibility for your unwilling participation in these practices and beginning a new life committed to the goal of achieving real racial equality. The ride will be rough, but after your eyes have been opened, there is no point in standing still" (2010: 15–16). Whites have to embrace the reality of their privileged standing in a white-dominated society as a first step.

Using data from the 1997 Survey on Social Attitudes of College Students and the 1998 Detroit Area study, Bonilla-Silva found that white, working-class women were the most likely to have antiracist beliefs. He concluded that because these women are more likely than middle-class whites to face discrimination based on their vulnerable status in society, they were more likely to empathize with the situation for people of color. This awareness by white women of the racial hierarchy and their place, as well as their own experiences with discrimination, were important aspects of developing antiracist attitudes.

Several scholars, including Bonilla-Silva, emphasize the importance of overcoming denial about how racism operates in society. In addition to raising individual awareness, it is important to also tie that to changing the structures in the society that maintain and reproduce racial inequality. Johnson, Rush, and Feagin note, "A nonracist society cannot be achieved if whites continue to deny the reality of the racist society and of racism within themselves. The painful emotional work of actually undoing individual racism must be accomplished in combination with collective efforts for structural change . . . a useful place to begin undoing racism is to address the social, economic, and political embeddedness of white racism within the foundation of the U.S. political system" (2000: 101). Racism is foundational in the United States, as this quotation suggests; therefore working to change the way institutions function is important in order to ensure that anti-racism is long reaching. Johnson et al. suggest that reeducation is a key aspect of creating this change. Not only must this education occur in formal academic settings, but also must occur in "all structures that actively communicate and reinforce information about racial matters and racial ideology" (2000: 102). This level of change would require the mass media and even families to teach anti-racism.

One of the challenges regarding anti-racism is convincing whites that this is the correct path. As the majority group, whites enjoy the spoils of a system that benefits them. Though they may not be actively racist, most whites benefit from white privilege in the United States, so they experience gains based on the system of racism that exists. Therefore, it is critical to push whites to see the advantages of being an antiracist and to fight against systems that ultimately benefit them. This means that whites must move out of their present comfort zones to confront personally the painful and usually emotional work of doing anti-racism every day. We also envision the widespread formation of cross-racial coalitions with others who are devoted to doing anti-racism. Overall, we visualize many white individuals actively, consciously, and consistently working to eliminate racism by rejecting systems of privilege-maintenance in favor of human dignity, mutual respect, and liberty. The task of doing this is ultimately a great challenge. It is important then to research those that are antiracist in order to determine what makes them reject the social order as it is. Also, Wise (2011) suggests that the history of anti-racism is not well explored or understood, resulting in few role models for whites.

Kathrin A. Parks

See also

Biological Racism; Color-Blind Racism; Cultural Racism; Ideological Racism; Institutional Racism; Internalized Racism; Modern Racism; Non-white Racism; Racism; Reverse Racism

Further Reading:

Bonilla-Silva, E. *Racism without Racists: Color-Blind Racism and Racial Inequality in Contemporary America.* 3rd ed. Lanham, MD: Rowman and Littlefield Publishers, 2010.

Johnson, Jacqueline, Sharon Rush, and Joe Feagin. "Doing Anti-racism: Toward an Egalitarian American Society." *Contemporary Sociology* 29 (2000): 95–110.

Wise, T. *White Like Me: Reflections on Race from a Privileged Son.* Berkeley, CA: Soft Skull Press, 2011.

Anti-Semitism in the United States

Anti-Semitism refers to hateful beliefs about or actions taken against the Jewish people, individual Jews, or non-Jews who are perceived as Jewish. This hate can be based on Jewish people as a race, a culture, or an ethnic group, and has existed for most of Judaism's more than 4,000-year history. In the United Nations' 1950 *Statement on Race*, anti-Semitism was acknowledged as a form of racism.

Anti-Semitism began like any other kind of nativism or xenophobia (fear and/or hatred of foreigners): nations surrounding the Middle Eastern areas in which Jews lived conquered and subjugated or enslaved them. A normal part of this subjugation was the requirement that Jews stop practicing their religion, often enforced through laws that specified that Jews who did not convert or stop engaging in Jewish practice would be put to death, or at least forced to pay special high taxes. Many polytheistic religions were able to incorporate the old and new religions together; for instance, by finding equivalencies between their traditional gods and the gods of the new religion. The Jewish religion and people set themselves apart from other religions and people surrounding them, however, through their adoption of monotheism and their unique rules of ritual and dietary purity. Later, the Jews' use of a language different from that which the local people spoke was also a source of distinction. They were not ready to convert after being conquered, which resulted in many massacres and expulsions, as well as the development of a hatred against Jews on the part of many conquering states. Before the emergence of Christianity, Jews had already faced such subjugation from Egypt, Babylonia, Greece, and Rome.

Christianity, and later Islam, intensified religious anti-Semitism because their adherents saw their own religions as improving on Judaism, while Jews did not agree. Throughout the history of Christianity, various denominations have blamed Jews for the crucifixion of Jesus (who was born a Jew). This blame has been closely tied to the fact that the Jewish holiday of Passover occurs near the time of Easter and involves special foods, which Christian anti-Semitics libelously believe to be made with the blood of Christian children. Throughout the history of Christian Europe, countries and towns have expelled their Jewish residents, launched programs of violence and theft against them, and forced conversions. In most areas, Jews were not allowed to own property and were confined to certain specific professions, such as traveling sales and banking. Their association with banking would come back to haunt them in accusations of usury and world domination made in literature ranging from Shakespeare's *The Merchant of Venice* to anti-Semitic tracts like *The Protocols of the Elders of Zion*.

Jews came to the New World from the beginning of its colonization. Jews were among the early residents of the Dutch colonies in North America, having arrived by 1654. Other early areas of Jewish settlement were Philadelphia, Pennsylvania; Newport, Rhode Island; Charleston, South Carolina; and Savannah, Georgia. Early Jewish settlers were primarily assimilated Jews from European countries such as England, Holland, Germany, Spain, and Portugal, and they were able to be active participants in colonial life in those colonies that granted religious freedom. Among these immigrants were Spanish Jews fleeing the Inquisition, including some whose families had converted to Catholicism in the earlier waves of the Inquisition but were now under scrutiny again. Jews who attempted to settle in other colonies, particularly the Puritan New England ones, faced severe religious persecution. Many of these early immigrants were Sephardic Jews, or descendents of those Jews who had settled in Spain and other Mediterranean areas of the Jewish diaspora.

Steady numbers of Jews immigrated to the United States throughout its early history, but immigration was most intense during the period that has become known as the first mass migration, spanning the years 1881 to 1928. During this time, more than 2.3 million Jewish immigrants arrived and stayed in the United States. As compared with the earlier immigrants, these Jews were less assimilated, less educated, and poorer. They were Ashkenazi Jews, who came from eastern European countries such as Russia, the Ukraine, and Lithuania, had names that were more clearly Jewish in origin, and spoke Yiddish, a mix of German and Hebrew. The assimilated Jews already in the United States founded organizations such as the Hebrew Immigrant Aid Society to help the new immigrants assimilate to life in the new country, partially because they feared that these more recognizably Jewish immigrants would draw more attention to Jews in general and bring on more anti-Semitism and discrimination.

This wave of migration came to an end with the passing of restrictive immigration legislation, including entry taxes that were hard for impoverished refugees to pay; a literacy requirement that was difficult for many Jewish women who were never taught to read; tests of mental capability that were often culturally or linguistically biased; and, finally, the National Origins Acts of 1921 and 1924. These laws restricted immigration to no more than 2 percent of the number of individuals of each nationality living in the United States as of 1890. Because Jews were not counted as a separate nationality, they were forced to try to enter the country on the miniscule quotas allocated to the eastern European nations they were fleeing. No exception was made for refugees.

The result of these laws was that when Hitler and the Nazis came to power in Germany in the 1930s, few Jewish refugees were able to flee. Those who could, traveled to countries with bigger immigration quotas and tried to obtain papers there, but this was a risky and expensive effort. Legislators in the United States refused to allow Jews to enter during Nazi rule, even as evidence of concentration camps came to light. President Franklin Delano Roosevelt, who, because of his involvement in fighting against Nazi Germany in World War II, has come to be seen as a savior of the Jews, was also complicit in the decision to refuse Jewish refugees' entry. The most horrific result of this decision was the turning away in 1939 of the USS *St. Louis*, a ship filled with 900 Jewish refugees. The ship was refused entry in American waters in New York and was surrounded by Coast Guard ships to prevent the refugees from jumping to freedom. After the ship returned to Europe, the passengers sought refuge in other countries. Most of them, however, were later killed in Nazi concentration camps.

It was not only in terms of immigration that anti-Semitism affected Jews in the United States during this period, however. Many well-known public figures in politics, business, and religion espoused anti-Semitism, including Henry Ford (creator of the Ford automobile) and Father Charles Coughlin, a Royal Oak, Michigan, radio priest who advocated social justice for the poor and blamed the Jews for economic problems. Additionally, white supremacist hate groups such as the Ku Klux Klan (KKK) emerged during these years. The KKK is strongly nativist and blamed both Jews and blacks for the economic woes of the Great Depression. KKK violence over the years has included severe beatings, lynchings, arson, and cross-burnings, each of which has been directed against Jews. Jews also experienced violence from other immigrant groups, Irish gangs for example.

Revisions to immigration laws after the Nazi Holocaust in World War II did eventually allow for refugees to come to the United States, and Jews continue to make use of this method for immigration. Jewish refugees today come primarily from Muslim countries in the Middle East and from the countries making up the former Soviet Union. These new Jewish refugees tend to be less educated than their counterparts already in the United States. Refugees from the former Soviet republics face particular challenges, as the anti-Semitic regimes there prohibited most Jews from learning anything about their religion. These changes in refugee laws were accompanied by the end of legal discrimination against Jews. In the United States, no legal measures openly discriminate against Jews, which is not the case in many other countries. These changes reduced anti-Semitism, though they did not eliminate it.

Nonviolent anti-Semitism was even more prevalent. Many social clubs were closed to Jewish members. Elite colleges and universities established quotas limiting the percentage of Jewish students who would be admitted. For instance, Harvard University's quota, adopted in the 1920s, limited Jews to 15 percent of the student body. In the 20 years from 1920 to 1940, the percentage of Jews in Columbia University's medical school fell from 50 percent to less than 7 percent, and in 1940 Jews had one-tenth the chance of admission to Cornell's medical school that non-Jews had. Discrimination was also common in employment, with as many as 20 percent of job openings in the 1950s requesting non-Jewish applicants. Jewish applicants were also disproportionately rejected for executive jobs at leading industrial corporations.

Organized hate groups that espouse anti-Semitism still exist in the United States. One of these groups is Christian Identity, a conservative coalition of groups calling for a Christian nation and violence against Jews, blacks, and homosexuals. This group believes Jews are descended from Satan and are the enemies of all humanity. Other anti-Semitic groups include Nazis and Neo-Nazis, skinheads, white women's groups, and far-right conservative political groups. A number of these groups are Holocaust Revisionists, which means that they believe that the Nazi killings of 6 million Jews were invented by Allied governments or Zionist activists as propaganda, or else that Jews invented the Holocaust to get sympathy and enhance their ability to dominate world affairs. Some revisionists do accept the idea that the Nazis wanted to rid their lands of Jews but do not believe that concentration camps existed to kill their internees; others believe that the entire subject is a fiction. Some anti-Semitic groups have also blamed Jews for the terrorist attacks on September 11, 2001, even though those who committed the attacks were part of anti-Semitic groups. It is not only white supremacist groups that are anti-Semitic. There are organized anti-Semitic groups among African Americans, as well. The most well known of these is Louis Farrakhan's Nation of Islam. Claims made by black anti-Semitic groups have included the charge that Jewish doctors deliberately infect black children with HIV, that Jews themselves inspire genocide, and that Jews in Hollywood deliberately conspire to subjugate blacks.

Bias crimes and hateful acts committed against Jews by organized anti-Semitic and hate groups as well as by isolated individuals made up over 10 percent of all hate crimes reported to the FBI in the year 2001, and 57 percent of religion-related hate crimes. These crimes range from physical assaults to arson and vandalism (including spray painting swastikas and other symbols and messages of hate) of synagogues and private homes. In 2002, anti-Semitic bias crimes overall increased by 17 percent, but vandalism declined by 4 percent. Incidents on college campuses have also increased, and there is a large number of anti-Semitic Web sites and chat rooms on the Internet, some of which propagate anti-Semitic e-mail chains.

According to a 1999 Gallup poll, 8 percent of American adults would not vote for a Jewish candidate for president if their party were to nominate one (as compared to 63 percent in 1937 and 18 percent in 1978), so there has been a decline in anti-Semitism with time. Jews are more electable than homosexuals (41 percent would not vote for the latter) or atheists (51 percent), and are on a par with women. However, Americans are more willing to vote for blacks, Baptists, Mormons, and Catholics. There are still private clubs, especially country clubs, that exclude Jews. And some colleges still try to limit the percentage of Jews in their student bodies, though the quotas they once used are now illegal. Instead, they look for geographic diversity and limit the number of students they admit from certain areas with high Jewish populations. However, there are instances where Jews must resort to court action to stop colleges or employers from discriminating against them. As a result of settlement agreements some colleges have been forced to establish special sensitivity training and learning centers to counter anti-Semitism on their campuses.

Some of the anti-Semitism in the United States today is related to the existence of Israel as the state of the Jewish people. The ongoing conflict in the region between Israel, its Muslim Arab neighbors, and the Palestinian people has led to events in the United States where Zionists (supporters of Israel as the homeland for the Jewish people) and Jews have been targeted by anti-Israel protesters. These events have been common at antiwar demonstrations, as well as on college campuses. In the United States, it is not only Muslims but a wide variety of people who are anti-Zionist. Zionism and Judaism, like anti-Semitism and anti-Zionism, are not synonymous, and it is possible for people to disapprove of Israel, Israeli policies, and the actions of the Israeli state without being anti-Semitic. Anti-Zionist feelings and actions, however, often turn into anti-Semitic feelings and actions because of the close connection between Jews and the state of Israel.

It is important to take note of the connections between anti-Semitism and other forms of racism and hatred. Many different forms of hatred spring from the same sources, as can be seen by the views espoused by the hate organizations discussed above. The continuing existence of anti-Semitism is not merely an annoyance in the life of Jewish Americans but also a legitimating of the practice of other forms of hate. Anti-Semitism is also tied to the anti-Americanism of international terrorist groups and to anti-Israel actions of many Palestinian and Muslim activists. While these different kinds of hate are separate entities, the links between them clarify the need to act against racism, prejudice, and discrimination as an interrelated set of beliefs and actions, rather than targeting individual groups or kinds of hate one at a time. Jews have long experienced the fact that when one source of hate is suppressed (for instance, Nazi Germany), another may spring up in its place (the anti-Jewish policies of Stalinist Russia).

Jews in the United States have acted to combat anti-Semitism in many ways. They have organized groups such as the Anti-Defamation League, the American Jewish Committee, and the Simon Wiesenthal Center that work to combat anti-Semitic activity both in the United States and around the world. These organizations conduct research on the current state of anti-Semitism, educate individuals and governments about what can be done, and contact the news media to ensure fair reporting about anti-Semitic incidents. Jewish organizations, including those whose primary mission is combating anti-Semitism as well as others, also conduct political activism in favor of laws and policies that help reduce anti-Semitism. Some of these laws include those against hate crimes, prohibiting prayer in schools, and requiring education about tolerance. Many of these laws are helpful to other minority ethnic and religious groups in the United States. Jewish groups also support actions to ensure diversity in higher education, though some affirmative action policies are not supported because of their similarity to the discriminatory quota systems that once kept Jewish students out of elite institutions. Rarely, Jews have turned to terrorist activity to try prevent anti-Semitic activity or to retaliate for actions that have already been taken. The most notable group of this kind is the Jewish Defense League. However, most Jewish groups that work against anti-Semitism are nonviolent and are eager to work with other ethnic and religious groups to further civil rights and nondiscrimination for everyone.

MIKAILA MARIEL LEMONIK ARTHUR

Further Reading:

Carr, Steven Alan. *Hollywood and Anti-Semitism: A Cultural History Up to World War II*. Cambridge: Cambridge University Press, 2001.

Chesler, Phyllis. *The New Anti-Semitism: The Current Crisis and What We Must Do About It*. San Francisco: Jossey-Bass Publishers, 2003.

Jaher, Frederic Cople. *A Scapegoat in the New Wilderness: The Origins and Rise of Anti-Semitism in America*. Cambridge, MA: Harvard University Press, 1994.

Lipstadt, Deborah E. *Denying the Holocaust: The Growing Assault on Truth and Memory*. New York: Free Press, 1993.

Mayo, Louise A. *The Ambivalent Image: Nineteenth-Century America's Perception of the Jew*. Rutherford, NJ: Fairleigh Dickenson University Press, 1988.

Slavin, Stephen L., and Mary A. Pratt. *The Einstein Syndrome: Corporate Anti-Semitism in America Today*. New York: World Publishers, 1982.

Sleznick, Gertrude Jaeger, and Stephan Steinberg. *The Tenacity of Prejudice: Anti-Semitism in Contemporary America*. New York: Harper & Row, 1969.

Arab American Institute (AAI)

The Arab American Institute (AAI) was established in 1985 to represent the interests of Americans of Arab descent in politics, notably on Capitol Hill, and to foster their civic and political empowerment through policy, research, and public affairs services. AAI offers training and strategies for candidates who want to run for political office at the local, state, and national level; conducts constituency research; and monitors U.S. opinion and policy makers on issues that are of concern to Arab Americans, including the U.S. government's Middle East policy. Like most Middle Eastern advocacy organizations, AAI's agenda focuses on both domestic and foreign policy issues. Since its inception, AAI has been active in debunking stereotypes of Arabs and Arab Americans in the media and the general public. To this end, it has published a pamphlet entitled "Arab Americans: Making a Difference," which highlights the lives of prominent Arab Americans, such as former Senate majority leader George Mitchell, former secretary of health and human services Donna Shalala, and the Green Party presidential candidate in 2000 and 2004, Ralph Nader.

After the events of September 11, 2001, AAI was, like most Arab and Muslim American organizations, overwhelmed with the increased demand for its services in fighting the backlash. Its president, James Zogby, appeared regularly on the media, advocating for his constituents and educating the American public about Arab Americans and the Arab world. AAI collaborated with civil rights groups and other sympathizers in fighting the various government initiatives that targeted Arab Americans, especially immigrants. It also tried to increase its membership across the nation by energizing chapters and establishing new ones. These chapters were especially visible in organizing "know your rights" forums for those in the immigrant communities, encouraging them to register to vote and become more active politically.

Since 1996, AAI's nonprofit arm, the Arab American Institute Foundation, has been supporting public information and education programs and sponsoring outreach. The goal of the foundation is to promote a fuller and deeper public understanding of this ethnic community, its present and future goals, and its role in the ever-expanding diversity of America. The annual Kahlil Gibran: Spirit of Humanity Awards Gala in Washington, D.C., is symbolic of the foundation's mission. Named after the author of *The Prophet*, individuals and institutions that have demonstrated a profound commitment to values of equality, responsibility, understanding, and generosity are honored. Honorees have included Queen Noor of Jordan, rock star Sting, and the Aga Khan Foundation.

MEHDI BOZORGMEHR AND ANNY BAKALIAN

See also

Arab/Muslim American Advocacy Organizations

Further Reading:

Ameri, Anan, and Dawn Ramey, eds. *The Arab American Encyclopedia*, Woodbridge, CT: U.X.L, 2000.

Arab American National Museum. *Telling Our Story*. Dearborn, MI: Arab American National Museum, 2007.

Boosahda, Elizabeth. *Arab-American Faces and Voices: The Origins of an Immigrant Community.* Austin: University of Texas Press, 2003.
Orfalea, Gregory. *The Arab Americans: A History.* Northampton, MA: Olive Branch Press, 2006.

Arab/Muslim American Advocacy Organizations

Arab and Muslim immigrants have experienced discrimination throughout most of their history in the United States, but they did not mobilize politically or establish advocacy organizations until the 1970s. A number of factors influenced this timing. One is the change in immigration laws in 1965, which brought a new wave of highly educated Arab/Muslim immigrants who found U.S.–Middle East relations to be skewed. The oil boom in the 1970s increased further the large-scale influx of college students from oil-rich Arab countries and Iran. As educated immigrants, these newcomers were more responsive to events in the Middle East. Another factor is the emergence of ethnic identity politics in the post–civil rights era, which particularly benefited the native-born Arab Americans. Yet another factor that contributed to the creation of advocacy organizations is the series of violent attacks on American interests by various Middle Eastern groups after the 1970s, and the way these were played out by U.S. media and politicians, which created stereotypes of Arab terrorists and by association of Arab/Muslim Americans. Finally, a new generation of civic-minded professionals of Arab descent has come of age.

Arab and Muslim American organizations were established to educate the American public about their ethnic origin and culture and to address the bias they saw in U.S. foreign policy. They mobilized their constituents to take a more active political and social role at the local and national levels. They started a variety of programs, published news reports, organized conferences, created internships, and encouraged their members to write to their congressional representatives on specific issues and support the campaigns of "friends" of the Middle East, at home and abroad.

Undoubtedly, the post–9/11 backlash was the biggest test for Arab/Muslim American advocacy organizations. The scale of hate crimes and government initiatives necessitated that most of these organizations, regardless of their original mission and goals, engage in some advocacy on behalf of their constituents. The ethnic/religious professional organizations responded to the backlash as experts in their specific field. For example, the Arab American Bar Association in Chicago issued a "white" or position paper about the backlash, members of the American Muslim Law Enforcement Officers Association made public appearances at community forums and town meetings to speak about relations with the police, and the American Arab Chamber of Commerce in Dearborn, Michigan, the largest Arab American enclave, educated its members to be proactive with their customers.

Many organizations grew in size, in the number of programs they offered and, in a few cases, even branched into social services. Much of this growth was the result of unprecedented grants they received from major American philanthropic organizations soon after the backlash started. Until September 11, Arab and Muslim American communities were generally not on the radar screen of the foundation world, and this is another reason for the foundations' reaction to the crisis. Several new organizations were established as a result of the gaps and needs observed after 9/11. Mostly young, U.S.-educated men and women who were able to galvanize their peers in the community established these organizations. For example, the Association of Patriotic Arab-Americans in the Military was created by a U.S. marine of Arab descent.

The goal of most Arab/Muslim American organizations was to mobilize their respective communities. They encouraged their members to be politically savvy, know their rights, and exercise them. They organized public forums and town hall meetings, offering "know your rights" presentations by public officials and experts. For example, in Brooklyn, New York, home to many immigrants of Arab descent, various groups hosted about a dozen such events in the 18 months following 9/11. Voter-registration campaigns became more frequent in this population as well, and young, second-generation activists led the way as volunteers. The Network of Arab-American Professionals, New York chapter, was exemplary in strategically canvassing New York City's five boroughs, as well as New Jersey, to register voters.

A major emphasis of almost all the Arab/Muslim American advocacy organizations, irrespective of their mission,

American Arab Anti-Discrimination Committee (ADC)

James Abourezk, the first person of Arab descent to serve in the U.S. Senate, established the American-Arab Anti-Discrimination Committee (ADC) in 1980 as a membership-based civil rights advocacy organization. The ADC's mission is to defend the rights of men and women of Arab descent and promote their cultural heritage. Through educational programs, media monitoring, and other efforts, the ADC fights negative stereotypes of Arab Americans. It also provides legal services and counseling in cases of discrimination and defamation. Because many of the ADC's members are concerned with establishing a more balanced U.S. Middle East policy, the organization's goals go well beyond the domestic issues implied by its name. Abourezk, a Democrat, who was a senator for South Dakota from 1973 to 1979, created the ADC in response to several trends, including the large influx of Arab immigrants brought about by changes in immigration policy in 1965, the increasing tensions and anti-American rhetoric in the Middle East, and the prevalence of anti-Arab bias in the American media and popular culture.

One of the ADC's major contributions has been compiling and analyzing evidence of hate crimes and incidents of discrimination against Arab Americans in periodic reports (six since 1991). Its report "The Post–September 11 Backlash: September 11, 2001–October 11, 2002" revealed that in the nine weeks following the attacks, more than 700 violent incidents and 800 cases of employment discrimination were aimed at Arab or Muslim Americans, a marked escalation from previous years. Also of significance were the "new discriminatory immigration policies" that resulted in the detentions and selective deportation of immigrants from the Arab World and the monitoring of students and young men from that Middle East. The report concluded that "Arab Americans suffered a serious backlash following September 11, 2001." Undoubtedly, immigrants of Arab origin were the targets of ethnic and religious profiling by the U.S. government.

The ADC has joined coalitions of civil rights organizations in Washington, D.C., and others across the country to advocate for Arab immigrants. The backlash has galvanized many to join the ADC and fight for their civil rights. The organization has grown to about 40 chapters in more than 24 states, and there are ADC members in every state in the union. Second-generation Arab Americans have been particularly active in energizing the ranks of the ADC, as well as other advocacy organizations, in the post-9/11 period. Their mobilization has not only aimed at improving the civil rights of people of Arab descent in the United States, they have vociferously called for changes in U.S. policy toward the Palestinian people, the war in Iraq, and other conflicts in the Middle East.

Mehdi Bozorgmehr and Anny Bakalian

was to educate the mainstream American public about Islam, Arabs, and the Middle East. Some undertook long-term, labor-intensive projects. For example, the Council on American Islamic Relations launched the "library project" and solicited sponsors to donate to local libraries a set of recommended books about Islam. A year after the launch of this project, about half of the libraries in the major states where Arabs and Muslims reside in large number had received books on Islam.

No matter how successful these organizations were, they could not possibly meet their mission without building coalitions with civil rights/liberties organizations, interfaith initiatives, and other advocacy organizations, both within the same ethnic/religious group and with others. They also established ties with government officials and agencies at the local and national level. Organizations located in Washington, D.C., that serve the national interests of Arab/Muslim Americans tended to focus on policy issues. Many had a government-affairs officer or staff person devoted to meeting with congressional leaders and staffers and other government officials, but almost all of them allocated a proportion of their budget and time to policy.

Overall, the Arab/Muslim American advocacy organizations scrambled to meet the challenge by relying on material and connections they had already established. Yet they were also transformed, branching into uncharted territory and forging new ties. Yet, no matter how well established and endowed some of these organizations were, they were

Arab Community Center for Economic and Social Services (ACCESS)

Based in Dearborn, Michigan, the Arab Community Center for Economic and Social Services (ACCESS) is one of the oldest and largest Arab American support and advocacy organizations in the United States. ACCESS provides a range of social, legal, employment, health, and education services. In 1971, a group of community activists united around domestic issues, such as urban renewal, immigration discrimination, and the inclusion of Arab autoworkers in the union. They were also concerned about foreign policy in the Middle East, and the misrepresentation of Arabs in the media. They came together to establish ACCESS, electing George Khoury as the organization's first president. Today, ACCESS is an advocate for pan-Arab causes, promotes fairness in the Middle East, and works toward equity within the Arab American community. It tries to mainstream Arabic culture through its cultural arts program, gives clients a chance to compete more equitably in the labor force through its youth and employment programs, and offers families greater prospects for healthy lives through its managed-care program.

ACCESS undeniably achieves its goal as the premier Arab American human services center. Its budget exceeds $10 million a year, its programs are comprehensive, it serves over 50,000 clients, it comes into contact with about a quarter of a million people annually, and it has won recognition as a national leader among nonprofit organizations. Through national outreach programs, ACCESS is building a national network of Arab American organizations, trying to empower this ethnic community, especially the new immigrants. This goal has become particularly pressing in light of the backlash that followed the events of September 11, 2001.

Mehdi Bozorgmehr and Anny Bakalian

overwhelmed and stretched by the exponential increase in demand for their services, participation in public events, interaction with the media, and their need to establish coalitions. It is noteworthy that most of the Arab/Muslim American advocacy organizations successfully managed to walk a fine line as they addressed two somewhat contradictory goals: expressing loyalty to the United States and proving their patriotism and, at the same, defending their constituents against government initiatives.

In the post–9/11 era, if there is a silver lining to this otherwise sad episode in American history, it is an attempt on the part of the American public to better understand Arab culture and the Muslim faith. Here, too, representatives of advocacy organizations played a role in disseminating knowledge. They distributed books and other publications, participated in interfaith events, and appeared in schools, libraries, churches, and temples. It is remarkable that many ordinary Americans were receptive and even went out of their way to show tolerance and understanding.

Mehdi Bozorgmehr and Anny Bakalian

See also

Arab American Institute; Islamophobia; September 11, 2001, Terrorism, Discriminatory Reactions to

Further Reading:

Ameri, Anan, and Dawn Ramey, eds. *The Arab American Encyclopedia*, Woodbridge, CT: U.X.L, 2000.

Arab American National Museum. *Telling Our Story*. Dearborn, MI: Arab American National Museum, 2007.

Boosahda, Elizabeth. *Arab-American Faces and Voices: The Origins of an Immigrant Community*. Austin: University of Texas Press, 2003.

Orfalea, Gregory. *The Arab Americans: A History*. Northampton, MA: Olive Branch Press, 2006.

Archie Bunker Bigotry

Archie Bunker was a television sitcom character featured in the controversial, groundbreaking show *All in the Family*, which was created by writer-producer Norman Lear and inspired by the British television series *Till Death Do Us Part*. ABC originally commissioned the pilot but then rejected it. Lear took the show to CBS, and it premiered there on January 12, 1971; its final episode aired in 1979. The show sparked controversy with its handling of previously taboo subjects, such as breast cancer, impotence, and rape, and

Jean Stapleton (as Edith Bunker) and Carroll O'Connor (as Archie Bunker) during an episode of *All in the Family*. (Photofest)

with its handling of hot political topics, including the Vietnam War, gun control, and racism. For many Americans, Bunker personified the image of an endearing bigot.

In the show, Bunker, played by actor Carroll O'Connor, depicted an uneducated, prejudiced, conservative, white, working-class guy who lived at 704 Houser Street in the Corona neighborhood of Queens, New York, with his sweet, bumbling wife, Edith (whom he called Dingbat); his daughter, Gloria; and his ultraliberal, Polish American son-in-law, Mike Stivic, a graduate student (also known as Meathead).

An unabashed bigot, Bunker loathed virtually every minority group and, in unrestrained diatribes, called blacks "jungle bunnies," "coons," and "spades"; Puerto Ricans "spics"; and Chinese people "chinks." Though he loathed minorities, they were often nearby, both at work and at home. His next-door neighbors, the Jeffersons, were a black family. Louise Jefferson was one of Edith's close friends, while her husband, George, the owner of a small dry-cleaning business, despised Archie; their son, Lionel, a good friend of Mike's, often visited the house and enjoyed teasing Archie about his racist beliefs. The Jeffersons later spun off into their own series, building on the premise that the family's dry-cleaning business had produced enough wealth for them to move into tony Manhattan. A 1972 episode, in which the black singer/dancer Sammy Davis Jr. kissed Archie, is often cited as a historic moment in American race relations.

When the show was launched, network executives, including CBS president William Paley, who was Jewish, were so concerned about its potentially offensive nature that the network took the unusual step of introducing it with the following disclaimer: "The program you are about to see . . . seeks to throw a humorous spotlight on our frailties, prejudices, and concerns. By making them a source of laughter we hope to show—in a mature fashion—just how absurd they are." While some viewers complained about its "liberal bent," the show, which was written by Lear and Bud Yorkin, also Jewish, turned out to be extremely popular and was ranked number one in ratings for five consecutive years, becoming an anchor for the CBS network. Further expressions of the show's success were an "Archie for President" campaign launched in 1972 and the enshrinement of "Archie's chair," a prop in which he regularly sat in the show, at the Smithsonian Institute in Washington, D.C.

Although the show received much critical and popular praise for its frank, humorous handling of emotionally and politically charged topics, some scholars criticized it for reinforcing prior prejudices and stereotypes. By presenting Bunker as a cultural archetype, the series can be seen as inadvertently validating such beliefs. Black psychologist Alvin Poussaint condemned the show, saying its "disarming" nature was its danger: "Blacks, for their own survival, should be in a posture of being very angry with bigots." Television executives commissioned a study on the show's impact, hoping to prove its claim that the show promoted positive race relations; but when the study's researchers concluded otherwise, saying that the show in fact reinforced bigoted beliefs, television executives ended up ditching the report's findings.

After the show ended in 1979, the creators reshaped the focus, centering a new show on a bar in Astoria, Queens, that Archie purchased after his retirement, and it renamed the show *Archie's Place*, which aired until 1983. Other spinoff series from the show included *Maude*, whose title character, a liberally minded feminist played by actress Beatrice Arthur, was first introduced as Edith's cousin on *All in the Family*. *The Jeffersons* and *Gloria* were other spinoffs. When O'Connor died in June 2001, he was remembered as television's Archie Bunker, despite a varied career that spanned films and stage.

Rose Kim

See also

Discrimination; Television and Racial Stereotypes; Television Drama and Racism

Further Reading:

Entman, Robert M., and Andrew Rojecki. *The Black Image in the White Mind: Media and Race in America*. Chicago: The University of Chicago Press, 2001.

Graves, Sherryl Browne. "Television and Prejudice Reduction: When Does Television as a Vicarious Experience Make a Difference?" *Journal of Social Issues* 55, no. 4 (1999): 707–727.

Arizona House Bill 2281 (HB 2281) (2010)

Arizona House Bill 2281 (2010) was a controversial law that banned ethnic studies courses at the secondary school level throughout the state. The law was specifically designed to eliminate Mexican American studies in the Tucson Unified School District (TUSD). Notably, HB 2281 was passed a month after the polemic Arizona SB 1070—known as the Support Our Law Enforcement and Safe Neighborhoods Act—legislation that required state law enforcement to determine the immigration status of detained individuals if there was reasonable suspicion that the suspect was an illegal immigrant. Both laws were seen as evidence that the Arizona Republican Party, influenced by the Tea Party movement's ideological views in regards to immigration and ethnic empowerment, sought to target the Latino population of Arizona.

On May 11, 2010, Arizona governor Jan Brewer signed House Bill 2281, legislation that was aimed at prohibiting school districts in the state from including in their programs of instruction any course that promoted the overthrow of the federal and/or state government and/or the U.S. Constitution, created resentment toward any class or race, promoted ethnic solidarity instead of individuality, and were specifically designed for any one ethnicity.

State Superintendent of Public Instruction Tom Horne, author of the legislation, had stated that the bill was written specifically to target the Mexican American studies program in the TUSD. Horne was especially critical of the use of the textbook *Occupied America: A History of Chicanos* (1972), by Rodolfo Acuña, professor and founder of the Chicano studies program at California State University, Northridge. In regard to that particular book, Horne stated, "To begin with, the title of the book implies to the kids that they live in occupied America, or occupied Mexico." Horne and other supporters of HB 2281 argued that ethnic studies courses fostered divisiveness and disloyalty by communities of color towards the United States as well as resentment towards white people.

In January 2011, Horne reported that the TUSD was out of compliance with the law. At that point, Horne had taken office as Arizona attorney general. Later that year, his successor as Arizona state superintendent, John Huppenthal, ordered an audit of the TUSD. Huppenthal had run for office promising to "stop La Raza" and advocating HB 2281. The

TUSD was ruled noncompliant in December 2011 for having such texts as William Shakespeare's *The Tempest* and Bill Bigelow's *Rethinking Columbus: The Next 500 Years* (1998) used in its Mexican American Studies program. The following month, TUSD voted to cut the program.

The backlash to HB 2281 resulted in various Chicano advocacy groups, such as Librofícante, protesting the law by providing the newly banned books. The Librofícante project is aimed at creating awareness of the prohibition of the Mexican American Studies program and ethnic studies literature in Tucson. Student-led marches and protests also followed the state's initial decision to pass HB 2281. Moreover, the law inadvertently made the banned books more popular as Chicano students embraced them after they were removed, in some instances publicly, from the classroom.

Abraham O. Mendoza

See also

Arizona Senate Bill 1070 (SB 1070) (2010); Ethnic Studies. Document: Arizona Senate Bill 1070 (2010)

Further Reading:

Arizona House Bill 2281 (2010). http://www.azleg.gov/legtext/49leg/2r/bills/hb2281s.pdf.

Billeaud, Jacques. "Ariz schools' ethnic studies program ruled illegal." Associated Press, December 27, 2011. http://news.yahoo.com/ariz-schools-ethnic-studies-program-ruled-illegal-021635252.html.

Santa Cruz, Nicole. Arizona bill targeting ethnic studies signed into law. *Los Angeles Times*, May 12, 2010. http://articles.latimes.com/2010/may/12/nation/la-na-ethnic-studies-20100512.

Arizona Senate Bill 1070 (SB 1070) (2010)

On April 19, 2010, the Arizona state legislature passed Arizona Senate Bill 1070 (SB 1070), the Support Our Law Enforcement and Safe Neighborhoods Act, and Arizona governor Jan Brewer signed the bill into law on April 23. The act, which provides for broader policing of illegal immigration by state and local law enforcement in Arizona, ignited a firestorm of controversy in the wake of its passage. On July 28, a day before it was scheduled to go into effect, U.S. District Judge Susan Bolton temporarily blocked key parts of the new law, including a provision that would require police to check a person's citizenship or immigration status at the time of a traffic stop, detention, arrest, or other police action if there is reasonable suspicion that the person is not a U.S. citizen or legal immigrant. Judge Bolton also put on hold a component that would make it a state crime for an immigrant to be without papers indicating legal immigration status. Though the law also includes several other provisions that attempt to crack down on illegal immigration in other ways, these elements provoked the most controversy, as critics charged that they mandate or reinforce racial profiling by police and will lead to unconstitutional infringement of the civil rights of many U.S. citizens. Supporters of the law claim that inadequate federal immigration enforcement has made such state-level measures necessary due to economic and safety concerns associated with illegal immigrants.

There has been significant public outcry against SB 1070, particularly by advocacy groups concerned about the prospect of targeted profiling of Hispanics, and boycotts have been organized in an effort to economically ostracize Arizona—even the governments of major U.S. cities like Los Angeles and San Francisco have terminated or stopped pursuing contracts with Arizona-based firms. Legal challenges to the law on constitutional grounds have also been filed by such civil rights groups as the American Civil Liberties Union, the National Association for the Advancement of Colored People, and the Mexican American Legal Defense and Educational Fund. On July 6, 2010, in a widely anticipated move, the Justice Department officially joined the fray and filed suit against the state of Arizona and Gov. Brewer, aiming to block enforcement of the new immigration law on the grounds that it usurps the federal government's authority on immigration policy. Even after Judge Bolton issued her injunction in response to this legal challenge, which Gov. Brewer said she would appeal, protesters against the law, in an act of civil disobedience, gathered in Phoenix on the morning it went into effect and blocked a street near city hall.

Arizona's new law and the events surrounding it have reenergized the national debate over immigration reform and drawn attention to a larger movement taking place in many states to expand upon federal efforts to combat illegal immigration. Shortly after Gov. Brewer signed SB 1070 into law, a number of other states—including Utah, South Carolina, and Oklahoma—announced that they would consider passing similar measures. Though the enactment of SB 1070 may have catapulted Arizona to the forefront of this movement, the state is by no means the only battleground in the ongoing debate over immigration in the United States.

ABC-CLIO

See also

Arizona House Bill 2281 (HB 2281) (2010); Ethnic Studies. Document: Arizona Senate Bill 1070 (2010)

Aryan Brotherhood

The Aryan Brotherhood, also known as the Brand, Alice Baker, or the One-Two, is a white supremacist prison gang that was founded in the maximum security prison in San Quentin, California, in 1964 by racist neo-Nazis and biker inmates. Despite the fact that members of the Aryan Brotherhood make up less than one tenth of 1 percent of the United States prison population they are estimated to be responsible for 18 percent of all prison murders. While it is difficult to gain an accurate count of Aryan Brotherhood membership, the FBI estimates that there are 15,000 members nationwide with one half in prisons and the other half out of prison. This white supremacist gang has members and associates in every major state and federal prison in the United States. They are considered to be the most violent and powerful prison gang in America.

Until the 1960s, in the United States the majority of prisons were racially segregated. Once they were desegregated gangs formed along racial and ethnic lines and became an increasing problem. The Aryan Brotherhood formed in 1964 by white inmates based on a neo-Nazi ideological framework, specifically the racial hatred of any nonwhite individual. After being established in the 1960s the gang expanded rapidly in the U.S. prison system throughout the 1970s and engaged in multiple acts of violence motivated by racial hatred. During this time period they also expanded their operations to include the trafficking of contraband into the prison system and control of gambling, drugs, and prostitution behind prison walls. Since the 1980s the Aryan Brotherhood has been split into two separate but cooperative factions, one of federal prisoners and one of state prisoners.

Individuals often join the Brotherhood after being sentenced to prison. The main reason for originally joining is for protection. Recruits are required to read *Mein Kampf* and "earn their badge" by attacking or killing black inmates. Once initiated, members adopt the blood in, blood out mentality where they take a blood oath to join and are only released from membership by their own death (SPLC). Members can often be identified by their close-shaven hair styles and tattoos of swastikas, shamrocks, the letters AB, and the numbers 666.

Members of the Aryan Brotherhood are involved in a significant amount of prison violence and murders, mostly against black inmates who are members of their rival gangs the Bloods, the CRIPS, and the Black Guerillas. Beginning in the 1970s the Aryan Brotherhood morphed into a criminal syndicate that became heavily involved in the trafficking of contraband, particularly methamphetamine and heroin, behind prison walls. Aryan Brotherhood members who have been released from prison are expected to help support their incarcerated brothers by producing and distributing drugs on the outside. Failure to provide for incarcerated members results in the death of that individual once they are incarcerated again. Wives and girlfriends of incarcerated members are also heavily involved in the smuggling of drugs into the prisons system. Incarcerated Aryan Brotherhood members have also been heavily involved in gambling and forced prostitution behind bars. Free members of the Aryan Brotherhood have been responsible for hate crimes against minority group members in the name of RAHOWA (racial holy war) such as the two brotherhood members who killed James Byrd Jr. in Jasper, Texas, by dragging him behind their pickup truck.

Law enforcement officers have attempted to curb the activities of the Aryan Brotherhood behind bars by isolating members, but the members have somehow always found a way to communicate. The threat of additional time for committing homicides behind bars has also not served as a deterrent as many members are already serving life sentences. Recently, however, some members have been brought up on capital charges under racketeering indictments for sanctioning murders to promote their gang status and control of the prison narcotics network.

Virginia R. Beard

See also
Hammerskin Nation; Hate Groups in America; Ku Klux Klan (KKK)

Further Reading:
Brooks, John Lee. *Blood In Blood Out: The Violent Empire of the Aryan Brotherhood.* London: World Head Press, 2010.
F.B.I. Records: The Vault. "Aryan Brotherhood." http://vault.fbi.gov/Aryan%20Brotherhood%20/Aryan%20Brotherhood%20Part%201%20of%201/view (accessed December 20, 2012).
Fleisher, Mark S., and Scott H. Decker. "An Overview of the Challenge of Prison Gangs." *Corrections Management Quarterly* 5 (2001): 1–9.
King, Joyce. *Hate Crime: The Story of a Dragging in Jasper Texas.* New York: Random House, 2002.
Southern Poverty Law Center. "Leaders of Racist Prison Gang Aryan Brotherhood Face Federal Indictment." http://www.splcenter.org/get-informed/intelligence-report/browse-all-issues/2005/fall/smashing-the-shamrock (accessed December 20, 2012).

Aryan Nations

The Aryan Nations has become the most important of the Christian Identity groups. Richard Girnt Butler founded the Aryan Nations in April 1974. Aryan Nations combined militant white supremacy with virulent anti-Semitism. Butler was able to build the Aryan Nations as America's primary white supremacist organization, replacing the Ku Klux Klan. Butler and his followers adopted from William Pierce, the leader of the National Alliance, the concept that the United States was under the control of the Zionist Occupational Government (ZOG). In Butler's view, the ZOG not only controlled the American government but also had as its goal the usurpation of Aryan liberties. He believed that "Jews controlled the news media and were descended from Eve and Satan, African-Americans were 'mud people,' and Hitler stood up for the white race."

Butler became acquainted with William Potter Gale, a former senior army officer, during the 1961 ballot initiative to ban communists from teaching in California schools. Butler worked with Gale in the early 1960s with the paramilitary group California Ranger. Gale then introduced him to Wesley Swift, the founder of the modern Christian Identity movement. Soon afterward, Butler became a convert to Swift's brand of Christian Identity and joined Swift's Church of Jesus Christ Christian in Los Angeles. After Swift died in 1970, Butler succeeded him as the lead minister of the Church of Jesus Christ Christian. Butler was not as successful a minister as Swift, so in April 1974, he transferred the church to a 20-acre compound in Hayden Lake, Idaho. Shortly after arrival in Idaho, he started a chapter of the Posse Comitatus with himself as its head, but within two years, he was expelled because members believed that he was trying to use it as a private army. After this failure, it took until June 1978 for him to establish the Aryan Nations with the goal of establishing a white homeland in the Pacific Northwest.

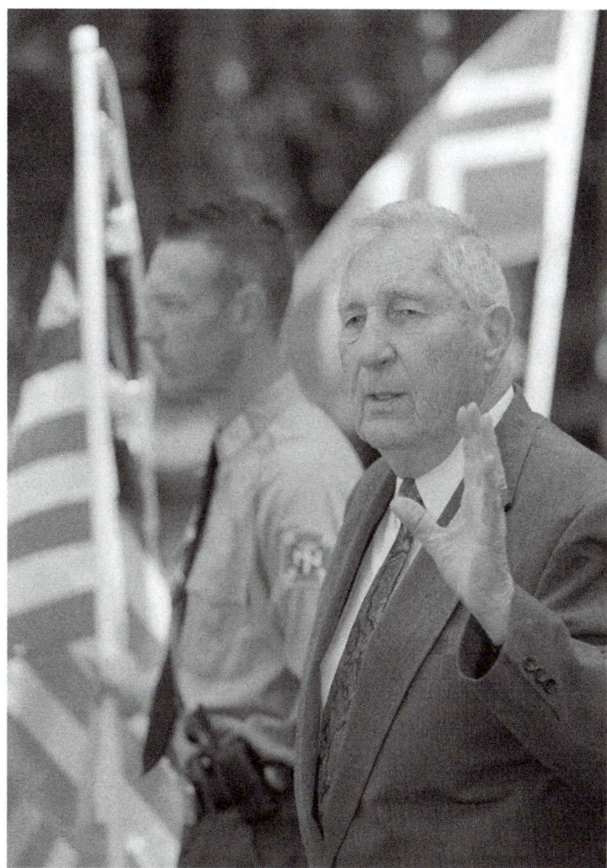

Founder of the Aryan Nations, Richard G. Butler, right, announced July 2, 1999, at a press conference at the Aryan Nations headquarters in Hayden, Idaho, 1999. (Associated Press)

Butler's church was always short of funding. To raise funds, Butler began to sell family memberships in the Aryan

Skinheads

The skinheads are an international movement of white, largely male youth gangs associated with neo-Nazi and white-power ideologies. Neo-Nazi skinhead groups are among the most militant advocates of white supremacy and are believed responsible for the commission of numerous hate crimes since the 1970s.

Originating in the late 1960s and 1970s in the United Kingdom, skinheads presented themselves as working-class, anti-establishment radicals and developed a subcultural dress code of closely shaved heads, combat boots, combat fatigues, swastika tattoos, and suspenders. The 1970s British Skinheads were associated with punk subculture and punk music as well as Nazi-inspired fashion, and some skinheads today remain primarily focused on music and subcultural style. Neo-Nazi skinheads, however, are considered the foot soldiers of white supremacism and have created a white-power youth movement that has a global reach. By 1995, the Anti-Defamation League estimated that there were approximately 70,000 skinheads worldwide. The skinheads movement reached the United States in the mid-1980s. Although skinheads are generally only loosely organized, U.S. neo-Nazi skinheads are affiliated with a number of more organized groups, especially the White Aryan Resistance (WAR), a neo-Nazi hate group founded in 1983 by Tom Metzger. WAR and its skinhead youth wing, the Aryan Youth Movement, advocate for individual and small-cell guerilla terrorism and violence against immigrants and minorities as well as police and other officials. The Anti-Defamation League estimates that skinheads were responsible for at least 43 hate-crime murders between 1990 and 1997.

Victoria Pitts

Nations for $15 a year, and taped sermons were sold for $2.50. By the 1980s, there were around 300 local members and 6,000 in the United States and Canada.

Butler developed the strategy of the "10 percent solution." His plan was to gain enough adherents in the five Pacific Northwest states of Idaho, Montana, Oregon, Washington, and Wyoming that the Aryan Nations could gain political power. Butler began a series of Aryan Nations conferences, with the Pacific States National Kingdom Identity Conference in 1979 being the first. The problem with the "10 percent solution" was that many of the potential recruits were from the South, and they had no desire to relocate to the Pacific Northwest.

Over the next 28 years, Butler led the Aryan Nations. He broadcasted through the Aryan Nations a militant message of white supremacy. At a gathering on April 20, 1996, members of the Aryan Nations published a manifesto in the language of the original Declaration of Independence that declared their independence from the United States. This was part of the Aryan Nations' campaign to build an Aryan homeland in the Pacific Northwest.

Most of the Aryan Nations' activities have been devoted to propaganda and the recruitment of new members. The audience most receptive to the message of the Aryan National has been white inmates in prison. Prisoners in many federal and state prisons formed an offshoot group called the Aryan Brotherhood.

Butler's lack of militant action resulted in a loss of Aryan Nations' members from time to time as more activist groups formed appealing to those with more violent tendencies in the white supremacist movement. Most famous of these was the Order, or the Silent Brotherhood, formed by Robert Jay Mathews to engage in direct action. Butler ended up repudiating him and his actions.

Another such case involved Buford Furrow. Furrow had been a member of Aryan Nations and a former guard at the Hayden Lake compound. Furrow went on a shooting spree at a Jewish Community Center in Southern California in 1999. He wounded a teacher and several students before killing a Philippine postal worker. After his capture, Furrow pleaded guilty to the offenses and received two life sentences.

Despite Butler's efforts to avoid violence, the Aryan Nations received a legal setback that bankrupted the organization. One day in 1998, a woman, Victoria Keenan, and her young son, Jason, drove past the compound. The car backfired, and the members of the Aryan Nations guards interpreted the noise as gunfire. These guards ran down the car and assaulted the woman. She sued with the help of the

Southern Poverty Law Center. A subsequent civil court judgment against both the Aryan Nations and Butler bankrupted them. Butler had to relinquish control of the Hayden Lake compound in the summer of 2001. A supporter, Vincent Bertollini, purchased a home for him in Hayden in October 2000.

This financial setback led Butler to resign as head of the Aryan Nations. Butler considered a number of candidates before picking Harold Ray Redfeairn as its new head. Redfeairn, a former roofer from Dayton, Ohio, has a checkered past. He served six years in an Ohio prison from 1986 to 1992 after a conviction for robbery and the attempted murder of a Dayton police officer in 1985. Redfeairn had control of the administration of the Aryan Nations until he resigned in January 2002, the day after he expelled Butler from the Aryan Nations. Then Redfeairn died on October 26, 2003, at the age of only 51. Despite his expulsion, Butler remained the spiritual leader of the Aryan Nations until his death on September 8, 2004.

After the deaths of Butler and Redfeairn, the Aryan Nations reorganized. Instead of a single leader, the remaining leaders selected a four-member leadership council to run the Aryan Nations and transferred the organization's headquarters to Lincoln, Alabama. Despite this reorganization and transfer of operations, the Aryan Nations has a leadership void, with several individuals eager to assume Butler's mantle, and the group has split into several factions.

Stephen E. Atkins

See also

Aryan Brotherhood; Hate Groups in America; Klu Klux Klan (KKK)

Further Reading:

Coates, James. *Armed and Dangerous: The Rise of the Survivalist Right.* New York: Hill and Wang, 1987.

Flynn, Kevin, and Gary Gerhardt. *The Silent Brotherhood: Inside America's Racist Underground.* New York: Free Press, 1989.

Wakin, Daniel J. "Richard G. Butler, 86, Dies; Founder of the Aryan Nations." *New York Times*, September 9, 2004.

Asbury Park (New Jersey) Riot of 1970

The 1970 Fourth of July holiday weekend began with a period of civil unrest for Asbury Park, New Jersey. Although the trouble started Saturday evening with a few groups of young people breaking windows, Asbury Park's West Side community had been plagued by a significant lack of jobs, adequate housing, and recreation facilities that contributed to the unrest for many years. The number of citizens involved in the riots steadily escalated over the following nights, as did the level of destruction. Before peace was to return, much of the West Side would be severely damaged. In brief, the seven nights of unrest resulted in $4 million of building and personal property damage, 167 arrests, 165 civilians wounded or injured, 15 police officers injured, the loss of an estimated 100 jobs, and an undetermined number of families made homeless.

The small disturbances of July 4 received little immediate attention from the local and national press, but the city's entire police force was called to duty. By the early hours of Monday, July 6, the number of Asbury Park residents involved in the rioting significantly increased, as did the amount and extent of property damage. At this time, Police Chief Thomas S. Smith called almost 100 police officers from surrounding communities into the West Side to assist Asbury Park's police force. Mayor Joseph F. Mattice declared a state of emergency and, later that day, ordered a curfew from 10:00 p.m. to 6:00 a.m. for the city. The curfew would remain in place for the following three days, but its starting time would change as the violence decreased.

On the morning of Tuesday, July 7, West Side African American leaders presented a list of 20 demands to the Asbury Park City Council. Two new demands would be added during the following days. Demands such as amnesty for those arrested and the immediate removal of outside police forces were directly related to the current period of unrest. Many of the demands, however, addressed the pressing needs that created the atmosphere in which such violence had erupted. For example, residents demanded the development of a Recreation Commission and the immediate employment of at least 100 West Side youths.

The economic disenfranchisement and lack of resources underlying the events had long been a reality for the city's African American West Side residents. In fact, citizens of the West Side made these pressing needs known to Mayor Mattice and the city council long before the events of the July 4 weekend. City officials also had recognized these growing problems. Unfortunately, requests for increased funding for the West Side remained unanswered from local, state, and federal levels. The state and federal government considered the needs of this community less pressing than those of other struggling cities.

By Wednesday, July 8, the majority of the West Side business district was damaged, and the city struggled to handle the increased demands resulting from the riots. The annex to the Monmouth County Jail in Asbury Park was at capacity, and conditions in the jail were described as almost unbearable at times. Reports from the local hospital indicated that at least 32 of the 56 injured in the previous night of violence were treated for gunshot wounds.

Citizen peace patrols started walking the most heavily damaged street on Wednesday. The citizen patrols encouraged members of the community to observe the imposed curfew. State police also remained in the West Side throughout the evening, patrolling the streets by car. When the sun rose the next day, the community had experienced a full night of calm. Throughout the rest of Thursday, July 9, the relative peace continued. New Jersey governor William T. Cahill toured the West Side and requested that President Richard Nixon declare Asbury Park a major disaster area.

Meetings between African American community leaders and the city council also took place on Wednesday. Although the parties involved succeeded in continuing the dialogue, the demands previously presented remained unanswered. Discussions of the West Side community's demands continued through Friday, July 10, but the city council failed to provide the answers promised the previous day. The city council's slow response to these demands and complaints of police misconduct added to the community's injury. West Side citizens felt disappointed by the failure of the local government to accept responsibility for its part in the underlying causes of the unrest.

Willie Hamm, the leading spokesman for the West Side, announced that further communication would be halted until the city council addressed the community's demands. Talks resumed later that day with a definitive goal of addressing the current demands. By late Friday evening, West Side leaders and the city council came to terms, and all demands were at least minimally addressed.

The West Side remained calm for the following two days, and the state police left the neighborhood on Saturday. Disheartened by the violence that destroyed their neighborhood and injured their friends and families, West Side citizens united in efforts to aid those left homeless. African American community leaders continued lobbying for much-needed resources, while still facing many of the same obstacles that existed prior to the riots.

Elizabeth M. Webb

See also

Race Riots in America. Documents: Report on the Memphis Riots of May 1866 (1866); Account of the Riots in East St. Louis, Illinois (1917); A Southern Black Woman's Letter Regarding the Recent Riots in Chicago and Washington (1919); The Cook County Coroner's Report Regarding the 1919 Chicago Race Riots (1920); The Final Report of the Grand Jury on the Tulsa Race Riot (June 25, 1921); Testimony from *Laney v. United States* (1923); The Governor's Commission Report on the Watts Riots (1965); Cyrus R. Vance's Report on the Riots in Detroit (1967); The Reports of the Oklahoma Commission to Study the Tulsa Race Riot of 1921 (2000–2001); Draft Report: 1898 Wilmington Race Riot Commission (2005)

Further Reading:

"City Council Lists Answers to 22 West Side Demands." *Asbury Park Evening Press*, July 14, 1970, 1.

"County Jail Overflowing." *Asbury Park Evening Press*, July 8, 1970, 4.

"Second Week of July in Retrospect." *Asbury Park Evening Press*, July 12, 1970, sec. C, 1.

Wheeling, John. "Shootings Erupt, 56 Are Hurt." *Asbury Park Evening Press*, July 8, 1970, 1.

Wolff, Daniel J. *4th of July, Asbury Park: A History of the Promised Land*. New York: Bloomsbury, 2005.

Asian American Legal Defense and Education Fund (AALDEF)

Founded in 1974, the New York–based Asian American Legal Defense and Education Fund (AALDEF) was the first organization on the East Coast to address the legal rights of Asian Americans. Over the years, AALDEF established itself as a leader on issues of voting rights, anti-Asian violence, labor and tenant rights, immigrant concerns, and most recently, the effects of 9/11 on the Asian American community in New York.

In 1985 AALDEF negotiated the first ever agreement with the New York City Board of Elections to provide Chinese-speaking voters with bilingual materials and assistance. In

1995, under terms of the federal Civil Rights Act, AALDEF successfully campaigned for the full translation of ballots in New York City into Chinese and English. Defending the rights of low-income tenants in Chinatown, an AALDEF lawsuit in 1986 blocked construction of a 21-story luxury condominium. In the decision, *Chinese Staff and Workers Association v. City of New York*, the New York Court of Appeals required an impact assessment of new development on small businesses and low-income tenants, establishing a legal foundation for preserving low-cost housing.

AALDEF's work for immigrant labor rights and against sweatshops has included workers' rights clinics and free legal assistance to garment and restaurant workers. In 1997, AALDEF successfully represented striking workers at Chinatown's Jing Fong Restaurant—one of the largest in New York—winning a $1.1 million settlement to recoup skimmed tips, unfair wages, and unpaid overtime. After 9/11, AALDEF represented the New York Asian population, managing legal and social-service claims, representing detainees, and documenting and advocating for victims of hate crimes, particularly South Asians and Filipinos. The organization continues its work to protect the civil rights of Asian Americans by litigating cases, providing legal resources and information clinics, educating Asian Americans about their legal rights, and providing a variety of programs on various issues.

KENNETH J. GUEST

See also

Mexican American Legal Defense an Education Fund

Further Reading:

Ho, Fred, ed. *Legacy to Liberation: Politics and Culture of Revolutionary Asian/Pacific America*. Edinburgh: AK Press, 2000.

Kwong, Peter. *Forbidden Workers: Illegal Chinese Immigrants and American Labor*. New York: New Press, 1997.

Lien, Pei-ti. *The Making of Asian America through Political Participation (Mapping Racism)*. Philadelphia: Temple University Press, 2001.

Lowe, Lisa. *Immigrant Acts: On Asian American Cultural Politics*. Durham and London: Duke University Press, 1996.

Ong, Paul. *Beyond Asian American Poverty: Community Economic Development Policies and Strategies*. Los Angeles: Leadership Education for Asian Pacifics, 1993.

Parreñas, Rhacel Salazar. *Servants of Globalization: Women, Migration, and Domestic Work*. Stanford, CA: Stanford University Press, 2001.

Zhou, Min. *Chinatown: The Socioeconomic Potential of an Urban Enclave*. Philadelphia: Temple University Press, 1992.

Assimilation

In its broadest use, the term *assimilation* refers to how groups of people integrate with each other into a unified society. In the 1920s, the sociologist Robert Park came out with a four-stage theory of race relations (the Race Relations Cycle) to explain how racial and ethnic groups in the United States interacted and accommodated each other. This theory became the basis of what is called "straight line assimilation," now thought of as classic assimilation theory. The steps of this model were: *contact*, *competition*, *accommodation*, and *assimilation*. Essentially, immigrants arrive in the host society and compete with other groups for resources. This competition sorts them into a hierarchy of accommodation within the host society, either as a dominant group or a dominated group. At this point the immigrants are considered part of the society and are therefore assimilated.

Among others, Milton Gordon continued Park's work. However, Gordon broadened the number of possible outcomes that could be called assimilation. His three working models of assimilation of immigrants into the host society in the United States were the Melting Pot, pluralism, and Anglo-conformity. In the Melting Pot, the traditions and cultures of both groups are blended to form a new cultural pattern taking on aspects of both groups and changing as new immigrants arrive. With pluralism, the traditions and cultures of both the host and immigrant populations are seen as equally valid and valuable and are allowed to co-exist while the national identity of the host society is still maintained. In contrast, in Anglo-conformity, immigrants to the United States adapt themselves to the traditions and culture of the dominant, host culture that they move into.

Anglo-conformity, along with some aspects of the Melting Pot, is most closely related to Park's model. Anglo-conformity is what Americans commonly think of when they think of the term *assimilation*—a system where immigrants have to abandon their ethnic or national customs and instead mold their behaviors to the norms of the dominant majority. As each new generation of immigrants arrive in this country, they feel the need to assimilate and become "American," a process that might only be completed by their children or grandchildren. This process of assimilation is how an English-speaking majority is even kept in the United States since the bulk of Americans are not from English-speaking ethnic backgrounds.

Gordon saw immigrants as passing through seven stages or subprocesses of assimilation: *cultural, structural, marital, identificational, attitude receptional, behavior receptional,* and *civic.* These subprocesses can be thought of as either a step in the assimilation process or a type of assimilation itself. Not every immigrant group manages to pass through every stage. They may stall along the way or they may skip parts of stages altogether.

Gordon notes that if there is a master cultural mold for American society, it is that of the white, Protestant middle class of Anglo-Saxon ethnicity. If this is the master pattern for assimilation in the United States then obviously some groups will have an easier time assimilating than others. Immigrants whose cultural differences with the host society lay basically with language will be able to assimilate easier than immigrant groups who have both a different language and a religion. Having a different racial identity would make this even more difficult.

To add even more complexity to this, those who espouse the theory of segmented assimilation would note that not everyone who assimilates to American culture necessarily uses white, middle class, Anglo-Saxon Protestants as their model. By its very nature, classic assimilation theory speaks of assimilation and upward mobility as though they were the same thing. However, immigrants today tend to not move into middle class neighborhoods when they first arrive in this country. The Americans that they and their children see may not be upwardly mobile. In cases like this, maintaining a level of ethnicity may actually be protective to the immigrants and the society as a whole as opposed to a downwardly mobile assimilation.

Robert Park described assimilation as achieving enough of a degree of cultural solidarity to maintain a national existence. Some people take this to mean the complete eradication of ethnic or cultural distinctiveness. While such an extreme view may be of historical use, it would appear that the more specific Anglo-conformity definition would be too narrow for use in the modern United States. Gordon's complete three model scheme may have more use for those thinking about the future development of ethnic and racial relations in the America, especially the cultural pluralism model.

DONALD P. WOOLLEY

See also

Melting Pot Theory; Pluralism; Segmented Assimilation

Further Reading:

Gordon, Milton. *Assimilation in American Life: The Role of Race, Religion and National Origins.* New York: Oxford University Press, 1964.

Gordon, Milton. *Human Nature, Class, and Ethnicity.* New York: Oxford University Press, 1978.

Park, Robert E. *Race and Culture.* Ann Arbor, MI: Free Press, 1950.

Assimilation Theory

Assimilation theory is a theory describing and explaining the process of assimilation—the blending together culturally, socially, psychologically, and biologically—that eventually occurs when diverse groups have contact with each other in a multiethnic society. This homogenization is a process of boundary reduction and a process of losing racial and ethnic distinctions. Theories of assimilation vary in their focus and in the explanations they provide. Two assimilation theories, Park's race-relations cycle and Gordon's theory of assimilation, have been influential in explaining intergroup relations.

Robert Park was one of the first theorists to suggest a cycle of race relations through which new immigrant groups would pass, a sequence of stages leading eventually to full assimilation. According to Park, the race relations cycle takes the form of *contacts, competition, accommodation,* and eventual *assimilation.* The cycle is progressive and irreversible. Customs regulations, immigration restrictions, and racial barriers may slacken the tempo of the movement or halt it altogether for a time, but the cycle cannot change its direction. He maintained that this four-stage cycle is a universal process; that is, it pertains to race relations everywhere, not just to those of the United States.

Critics of Park's theory of the race-relations cycle theory have pointed out that such a cycle may describe fairly well the experiences of most white European immigrant

Robert Park exerted a major influence on the development of American sociology. A professor at the University of Chicago in the 1920s, he became a leader of the "Chicago school" of sociology and pioneered in the study of race and ethnic relations. (University of Chicago)

groups in the United States but that it does not represent the experiences of the groups with distinctive physical markers who came to America either voluntarily or involuntarily. The experiences of African Americans and Native Americans are clear cases of groups not following his race-relations cycle.

Milton Gordon also contributed to an understanding of the assimilation process. He argued that multiple processes of assimilation occur to different degrees in different dimensions, that assimilation is not a single, distinct linear process. He identified seven different areas of assimilation: *cultural*, *structural*, *marital*, *psychological*, *attitudinal*, *behavioral*, and *civic*. This process is neither inevitable nor sequential. Any particular group may remain indefinitely at any one of these stages. According to Gordon, the cultural and structural stages of assimilation are the most important. *Cultural assimilation* refers to the adoption of cultural patterns of the dominant, or host, group by the subordinate groups. *Structural assimilation*, according to Gordon, refers to the integration of the subordinate immigrant group into the social institutions of the dominant group, especially at the primary group level. In other words, when subordinate groups, such as new immigrant groups, are well blended into cliques, clubs, friendships, and other primary social institutions, we may say that structural assimilation has occurred. Gordon argued that structural assimilation at the primary level is the key to all subsequent assimilation. Once structural assimilation has occurred, either simultaneously with or subsequent to acculturation, Gordon claimed that the other types of assimilation would naturally follow. It is possible, according to Gordon, that a group assimilates culturally but remains separate structurally.

Gordon's theory of assimilation, too, has been criticized on several different points. One serious shortcoming of his theory lies in its understanding of structural assimilation as entailing interaction with the dominant group only at the primary level. Structural assimilation, however, should occur at the secondary institutional level as well as at the primary level in intergroup relations. In other words, the integration of new immigrant groups in the areas of education, employment, and the political sector is crucial to determining eventual assimilation in other dimensions.

Both theorists place less emphasis on the situational variables affecting the assimilation process. But one important fact related to assimilation in the United States is that different groups encounter a variety of experiences during the process of assimilation, and many factors can affect the degree and forms of assimilation. Some of these factors are how and when a group enters a society, its size and dispersion, its cultural similarity to the dominant group, and its physical distinctiveness. For instance, when a large number from an immigrant group enter a society during a short period of time, are concentrated in certain geographic areas, and practice cultural patterns, such as language and religion, that are different from those of the dominant group or groups, they are less likely to assimilate. One of the key determining factors of assimilation in American society has been physical differences from the dominant group. When dominant groups do not allow subordinate groups to assimilate, those groups remain separate.

Milton Gordon's Stages

Stage or Sub Process	*Characteristics*
Cultural Assimilation	Change of ethnic cultural patterns to those of host society
Structural Assimilation	Large-scale entrance to host society clubs and institutions
Marital Assimilation	Large-scale intermarriage with host society
Identification Assimilation	Development of a sense of collective identity based on host society
Attitude Reception Assimilation	Absence of prejudice
Behavior Reception Assimilation	Absence of discrimination
Civic Assimilation	Absence of value and power conflict with the host society

Source: Adapted from Gordon (1964: 71).

HEON CHEOL LEE

See also

Americanization Movement; Chain Migration; Immigration Acts; Melting Pot Theory; Segmented Assimilation

Further Reading:

Gordon, Milton M. *Assimilation in American Life*. New York: Oxford University Press, 1964.

Park, Robert E. *Race and Culture*. New York: Free Press, 1964.

Atlanta Compromise, The

The so-called Atlanta Compromise derives its name from the famous speech by Booker T. Washington at the Cotton States Exposition in Atlanta in September 1895, where the eminent black educator and leader addressed a racially segregated audience and advocated that African Americans focus on economic advancement rather than social and political equality. In other words, according to Washington in the Atlanta Compromise, African Americans would accommodate themselves to segregation and disfranchisement.

Reflecting the worsening situation facing African Americans in the 1890s—the rise of Jim Crow, disfranchisement, lynching, and economic hard times—Washington firmly believed that African Americans should focus on learning trades and skills and thus build up the black community. Washington was heavily influenced by the educational and sociological theories of the day and the education he received at Hampton University in Virginia. Washington bought into the notion that industrial education and self-help would lead to success. At the Tuskegee Institute in Alabama, from 1881 onward, Washington put these ideas into practice with much success. For example, the graduates from Tuskegee played key roles at the local level in scores of black communities across the South and built up successful black businesses and prosperous farms. At Tuskegee, black students learned new farming techniques and skills that stood them in good stead for the future.

Although Washington was well known in the South by 1895, mainly through good press and close relations with leading white politicians as well as the fine reputation of Tuskegee, it was the Atlanta Compromise that brought Washington national acclaim. In his brief speech to hundreds of onlookers, including the governor of Georgia, Washington contended that African Americans should be given a chance to succeed in business and commerce, that African Americans had shown great loyalty to whites over the generations and therefore deserved the opportunity to be successful. He urged those who complained about the slow nature of change to focus on small improvements and the future, even if the pace of transformation was gradual. He believed that justice, peace, and economic opportunity would lead to a new era of prosperity for all in the South—black and white. Washington argued that cooperation between the races did not threaten segregation at all and, in the most famous quote from the speech, he postulated: "In all things that are purely social we can be as separate as the fingers, yet one as the hand in all things essential to mutual progress." In a nutshell, this was the Atlanta Compromise—accommodation with racism and Jim Crow and disfranchisement—for economic success. Washington also believed that economic prosperity would eventually lead the way to civil and political rights. Whites and African Americans in the crowd cheered the speech and rushed to congratulate Washington.

The Atlanta speech and Compromise propelled Washington into the position of the national spokesman and leader of African Americans in the United States—Frederick

As the head of Tuskegee Institute (a leading center of African American education), Booker T. Washington was a major spokesperson for African Americans during the late 19th and early 20th centuries. (Library of Congress)

Douglass had died earlier in the year. All across the nation, scholars, politicians, and industrialists praised Washington and his ideology. It has been noted that Washington gained ascendancy because his ideas reflected the time. For the next 20 years, until his death in 1915, Washington and the Atlanta Compromise dominated race relations in the United States. At the time, most whites in the South and North and most African Americans supported the tenets of the Atlanta Compromise. Millions of dollars from Northern philanthropists poured into the coffers of black colleges and businesses that adhered to industrial education and self-help programs. Washington became known as the Wizard of Tuskegee—indeed, the institution served as the model for the Atlanta Compromise. Washington built close relations with Republicans, particularly Theodore Roosevelt, as well as wealthy industrialists, such as John D. Rockefeller.

In private, Washington did not always follow the Atlanta Compromise of accommodation with racism and the second-class status of African Americans. Indeed, Washington often completely opposed his professed public pronouncements. It is clear that he rejected white racism. He spoke of his opposition to segregation, his outrage against lynching, and the illegality of disfranchisement. He supported black defendants (in private) with monies in cases dealing with discrimination. He lobbied hard for positions in the federal government for qualified black aspirants. However, due to his accommodationist approach, conciliatory attitude, and public deference to whites, these efforts were kept secret from most African Americans and whites.

The Atlanta Compromise made Washington the leading spokesman for African Americans, and his accommodationism made him very popular within the black community. This approach to racial progress at a very difficult time for African Americans did yield success—for example, increased spending on black schools and more black colleges in the South, as well as increased black business activity throughout the South. However, criticisms of the Atlanta Compromise did emerge. The voice of opponents in the 1890s was muted; perhaps the most famous black opponent at this time to the Atlanta Compromise was Bishop Henry McNeal Turner.

A more determined opposition to accommodationism formed as the new century dawned. It was clear to many black intellectuals and white liberals that the Atlanta Compromise did not lead to increased opportunities for African Americans. Successful black businesses and businessmen were often the target for racial violence—for example, in the Atlanta Riot of 1906—and the lives of the majority of African Americans were one of poverty and lack of opportunity. Self-help did not seem to work for many. Thus from 1900, the voices of opposition grew. William Monroe Trotter, a black leader from Boston, criticized Washington's ideology as delusional. The most famous critic was W.E.B. Du Bois, who advocated full civil rights and integration immediately and that African Americans needed to build up a talented tenth of well-educated men and women to lead the fight for equality. The death of Washington in 1915 and the changing nature of race relations in the United States also heralded the passing of the Atlanta Compromise and the policy of accommodation. The Atlanta Compromise had become discredited. A new approach of integration and full civil and political rights, exemplified by the National Association for the Advancement of Colored People, took the place of the Atlanta Compromise.

For 20 years, the Atlanta Compromise and accommodationism with racism was the leading black ideological and pragmatic position in the age of Jim Crow. Although it is now discredited by most scholars and civil rights activists, it is clear that the Atlanta Compromise both reflected the mood and beliefs of time and also enabled many African Americans to cope, economically, during the nadir of race relations in the United States. Washington's belief that African Americans should build up their own communities and support one another in economic advancement holds true today. Washington never agreed with the white racists who believed in the natural inferiority of blacks. Washington always believed in equality and advancement. He espoused hard work, self-help, and Christian morality. But his belief that this could come while civil and political rights remained on the back burner was misguided at best, and perhaps a product of black powerlessness at the height of Jim Crow.

JAMES M. BEEBY

See also

Du Bois, W.E.B.; Washington, Booker T.

Further Reading:

Harlan, Louis. *Booker T. Washington: The Making of a Black Leader, 1856–1901*. New York: Oxford University Press, 1972.
Harlan, Louis. *Booker T. Washington: The Wizard of Tuskegee, 1901–1915*. New York: Oxford University Press, 1983.
Meier, August. *The Negro Thought in America, 1880–1915: Racial Ideologies in the Age of Booker T. Washington*. Ann Arbor: University of Michigan Press, 1963.
Washington, Booker T. *Up from Slavery*. New York: Doubleday, 1901.

Atlanta (Georgia) Riot of 1906

On a humid September evening in 1906, in the shadow of the state capitol and three blocks from police headquarters, a race riot broke out in Atlanta that paralyzed the city for three days. While authorities scrambled to quell the violence, mobs of fierce white men roamed the streets attacking black citizens, vandalizing black businesses, and searching train stations, freight yards, trolley cars, and hotels for black workers.

Hundreds were beaten, dozens murdered. Hospitals overflowed with casualties, and undertakers received daily calls to retrieve bodies discovered in the morning light. The official death toll counted 10 black and two white victims. Unofficial reports estimated over 50 fatalities. How did one of the most populous cities in the country, known for its relatively progressive race relations, descend into mob rule and stall the cause of social reform in the South for decades?

Atlanta occupied an unusual place in the post-Reconstruction South. At the turn of the century, while much of the region was stagnating economically and culturally, Atlanta was one of the bustling metropolises of Progressive-era America. In 1900, the city's population was 90,000; by 1910, it was 150,000 (roughly one-third black). Eleven major railroads used it as a distribution center; its strategic location at the foot of the Appalachian Mountains made it a prime link between the Tennessee Valley and the Eastern Seaboard. Bank clearings in 1900 totaled $96 million; in 1906 they rose to $235 million. Among U.S. cities, only Los Angeles enjoyed faster growth.

In what was called the New South vision, Atlanta business leaders and politicians crafted a plan whereby the rural South would be complemented by centers of industry, commerce, and transportation—and these would be operated by a white management/black worker division of labor. In bringing black men into the industrial system, albeit at the bottom, the New South ensured the investment of Northern capital, promoted economic stability among the lower classes, and eased racial tensions by allowing blacks an acknowledged place in the economy while not infringing upon white supremacy in social and political matters. As a result, Atlanta in 1906 boasted a thriving middle-class black population and culture. Intellectual life for African Americans in Atlanta was vibrant as well. Atlanta had the largest concentration of black colleges in the world, and the churches there were large and active. Booker T. Washington also maintained a loyal following in the city. The visible signs of black success and interracial cooperation prompted Atlantans to claim to have solved the "race problem" in America.

And yet, alongside the genuine progress could be found all the customary troubles of urban growth, compounded by racial tensions. Downtown Atlanta was the hub of luxury hotels, the largest convention center in the South, state office buildings, and specialty shops, but certain sections open to African Americans catered to lower habits. In the backwash behind Marietta Street stood a dozen brothels, while along Decatur Street ran a series of saloons and "club rooms" offering corn whiskey and draft beer. Poolrooms, pawn shops, dance houses, and gambling dens were also prevalent, and fights and domestic disturbances happened nightly. Too many rural blacks searching for work found no gainful prospects and ended up joining the underworld economy.

Crime and punishment were an overt fact of life in early 20th-century Atlanta. In 1906, Atlanta recorded over 21,000 arrests. By contrast, Milwaukee, with three times the population of Atlanta, had only one-quarter as many arrests. Most of the cases were run through the City Recorder, a hasty trial court in which suspects were brought before a judge without counsel, and the credibility of witnesses and levying of punishment stood solely with the judge. Most cases lasted no more than a few minutes, with convicted persons paying a fine or serving short sentences in the city stockade. Longer sentences were passed to county courts, where criminals ended up doing time on the chain gang or in the convict lease camps. The chain gang and convict lease systems were an integral part of the city and state economy. Prisoners were either made to build roads, clean thoroughfares, and haul materials for public projects, or "rented" to private firms for a daily fee where the overseers worked prisoners mercilessly.

A growing city, an African American underclass, a penal system with perverse incentives, a prominent black intelligentsia, and a rising black middle class—these were some of the ingredients that led to race-based upheaval. Furthermore, early in 1906, a heated gubernatorial campaign inside the Democratic Party descended into race baiting and demagoguery. Two factions were fighting for control over the state, the conservatives, led by candidate Clark Howell, and the reformers, led by Hoke Smith. Trouble began when Smith started to cast his campaign as a crusade for white privilege and power. Touring the rural districts, he punctuated his speeches with racist battle cries, calling for the removal of the black man from the polling booth.

What this meant was that the very progress that Atlanta hailed as a marker of success became a target of reproach. A steady black middle class entailed a black political bloc, and with voters roughly divided between conservative and reform Democrats, the black vote could become a swing vote. With evidence of black uplift coming from Atlanta, and with politicians demonizing it into a grave challenge to white society, Negro disenfranchisement became the prime issue in the campaign. Howell disdained such demagoguery, but finding that Smith's white supremacism attracted cheers, he joined in decrying the black vote. By the end of spring, both candidates were calling themselves the white people's savior.

The candidates' racist speechifying was echoed in the newspapers. Rural periodicals always found race a profitable topic, and Smith's cautions of Black Power produced fittingly vivid headlines. As the election approached, editorials and headlines raised the black threat in ever-more-menacing terms. By mid-summer 1906, Atlanta had reached a fever pitch. A few cases of blacks attacking whites in the suburbs of Atlanta led to headlines in the newspapers harping on an "epidemic of Negro crime." Blacks who were caught were often lynched on the spot without trial or sentencing. After one such lynching, one Atlanta newspaper called the *Evening News* proposed a network of vigilantes to scout the countryside at night and seize wandering black men. Black leaders tried to curb Negrophobia with reasoned statements about every race having its share of criminals and lynch law being a travesty of civilized society, but the race feeling was too powerful.

The final weekend of the summer began with a visit from the Great Commoner, William Jennings Bryan. On Thursday, September 20, the Populist leader and presidential candidate stayed in Atlanta to speak on the issues of the day, attracting thousands of citizens from all around the state. That night, another assault outside Atlanta took place. Lynch parties were forming, and word of the incident was spreading around the city. The next day's *Atlanta Georgian* newspapers asked, "Negro Clubs the Cause of Assault?" and "Men of Fulton, What Will You Do to Stop These Outrages against the Women?" On Friday, stories circulated of a drunken black man invading a white family home the previous night, and police officers the next morning began a slow circuit through all the colored saloons in town.

Despite the crackdown, by midday on September 22, the sidewalks of shadier streets downtown were jammed. In black neighborhoods, parents expecting trouble advised their children to stay close to home, but the same expectation led many curious or angry white youths downtown. That afternoon, "Negro Attempts to Assault Mrs. Mary Chafin Near Sugar Creek Bridge" was the headline of the *Journal*'s first extra, cried out by dozens of newsboys scattering across the downtown area. A suburban dairyman's wife, it reported, barely escaped assault by a strange black man hiding in her barn. More newspaper extras circulated that day, all reporting on white assaults perpetrated by blacks. These reports traveled quickly around Atlanta, with newsboys selling hundreds of extras. Along Decatur Street, 2,000 white men congregated around one man who commenced a panicky diatribe on black rapists, haranguing the city for tolerating the crimes and allowing the perpetrators to escape immediate retribution.

People on the fringe of the gathering ran to tell friends and cohorts that a mob was forming. A black messenger boy passed by on a bicycle and was knocked down. Another black bystander on the edge of the crowd was taunted and pushed. When he struck back, a dozen men beat him senseless and left him bleeding on the pavement. Five thousand white men and boys soon made up the tumult. The mayor appeared and ordered water hoses turned on the crowd. Men split up into gangs of enraged whites, half-drunk observers, and rowdy boys racing down the streets and alleyways looking for black pedestrians to harass. Bars emptied as news of a riot in progress spread.

Policemen swarmed the area, but heavily outnumbered and, in some cases, in secret sympathy with the mob, they were helpless to stop the attacks. By 8:00 P.M., about 10,000 howling men and boys roamed the city blocks. Various white mobs invaded black saloons and clubs, destroyed storefronts and terrorized black customers, and attacked black passengers on streetcars. Some gangs inflicted minor violence on black victims, while others were immediately bent on murder. Mobs controlled the downtown area. Black men and women sought whatever refuge and hiding place they could find. With blacks in flight and white gangs on the prowl, it wasn't so much of a riot as it was a hunt. The atrocities accumulated for hours. A young man was clubbed to death on the Forsyth Street viaduct. A railroad porter was dragged out of his Pullman car and shot to death on the tracks. To handle the overflow of cases at Grady Hospital, police headquarters was turned into an emergency clinic. The night's carnage did not end until after midnight when state militia arrived in the city.

The morning of September 23 revealed an Atlanta never seen before. Small detachments of soldiers marched from corner to corner. Trolleys were running, but with extra cabmen armed with shotguns. Hundreds of citizens wandered along, gazing at signs of the night's disorder. Nobody thought the violence was over. Then, men who perpetrated the alleged assaults were still at large, a fact licensing hordes of white vigilantes to comb the suburbs with dogs and armaments. The newspapers advocated deputizing more white men to constrain the white gangs and to prevent black reprisal. In the black community, citizens were readying for another round of attacks once night fell. Soldiers monitored the downtown streets, but many neighborhoods remained defenseless. Furthermore, black citizens saw little evidence that the authorities would act preemptively against the gangs. The sheriff of Fulton County had spent most of the previous night at home. The newspapers still ranted about "Negro crime," blaming the sexual assaults for the killings, not the killers. Small incidents of violence began again soon after dusk.

On Monday, September 24, the authorities struck back. It was clear that the simple presence of soldiers in the downtown area would not halt the skirmishes in different neighborhoods or discourage the troublemakers roving around the freight yards and suburbs. In the City Recorder's Court, the judge started to work through a docket crowded with men arrested for rioting, looting, and drunkenness. A military order prohibited the further sale of firearms, and saloons were closed by order of the mayor. The police chief declared that any officers failing to suppress violence would be terminated, and no males under age 21 were allowed on the streets after 5:00 P.M. Six hundred state troops patrolled the streets, but citizens remained nervous.

On Tuesday, more state troops filed into the city as hundreds of black refugees were seen on the roads leading away from Atlanta. With blacks now armed and ready to shoot back, a stalemate had set in. Soldiers and police officers conducted some house-to-house searches in black neighborhoods to confiscate weapons, but sniping between white and black gangs continued.

On Wednesday, September 26, the *Constitution* headline announced, "Atlanta Is Herself Again; Business Activity

Restored and the Riot Is Forgotten." Officials and business leaders set about calming relations between the races and repairing the city's damaged reputation. The Fulton County Grand Jury begged witnesses to killings to come forward and testify. At a City Council meeting held on September 28, the mayor stated that he believed much of the violence was instigated by the seditious newspaper extras being aggressively spread through the city. A relief fund was set up for the families of victims, and white leaders visited black congregations to apologize for the outbreak and promise better protection in the future.

Legal action proceeded. A police board charged several officers with misconduct such as allowing assaults to take place and failing to disarm gangs. In the City Recorder's Court, dozens of white men were brought to the bar. Those guilty of misdemeanors received a 30-day term in the stockade or a $100 fine. More serious criminals were turned over to Superior Court. About 60 black men from one shootout were charged with murdering a police officer, but only one man was convicted. Of the others, the trial jury determined that since the black citizens were defending themselves from attack, they should not be punished. In November, a black man was acquitted of rape, even though a white woman on the stand identified him as her assailant.

The larger implications of the riot took months to materialize. For Atlanta's black intelligentsia, the riot was a disaster. They were intimidated and distraught. The editor of *The Voice of the Negro* was run out of town for having sent an anonymous telegram to the *New York World* accusing "sensational newspapers and unscrupulous politicians" (*New York World*, September 27, 1906) of stoking race hatred with trumped-up stories. W. E. B. Du Bois returned to his scientific work in Alabama and said little about the affair. Disillusioned with Atlanta, he left his post at Atlanta University a few years later and moved north to help manage the newly formed NAACP. Bishop Henry M. Turner renewed his call for mass emigration to Africa: "In the name of all that is good and righteous, what do you see in this country for the black man but constant trouble?" (*Atlanta Constitution*, November 10, 1906).

For Atlanta's white community, the riot was a mark of shame best overcome by returning the city to regular operations of commerce. A *Journal* editorial on September 24, 1906, urged, "Obey the Law and Get Back to Business." Business leaders worried that an exodus of black families would create a labor shortage and depress real estate values. In the ensuing months, business recovered, but the city's reputation for progressive race relations was shattered. In the coming years it would become just like any other Southern city in its periodic outbreaks of race-based incident. In 1915, Leo Frank was lynched a few miles north of the city, and later that year the Ku Klux Klan was resurrected in a midnight ceremony atop Stone Mountain, 10 miles east of downtown. For years, Klan headquarters would be located in an Atlanta suburb. It would take decades for Atlanta to become a home of racial progress once again.

Mark Bauerlein

See also

Atlanta (Georgia) Riot of 1967; Disenfranchisement; Race Riots in America; Rape as Provocation for Lynching. Documents: Report on the Memphis Riots of May 1866 (1866); Account of the Riots in East St. Louis, Illinois (1917); A Southern Black Woman's Letter Regarding the Recent Riots in Chicago and Washington (1919); The Cook County Coroner's Report Regarding the 1919 Chicago Race Riots (1920); The Final Report of the Grand Jury on the Tulsa Race Riot (June 25, 1921); Testimony from *Laney v. United States* (1923); The Governor's Commission Report on the Watts Riots (1965); Cyrus R. Vance's Report on the Riots in Detroit (1967); The Reports of the Oklahoma Commission to Study the Tulsa Race Riot of 1921 (2000–2001); Draft Report: 1898 Wilmington Race Riot Commission (2005)

Further Reading:

Baker, Ray Stannard. *Following the Color Line: American Negro Citizenship in the Progressive Era*. Reprint, New York: Harper Torchbooks, 1964. Originally published 1908.

Bauerlein, Mark. *Negrophobia: A Race Riot in Atlanta, 1906*. San Francisco: Encounter Books, 2001.

Crowe, Charles. "Racial Violence and Social Reform: Origins of the Atlanta Riot of 1906." *Journal of Negro History* 53 (1968): 234–56.

Harlan, Louis R. et al., eds. *The Booker T. Washington Papers*, vol. 9 of 11. Urbana: University of Illinois Press, 1972–1989.

Martin, Thomas H. *Atlanta and Its Builders: A Comprehensive History of the Gate City of the South*, 2 vols. Atlanta: Century Memorial Publishing, 1902.

Washington, Booker T. *Up from Slavery*. New York: University Books, 1989.

White, Walter, Jr. *A Man Called White*. New York: Viking Press, 1948.

Atlanta (Georgia) Riot of 1967

The summer of 1967 involved a series of high-profile racial riots in urban areas such as Tampa, Florida; Cincinnati, Ohio; Detroit, Michigan; and Newark, New Jersey, that sparked seemingly irrational violence and destruction of property. A riot in Atlanta, Georgia, that was sparked by a minor incident on June 17 of that year had a different outcome than the other cities mentioned. Efforts by police, community officials, and the mayor quickly brought a potentially volatile situation under control.

In 1967, Atlanta was in the process of positioning itself to be the model city for the New South. Rapid post–World War II industrialization along with the annexation of outlying communities turned the city into a vigorous metropolitan area. Atlanta, whose African American citizens in the city accounted for around 44 percent of the population by the mid-1960s, was in the process of racially integrating many of its municipal services; the number of black police officers was higher than those of most major cities in the nation. The Student Nonviolent Coordinating Committee (SNCC) along with its prominent and controversial president, Stokely Carmichael, was headquartered in Atlanta. The city, despite plans to be a progressive Southern metropolis, also maintained a very large membership of the Ku Klux Klan.

Despite its progressive posture in the 1960s, conditions in inner-city Atlanta had been less than desirable due to overcrowding, economic depression, discriminatory practices, and generally poor living conditions; these conditions were similar to those of Detroit and Newark that year. There was a very sharp differentiation between white and black salaries, and median incomes for black families were less than those of whites. Local newspapers continued to advertise job openings separately by race, and even when blacks were able to obtain decent employment, chances for advancement were still slim. In addition, overcrowding in residential areas and schools were daily realities in black communities. Education was substandard in the black schools as de facto segregation continued to separate students. Recreational resources that could reduce levels of restlessness and idleness were largely absent in the area. African American citizens began to vocalize their grievances over these conditions increasingly as tensions between blacks and whites in the city began to grow. With few acceptable outlets to vent frustrations, troubles began to brew at a shopping center that was an area gathering place in a community known as Dixie Hills.

In June 1967, when a black security officer refused to let a young black man carrying a beer can into a restaurant at the Dixie Hills Shopping Center, the two tussled and were soon joined by the young man's two friends. Police were called to the scene to assist the security guard and arrested the three youths outside the shopping center as a large crowd of 200 to 300 people grew to watch the activity. The crowd quietly dispersed when directed to do so by police.

The next day, another young African American man began banging on a fire alarm bell at the same shopping center where the other arrests were made; the alarm had apparently short-circuited and the youth was hitting it with a broom handle. Officers who were responding to the fire alarm directed the young man to refrain from hitting the bell. He refused to stop and a scuffle ensued. Soon, some onlookers who had gathered to observe the activity decided to jump into the fray. One of the officers fired his revolver into the crowd and shot the youngster, who received minor wounds during the confrontation.

A meeting that night in the community was attended by many local citizens and had several speakers, including Stokely Carmichael. Carmichael, who had just been bailed out of jail after an altercation with police the previous day, gave a rousing speech, and the audience poured out into the street in protest. The crowd grew to over 1,000 and threw rocks and bottles at police cars and broke car windows as acts of defiance against the police, who became concerned that they were being fired upon. Other officers quickly responded to the scene and fired their weapons over the heads of the crowd, which acquiesced. In the end, only 10 people were arrested, most of them young.

A few days later, another community gathering produced another fracas between residents and police. The citizen protestors numbered 200 and the strength of the officers was around 300. When a small incendiary device exploded near some of the officers, weapons were fired into a crowd, killing one man and seriously injuring one boy. Community workers quickly worked to deter any future violence and Mayor Ivan Allen Jr. paid a visit to the area to request calm. Efforts by militant activist H. Rap Brown to incite another demonstration by the residents failed, and politicians and black leaders desiring to remove Stokely Carmichael from the area drew up petitions for his ouster.

Improvements to the area that had been promised prior to the events of June 17 and 18 were put into place the next day. A black youth patrol similar to one that had begun earlier in Tampa, Florida, began in Atlanta although it was met with opposition by SNCC, which felt the idea was a sell-out to the white power structure. The establishment of the youth patrol possibly assisted in staving off future racial outbreaks in the city.

According to a 1968 commission that investigated the race riots of 1967, there were several factors that contributed to the violent outbreaks. These factors included crowded and unsafe inner-city living conditions made worse by the heat of that summer, a large number of unsupervised young people on the streets, unsatisfactory police–community relations, slow and inaccurate responses from the police, and the transmission of inaccurate information. During that "long, hot summer," Atlanta had these same contributing factors, but efforts made by city officials helped prevent the extensive destruction that was encountered in Detroit, Newark, and other areas.

LEONARD A. STEVERSON

See also

Atlanta (Georgia) Riot of 1906; Long Hot Summer Riots; Race Riots in America. Documents: The Report on the Memphis Riots of May 1866 (July 25, 1866); Account of the Riots in East St. Louis, Illinois (July 1917); The Cook County Coroner's Report Regarding the 1919 Chicago Race Riots (1919); A Southern Black Woman's Letter Regarding the Recent Riots in Chicago and Washington (November 1919); The Final Report of the Grand Jury on the Tulsa Race Riot (June 25, 1921); Testimony from *Laney v. United States* Describing Events during the Washington, D.C., Riot of July 1919 (December 3, 1923); The Governor's Commission Report on the Watts Riots (December 1965); Cyrus R. Vance's Report on the Riots in Detroit (July-August 1967); The Reports of the Oklahoma Commission to Study the Tulsa Race Riot of 1921 (2000-2001); The Draft Report of the 1898 Wilmington Race Riot Commission (December 2005)

Further Reading:

Report of the National Advisory Commission on Civil Disorders. Washington, DC: U.S. Government Printing Office, 1968.

B

Back to Africa Movement

The Back to Africa Movement, which dates back to the early 1600s, was a plan that attempted to return African Americans to Africa. Supporters of the movement believed that a return migration to Africa would provide African Americans the opportunity to establish an economic base, escape the discriminatory system that existed in America, and reconnect culturally with their heritage. Some of the most vocal early supporters included the wealthy African American philanthropist and ship captain Paul Cuffee, who in 1815 used his own funds to establish a colony in Sierra Leone, and the American Society for Colonizing the Free People of Color in the United States, which was later renamed the American Colonization Society (ACS).

The ACS made its first attempt to begin a return migration to Africa in 1820 when it sent a group of 86 African American workers and their families to establish a settlement on Sherbro Island off the west coast of Africa. The settlement eventually failed because of the settlers' exposure to diseases in the swampy land's unhealthy conditions and their lack of acceptance from the native people. In 1821, the ACS purchased a second piece of land that was 36 miles long and three miles wide from the Dey and Grand Bassa people. The land was used to establish the country of Liberia. The remaining settlers on Sherbro Island were relocated to Liberia, and the ACS continued to transport new settlers to the country.

In 1827, several slave states began to invest in Liberia. They organized themselves independently of the ACS and established colonies in an effort to transport free African Americans to the country. They believed that by transporting freed men and women, they could silence or limit any attempts to encourage enslaved African Americans to seek freedom. Due to the pooled efforts of these and other groups, approximately 11,000 African Americans were relocated to Liberia before the movement ended.

The failure of the Back to Africa Movement of the 1800s is attributed to a variety of factors. It began with the ACS's difficulty in finding enough funds to cover the cost of transportation, land grants, and other expenses that were associated with their voyages. It also suffered from the competing interests of proslavery supporters who were trying to remove the threat of a slave revolt, racist separatists and prejudiced individuals who believed African Americans were worthless and should be transported out of the country, and the views of prominent African Americans such as Frederick Douglass who adamantly opposed returning to Africa.

The Back to Africa Movement regained momentum during the early 1920s as Marcus Garvey and other Black Nationalists advocated the return of African Americans to Africa.

Garvey believed that a return migration to the motherland was the only way that people of African descent around the world could gain economic stability and respect. Garvey's views were adamantly opposed by many well-educated African Americans, such as W.E.B. Du Bois.

Barbara A. Patrick

See also

Abolitionist Movement; Abu-Jamal, Mumia; Black Nationalism; Black Panther Party (BPP); Black Power; Reparations; Slavery

Further Reading:

"History of Liberia: A Time Line." http://memory.loc.gov/ammem/gmdhtml/libhtml/liberia.html (accessed January 2013).

McCartney, John. *Black Power Ideologies: An Essay in African American Political Thought.* Philadelphia: Temple University Press, 1992.

Baldwin, James (1924–1987)

James Arthur Baldwin, author, activist, and critic, was born to Emma Birdis Jones on August 2, 1924, in Harlem, New York. Though Baldwin never knew his biological father, he was adopted by David Baldwin at three years of age. Baldwin's strained relationship with his stepfather was the core influence for the pseudo-autobiographical *Go Tell It on the Mountain* (1953), a story of the religious and spiritual development of a young black man in Harlem, New York. A religious fanatic, David Baldwin would often force his beliefs on young James. At the age of 14, Baldwin became a preacher but later denounced religion after moving to Greenwich Village in New York City. Focusing on his literary craft, Baldwin began to write stories, essays, and reflections on his life. While developing his writing, Baldwin also began to recognize and acknowledge his homosexuality. In order to escape racial and sexual intolerance, Baldwin moved to Paris, where he would spend the majority of his life.

Though he spent most of his time abroad, Baldwin was very active in the desegregation movement in the American South. He would eloquently speak out against the racial injustices blacks faced during the mid-20th century. In *Notes of a Native Son* (1955), Baldwin called for the racial injustices in American societies to cease. In the "Autobiographical Notes," Baldwin criticized the body of literature available about black society and culture. "From this point of view, the Negro problem is nearly inaccessible. It is not written about so widely; it is written about so bad," Baldwin wrote (6). Because of the lack of quality literature for and about African Americans, Baldwin used his own experiences as a black man and molded them into a literary art, both fictitious and critical. At the climax of the civil rights and Black Power movements, Baldwin released two powerful collections of essays—the best-selling *Nobody Knows My Name* (1961) and *The Fire Next Time* (1963). In these collections, Baldwin analyzed the race relations between blacks and whites and demanded racial justice and tolerance. The critical and biting essay "Down at the Cross" critiques the growing severance between Christianity and the Nation of Islam. Baldwin argues the need to eradicate the oppression of blacks through the joining of both religious camps. After returning to Europe and a vicious attack by Eldridge Cleaver in *Soul on Ice*, Baldwin's insight into the black American struggle was questioned.

Baldwin ignored his critics and continued to write. Heavily represented in the nonfiction genre during the 1960s and 1970s, Baldwin also continued writing works of fiction. Several novels were released during this time period, many focusing on and critiquing America's outlook on racial relations. *Another Country* (1962) focused on the role of race in interracial friendships. *If Beale Street Could Talk* (1974) looked at the relationship between black men and women, and the role of family against the socially oppressive system faced in Harlem.

Baldwin returned to the United States in 1983 to accept a teaching position at the University of Massachusetts–Amherst in the African American Studies Department. After his tenure at Amherst, Baldwin spent his remaining days in France, where he died in 1987 at the age of 62.

Regina Barnett

See also

American Literature and Racism; Desegregation

Further Reading:

Baldwin, James A. *Notes of a Native Son.* New York: Dial Press, 1955.

Baldwin, James A. *The Fire Next Time.* New York: Dial Press, 1963.

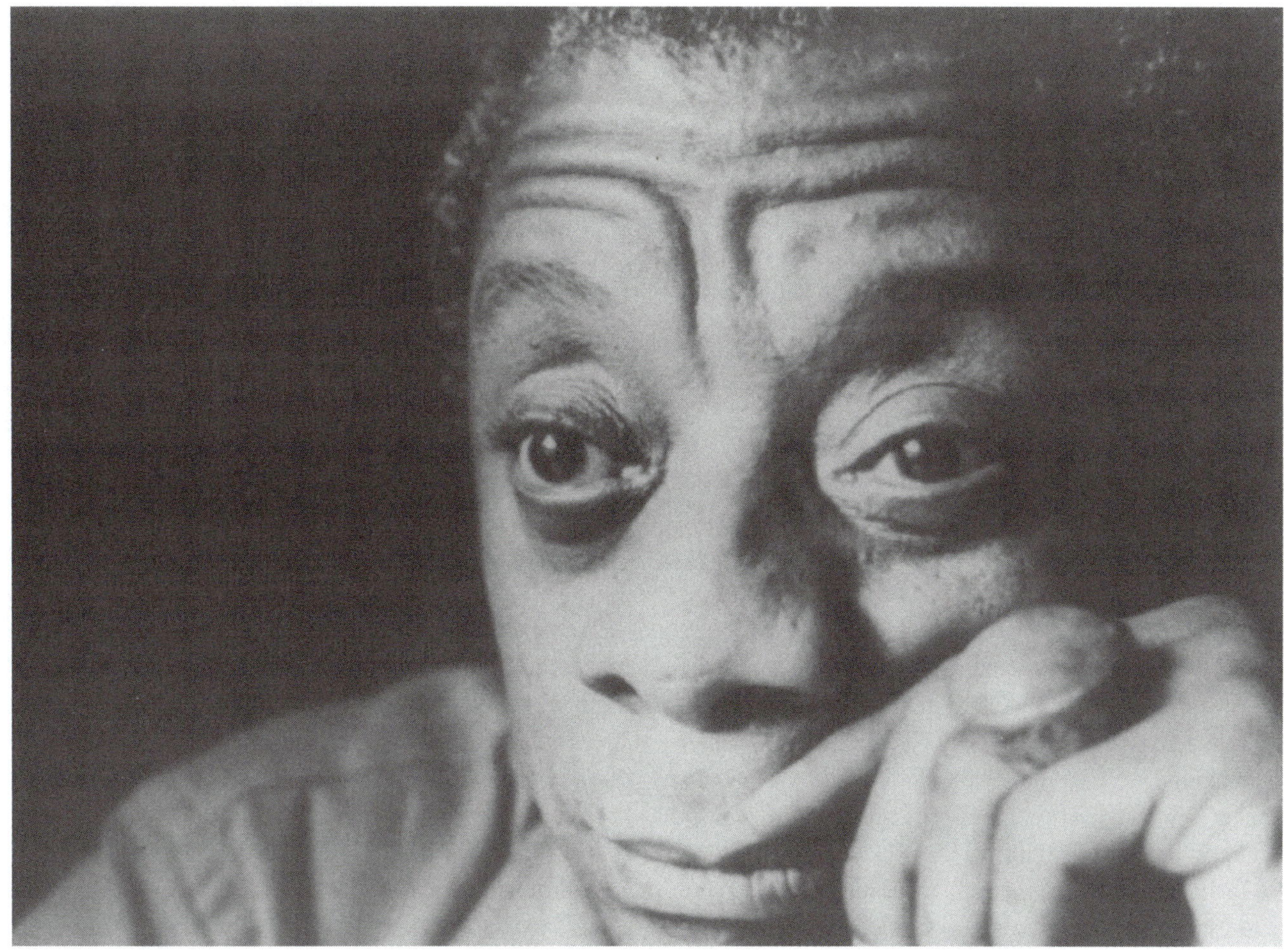

James Baldwin, author of the novel *Go Tell It on the Mountain* (1953), wrote about the effects of race, religion, and sexuality on personal identity. (Library of Congress)

Baraka, Amiri (b. 1934)

Amiri Baraka (originally LeRoi Jones), through poetry, essays, plays, fiction, and music criticism, has worked at institution building, at bridging the gap between the arts and the people, and at using the arts as catalysts to awaken black cultural pride. Baraka came to national prominence in the 1960s through his award-winning drama, his poetry, and his demonstration of fierce leadership in and passionate commitment to political change for African American people. Along with several other prominent figures, his philosophy and his polemical poetry have been credited with being primary shapers of the period known as either the Black Arts Movement or Black Aesthetics, associated with black cultural nationalism and the political revolution of the 1960s. This emphasis on the revolutionary and propagandistic potential of the literary arts was intended to fuel or to complement the civil rights movement in the 1960s.

Baraka was born to Coyette LeRoy and Anna Lois Russ Jones in Newark, New Jersey, in 1934. Baraka had recast his name "LeRoy" to the French spelling "LeRoi" during his high school years. Baraka was raised in a lower-middle-class family that included his maternal grandparents. He attended Rutgers University in 1951 on a science scholarship but then transferred to Howard University in 1952 and became an English major and philosophy minor. Baraka left Howard University in 1954 and spent nearly three years in the U.S. Air Force, stationed in Puerto Rico.

In 1958, he settled in New York City, where he found the East Village section of the city congenial and its predominantly white bohemian community supportive of his initial poetic impulses. He worked for *Record Changer* magazine and took graduate courses in comparative literature at Columbia University. In October 1958, he married Hettie Cohen, a young Jewish coworker at the magazine. Together they had two daughters. With her, he published and edited *Yugen*, a "little" literary magazine that brought Baraka in close contact with contemporary white Beat poets Allen Ginsberg, Jack Kerouac, Robert Creeley, and Charles Olsen. This literary community influenced Baraka's early poetry, especially through its emphasis on self-awareness.

His first volume of poetry, *Preface to a Twenty Volume Suicide Note*, consisted of poems composed between 1957 and 1961. Several of the poems reflected Baraka's disenchantment with what he perceived as the seduction of the African American middle class by white values. Baraka references popular culture from the comics, radio, and Hollywood. He nostalgically and ironically mourns the passing of the ideals they once offered. The images that convey the loss are vividly barren, and many of them use strong sexual images, a general characteristic of Baraka's poetry. The last poem in the volume, titled "Notes for a Speech," is significant in view of Baraka's eventual metamorphosis from questioning his identity to affirming his blackness.

In 1960 Baraka was part of a delegation of artists and scholars, through which he traveled to Cuba to commemorate Fidel Castro's coup of 1954. The political impact of the event awakened Baraka's own dormant political inclinations and the fervor of revolution in Cuba's youth ignited his own social consciousness. The emergence of Third World nations in Africa in the early 1960s and the beginnings of the civil rights movement at home were other events that weighed in on Baraka's conclusions.

The Dead Lecturer, Baraka's second volume of poetry, continued to document the poet's developing artistic and political identity but also suggested an ongoing dialogue with the first collection. Baraka's developing artistic identity was enhanced through the research and writing of *Blues People*, essays that Baraka worked on simultaneously with writing *The Dead Lecturer* poems. This artistic identity found an outlet through numerous references to music and its African American cultural traditions.

The changes in Baraka's artistic identity were reflected in his personal life. By fall 1965, he had left his Jewish wife and their children, along with his village friends, and moved to Harlem. The poems of *Black Magic*, a collection drawn from *Sabotage* (1961–1963), *Target Study* (1963–1965), and *Black Art* (1965–1967), reflected this period of metamorphosis in the poet's life and his embracing of Black Nationalism, although he wrote more drama than poetry between 1965 and 1970. *Black Magic* showed Baraka's complete withdrawal from white society and included two of his most anthologized and most widely discussed poems, "Black People" and "Black Art." The latter poem, in demanding that art should fuel political and violent action, had the language and incendiary tone that would become characteristic of the militant poetry of the decade. While "Black Art" is representative of the models of Black Aesthetics poetry that challenged passivity and aimed to energize a black nation, it was criticized for its anti-Semitic references.

Still another catalyst for Baraka's altering identity in 1967 was his year as a visiting professor at San Francisco State College, as the thrust toward Black Nationalism was well underway on the West Coast and offered him another model for personal and political potential. Later that year, he had relocated from Harlem to Newark and remarried. His second wife, Sylvia, an African American woman, was an actress, painter, and dancer. In 1968, he affirmed his identity through the name Imamu Amiri Baraka. However, he would continue with slight recastings of himself in the years to come. In 1974, Baraka dropped Imamu, a Muslim spiritual title. Sylvia, too, recast herself as "Bibi Amina." Baraka and Bibi Amina had five children. During the Newark Riot of 1967, Baraka was beaten by the police and arrested for illegal possession of firearms. Baraka was convicted of a misdemeanor and imprisoned, but the conviction was overthrown during appeal.

In Harlem, Baraka had established the Black Arts Repertory Theatre/School, which became a model for black theaters in other cities, and in Newark, he continued this work by opening Spirit House, a black repertory theater and cultural center, and continued writing poetry. In 1974 he underwent yet another political transformation by deemphasizing Black Nationalism and became a socialist through accepting Marxist-Leninist thought. In this identity, capitalism was the greatest enemy of black people.

Baraka has continued to advocate social change and to use his art and voice as primary instruments to that end. He has also turned his talents to the service of poetry through editing anthologies of poetry. His status as a revered revolutionary poet and speaker in African American literary circles has remained constant well into the present. Moreover, he has also appeared as himself in multiple films, as recently as 2009. However, he has also generated much controversy through his poem "Somebody Blew Up America," which was about the September 11, 2001, attacks, which he wrote as Poet Laureate of New Jersey in 2001. Critics alleged that this poem was anti-Semitic, given its allegation of Israeli involvement in the attacks. In 2003, he published *Somebody Blew Up America and Other Poems.*

In 2003, Baraka also published *The Essence of Reparations*, a collection of essays on the issue of reparations. In 2005, Baraka published *The Book of Monk*, followed by *Tales of the Out & the Gone* in 2006. Baraka continues his political activism through his writings and public speaking.

JOYCE PETTIS

See also

Black Arts Movement (BAM)

Further Reading:

Benson, Kimberly W. *Baraka: The Renegade and the Mask*. New Haven, CT: Yale University Press, 1976.

Harris, William J. "Amiri Baraka." *In African American Writers*, edited by Lea Baechler and A. Walton Litz. New York: Charles Scribner's, 1991.

Hudson, Theodore R. *From LeRoi Jones to Amiri Baraka*. Durham, NC: Duke University Press, 1973.

Reilly, Charles, ed. *Conversations with Amiri Baraka*. Jackson: University of Mississippi Press, 1994.

Basketball

Basketball, a team sport invented by James Naismith at the YMCA in Springfield, Massachusetts, in 1891, was an important venue for interracial team sports competition throughout the 20th century. Designed as a way to encourage physical fitness during the winter months, the first game of basketball involved players dribbling a soccer ball in a gymnasium and shooting at peach baskets suspended at either end of the playing floor. Over time, the sport developed its own equipment, and its rules evolved considerably. Although the sport started in the northeast, it quickly made its way across the country, spreading rapidly through the network of nationwide YMCAs. African American players, although initially restricted in many ways from playing with or against whites, gradually changed the contours of the game and came to dominate the sport nationwide.

Basketball was originally intended as a sport for whites interested in the tenets of "Muscular Christianity," a nationwide fitness movement that linked personal health to godliness. However, basketball quickly became popular with African Americans as well. Edwin B. Henderson, a black Harvard graduate, was a key figure who promoted black athletics, including basketball, as a way to uplift African Americans. Henderson helped establish interscholastic athletics leagues for black high schools in the mid-Atlantic region in 1906, setting an example that would be mimicked nationwide, and published pro-athletic articles in national publications (such as *The Crisis*) from the 1910s through the 1960s. Women's schools also founded basketball teams for their students, although rules were often changed to limit the amount of running and jumping required of players. In men's colleges, the first intercollegiate conference for black schools was the Central Interscholastic Athletic Association, formed in 1916 by Hampton Institute, Shaw University, Lincoln University, Virginia Union University, and Howard University. The popularity and success of this conference, which featured schools in the Maryland–Virginia–North Carolina region, inspired other black schools to set up their own conferences, since competition against white schools was strictly prohibited across the South (and, indeed, in many schools across the nation). There were some black players on majority white schools in the North and West (such as Paul Robeson at Rutgers College from 1915 to 1919), but they were few and far between.

Professional options for black players in the early years of the game were limited as well. Because professional leagues struggled to stay afloat, professional barnstorming teams were black athletes' best chance of making a living playing basketball. Particularly important were the New York Renaissance (usually called the "Rens") and the Harlem Globetrotters, whose differing trajectories suggest the limits to integrated basketball competition in the first half of the 20th century. The Rens, run by African American Robert L. Douglas, were an all-black team that first gained fame in the 1920s. Playing against both black and white teams, the Rens were remarkably successful, consistently defeating the top club teams in the nation, and even winning over 90 percent of their games in one stretch of the 1930s. Players such as Charles "Tarzan" Cooper excelled on the court, and the Rens won a tournament of professional teams in 1939, beating an all-white team from Wisconsin to claim a "national championship" of sorts. However, the team faced financial troubles in later years, as white teams hesitated to play them for fear of being embarrassed, and arenas refused to give the team a healthy share of the box office because of the team's racial makeup.

In contrast, the Harlem Globetrotters, a team run by white Jewish entrepreneur Abe Saperstein, enjoyed considerable financial success from the mid-1920s through the 1950s. By incorporating "clowning" in their performances, the all-black Globetrotters were more palatable to white audiences, who could fall back on stereotypes of African Americans as intellectually feeble. As a result of their comedic performances, and the presence of a white manager, the team earned considerably more money, and had many more opportunities, than the Rens. Although the Globetrotter players were well paid in comparison to other black players, it was also clear that Saperstein pocketed more money than anyone, and many players resented his exploitation of their athletic abilities and his paternalistic attitude towards them. Still, the Globetrotters team was the best professional opportunity for black basketball players until the late 1950s, when the National Basketball Association (NBA) welcomed more black players into the league and provided better financial compensation to its players.

Although the game of basketball evolved in a number of ways over the years, African Americans, including the members of the Rens and the Globetrotters, played the game in a distinct fashion that ushered in sweeping changes when integrated competition began. First, black players tended to play a more improvisational style than whites, borrowing from jazz a sense of individual virtuosity. Second, black players also played a faster version of the game, often pushing the ball up the court more quickly than their white counterparts. African American coach John McLendon, who learned the game from Naismith while a student at the University of Kansas, played a particularly important role in speeding up the game and emphasizing the fast break. McLendon was a highly successful head coach at North Carolina College for Negroes in Durham (now known as North Carolina Central University), Hampton Institute, and Tennessee A&I (now known as Tennessee State) in the 1940s and 1950s. He also coached Tennessee A&I to a national championship in the 1957 National Association of Intercollegiate Athletics tournament, the first time a sports team from a black school had ever won a national championship in interracial team competition. The innovations developed by McLendon and others changed the game from one focused on set plays with little player movement to one in which players constantly maneuvered on the court, looking for space to receive passes. Black players also made the game more vertical, jumping high into the air to retrieve missed shots and "dunking" the ball through the hoop for easy scores.

The innovations black players brought to the game infiltrated the broader culture, as the walls of segregation crumbled at the professional and collegiate levels. Although some of the early struggling professional leagues featured integrated teams in the 1940s, the NBA, which eventually became the most successful professional league, had exclusively all-white teams when it officially organized in 1949. However, one year later, Boston Celtics owner Walter Brown selected Chuck Cooper, a black player from Duquesne University, in the second round of the college draft. The Washington Capitals then selected Earl Lloyd of West Virginia State in the ninth round, and the New York Knicks purchased the contract of Nat "Sweetwater" Clifton from the Globetrotters. Since Cooper was the first black player drafted into the NBA, Lloyd the first to play in a game, and Clifton the first to sign a contract, all have some claim as the first black player in the league. Gradually, more African Americans were able to enter the NBA, although many of the early players complained in later years that they were told by coaches to focus on defense and rebounding, leaving the more high-profile role of scorer to white players.

At the collegiate level, black players gradually became more prominent members of previously all-white teams, starting on the East Coast, where black players helped lead the City College of New York to the NCAA championship in 1950. Other important black players who starred for integrated teams in the 1950s included Bill Russell and K. C. Jones, who led the University of San Francisco Dons to back-to-back NCAA national championships in 1955 and 1956;

Wilt Chamberlain, who led the University of Kansas to a runner-up finish in 1957; and Oscar Robertson, who starred for the University of Cincinnati in the late 1950s. Texas Western (now known as the University of Texas at El Paso) featured the first all-black starting five to win an NCAA championship when its squad defeated the all-white team from the University of Kentucky in 1966. Another important moment occurred in 1963, when the all-white Mississippi State team defied a court order by appearing in an NCAA tournament against the integrated Loyola University of Chicago team.

Although traditionally white Southern schools were more intransigent in their stance against black athletes, stars such as Charlie Scott at the University of North Carolina debuted in the late 1960s, and all college teams were integrated by the mid-1970s.

Over time, African Americans came to dominate the sport at the collegiate and professional levels, changing the style of play in the process. Some have lamented the damage done to black basketball powerhouses as a result of integration, as schools such as Tennessee A&I and others find it difficult to compete for the top African American players. Evidence of exploitation of black college players—such as Texas Western's stars, who were essentially given a free pass on schoolwork—also have caused some to worry that integration has neglected the educational uplift often emphasized at black schools. These issues continue to be debated into the present day.

Gregory Kaliss

See also

Historically Black Colleges and Universities; Sports and Racism

Further Reading:

George, Nelson. *Elevating the Game: Black Men and Basketball.* Lincoln: University of Nebraska Press, 1992.

Gorn, Elliott, and Warren Goldstein. *A Brief History of American Sports.* New York: Hill and Wang, 1993.

Henderson, Russell J. "The 1963 Mississippi State University Basketball Controversy and the Repeal of the Unwritten Law: 'Something More Than the Game Will Be Lost.'" *Journal of Southern History* 63, no. 4 (November 1997): 827–54.

"John McLendon." North Carolina Central University Web site http://www.nccu.edu/campus/athletics/jmhofbio.html (accessed June 9, 2008).

Thomas, Ron. *They Cleared the Lane: The NBA's Black Pioneers.* Lincoln: University of Nebraska Press, 2002.

Bates, Daisy (1914–1999)

Daisy Bates was an African American civil rights activist, journalist, author, and National Association for the Advancement of Colored People (NAACP) leader during the Little Rock desegregation crisis of 1957. As president of the Arkansas NAACP, Bates helped direct negotiations between the Little Rock School Board, the state, and federal authorities, while focusing primarily on the well-being of the nine black students who were integrating the high school.

Bates was born Daisy Lee Gatson in tiny Huttig in southern Arkansas on November 11, 1914. She grew up with friends of her parents after her mother was killed by whites and her father fled town. This background inspired Bates to fight for racial equality throughout her life. When she was 15 years old, she began dating L. C. Bates, and they were married three years later. He was an insurance salesman when they first met, but he studied journalism and worked for several black-owned newspapers.

Civil rights activist Daisy Bates, then 82, recalls her role in the 1957 integration of Central High School in her Little Rock, Arkansas, home, near a portrait of her late husband L. C. Bates, 1997. (Associated Press)

The Bateses leased a struggling church-owned press and began printing the *Arkansas State Press*, a Little Rock newspaper focused on civil rights issues. Besides journalism, the Bateses worked for the NAACP. Bates was not a member of Little Rock's black upper crust. She never completed college, had no significant role in the African American church, and was not wealthy. Yet she still managed to rise in the NAACP, eventually becoming president of the state's confluence of local branches in 1952.

After the *Brown v. Board of Education* (1954), school desegregation became the Arkansas NAACP's primary focus. Bates and the NAACP Legal Defense Fund brought a lawsuit against the Little Rock School Board in 1956. In *Aaron v. Cooper*, the U.S. Supreme Court established that Central High School would desegregate in the fall of 1957. Thereafter, more black students and schools would be integrated. On September 2, 1957, the day before school was scheduled to begin, Orval Eugene Faubus, Arkansas's segregationist governor, ordered the Arkansas National Guard to surround Central High School to keep the peace as an angry white mob had gathered to protest and harass the black students. Desegregation did not begin on September 3 as scheduled.

After more judicial activity, Faubus removed the National Guard and city police took over on September 20. On September 23, the nine black students entered Central High through a side door. With a mob of angry whites growing larger and more unruly, police removed the black students from school. The next day, President Dwight D. Eisenhower sent the 101st Airborne Division to keep order in Little Rock. The following day, soldiers escorted the "Little Rock Nine" to school.

Throughout this period and during the school year, Bates served as a liaison between the students, NAACP lawyers, public officials, and the media. The NAACP's local lawyer, Wiley Branton, relied on Bates to communicate with the students and their families who did not have legal representation of their own. The Bates home became an unofficial meeting place for members of the media from the North who descended on Little Rock and had also been attacked by segregationist protesters.

Bates continued to be harassed on a nightly basis, becoming a lightning rod for attack from white supremacists. The Bateses did not believe in the nonviolent tactics of Martin Luther King, Jr.'s Southern Christian Leadership Conference and were heavily armed at home. Several crosses were burned on her lawn, her windows were shot out repeatedly, and threatening phone calls offered her little rest at night from 1956 until she moved to New York in 1960 to work on her memoir of the Little Rock crisis. *The Long Shadow of Little Rock* was published in 1962 with a foreword by former first lady Eleanor Roosevelt. The account of her enduring work won much acclaim and later the American Book Award for a version republished by the University of Arkansas Press in 1982.

Bates lived in Washington, D.C., and worked with President Lyndon B. Johnson's War on Poverty initiative until she had a stroke in 1965. She moved back to Arkansas in 1968 but continued working on local poverty issues in Mitchellville. After the death of her husband, Bates focused on restarting the *Arkansas State Press*. The newspaper reappeared in 1984, with Ernest Green, one of the Little Rock Nine, working as its national marketing director. In 1984, Bates also received an honorary law degree from the University of Arkansas–Fayetteville, where her papers were later deposited. On November 4, 1999, Bates died of a heart attack in Little Rock.

Bates is known for her unwavering devotion to fighting discrimination against African Americans. Her presence also challenged the domination by black male clergymen in the NAACP's leadership roles. She broke the mold of most female civil rights supporters and did not have the deep religious background of other women working in the movement. Unlike Ella Baker, Bates worked in the foreground, becoming a public face of activism. Most important, Bates did not permit the Little Rock Nine to become sacrificial lambs for the civil rights movement. The actions by Bates and President Eisenhower's federal intervention ensured that massive resistance never became an accepted practice and pushed the civil rights movement in new directions.

Peter Carr Jones

See also

Brown v. Board of Education (1954); Little Rock Nine; National Association for the Advancement of Colored People (NAACP). Document: *Brown v. Board of Education* (May 1954)

Further Reading:

Bates, Daisy. *The Long Shadow of Little Rock*. Little Rock: University of Arkansas Press, 1986.

Jacoway, Elizabeth. *"Turn Away Thy Son": Little Rock, The Crisis That Shocked the Nation.* New York: Free Press, 2007.
Stockley, Grif. *Daisy Bates: Civil Rights Crusader from Arkansas.* Jackson: University Press of Mississippi, 2005.

Baton Rouge Bus Boycott

The Baton Rouge Bus Boycott in 1953 was the first bus boycott in the American South that attempted to end segregation on city buses. The boycott served as an illustration of what could be achieved through peaceful resistance. The methods adopted in Baton Rouge were taken up by the bus boycott that occurred in Montgomery, Alabama, in 1955, which many historians view as the beginning of the civil rights movement in the American South.

African Americans made up the vast majority of bus passengers in Baton Rouge, Louisiana, yet they were consigned to seats on the back of the bus while the first 10 rows of all city buses were reserved for white passengers. Frequently, seats on the front of the bus remained empty while African Americans went toward seats in the rear. A fare increase served as the spark for the protest. Shortly after the city council instituted the increase, which of course hit African Americans harder as they were the buses' primary passengers, Baptist minister T. J. Jemison spoke against the city council's fare increase and proposed ending segregation on Baton Rouge buses. The city council on March 19, 1953, instituted Ordinance 222 for Baton Rouge buses that allowed blacks to sit in the front seats so long as they did not take any seats in front of white passengers. In addition, African Americans had to enter the bus from the rear rather than the front.

Despite the city council's change of policy, bus drivers failed to observe the new rules. Reverend Jemison tested the new policy by refusing to give up his seat when ordered to by a driver. The driver then took the bus to the police station, but given the city council's ordinance, the police failed to take action against Jemison. Given the decision of the city of Baton Rouge's authorities, the bus drivers then chose to go on strike to protest Ordinance 222. The Louisiana attorney general found the Baton Rouge ordinance to be in violation of state segregation law, whereupon the strike ended.

In reaction, Jemison and the African American community of Baton Rouge formed the United Defense League, which on June 19, 1953, called for a boycott of the Baton Rouge public transportation system. The United Defense League grew out of the African American churches. Church buildings also served as nightly meeting places during the bus boycott. At these meetings, money was raised for the boycott and the United Defense League organized a system of rides for those engaged in the boycott, though many chose to walk. The United Defense League politically united the African American community of Baton Rouge. The United Defense League and the city of Baton Rouge quickly reached an agreement, and the boycott ended on June 24, 1953. Despite Jemison and the United Defense League's agreement, many people who had engaged in the boycott were disappointed with the settlement, which preserved segregated seating and reserved the first two rows for white passengers, though the back seat was also reserved for African American passengers. Still, despite the limited achievements of the boycott, the methods adopted in Baton Rouge would be utilized in Montgomery in 1955 and later boycotts.

Michael Beauchamp

See also
Busing; Civil Rights Movement

Further Reading:

Parent, William. *Inside the Carnival: Unmasking Louisiana Politics.* Baton Rouge: Louisiana State University Press, 1996.
Williams, Juan. *Eyes on the Prize: America's Civil Rights Years, 1954–1965.* New York: Penguin, 1988.

Batson v. Kentucky (1986)

Batson v. Kentucky was a landmark case dealing with the relationship between race and jury selection. Specifically, the *Batson* decision, as it is called, set precedents about how peremptory challenges may be used in a criminal case. During the jury selection, or voir dire, phase of a trial, both prosecutors and defense attorneys have the right to a certain number of peremptory challenges, meaning they can dismiss a prospective juror without giving a reason. These decisions may be challenged, and the judge decides whether the exclusion will stand. In *Batson v. Kentucky*, the U.S.

Supreme Court ruled that peremptory challenges cannot be used to dismiss jurors based solely on their race.

The Batson case started in 1982 when an all-white jury in a Louisville, Kentucky, circuit court found African American James K. Batson guilty of burglary and of receiving stolen goods. He was sentenced to 20 years in prison. Four potential black jurors had been dismissed from jury duty during the jury selection process of this trial. After a lengthy appeals process based primarily on the voir dire phase of the trial, *Batson v. Kentucky* went to the Supreme Court. In 1986, the Supreme Court decided with a vote of 7–2 that peremptory challenges cannot be used to exclude African Americans from juries in cases with African American defendants unless there is a neutral explanation; that is, race is not the reason given for dismissal. The decision was later expanded to hold for ethnicity and gender.

The Supreme Court drew on the Sixth Amendment and Fourteenth Amendment in their ruling on the *Batson* decision. Both amendments are designed to guarantee a fair trial. The Sixth Amendment, part of the Bill of Rights enacted in 1791, states, "In all criminal prosecutions the accused shall enjoy the right to a speedy and public trial, by an impartial jury. . . ." If there are racist preconceptions about a defendant this impartiality is undermined. The Fourteenth Amendment, enacted in 1868, states that all citizens shall have "due process." Specifically, the Supreme Court decided in *Batson v. Kentucky* that the practice of excluding jurors because of their race violated the Equal Protection Clause of the Fourteenth Amendment, which guarantees that no person shall be denied equal protection under the law. Where African Americans are concerned, these constitutional rights have historically been denied. The Supreme Court has sometimes been party to this denial, but in such cases as *Batson v. Kentucky*, the Court has stated that *all* citizens, regardless of race, should be guaranteed their constitutional rights.

The *Batson* decision has gone a long way in combating racial prejudice in the jury selection process, which in turn has positively impacted the fairness of trials for African Americans. For decades, attorneys—especially prosecutors—were more likely to dismiss potential black jurors when that was the race of the defendant. There is ample evidence that, without being consciously racist, many whites have stereotyped conceptions of African Americans, seeing them as violent and dangerous. This includes judges and attorneys, as well as citizens called to jury duty. There is also experimental data indicating that in spite of using "race-neutral" terms, subjects often use race as a criterion in making decisions. This history of prejudice and discrimination against blacks in the United States makes it less likely that African Americans will be able to become jurors, leading to the underrepresentation of blacks on jury trials. African Americans are statistically more likely than whites to have been in prison, and a prison record can be a reason to exclude a person from jury duty. Stereotypes about blacks can lead to their being excluded for not being of "good character." Since more African Americans are likely to be in low-paying jobs, many can reasonably claim that jury duty is an economic hardship. However, many African Americans are both eligible and eager to serve. Surveys of excluded black jurors have revealed feelings of humiliation and of not being regarded as full citizens. While the Batson decision has done much to increase the racial impartiality of jury trials, there are still limitations to its implications. Although the decision prohibits peremptory challenges being used to dismiss jurors based solely on their race, it is rare that either an attorney or someone in the jury pool will actually state that race will influence their decisions. However, attorneys know that a juror's ability to empathize with the accused can affect their verdict, and lawyers want to win their cases. In fact, manuals for lawyers still instruct them on how to use race when considering whether to accept a person for jury duty.

While concurring with the *Batson* decision, Justice Thurgood Marshall correctly predicted that race-based exclusions would continue. As Marshall explained, any prosecutor can easily cite nonracial reasons for excluding a juror, even if race is in fact the primary reason for him or her using a peremptory challenge. It is up to the defense attorney to prove *intentional* discrimination to the satisfaction of the presiding judge, and it has been rare that judges decide race was the factor leading to juror dismissal. For example, in one case, a prosecutor dismissed a potential black juror saying he had facial hair when no others did. An appeals court found that this violated the *Batson* decision. However, when the case went to the Supreme Court, the decision was reversed on the grounds that the prosecutor had used race-neutral criteria.

Furthermore, the *Batson* decision was not retroactive and therefore could not help already imprisoned African

Americans, some of whom have been executed. Especially in the South, race-based exclusions have continued. Prosecutors have successfully justified their dismissal of black jurors by pointing to the demeanor of the prospective juror, their lack of intelligence, coming from a high crime neighborhood, being unemployed or a single parent, or, in one case, resembling a drug dealer. Rarely are there consequences for such prosecutors.

Combating discrimination in jury selection requires changes to the process. Justice Marshall wanted to eliminate peremptory challenges altogether in order to guarantee race-neutral jury selection. Other recommendations have included demands that the federal government investigate more vigorously cases of suspected discrimination, calls for a more racially diverse justice system, and suggestions that community groups and civil rights organizations be called on to monitor the racial impartiality of the courts. The evidence suggests that despite the *Batson* decision, until effective measures are taken to prevent racial bias in jury selection, it is likely to continue.

Barbara Chasin

See also

Sentencing Disparities. Document: *Furman v. Georgia* (1972)

Further Reading:

Equal Justice Initiative. "Illegal Racial Discrimination in Jury Selection: A Continuing Legacy." August 2010. http://www.eji.org.

Marshall, Thurgood. Justice Marshall, concurring. *Batson v. Kentucky*, Supreme Court, 476 U.S. 79, April 30, 1986.

Sommers, Samuel R., and Michael I. Norton. "Race-Based Judgments, Race-Neutral Justifications: Experimental Examination of Peremptory Use and the *Batson* Challenge Procedure," *Law and Human Behavior* 31 (2007):261–273.

Watts, Mikal C. and Emily C. Jeffcott, "A Primer on Batson, Including Discussion of *Johnson v. California, Miller-El v. Dretke, Rice v. Collins, and Snyder v Louisiana,*" *St. Mary's Law Journal* 42: (2011): 337–410.

Beauty Standards

Beauty is generally considered a gendered trait and is therefore deemed a phenomenon exclusive to women's experiences. The feminist literature on beauty standards tends to gravitate towards two perspectives. The first focuses on the oppressive nature of beauty standards. Bartky (1988), for example, argues that women are coerced into conforming to beauty standards created by and for men. This hegemonic "male gaze" forces women to judge themselves and engage in beauty work to alter their appearance for male desires. The second perspective, in contrast to the first, presents a picture of women who engage in beauty work as active agents rather than victims or cultural dupes of patriarchal ideology. In *Body Work: Beauty and Self-Image in American Culture*, Gimlin (2002) argues that women are rational decision makers who strategically engage in beauty work to achieve positive physical, psychological, or social results.

Although the work of these theorists contributes greatly to feminist understandings of beauty, they take for granted that the image of feminine beauty is often racialized and defined by Eurocentric or white supremacist aesthetic standards. These bodies of work fail to recognize, as Collins' (1990) intersectionality theory so deftly explains, that viewing beauty as solely a women's issue does not take into account interacting and converging biographical factors that create unique experiences and understandings of beauty.

Because black women are constructed contra white femininity, the value of black women's beauty is measured by their proximity to white feminine beauty standards. During slavery, one's physical appearance could determine whether you worked indoors as a house servant or were relegated to the field. That is, darker-skinned individuals, by virtue of select religious ideologies and the burgeoning scientific racism of the day, were thought too dangerous, and/or both morally and mentally ill-equipped, to work in close proximity to upper-class property owners and administrators. This labor arrangement also assisted the reproduction of the status color hierarchy: those that worked under the sun became darker, and darker skin was translated as a sign of lower social status, whether enslaved blacks or "redneck" or "white trash" whites. This color/labor hierarchy, also known as colorism, was born out of the raced, gendered, and classed antebellum plantation system. Yet the social and ideological dominance of this system still holds the ability to stigmatize black women's appearance today.

Scholars writing on issues of body image and beauty among women of color have described the potentially corrosive and stigmatizing effect of white beauty standards. Minority women in general and black women specifically face a unique obstacle because a definition of beauty based on a white model effectively excludes black women from achieving the ideal. Scholars emphasizing the negative impact of white beauty standards point to practices such as skin lightening and cosmetic surgery.

While there are scholars who argue that black women are negatively impacted by the white beauty ideal, there are others who believe that minority women are unaffected because of the presence of a black beauty standard. The "Black Is Beautiful" movement in the 1960s insisted that black women challenge the white ideal by developing an alternative beauty standard. Research examining body image and self esteem among black women suggests that many young black females do not identify or evaluate themselves according to white media images and may in fact use alternative beauty standards. Scholars such as Meg Lovejoy (2001) argue that because femininity is constructed differently within the black community, women are more likely to express traditionally feminine as well as traditionally masculine characteristics. While scholars believe that traits such as assertiveness, independence, and self-reliance contribute to higher esteem in black women, the closer association of black women with masculinity may work to further stigmatize black women in the eyes of mainstream society.

Sheena Kaori Gardner and Matthew W. Hughey

Further Reading:

Bartky, Sandra L. "Foucault, Femininity, and the Modernization of Patriarchal Power." In *Feminism and Foucault*, edited by Irene Diamond and Lee Quinby, 61–87. Boston: Northeastern University Press, 1988.

Blay, Yaba Amgborale. "Skin Bleaching and Global White Supremacy: By Way of Introduction." *Journal of Pan African Studies* 4 (2011): 4–46.

Collins, Patricia Hill. *Black Feminist Thought*. New York: Routledge, 1990.

Gimlin, Debra. *Body Work: Beauty and Self-Image in American Culture*. Berkeley: University of California Press, 2002.

Lovejoy, Meg. "Disturbances in the Social Body: Differences in Body Image and Eating Problems among African American and White Women." *Gender and Society* 15 (2001): 239–61.

Belafonte, Harry (b. 1927)

Although immortalized in the collective consciousness of popular culture for his signature tune the "Banana Boat Song" and its popular lyric "Day-O," musician, actor, writer, and entertainer Harry George Belafonte Jr. has become equally noted for his tireless efforts as a social activist over the span of his five-decade-long career. Born in Harlem, New York, on March 1, 1927, Belafonte was raised by his mother. For a time in his early youth, the family lived in the village of Aboukir in his mother's native homeland of Jamaica. Spending his formative years abroad, life in Jamaica served as a cultural reservoir for Belafonte, as his artistic prowess would later develop in part from his exposure to the native music heard across the island. In his teenage years, Belafonte returned to New York City to attend high school, yet dropped out to enlist in the U.S. Navy, serving a tour of duty during World War II. Upon his return to New York City in the late 1940s, Belafonte began to explore fully his artistic side and embarked on an acting and musical career with the American Negro Theatre troupe. Performing on stage, Belafonte secured his status as a gifted performer in his first Broadway musical *Almanac*, winning the Tony Award, and establishing himself as a marketable and multifaceted entertainment talent.

Belafonte has continued over the years a long-standing recording and acting career that has included numerous awards and honors. His 1956 album *Calypso* became the first album in recording history to sell over one million copies in its initial release. Belafonte also worked in several films, securing his role as an internationally known, crossover talent. With his fame, Belafonte became an outspoken opponent of racial discrimination, and over the years he has been affiliated with a number of humanitarian and civil rights causes. Belafonte's fame initially occurred during the height of Jim Crow segregation, and this legalized discrimination informed Belafonte's artistic and humanitarian ideals. Artistically, Belafonte chose roles that focused on the issues of racism, such as Robert Wise's 1959 film *Odds Against Tomorrow*. A critic of Southern racist politics, Belafonte also boycotted the South from 1954 to 1961, refusing to play for segregated audiences. Belafonte also refused roles that catered to racial stereotyping and turned down roles such as *Porgy and Bess* in accordance with his ideals. Inspired by his mentor, activist and performer Paul Robeson, Belafonte

Singer Harry Belafonte appears on the Broadway stage in *Belafonte at the Palace*, January 5, 1960, in New York. (AP/Wide World Photos)

worked throughout his career to focus his art from a perspective that would champion the cause of civil rights and racial equality.

Belafonte has been politically active throughout his career. As a long time associate and friend of Martin Luther King, Jr., Belafonte used his fame and money to help finance the modern civil rights movement, bailing out King on occasion and providing monetary support for a variety of organized events, including the 1963 March on Washington. Belafonte was also appointed by President John F. Kennedy to serve as a cultural advisor to the Peace Corps, traveling to a number of countries as an ambassador of goodwill to foreign nations. Although awarded honors and prizes for his efforts, Belafonte has been a long-standing critic of American foreign policy, issuing attacks on various administrations as recently as that of George W. Bush and the Iraq War. Belafonte continues his efforts to this day, using art to influence politics and pursuing causes that reflect his humanitarian ideals.

KEVIN STRAIT

See also

Magical Negro Films; Narrowcasting

Further Reading:

Fopelson, Genia. *Harry Belafonte*. Los Angeles: Holloway House Publishing Company, 1991.

Remarks by Harry Belafonte about Paul Robeson to the Veterans of the Abraham Lincoln Brigade. http://www.cpsr.cs.uchicago.edu/robeson/belafonte.html (accessed June 9, 2008).

Bell Curve: Intelligence and Class Structure in American Life

Published in 1994, *The Bell Curve: Intelligence and Class Structure in American Life* is a controversial analysis concerning factors that influence human intelligence. Richard Herrnstein and Charles Murray argue that racial differences in intelligence are due to biological and environmental factors. To argue this claim, the authors discuss several different studies, but one study they examine in depth is Scarr and Weinberg's (1976) study of "IQ Test Performance of Black Children Adopted by White Families." While Herrnstein and Murray use this study to back up their claim—that racial differences in intelligence tests (IQ) are partially explained by genetics—those were not Scarr and Weinberg's conclusions (Sternberg 1995). Thus, the validity of Herrnstein and Murray's claim has often been criticized, attacked, and refuted by a number of different scholars.

Throughout their book, the authors argue that high levels of cognitive ability are associated with positive outcomes, such as high educational attainment, income, and prestigious jobs, while lower levels of cognitive ability are associated with societal issues, such as unemployment and poverty. To depict this relationship, the authors use data from the National Longitudinal Survey of Labor Market Experience of Youth (NLSY), a nationally representative sample of youth ages 14–22. Initiated in 1979 by the Department of Education, the NLSY is a comprehensive data set concerning familial background, educational and occupational outcomes, and cognitive ability.

Beginning in Part II of their book, Herrnstein and Murray claim that intelligence scores, measured by IQ, are strong predictors of the likelihood of: poverty; high school retention; college attainment; unemployment; having children out of wedlock; high divorce rates; low marital rates; the reception of welfare; among children of mothers with low IQ—low birth weight, poor motor skills and behavioral problems; participation in criminal behavior; and lack of voter participation.

In Part III, the authors turn to ethnic differences in intelligence and social behaviors, the most controversial component of their book. In terms of cognitive ability, East Asians (e.g., Chinese and Japanese) normally perform better on achievement and intelligence tests compared to their white counterparts. Whites, however, have higher IQs compared to blacks. This difference exists at every level of the socioeconomic spectrum. And since lower levels of cognitive ability explain the likelihood of participating in undesirable behaviors, Herrnstein and Murray argue that the low IQ scores among blacks and other racial minorities partially explain their lack of educational and occupational mobility and high levels of involvement in societal problems. Since high intellectual scores are associated with increased chances of mobility, the authors argue that our society will become like a caste system, where those with superior intellectual skills are concentrated at the top of the economic hierarchy and those at the bottom will be surrounded and involved in a number of social problems.

This argument, however, has been heatedly debated since it was first published. First, how intelligence is measured has been criticized. Herrnstein and Murray use IQ tests as predictors of a number of factors; however, IQ tests do not measure all aspects of what it means to be intelligent. According to Gould, the author of *Curveball*, since Herrnstein and Murray's measure of intelligence and its premises are flawed, the authors' arguments are inherently false. For instance, the main premise of their measure of intelligence is that it is genetically based, and can be measured as a single number. Social scientists and other scholars, however, often argue that intelligence is influenced by a number of societal variables (e.g., poverty, racial segregation, and education) and that there are a number of ways to measure intelligence, not just an IQ score. By stating that genetics is a main variable influencing one's likelihood of educational and occupational mobility, Herrnstein and Murray ignore how societal institutions influence individuals' access to pathways of mobility. By doing so, their argument reflects that of Charles Darwin, where only the fittest individuals and/or societies will survive.

This argument, that intellect is influenced by genetics, is not popular within the social sciences. Sternberg (1995) cites how this book, intentionally or not, blames people with low IQs for societal ills. However, Herrnstein and Murray did not and cannot prove that IQ *causes* a number of positive or negative social behaviors (IQ is correlated with a number of factors, which is different than causation). It may be that society's treatment of individuals with low IQs influences them to participate in more undesirable behaviors. Yet, this argument will not subside, as scholars in all fields remain adamant at finding a main reason for a number of economic and occupational outcomes.

Bobette Otto

See also

Academic Racism; Education and African Americans; *End of Racism, The*

Further Reading:

Gould, Stephen Jay. "Curveball." *New Yorker*, November 28, 1994. http://www.dartmouth.edu/~chance/course/topics/curveball.html.

Herstein, Richard J., and Charles Murray. *The Bell Curve: Intelligence and Class Structure in American Life*. New York: Free Press, 1994.

Jacoby, Russell, and Naomi Glauberman, eds. *The Bell Curve Debate: History, Documents, and Opinions*. New York: Three Rivers Press, 1995.

Lemann, Nicholas. "The Bell Curve Flattened: Subsequent Research Has Seriously Undercut the Claims of the Controversial Best Seller." *Slate*. 1997. http://www.slate.com/articles/briefing/articles/1997/01/the_bell_curve_flattened.html.

Scarr, Sandra, and Richard A. Weinberg. "IQ Test Performance of Black Children Adopted by White Families." *American Psychologist* 31 (1976): 726–39.

Sternberg, Robert J. "For Whom the Bell Curve Tolls: A Review of *The Bell Curve*." *Psychological Science* 6 (1995): 257–61.

Bellecourt, Clyde (b. 1939)

A Native American activist for over four decades, Clyde Bellecourt is best known for cofounding, with Dennis Banks and other Native American community leaders, the American Indian Movement in Minneapolis, Minnesota, in July 1968.

An Anishinabe, Clyde Howard Bellecourt was born on May 8, 1939, on the White Earth reservation in Minnesota. He had frequent run-ins with the law throughout his youth, and by 1962 he had been sent to the Stillwater State Penitentiary for eight months, where he completed a high school equivalency program. In 1964, he was released on parole and began to network with other Native rights activists, which culminated in the formation of the American Indian Movement (AIM) in 1968.

AIM was originally formed to improve government-funded social services to urban neighborhoods and to prevent the harassment of Native Americans by police. During the 1972 occupation of the Bureau of Indian Affairs building in Washington, D.C., Bellecourt helped draft the 20-point document presented to the government. Although AIM demands were ignored, the government did establish a task force that met with movement leaders and promised to make no arrests in connection with the occupation. Bellecourt also worked extensively to raise funds for AIM-sponsored projects and was briefly associated with militant black activist Stokely Carmichael.

Increasingly confrontational, Bellecourt and other AIM leaders implemented an armed occupation of the tiny South Dakota hamlet of Wounded Knee on February 27, 1973. Bellecourt was elected to the council of the AIM-declared "Nation of Wounded Knee" and eventually cosigned the peace agreement that ended the confrontation. Not long after Wounded Knee, Bellecourt was wounded when shot in the stomach by Carter Camp, another occupation leader.

In the 1990s, Bellecourt lobbied energetically on behalf of the Mille Lac Chippewa during their struggle to maintain traditional walleye pike harvests along the shores of Flathead Lake in Minnesota. (Earlier successes in Wisconsin had allowed Native Americans there to continue their treaty-guaranteed right to maintain a traditional subsistence fishing economy.) Powerful opposition in Minnesota, led by former Minnesota Viking football coach Bud Grant, persuaded the state legislature to reject an agreement that would have allowed the tribe to harvest about half of the walleye pike in Flathead Lake.

Into the 21st century, Bellecourt continues to fight for Native American rights, still active as the national director of AIM, as well as the director of the Peacemaker Center for Indian Youth. He also serves as a leading figure of the National Coalition on Racism in Sports and Media and founded the Board of American Indian OIC, an organization devoted to finding employment for American Indians. On Christmas Eve December 2013, he was arrested while shopping at a mall during an Idle No More event; in September 2013, the judge in the case declared a mistrial after a jury deadlock.

David Ritchey

See also

American Indian Movement (AIM); Means, Russell; Native Americans, Conquest of; Native Americans, Forced Relocation of; Native American Graves Protection and Repatriation Act (1990); Occupation of Alcatraz Island; Peltier, Leonard; Red Power Movement

Further Reading

Knox, Margaret L. "The New Indian Wars: A Growing Movement Is Gunning." *Los Angeles Times*, November 7, 1993.

Lazarus, Edward. *Black Hills, White Justice: The Sioux Nation versus the United States, 1775 to the Present.* New York: Harper Collins, 1991.

Lyman, Stanley David. *Wounded Knee, 1973: A Personal Account.* Lincoln: University of Nebraska Press, 1991.

Stern, Kenneth. *Loud Hawk: The United States versus the American Indian Movement.* Norman: University of Oklahoma Press, 1994.

Weyler, Rex. *Blood of the Land: The Government and Corporate War against the American Indian Movement.* New York: Vintage Books, 1982.

Bellingham Riots (1907)

On September 4, 1907, a Hindu community in Bellingham, Washington, was attacked by an angry mob of 500 white men, most of whom were locals working in the lumber mills. The mob invaded the homes of the "ragheads"—the racial slur they used to describe the people from South Asia—and dragged people onto the streets, beat them, and drove them from town. The attacks became known as the Anti-Hindu riots, or more generally, the Bellingham riots, and the conditions that gave rise to the Bellingham riots were part of a larger pattern of race riots across the United States during the early part of the 20th century: angry white workers, concerned about losing their jobs to "nonwhite" immigrants, resorted to violence to exclude certain groups from the local job market. Racial conflict among workers was oftentimes encouraged by their employers, who purposely used "non-white" workers as strike breakers and scabs in attempts to bust unions. Many white union rank-and-filers were members of the Asian Exclusion League, whose motto was, "The preservation of the Caucasian race upon American soil."

In the 1890s, many South Asians—most of whom were Hindu—fled the exploitation of British colonial rule in India for the United States. Between 1899 and 1913 more than 7,000 "Hindus" settled in the Pacific Northwest, seeking work in booming lumber and railroad industries. Once there, Hindu immigrants faced the same kind of hostility by white workers and their unions in the lumber mills as Chinese workers faced in California. At the time, many unions practiced racial exclusion as a way to monopolize the best jobs in the area for their white members. When threats and intimidation against immigrant workers failed to drive them out of the industry, white workers resorted to violence.

But racial tensions did not come to violence in all communities. For example, Astoria, Oregon, was similar to Bellingham, Washington, in that the economy there was also based on the timber and railroad industries, but immigrants from South Asia were welcome there. According to a *Daily Astorian* article, dated April 26, 1976 (9B), one man was quoted as saying, "We were afraid of them [South Asians] at first, but my dad said, 'They have to make a living the same as the rest of us. We are foreigners too.'"

MICHAEL ROBERTS

See also

Race Riots in America. Documents: The Report on the Memphis Riots of May 1866 (July 25, 1866); Account of the Riots in East St. Louis, Illinois (July 1917); The Cook County Coroner's Report Regarding the 1919 Chicago Race Riots (1919); A Southern Black Woman's Letter Regarding the Recent Riots in Chicago and Washington (November 1919); The Final Report of the Grand Jury on the Tulsa Race Riot (June 25, 1921); Testimony from *Laney v. United States* Describing Events during the Washington, D.C., Riot of July 1919 (December 3, 1923); The Governor's Commission Report on the Watts Riots (December 1965); Cyrus R. Vance's Report on the Riots in Detroit (July-August 1967); The Reports of the Oklahoma Commission to Study the Tulsa Race Riot of 1921 (2000-2001); The Draft Report of the 1898 Wilmington Race Riot Commission (December 2005)

Bensonhurst (New York) Incident (1989)

The widely publicized death of Yusef Hawkins, a young African American man killed by a group of whites in Bensonhurst, New York, in August 1989, created outrage across the country and severely aggravated racial tensions in New York City.

On August 23, 1989, 16-year-old Hawkins and a group of his friends traveled from his Brooklyn neighborhood to the Italian-American neighborhood of Bensonhurst to respond to an advertisement for a car for sale. While he was traveling to Bensonhurst, a woman of the neighborhood was arguing with Keith Modello, telling him that he was going to be beaten up by her black boyfriend and a group of his friends who were en route to the neighborhood. Modello gathered a group of his friends armed with sticks and a bat and waited for the black men to arrive. When Hawkins and his friends arrived, they were met by the angry white men, but Hawkins explained why they were in the neighborhood. As Modello and his friends were about to let Hawkins and his friends proceed with their mission of seeing a car for sale, another teen came on the scene with a gun and began firing shots.

Hawkins was hit and died before paramedics arrived on the scene. The alleged shooter was Joey Fama. Black leaders and community activists, led by the Rev. Al Sharpton, marched through Bensonhurst to protest Hawkins's death. The protesters were met by angry whites, who shouted death threats at the marchers. During the trial, both Keith Modello and Joey Fama were acquitted. Protesters marched from the courthouse to Hawkins's house, looting some stores and throwing rocks at TV news vans. Citizens of New York, especially those of the black community, were outraged by the verdicts. Tensions were already high over earlier incidents like the 1986 Howard Beach incident. Many of the black protestors felt justice was not served and that the outcome of the incident was another example of the inherent racism in a judicial system that provided unequal protection under the law for blacks. The incident later inspired Spike Lee's film, *Jungle Fever*.

CATHERINE ANYASO

See also

Hawkins, Yusef. Documents: The Report on the Memphis Riots of May 1866 (July 25, 1866); Account of the Riots in East St. Louis, Illinois (July 1917); The Cook County Coroner's Report

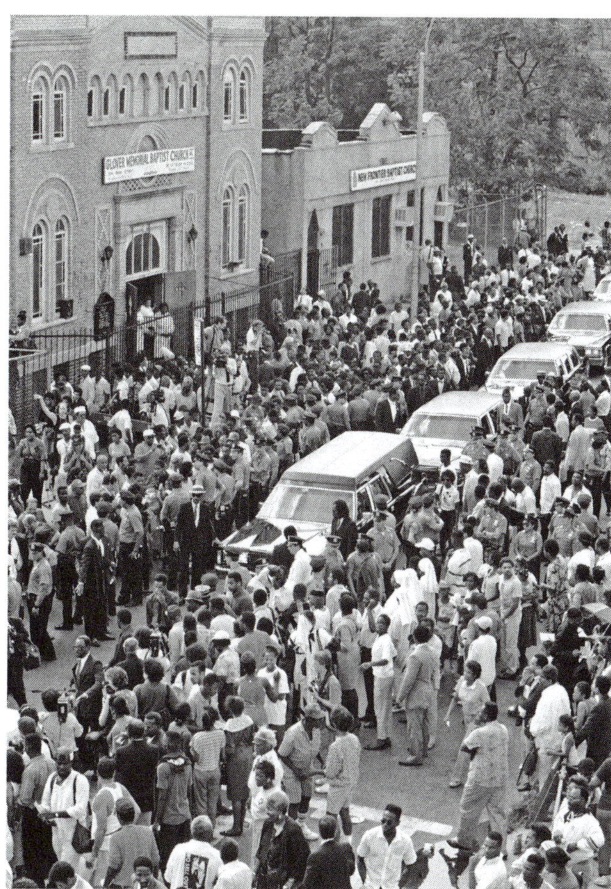

A crowd looks on as the coffin containing Yusef Hawkins is carried out of Glover Memorial Church in Brooklyn, New York, on August 30, 1989. Hawkins, 16, was shot to death in Bensonhurst. (AP Photo/Mario Cabrera)

Regarding the 1919 Chicago Race Riots (1919); A Southern Black Woman's Letter Regarding the Recent Riots in Chicago and Washington (November 1919); The Final Report of the Grand Jury on the Tulsa Race Riot (June 25, 1921); Testimony from *Laney v. United States* Describing Events during the Washington, D.C., Riot of July 1919 (December 3, 1923); The Governor's Commission Report on the Watts Riots (December 1965); Cyrus R. Vance's Report on the Riots in Detroit (July-August 1967); The Reports of the Oklahoma Commission to Study the Tulsa Race Riot of 1921 (2000-2001); The Draft Report of the 1898 Wilmington Race Riot Commission (December 2005)

Further Reading:

Anderson, Lorrin, and William Tucker. "Cracks in the Mosaic." *National Review* 42 (1990).

Perry, Barbara. *In the Name of Hate: Understanding Hate Crimes.* New York: Routledge, 2001.

Berea College v. Kentucky (1908)

Berea College, located in Berea, Kentucky, was founded to educate former enslaved African Americans and poor Appalachian whites. In 1859, the college obtained its charter from the state. However, no classes were offered at the facility until 1866, after the Civil War ended. Initially the college was started as an independent, nonsectarian Christian institution by John G. Fee, an evangelical, abolitionist minister from Bracken County who had moved to the area when he received several acres of land from Cassius M. Clay, a fellow Kentucky abolitionist. Because the college held close ties with numerous Presbyterian, Congregational, and Baptist churches, between 1855 and 1859, the institution merely functioned as a nondenominational mission school.

Simultaneously, the founders of Berea introduced a completely integrated curriculum to try to attract men and women, as well as African American and Caucasian students, to its facility. However, before the college could implement its educational plan, the fear of abolitionist-led uprisings, similar to John Brown's assault on the federal armory in Harpers Ferry, Virginia, in 1859, led many local citizens to organize a grassroots group that forced Fee and his supporters to leave the city of Berea. It was not until the early years of Reconstruction, on March 6, 1866, when Berea opened an integrated elementary school with the enrollment of three African American female students, that Fee returned and the college quickly enacted its integrated educational plan. The following year, the first completely integrated class, taught by Ellen P. T. Wheeler, the wife of a missionary Fee had known during his visits to Camp Nelson, Kentucky, was offered at the institution.

In 1869, Edward Henry Fairchild, a graduate of Oberlin College, became the first president of Berea College. Under his leadership, several buildings were constructed and an enormous endowed funding campaign was started, led by money donated by the American Missionary Association as well as various private donors. During these years, Berea's enrollment also flourished with its highly ambitious educational philosophy that rested on the creation of an entirely integrated and socially equal instructional experience for all races, from kindergarten through college. For example, from 1866 to 1889, at least half of Berea's student body was African American. However, in late 1889, with the departure

Berea Court Case (1904)

On October 8, 1904, the grand jury of Madison County, Kentucky, presented in the circuit court of that county an indictment, charging:

> The said Berea College, being a corporation duly incorporated under the laws of the state of Kentucky, and owning, maintaining, and operating a college, school, and institution of learning, known as "Berea College," located in the town of Berea, Madison county, Kentucky, did unlawfully and wilfully permit and receive both the white and negro races as pupils for instruction in said college, school, and institution of learning.

This indictment was found under an act of March 22, 1904, whose 1st section reads:

> Sec. 1. That it shall be unlawful for any person, corporation, or association of persons to maintain or operate any college, school, or institution where persons of the white and negro races are both received as pupils for instruction, and any person or corporation who shall operate or maintain any such college, school, or institution shall be fined $1,000, and any person or corporation who may be convicted of violating the provisions of this act shall be fined $100 for each day they may operate said school, college, or institution after such conviction.

The ruling, read by Justice Brewer [excerpt]:

> There is no dispute as to the facts. That the act does not violate the Constitution of Kentucky is settled by the decision of its highest court, and the single question for our consideration is whether it conflicts with the Federal Constitution. The court of appeals discussed at some length the general power of the state in respect to the separation of the two races. It also ruled that "the right to teach white and negro children in a private school at the same time and place is not a property right. Besides, appellant, as a corporation created by this state, has no natural right to teach at all. Its right to teach is such as the state sees fit to give to it. The state may withhold it altogether, or qualify it. . . ."
>
> There is no force in the suggestion that the statute, although clearly separable, must stand or fall as an entirety on the ground the legislature would not have enacted one part unless it could reach all. That the legislature of Kentucky desired to separate the teaching of white and colored children may be conceded; but it by no means follows that it would not have enforced the separation so far as it could do so, even though it could not make it effective under all circumstances. In other words, it is not at all unreasonable to believe that the legislature, although advised beforehand of the constitutional question, might have prohibited all organizations and corporations under its control from teaching white and colored children together, and thus made at least uniform official action.

Justice Harlan, dissenting [excerpt]:

> The capacity to impart instruction to others is given by the Almighty for beneficent purposes; and its use may not be forbidden or interfered with by government,—certainly not, unless such instruction is, in its nature, harmful to the public morals or imperils the public safety. The right to impart instruction, harmless in itself or beneficial to those who receive it, is a substantial right of property,—especially, where the services are rendered for compensation. But even if such right be not strictly a property right, it is, beyond question, part of one's liberty as guaranteed against hostile state action by the Constitution of the United States. This court has more than once said that the liberty guaranteed by the 14th Amendment embraces "the right of the citizen to be free in the enjoyment of all his faculties," and "to be free to use them in all lawful ways." If pupils, of whatever race,—certainly, if they be citizens,—choose, with the consent of their parents, or voluntarily, to sit together in a private institution of learning while receiving instruction which is not in its nature harmful or dangerous to the public, no government, whether Federal or state, can legally forbid their coming together, or being together temporarily, for such an innocent purpose. If the common-wealth of Kentucky can make it a crime to teach white and colored children together at the same time, in a private institution of learning, it is difficult to perceive why it may not forbid the assembling of white and colored children in the same Sabbath school, for the purpose of being instructed in the Word of God, although such teaching may be done under the authority of the church to which the school is attached as well as with the consent of the parents of the children.

Source: Excerpts from *Berea College v. Kentucky*, 1908, pp. 1, 3, 10–11.

of President Fairchild, the educational environment of the institution began to change. For instance, with the appointment of William Goodell Frost as Berea's third president, more emphasis was placed on the recruitment and retention of poor white Appalachians, not the enhancement of the institution's integrated educational curriculum and overall plan. Soon, segregated classrooms and dorms began to appear. Also, the percentage of African American students who enrolled and continued their education at Berea College declined greatly.

On October 8, 1906, a grand jury in Madison County, Kentucky, indicted Berea College for violating the state's Day Law. The Day Law, proposed by State Representative Carl Day of Breathitt County in 1904, made it illegal to educate African American and Caucasian students in the same facility. Despite its conviction, Berea continued to challenge Kentucky's Day Law in court until the U.S. Supreme Court ruled in *Berea College v. Kentucky* (1908) that the Commonwealth of Kentucky had the right and authority to alter any educational charter it issued. Moreover, the Court also noted that Berea still had the ability to educate any students who enrolled at its institution, just not at the same time or place.

Eric R. Jackson

See also

Affirmative Action; College Admission, Discrimination in; Education and African Americans; Educational Achievement Gap; Historically Black Colleges and Universities; UC Berkeley Bake Sale; *Williams v. Mississippi* (1898)

Further Reading:

Harrison, Lowell H., and James C. Klotter. *A New History of Kentucky*. Lexington: University Press of Kentucky, 1997.

Heckman, Richard A., and Betty Jean Hall. "Berea College and the Day Law." *Register of the Kentucky Historical Society* 66 (1968): 35–52.

Nelson, Paul David. "Experiment in Interracial Education at Berea College, 1858–1908." *Journal of Negro History* 59 (1974): 13–27.

Peck, Elisabeth S. *Berea's First Century, 1855–1955*. Lexington: University of Kentucky Press, 1955.

Sears, Richard. *A Utopian Experiment in Kentucky: Integration and Social Equality at Berea, 1866 to 1904*. Westport, CT: Greenwood Press, 1996.

Bernhard Goetz Case

Bernhard Goetz, a white American of German descent, successfully claimed that his shooting of four black teenagers in a New York City subway car was self-defense, making him one of the most widely discussed white criminal defendants of the late 1980s. The case began with the original shooting incident in 1984 and went to trial the following year. The Goetz case became the center of a nationwide spotlight, sparking a widespread debate on the relationship between race and crime in major American urban centers. Goetz, who was labeled as "the subway vigilante" by the media, came to stand for the frustration of many Americans during the 1980s with the high crime rates of large cities. Alternately commended and vilified by the American public, Goetz and his trial did much to define the legal limits of self-defense, especially when race is a contributing factor.

The initial incident in the Bernhard Goetz case took place on December 22, 1984, when two young men, Troy Canty and James Ramseur, asked Goetz for money on a New York City subway train in Manhattan. Goetz, without provocation, then shot at them and their companions, Barry Allen and Darrell Cabey. Goetz subsequently fled the subway, drove to New England, and concealed evidence of the crime. On December 30, he turned himself in to police

Michael Dunn Case (2012)

In November 2012, during a confrontation at a Florida gas station, Michael Dunn, a white man, fired at least eight shots at a car of unarmed teens, killing Jordan Davis, a 17-year-old black male. Dunn told police that he felt threatened and thought he saw a gun in the teens' car, though no guns were ever found. Dunn's attorney is currently contemplating a self-defense strategy using Florida's "Stand Your Ground" law, which allows the use of deadly force when a person perceives a threat to their safety. Though this incident has been compared to the Trayvon Martin murder, it may actually be more applicable to the Bernard Goetz case in terms of the way in which a white perpetrator shot multiple times at four unarmed teenagers in a public space and is claiming that he did so because he feared for his personal safety.

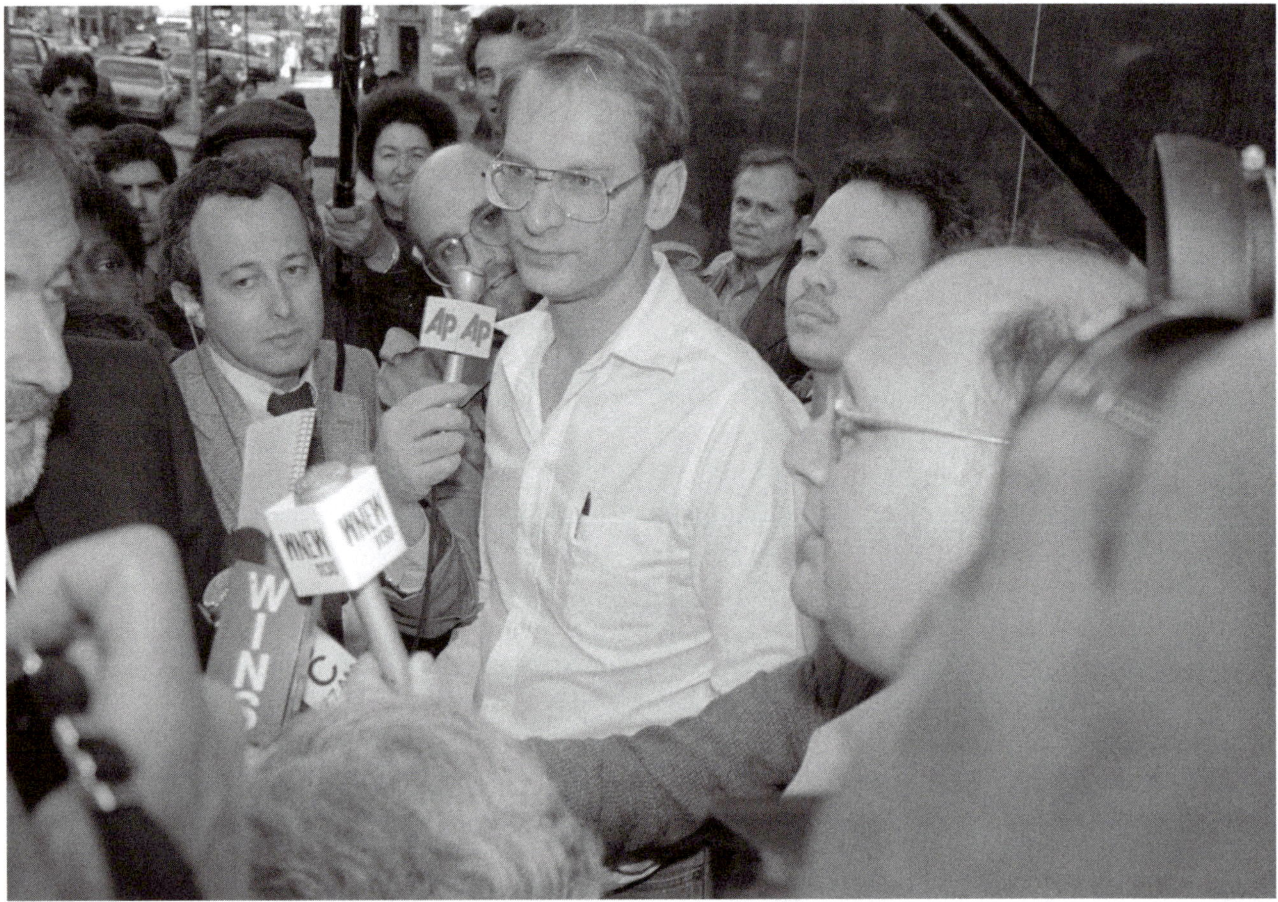

Accused subway vigilante Bernhard Goetz, who shot four young black men whom he believed were intent on robbing him on the subway, is surrounded by newsmen in New York, 1987. (Associated Press)

in Concord, New Hampshire. Goetz was eventually charged with attempted murder, assault, and reckless endangerment; however, a jury found him not guilty of all charges except an illegal firearms possession, for which he served two-thirds of a one-year sentence. In 1996, one of the men Goetz shot and badly injured obtained a civil judgment of $43 million against Goetz.

Goetz alleged that the four young men had tried to mug him and that he was acting in self-defense. Because Goetz was a white man allegedly defending himself against four black men, there were significant racial implications in the case. Goetz was generally supported by the white public as a hero asserting his right to self-defense. At the time of the incident during the 1980s, the American public was frustrated by high rates of crime in large cities and were calling for transgressors to be punished. The public and media fashioned and admired Goetz as that punisher, rather than as a racist who fired an illegally obtained weapon multiple times at four black unarmed teenagers. According to police transcripts, Goetz stated that his intention was to do anything he could to hurt the victims, to murder them, and to make them suffer as much as possible. This sentiment is exemplified by Goetz's statement of aiming for the center of the body when he shot each of the victims. In his confession, Goetz also stated that he did not have a permit to carry the weapon he used in the shooting.

Scholars explain that despite this confession, the white public rallied around Goetz as a shining example of someone exerting his or her individual control over crime—a control which the government did not appear to have during that time. In the 1980s, there was nationwide skepticism about the police and their ability to protect the general citizenry, especially with rising crime rates in major U.S. cities. In order to turn Goetz into a hero, the public excused racial explanations of the crime under the guise of justice, deeming Goetz's white skin and the black skin of the victims as mere coincidence. This, in turn, justified the coincidental white public support for Goetz. However, scholars argue that it was in fact a racially conscious decision to revere Goetz since the public was generally unaware of most of the factual events in the case. Indeed, no one except for those in the subway car could know with any certainty if Goetz's actions were justified by self-defense.

Despite these claims of racial impartiality, race was a major factor in the outcome of the Goetz case. During Goetz's trial, several racial tactics were utilized by the defense. For instance, the defense recreated the shooting using four black males to act as the teenage victims. Typically, the purpose of this type of demonstration is to illustrate the way in which each bullet entered the body of the victims. However, the police transcripts already showed Goetz's intent to do the most damage possible with his aim. Scholars argue that the real motivation behind this demonstration was to dramatically recreate the scene of Goetz surrounded by four black males, conceivably to incite fear in the jury of how they might feel in Goetz's position. This is exemplified by the fact that the defense selected four large, muscular, imposing young black men to play the part of the victims.

The defense also exploited this sense of fearfulness in the jurors by describing the victims as savage predators and gang members. This was a major characteristic of the defense's trial tactics: to paint the victims as more than just four black teenagers, but rather as representations of a class and group of people symbolizing a threat to white society. The racialized nature of Goetz's trial is further demonstrated by the way the case revolved around questions that should not have mattered but arguably did because of race. For example, the defense presented evidence of how close the victims were standing to Goetz before he shot them, whether or not he fired at one of them in the back, and the motivations for his actions.

Despite public perception of the Goetz shooting as a nonracialized coincidence, scholars agree that the case was in fact a highly racialized event. Ultimately, the initial incident, subsequent white support of Goetz, and Goetz's acquittal should all be understood in a racial framework. This framework shows that in the United States, race can and does influence the social construction of who can be named a hero, a victim, or a perpetrator and who is deemed guilty and innocent.

Adrienne N. Milner

See also
Hate Crimes in America; Trayvon Martin Case

Further Reading:

Armour, Jody D. "Race Ipsa Loquitur: Of Reasonable Racists, Intelligent Bayesians, and Involuntary Negrophobes," *Stanford Law Review* 46 (1994): 781–816.

Barnes, Robin D. "Interracial Violence and Racialized Narratives: Discovering the Road Less Traveled," *Columbia Law Review* 95 (1996): 1301–42.

Carter, Stephen L. "When Victims Happen to Be Black," *Yale Law Journal* 97 (1988): 420–47.

CNN. "Michel Dunn, Jordan Davis Loud Music Shooting Case: Dunn Pleads Not Guilty." http://www.wptv.com/dpp/news/state/michael-dunn-jordan-davis-loud-music-shooting-case-dunn-pleads-not-guilty.

Fletcher, George P. *A Crime of Self-Defense: Bernhard Goetz and the Law on Trial.* Chicago: University of Chicago Press, 1988.

New York Times. '*. . . You Have to Think in a Cold-Blooded Way.*' http://www.nytimes.com/1987/04/30/nyregion/you-have-to-think-in-a-cold-blooded-way.html?pagewanted=all&src=pm.

Bethune, Mary McLeod (1875–1955)

Mary McLeod Bethune was one of the most prominent educators and civil servants of the twentieth century. "The First Lady of the Struggle," as she was known, worked indefatigably to guarantee the right to education and freedom from discrimination for African Americans. She was the 15th of 19 children born to former slaves in Maysville, South Carolina, on July 10, 1875. Growing up on her parents' farm, where she picked cotton, Bethune did not attend school until she was 11 years old, at the Presbyterian mission school in Maysville. Then she attended Scotia Seminary, an African American girls' school in Concord, North Carolina, and subsequently attended the Moody Bible Institute in Chicago.

Upon receiving her degree, she taught at the Presbyterian mission school in Maysville and then the Haines Institute in Augusta, Georgia, in 1896. At the Kindell Institute in Sumpter, South Carolina, she met Albertus Bethune, whom she married. In 1904, she opened a school for African

American girls in Daytona Beach, Florida. Starting with five girls and her son, she began the school with virtually nothing: crates were used for desks, charcoal for pencils, and crushed elderberries for ink. To raise money for the school, she and her students held many bake sales. As the school developed, Bethune sought financing help. She was able to get James M. Gamble, of Proctor & Gamble in Cincinnati, Ohio, to become a benefactor. He would contribute to the school until his death.

In 1923, her Daytona Literacy and Industrial School for Training Negro Girls merged with the all-boys Cookman Institute of Jacksonville, Florida, to form a coeducational high school. In 1924, the school became affiliated with the Methodist Church. In 1931, it became Bethune-Cookman College, a junior college. Bethune-Cookman became a four-year college in 1941. Bethune was president until 1942 and from 1946 to 1947. By 2007, the school achieved university status. As of 2007, the school had an enrollment of close to 3,000 students and an endowment of over $37 million.

As president of the National Association of Colored Women, Mary McLeod Bethune was also a leader of the National Council of Women. In 1927, at a luncheon she hosted, Bethune met Eleanor Roosevelt and began a lifelong friendship. As a result of this contact, Bethune was named director of Negro Affairs in President Franklin D. Roosevelt's National Youth Administration (NYA) in 1936, a position she held until 1944. This organization, a part of Roosevelt's second New Deal, helped youth obtain employment. Thus she became the highest-ranking African American in the Roosevelt administration. She also was part of Roosevelt's Black Cabinet, an informal group of prominent African Americans that included Ralph Bunche, Eugene K. Jones, Rayford Logan, and Truman K. Gibson Jr. Their goal was to plan strategy and set priorities regarding African Americans for the Roosevelt administration. She was a champion of civil rights and pressed for anti-lynching legislation and abolition of the poll tax. During World War II, she also served as a special assistant to the secretary of war and assistant director of the Women's Army Corps (WAC). She left government in 1944 when the NYA disbanded. As president of the National Council of Negro Women, a position she held until 1949, she attended the founding conference of the United Nations. Even in her retirement, she spoke out on civil rights issues until her death on May 18, 1955. She was buried on the campus of Bethune-Cookman College.

Sanjeev A. Rao, Jr.

See also

National Association for the Advancement of Colored People (NAACP)

Further Reading:

Gelders, Sterne Emma. *Mary McLeod Bethune*. New York: Alfred A. Knopf, 1957.

Holt, Rackham. *Mary McLeod Bethune: A Biography*. Garden City, NY: Doubleday, 1964.

McCluskey, Audrey Thomas, and Elaine M. Smith, eds. *Mary McLeod Bethune: Building a Better World*. Bloomington: Indiana University Press, 2000.

Bigotry

Bigotry is prejudice against an individual or group of people based on real or perceived characteristics; in the case of race, bigotry most often manifests itself as white prejudice against people of color. A bigot is an individual who harbors negative attitudes and emotions towards another individual or group. Traditionally, bigots are unashamed of their views and somewhat embrace the idea that they are smart enough to know the difference between inferior and superior groups. A famous image of a bigot is Archie Bunker from the show *All in the Family*; in almost every episode he insulted blacks, Puerto Ricans, women, and other minorities. Some contemporary celebrities have been confronted for having bigoted attitudes. Mel Gibson has made anti-Semitic comments; Don Imus called the black players of the Rutgers women's basketball team "nappy-headed hos"; and Michael Richards lashed out at four black audience members with the N-word and alluded to the historic practice of lynching.

Bigotry stems from stereotypes, media depictions, inherited familial attitudes, and/or from residing in homogenous groups. Usually, bigotry is prejudiced attitudes held by the powerful about the powerless. Bigotry, traditionally, is overt racial attitudes that operate on the individual level such as the examples above with Gibson, Imus, and Richards; however, bigotry can also be subtle or work on the macro level. On the subtle level, bigotry can manifest itself in covert, unintentional, and automatic ways—what Anderson (2010) terms "benign bigotry." In this type of bigotry, an individual may not believe that s/he is prejudiced but in fact still holds discriminatory attitudes and beliefs. These attitudes and beliefs can be measured using Implicit Association Tests (IAT). These tests measure the strength of association between mental constructs. For example, a computerized test will quickly flash images of black and white faces along with the words "good" and "bad"; associations between white and good or black and bad reveal unguarded, subconscious beliefs about racialized others. On the macro level, bigotry can be seen when individual prejudiced attitudes coalesce among groups and result in action. For example, the Ku Klux Klan is a group of bigots brought together by their common disregard for blacks and other nonwhites. Another example of bigotry operating on the macro level can be seen during times of war when individuals adopt prejudiced attitudes towards the nationality or race of the enemy. For instance, during the Vietnam War the Vietnamese were labeled "gooks," during WWII Japanese were called "Japs," and in heightened times against communism Chinese were called "Chinks."

Contemporary examples of bigotry can be seen particularly around tensions with terrorists and undocumented immigrants. After 9/11 some assumed that anyone of Middle Eastern descent was a potential terrorist, and in particular the turbans of the Sikh and Muslim faiths were conflated with the head coverings of al-Qaeda. In 2009, when an attempt was made to open a Muslim mosque and community center in downtown Manhattan near the site of Ground Zero, there were numerous protests as Muslims were seen as terrorists and un-American. Arabs in America have long been depicted as one homogenous group, so it is not surprising that people assume all Muslims are Arab and all Arabs are Muslim. In fact, only 12 percent of the world's Muslims are Arab, and the Sikhs had nothing to do with 9/11 or terrorism against the United States. In a similar vein, just as some see all Arabs or Muslims as terrorists, some view all Mexicans, or Latinos in general, as "aliens"—immigrants in the United States without legal documentation. Anti-immigration and specific anti-Latino legislation has been increasingly popular within the last 5 to 10 years.

Bigotry as a form of prejudice and discrimination is still a problem today and is scientifically analyzed in the field of social psychology. Social psychologists aim to understand the links between individual attitudes and beliefs with individual and collective action. Bigotry, particularly overt bigotry, can be difficult to overcome, but increasing contact with others by creating diverse environments where people can learn about one another has been shown to help. Another tactic is "stereotype suppression," where people are encouraged to actively dispel any stereotypes that may enter their minds. Subtle or benign bigotry, particularly of the type that people don't even realize they possess, has shown to be successfully counteracted by simply making individuals aware of their prejudices so they can educate themselves and consciously overcome them. In general, teaching people compassion for others helps, so that rather than making assumptions about other people's worth there is an effort to understand their circumstances.

Hephzibah Strmic-Pawl

See also

Discrimination; Implicit Bias; Prejudice; Racism

Further Reading:

Anderson, Kristin J. *Benign Bigotry: The Psychology of Subtle Prejudice.* Cambridge: Cambridge University Press, 2010.

Child, Ben. "Mel Gibson 'Hates Jews' Says Screenwriter, Joe Eszterhas." *The Guardian.* http://www.guardian.co.uk/film/2012/apr/12/mel-gibson-jews-joe-eszterhas.

CNN Wire Staff. "Protestors Descend on Ground Zero for Anti-Mosque Demonstration." *CNN US.* http://www.cnn.com/2010/US/06/06/new.york.ground. zero.mosque/index.html.

Gordon, Ian, and Tasneem Raja. "164 Anti-Immigration Laws Passed Since 2010? A MoJo Analysis." http://www.motherjones.com/politics/ 2012/03/anti-immigration-law-database.

Guttenberg, Steve. "CBS Fires Don Imus Over Racial Slur." *CBS News.* http://www.cbsnews.com/2100-201_162-2675273.html.

Takaki, Ronald. *A Different Mirror: A History of Multicultural America.* Boston: Back Bay Books, 1993.

TMZ Staff. " 'Kramer's' Racist Tirade—Caught on Tape." *TMZ.* http://www.tmz.com/2006/11/20/kramers-racist-tirade-caught-on-tape/.

Bilingual Education

Bilingual education in the United States can be traced back to the eighteenth and nineteenth centuries in communities where German, French, Spanish, and other minority language speakers were concentrated (e.g., New Mexico, California, Louisiana, northern New England, the Midwest, and the East). However, bilingual education as a national policy did not emerge until 1968, as a result of the Bilingual Education Act (BEA) of 1968 enacted by Congress. This act legitimized bilingual education programs at the national level and allocated funds for teaching limited-English-proficiency (LEP) children of low-income families in their native languages while they were learning English. Over time, bilingual education programs have been expanded by a series of amendments to or reauthorization of the 1968 BEA.

Bilingual education means education in two languages. In the United States, this term describes a number of educational approaches using students' native language and English in instruction. There are four basic types of bilingual education programs.

(1) *Transitional bilingual education.* In this model, children learn school subjects (e.g., math, literature, arts, science, and social studies) in their native language while studying English in programs designed for second-language learners. The goal is to prepare students to enter mainstream English classrooms. (2) *English immersion.* The goal of this model is to assist students in achieving proficiency in English. Students are "immersed" in English, which is the language of instruction. Teachers deliver lessons in simplified English so that students learn English and academic subjects. (3) *Two-way bilingual education.* Its purpose is to help all students achieve proficiency in both English and their native language. Instruction is given in both languages. (4) *English as a Second Language.* This program uses a combination of methods to teach English to non-English-speaking students of different language backgrounds.

Bilingual education has been an issue of ongoing controversy. Proponents argue that bilingual education helps LEP students ease the transition to the regular English program; gives bilingual children advantages over monolingual

California Ballot Proposition 227 (1997)

In November 1997, California voters passed Proposition 227 (the English Language Education for Children in Public Schools Initiative) with a large margin (61 percent yeas vs. 39 percent nays). The proposition was aimed at eliminating bilingual education in California public schools. It proposed the following key provisions: "All children in California public schools shall be taught English by being taught in English"; all children with limited English proficiency shall be placed in a sheltered English immersion program for a temporary period of no more than one year; under parental-waiver conditions (e.g., already with English proficiency, the child is age 10 or older, or there are special physical, emotional, psychological, or educational needs), parents could request that their children be transferred to classes where children are taught through bilingual-education techniques permitted by law; and $50 million a year for 10 years shall be allocated to fund programs of adult English-language instruction.

Cosponsored by Silicon Valley millionaire Ron Unz and Latino teacher Gloria Tuchman, Proposition 227 was an attempt to fix the problems of existing bilingual education in California, such as lengthy stays in bilingual-education programs, a lack of qualified bilingual teachers, and a deficiency in students' English proficiency, which is needed to compete in college and the labor market. However, there is no indication that the proposition's prescription has worked. Many parents have chosen to keep their children in bilingual-education programs. According to the California Department of Education, in the 1998–1999 school year, nearly 170,000 children remained in bilingual classrooms, down from 410,000 in the previous school year. Another 472,000 English learners received at least some "support" in their native language, compared to 306,000 in 1997–1998, despite threats of lawsuits by English-only advocates. Furthermore, Proposition 227 is seen to be shortsighted because it will turn potential bilinguals and multilinguals into monolinguals in an increasingly global economy. Some believe a legislative mandate for instructional programs is not needed and the choice should be left to parents and children.

Philip Yang

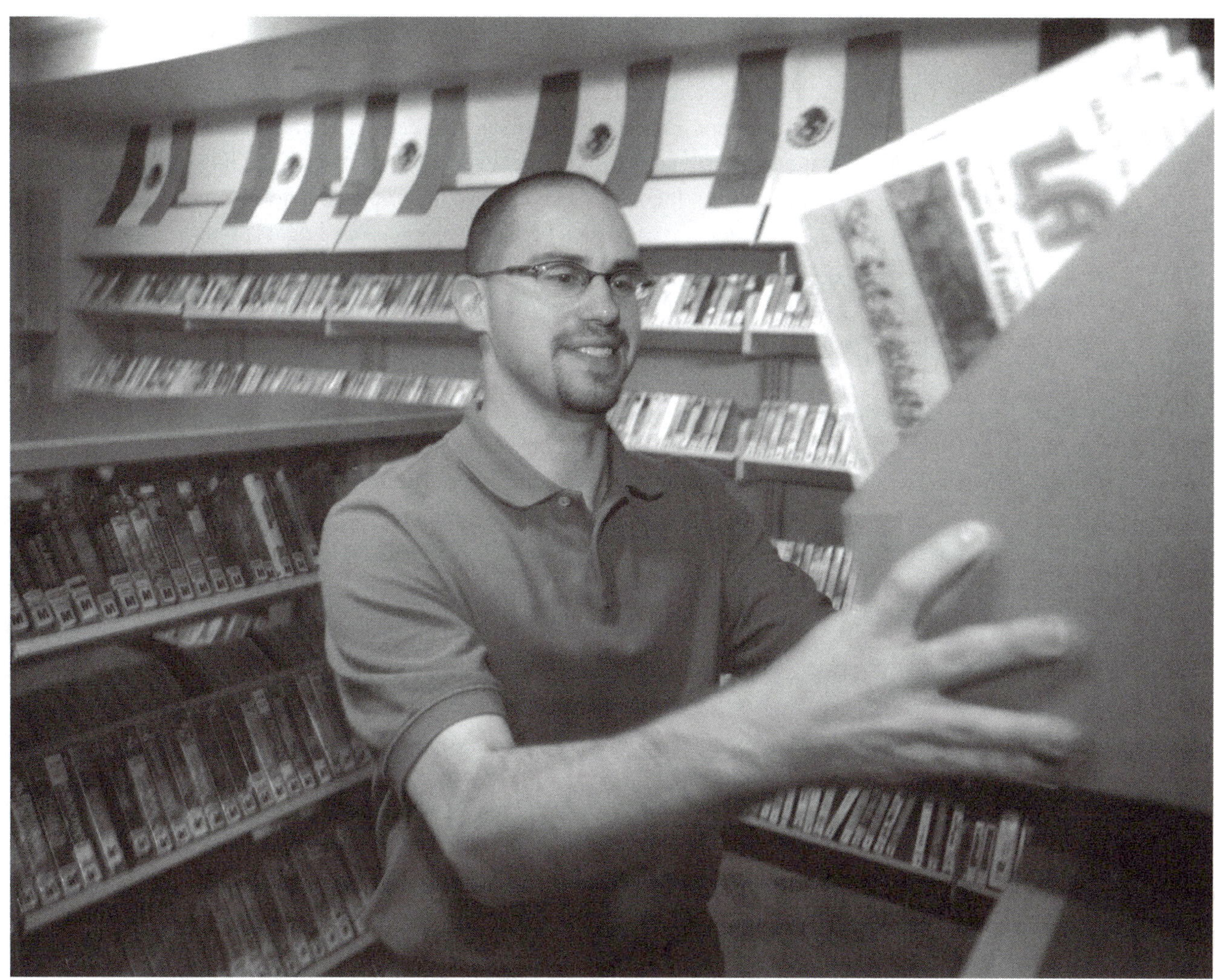

In spite of the diminishing popularity of bilingual education, bilingualism is still a common cultural reality. Here, Mike Eitner, a librarian at the Denver Public Library's main branch, stacks copies of Spanish-language newspapers in the El Centro section, catering to Spanish readers. (Associated Press)

children in cognitive skills, especially in the ability to analyze the form and content of language and knowledge; helps children develop language and literacy skills that are transferable to learning a second language, such as organization of a paragraph and arguments; and helps non-English-speaking students maintain their native language and culture. Opponents contend that bilingual education is not needed because, historically, non-English-speaking European immigrants in the late nineteenth and early twentieth centuries succeeded without federally sponsored bilingual education programs; because it slows down the transition of LEP students to the regular English program by totally or almost totally separating LEP students from other English-speaking children and by reducing the amount of time spent on learning English; and because it encourages ethnic separation and ethnic tribalism in schools and in society by reinforcing the loyalty of LEP students to their native languages and by delaying their integration into the English-speaking society.

In recent years, public sentiment against transitional bilingual education programs has been rising. In 1997, California voters endorsed Proposition 227, which largely eliminated bilingual education in California public schools. In 2000, Arizona voters passed Proposition 203, an initiative similar to Proposition 227. In both states, the proportion of LEP students in bilingual education classes declined from about one-third to 11 percent after the initiatives became

Lau v. Nichols (1973)

In 1973, the U.S. Supreme Court issued its decision in *Lau v. Nichols*, ruling that the San Francisco public school system violated the Civil Rights Act of 1964 by denying non-English-speaking students of Chinese ancestry a meaningful opportunity to participate in the public educational program. The decision stated that "merely by providing students with the same facilities, textbooks, teachers, and curriculum," the school district failed in its obligation to ensure that they received an equal educational opportunity. The Lau decision was important because it extended civil rights protections to linguistic minorities, that is, to students who did not speak English, by applying the Civil Rights Act's prohibition on discrimination based on "national origin." If English is the mainstream language of instruction, the high court reasoned, then measures must be taken either to ensure that English is taught to students who have limited English proficiency, or to provide such equal opportunities by holding instruction in students' native language.

Lau was a class-action lawsuit filed on behalf of 1,800 Chinese immigrant students who were not receiving English-language instruction but were forced to attend academic classes offered only in English. It followed meetings between the growing multigenerational Chinese American population and school administrators. Chinese American advocates had conducted studies that demonstrated the needs of non-English-speaking children were not being met, but the school system had not responded with policy changes. At that time, the population of Chinese immigrant students was growing and large numbers of them were becoming disengaged from the educational process because they could not understand the language of instruction.

Khyati Joshi

law. As in the cases of California and Arizona, Ron Unz, a Silicon Valley millionaire, also financed and launched campaigns in Colorado and Massachusetts that placed anti-bilingual-education initiatives on their state ballots. While Massachusetts voters ratified the ballot measure, Colorado voters rejected the initiative in their state.

Overall, available empirical evidence seems to provide some support for bilingual education as a proper education *option* for LEP students. Well-designed bilingual educational programs seem to be as effective as other methods in some learning settings, but there is no clear evidence that they are more effective than other programs. The controversy over bilingual education has more to do with social and political concerns than with pedagogical concerns. Bilingual education is a political issue as much as it is an educational one, maybe even more so. Some believe that whether to participate in a bilingual education program should be the choice of parents and students. In this vein, to achieve the maximum from bilingual education, educators ought to move in the direction of enrichment programs to make all students truly "bilingual."

Philip Yang

See also

English-Only Movement; Immigration Acts. Documents: Bilingual Education Act (1968); Proposition 227 (1998)

Further Reading:

August, D., and E. E. Garcia. *Language Minority Education in the United States: Research, Policy, and Practice.* Springfield, IL: Charles Thomas, 1988.

Crawford, James. *Bilingual Education: History, Politics, Theory, and Practice.* 2nd ed. Los Angeles: Bilingual Education Services, 1991.

Biloxi Beach (Mississippi) Riot of 1960

The 1960 Biloxi riot represented the first indigenous African American protest in Mississippi during the civil rights movement era and began when local blacks attempted to use segregated beaches. In 1955, Dr. Gilbert Mason opened a medical practice in the coastal town of Biloxi. The area's beautiful manufactured beach immediately appealed to the young physician, a Mississippi native, and his new family. Yet Mason quickly discovered that local police only allowed whites to use the 26-mile shoreline. He joined the National Association for the Advancement of Colored People (NAACP) branch in nearby Gulfport and tried to make beach integration its primary objective. For several summers, Mason repeated his appeals at group meetings but never received a satisfactory response. On May 14, 1959, Mason decided to act without NAACP support. He and six of his black neighbors went to the forbidden beach and entered the surf. A city policeman made them leave, but Mason met Biloxi's mayor Laz Quave later that day to inquire about the specific laws he had violated. The mayor could cite no existing statutes but threatened Mason with arrest if he used the beach again. Undaunted, Mason asked the local board of supervisors why blacks could not use the facility. The group claimed that beachfront property was privately owned and that neither the city nor county, therefore, could determine who used it. Yet Mason investigated the claim and discovered that the county obtained federal funding to construct the recreational area. To ensure receipt of the needed financing, the state senate passed a bill promising to open coastal beaches to all citizens. Ironically, then, a Mississippi law made segregation of state beaches illegal. For the remainder of 1959 and into 1960, Mason prepared organized local blacks to use the beach during the coming summer. He named the project Operation Surf.

On April 17, 1960, Mason's plan commenced. Numerous blacks promised to participate in the so-called wade-in, but none appeared and Mason carried out the protest alone. After Mason swam in the gulf for nearly 20 minutes, two Biloxi police officers arrested Mason for disorderly conduct. The apprehension represented a turning point in the Biloxi civil rights movement because most local blacks reacted to it with shock and anger. An unshakable Mason planned to use the beach again the following Sunday, but this time he had the help of an inspired community. On the night before the demonstration took place, a cross was burned on the beach as an ominous warning to blacks who wanted the area integrated. The threat only galvanized the resolve of area African Americans.

At approximately 1:00 P.M. on April 24, 1960, over 100 black men, women, and children walked upon Biloxi beach to hold a "wade-in" in the Gulf of Mexico. It was the first locally organized nonviolent direct action protest in Mississippi during the post–World War II period. A mob of agitated whites met the group and told them to leave the area. When blacks ignored the warnings and stepped into the water, whites attacked them with pool sticks, clubs, chains, blackjacks, lead pipes, and a wire cable made into an 18-inch whip. The incident began what the *New York Times* called "the worst race riot in Mississippi history" (April 26, 1960). Local law enforcement officers watched approvingly and directed traffic while whites beat elderly blacks unconscious, hit women in the face with brass knuckles, and attacked teens with baseball bats. White airmen from nearby Keesler Air Force Base were attacked when they tried to protect fallen blacks. One white crowd even set fire to items that protestors left on the beach when they fled their assailants. Mason was patrolling the area in his car when he witnessed the violence begin. As the doctor exited his vehicle, five whites attacked, but Mason wrestled a pool cue from one ruffian and fought off the men. An officer who witnessed the incident arrested only Mason for disturbing the peace and obstructing traffic.

As the initial beachfront violence subsided, violence spread throughout Biloxi. Hostile whites surrounded the city police department, bus stations, restaurants, and bars to assault Negro passersby. Gunshots wounded four blacks, three of whom were women, while whites pulled others from their vehicles and left them bloodied in the streets. At dusk, nearly 500 blacks met in front of Mason's home to protect the doctor. Yet Mason turned himself into city police after treating injured blacks at his office and spent the night in a nearby city to avoid potentially deadly situations. As the night progressed, those present at Mason's home refused to leave. Others flooded the police station with calls requesting protection for their families and property. Deputies spent the night escorting blacks from their jobs to their homes, and many who could not obtain rides remained at their workplaces. Arsonists even tried to destroy Mason's medical office. Some blacks, though, exchanged gunfire with whites and wounded two attackers. Before the tumultuous night ended, officers arrested 22 blacks and two whites.

On the morning after the Biloxi riot, NAACP President Roy Wilkins sent Mississippi Field Secretary Medgar Evers to the coast to investigate the incident. The visit resulted in the formation of a Biloxi NAACP branch and initiation of a legal battle to open local beaches to people of all races. On May 17, 1960, exactly six years after the release of the *Brown v. Board of Education* verdict, the U.S. Department of Justice filed a lawsuit against public officials in Harrison County and Biloxi to desegregate area beaches. The case marked the first of its kind filed by the federal government due to the acceptance of federal funds by a state in exchange for a public recreation area. In 1972, over six years after the original trial occurred, the long battle to desegregate Mississippi beaches ended with all citizens legally free to use the public area. The final verdict represented a formality, as local officials had long accepted the inevitability of beach integration and had allowed blacks use of the facilities since the mid-1960s.

J. Michael Butler

See also

Medgar Evers Assassination. Documents: The Governor's Commission Report on the Watts Riots (1965); Cyrus R. Vance's Report on the Riots in Detroit (1967)

Further Reading:

Butler, J. Michael. "The Mississippi State Sovereignty Commission and Harrison County Beach Integration, 1959–1963: A Cotton-Patch Gestapo?" *Journal of Southern History* 68 (February 2002): 107–48.

Mason, Gilbert R., with James P. Smith. *Beaches, Blood, and Ballots: A Black Doctor's Civil Rights Struggle*. Jackson: University Press of Mississippi, 2000.

Biological Determinism

The idea that race is a biologically fixed category is a pervasive one around the world. Biological determinism holds that stemming from the apparently embodied nature of race it follows that moral and intellectual capacities are also inherited. Hence, different races are believed to have different aptitudes and inclinations, making them more or less suited to particular occupations, for instance. As different occupations are differently compensated, social stratification is believed to result from and provide evidence for a natural racial hierarchy. This has also played a major role in criminological explanations that argue that some races are more apt to break the law than others, as well as in medicine where it has been argued that different races respond differently to disease and treatment.

French naturalist Count Georges-Louis Leclerc de Buffon (1707–1788).

Generally speaking, biological determinism is the result of a transformation of authority in Western culture occurring between the 17th and 20th century in which religious definitions of savagery gave way to scientific definitions of race. During the European Enlightenment science and reason were ascendant but still circumscribed by dominant Christian theology. The fact that most non-Europeans were also non-Christian was perceived to be a deficit of their character. To be ignorant of Christianity was synonymous with savagery, whereas to be saved was to be civilized. In contrast to religious and folk beliefs about race, science saw itself as eminently rational, immune to emotion, and unfettered by superstition. The "fact" of race was established by such continental scholars as Georges-Louis Leclerc, Comte de Buffon, and Johann Blumenbach. The institution of slavery was a crucial economic force driving this transformation, particularly in the Americas where legislators used law and policy to reduce Africans to chattel slavery, with religion and science providing the justification.

By the mid-19th century, around the time the social sciences of anthropology, psychology, and sociology were coming into being as formalized academic disciplines, biological determinism was prevalent. In the United States science was deployed to attack the claims of the abolitionists who claimed that slavery was immoral through studies that proved that blacks and Indians were inferior. For example, the earliest physical anthropologists such as Samuel Morton and Louis Agassiz claimed there was a connection between cranial capacity and intelligence. They felt that culture was biologically determined and physical measurements of skulls could be used to devise a ranking of cultures. Josiah Nott, Morton's student, carried this line of thinking a step further by arguing that blacks and whites were of separate species. Still others argued that nonwhite races were morally and intellectually like children, with whites taking up the role of parent by guiding and disciplining their wards. Africans were thus better off under slavery than freed. All of this scientific debate was especially useful to proslavery forces in their efforts to lobby against the abolitionists. The longstanding belief in a hierarchy of races was echoed by science and codified in law by the Supreme Court of the United States in *Dred Scott v. Sandford* (1857). Writing for the majority Chief Justice Roger Taney framed his argument by noting that blacks were "far below" whites in the "scale of created beings."

After the Civil War science and biological determinism were used to justify Jim Crow legislation, segregation, and American imperialism in the Pacific, particularly through social Darwinism, which became an increasingly dominant ideology as legislators and business moguls poured money into university studies and magazine features to convince a public ready to believe in the powers of science. Returning to Thomas Hobbes's notion of man in the state of nature as a war of all against all, the social Darwinists argued that those with the most privilege in life were at the top because they deserved to be. Since structural inequality was natural, stemming from the biological inferiority of the lower classes, government intervention to provide public services like education and health care or to provide for a minimum wage was morally wrong because it prevented the weak from being weeded out. This illustrates how arguments for superior and inferior races coincided with American cultural beliefs about personal responsibility and individualism.

The most vocal proponent of social Darwinism was Herbert Spencer, an Englishman and acquaintance of Charles Darwin, who coined the phrase "survival of the fittest." The principal tenet of Spencer's argument was that society was like a living organism. Social institutions like families and government could be made to fit into an evolutionary framework. It was possible then for the social sciences to dispassionately compare human cultures to one another and accurately measure the relative degrees of superiority between them. Biologically deterministic theories were not only useful in maintaining racist structural inequalities; they also helped to uphold patriarchy by explaining the inherent inferiority of women to men. Additionally, as the American economy shifted from one based on agriculture to industrial capitalism, social Darwinism explained class differences and how the fittest individuals became the wealthiest while the poor were to remain laborers because of their natural inferiority.

Biological determinism in science was not only a response to cultural norms; it served to intensify them and the significance of a belief in races. The rather weak science behind biological determinism appears more substantial than it really is because it echoed the cultural beliefs of its audience.

MATTHEW D. THOMPSON

See also

Bell Curve: Intelligence and Class Structure in American Life; Racial Taxonomy

Further Reading:

Baker, Lee D. *From Savage to Negro: Anthropology and the Construction of Race, 1896–1954*. Berkeley: University of California Press, 1998.

Blakey, Michael L. "Skull Doctors: Intrinsic Social and Political Bias in the History of American Physical Anthropology." *Critique of Anthropology* 2 (1987): 7–35.

Gossett, T. F. *Race, the History of an Idea in America*. Dallas: Southern Methodist University Press, 1963.

Gould, Stephen J. *The Mismeasure of Man*. New York: W. W. Norton, 1981.

Greene, J. C. *Science, Ideology, and World View*. Berkeley: University of California Press, 1981.

Biological Racism

Biological racism refers to the idea that the races are biologically different and that some races are superior to others in intelligence and moral characteristics. Biological racism was most popular in the United States in the 1920s, when IQ tests were first developed. It also took the form of anti-immigrant reactions to the influx of non-Protestant immigrants from Southern, Central, and Eastern European countries, the influx that peaked in the first decade of the 20th century. Biological racism thus provided the intellectual justification for the Immigration Act of 1924, which drastically restricted immigration from these regions of Europe, as well as for the eugenics movement and antimiscegenation laws.

Madison Grant was the champion of the idea of biological differences among racial groups. In his 1916 book, *The Passing of the Great Race*, he argued that the races were in fact subspecies of man and that the "Nordic" race—those with light hair and eyes—was superior to "Negroid" and "Mongoloid" races. Grant argued against the idea that all people are created equal. Instead, he maintained that there were clear and immutable differences among the races that were reflected in physical attributes such as height, skin and eye color, and skull shape. He further argued that these physical characteristics were associated with spiritual, intellectual, and temperamental traits. He argued that the "white race"—the so-called great race of the title of his book—was in jeopardy of being dominated by what he considered to be the inferior races.

A foundation of biological racism is the idea of hereditarianism. Hereditarianism dates back to the late 19th and early 20th centuries, when Charles Darwin's ideas of evolution dominated much of the intellectual world. Darwin's theory of evolution posited that beneficial traits evolved through natural selection and that only the fittest species survive. This idea was later applied to human beings and called social Darwinism. Social Darwinism held that people who were successful were fundamentally more "fit" than people who were not successful; that is, nature rewarded those who were biologically superior. The rich, therefore, were argued to be biologically different, and superior, from the poor overall.

Social Darwinists further argued that biologically inferior people passed that inferiority to their children. Similarly, they thought that biological superiority was also inherited. Based on this idea, hereditarians of the late 19th and early 20th centuries supported both limiting the reproduction of those thought to be biologically inferior and antimiscegenation laws that would prevent the race mixing they feared would degrade the white race. The attempt to limit reproduction of people deemed unfit—and in extreme cases such as Nazi Germany, the mass murder of such people to promote biological "purity"—is known as eugenics.

Social Darwinism has little to do with Darwin's ideas. Social Darwinism, particularly as it was understood in the Progressive Era, has more in common with the theories of Jean-Baptiste Lamarck. Lamarck, a French naturalist who achieved prominence during the early 1800s, developed a theory of evolution based on transmutation and the ability of each generation to inherit the traits acquired by its ancestors. Lamarck's theories had largely been discredited by the 1900s. Nonetheless, social Darwinists such as Herbert Spencer and Sir Francis Galton had popularized the idea that human character is inherited. This social theory provided so-called scientific facts used to define the political debates over race, poverty, and immigration. One of the unique features about biological racism is its appeal to science to answer questions that normally are viewed as political or moral. Political and moral judgments are always subjective. Science is supposed to be objective. Biologically based arguments about racial differences can be particularly powerful because they claim to be objective fact. If specific racial groups are inherently inferior, for example, as some scientists at the turn of the century argued, then politicians who wanted to limit immigration could claim that what they were advocating was common sense, based on science, not political ideology.

In the early 20th century, Lewis Terman, a Stanford University psychologist, popularized widespread IQ testing in the United States. Following the eugenicist movement of the time, Terman worried that individuals with low IQ scores could lower the quality of American "stock"—the biological fitness of the American population. As a result, he was a strong supporter of immigration restrictions and of sterilizing men and women with low IQ scores or other "undesirable" traits, such as mental illness. Like many eugenicists of the time, Terman believed that intelligence, morality, and other human traits were linked and heritable; therefore, he viewed limiting or eliminating the reproduction of people with those characteristics as sound goal for social policy.

Persuaded by the hereditary argument of Terman and other psychologists, the U.S. Congress passed the National

Origins Act in 1924. A decade after the immigration act, fascism dominated much of Europe. Jewish refugees—one of the restricted groups—were turned away from the United States even though the total quota of immigrants had not been met. It has been estimated that 6 million Southern, Central, and Eastern Europeans were barred from admission to the United States in the 1930s on the basis of their nationality or "race."

Eugenics and the argument that there are significant biological differences among the "races" began to become socially and politically unacceptable after World War II. The Nazis in Germany justified the Holocaust on alleged biological inferiorities of Jews and other groups. The Nazi quest to produce a "super race" of so-called Aryans left many people deeply wary of claims that some "races" are biologically superior to others. Biological racism, however, has occasionally reemerged, particularly around social policies such as the Head Start program in the 1960s, which aims to improve the academic performance of low-income, often minority, children.

In 1969, educational psychologist Arthur Jensen published a controversial article titled "How Can We Boost IQ and Scholastic Achievement?" In it, Jensen argued that different racial groups have different average intelligence levels. Based on tests that he performed in the 1960s on school children, Jensen divided cognitive ability into two groups, level 1, simple functioning, and level 2, higher-level thinking. Jensen argued that level 1 abilities were distributed across racial groups but that level 2 abilities were not. He wrote that Asians as a group have the highest level 2 abilities, and blacks the lowest, with whites in the middle. Jensen argued that the differences that he found reflected fundamental biological difference only slightly affected by environmental factors. Therefore, programs aimed at improving the academic functioning of minority children would have a very limited impact.

Some contemporary scholars continue to argue that race is a biological category and that differences in ability observed among racial groups are inborn. These researchers are often called racists by their critics, a label that they strongly resist and view as detrimental to open academic debate. One of the most prominent and controversial contemporary books on race and IQ is *The Bell Curve* (1994) by Richard J. Herrnstein and Charles Murray. Herrnstein and Murray, like the social Darwinists of the late 19th and early 20th centuries, argue that social hierarchies reflect real differences in ability. In other words, smarter people are more likely to be rich and powerful. Moreover, they argue that this is not just true for individuals, that some groups, on average, have lower IQs than others. We therefore should not be surprised that some groups, notably blacks, do not do as well economically as other groups. Herrnstein and Murray do not argue that *all* blacks are less intelligent than whites. However, they do argue that there are real differences between the *average* cognitive abilities of East Asians, whites, and blacks that account for some of the social stratification that we see in the United States.

Critics of Herrnstein, Murray, and Jensen, notably Stephen Jay Gould, argue that their perspective ignores the well-documented effects of culture, racism, and testing bias in accounting for differences in IQ scores and social position. In his essay "Curveball" (1994), Gould accuses Murray and Herrnstein of omitting important facts, distorting statistics, and denying the political implications of their work. To Gould, much of the research on racial differences is politics disguised as science. Practitioners of this research, such as Jensen, counter that what they are doing is pure science that should not be constrained by political concerns. Being able to identify the biological basis of "racial" differences, however, depends on identifying the existence of distinct racial groups, which to date no one has been able to do. Race remains an important social and cultural category, but the most advanced genetic research casts doubt on the idea that it is a biological category. Thus, at this time observed differences in the IQ test scores and social status among the "races" cannot be attributed to biological differences.

Although biological racism typically targets blacks as an inferior race, this is not always the case. For example, in 1991 Leonard Jeffries, a professor of black studies at City College of New York (CUNY), made a controversial speech entitled "Our Sacred Mission." He claimed that Africans were the only true race and that all other races were a genetic mutation. He also argued that blacks were "sun people"—peace loving and community oriented—whereas whites were "ice people"—individualistic and aggressive. This idea is also based on the assumption of a biologically based racial hierarchy.

Gould has argued that the science behind biological racism is deeply flawed and that it serves primarily to perpetuate social inequality. In Gould's well-known book, *The Mismeasure of Man* (1981), he uses the example of intelligence testing and immigration policy to illustrate this point. At the end of the 19th century, Gould notes, H. H. Goddard, an early popularizer of intelligence testing in the United States, went to the Ellis Island Immigration Station in the New York Harbor, to test the various races. Groups that today are considered different ethnic groups, such as Italians and the Irish, were at that time thought of as different races. The concept of race—with its undertone of fundamental difference—implies much greater difference than the more culturally dependent concept of ethnicity does. Goddard found that, according to his measures, 83 percent of Jews and 79 percent of Italians were feeble minded. Several years later Robert Yerkes, a Harvard professor, tested people drafted into the army and found that they had an average mental age of 13. Yerkes attributed the decline in American intelligence to the infusion of inferior races through immigration. He was particularly concerned about Jews, Italians, and Greeks—identified by Goddard as inferior races—and advocated a restriction on immigration to prevent inferior races from diluting the intelligence of Americans.

Yet, as Gould notes, the low scores obtained by Goddard on Ellis Island could easily be attributed to the fact that many of those being tested had never seen the objects that the tests asked about. For example, the tests had questions about bowling, pocket knives, and other objects that may not have been familiar to the new immigrants being tested. The testing environment was also less than ideal. An illiterate peasant from Italy might have great difficulty understanding a test being administered in a new country the moment he or she stepped off the boat, regardless of his or her intelligence.

The idea that there are biologically based differences among "the races" has lost credibility among academic researchers. Some researchers have argued that there is little reason to see "the races" as distinct biological groups at all. Classifications such as male and female, for example, have a biological basis. It is possible to identify an individual's sex based on his or her chromosomal makeup, if not through visual inspection. There is no comparable test for race. If there is no biological marker—only a socially based visual classification—then how can we claim this category is primarily biological?

Legally, race has been defined in many ways. In the South, there was the infamous "one drop rule." This rule held that a person could not be classified as white if he or she had one drop of "black blood," meaning an African American blood relative. In the Jewish tradition, Judaism passes through the maternal line. The Japanese consider only those with Japanese paternity to be Japanese. Today, on the U.S. census form, a person can choose his or her own race. Race, most researchers agree, is a subjective, cultural category and not a biological one.

Biological racism is currently rejected by mainstream scientists, many of whom question whether there is any biological basis to the classification of "race" at all. In the popular debate, however, a weaker notion of biological differences among the races has persisted, and many people are surprised to learn that there is little biological basis to the idea of race.

Robin Roger-Dillon

See also
Biological Determinism; Racism

Further Reading:

Gould, Stephen Jay. *The Mismeasure of Man*. New York: Norton, 1981.
Gould, Stephen Jay. "Curveball." *New Yorker*, November 28, 1994.
Grant, Madison. *The Passing of the Great Race*. New York: Charles Scribner's Sons, 1916.
Herrnstein, Richard J., and Charles Murray. *The Bell Curve: Intelligence and Class Structure in American Life*. New York: Free Press, 1994.
Jensen, Arthur R. "How Can We Boost IQ and Scholastic Achievement?" *Harvard Educational Review* 39, no. 1 (1969): 1–123.
Jensen, Arthur R. "The Debunking of Scientific Fossils and Straw Persons." *Contemporary Education Review* 1, no. 2 (1982): 121–35.
Leslie, Mitchell. "The Vexing Legacy of Lewis Terman." *Stanford Magazine*, July/August 2000.

Birth of a Nation, The

The Birth of a Nation, a film by director D. W. [David Wark] Griffith, represented a watershed for both the entertainment industry and race relations in the United States. It debuted in 1915 and is recognized as one of the most important films in American history. The movie displayed unprecedented artistic mastery and pioneered such techniques as the close-up, long shot, chase scene, and climactic triumph of the hero. Yet, it also depicted Reconstruction as a lawless period because it politically empowered blacks, who were intellectually incapable of self-rule and consumed by their lust of white women. *The Birth of a Nation*, therefore, continued the dehumanization of African Americans that characterized national culture in the early 20th century and fueled the rise of organized terror against blacks, particularly in Southern states.

D. W. Griffith, a Southerner whose father served as a colonel in the Confederate Army, based *The Birth of a Nation* on two novels that North Carolina minister Thomas Dixon authored. Those works, *The Clansman* and *The Leopard's Spots*, portrayed the Ku Klux Klan (KKK) as a heroic organization that saved white Southerners from the clutches of sex-starved black rapists and the North's Republican rule. Griffith used the books as inspiration for his epic drama in part because the nation prepared to commemorate the 50th anniversary of the Civil War's end.

When filming completed, Griffith had produced the longest and most expensive movie ever made. It featured large outdoor battle scenes, nighttime fighting, and a celebrated 20-minute ride by hooded Klansmen. The spectacle recreated cotton fields and an exact replica of Ford's Theater, employed thousands of extras with hundreds of horses, and used over 23,000 square yards of white sheeting. Yet, it also conveyed the clear message that blacks could not be trusted with basic freedoms. *The Birth of a Nation* championed Klansmen as the heroes of Reconstruction who returned order and stability to a region ravaged by the Republican Party in the war's aftermath. The film also demonized blacks as the reason national reunion in the post–Civil War era took as long as it did, and provided justifications for the atrocities whites committed against blacks during the period. In various scenes, freed slaves assaulted whites on the streets, attempted to rape white women, prevented whites from voting, and used their political power to pass laws that legalized interracial marriage. The film's final version ran for 90 minutes and used 12 reels at a time when most movies were no longer than five reels. It cost over $110,000 to complete, but Griffith had his masterpiece.

The movie debuted on February 8, 1915, at Clune's Auditorium in Los Angeles under the title *The Clansman*. The local NAACP protested the picture because of its inflammatory and racist content and obtained a court order that delayed the initial screening. Several blacks boycotted the premier of *The Clansman*, but over 100 police officers stationed at the theater prevented violence. The presence of actors dressed as Klansmen who rode horses outside of the theater undoubtedly infuriated the demonstrators. Yet, audiences and critics responded with such enthusiasm to Griffith's project that he changed its name to fit its grandiose vision before the film premiered in New York City. He now called his work *The Birth of a Nation*.

In the days before its New York premier, an enormous billboard that portrayed a hooded Klansman overlooked Times Square and deemed the film "a red-blooded tale of true American spirit." But the National Association for the Advancement of Colored People (NAACP) tried desperately to have the film banned in their city before it arrived and produced numerous pamphlets that attacked the movie as racist propaganda. One such piece was titled "Fighting a Vicious Film: Protest Against *The Birth of a Nation*" and called the film "three miles of filth" (Lavender, 2001). New York Mayor John Mitchell, however, ignored the protests. As black denouncements of the film mounted, Thomas Dixon planned to undermine his critics. He asked President Woodrow Wilson, a former classmate at Johns Hopkins, fellow Southerner, and published historian, to view the film. On February 18, Wilson hosted the first private screening of a movie at the White House.

He concluded that *The Birth of a Nation* "is like writing history with lightning. And my only regret is that it is all so terribly true" (Chadwick, 2001: 122). The film opened on March 3 in New York City to organized protests, but became the city's most financially successful film during the era of silent movies.

In some areas, black protests proved more successful than they did in New York. In Chicago, for instance, the mayor refused to give the film a viewing permit. Cities such as Denver, Minneapolis, San Francisco, and Philadelphia followed suit, if only for a temporary period. Yet, it was during the Boston screening where opposition to *The Birth of a Nation* sparked a violent confrontation between blacks, whites, and local police. The Boston NAACP, in imitation of branches throughout the United States, tried but failed to obtain an injunction against any presentation of the film in the city. When the film premiered at the Boston Tremont Theater on April 17, approximately 500 blacks protested its arrival. Some blacks bought tickets to the show and pelted the screen with eggs when Klansmen appeared. Others ignited stink bombs near the movie's finale. When blacks refused to leave the lobby of the Tremont after the film concluded, police moved among the crowd swinging their nightsticks. The interracial brawl rapidly spun out of control as other blacks and whites quickly joined the fray. Mayor James M. Curley deployed 260 officers to stop the riot. The following day, Curley held a public hearing to discuss the film's future, which D. W. Griffith and approximately 25,000 blacks attended.

Curley decided to ban the movie for one day, but NAACP leaders wanted it banished permanently. When the meeting concluded, the unsatisfied blacks moved to the Massachusetts State House and demanded that Gov. David Walsh make *The Birth of a Nation* illegal throughout the state. Walsh initiated a bill to ban the film and all racially provocative films, but the bill did not pass a legislative vote. The Boston NAACP organized no other protests of the feature.

The Birth of a Nation had its most immediate impact on American race relations when it opened in Atlanta, Georgia. On November 24, 1915, a week before the film premiered in the Peach City, William J. Simmons revived the Ku Klux Klan by burning a 15-foot cross on nearby Stone Mountain. The group had virtually ceased operations when Reconstruction ended in 1877. On the morning the film opened in Atlanta, Simmons placed an advertisement soliciting members for his new organization in the *Atlanta Constitution* next to information concerning *Birth of a Nation*'s premiere. Simmons and fellow Klan members paraded in front of the theater where the movie opened and gave a 21-gun salute before the viewing began. Trains even brought rural residents to the city en masse to the event. Inside of the theater, vendors sold Klan hats and other related souvenirs. The movie inspired newly formed Klan chapters to redesign their costumes and adopt the practice of cross burning in imitation of the heroes of *The Birth of a Nation*. In 1920, the Ku Klux Klan claimed 4.5 million members.

The Birth of a Nation became the highest grossing silent film in cinema history, earning more than $10 million at the box office in 1915. By 1949, it had earned $50 million (Chadwick, 2001: 132). Yet it continued to attract protests in many cities after its original run ended. In 1938, a manager of an East Orange, New Jersey, theater planned to show the movie for a week at his facility. He stopped playing the film four days early because two prominent black physicians gathered a petition signed by 609 residents that demanded he cease. The petition claimed that interracial fighting erupted in local schools each day that *The Birth of a Nation* was shown. During the 1940s, the national NAACP continued to boycott any theater that screened the picture. Even its presence at film festivals and historical presentations sparked controversy. In 1978, a museum in Riverside, California, scheduled a viewing of the film, but local blacks pressured city leaders to cancel it. An area Klan chapter decided to show the film in a nearby park as part of a recruitment drive, but over 200 citizens disrupted the viewing and attacked Klansmen with baseball bats and tire irons. The melee lasted over five hours and resulted in the hospitalization of five policemen. Two years later, 12 protestors stormed a San Francisco theater where *The Birth of a Nation* played, chased over 100 audience members out of the auditorium, and destroyed the film. In 1995, Turner Classic Movies canceled their broadcast of a restored version of the film because of the racial tensions that engulfed the nation in the wake of the O. J. Simpson murder verdict.

The Birth of a Nation has been selected for preservation in the United States Film Registry, but its importance far exceeds its artistic innovation. The movie seemingly justified white racism, perpetuated an atmosphere of racial hatred that lasted for decades, and inspired the rebirth of the Ku Klux Klan. Few elements of popular culture have had the effect, positively or negatively, that *The Birth of a Nation* continues to have on American race relations.

J. Michael Butler

See also

Films and Racial Stereotypes; Griffith, D. W.; Ku Klux Klan (KKK)

Further Reading:

Chadwick, Bruce. *The Reel Civil War: Mythmaking in American Film*. New York: Alfred A. Knopf, 2001.

Dray, Phillip. *At the Hands of Persons Unknown: The Lynching of Black America*. New York: Modern Library, 2003.

Lang, Robert, ed. *The Birth of a Nation*. New Brunswick, NJ: Rutgers University Press, 1994.

Lavender, Catherine. "D.W. Griffith, *The Birth of a Nation* (1915)." College of Staten Island of the City University of New York, 2001. http://www.library.csi.cuny.edu/dept/history/lavender/birth.html.

Williamson, Joel. *The Crucible of Race: Black–White Relations in the American South Since Emancipation.* New York: Oxford University Press, 1984.

Birthers

Birthers is the name given to the group of people who believe that Barack Obama was born outside of the United States, typically in Kenya, and is therefore, under Article Two of the U.S. Constitution, ineligible to hold the office of president. This assertion is one of the most recent conspiracy theories to emerge in American politics. It has resulted in many lawsuits against Obama, which were designed to prevent him from assuming the presidency and later, to invalidate his actions since taking office. Many believe that racial prejudice is responsible for the strength and longevity of the birther theory.

According to scholars, the birther line of attack against Barack Obama began during his successful 2004 campaign in Illinois for the U.S. Senate. The attacks were started by Andy Martin, a perpetual candidate in the state who accused Obama of secretly adhering to Islam. In 2008, when Senator Obama was campaigning for the Democratic presidential nomination, his opponents began to question his citizenship and therefore his eligibility to be president. The charge against Obama originated in an anonymous April 2008 e-mail circulated by supporters of his chief Democratic opposition, Hillary Clinton, and it was made more forcefully in the general election against Senator John McCain when Obama's election began to appear more likely.

Despite being refuted by leaders in both the Democratic and Republican parties, the rumors of Obama being born outside the United States resonated with a significant number of Americans in 2010. An August 2010 poll conducted by CNN found that more than a quarter (27 percent) of the American public doubted that Obama was born in the United States and 11 percent reported that he definitely was not. The disbelief persisted in spite of the Obama campaign releasing his Hawaiian birth certificate during the 2008 campaign.

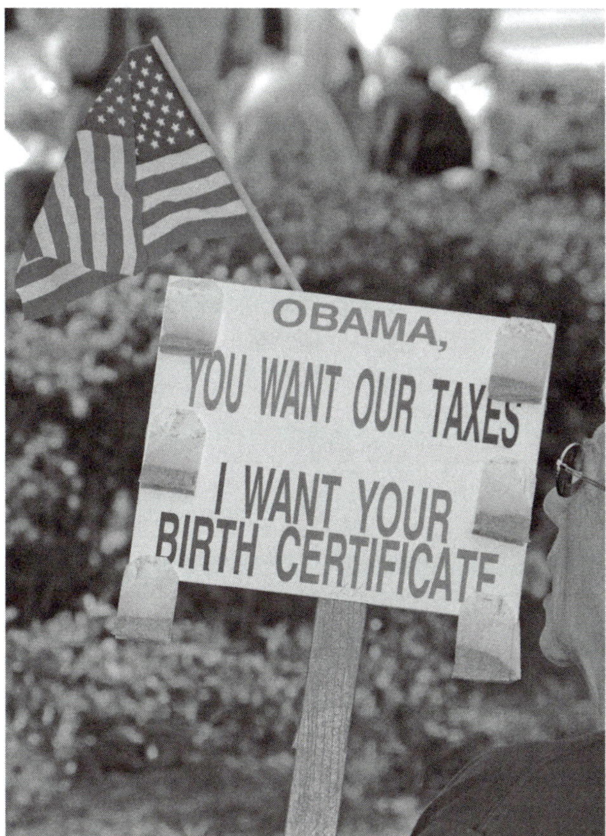

A Tea Party supporter holds a sign demanding President Obama's birth certificate. Tea Party supporters have been some of the most outspoken birther bill supporters. (Cheryl Casey/Dreamstime.com)

The document was deemed a forgery by the believers in the birther movement even though officials in the state of Hawaii confirmed its authenticity.

Those dismissing Obama's birth certificate insisted that only the long-form birth certificate, the release of which is prohibited by Hawaiian law, would prove him to be a native of the United States and therefore eligible to be president. In April 2011, President Obama released the long-form birth certificate in an attempt to put to rest issues pertaining to his birthplace and his eligibility to serve as president, claiming that focusing on these matters were distracting elected officials from focusing on the problems facing the United States. Obama's release of his long-form birth certificate followed intense media coverage of real estate tycoon and reality television star Donald Trump's questions pertaining to the president's citizenship. At the time, Trump was flirting with a bid for the Republican presidential nomination.

Birther-Inspired Legislation

As a result of the birther theories, several Republicans endorsed legislation to require presidential candidates to release their birth certificates to the public. In April of 2011, Arizona's legislature passed a bill requiring presidential candidates to prove that they are citizens of the United States before their names can appear on ballots. This requirement is for all candidates, but the text of the bill mentions President Barack Obama by name. Gov. Jan Brewer vetoed the bill. Similar legislation was under consideration in 13 other states at the time.

Many scholars believe that racial prejudice plays a part in leading people to question Barack Obama's birthplace. This is a claim that supporters of the birther theory, specifically Donald Trump, adamantly deny. Studies have found that whites demonstrating higher levels of racial prejudice are more likely to evaluate Obama's job performance as poor and are also more likely to view Barack Obama the person as less American. Low-prejudice whites more frequently give the president high marks for his job performance and are less likely to see him as un-American.

Birther theories have led to multiple lawsuits attempting to prevent Barack Obama from assuming the presidency or to invalidate actions he has taken since assuming the office. Every suit has been dismissed. Perhaps the most insistent birther is Orli Taitz, a California attorney who has filed multiple lawsuits challenging Obama's citizenship. In 2009, Taitz attempted to have two forged Kenyan birth certificates admitted into court as evidence. Both forgeries were rejected by the courts. In August of 2010 Orli Taitz was fined $20,000 for her suit.

In 2010, army doctor Lieutenant Colonel Terry Lakin refused deployment to Afghanistan based on suspicion that Barack Obama is not a natural-born citizen. Therefore, according to Lakin, his deployment orders were illegal. The doctor claimed that he deliberately invited his own court marshal, in order to force the president to show his birth certificate. Lakin was sentenced to 18 months of incarceration and dismissed from the army. To date, it is unclear what the personal costs of these legal actions have been to Barack Obama.

During the 2010 midterm election cycle, some Republican candidates expressed doubt about the president's birthplace, but the party leaders, including eventual 2012 Republican presidential nominee Mitt Romney, would not entertain the questions publicly. They attempted to steer their party away from the conspiracy theory, and on prominent conservative Web sites and blogs expressed concerns that the birthers' disrespect for facts were discrediting right-wing thought. Erick Erickson, editor of the RedState blog, declared that his Web site was not the place for people questioning Obama's birthplace, and talk show host Michael Medved speculated that the entire birther conspiracy might even be a conspiracy to make conservatives look foolish and disgrace themselves.

Deeb Paul Kitchen

See also

Tea Party

Further Reading:

Hehman, Eric, Samuel L. Gaertner, and John F. Dovidio. "Evaluations of Presidential Performance: Race, Prejudice, and Perceptions of Americanism." *Journal of Experimental Psychology* 47, no. 2 (2011): 430–35.

"My Fox Phoenix." *My Fox Phoenix Web site.* April 18, 2011. http://web.archive.org/web/20110428103934/http://www.myfoxphoenix.com/dpp/news/politics/state_politics/brewer-vetoes-birther-bill-guns-on-campus-4-18-2011 (accessed December 19, 2012).

Shear, Michael D. "With Document, Obama Seeks to End 'Birther' Issue." *New York Times*, April 27, 2011.

Smith, Ben, and Byron Tau. "Birtherism: Where It All Began." *Politico.* April 22, 2011.

Travis, Shannon. *Quarter Doubt Obama was Born in U.S.* August 9, 2010.

Verango, Dan. "Study: Racial Prejudice Plays Role in Obama Citizenship Views." *USA Today*, April 27, 2011.

Black and Non-Black Hierarchy

The concept of a black and non-black hierarchy refers to a social system in which being black is stigmatized and holds negative connotations, while being non-black allows for more opportunities and privilege. For example, in a black and non-black racialized social system, arriving immigrants might understandably distance themselves from African Americans, especially in social circumstances where being black or African American removes life opportunities. In such a system, being non-black signifies a less stigmatized, punished, or oppressed status. In this black-on-bottom\ everyone-else-on-top social system, blacks are thought of as a "polluted" class. Consequently, when given the choice, non-black individuals or groups would reject identity associations with African Americans, since their black racial designation leads to social subordination.

Sociologists and U.S. social historians have traditionally described the American social system as a white/nonwhite social hierarchy of race relations, where whites are at the top of this hierarchy. This designation comes from analyzing the results of slavery, slavery's subsequent legacy of discrimination, and the U.S. history of black social and economic disadvantage. However, the civil rights movement of the 1950s and 1960s did much to break down legal and social barriers excluding nonwhites from participating equally in American society. Consequently, the nation's demographic profile has increased in racial and ethnic diversity, shifting towards a more complicated demographic social pattern than merely white and nonwhite. Since there are now many more races and ethnic groups in America than ever before, the racial hierarchy today is a bit more unclear than it was before 1965. Sociologists have understandably begun to wonder where these other groups fall in the prevailing racial hierarchy, proposing that perhaps the racial binary of white/nonwhite is changing as a result of this increased diversity.

In American society, whites socially and numerically dominated all sectors of political, economic, and cultural life before 1965. It is therefore understandable why social theorists have classified the U.S. social system as a white/nonwhite hierarchy. However, perhaps this characterization made more sense before 1965 than it does now, as prior to 1965 the national population was almost entirely composed of non-Hispanic whites (85 percent) and blacks (11 percent), contained few Native Americans (<1 percent), and had very few Asian or Latin-American immigrant groups (<5 percent). Today, however, the U.S. population is not so obviously white and black, as it stands today at 63.7 percent white, 12.6 percent black, 16.3 percent Hispanic, and 4.8 percent Asian, with other groups composing the rest.

This rapid demographic and social change occurring since 1965 calls into question the now somewhat dated sociological description of the United States as a white/nonwhite binary system. However, characterizing the evolving structure of the racial hierarchy in the United States remains difficult. This is in part because recent immigrants and immigration streams since 1965 have effectively introduced a host of new demographic types and categories into American social structures. These new types include new demographic categories that were relatively nonexistent before 1965, such as "Asian" and "Hispanic." There have also emerged new racial phenotypes, including Asian and Latin American multiracial facial features. Finally, since 1965, new ethnic populations and cultural forms have emerged; for example, the socio-behavioral patterns of Asian or Hispanic language, dress, and political identities. All of these demographic shifts and newly observable racial and ethnic characteristics have made it difficult to uphold the black/white binary that traditionally dominated characterizations of American society.

However, despite the recent diversification of American society, most U.S. whites today display broadly similar attitudes, social patterns, and political orientations, exhibiting few ethnically variable differences. Such white socioeconomic homogeneity did not always exist but was instead achieved across nearly three generations, through what researchers call "classical" or "straight-line" assimilation. This is a theory developed mainly by sociologists Richard Alba and Victor Nee which argues that, over time, arriving immigrants follow a three-generation assimilation pathway into the American mainstream middle class; which is to say, into middle-class whiteness. This pathway occurs as the children of immigrants learn English and the grandchildren of immigrants fail to speak and display the languages and cultures of their immigrant grandparents' homelands. Assimilation research demonstrates historically and statistically that racial categories of whiteness, though once exclusive even for certain European immigrants between 1920 and 1970, have been subject to striking change. Indeed, U.S. racial boundary lines that formerly excluded from whiteness certain European ethnic groups such as Irish and Italian immigrant groups in the late 19th and early 20th centuries have been subject to what sociologists call "boundary blurring." In this blurring process, Italian, Irish, and Jewish immigrant groups have become structurally indistinguishable from U.S. Anglo Saxon whites. Essentially, this means that "white-ethnic" European immigrant groups, which were once not at all considered "white," have moved into the white socioeconomic and political niches that formerly excluded them. Ultimately, sociologists agree that the category of whiteness has been steadily expanding over the last century to incorporate ever more immigrant groups, blotting out many indicators of racial and ethnic difference in the process.

If new immigrants such as Asians and Indians from the subcontinent follow this path, then scholars have hypothesized that the United States will become a black/non-black hierarchy. In this system, blackness will continue to be stigmatized as whiteness expands to include more non-black Asian and Latin American groups. Statistical evidence shows that this black/non-black hierarchy is indeed expanding, as new immigrants from Latin America, especially multiracial and black immigrants, are not being assimilated into the white middle class. Instead, sociologists such as Min Zhou have pointed out that "downward assimilation" patterns are developing, where these immigrants are becoming enveloped under non-black racial categories. Further complicating the matter is that Asians in American society have been thought of as "honorary whites," as their socioeconomic status has in some cases outpaced whites. One example is in the area of educational attainment, as today, 42 percent of Asians and only 26 percent of whites hold college degrees. Because of these changes in the way new ethnic groups are assimilated or excluded from the category of whiteness, it seems more apt today to describe the American social system as a black/non-black hierarchy rather than a white/nonwhite one.

In the United States today, it is common for new multiracial immigrants who appear black to become stigmatized alongside African Americans. For this reason, scholars have begun to describe the U.S. social system as a black and non-black hierarchy, where blackness is penalized and being non-black is privileged. Many scholars, however, still refer to America as a white/nonwhite hierarchy where whiteness and being white is what counts. In either case, it is clear that race in America has much to do with the social status and economic prosperity one is able to attain, with racial groups designated as white enjoying much more freedom and mobility than those designated nonwhite.

Salvatore Labaro

See also
Racism; Social Construction of Race; Tri-racialization

Further Reading:

Alba, Richard D. 1990. *Ethnic Identity: The Transformation of White America.* New Haven, CT: Yale University Press, 1990.

Alba, Richard D. *Blurring The Color Line: The New Chance for a More Integrated America.* Cambridge, MA: Harvard University Press, 1991.

Alba, Richard, and Victor Nee. "Rethinking Assimilation Theory for a New Era of Immigration." *International Migration Review* 31 (1997): 826–74.

Alba, Richard, and Victor Nee. *Remaking the American Mainstream: Assimilation and Contemporary Immigration.* Cambridge, MA: Harvard University Press, 2003.

Feagin, Joe R. *Racist America: Roots, Current Realities, and Future Reparations.* New York: Routledge, 2000.

Lee, Jennifer, and Frank D. Bean. "Reinventing the Color Line: Immigration and America's New Racial/Ethnic Divide." *Social Forces* 86, no. 2 (2007): 561–86.

Zhou, Min. "Segmented Assimilation: Issues, Controversies, and Recent Research on the New Second Generation." *International Migration Review* 31, no. 4 (1997): 825–58.

Black Anti-Semitism

Among certain segments of the African American population in the United States, anti-Semitism and anti-Semitic groups can claim a large following. Claims made by black anti-Semitic groups have included the charge that Jewish doctors deliberately infect black children with HIV, that Jews themselves inspire genocide, and that Jews in Hollywood deliberately conspire to subjugate blacks. This black anti-Semitism probably arose out of the need for African Americans to hold the perpetrators of slavery responsible for their actions, and the leaders of various groups arrived at the Jews as a suitable culprit. However, only about 50,000 Jews lived in the United States before 1850, and most of these lived in the North, where slavery was already outlawed. If they did live in the South, many were urban merchants rather than slave owners. The number of Jewish families who owned slaves is estimated at a few hundred, at the most. Jews in the United States in the civil rights era were particularly involved in the civil rights movement's efforts to address some of these very problems, though the emergence of Black Nationalism was disruptive to this coalition.

Black anti-Semitism is also linked to general Christian anti-Semitic attitudes. Many American blacks are members of evangelical Christian denominations that hold that Jews, and all non-Protestants, are heathens who are straight on the road to hell unless they convert. Many of these denominations pick up on the anti-Semitism of the Middle Ages that blamed Jews for poisoning wells, spreading the plague, and murdering Christian children. Evangelical Christians are encouraged to proselytize Jews. Black anti-Semitic beliefs began to spread in earnest after Israel became the Jewish state. African Americans came to identify with the Palestinian people living in the region and saw Israeli attempts to solidify control over the region and protect themselves from Arab terrorism as domination over people of color in general. This attitude was intensified as greater numbers of African Americans began to convert to Black Nationalist Islam, thereby becoming coreligionists with the Palestinians. African American feelings about Israel, however, are not indicative of their feelings toward Jews in the United States.

A final source of black anti-Semitic sentiment is the fact that, historically, many of the merchants operating in predominantly African American neighborhoods have been Jews. This was particularly true before the mass immigration from Asia, as these merchants have increasingly been replaced by Korean immigrants, while the Jews have become wholesalers and landlords. The residents of these neighborhoods blame the Jewish merchants, and by extension all Jews, for the inflated prices, lack of selection, and disruptive shoplifting suspicions in operation in the stores. At times, the residents of these neighborhoods have responded to their dissatisfaction with riots. To some extent, the merchants in these neighborhoods are responsible for these policies. However, other conditions of doing business are also responsible.

One of the most well-known, and violent, incidences of black anti-Semitic behavior was the murder of Yankel Rosenbaum in the Crown Heights section of Brooklyn, New York, in the summer of 1991. Rosenbaum was an Australian student in yeshiva (an institute for the study of Jewish religion and texts) who was stabbed to death by Lemrick Nelson, an African American man, as a mob shouted "Get the Jew!" This event was part of race riots in the area between African American and Jewish residents that included destruction of property and muggings as well as this brutal murder. The riots began after an African American child, Gavin Cato, was killed in an automobile accident, but Rosenbaum had nothing to do with this accident and was just an innocent Jew who happened to be chosen by the mob as the person through whom they would vent their rage. Additionally, the mayor of New York, David Dinkins, who was black, did nothing to stop the riots.

Black anti-Semitic groups have picked up on such classic anti-Semitic literature as *The Protocols of the Elders of Zion* as well as publishing their own works, such as *The Secret Relationship between Blacks and Jews*. They have tried to claim, however, that they are not anti-Semitic, by saying that they do not believe in genocide or concentration camps. In other words, many of these groups believe that only the most extreme forms of anti-Semitism count as anti-Semitism. These groups also try to ignore the many examples of Jews who have dedicated themselves to working for black civil rights.

One of the most well-known black anti-Semitic groups is the Nation of Islam, a Black Nationalist Islamic group founded by Wali Farad Muhammad (born Wallace Dodd Fard) in 1930 and now run by Louis Farrakhan. This organization was originally set up as a religious movement aiming to help African Americans develop a sense of pride and civil rights. However, under the leadership of Farrakhan, beginning in 1977, the organization added outspoken anti-Semitism to their prior motive of fighting white domination. During and before the Million Man March in Washington, D.C., to strengthen the black community in 1995, Farrakhan made statements about Jews (as well as Asians) sucking the lifeblood out of the black community.

Mikaila Mariel Lemonik Arthur

See also

Anti-Semitism in the United States

Further Reading:

Baldwin, James. *Black Anti-Semitism and Jewish Racism*. New York: R. W. Baron, 1969.

Brackerman, Harold. *The Truth behind the Nation of Islam's "The Secret Relationship Between Blacks and Jews."* New York: Four Walls Eight Windows, 1994.

Black Arts Movement (BAM)

The Black Arts Movement (BAM) lasted from approximately 1965 until 1976. Its inception has been associated with poet and social critic Amiri Baraka's 1965 founding of the Black Arts Repertory Theatre/School (BART/S) in Harlem and with Fisk University's 1967 Second Black Writers' Conference, at which many BAM writers first connected. The BAM was the second major 20th-century movement, after the Harlem Renaissance (HR), in which African American writers and visual artists sought to define black creativity. Both BAM and the concurrent Black Power Movement operated under the auspices of a black aesthetic. Black Power participants were committed to the concrete ways, such as the Black Panther Party's free-breakfast program, in which black solidarity enabled independence from mainstream institutions. BAM members argued through their writing and visual creations that art was a means of affirming black cultural elements. Both groups articulated their notion of a black aesthetic through political statements, distinctive rhetoric, and Black Nationalist sentiments. For BAM, creative activities served to publicize debates about black identity and American race relations.

In part BAM extended the work of the HR. Commentators have described it as both a project that started where HR efforts ended and an attempt to revise the assimilationist attitude of some 1920s artists. BAM participants shared social perspectives with HR artists, including beliefs in the unique qualities of black creativity and in art's potential for expressing political views. Writers from both movements experimented with linguistic and thematic innovations, as in Jean Toomer's *Cane* (1923) and poet Sonia Sanchez's *We a BaddDDD People* (1970). However, BAM writers, particularly the poets, found public performances of their works and broadsides of individual pieces an effective way of communicating with a large audience.

Poetry dominated BAM writing, perhaps because it was relatively short and easy to publish. It also represented a malleable forum for political critique. The civil rights movement of the 1950s forms an important historical backdrop to BAM. The social and legal advances gained during that period seemed to lessen in the face of following events: the assassination of Malcolm X, the crimes committed against Mississippi's Freedom Riders and voter registration organizations, and Federal Bureau of Investigation scrutiny of writers with "seditious" leanings. Sanchez was under surveillance after she supposedly taught subversive materials, although in 1969 she helped to found the country's first Black Studies department and taught the first college seminar on literature by African American women. BAM poets explored the limits of U.S. democracy and defied conventional decorum in books such as Nikki Giovanni's *Black Feeling, Black Talk/Black Judgment* (1968), Haki Madhubuti's *Don't Cry, Scream* (1969), Larry Neal's *Hoodoo Hollerin' Bebop Ghosts* (1968), and Carolyn Rodgers' *Songs of a Blackbird* (1969).

Several BAM poets participated in writing collectives. The Umbra writers' workshop, a short-lived group that included Tom Dent, Calvin Hernton, and Ishmael Reed, emphasized the productive directions in which writing could shape the black aesthetic; they published *Umbra Magazine* and introduced live performance to BAM associates. Some members of the Beats, such as Jack Kerouac, imitated the performance techniques popularized by Amiri Baraka and Sanchez, unconsciously parodying as well as paying tribute to BAM innovations. Such innovations also overlapped with the experimental creations of high-modernist and language poets. BAM writers provided a structural bridge between avant-garde movements and unsettled the concept of "black poetry."

BAM included dramatists, novelists, and essayists who interrogated the movement's politics. Adrienne Kennedy's play *Funnyhouse of a Negro* (1964) examines the spiraling effects of racist social relations. Several books also commented on BAM's effectiveness: Ishmael Reed's novel *Mumbo Jumbo* (1972), Alice Walker's novel *Meridian* (1976), and Michele Wallace's cultural study *Black Macho and the Myth of the Superwoman* (1978). These works identify the sources of BAM activism and its drawbacks. In the mid-1970s a split between political activists and artists as well as government manipulations led to BAM's dissolution. Its legacy endures in the efforts of later African American writers to reconcile past social and creative triumphs with future goals.

Emmanuel S. Nelson

See also

Baraka, Amiri

Further Reading

Collins, Lisa Gail, and Margo Natalie Crawford. *New Thoughts on the Black Arts Movement.* New Brunswick, NJ: Rutgers University Press, 2006.

Gabbin, Joanne, ed. *Furious Flower: African American Poetry from the Black Arts Movement to the Present.* Charlottesville: University of Virginia Press, 1999.
Neal, Larry, Amiri Baraka, and Michael Schwartz. *Visions of a Liberated Future: Black Arts Movement Writings*, edited by Michael Schwartz. New York: Thunder's Mouth Press, 1989.
Smethurst, James Edward. *The Black Arts Movement: Literary Nationalism in the 1960s and 1970s.* Chapel Hill: University of North Carolina Press, 2005.

Black Bourgeoisie

The black bourgeoisie in the United States consists of members of the upper and upper-middle classes among African Americans. In 1957, sociologist E. Franklin Frazier's *Black Bourgeoisie* delivered what many thought to be a scathing exposé of the black upper class. Frazier's labeling of the black upper class as bourgeoisie is likely an indication of his critique of the group because of his Marxist orientations. He was skeptical of the black bourgeoisie's motives in leading the black community as he observed the group to have exploited the black lower classes as much as have whites, finding them to be narrow and opportunistic. Lifestyle distinctions, middleman politics, and specifically bourgeois interests defined what Lacy (2007) refers to as the "black elite." Frazier argued that politicians attempted to accommodate the needs of their constituencies, mostly poor blacks, to the interests of the white political machines in which they were embedded, or promoted a specifically middle-class black agenda, rather than incorporating the issues of interest to poor blacks into the political landscape.

The black elite has undergone some transformation since the first free blacks lived in the early 1600s. The distinction between house slaves and field slaves became the basis for the creation of an upper class of African Americans. Biracial children resulting from nonconsensual and consensual relationships between slave owners and slaves, often called mulattos, were often used in the house, rather than in the field, and were sometimes manumitted by their slaveholding fathers. Having such close proximity to slave owners, the often lighter-skinned house slaves were trained to speak differently and developed different skills than those of the field workers. These skills and advantages would later enable them to begin successful entrepreneurial efforts in the skilled trades, such as tailoring and blacksmithing, as well as domestic endeavors, post-Emancipation. House slaves were much more likely to be able to be educated, and as a result blacks with white ancestry had access to college educations post-Emancipation more readily than descendants of field slaves, and were able to begin a tradition of college attendance.

Jack and Jill of America

Jack and Jill of America, Inc., is a social organization of black mothers founded to expose their children to cultural experiences and to socialize with children of other like-minded parents. It was founded as a playgroup on January 24, 1938, in Philadelphia, Pennsylvania, by Marion Stubbs Thomas and 19 other upper-class black mothers who wanted to get together to provide their children with the social and cultural experiences in which they could not participate as a result of segregation. The organization grew over time as chapters were started across the entire United States. The group features cultural trips, activities, and programs, and is perhaps most known for its debutante cotillions, an elaborate coming-of-age ceremony common in upper-class society. Membership in the club is attained exclusively by invitation from a family who already belongs to the organization, or by marrying a person who is a member.

There is great distinction socially between the black bourgeoisie and lower classes. Attending different churches, socializing in different circles, and sometimes living in different sections of the black neighborhoods, the black bourgeoisie became increasingly distant from the majority of blacks, both physically and culturally. For instance, the black bourgeoisie were usually Episcopalian and Congregational church members, unlike the majority of the black lower classes who tended to be Baptist or charismatic. Drake and Cayton (1945) detail the distinctions among the Bronzeville, Chicago, black community's numerous social clubs and organizations among the black upper classes.

Higher education is very important to the black elite, but the choice of school is vital. Preferred historically black colleges and universities (HBCUs) include Howard University,

Dr. E. Franklin Frazier, head of the Sociology Department at Howard University, Washington, D.C., poses at his desk in Douglas Hall at the university, 1957. Dr. Frazier is the author of the highly controversial book *Black Bourgeoisie*. (Associated Press)

of which E. Franklin Frazier was an alumni; Fisk University; Hampton University; Dillard University; Spellman College; and Morehouse College. However, students from the black upper class are increasingly attending prestigious traditionally white institutions, as HBCUs increasingly serve black students with lower family incomes, less preparation for college, and no family history of college attendance.

Social clubs—fraternities and sororities—are also extremely important to the socialization of the black upper class. Lifelong public service is a large component of the expectation of members of black sororities and fraternities; much more so than that of white fraternal organizations. Despite the commitment to public service, social clubs were maligned for upholding their social mission by hosting balls and cotillions, arguably mimicking white upper-class social activities. The social mission of the social clubs and tendency to avoid activism are among the characteristics that prompted Frazier (1957) to argue that blacks' lives lose content and significance upon attainment of middle-class status. He characterized the black bourgeoisie as suffering from "nothingness," being without cultural roots and rejecting being identified with other blacks.

> **The Paper Bag Test**
>
> Preference for lighter skin among African Americans influenced many aspects of social, family, and professional life, especially among blacks in the upper classes. Around the turn of the 20th century, black social clubs and organizations used a number of methods to exclude dark-skinned people from participating in their groups. One method, referred to as the paper bag test, required applicants to place their arm inside a brown paper bag. The individual's skin color in relation to the color of the paper bag was used to determine whether the applicant's skin tone was acceptable. Those with skin darker than the paper bag were denied entry to the club or organization.

Lawrence Otis Graham's (1999) book *Our Kind of People: Inside America's Black Upper Class* can be seen as a response to Frazier's claim of the black bourgeoisie suffering from "nothingness." Graham, a member of the black upper class himself, provides a comprehensive history of the black upper class, detailing the important social organizations, educational institutions, neighborhoods, and industries that have shaped the black upper class as it has grown. New money and old money distinctions well known among the white upper classes are also salient among the black upper class. Careers in medicine, law, and business are deemed appropriate ways of amassing wealth, rather than entertainment and sports. Graham argues that the black upper classes in Northern cities were more fluid in terms of membership than were those in Southern cities, with Southern upper-class blacks. He also noticed that colorism among the black elite was less prevalent in the North than in the South.

Sociologist Karyn Lacy's (2007) studies of the black lower-middle, middle, and upper-middle class underscores the importance of a uniquely black identity to members of the black elite. Members of the black elite are both economically and culturally distinct from members of the black middle class, and with the growing black upper-middle class carving out a distinctly black middle-class identity, there may be more distance between the classes in the future.

Renee S. Alston

See also

Black Middle Class; Du Bois, W.E.B.

Further Reading:

Book Discussion on "Our Kind of People" http://www.c-span.org/program/Kind.

Drake, St. Clair, and Horace Cayton. *Black Metropolis: A Study of Negro Life in a Northern City*. New York: Harcourt, Brace and Company, 1945.

Frazier, Franklin, E. *Black Bourgeoisie*. New York: Free Press, 1957.

Graham, Lawrence Otis. *Our Kind of People: Inside America's Black Upper Class*. New York: Harper Perennial, 1999.

Lacy, Karyn. *Blue-Chip Black: Race, Class, and Status in the New Black Middle Class*. Berkeley: University of California Press, 2007.

Lacy, Karyn. "All's Fair? The Foreclosure Crisis and Middle-Class Black (In) Stability." *American Behavioral Scientist* 56, no. 11 (2012): 1565–80.

Teele, James E., ed. *E. Franklin Frazier and Black Bourgeoisie*. Columbia: University of Missouri, 2002.

Black Cabinet

Officially known as the Office of Negro Affairs, the Black Cabinet, or "Black Brain Trust," was a group of African American public policy advocates informally established during the first term of President Franklin D. Roosevelt. Originally created under the direct auspices of Secretary of the Interior Harold L. Ickes, the Black Cabinet came to serve the U.S. government from the early to mid-1930s and sporadically, and often unofficially, during the following decade. Consisting of a number of associates with diverse expertise in fields ranging from law, education, and political science, the Black Cabinet boasted as many as 45 members in 1935 and worked within the departments of the executive branch towards strengthening New Deal agencies to provide federal relief and civil justice for African Americans in the midst of a racially segregated nation.

The Black Cabinet originated largely as a response towards the racially polarizing effects of Jim Crow segregation, as well as the lingering outcome of the Great Depression and its ravaging consequences for the African American community. Stemming from the stock market crash of 1929, rural African Americans were devastated as cotton prices dropped dramatically from 18 cents a pound to six cents a pound. As more than 2 million African American farmers went into enormous debt, a number of Southern black sharecroppers left the fields for the cities of the North in order to find work. Occupying largely menial jobs such as train porters, maids, sanitation workers, and cooks, African Americans competed directly with whites, leading towards increased economic and racial tensions within the tumultuous and segregated environment of the United States.

Although largely neglecting the plight of African Americans during the first half of his first term, President Roosevelt began to take notice and acted to address the instability that resulted from this cultural convergence. To work within his New Deal programs, Roosevelt sanctioned the Black Cabinet to directly address the issues of African Americans in the age of the Depression. President Roosevelt's motives for endorsing the Black Cabinet were numerous in their design. Inspired by the words and actions of black orators such as Sojourner Truth and the grace and dignity of Marian Anderson, an African American singer who performed for state functions in spite of segregation, First Lady Eleanor Roosevelt became an effective anti-lynching activist and advocate for ending Jim Crow segregation. The first lady also served as a primary influence on President Roosevelt, compelling him towards the cause of racial justice as well as addressing the social, economic, and political inequalities of Jim Crow segregation. President Roosevelt's authorization of the Black Cabinet was a controversial yet distinctly political move. The creation of a Black Cabinet conflicted directly with the interests of Southern senators, angering those who were to serve as potential allies for Roosevelt as he doggedly pursued his New Deal plan for Depression relief. However, the formation of the Black Cabinet effectively secured Roosevelt's growing interest in acquiring the African American vote, as the cabinet came to represent among African Americans a viable and concerted effort to integrate blacks within the working political, economic, and social spheres of mainstream society.

The Black Cabinet worked directly with various government programs for farm subsidies, wider employment opportunities, and better housing and education options for poor and disenfranchised African Americans. The Black Cabinet also worked within the judicial branch to effectively challenge Jim Crow's grip on the legal system. Among its more prominent members were Ralph Bunche and Mary McLeod Bethune, both of whom served successfully as international representatives of the U.S. government. Other members included the National Urban League's Eugene K. Jones, and Robert Weaver, who would become the first U.S. secretary of housing and urban development. The Black Cabinet ended upon President Roosevelt's death in 1945.

KEVIN STRAIT

See also

Anti-Lynching Legislation; Roosevelt, Eleanor

Further Reading:

Gibson, Truman Jr., and Steve Huntley. *Knocking Down Barriers: My Fight for Black America*. Evanston, IL: Northwestern University Press, 2005.

"New Deal Agencies and Black America." http://www.lexisnexis.com/documents/academic/upa_cis/1399_NewDealAgenciesBlackAm.pdf (accessed January 2013).

Black Church Arsons

Black church arsons are slowly becoming a reemerging problem across the American South. Civil rights activists are confronted with terrorist acts by groups such as the Ku Klux Klan (KKK) and other white supremacist organizations that seek to regain the absolute power that whites held prior to the civil rights movement. White supremacists have targeted black churches because they consider any type of African American community practice a detrimental threat to white culture.

In 1866, the KKK originated in Pulaski, Tennessee, as a social group for Civil War veterans. On August 16, 1996, a federal indictment charged the KKK with a string of black church arsons in South Carolina, and more than 70 since 1995. Klan members Gary Cox and Timothy Welsh both confessed their violation of civil rights laws when admitting their role in the torching of the Mount Zion AME Church in Greelyville, South Carolina. Cox and Welsh were also implicated in the burning of Macedonia Baptist Church in Bloomville, South Carolina.

Arthur Allen Haley and Hubert Lavon Rowell were arrested on conspiracy and arson charges for a black church, labor camp, a Claredon County Service Center, and a black man's automobile. Haley and Rowell were also suspected of providing Cox and Welsh with deadly explosives. South Carolina's attorney general's office claimed that the KKK instructed their members to regard black churches as a threat to white power because black community actions advocate racial equality. Recent statistics show that the KKK has burned approximately 57 churches with black congregations over the past decade. Although cases of black church arsons are on the rise, they typically receive scant media attention. News groups usually cover a story of vandalism against sacred African American grounds with few follow-up reports.

In contrast, the Atlanta-based Center for Democratic Renewal (CDR) is the main group that conducts research on patterns of black church arsons. The CDR is an organization whose primary goal is to work with "progressive activists and organizations to build a movement to counter right-wing rhetoric and public policy initiatives" (Fumento, 1996). Mainstream conservatives are portrayed as racist criminals by the CDR. CDR researchers discovered that the great majority of individuals that are detained or arrested in connection with black church arsons are black. Racially skewed studies conducted by the CDR have labeled accidental fires as intentional. Furthermore, the CDR failed to report blazes set by African Americans themselves.

The National Association for the Advancement of Colored People (NAACP) plays a significant role in highlighting cases of arson against African Americans. On Thursday, February 8, 1996, the Department of Justice launched a civil rights investigation into a string of arsons across Alabama and Tennessee. The investigation was launched one day after the NAACP released a statement that they delivered to U.S. Attorney General Janet Reno asking the federal government to probe into how black church arsons violate civil rights laws. According to Wade Henderson, director of the NAACP's Washington, D.C., division, black church arsons are resurrections that bring back historically troubling memories for African Americans (Fletcher, 1996: A04). The work of the NAACP demonstrates a sharp rise in black political power in the United States.

NationsBank Corporation offered a prize of $50,000–$100,000 for information leading to the arrest and conviction of those involved in over 10 incidents of arson in the American South. NationsBank's efforts were meant to eliminate any possibility of future arson against black churches.

The Christian Coalition joined forces with black church officials to offer a repentant gesture for centuries of senseless violence. Uniting two powerful organizations brought peace between black pastors and the Southern Baptist Convention. The Southern Baptist Convention was created by an antebellum division between Northern and Southern Baptists over slavery. An apology was later issued by the Southern Baptist Convention for its racist perspective on black bondage. Ralph Reed, executive director of the Southern Baptist Convention, asked that its affiliate churches run a special charity collection on July 14, 1996, in an effort to raise approximately $1 million to rebuild several burned churches. Black pastors have received assistance from the National Council of Churches—a New York City–based faction composed of 33 Protestant and Orthodox denominations. Widespread cooperation among predominantly white religious groups and black churches is a symbol of a growing trend to terminate racial conflict in the United States.

A great debate exists on whether most black church arsons are intentional or accidental. Investigators often interrogate pastors and other church officials of their whereabouts when a particular blaze commenced. Judiciary committees are usually skeptical about how moral the research methods used by investigative groups like the Bureau of Alcohol, Tobacco and Firearms (ATF) are. Government officials noted that 10 ATF agents were discovered participating in an annual "Good O' Boy" meeting featuring Uncle Tom shows. Such practices have generated great distress among Americans residing in the Southern states concerning whether their civil rights are being safeguarded by responsible officials.

Gerardo Del Guercio

See also

Ku Klux Klan (KKK); National Association for the Advancement of Colored People (NAACP); White Supremacy. Documents: Report on the Memphis Riots of May 1866 (1866); Account of the Riots in East St. Louis, Illinois (1917); A Southern Black Woman's Letter Regarding the Recent Riots in Chicago and Washington (1919); The Cook County Coroner's Report Regarding the 1919 Chicago Race Riots (1920); The Final Report of the Grand Jury on the Tulsa Race Riot (June 25, 1921); Testimony from *Laney v. United States* (1923); The Governor's Commission Report on the Watts Riots (1965); Cyrus R. Vance's Report on the Riots in Detroit (1967); The Reports of the Oklahoma Commission to Study the Tulsa Race

Riot of 1921 (2000–2001); Draft Report: 1898 Wilmington Race Riot Commission (2005)

Further Reading:

Fehr, Stephen C. "U.S. Historic Trust Puts Black Churches on Endangered List." *Washington Post*, June 18, 1996, A03.

Fletcher, Michael A. "U.S. Investigates Suspicious Fires at Southern Black Churches." *Washington Post*, February 8, 1996, A03.

Fumento, Michael. "A Church Arson Epidemic?: It's Smoke and Mirrors." *Wall Street Journal*, July 8, 1996. http://www.fumento.com/wsjfire.html.

Mississippi Burning. Directed by Allan Parker. MGM, 1988.

Ortiz, Paul. *Emancipation Betrayed: The Hidden History of Black Organizing and White Violence in Florida from Reconstruction to the Bloody Election of 1920*. Berkeley: University of California Press, 2005.

Black Churches

The history of black churches and legalized discrimination predates both the mid-19th-century minstrel show, from which the term "Jim Crow" was derived, and the U.S. Supreme Court's legalization of "separate but equal" in *Plessy v. Ferguson* (1896). It is tied to the complex relationship between racial oppression and black resistance to it, as well as in the quest among blacks for self-determination and valuation. Black churches of the 18th and 19th centuries mounted their first collective act of resistance by embracing their own interpretation of the Bible, one distinct from that of white slaveholders. Slaveholders contended that the system of slavery reflected divine order. They based their supposition on "the Hamitic curse," according to which Africans were the descendants of Ham, the son whom Noah had cursed for mocking rather than covering Noah as he lay naked in a drunken stupor. Noah vowed that Ham would serve his brothers, Shem and Japeth, for failing to conceal his shame. The Hamitic curse laid the foreground for white slaveholders to stress biblical passages in the Old and New Testaments that seemed to sanction slavery and separatism, or verses that implied a hierarchy privileging whiteness and condemning blackness. Blacks, by contrast, embraced passages and narratives that emphasized liberation and egalitarianism, particularly Exodus in the Old Testament, and New Testament themes of redemption and inclusion. Despite the theological differences expressed over time in the proliferation of black churches and denominations, black Christians reflected a collective commitment to autonomy and valuation by establishing religious organizations that addressed their spiritual, social, and political needs, and afforded them unprecedented opportunities to develop leadership skills, musical gifts, and myriad talents.

African American resistance to racism and appreciation for autonomy is readily expressed in the establishment of the African Methodist Episcopal Church (AME). In the aftermath of the American Revolution, Richard Allen precipitated the first wave of independent black religious expression among mainline worshippers by establishing the Bethel AME Church in 1793 in Philadelphia. Allen and a fellow worshipper were told that a room in which they prayed was off-limits to blacks. Allen responded to discriminatory treatment by establishing a church where African Americans could worship freely. Although Allen's vision unfolded in a barn, by 1816 it had engendered the first independent black denomination in the country, one that by the dawn of the 20th century claimed congregations throughout the United States, Africa, and the Caribbean. The separation Allen initiated was based on social as opposed to theological differences and was a harbinger of the commitment to social justice and uplift that remained important tenets of the Black Church from the birth of the AME onwards.

Subsequent willing separations of blacks from predominantly white churches and denominations occurred after the Civil War, when thousands of African American Southerners, especially Baptists and Methodists, initiated a grand exodus from white congregations. From the late 19th century onwards, blacks continued to form denominations independent of white hierarchy and control. The seven largest independent black denominations include the African Methodist Episcopal Zion Church; Christian Methodist Episcopal Church; National Baptist Convention, USA, Inc.; National Baptist Convention of America, Unincorporated; Progressive National Baptist Convention; and the Church of God in Christ. The establishment of all but the latter two predated the legal birth of Jim Crow.

In the immediate aftermath of slavery, black churches focused on education, which they believed offered the surest defense against poverty and exploitation. They worked to establish educational institutions to serve newly emancipated African Americans. By 1952, independent black denominations had established numerous church-affiliated historically black colleges and universities, including Wilberforce (AME), Paul Quinn (AME), Tyler College (AME), and others. These institutions were springboards for a variety of social, civic, and self-help organizations. They were also cauldrons of social and political activity, where members were encouraged to engage in the political process. For example, members of the AME church in Florida played a key role in the election of black political officials during Reconstruction.

Black Methodist, Baptist, and Pentecostal women were indispensable parties to projects initiated by their respective denominations. They helped raise funds for educational institutions, mission projects, orphanages, convalescent homes, and other social outreach efforts at home and abroad despite their persistent encounter with various degrees and expressions of gender discrimination within the polities they served. The long-term impact of their involvement and the complexity of the projects they initiated usually depended on the general economic and educational standing of the church or organization to which they belonged. Generally, the richer and more educated the church, the more sophisticated the outreach.

When African American members of the various denominations traveled to state and national conventions, they had to make prior arrangements to live in the homes of blacks residing in the area of a given convention. Within the Church of God in Christ, for example, members attending conventions would agree to attend the services in shifts. Some attended the night services and slept during the day; others attended the daytime meetings and slept during the night. Regardless of the position held within the denominations served, blacks were expected to respect the rules of Jim Crow. Just as members endured the day-to-day indignities of Jim Crow, independent black denominations were barred from joining predominantly white religious organizations.

This unyielding backdrop of racism and bigotry helped precipitate the Great Migration, a period during which individuals, families, and sometimes even entire churches decided to leave the South. Black pastors, sometimes following their members, headed to the Midwest and West, where all hoped to find greater social, political, and economic opportunity. Black Southerners in migration helped create the progressive social era that emerged with the election of Franklin D. Roosevelt, whose administration set the stage for future civil rights reform. Black churches in Chicago were challenged to establish a variety of programs to assist new arrivals. Churches and denominations that offered adequate responses to the needs of migrants experienced phenomenal growth during the Great Migration. Those that failed to adapt to the changing needs of Chicago's black migrant community experienced a notable decline.

The gospel music tradition was one of the most dynamic examples of cultural creativity and resistance to emerge during the Jim Crow era. Black church musicians and songsters, particularly of Pentecostal and Baptist traditions, began to shy away from the accepted repertoire of sacred music approved by leaders of mainline churches, who at the turn of the century generally sought to facilitate black assimilation into American culture. This new generation of church musicians opted to compose songs that reflected the cultural and spiritual experiences of African American Christians. Using fast-paced rhythms and expressive lyrics, they treated a variety of themes in their songs, including struggle and triumph, suffering and healing, and, perhaps most importantly, power, especially the transcendent nature of divine power.

Black churches of the Jim Crow era experienced perhaps some of their greatest triumphs and trials during the civil rights movement, when ministers, churches, laymen, and organizations responded to the call for civil rights. Baptist ministers and others founded the Southern Christian Leadership Conference in response to the Montgomery Bus Boycott, with Martin Luther King, Jr. serving as the first president of the organization. Although black Baptist ministers were at the forefront of the movement, members and individual churches affiliated with the Church of God in Christ (COGIC), the largest predominantly black Pentecostal organization, made important contributions to the pre–civil rights and civil rights efforts as well.

Mamie Till Mobley, the mother of Emmett Till and a member of Robert's Temple COGIC in Chicago, fueled the movement when she permitted *Jet* magazine to publish a photograph of her son's mutilated remains. Mason Temple

COGIC in Memphis, Tennessee, the headquarter church of the COGIC, organized musicals and political rallies in support of the Sanitation Workers Strike. Suggesting the role Martin Luther King, Jr. thought the COGIC organization might play in the continued struggle for justice, it was at Mason Temple COGIC that King roused the audience with his famous "mountaintop" address, the last speech he gave before his assassination.

In essence, black churches of the Jim Crow era provided refuge against the social, political, and economic storms confronting blacks throughout the period of legalized discrimination. Churches fostered important opportunities for blacks to exercise leadership and organizational skills as they established churches, schools, and organizations to address the needs of the communities they served. They also provided critical space for aspiring soloists, groups, and musicians to nurture and hone their creative musical gifts despite the opposition.

Karen Kossie-Chernyshev

See also

Civil Rights Movement

Further Reading:

Best, Wallace. *Passionately Human, No Less Divine*. Princeton, NJ: Princeton University Press, 2005.

Butler, Anthea D. *Women in the Church of God in Christ: Making a Sanctified World*. Chapel Hill: University of North Carolina Press, 2007.

"Churches v. Jim Crow." *Time*, December 13, 1948. Printed at Time Incorporated, 2008, http://www.time.com/time/magazine/article/0,9171,799481,00.html (accessed June 12, 2008).

Cornelius, Janet Duitsman. *Slaves Missions and the Black Church in the Antebellum South*. Columbia: University of South Carolina Press, 1999.

Gomez, Michael A. *Reversing Sail: A History of the African Diaspora: New Approaches to African History*. New York: Cambridge University Press, 2005.

Kossie-Chernyshev, Karen. "A Grand Old Church Rose in the East: The Church of God in Christ in East Texas." *East Texas Historical Journal* 41, no. 2 (2003): 26–36.

Kossie-Chernyshev, Karen. "Constructing Good Success: The Church of God in Christ and Social Uplift in East Texas." *East Texas Historical Journal* no. 1 (2006): 49–55.

Rivers, Larry Eugene, and Canter Brown. *Laborers in the Vineyard of the Lord: The Beginnings of the AME Church in Florida, 1865–1895*. Gainesville: University Press of Florida, 2001.

Robeck, Cecil M., Jr. *The Azusa Street Mission and Revival: The Birth of the Pentecostal Movement*. Nashville, TN: Thomas Nelson Reference and Electronic, 2006.

Sernett, William. *Bound for the Promised Land: African American Religion and the Great Migration*. Durham, NC: Duke University Press, 1997.

Black Codes

The Black Codes was the term applied to laws enacted throughout the former Confederate states between 1865 and 1867. The Black Codes set out the specific rights of blacks following the end of the Civil War; in practice, they were used to restrict and control the activities of black people in these states, particularly in relation to their labor. The Black Codes were gradually ended by the actions of the federal government, including through the Freedmen's Bureau, and the establishment of Reconstruction governments. The creation of new state constitutions erased the Black Codes from the statutes. Nonetheless, the motivation that underlay the Black Codes survived and continued to shape the development of black-white relations in the years after Reconstruction. The Black Codes were distinct from the Jim Crow laws that succeeded them after Reconstruction, although both sought to limit the behavior of black people, and there were significant similarities.

In the chaos that followed defeat in the Civil War, the South struggled to make sense of its new reality. Of particularly grave concern to the white South was the position of blacks, particularly those who had recently been emancipated. Across the former Confederate states, whites were concerned that blacks would take revenge for slavery, and rumors of uprisings like those fomented by free blacks in Haiti were rife. At the same time, many former slave owners believed that blacks owed them gratitude and loyalty for the perceived benefits extended to them in slavery. Many planters felt betrayed when freed slaves left their plantations; the return of former slaves to a plantation was a source of particular satisfaction, an apparent endorsement of the benevolence of Southern slavery. Nonetheless, former slaves were at pains to distinguish between their slave lives and their new freedom; although most were polite and courteous to former masters, they now expected the same in return, a courtesy that many whites were loath to extend. Blacks who continued to live on plantations often preferred to create new houses, rather than to live in former slave quarters, and few were keen to establish close relations with former masters.

While concerns over the potential for black revenge and the loss of the Southern way of life were tangible, at the heart of the South's concerns was that emancipation would lead to the loss of the majority of the region's agricultural labor force. The antebellum Southern economy had relied on slave labor, and without that workforce, Southern agriculture was stymied. After the Civil War, many whites assumed that former slaves would leave the South, as, indeed, many did, draining the region of agricultural labor. More, however, remained in the South, and this raised different anxieties. Antebellum attitudes persisted, and fears that blacks were naturally inclined to idleness and vagrancy increased doubts over their willingness to work without coercion. Many farmers were reluctant to plant a crop when they did not know whether there would be a labor force to harvest it. While many whites complained that blacks were indolent and reluctant to work, it is perhaps more true that blacks recognized the parallels between paid agricultural work and slavery, and were reluctant to enter into agreements whereby they would work on the same plantation as they had during slavery, growing the same crop for the same planter.

Whites failed to acknowledge this fear. Agricultural labor was considered to be the only purpose for which blacks were fit, and most whites assumed that the natural inclination of black people was to idle, unless put to work specifically. The prospect of using white labor on a large scale was never considered seriously; indeed, a more serious prospect was the importing of Chinese labor or other immigrants, such as Germans and Irish. However, such ideas were contrary to Southern orthodoxy, and, in any case, the preference of the white South was for the slave labor force to be reestablished in freedom. The example of the West Indies, where former slaves had taken up small plots of land, causing the decline of the plantation system, was further reason to ensure that blacks were compelled to work on large plantations. However, the need for a guaranteed labor force, even more than the need to reinstate antebellum social and cultural norms, was the key determinant in the creation of the Black Codes.

Despite emancipation and its attendant fears, many Southerners assumed that the patterns of antebellum life would be reestablished quickly. Slavery may have been abolished, but white people continued to believe that blacks were inferior and should be subordinate to white society, and thus expected to retain control over their activities. Moreover, the abolition of slavery and the presence of so many freedmen threatened to undermine both the traditional Southern social structure and the South's main economy. Many arguments that had been used to defend slavery were once again brought to bear. Emancipation was derided as a Northern folly that had misjudged the disposition of blacks and given them unrealistic hopes and ambitions. Southerners argued that the North understood nothing of the black character, which was inherently unsuited to freedom without the paternalistic framework of slavery or some other form of white supervision. Blacks, particularly those who had been emancipated recently, would struggle to survive. Thus, they contended, it fell to the South to once again intervene to provide the necessary direction required by black people.

Presidential Reconstruction made it easy for Southern state legislatures to pass laws that placed blacks into a twilight world between slavery and freedom. The Black Codes set out the rights of blacks, but they also established pernicious labor requirements that severely limited their freedoms. Northerners accused Southern states of attempting to reestablish slavery, but the Black Codes, while impinging on many aspects of freedmen's lives, never went that far. Instead, freedmen in the South found themselves in an awkward position between the full freedom that they expected upon emancipation and the complete subordination of slavery. The Black Codes were a stern response to concerns in the aftermath of the Civil War, but they drew on diverse legal precedents. The slave codes and the laws that had governed the behavior of free blacks during slavery were easy models to reach for. So, too, were the codes that had been implemented in the British West Indies after the abolition of slavery there. Other existing laws, particularly vagrancy statutes, were used in the formulation of the Black Codes.

The first Black Codes were introduced in Mississippi and South Carolina in late 1865, and these two states had the most far-reaching codes. As well as being the first, they were also amongst the harshest, since the lack of agricultural labor would be hardest felt in these states. The Mississippi Black

The plantation police, or home guard, examine African American passes on the levee road in the South. Black Codes were used during Reconstruction to control and regulate the movement of former slaves. (Bettmann/Corbis)

Codes applied to anyone who was one-eighth or more black. In setting out the rights of blacks in Mississippi, the Black Codes recognized slave marriages, allowed black people to own property (although with limitations on where they could own land), make contracts, sue and be sued, and be witnesses in cases in which a black person was involved. However, the Black Codes also set out that Mississippi blacks could not hold public office, serve on juries, or bear arms. Interracial marriage and cohabitation was forbidden. As in other former Confederate states, blacks were not given the vote. Mississippi also reenacted laws that had formerly applied to slaves, but extended them to all blacks.

The specific details of the Black Codes in each state differed, but across the South as a whole, the purpose and operation of the codes was the same (in North Carolina, no formal Black Codes were passed). The Black Codes set out particular rights and freedoms that could be expected by blacks, but these were in essence restrictive measures that underlined the fact that the South intended to maintain the distinction between the races, with blacks in a position of impotent subservience. The Black Codes left no doubt that former slaves had become not free men, but free blacks, while the position for blacks who were not freedmen invariably became worse. This was most true in relation to labor, where states sought to ensure an adequate agricultural workforce. In all Southern states, the Black Codes were expressed in such a way that freedmen had little choice but to enter into agricultural labor contracts, and despite protestations to the contrary, there was no doubt that the white South considered blacks to be suitable for nothing other than field work.

Nonagricultural work was not closed to blacks, but was severely restricted, even for those who were not freedmen. In South Carolina, a license was required, along with a certificate signed by a local judge to guarantee the skill and moral character of the bearer. Furthermore, the employment opportunities of blacks in South Carolina were limited by a tax of between $10 and $100 for anyone who wished to engage in an occupation outside agriculture. This tax applied to all blacks and had a damaging effect on the well-established black artisan community in places like Charleston. In Mississippi, blacks who wished to engage in "irregular" work required a certificate. In conjunction with laws that prevented them from renting or leasing land outside towns or cities, and the refusal of the Freedmen's Bureau to provide relief rations to blacks who refused to sign labor contracts, these requirements left agricultural labor as the only option for blacks in several Southern states.

In seeking to protect the interests of planters in Mississippi, anyone who sought to entice a contracted black worker to break his or her contract could be imprisoned or fined $500. Various other aspects of the Black Codes served the same purpose. Blacks who broke labor contracts would forfeit wages already earned, and could be arrested by any white person. While protecting employers, this also severely limited the options available to black workers, who, despite their freedom, were denied economic mobility and were faced with little choice other than agricultural labor. The parallels with slavery were clear, and in most states, these were underlined by codes of behavior expected of black agricultural workers, and the definition of the hours of work from sunup to sundown. In South Carolina, the line between slave labor and free labor was blurred further through references to "masters" and "servants" on employment contracts. The Freedmen's Bureau rarely sought to prevent such obviously biased contracts, not because it favored the planters, as some blacks suggested, but because it viewed them as a temporary measure required to establish blacks in free labor.

The primacy of the South's concerns over labor, as well as its conviction that it could continue to intervene in the lives of blacks, was demonstrated amply by the introduction of apprenticeships. Apprenticeships allowed planters to compel black children to work for them if they were orphaned or were not being supported by their parents. Courts had the power to bind a child to an apprenticeship, for which the consent of the child's parents was not required. Former slave masters had first option on such children, and much about the system perpetuated white beliefs that they had the right to control the lives of blacks. The apprenticeship system was abused widely, and many children were bound into apprenticeships by Southern courts against the wishes of their parents. Since these children were bound under apprenticeships, planters were not required to pay them, further compounding the system's similarities to slavery. The apprenticeship system was a particular source of angst for freedmen, many of whom petitioned the Freedmen's Bureau and other federal officials for the return of children bound to such contracts.

In all states, blacks were required to have legitimate employment; those who did not were considered vagrants and could be fined or jailed. Vagrancy laws worked in conjunction with restrictions on the employment opportunities of blacks to further ensure a ready supply of agricultural labor. In many cases, people arrested under vagrancy laws were forced to work to pay off fines, thus further perpetuating the South's manipulation of free blacks for its own labor needs. In Mississippi, the vagrancy laws were expanded to include any black person who had run away, was found drunk, considered wanton in conduct or speech, had neglected his or her job or family, handled money carelessly, or was considered to be idle or disorderly. Similarly, anyone unable or unwilling to pay a new tax, the purpose of which was to support poor blacks, was considered a vagrant. Blacks were required at the beginning of each year to present written evidence of employment for the forthcoming year, or risk being classed as vagrants. In Alabama, vagrancy laws extended to runaway or stubborn servants and children, workers who worked too slowly, and workers who failed to adhere to the terms of their employment contract.

The introduction of the Black Codes established particular limitations to the employment opportunities available to blacks. As white Southerners sought to tighten their control over the means of production and force blacks into labor contracts, they also restricted activities and freedoms that had existed during slavery and that gave blacks some means of economic independence. In some states, hunting and fishing, as well as the grazing of livestock, were banned by the Black Codes. Some states ended the free ranging of livestock, requiring instead that animals be grazed on fenced land; such laws excluded those who did not own land from keeping animals. Other states banned blacks from owning guns and dogs, or imposed taxes on them. All of these laws were designed to further separate blacks from the ability to provide for themselves, compelling them ever further into agricultural labor contracts.

Other laws that supported the spirit and letter of the Black Codes were introduced across the South. Tax laws were reformed, ostensibly to assist planters amidst concerns over the availability of labor, so that even the largest landowners were required to pay only extremely small taxes—as small as one-tenth of 1 percent in Mississippi. At the same time, high poll taxes were applied to freedmen. As with many crimes during this period, failure to pay was punishable by enforced labor. Those who did not pay the tax could be hired out to any planter willing to pay the outstanding tax. This system led to the development of peonage—whereby people (predominantly black) were required to work to pay off a debt. The peonage system was open to abuse by planters, and many blacks found themselves in virtual slavery, forced to work to pay off debts with no way of knowing how much they still owed, or even if they had paid the debt in full. Thus, the Black Codes were part of a system designed to keep blacks powerless and economically dependent.

Despite emancipation, Southern institutions continued to be set against blacks. The Black Codes expressly set out the rights that blacks could expect. In most Southern states, blacks were now able to testify in court, although often they could not sit on juries. This did not change the way in which justice was served, and courts routinely found in favor of white people and against black people. In cases in which whites were accused of crimes against blacks, typically the accused were acquitted. Where whites were found guilty, sentences tended to be lighter than those given to blacks for similar crimes, and in several states, including Mississippi, South Carolina, and Louisiana, convicted blacks could be whipped, but convicted whites could not. Just as during slavery, the murder of a black person by a white person was rarely punished: of 500 whites tried for the murder of a black person in Texas between 1865 and 1866, none were convicted.

Although the Black Codes provided a range of laws intended to ensure an adequate agricultural workforce, planters continued to experience labor shortages, particularly through workers being attracted elsewhere by better conditions. In response, some planters tried different means of keeping workers on the land. This included paying laborers a share of the crop instead of a monthly wage, in the hope that workers would remain on the plantation until the crop was harvested, lest they lose what they had already earned. This system was ripe for exploitation, and many laborers complained that they were given a smaller share of the crop than that to which they were entitled. This system would develop into sharecropping, which would be used to keep many blacks landless and poor during the Jim Crow years. Indeed, aspects of many of the Black Codes were identifiable in Jim Crow laws.

The Black Codes were aimed primarily at ensuring that the South maintained an adequate agricultural labor force, but few Southerners were willing to accept that freed blacks should have access to the rights they assumed would be theirs upon emancipation. Many states created Black Codes that went beyond controlling the employment status of free blacks. In Louisiana, the behavior expected of agricultural workers bore strong resemblance to slavery. Bad work, failing to obey reasonable orders, and leaving home without permission were considered acts of disobedience, as were acting impudently or using bad language to or in the presence of the employer or his family. A sliding scale of punishments existed for transgressing these rules.

Restrictions were also imposed outside of work. In the town of Opelousas, Louisiana, freedmen needed the permission of their employer to enter town; any black person found without a pass after 10:00 at night was subject to imprisonment, and no black person was allowed to have a house within the city. In most parts of the South, large gatherings of blacks were forbidden for fear of fomenting sedition or inciting riots. In Mississippi, Black Codes made it a misdemeanor for blacks to engage in a host of activities, including making insulting gestures, preaching the gospel without a license, and selling alcohol. Similar restrictions were imposed by Black Codes throughout the South.

Black Southerners did not allow the Black Codes to go unchallenged. In Mississippi, freedmen petitioned the governor to assure him of their desire to work and to point out that they had no desire to rise up against former masters. The Mississippi petition asked the governor for clarification of the status of blacks in the state, given the apparent contradiction between the abolition of slavery and the terms of the Black Codes. In South Carolina, too, blacks requested recognition of their status as free men and asked for equal treatment. Despite the moderate language of such petitions, they were easily ignored by Southern legislatures in which planters had significant influence, but such petitions were noticed in the North and were a key factor in Northern criticism of the Black Codes.

The Black Codes were short lived as a legal entity. The large number of laws enacted throughout the South, and their openly prejudiced nature, made them an easy target for the Freedmen's Bureau and the federal government. From their introduction, many Black Codes had been struck down throughout the South, mainly as a result of being too blatantly discriminatory. From their inception, the Black Codes had provoked ire outside the South. Northerners considered them to be a barefaced attempt to re-create slavery and so contrary to the spirit of emancipation that many people, even those who did not necessarily support civil rights for blacks, demanded that the South respect the ideology of free labor. The pleas of Southern blacks for evenhanded treatment and recognition of their status were well publicized in the North, and helped to galvanize support for action.

Even within the South, there had been some concern over the Black Codes, at least over the speed and severity with which they had been applied, if not necessarily their purpose. In 1866, several Southern legislatures had reduced the severity of some Black Codes, largely as a response to the failure of the anticipated outward migration of former slaves, but also in response to concerns that their continued operation would attract unwanted Northern intervention.

The Civil Rights Act of 1866, which defined citizenship and established the civil rights of citizens, and the Fourteenth Amendment were intended in part to check the effects of the Black Codes. The establishment of full Congressional Reconstruction from 1867 onward saw the formal end of the Black Codes throughout the South, and Reconstruction governments removed the remains of the Black Codes from the statutes. Of particular significance, and as a reminder of the extent to which the Black Codes had been driven by a desire to control black activity in the labor market, the last vestiges of controls over black employment opportunities were removed.

Black children could no longer be apprenticed to an employer without parental consent. Perhaps the most insidious example of the Black Codes, vagrancy laws were rewritten to remove many existing definitions that had been used to ensnare innocent blacks, and it was no longer permissible to put someone to work to pay off a debt. Reconstruction laws also relaxed statutes concerning the enforcement of labor contracts, removing, for example, punishments for enticing a black laborer to break his or her contract.

Nonetheless, the Black Codes continued to have effect in many parts of the South, even when they had been abolished officially; this was particularly true where the Freedmen's Bureau and other federal officials had little presence. While the rescinding of many Black Codes prevented them from being acknowledged and advertised publicly, they often continued to be exercised. Vagrancy laws were particularly persistent, and blacks who refused to enter into a labor contract or who broke such a contract could still expect to be punished as though the Black Codes remained untouched.

While the legal instruments of the codes had been dismantled, the spirit that had driven them remained. Throughout the South, arguments continued to be put forth that blacks would not work without being compelled to do so, lacked the skills and temperament to work for themselves, and, perhaps most significantly for planters, were required as agricultural labor to sustain the Southern economy. It is undeniable that the Black Codes and their application were driven by more than a desire to maintain the Southern economy. Nonetheless, the demands of Southern agriculture and the influence of planters allowed the Black Codes to continue being applied, legally or otherwise, in the face of black protests and Northern condemnation.

The Black Codes sought to continue to hold blacks in a state of powerlessness and dependence on whites. The need for labor was urgent, but arguments to suggest that blacks would not work unless compelled to do so were largely fallacious and a convenient prop for the white South, which also wanted to perpetuate antebellum socioeconomic patterns. That the Black Codes reached into areas of black life beyond work was a clear indication that the South refused to recognize the freedom of blacks and expected to continue to treat them as they had during slavery. After Reconstruction's end, the Jim Crow laws that were instituted throughout the South bore many similarities to the Black Codes, particularly those that sought to keep blacks as a landless servile class. Although short-lived, the underlying impetus of the Black Codes belonged to a deep-rooted racial ideology that continued to shape the lives of Southern blacks well into the 20th century.

SIMON T. CUTHBERT-KERR

See also
Jim Crow Laws; Segregation

Further Reading:

Foner, Eric. *Politics and Ideology in the Age of the Civil War*. New York: Oxford University Press, 1980.

Foner, Eric. *A Short History of Reconstruction*. New York: Harper and Row, 1988.

Franklin, John Hope. *From Slavery to Freedom: A History of American Negroes*. New York: Alfred A. Knopf, 1974.

Litwack, Leon F. *Been in the Storm So Long: The Aftermath of Slavery*. London: Athlone Press, 1979.

Litwack, Leon F. *Trouble in Mind: Black Southerners in the Age of Jim Crow*. New York: Alfred A. Knopf, 1998.

Woodman, Harold. "The Reconstruction of the Cotton Plantation in the New South." In *Essays on the Postbellum Southern Economy*, edited by Thavolia Glymph and John J. Kusma. College Station: Texas A&M University Press, 1985.

Woodward, C. Vann. *The Strange Career of Jim Crow*. New York: Oxford University Press, 1966.

Black Family Instability Thesis

The black family instability thesis is a theoretical framework rooted both in the culture of poverty thesis and a pathology model that suggests that black poverty is largely a result of the instability of black families. Daniel Patrick Moynihan's report "The Negro Family: The Case for National Action," released in 1965, is largely associated with the black family instability thesis. In the report, Moynihan argued that the disintegration of black families was the main cause of black poverty. He presented the following data from the 1960 census to illustrate the instability of the black family: nearly one-quarter of urban black marriages were dissolved; nearly one-quarter of black births were out of wedlock; almost one-quarter of black families were headed by females; and increasing numbers of black families were welfare dependent. According to Moynihan, black family instability was the primary cause of their poor economic conditions. His study included comparative data for blacks and whites on factors such as marital status and birth rates, as well as statistics on nonwhite unemployment rates and Aid to Families with Dependent Children cases, to illustrate the growing number of female-headed families among blacks.

According to Moynihan, female-headed families are more welfare dependent and their children's educational chances are more limited, which contributes to their poverty. Because of the legacy of slavery, he argued, black families are far more unstable—that is, far more likely to be headed by females—than white families. As a result, family instability and poverty maintain a vicious cycle in the black community. Therefore, he recommended that the government should take action to strengthen black families so that they can escape from poverty. If poor black families were to experience stability similar to their white and black middle-class counterparts, national interventions were needed to alter the "tangle of pathology" that prevented them from maintaining nuclear families and experiencing economic stability.

Although the 1965 Moynihan report is mainly associated with the black family instability thesis, similar findings were intimated much earlier by W.E.B. Du Bois in *The Philadelphia Negro* (1899) and by Gunnar Myrdal (1944) in *An American Dilemma: The Negro Problem and Modern Democracy*. E. Franklin Frazier's chapter "Family Disorganization" in his 1957 *The Negro in the United States* also recognized the socioeconomic success of middle-class blacks and correlated poverty among blacks to matrilineal black families, negative urban conditions, and aberrant lifestyles. Moynihan cited Frazier's findings in his 1965 study.

Moynihan's black family instability thesis has been widely known to social scientists mainly because it has been subjected to severe criticism. The major critiques can be summarized into the following three categories. First, they have indicated that Moynihan stereotyped black families. Although his 1960 census data showed only one-fourth of black families were female headed, he emphasized the "pathological" nature of black families as if all black families were female headed. Second, he used white middle-class families as a norm in evaluating black families. Since 1960, the proportion of female-headed families has significantly increased for both the black and the white communities. Thus, there is a far greater diversity in family systems, and a two-parent family should not be a norm for evaluating other types of families. Third and most importantly, Moynihan focused on the effects of family instability on poverty when the two variables mutually affect each other. As has been adequately pointed out, black men's joblessness is the main determinant of black family instability. As a result of racial discrimination, black men have difficulty finding jobs, which undermines black family stability. Therefore, Moynihan's critics have pointed out that by focusing on family instability as the main cause of black poverty, Moynihan provided the blaming-the-victim argument. Although Moynihan was well intentioned in his attempt to help eliminate poverty in the black community, his cultural argument has conservative implications.

Sandra L. Barnes

See also
Illegitimacy Rates; Moynihan, Daniel Patrick

Further Reading:
Du Bois, W.E.B. *The Philadelphia Negro*. Philadelphia: University of Pennsylvania Press, 1899.
Fine, Mark, Andrew I. Schwebel, and Linda James-Myers. "Family Stability in Black Families: Values Underlying Three Different Perspectives." *Journal of Comparative Family Studies* 18, no. 1 (1987): 1–23.
Frazier, E. Franklin. *The Negro in the United States*. New York: Macmillan, 1957.
Moynihan, Daniel Patrick. "The Negro Family: The Case for National Action." Washington, DC: Office of Policy Planning and Research, U.S. Department of Labor, 1965.
Myrdal, Gunno. *An American Dilemma: The Negro Problem and Modern Democracy*. New York: Harper & Row, 1962.

Black Feminist Thought

Black Feminist Thought (BFT) or "afrocentric feminist thought," refers to a set of ideas produced by black women that comes out of the unique historical, political, and sociocultural experiences of black women in the United States. These ideas make up a social theory of and for black women. Essentially, BFT explains black women's understandings of their experiences in American society. Although there are certain commonalities that underlie BFT, the theory also allows space for the social variables of race, sex, and class. Thus, while there are universal themes expressed through BFT, these themes may be expressed differently by distinct groups of black women depending on their individual experiences with social oppressions and liberation struggles.

BFT explains that black women collectively experience a distinct world of social relations. This collective experience can be referred to as a "standpoint." As a sociological theory, this particular standpoint of black women derives from the communities and conditions in which black women typically live. It encompasses things like black women's unpaid and paid labor activities, and the unique social relationships black women tend to have with others at home and work.

The primary perspective encompassed by the BFT standpoint is a worldview of disadvantage. This perspective is historically differentiated from the more privileged positions enjoyed by populations that are not black and not female—specifically, the white and the male populations. BFT explains why this unique worldview of disadvantage is only available to those occupying the black-American-female's unique standpoint in American society. According to BFT, an individual's life is lived firmly within and according to the unique standpoints afforded their group based on gender, race, and class. These distinctions are socially constructed and often consist of experiences of oppression, including racism, sexism, and classism. Furthermore, BFT emphasizes the possibility that black women can have unique structural insights about society and social structure because of their very position of disadvantage. These particular insights are only possible from the bottom of the social hierarchy looking up.

In BFT, discrimination based on race, class, and gender are not seen as separate occurrences, but instead, are understood as interlocking systems of oppression. Black women have historically experienced all three of these levels of discrimination, leading to their general worldview from a position of disadvantage. Historically, black women have been marginalized by gender and often face sexism within the black community. They are consistently marginalized by race and class among white women, and are variously marginalized by class, race, and sex by everyone else. From experiencing this triple form of gender-race-class oppression, black women have come to know through lived experience that certain kinds of knowledge are only available based on the position of social privilege one occupies. Based on this recognition, BFT has created a theory of knowledge and society that reconceptualizes the social relations of power, knowledge, and resistance in U.S. society. Rather than upholding the utopian belief that power and knowledge are equally available to all American citizens, regardless of race, class, and gender, BFT holds that the level of power and knowledge one can attain is in fact highly dependent on race, class, and gender.

Because black women occupy a distinct social standpoint—one that is unique from black men or white women—BFT holds that black women experience oppression very differently than other groups. For example, black men are not subjected to the type of sexualized racism often directed at black women, meaning that black women experience oppression in their dual marginalized positions of being both female and black. Racism is evidenced as gendered when considering how many racially controlling images are also sexualized; for example, the stereotypes of the welfare queen, the jezebel, the mammy, and the hoochie. These stereotypes cannot apply to black men, demonstrating that racism is quite often gendered. Moreover, black women who are the specific targets of these racialized sexist labels experience sexism differently than their white female counterparts. The welfare queen, the mammy, the jezebel: there are no equivalent sexualized, racist stereotypes for white women. White women cannot be described by the racism of the sexist controlling images reserved for women of color, demonstrating that sexism is racialized. BFT, therefore, has two main premises. First, that sexism is always racialized, and second, that racism is always sexualized. This line of thinking allows BFT to reveal new sociological insights into theories of gender, race, and class.

There are four major consequences of BFT that lead to new ways of understanding how American society operates in regards to race, class, and gender. First, BFT rationalizes why there can be no universal, bias-free, or "objective" knowledge. Second, BFT explains that what is knowable depends upon *who* tries to know *what* and *why*. Third, BFT emphasizes that the creation, perception, and meaning of knowledge—whether that knowledge be scientific, social, personal, or political—depends upon the knower's own standpoint and assumptions, many of which are determined by race, class, and gender. Finally, BFT holds that these intersecting social variables of gender, race, class, and their corresponding social oppressions of sexism, racism, and classism are the very lens through which both individuals and groups come to perceive themselves, others, society, and culture. Essentially, BFT holds that how we come to understand ourselves and our society, along with the knowledge we are able to gain and the corresponding levels of social power available to us, are all inextricably linked to our race, gender, and class.

Perhaps expressed most completely and succinctly by *The Combahee River Collective Statement*, academic BFT largely originates from the discontent of black women's politically marginalized positions within U.S. society, academia, and the activisms of the 1960s and 1970s. In her 2000 book titled *Black Feminist Thought*, Patricia Hill Collins explains the history of subtle and blatant racisms which black women have faced while working within the male-dominated black liberation and black civil rights movements, and within the white-dominated feminist and women's liberation movements of past eras. These two experiences of half-hearted inclusion led women of color to the creation of academic BFT.

Essentially, mainstream first- and second-wave feminisms were dominated by white women. Because of this emphasis on white women's middle-class aspirations, these prior waves of feminism did not sufficiently address the needs or experiences of black women who had been racialized and concentrated into the lowest social class. Meanwhile, male-dominated black civil rights movements from the 1960s through the 1980s were liberation struggles dominated by the sexisms of its all-male church leadership. There was no room in these movements for the aspirations of black women seeking liberation from sexism and male domination. In fact, according to some Christian dictums followed by church organizers, a woman's place is subservient to men, explaining why women held almost no leadership positions even in the black civil rights demonstrations powered by women's efforts. Both Patricia Hill Collins and the authors of the Combahee River Collective Statement have used these histories of exclusion to justify the origins and functions of BFT, providing insight to those studying gender, race, and class and the social inequality, biases, and discrimination based upon these categories.

Salvatore Labaro

See also
Combahee River Collective (CRC); Discrimination

Further Reading:

Brown, Irene, and Joya Misra. "The Intersection of Gender and Race in the Labor Market." *Annual Review of Sociology* 29 (2003): 487–513.
Collins, Patricia Hill. "The Social Construction of Black Feminist Thought." *Signs* 14, no. 4 (1989): 745–73.
Collins, Patricia Hill. "Moving Beyond Gender: Intersectionality and Scientific Knowledge." In *Revisioning Gender*, ed. Myra Marx Ferree, Judith Lorber, and Beth B. Hess, 261–84. Thousand Oaks, CA: Sage, 1989.
Collins, Patricia Hill. *Black Feminist Thought: Knowledge, Consciousness, and the Politics of Empowerment*. New York: Routledge, [1990] 2000.
Hurtado, Aida. "Relating to Privilege: Seduction and Rejection in the Subordination of White Women and Women of Color." *Signs* 14 (1989): 833–55.

Black Like Me

In late 1959, John Howard Griffin (June 16, 1920–September 9, 1980), a white author, writer, and journalist, traveled through Louisiana, Mississippi, and Alabama disguised as an African American. His account of the journey was serialized in *Sepia* magazine and published in 1961 as *Black Like Me*, the title of which comes from Langston Hughes's poem "Dream Variations." Griffin's stated reason for the trip was to investigate suicide among black men in the South, but his real reasons were more complex. In experiencing life as a black man, he believed that he was bridging a gap between white society's perception of the black experience and the reality to which few white people were exposed. Griffin also regarded the journey as a challenge to his own beliefs and to his understanding of his own culture and, indeed, his own self.

Griffin was born into a middle-class Texas family, whom he regarded as "genteel southerners." His family considered themselves above the brutal racism of many white Southerners, but Griffin was nonetheless raised in an air of prejudice in which blacks were considered to be different from whites and therefore inferior. This sense of the otherness of black people would stay with him for many years, and would be

Author John Howard Griffin in 1964, known for his controversial and best-selling book *Black Like Me*. (Bettmann/Corbis)

both a motivation for and a theme of *Black Like Me*. For much of his life, Griffin wrestled with his own attitude to race and that of white society. At age 15, he traveled to France to take up a place at the Lycée Descartes in Tours. There, he prided himself on the fact that he shared the classroom with black Africans—something that would not happen in Texas—yet he was uncomfortable with their presence in the dining room, which his white peers accepted unquestioningly. Griffin reconciled this by accepting the French attitude to race as a cultural difference. When the Nazis invaded France, Griffin helped to smuggle Jews out of the country and recognized the Nazis' persecution of the Jews as groundless and inherently wrong, although he did not see parallels with the treatment of blacks in the United States.

While serving in the Army Air Force during World War II, Griffin was tasked with studying a remote island tribe, to ensure that they would ally themselves with the United States and not the Japanese. Griffin was fascinated by the islanders' society and fully immersed himself in their way of life, although he regarded them as he had black people in Texas, and as a white man considered himself to be superior. He accepted that the islanders had knowledge and skills that he lacked to survive on the island, but concluded that this was merely a cultural superiority, borne from their knowledge of that specific way of life. As nonwhites the islanders were "other," just as blacks were in the United States, and he remained convinced of the inherent superiority of white people.

After the war, Griffin returned to Texas. His eyesight had been damaged in a bombing raid during the war, and in 1946, he lost the use of his eyesight completely. Griffin did not allow his blindness to restrain him: during this period he married, had two children, and published two novels. Arguably the most important event of this period was that Griffin came to realize that he could judge people only by how he interacted with them, not by their skin color. Moreover, as a blind person, Griffin himself became the "other" that he had always considered black people. In 1957, Griffin's eyesight returned, and in 1959, he decided to undertake a trip into the South, disguised as an African American, an idea that had gestated during his sightlessness.

Griffin darkened his skin by using medicine typically used to treat vitiligo and exposing himself to sunlamps for up to 15 hours each day. In facing his own racial attitude, Griffin was anxious about confronting his own image with different colored skin. He was particularly concerned by what his new appearance would mean for his relationship with his family, and wondered whether their racial prejudice—however mild—was so deep that they would be unable to accept his new self. Indeed, Griffin's first glimpse of himself as a black man forced him to confront his own racial prejudices; so stunned was he by his transformation, Griffin struggled to reconcile his appearance with his own sense of self. This loss of self is a recurring theme throughout the book.

Griffin began his journey in Louisiana in November 1959. During his time in disguise, one of Griffin's stiffest challenges was to stop thinking as a white person and to experience life as a black Southerner. He was skeptical that he would pass as an African American, not least because he believed that he did not have typically African American features. Griffin soon realized the diversity of face shapes, eye colors, and bone structures in the African American community, and he was accepted unquestioningly as an African American by everyone he encountered. Griffin disclosed his identity only to Sterling Williams, a black shoeshiner whom Griffin had befriended in New Orleans before he made his transformation. Although Williams accepted that Griffin had to be the white man to whom he had spoken several times in the past few days, he continued to doubt that Griffin was, in fact, white. Nonetheless, Williams became Griffin's mentor in entering into black life.

Griffin's account of his experience reveals his horror at both the nature of the black ghetto and the open racism he encountered from almost every white person he met. He struggled to cope with the character of black life he experienced, even though he recognized that this was a reality forced upon black people by Jim Crow. The poverty and desperate situations in which he found himself regularly led him to despair and doubt about his ability to complete the trip (indeed, on at least two occasions, Griffin took brief breaks from his journey, spending time with P. D. East, a liberal white Mississippian, in his home in Hattiesburg, and with an Episcopalian priest in New Orleans). Many of Griffin's bleakest moments were a result of his treatment at the hands of white people, and he encountered regularly the humiliation that attended the daily experiences of black Southerners.

Trying to find work, he was rejected out of hand, often told bluntly that he would not be hired because of his race. His experiences of segregation—often de facto—saw him moved on in public spaces and making use of inadequate separate facilities. On a bus journey into Mississippi, he was prevented from leaving the bus to use the bathroom at a rest stop and came to recognize these humiliations in the faces and behavior of the black people he met. His encounters with white men often revealed their level of sexual depravity and fascination with the sex lives of black people. On one occasion, he was tacitly, but clearly, threatened with murder. In particular, he was stunned by the racism he encountered from white women, having believed strongly in the inherent virtuousness of Southern womanhood.

Griffin's experience left him despairing for white people who subjected blacks to a reality that was founded entirely on prejudices based on skin color. Griffin found that by the end of his trip, he had become reconciled with his appearance and his place in society as a black man. While he had not lost his sense of self as he feared he might, he had been transformed by his experience—he recognized that he had started to look and think differently, hardening himself against the next expected indignity. With black skin, he found that he struggled to talk to his wife, having assimilated the understanding that black men did not address white women. Just as Griffin's entry into black society had been anxious, so was his reentry into white society. However, just as he found that he was immediately accepted as black because of his skin color, so he found that his white skin instantly gave him access to all that had been denied him as a black man.

Although *Black Like Me* received generally positive reviews, and entered the best-sellers list, *Negro Digest*—the only black publication to review the book—was lukewarm, wondering whether a white man could truly understand what it meant to be an African American in the South. The publication of *Black Like Me* led to Griffin and his family being subjected to death threats to the extent that they spent nine months living in Mexico during 1960 and 1961. In the years following its publication, there was strong media interest in the book, and Griffin became a spokesman on race issues for much of the rest of his life. Until his death in 1980, Griffin continued to write and lecture on the question of race in various contexts, including the Christian faith.

Simon T. Cuthbert-Kerr

See also

Jim Crow Laws; Whiteness Studies

Further Reading:

Bonazzi, Robert. *Man in the Mirror: John Howard Griffin and the Story of* Black Like Me. New York: Orbis, 1997.

Griffin, John Howard. *Black Like Me*. San Antonio, TX: Wings Press, 2004.

Black Manifesto

The Black Manifesto, which was created in 1969, includes a demand for monetary reparations; a summary of the violence, crimes, and other oppressive acts that justify redress; and an outline of how the reparations ought to be spent for the creation of numerous black self-help programs, businesses, and institutions. The contents of the manifesto, as well as the way in which it was presented to the general public by James Forman, the director of international affairs for the Student Nonviolent Coordinating Committee, generated harsh criticism rather than sympathy. The objectives of the manifesto were never brought to fruition.

The Black Manifesto reflected the radical switch from nonviolence to Black Power in the mid-1960s. The Black Power movement ushered in a new era of black assertiveness and militancy. Also during this period, black youth rioted to protest the gross wrongs of racism, racial violence, and oppression in the ghettos. Thus, the Black Manifesto was a radical response to centuries of racism and a demand for atonement by whites, particularly white churches and Jewish synagogues, whom Forman believed were largely to blame. Reiterated throughout the document are statements that express a willingness to seize reparations through violence. The actual document is addressed "to the white Christian churches and the Jewish synagogues in the United States of America and all other racist institutions."

The introduction of the Black Manifesto was written by Forman himself. It includes an assertion of black consciousness and black achievement, and statements regarding the need for black self-determination and empowerment and the importance of bettering the lives of Africans around the world. He criticizes wealthy whites, capitalism, and imperialism. Forman also alludes to his reason for singling out Christians, whom, he states, "have been involved in the exploitation and rape of black people since the country was founded" (Schuchter 1970: 195).

The list of demands was written by an unknown author. It begins with a demand for $50 million and includes a list of programs that the money will fund, such as a Southern land bank to help blacks acquire land, publishing and printing companies, TV networks, a research-skills center, and a national black labor strike and defense fund. There is also an appeal made for black support of these programs and a proposal for the election of a steering committee to lead the "battle" to "implement these demands" (Schuchter 1970: 200).

In the final paragraphs of the Black Manifesto, it is acknowledged that violence is not desirable; however, blacks "are not opposed to force . . . We were captured in Africa by violence. We were kept in bondage and political servitude and forced to work as slaves by the military machinery and the Christian church working hand in hand" (Schuchter 1970: 202).

On May 4, 1969, Forman intentionally interrupted the services of the Riverside Church in New York. Although Dr. Ernest Campbell, the minister, had agreed to allow Forman to present the Black Manifesto to the congregation, he was taken aback when Forman intruded during the communion service, which Forman had specifically been requested not to do. As Forman read the Black Manifesto, numerous members of the church walked out. News of the Black Manifesto was publicized across the nation. Dr. Campbell wrote a letter in which he asserted that "it is just and reasonable that amends be made by many institutions in society—including, and perhaps especially, the church" (Schuchter 1970: 6). Amidst the clamor of protests from numerous churches and synagogues, his was the lone voice of empathy.

Gladys L. Knight

See also
Black Power; Forman, James

Further Reading:

Schuchter, Arnold. *Reparations: The Black Manifesto and Its Challenge to White America.* New York: J. B. Lippincott, 1970.

Black Middle Class

The development, transition, and precariousness of the black middle class is inextricably related to racialized processes in the economy, education, legislation, and urbanization. There are a number of ways in which middle class can be defined. Income is the most common, with the middle range of the income distribution being defined as middle class. White-collar professions, high educational attainment (college and above), and homeownership are other characteristics used to define members of the middle class. Comfortable lifestyle, mainstream values, and mannerisms are also used to determine class status. These are all criteria for the middle class in general; however, lifestyle, tastes, and behavior are particularly salient subjective measures of membership in the black middle class, primarily because of the black middle class' unique history.

In its infancy, the black middle class was primarily based on values and affiliations, because the vast majority of blacks had relatively modest economic resources, compared to whites. Sociologists Drake and Cayton (1945) were among the first researchers to study the black middle class, finding that patterns of behavior, family structure, concern for respectability and aesthetics, and striving for upward mobility were the true measures of middle-class status. As more opportunities were available to blacks in education and the workforce after the passage of civil rights legislation, the black middle class was able to expand beyond the ghettos and rural areas into the suburbs, and expand professionally into integrated work settings.

Landry (1987) separates the black middle class into the old black middle class and the new black middle class, with the new black middle class referring to the middle class that developed as a result of civil rights gains. Using income, wealth and lifestyle criteria, Karyn Lacy (2007) identifies three distinct groups: the elite black upper-middle class, the core black middle class, and the black lower-middle class. Members of the elite black middle class tend to live in elite suburbs, far from low- and mixed-income city neighborhoods, and distinct from the core middle-class suburbs. Though the black middle class is charged with abandoning the black poor in many academic studies and policy papers, there is little empirical evidence that that is the case, because racial segregation ensures that the black middle class continues to live close to and in the same neighborhoods as poor blacks. The black lower middle class, which makes up the largest portion of the black middle class, tends to reside adjacent to or with lower-class blacks. Recent observations of an increase in class segregation among African Americans can be accounted for by the numerical increase in the size of the black middle class and a spatial enlargement of their residential enclaves. The increase in the size of the black middle class caused the residential changes in its relationship with the black poor, rather than the specific desire to move away from the black poor.

Members of the black middle class grapple with barriers to acquiring the trappings of middle-class status, including homes in resource-rich neighborhoods with high-quality K–12 education, low crime rates, and good services. In comparison to middle-class whites, middle-class blacks remain at a disadvantage in a number of outcomes. Middle-class blacks have been shown to experience neighborhood conditions worse than poor whites, on average, including neighborhoods with higher poverty, more crime, less political

Black Wealth/White Wealth: A New Perspective on Racial Inequality

Melvin L. Oliver and Thomas M. Shapiro, in their 1995 book *Black Wealth/White Wealth: A New Perspective on Racial Inequality*, systematically detailed the distribution of wealth for black and white Americans, paying particular attention to the inequities between the two groups. They argued that it is necessary to examine wealth as well as income to determine how well black families fared in comparison to white families, because wealth disparities between blacks and whites are much greater than income disparities. Three measures of wealth—income, net financial assets, and net worth—were examined to determine how total wealth for blacks compared with that for whites. Net worth consists of the value of all assets minus debts; net financial assets exclude home and vehicle equity.

Oliver and Shapiro found considerable differences in wealth between whites and blacks of all income levels. But they focused on the disparities between middle-class blacks and whites, as there was the perception that a strong and stable black middle class had emerged in the United States. Middle-class status was measured in multiple ways, but in each instance whites fared better than blacks in terms of income and wealth distribution.

The authors also demonstrated how precarious the black middle class was by illustrating that the typical white middle-class family could survive without income at its present standard of living for slightly more than four months, whereas the typical black middle-class family would be unable to survive for even a month. One very notable finding was that net financial assets held by poverty-level whites were almost equal to those held by the highest-earning blacks. Oliver and Shapiro contended that past inequities, such as laws, that prevented blacks from accumulating wealth or participating in mainstream business endeavors had a cumulative effect that continues to be felt in the present.

Romney S. Norwood

clout, fewer well-funded schools, and fewer services. In addition to neighborhood disadvantages, wealth creation for middle-class blacks lags dramatically behind that of whites. In fact, the ratio of wealth for whites compared to blacks is 20:1. This gap in wealth has significant consequences for the quality of life among middle-class blacks.

A number of interesting trends are occurring among the black middle class currently. Declines in the marriage rates among blacks have generated a great deal of discussion about the precariousness of the black middle class as a result of a decline in married-couple families. However, an increasing number of black professionals are choosing to live alone rather than marry, and this household type is coming to comprise a significant segment of the black middle class. Also, many blacks are choosing to move to disadvantaged black neighborhoods in what has been referred to as black gentrification. Black gentrifiers report different motivations for moving to these kinds of neighborhoods than do white gentrifiers, including feeling responsible for the improvement of black communities. Ellis Cose uncovered the frustration common among the black middle class despite being able to take advantage of increased opportunities, in his 1994 book *The Rage of A Privileged Class*. However, his recent work *The End of Anger: A New Generation's Take on Race and Rage* reveals a hopeful and optimistic black middle class, one skilled at negotiating institutions in order to succeed despite continuing discrimination.

Renee S. Alston

See also

Black Bourgeoisie; Intergenerational Social Mobility

Further Reading:

Cose, Ellis. *The Rage of a Privileged Class: Why Do Prosperous Blacks Still Have the Blues?* New York: Harper Perennial, 1994.

Cose, Ellis. *The End of Anger: A New Generation's Take on Race and Rage.* New York: Ecco, 2011.

Drake, St. Clair, and Horace R. Cayton. 1945. *Black Metropolis: A Study of Negro Life in a Northern City.* New York: Harcourt, Brace and Company, 1993.

Lacy, Karyn R. *Blue-Chip Black: Race, Class, and Status in the New Black Middle Class.* Berkeley: University of California Press, 2007.

Landry, Bart. *The New Black Middle Class.* Berkeley: University of California Press, 1987.

Marsh, Kris, William A. Darity, Philip N. Cohen, Lynne M. Casper, and Danielle Salters. "The Emerging Black Middle

Class: Single and Living Alone." *Social Forces* 86, no. 2 (2007): 735–62.

Moore, Kesha S. "Gentrification in Black Face? The Return of the Black Middle Class to Urban Neighborhoods." *Urban Geography* 30, no. 2 (2009): 118–42.

Oliver, Melvin L., and Thomas M. Shapiro. *Black Wealth/White Wealth: A New Perspective on Racial Inequality*. New York: Routledge, 1995.

Pattillo, Mary. *Black on the Block: The Politics of Race and Class in the City*. Chicago: University of Chicago Press, 2007.

Taylor, Paul, Rakesh Kochhar, Richard Fry, Gabriel Velasco, and Seth Motel. "Wealth Gaps Rise to Record Highs between Whites, Blacks and Hispanics." *Pew Research Center, Social and Demographic Trends* (2011).

Black Nationalism

Black Nationalism comprised diverse movements that advanced black social, economic, and political independence from whites. Violence, as well as the degrading social conditions for blacks in America, was a major reason blacks embraced the notion of self-autonomy. At other times, Black Nationalism was a voluntary or involuntary reflex to persistent racism and discrimination.

Black Nationalism movements began in the North in the early 1800s. Frustrated by white resistance to endow blacks with full rights and freedoms, Paul Cuffe spearheaded a plan to send blacks to Africa. In 1815, he transported 34 blacks to Sierra Leone in West Africa. In 1816, several prominent white leaders met in Washington, D.C., to establish the American Colonization Society (ACS). Their objective was to help abolish slavery and send free blacks and newly emancipated slaves to Africa. In 1821, the ACS established the colony of Liberia in West Africa.

Some blacks scorned the ACS and all back-to-Africa movements. They felt culturally removed from Africa and unable to claim it as their home. Others expressed contempt toward Africans. But some blacks supported the ACS. In 1820, Bishop Daniel Coker of the African Methodist Episcopal (AME) Church led 86 blacks to Liberia. In 1824, 200 blacks left their homes in Philadelphia, New York City, and Baltimore and journeyed to Haiti. Blacks leaped at the opportunity to Christianize Africans, govern themselves, and reconnect with their ancestral heritage. However, these trips were not always successful. Many blacks returned to the United States. Failure to get along peaceably with the native inhabitants and to acclimate to the often harsh environments were common reasons for their return.

Departure of the Danish steamer *Horsa* from Savannah, Georgia, on March 19, 1895. The 200 African Americans aboard were bound for Liberia under the auspices of the American Colonization Society. (North Wind Picture Archives)

As a result of antiblack and antiabolitionist sentiments, a maelstrom of race riots hit many northern cities starting in 1829 and continuing into the late 1850s. The most intense riots occurred in Cincinnati, Ohio; Providence, Rhode Island; New York City; and Philadelphia, Pennsylvania. In 1829, local politicians incited a three-day riot in Cincinnati, Ohio. In 1831, white sailors instigated a riot in Providence, Rhode Island, that obliterated a black neighborhood. In 1834, a white mob ravaged black homes, a black church, a black school, and the home of a white abolitionist. Philadelphia experienced riots in 1820, 1829, 1834, 1835, 1838, 1842, and 1849.

In the face of the sweltering violence of the mid-1800s, Martin R. Delany's Black Nationalism was a balm to many horrified blacks. Delany, a prominent black leader, physician, and novelist, believed blacks must form a separate

Afrocentrism

Afrocentrism is a political and cultural movement that seeks to establish the primacy of African tradition over European culture in historiography and education. Conceived as a corrective to Eurocentrism, the chauvinistic claim to the superiority of European culture, Afrocentrism developed with a variety of black nationalist movements in the mid-1960s, such as the Moorish Science Temple, the Nation of Islam, and the Black Power movement. Afrocentrists strived to reexamine and reevaluate the history and culture of Africans and their descendants from their own perspective, creating an understanding of them not merely as passive objects but as active agents. But Afrocentrism has not been a unified movement at all. Some religionists created the myth of black supremacy, the exact reversion of the myth of white supremacy, in which blacks were the original creation of God and whites the depredated race. Some historiographers argued that ancient civilization was indebted to the northeastern African civilizations, that is, Kemet (Egypt), Nubia, Axum, and Meroe. Martin Bernal, for example, proposed in his work *Black Athena: The Afroasiatic Roots of Classical Civilization* (1987) that ancient Greek civilization had its roots in Africa. Many schools, from elementary to college level, incorporated Afrocentrism into school curriculum. Research institutes were established in and outside universities, such as the Kemetic Institute in Chicago and the Association for the Study of Classical African Civilizations. Afrocentrism contributed to reclaiming the sense of dignity of African descendants and rediscovering the lost legacy of African civilization. But many criticized the movement as the retrospective projection of contemporary racial rhetoric onto ancient civilizations rather than truly illuminating historical scholarship.

Dong-Ho Cho

nation, whether it be in Africa, Latin America, or the American West. Frederick Douglass, a former slave and influential black abolitionist, opposed Delany. He supported an integrationist ideology, believing that blacks would eventually assimilate into American society and achieve equality. The imminent Civil War of 1861 and the subsequent emancipation of slaves thwarted Delany's movement. With the advent of civil rights legislation and the promise of unprecedented freedoms, blacks were filled with optimism.

Expectations were crushed when the U.S. Supreme Court reneged on pivotal civil rights they had previously granted blacks, and the federal government failed to enforce the Fourteenth Amendment, abandoning blacks during the tumultuous period when white Democrats seized control over Republican governments at the end of Reconstruction. White mobs tormented blacks and assailed them with all manner of violence. AME bishop Henry McNeal Turner responded to the atrocities in the South by calling for a return to Africa. He believed Africa offered an opportunity for safety, dignity, equality, self-determination, and economic development. A few blacks, mainly poor farmers, rallied behind him.

The turn of the century ushered in another era of violence. Many riots took place, notably in Springfield, Ohio (1904); Chattanooga, Tennessee (1906); Greensburg, Indiana (1906); Palestine, Texas (1910); and Chester and Philadelphia, Pennsylvania (1918). Ku Klux Klan violence raged, and racist conditions flourished in northern cities. These conditions preceded Marcus Garvey's Black Nationalism and persisted long after the demise of his movement. Garvey garnered several million exuberant supporters and established the Universal Negro Improvement Association (UNIA), multiple black businesses, and a newspaper. His economic pursuits and ability to engender racial pride and empowerment were more successful than his back-to-Africa efforts. He supported Pan-Africanism, desiring to empower the descendants of Africa from around the world. He also wanted to create a unified, black-controlled nation. Many black leaders and whites objected to Garvey's ideas and influence. At the height of his popularity, the U.S. government infiltrated Garvey's organization. In 1925, Garvey was imprisoned for mail fraud and deported to England, where he died in 1940. Without Garvey, UNIA collapsed.

A massive, nonviolent grassroots movement sprang up in the 1950s, largely for the purpose of challenging discrimination and Jim Crow laws. Blacks and whites worked side by side, engaging in nonviolent protests, such as sit-ins, boycotts, and marches. More often than not, these protestors faced hostile white mobs and police violence. Fed up with the mounting and unrestrained violence, some originally nonviolent organizations, such as the Congress of Racial Equality and the Student Nonviolent Coordinating Committee, turned militant. They ousted their white members and transformed themselves into separatist organizations and institutions. Like the ensuing Black Panther Party, they adopted a new doctrine of Black Power and Black Nationalism. The Student Nonviolent Coordinating Committee declined not long after that, and the Black Panther Party met its end after federal operatives infiltrated it.

Altogether, these efforts to unite and empower blacks achieved some success. They spawned hope and relieved, albeit temporarily, the plight of blacks. However, they did not eliminate violence or racism in the United States or abroad. Blacks who escaped to Africa or other parts of America often faced adversity tantamount to their former conditions. Their separatist views, although a form of self-preservation and a reaction to racist institutions, bred suspicion and retaliation. Among blacks, nationalism never achieved mass acceptance. In the end, lack of funds and other extenuating circumstances shortened the life of Black Nationalism.

Gladys L. Knight

See also

Black Manifesto; Black Panther Party (BPP); Garvey, Marcus; Nation of Islam

Further Reading:

Bernal, Martin. *Black Athena: The Afroasiatic Roots of Classical Civilization.* New Brunswick, NJ: Rutgers University Press, 1987.

Moses, Wilson Jeremiah. *Classical Black Nationalism: From the American Revolution to Marcus Garvey.* New York: New York University Press, 1996.

Van Deburg, William L. *Modern Black Nationalism: From Marcus Garvey to Louis Farrakhan.* New York: New York University Press, 1997.

Black Panther Party (BPP)

The Black Panther Party (BPP) was a black empowerment organization that promoted social, political, and economic equality in American society through socialist reform and tactical resistance against state repression. Originally named the Black Panther Party for Self-Defense, Merritt Junior College students Huey P. Newton and Bobby Seale founded the BPP in October 1966. In the late 1960s, the BPP achieved international prominence, with vocal leaders, famed community service programs, and highly publicized standoffs with police officers. The organization dissolved in the late 1970s after withstanding infiltration, arrests, assassinations, and internal tensions directly and indirectly resulting from the COINTELPRO activities of the Federal Bureau of Investigation (FBI).

Backdrop and Background

In the 1960s, civil unrest mostly among college-aged adults who were ideologically socialist and opposed to the Vietnam War threatened the stability of the United States in the Cold War era. The BPP was established one year after the murder of Malcolm X and two months after race-related riots erupted in 43 U.S. cities within a two-month period (*see* Long Hot Summer Riots, 1965–1967).

Newton and Seale were members of Merritt Junior College's Afro-American Association, led by their mentor Donald Warden. In 1965, they participated in Warden's "Economic Night" at a storefront that later became the BPP headquarters. In October 1966, Newton, Seale, and David Hilliard drafted a blueprint for the BPP. They adopted the panther as their symbol from Stokely Carmichael's Lowndes County Freedom Organization in Alabama.

The six original Black Panthers were Reggie Forte, Sherman Forte, Elbert "Big Man" Howard, "Little" Bobby Hutton (treasurer), Newton (defense minister), and Seale (chairperson). Released from prison in December 1966, Eldridge Cleaver joined the BPP in February 1967.

Early Development

From its onset, the BPP was recognized as an exemplary revolutionary organization among antiestablishment groups of all races. With a solid platform built on a well-crafted 10-point plan the BPP summarized the needs of the black community by declaring as follows:

1. We want freedom. We want power to determine the destiny of our black community.
2. We want full employment for our people.

3. We want an end to the robbery by the white man of our black community.
4. We want decent housing, fit for shelter of human beings.
5. We want education for our people that exposes the true nature of this decadent American society. We want education that teaches us our true history and our role in the present-day society.
6. We want all black men to be exempt from military service.
7. We want an immediate end to police brutality and murder of black people.
8. We want freedom for all black men held in federal, state, county, and city prisons and jails.
9. We want all black people when brought to trial to be tried in court by a jury of their peer group or people from their black communities, as defined by the Constitution of the United States.
10. We want land, bread, housing, education, clothing, justice, and peace. (Black Panther Party, 1)

Early in the BPP's development, its founders established sophisticated strategies to defend black communities against police oppression. By studying gun laws, Newton and Seale developed Panther police patrols—civilians armed with rifles—who publicly monitored police activity and defended citizens against police brutality. In 1967, Panther police patrols motivated California state legislators to pass the Mulford Act, which outlawed carrying firearms in public places. Twenty-six Panthers protested the bill by marching to the California State Capitol in Sacramento with firearms. The same year, Newton was arrested after he responded to a citizen's complaint against a police officer in Oakland. Seale was arrested for carrying a gun while trying to post bail for Newton.

Less than a year after its inception, the BPP organized an antiwar rally at the United Nations in New York and released its first publication, *The Black Panther Party: Black Community News Service*. The BPP nearly doubled its membership in 1968 after Newton recruited Alprentice "Bunchy" Carter while in prison. Carter was a former gang leader who started the Southern California BPP branch.

By the end of 1968, the BPP had 45 chapters and over 5,000 members. Branches were established in Chicago, New York, Baltimore, Denver, and New Orleans. New leaders emerged including Fred Hampton, Lumumba Shakur, and Kwame Ture (Stokely Carmichael). The BPP's national Serve the People Programs included the Free Breakfast for Children Program, which served more than 10,000 students, and a sickle-cell testing program, which was responsible for testing more than 500,000 African Americans. The Serve the People Programs received support from a cross-section of the population, spanning from black activists and white religious leaders, to industry giants such as Safeway Foods and the Jack-in-the-Box Corporation. The BPP also organized rent strikes, "liberation schools," free clothing drives, and campaigns for community schooling and policing.

Rise to International Prominence

The BPP achieved international prominence in late 1968 and early 1969. *The Panther*, the BPP weekly newsletter, reached an estimated circulation of 139,000 copies per week. In addition, ABC's 1969 TV special, "The Panther," revealed that 62 percent of the black community supported the BPP's philosophy.

In 1968, Eldridge Cleaver became the Panthers' minister of information and released his acclaimed prison memoirs, *Soul on Ice*. BPP leaders lectured at the nation's most prestigious universities, including the University of California at Berkeley and Boston College. Panther member George Murray taught classes at the University of San Francisco, and Cleaver offered a lecture series at UC Berkeley, despite the opposition of then governor Ronald Reagan. Panther chief of staff David Hilliard delivered a speech before an estimated 250,000 people in November 1969.

Alliances quickly emerged between the BPP and liberal political groups, as well as with inner-city black street gangs. White auxiliary organizations, such as the Los Angeles-based Friends of the Panthers (FoP), and the Portland-based White Panther Party, amplified BPP support among the New Left and the white counterculture. Academy Award–winning actress Jane Fonda and acclaimed playwright and college professor Donald Freed were among the more visible FoP members. In 1968, the mixed-race Peace and Freedom Party endorsed Eldridge Cleaver for president. Later that year, Chicago BPP leaders Fred Hampton and Bobby Rush negotiated a truce between Chicago street gangs and initiated talks with the P. Stone Rangers. A successful merger between the

Chicago BPP and the P. Stone Rangers would have instantly doubled the BPP's national membership.

COINTELPRO

In 1968, J. Edgar Hoover, director of the FBI, expanded his COINTELPRO-Black Nationalist Hate Groups operation. Later that year, he initiated COINTELPRO-BPP, specifically targeting BPP members for assassination, arrest, and infiltration. In June 1969, he pledged to eradicate the organization by the end of the year.

The FBI primarily used local police officers and informants to carry out assassinations against BPP members. In 1968, Oakland police initiated a shoot-out with Panthers resulting in the murder of 17-year-old Bobby Hutton. Months later, Los Angeles police killed five BPP members in two separate incidents. The event sparked four days of rioting at the Democratic National Convention of 1968 in Chicago. One month later, San Francisco police officer Michael O'Brien killed BPP member Otis Baskett. Random killings of BPP members continued over the next two years, including the Los Angeles metro squad killing of BPP member Walter Pope as he delivered BPP newspapers.

In 1970, many in the Black Power movement and the New Left believed George Jackson's murder in San Quentin Prison was COINTELPRO-related. George Jackson became a BPP member while serving a highly contested prison sentence at Soledad Prison in Salinas, California. He and two other inmates were collectively known as the Soledad Brothers. They became internationally known for exposing prison cruelty and admonishing capitalist oppression. George Jackson was killed three days before his highly publicized trial.

During COINTELPRO, BPP arrests were prevalent and usually unsubstantiated. Military-style police raids of BPP headquarters and homes were common during the COINTELPRO era. A BPP attorney noted that between 1967 and 1970 in Los Angeles alone, 87 BPP members who had been arrested were exonerated before they went to trial. Although most charges were eventually repealed, the string of arrests greatly marginalized BPP leadership. In addition, nearly 100 Panthers and BPP affiliates, including Mumia Abu-Jamal, Sundiata Acoli, and Mululu Shakur remain in prison today.

In the summer of 1967, 111 Panthers were arrested in Chicago, a sweep resulting in only a few minor charges. In the New York 21 case of 1969, Panthers, including Sundiata Acoli and Afeni Shakur, were arrested in New York for conspiring to detonate bombs at New York department stores and the New York Botanical Gardens. All charges against the New York 21 were dropped, but only after members were detained for more than two years.

A tide of high-profile arrests, which seemed to target the more influential BPP members, continued throughout the late 1960s to early 1970s. Celebrated Panther Angela Davis was indicted and placed on the FBI's most wanted list for conspiring to free George Jackson from a courtroom in Marin County, California. In 1968, San Francisco police ransacked the home of Eldridge Cleaver and his wife, BPP member Kathleen Cleaver. Eldridge Cleaver was eventually arrested for violating parole and went into exile to avoid prison. David Hilliard was arrested and held on $30,000 bail for threatening President Richard Nixon's life because of a benign comment he made during a speech. Bobby Seale, along with seven white men he recently had met, was arrested for organizing the Chicago riots at the 1968 Democratic National Convention. Huey Newton was convicted of voluntary manslaughter for the murder of Officer John Frey. His ruling was overturned in 1970, but only after he spent more than two years in prison. Panther leader Geronimo Pratt was arrested in 1970 for kidnapping and murdering Caroline Olsen. He spent 27 years in prison after being framed by Julius Butler, an FBI informant who had been previously suspended from the BPP for advocating violence.

By the time COINTELPRO-BPP officially dissolved in 1971, an estimated 7,500 BPP members were government informants. Figuratively speaking, there appeared to be a "weed and seed" initiative, whereby the FBI uprooted principled BPP members through assassinations and arrests, and planted ignoble infiltrators who corrupted the BPP with misinformation and criminal values. In 1969, the FBI paid out an estimated $7.4 million to BPP informants.

Informants were credited with instigating tensions that prompted Elijah Muhammad to pull the BPP's newsletter from newsstands that he directed. FBI informants also created the conditions that led to the highly publicized feud between the BPP and Ron "Maulana" Karenga's United Slaves (US) Organization. Infiltrators within the US Organization were responsible for assassinating BPP leaders "Bunchy" Carter and Jon Huggins. The murders preceded a series of phony memos, bogus cartoons, and other feigned incidents that ultimately led to genuine animosities between the US Organization and the BPP, as well as the public perception that both organizations were violent.

The copious presence of informants also led to a witch hunt within the organization. Accordingly, the FBI exploited suspicions within the organization by circulating rumors that true members were informants. The most extreme case was when FBI informant George Sams tortured and murdered BPP recruit Alex Rackley after convincing the New Haven, Connecticut, BPP chapter that Rackley was an informant.

Informants were also responsible for assisting the FBI and police with assassinating key BPP leaders. William O'Neal, FBI informant and Fred Hampton's personal bodyguard, provided the FBI with a detailed floor plan of Hampton's home. Officers used O'Neal's information to assassinate 17-year-old Panther Mark Clark and 21-year-old Hampton as they slept. Police officers unloaded approximately 99 rounds into the home, including one point-blank into the head of Hampton after he was wounded.

By 1970, the wave of informants within the BPP ultimately led to a culture of paranoia within the organization, culminating with a feud between Huey Newton and Eldridge Cleaver. Cleaver had been in exile for almost two years. He fled to Cuba to avoid prison for parole violation, did a stint in France, and eventually settled in Algeria, where he established the first international BPP chapter. During the same period, Newton spent more than two years in prison for manslaughter of a police officer. His ruling was overturned in 1970, and he immediately returned to the BPP, which was now replete with infiltrators. A substantial percentage of its members had been murdered or were in jail.

In 1970, the BPP was trying to reorganize and resolve the tyranny they were facing from the FBI. Many members of the New York chapters, some recently acquitted from the New York 21 case, favored enhancing BPP resistance to oppression by building an underground paramilitary infrastructure. At the time, New York chapters aligned with Cleaver who drew parallels between the BPP struggles and the revolutionary battles for Algeria. California chapters, which remained loyal to Newton, preferred to deemphasize the military structure and focus on community service.

The FBI quickly capitalized on the opportunity to drive a wedge between chapters by using informants to deliver bogus messages to Newton and Cleaver. Cleaver received a series of messages in Algeria suggesting that California BPP leaders were trying to undercut his influence, and were generally disorganized. Cleaver responded by expelling three members, including interim leader David Hilliard. In turn, Newton received anonymous letters warning him that Cleaver and members of the New York chapter were plotting to murder him. Newton responded by expelling the New York 21.

Months later, Newton expelled Cleaver and the entire international chapter for disloyalty. Cleaver responded by asserting that he was the true leader of the BPP and suspended Newton. More bogus communiqués followed, even after Newton and Cleaver publicly denounced one another. The FBI's puppet show between the East and West Coast Panthers did not end until violence erupted between the New York and California chapters. The New York chapter, convinced that Newton was cooperating with the FBI, eventually abandoned the BPP.

The Aftermath

As the FBI's two primary targets, Newton and Cleaver both showed emotional scars from years of harassment, intimidation, and psychological trickery. By 1971, the once flourishing BPP was reduced to a small, predominantly female-led group of Newton loyalists in California. Newton's faction was rumored to engage in sexual indiscretions, extravagant spending, and illicit drug use. Newton eventually fled the country to Cuba, after being arrested for pistol-whipping a tailor and killing a prostitute. He eventually returned to the United States and was acquitted of all charges in 1978. Newton returned to the University of California in 1980 and received a PhD in social philosophy. His dissertation was titled "War Against the Panthers: A Study in Repression in America." He was murdered in 1989, allegedly over a drug dispute.

Eldridge Cleaver returned to the United States with his wife, Kathleen Cleaver, in 1974. In a plea agreement, he avoided additional prison time. He became a born-again Christian and released an account of his religious transcendence in *Soul on Fire*. He also became politically conservative, and endorsed Ronald Reagan's 1980 presidential bid. In the 1980s, he was arrested for drugs. Cleaver died in 1998 of unknown causes.

Bobby Seale formally left the BPP in 1974. In 1989, Seale and David Hilliard formed a community group to assist disadvantaged Oakland neighborhoods after the Loma Prieta earthquake. Seale is currently an author, lecturer, and community activist.

Members of the BPP and their families filed several lawsuits against the FBI. In 1970, Huey Newton filed suit, claiming that his civil rights were violated in the 1968 raid of his home. In 1975, the BPP sued the FBI for $100 million for their COINTELPRO activities against them. In 1983, a Federal District Judge awarded $1.85 million to the estate of Fred Hampton for wrongful death.

The FBI's annihilation of the BPP affected the poor black community in many ways. The FBI's reliance upon social degenerates within the black community to infiltrate the BPP, in effect, increased the capacity of criminals, particularly drug dealers, in the black community. Other black nationalists, disenchanted with the BPP's new agenda and convinced the federal government would not allow them political freedom, joined underground guerrilla organizations such as the Symbionese Liberation Army (SLA) and the Black Liberation Army (BLA). The SLA and BLA were both allegedly responsible for several bank robberies, police officer assassinations, police station firebombings, and high-profile kidnappings—incidents the FBI during COINTELPRO falsely accused the BPP of plotting.

Conclusion

The BPP was the indocile superego of American culture during one of the worst periods of international imperialism and social inequality in U.S. history. In a sense, the BPP split the conscience of U.S. society, shedding light on a silent majority ready to embrace the universality of liberation and a sinister force fanatically committed to maintaining the status quo. The rise and extirpation of the BPP bears lessons and antidotes to many problems facing the black community today. The explosive number of black men in the criminal justice system, the rise of crack and the subsequent war on drugs, and the marginalized presence of black male leadership in the poor black community are the natural degenerative effects of the federal government's overthrow of the BPP. More importantly, the BPP's legacy lays bare the universal potential of black empowerment and the undaunted spirit of a community responding to oppression.

Ivory Toldson

See also

Black Nationalism; Black Power; COINTELPRO (Counter Intelligence Program); Forman, James

Further Reading:

Black Panther Party. "The Ten Point Plan." http://www.blackpanther.org/TenPoint.htm.

Churchill, Ward, and Jim VanderWall. *Agents of Repression: The FBI's Secret Wars against the Black Panther Party and the American Indian Movement.* Boston: South End Press, 1988.

Cleaver, Eldridge. *Soul on Ice.* New York: Dell Publishing, 1968.

Handman, Gary. *UC Berkeley Library Social Activism Sound Recording Project: The Black Panther Party.* Berkeley: University of California Berkeley Library, 1996.

Hilliard, David, and Lewis Cole. *This Side of Glory: The Autobiography of David Hilliard and the Story of the Black Panther Party.* Boston: Little, Brown and Company, 1993.

O'Reilly, Kenneth. *Racial Matters: The FBI's Secret File on Black America, 1960–1972.* New York: Free Press, 1989.

Seale, Bobby. *Seize the Time: The Story of the Black Panther Party and Huey P. Newton.* Baltimore: Black Classic Press, 1991.

Black Power

The term *Black Power* was first used as a slogan and later expanded to encompass an ideology, a movement, and a cultural revolution. However, blacks were not unified in their expression of Black Power. Some blacks advocated black pride and political, social, and economic self-determination and empowerment; others advanced a militant activism. These responses reflected black frustration with the violent white riposte to the civil rights movement, the approach of the civil rights leaders, and the conditions that remained unchanged after the historic Civil Rights Act of 1964.

The civil rights movement began in the 1950s. Although it was a predominantly black-led movement, whites also participated. These participants consisted of ordinary, largely middle-class men and women as well as churches, women's clubs, and college students. Prominent organizations included the National Association for the Advancement of Colored People (NAACP), the Southern Christian Leadership

Conference (SCLC), the Student Nonviolent Coordinating Committee (SNCC), and the Congress of Racial Equality (CORE). The movement's main objective was to eliminate segregation and gain equal rights through nonviolent methods of protest such as boycotts, sit-ins, and marches.

These demonstrations occurred in the South. Determined to maintain the status quo, white mobs intimidated, terrorized, lynched, and beat the participants. Police officers attacked the protestors with clubs, fire hoses, and dogs. Nevertheless, the nonviolent tactics brought about incremental gains toward integration.

In the 1960s, CORE and SNCC led the Freedom Rides to challenge segregation on public transportation and in public facilities and initiated the Freedom Summer (Mississippi) of 1964 to garner black suffrage. Both types of demonstrations took place in the South. During the Freedom Rides, both black and white protestors were beaten and attacked by white mobs and the Ku Klux Klan. During the Freedom Summer, one black and two white volunteers were shot and killed. Also, "thirty homes and thirty-seven churches were bombed, thirty-five civil rights workers were shot at, eight people were beaten, six were murdered, and more than 1,000 arrested" (Hine et al. 2000: 521). Despite heavy resistance, the Civil Rights Act of 1964 was passed on July 2, 1964, thereby eradicating segregation. While middle-class blacks in the South enjoyed greater freedoms, frustrations mounted for blacks in the North as conditions in the ghettos worsened.

Disillusioned by the violence of the civil rights era, the philosophy of integration and nonviolence, and continuing racism and oppression, blacks looked for another solution.

Black Power was a term coined by Robert F. Williams to signify political empowerment. In 1966, Rep. Adam Clayton Powell used the expression in an address at Howard University to encourage the emergence of black institutions. But when Stokely Carmichael, the chairman of SNCC, used the term at a rally in 1966 in Greenwood, Mississippi, he sparked a major movement. Carmichael defined Black Power as "a call for black people in this country to unite, to recognize their heritage, [and] to build a sense of community" and urged blacks "to define their own goals, to lead their organizations, and to reject the racist institutions and values of American society" (Dulaney 2003: 54–55). The SNCC and CORE ousted their white members and developed new strategies to match their new philosophy and its abandonment of nonviolence.

Blacks also experienced a major physical and artistic transformation during this period. Blacks "took pleasure in wearing African-inspired hairstyles and fashions, particularly with the colors green, black, and red, symbolizing Africa, black people, and blood or revolution" (Altman 1997: 31). Also, "the expression '*Black is Beautiful*' became popular everywhere, and the 'Black Power salute' was raised by athletes Tommy Smith and John Carlos during the presentation of their medals at the 1968 Mexico City Olympic Games" (Altman 1997: 31). Black Power encouraged blacks to solidify their relationships by calling one another brother and sister. It inspired new forms of communication and a new sense of pride that blacks had been deprived of for centuries. For the first time in history, blacks unashamedly embraced their blackness and their heritage. In 1967, blacks inaugurated the eminent Black Arts movement. Larry Neal stated that this movement was "radically opposed to any concept of the artist that alienates him from his community" and proclaimed it to be "the aesthetic and spiritual sister of the Black Power concept" (Hine et al. 2000: 547).

A key aspect of the Black Power ideology was militancy. This was not a new concept for blacks. Prominent leaders such as Henry McNeal Turner (1834–1915), Ida B. Wells-Barnett (1862–1931), and W.E.B. Du Bois (1868–1963) had advocated black self-defense. During the Black Power movement, organizations that were willing and able to confront white violence flourished. The Deacons for Defense and Justice, composed of war veterans, patrolled their communities and boldly challenged the Ku Klux Klan. Malcolm X, during the early years of his leadership in the Nation of Islam, not only promoted Black Nationalism but rallied young blacks to his call for retaliatory violence.

Young blacks in the ghettos joined rifle clubs. In 1966, Huey P. Newton and Bobby Seale founded the Black Panther Party for Self-Defense in Oakland, California, largely in response to police brutality. They engaged the police in several violent confrontations. In 1967, H. Rap Brown was arrested for inciting a riot when, after encouraging blacks in Cambridge, Maryland, to revolt, "a fire erupted in a dilapidated school" (Hine et al. 2000: 534).

Black Power: The Politics of Liberation in America

Published in 1967, *Black Power: The Politics of Liberation in America* by Stokely Carmichael and Charles V. Hamilton articulated a new direction of black freedom struggle beyond the traditional nonviolent civil rights movement. The book was written in a heightened sense of urgency amid the state violence against civil rights activists, the increasing disillusionment about the civil rights movement, and the explosion of ghetto riots. "Black Power" had already become a powerful rallying slogan and a controversial issue in the mass media before the book was published in 1967. The authors offered their book as the only viable hope for avoiding the destructive guerilla warfare. Although the media portrayed "Black Power" as reverse racism and a black supremacy movement, Black Power meant nothing other than black people's self-determination, self-definition, and control over the most important issues affecting their lives. To achieve this goal, Black Power asked for all blacks to unite, recognize their heritage, and create a community. It sounded like a separatist movement, but only superficially so. Only the restriction of membership to blacks would give substantial bargaining power to blacks as a group. A true coalition would be possible only on the basis of blacks' autonomous power. This would be, then, the prerequisite for the full participation of blacks in the democratic decision-making process of an open, pluralistic society. Black Power did not refute or oppose the ideas of democracy and open society, but it did see the current form of representative democracy and the idea of assimilation falling short regarding the self-determination of racial minorities. The book also underlined the deep connection between the struggle for the liberation of blacks in America and that of the Third World for national liberation in Africa and Asia.

Dong-Ho Cho

As the popularity of Black Power grew, a series of unprecedented riots (1965–1967) broke out in the nation's black ghettos. Among the most devastating riots were those that took place in Newark, New Jersey (1967), and Detroit, Michigan (1967), during what came to be known as the Long Hot Summer Riots. Young blacks incited these riots within their own communities as a response to real or rumored police attacks on residents. They attacked homes and businesses as well as white bystanders. A significant distinction between black violence and white violence was that blacks generally did not kill their victims. Most of the deaths that occurred came about when law enforcement attempted to restore order. The extent and validity to which radical organizations and activities within the ghettos may have influenced or participated in the rising incidence of such riots remains under debate.

White and black reactions to the raging violence that swept the urban North, and to the Black Power movement in general, differed. Many whites faulted blacks—not the circumstances that triggered the violence. Consequently, the black riots reinforced their preexisting stereotypes, and whites responded by calling for tighter restrictions and increased law enforcement in the ghettos. President Lyndon Johnson established a commission that determined that racism was the main cause of the riots. He proposed several programs to alleviate the problems affecting blacks, such as crime, unemployment, drugs, and poverty. At the same time, the government was responsible for the dismantling of many black vigilante organizations such as the Black Panther Party, which had attempted to better the community with social programs and to provide protection to the residents.

Generally, whites were suspicious of the Black Power movement. Blacks who wore their hair naturally and sported Afrocentric clothing were regarded as radicals and racists. Many whites were intimidated by blacks who no longer strove to be assimilated into mainstream society. In "An Advocate of Black Power Defines It," Charles V. Hamilton explained that some people believed Black Power was "synonymous with premeditated acts of violence to destroy the political and economic institutions of this country." He also stated that "the concept is understood by many to mean hatred of and separation from whites" (Hamilton 1969: 124).

Dr. Martin Luther King, Jr., the spokesperson for the civil rights movement, was distressed by the rioting and condemned the separatist ideology of the Black Power movement. However, he did support black economic, political, and social empowerment, and the expression and promotion of racial pride and dignity. However, the extreme militants celebrated the riots and warned of more. Other proponents of Black Power empathized with the rioters but desired "to establish solid, stable organizations and action programs" led by blacks (Hamilton 1969: 125) rather than to promote violence.

Furthermore, they believed "Black Power must (1) deal with the obviously growing alienation of black people and their distrust of the institutions of this society; (2) work to create new values and to build a new sense of community and belonging; and (3) work to establish legitimate new institutions that make participants, not recipients, out of a people traditionally excluded from the fundamentally racist processes of this country" (Hamilton 1969: 126). Within this framework, many blacks felt that they could work with, though separately from, whites.

In 1967, Black Power advocates held a conference in Newark (at the location of a riot that had occurred four days prior) to merge the factions within the black community and generate resolutions for the movement. Among the 286 organizations represented were the Abyssinian Baptist Church, the Black Muslims, CORE, the East Orange Housing Authority, the Fisk University Poverty Research Group, the NAACP, the New York Police Department, SCLC, and the Zimbabwe African People's Union. Out of over 80 resolutions concerning economic, political, educational, international, and other goals, the participants chose the Black Manifesto, which advanced Black Nationalism and self-determination.

During the Black Power movement, blacks were responsible for a number of changes in the black community and in the nation. Following in the steps of historical icons such as Carter G. Woodson, blacks helped establish black history programs in schools and black studies departments at colleges and universities. Television programs, commercials, and magazines represented more blacks, while "movies depicting black heroes (and heroines) who beat up evil whites were popular, though a number of people referred to these contemptuously as 'blaxploitation' films" (Hamilton 1969: 126). Also significant was the fact that blacks felt better about themselves as a result of "[rejecting] the lessons of slavery and segregation that caused black people to look upon themselves with hatred and disdain" (Hamilton 1969: 127). John Zippert, a CORE Task Force member, organized a sweet potato cooperative in Opalousa, Louisiana, and Antoine Perot, a CORE field secretary, established a freedom school "with thirty teachers and 200 students, ranging in ages from eight to eighty" including "Negro history, art, music, and other aspects of black culture" (McKissick 1968: 180). Other programs trained black leaders. Also, blacks made great artistic and literary contributions.

In contrast, many other blacks were more willing than ever to use violence as a means to revolt against racism. Although many of the more militant organizations helped defend blacks against police brutality and racist attacks, some helped fuel racial hate and the self-destructive violence that ignited in the ghettos.

GLADYS L. KNIGHT

See also

Black Manifesto; Black Nationalism; Black Panther Party (BPP); Race Riots in America

Further Reading:

Altman, Susan. "Black Power Movement." In *The Encyclopedia of African American Heritage*, edited by Susan Altman, 31–32. New York: Facts on File, 1997.

Carmichael, Stokely, and Charles V. Hamilton. *Black Power: The Politics of Liberation in America*. New York: Vintage Books, 1967.

Dulaney, W. Marvin. "Black Power." In *The Greenwood Encyclopedia of American Civil Rights*, edited by Charles D. Lowery and John F. Marszalek. Westport, CT: Greenwood Press, 2003.

Hamilton, Charles V. "An Advocate of Black Power Defines It." In *Black Power: The Radical Response to White America*, edited by Thomas Wagstaff, 132–37. Beverly Hills, CA: Glencoe Press, 1969.

Hine, Darlene Clark, William C. Hine, and Stanley Harrold, eds. *The African American Odyssey*. Englewood Cliffs, NJ: Prentice Hall, 2000.

King, Martin Luther, Jr. "Black Power Defined." In *I Have A Dream: Writings & Speeches That Changed the World*, edited by James M. Washington, 153–65. New York: HarperCollins, 1986.

McKissick, Floyd B. "Programs for Black Power." In *The Black Power Revolt*, edited by Floyd B. Barbour, 179–88. Manchester, NH: Porter Sargent Publishers, 1968.

Stone, Chuck. "The National Conference on Black Power." In *The Black Power Revolt*, edited by Floyd B. Barbour, 189–98. Manchester, NH: Porter Sargent Publishers, 1968.

Black Self-Defense

Many Americans associate the doctrine of black self-defense with the young male militant leaders of the Black Panther Party for Self-Defense and other groups that captured national attention in Northern urban centers in the latter part of the modern civil rights movement. These groups often defined themselves in opposition to the predominantly Southern-based nonviolent civil rights struggle. The tradition of black self-defense, however, emerged long before the modern civil rights movement. Black leaders argued for self-defense in response to the lynchings and race riots that plagued blacks during the Jim Crow era, phenomena that reached their apex during the Red Summer Race Riots of 1919. Blacks with political views as divergent as W.E.B. Du Bois, A. Philip Randolph, and Cyril Briggs used their media platforms, *The Crisis*, *The Messenger*, and *The Crusader*, respectively, to advocate black self-defense in these years. Even among blacks who subscribed to the tenets of nonviolence in their public political protest, there were few who extended this logic into their private lives, and many vowed to protect their families if attacked. Historians recognize the profound influence that civil rights activist and the most influential proponent of self-defense, Robert F. Williams, had on groups like the Black Panther Party and the lesser-known Revolutionary Action Movement (RAM), an important group in the development and dissemination of Black Power ideology.

Though women are often invoked as part of the justification for man's right to defend himself and what "belongs" to him, a woman is not usually the first person that comes to mind when one pictures an advocate of self-defense. Ida B. Wells-Barnett, however, was an important early advocate. Wells-Barnett, among the more radical members of the middle-class black women's club movement and an often-overlooked founder of the National Association for the Advancement of Colored People (NAACP), was, for many years, the entirety of the anti-lynching campaign in the United States and abroad. In 1892, one of her friends was among three men lynched for daring to open a grocery store in Memphis and taking business from a nearby white store. Wells-Barnett, in her paper, *Free Speech*, urged blacks to leave Memphis, and many blacks heeded her call. The incident also propelled her to write "Southern Horrors: Lynch Law in All Its Phases," an analysis of the ideology surrounding lynching, and "A Red Record," a phenomenal investigation of the practice of lynching in the United States. Wells-Barnett found that even though white mobs used rape as the public justification for lynching, most lynching did not occur after a black man was accused of rape. Worse, she made the bold assertion that among the times that rape was the actual charge, there were instances when white women entered into voluntary sexual relationships with black men. Livid Memphis whites ransacked her paper. Luckily, Wells-Barnett was on her way to New York at the time. Famously, she promised to "sell [her] life as dearly as possible" if attacked (Wells-Barnett 1970).

As blacks migrated to urban centers, race riots joined the largely rural phenomenon of lynching in the theater of American racial terror. There were 40 riots between 1898 and 1908 and 25 riots during the Red Summer of 1919 alone. W.E.B. Du Bois, in the pages of the NAACP's *The Crisis*, condemned the cowardice of Gainesville, Florida, blacks who did not fight back against a white mob, a mob that blacks outnumbered. Du Bois was furious that Gainesville blacks allowed their women and men to be murdered and that they had finally surrendered the man the mob sought (Du Bois 1916). Du Bois did more than write about defending the race; 10 years earlier, in response to an Atlanta riot, he had purchased a Winchester rifle to protect his family (Tyson 1998). The socialist publication *The Crusader*, coedited by A. Philip Randolph, who was later president of the Brotherhood of Sleeping Car Porters, and Chandler Owen, ran an editorial lauding black people's resort to self-defense in racial incidents in Memphis, Tennessee, and Longview, Texas. Although blacks were outnumbered, *The Crusader* argued that a significant factor bolstering the willingness of whites to take part in mob violence was the fact that whites believed that they would attack defenseless blacks. According to *The Crusader*, if any man in the mob thought that he might lose his life, he thought better of the attack. Moreover, law enforcement officials, who often argued that they were powerless in the face of the mobs, were more likely to intervene when blacks were armed and there was a chance that a real battle might break out (*Crusader*, September 1919).

Black Marxist Cyril Briggs was also moved by the spike in racial violence in 1919. The year before, he had formed a secret organization, the African Blood Brotherhood (ABB). The Marxist organization, because of the future orientation of Marxist theory, was not fond of concomitant black

Deacons for Defense and Justice

The Deacons for Defense and Justice were an armed African American group formed in Louisiana in 1964 to protect civil rights workers from the violence of the Ku Klux Klan (KKK).

The Deacons for Defense and Justice began in Jonesboro, Louisiana, in 1964 as a response to the growing crisis of white terrorism arising from the lack of local enforcement of the Civil Rights Act of 1957, Civil Rights Act of 1964, and the Constitution. As part of the Freedom Summer (Mississippi) of 1964, the Congress of Racial Equality (CORE) sent volunteers to Jonesboro. White members of the community felt that CORE volunteers would stir up trouble and threaten the system of white supremacy that was entrenched in the community. A mill worker and Korean War veteran, Ernest "Chilly Willy" Thomas, gathered a small group of men to act as armed security outside CORE's Freedom House. A high school teacher, Fred Kilpatrick, convinced the police to let him set up a volunteer black police force.

Upset by CORE's protest over the segregated pool and library in Jonesboro (*see* Segregation), the KKK, aided by police, drove a 50-car caravan through the black community. After this incident, Kilpatrick and Thomas adopted a formal structure for community defense and created the Deacons for Defense and Justice. After this, the number of protesters grew, and by December 1964 Jonesboro desegregated the library. In retaliation, the Klan burned crosses. In response, the Deacons issued a leaflet, left in white homes by black domestic workers, stating that anyone burning crosses in the black community would be killed.

By 1966, the Deacons had branches in 21 communities in the South. They were unsuccessful in creating branches in the North and the West. Even though they were armed, the Deacons for Defense and Justice were not a militant group that advocated violence like the Black Panther Party. The Deacons were seen more as the security arm of the nonviolence movement. They were made up of a lot of black war veterans and their purpose was to protect civil rights leaders and activists from violence and to act as a deterrent to the Klan. By 1968, they had faded out of existence.

Catherine Anyaso

political efforts that looked to the past. The ABB is perhaps best known for its critical stance regarding the nostalgic pageantry of Marcus Garvey's United Negro Improvement Association. But unlike mainstream Marxism, the group supported black self-government as well as black self-defense (Kelley 2003). Years later, Robert F. Williams would honor the organization when he named his popular newsletter after the ideological organ of the ABB, *The Crusader* (Tyson 1998).

The Deacons for Defense and Justice, a group that formed in 1964 in Jonesboro and Bogalusa, Louisiana, with a mission of defending Congress of Racial Equality (CORE) volunteers from Ku Klux Klan attacks, stand as evidence that the black self-defense tradition and the nonviolent arm of the modern civil rights movement could stand side by side. Nonviolent leaders did more than accept protection from those who believed in self-defense. Little Rock, Arkansas, NAACP president Daisy Bates, who oversaw the integration of Central High School, often bragged about her .32 automatic (Tyson 1998). Amzie Moore, a Mississippi NAACP leader who suggested and helped Student Nonviolent Coordinating Committee activist Bob Moses organize the voter registration drive that became known as Freedom Summer, carried a gun and kept his house well stocked and well lit, should he be attacked. Significantly, Moses, the quiet activist with an unmatched commitment to pacifism, was tested in one of the most brutal caldrons of unprovoked racial violence during the civil rights movement—Mississippi, which was well aware of Moore's arsenal (Tyson 1998).

Robert F. Williams, one of the most important proponents of black self-defense, began his career in black politics with the NAACP, although he had participated in the organized labor movement during his time in Detroit and even penned an article for the *Daily Worker*, so he cannot be claimed solely within civil rights history. Williams, a war veteran, managed to assemble an NAACP chapter in Monroe, North Carolina, that was composed largely of working-class blacks. Others had abandoned the NAACP after black gains in *Brown* and the Montgomery Bus Boycott inflamed white passions in the area. Williams's first campaign with the NAACP was to integrate Monroe public swimming pools. This ran counter to the practice of the NAACP, which had, since the Scottsboro case, shied away from interracial conflict at the intersection of race and sex. Predictably, the Ku Klux Klan came after Williams and his associates, but he and his veteran allies demonstrated that they were armed, a move that deterred Klan attacks. The infamous "Kissing Case," in which two 10-year-old boys were imprisoned after one kissed an eight-year-old white girl, brought the Monroe chapter into the spotlight and Williams onto the national and international scene. Malcolm X told his congregation that they had to support Williams's efforts on the war front. Sex and race were also at the center of the controversy that led to Williams's expulsion from the NAACP. After two trials in which the courts failed to punish white men after they attacked black women, Williams pledged to fight "lynching with lynching" a statement he later clarified (Tyson 1998).

Williams, still active after his expulsion, was content to follow the student activists during the North Carolina sit-in campaign. In the confusion surrounding white backlash over a CORE demonstration in Monroe, Williams was charged with kidnapping a white couple he had in fact sheltered during the fray. He and his family fled to Cuba. There, he broadcast his program, *Radio Free Dixie*, which reached blacks in New York and Los Angeles. He also continued to publish his newsletter, *The Crusader*, which he had started in 1959, and it reached many of the young black radical intellectuals today's students recognize from posters and movies. His book, *Negroes with Guns*, had a profound impact on Merritt College student Huey P. Newton. Williams and Malcolm X are cited as the two biggest inspirations for the formation of the Black Panther Party for Self-Defense. Williams also influenced another organization, RAM, considered one of the key organizations in developing the ideology of Black Power. The young radicals did not fail to honor their debt to Williams. In 1968, when the BPP asked him to become its foreign minister, he was already the president-in-exile of RAM (Tyson 1998).

SHATEMA A. THREADCRAFT

See also

Black Panther Party (BPP); Civil Rights Movement; Congress of Racial Equality (CORE); Ku Klux Klan (KKK); *Negroes with Guns*

Further Reading:

De Jong, Greta. *A Different Day: African American Struggle for Justice in Rural Louisiana, 1900–1970.* Chapel Hill: University of North Carolina Press, 2002.

Du Bois, W.E.B. "Cowardice." *The Crisis* (October 1916).

Hill, Lance. *The Deacons for Defense: Armed Resistance and the Civil Rights Movement.* Chapel Hill: University of North Carolina Press, 2004.

Kelley, Robin D.G. *Freedom Dreams: The Black Radical Imagination.* Boston: Beacon Press, 2003.

Marqusee, Mike. "By Any Means Necessary." *The Nation* 279 (July 5, 2004).

Randolph, A. Philip. "How to Stop Lynching." *The Messenger* (August1919).

Tyson, Timothy B. "Robert F. Williams, 'Black Power,' and the Roots of the African American Freedom Struggle." *Journal of American History* 85, no. 2 (September 1998): 540–70.

Wells-Barnett, Ida B. *Crusade for Justice: The Autobiography of Ida B. Wells*, edited by Alfreda M. Duster. Chicago: University of Chicago Press, 1970.

Wells-Barnett, Ida B. *On Lynchings.* Amherst, NY: Humanity Books, 2002.

Black Separatism

Black separatism is a social movement with the goal of black political, economic, and cultural autonomy either within or from white America. Adherents to the black separatist movement argue that blacks cannot gain true equality in societies where whites hold power and seek to create a new homeland. Many contemporary strains of black separatism hold racist ideologies, particularly antiwhite and anti-Semitic views. Current black separatist movements include the Nation of Islam, the New Black Panther Party, the United Nuwaubian Nation of Moors, and the Nation of Yahweh.

The history of black separatism in the United States can be traced back to the late 18th and early 19th century. During this time period the first proposals for recolonizing black Americans either on separate lands in the United States or in a separate country were espoused by white Americans, and during this time period there was substantial black opposition to recolonization proposals. In the early part of the 20th century the black separatist movement was reignited by Marcus Garvey who attracted the support of many blacks with his back-to-Africa approach of freeing blacks from white oppression in the United States. Garvey founded the Universal Negro Improvement Association and African Communities League to advance the position of black people within the United States. He also founded the Black Star Shipping Line that was designed to transport black people back to Africa. The black separatist ideas of Garvey also attracted white support during this time period, particularly from white supremacist groups as he opposed intermarriage and advocated for racial purity. Perhaps the most well-known resurgence of the black separatist movement in the United States is the Nation of Islam that was founded by Elijah Mohammed and later led by Louis Farrakhan and Malcolm X. Like previous black separatist movements before them, the Nation of Islam calls for several independent black states on American soil where whites and blacks will be totally separated. Louis Farrakhan has become infamous for bringing a racist, black supremacist element to the black separatist ideology. Regardless of the time period, all strains of black separatism from Marcus Garvey to the Nation of Islam have all asked the U.S. government to deed the historical "black belt" Deep South states to blacks so that they may establish a separate land that is politically, culturally, and economically independent from the white-dominated United States.

Marcus Garvey launched the first mass movement of African Americans in the United States that was based on racial pride, self-help, and separatism. (Library of Congress)

Black separatists argue that the dominant political institutions in the United States have historically promulgated inequality and injustice against blacks and therefore blacks cannot continue to live under the legal control of the white government. Adherents of the black separatism ideology advocate for political, economic, and cultural separation of whites and blacks in the United States. Politically they advocate for African American elected officials that are accountable to their black constituencies and they back politically progressive candidates such as Reverend Jesse Jackson. Economically they advocate for the patronage of black-owned business to enforce economic segregation from white society. Finally, they support cultural autonomy through the separation of the races through ideological stances against racial intermarriage and the call for land that black people can call their own. Some contemporary and more radical branches of black nationalism, particularly those associated with Louis Farrakhan's Nation of Islam, have adopted an antiwhite, anti-Semitic, anti-Catholic, and antigay stance based on statements made by the Nation of Islam's previous leader Elijah Mohammed. Mohammed believed that a renegade black scientist by the name of Yacub created whites 6,600 years ago as an inherently evil and ungodly people. He further argued that Catholics and Jews are "blue eyed devils" who practice "gutter religion" and prey on blacks. Thus, those who adopt these viewpoints have come to believe that blacks are the biblical chosen people, not Jews, and those blacks are not only equal to whites but surpass them in all respects. Thus, their views are considered to be black supremacist in nature. As a result of these black supremacist views and the continued inequality of blacks in American society relative to whites, some followers of the black separatist movement have advocated the use of violence as a means of achieving racial progress.

Virginia R. Beard

See also

Black Nationalism; Black Panther Party (BPP); Nation of Islam; *Plessy v. Ferguson* (1896). Document: *Plessy v. Ferguson* (1896)

Further Reading:

Brown, Robert A., and Todd C. Shaw. "Separate Nations: Two Attitudinal Dimensions of Black Nationalism." *Journal of Politics* 64 (2002): 22–44.

Feagin, Joe R. "White Separatists and Black Separatists: A Comparative Analysis." *Social Problems* 19 (1971): 167–80.

Hahn, Harlan. "Black Separatists: Attitudes and Objectives in a Riot-torn Ghetto." *Journal of Black Studies* 1 (1970): 35–53.

Southern Poverty Law Center. "Black Separatist." http://www.splcenter.org/get-informed/intelligence-files/ideology/black-separatist (accessed December 20, 2012).

Black Soldiers and Lynching

Lynching, or mob violence, was originally a system of punishment used by whites against African American slaves. The term *lynching* probably derived from the name Charles Lynch, a justice of the peace who administered and condoned mob vigilantism in Virginia during the 1700s. Historically, records show that black men were the main targets of lynching, and during and after wartime, black soldiers were singled out for this cruel system of punishment. More than 4,700 Americans—most of them black—were lynched between 1890 and 1960, according to figures from America's Black Holocaust Museum located in Milwaukee, Wisconsin.

Journalist Ida B. Wells-Barnett was one of the first antilynching advocates. She attacked the notion that lynching protected white women, proving with statistics that most black men who were lynched were never accused of rape but were hung for a variety of real or concocted offenses. The National Association for the Advancement of Colored People (NAACP) also launched a major campaign against lynching. In 1919, the organization published *Thirty Years of Lynching in the United States: 1889–1918*.

According to historians, there was a decline in lynching during World War I, but numerous blacks were murdered by lynching in the year after the war ended. Reportedly, more than 70 blacks, including 10 black soldiers—some still in their Army uniforms—were among those lynched.

In 1917, President Woodrow Wilson issued a call for Americans to enter World War I to make the world secure for the sake of democracy. More than 200,000 Americans went to Europe in support of the war. Because of the strict segregationist policies of the U.S. Army at this time, many blacks went to France and joined the French forces. Despite heated debates about whether they should participate in a war abroad when they could not exercise their rights at home, many black men went to war out of the belief that when the war ended, justice would reign.

At the end of the war when black soldiers returned to the United States, they were shocked and unprepared for the greeting they received. Reportedly, some black soldiers were beaten by angry white mobs. Race riots erupted across the country in cities such as New York; Washington, D.C.; and St. Louis.

Additionally, a disproportionate number of black soldiers were lynched during World War II, sometimes as Europeans and white American soldiers looked on. According to newspaper reports, most of the U.S. soldiers executed for capital crimes in Europe were black, and military courts sentenced a large number of black soldiers to be hanged in public between 1943 and 1946. At the time, less than 10 percent of the segregated Army was African American. For some black soldiers, postwar time brought continued lynching and beatings of blacks across the country, and such acts continued into the 1960s.

Some historians point out that the history of the lynching of blacks began with one incident at Fort Pillow, Tennessee, during the Civil War. According to numerous accounts, Confederate slaughter of black federal troops stationed at Fort Pillow took place in the mid-1800s. The action stemmed from Southern outrage at the North's use of black soldiers. From the beginning of the war, the Confederate leadership was faced with the question of whether to treat black soldiers captured in battle as slaves in insurrection or, as the Union insisted, as prisoners of war. In 1864, Confederate Col. W. P. Shingler ordered those in his command to take no more black prisoners. In what proved to be one of the most heinous racial incidents of the war and in American history, Confederate forces under General Nathan B. Forrest captured Fort Pillow on April 12, 1864, and took every effort to wipe out the black troops. Some were shot to death; others were burned or buried alive. A federal congressional committee investigation subsequently verified that more than 300 blacks, including women and children, had been slain after the fort surrendered. After the incident, black soldiers going into battle used the cry "Remember Fort Pillow!" Soon after the Fort Pillow Massacre, the South agreed to treat blacks as prisoners of war.

Frances Ward-Johnson

See also

Lynching; Veterans Groups; World War I; World War II

Further Reading:

Lockett, James D. "The Lynching Massacre of Black and White Soldiers at Fort Pillow, Tennessee, April 12, 1864." *Western Journal of Black Studies* 22 (Summer 1998).

Royster, Jacqueline Jones, ed. *Southern Horrors and Other Writings: The Anti-Lynching Campaign of Ida B. Wells, 1882–1900.* Boston: Bedford Books, 1997.

Black Women and Lynching

Lynching, or mob violence, was originally a system of punishment used by whites against African American slaves. The term *lynching* probably derived from the name Charles Lynch, a justice of the peace who administered and condoned mob vigilantism in Virginia during the 1700s.

Black women in the late 19th century were among the first to publicly protest racially motivated lynching, beginning a challenge that eventually turned into a key movement. Journalist Ida B. Wells-Barnett was one of the first anti-lynching advocates. She attacked the notion that lynching protected white women, proving with statistics that most black men who were lynched were never accused of rape but were hung for a variety of real or concocted offenses. Wells-Barnett's stand against lynching involved a strategy of investigation and exposure that eventually became the guide for all anti-lynching activism.

One of America's earliest and most successful anti-lynching campaigns was launched by Wells-Barnett from 1892 to 1900 by way of a writing campaign that included newspaper editorials and pamphlets and national and international public speaking platforms. Through her pamphlets and other writings, she portrayed lynching as acts of terrorism and oppression.

Several incidents that changed Wells-Barnett's life and propelled her understanding of lynching began when three of her close friends were murdered. On the morning of March 9, 1892, the bodies of Thomas Moss, Calvin McDowell, and Lee Stewart were found shot to death in a field a mile north of Memphis, Tennessee. The men had owned and operated the People's Grocery Store, a store in competition with a grocery owned and operated by a white man. After writing an explosive editorial, Wells-Barnett was threatened with lynching if she returned to Memphis from her vacation in the North.

Once she experienced the horrors of lynching first hand, Wells-Barnett was determined to launch a campaign to terminate the violence. Her pamphlets painted vivid pictures of lynchings, describing them as incredibly brutal acts at the hands of a lawless mob. She chronicled and cataloged specific examples, documenting hundreds of cases in her pamphlet, *A Red Record.* She revealed racial and regional patterns in the numbers, highlighting, for example, that 160 of the 241 lynchings reported in 1892 were of African Americans and that 180 of the 241 occurred in Southern states. She noted that the victims included five African American women; and that at least one group of victims was a 14-year-old girl and her 16-year-old brother, who were hanged alongside their father, the alleged criminal.

Wells-Barnett chronicled lynchings from January 1882 to January 1892 and identified the charges for which the 728 black men were killed. She also described the lynching in 1886 of one black woman in Jackson, Tennessee, accused of poisoning her white mistress. According to Wells-Barnett, the woman was dragged from jail, had the clothes torn from her body, and was hung in the public courthouse square.

More black women joined Wells-Barnett in her fight against lynching when the black women's club movement began in the 1890s. Clubwomen supported Wells-Barnett morally and financially in her efforts to publish two of her anti-lynching pamphlets, *Southern Horrors: Lynch Law in All Its Phases* and *The Red Record.*

Moreover, after the founding of the National Association for the Advancement of Colored People (NAACP) in 1909, scores of black women participated in anti-lynching activities. In the 1920s, the NAACP began an unsuccessful two-decade battle for federal anti-lynching legislation. An important part of black women's contribution to the

NAACP campaign for the anti-lynching bill—the Dyer Bill—was the establishment of an organization that publicized the horrors of lynching and provided a focus for campaign fundraising. The Anti-Lynching Crusaders, founded in 1922 under the NAACP umbrella, was a women's organization that focused on raising money to promote the passage of the bill and the prevention of lynching in general. The crusaders, led by educator Mary Talbert, sought to include white women but were largely unsuccessful. The crusaders' slogan was "A Million Women United to Stop Lynching" and their aim was to get 1 million women to donate at least one dollar each toward the NAACP anti-lynching campaign. The Anti-Lynching Crusaders never achieved their fundraising or legislative objectives but did successfully publicize the issue of lynching. They continued a tradition of campaigning begun by Wells-Barnett in the 1890s and later taken up by white women in the 1930s through Jessie Daniel Ames's Association of Southern Women for the Prevention of Lynching.

Black women, with Ida B. Wells-Barnett at the helm, catapulted the anti-lynching issue into the spotlight of American public sentiment and, for the first time, placed mob violence on the American agenda. Their anti-lynching campaigns revealed that the role of African American women, some of whom were former slaves, transcended boundaries as they used a public campaign to become champions of truth and justice and pioneers against violence, disorder, and lawlessness.

Frances Ward-Johnson

See also

Lynching; Rape as Provocation for Lynching; Women of All Red Nations (WARN)

Further Reading:

Brown, Mary Jane. *Eradicating This Evil: Women in the American Anti-Lynching Movement, 1892–1940* (Studies in African American History and Culture). New York: Garland Publishing, 2000.

Guy-Sheftall, Beverly. *Reader's Companion to U.S. Women's History*. New York: Houghton Mifflin Company, 1998.

Royster, Jacqueline Jones, ed. *Southern Horrors and Other Writings: The Anti-Lynching Campaign of Ida B. Wells, 1882–1900*. Boston: Bedford Books, 1997.

Schechter, Patricia. *Ida B. Wells-Barnett and American Reform, 1880–1930*. Chapel Hill: University of North Carolina Press, 2001.

Blackface

Blackface is a style of theatrical makeup used to caricaturize black people. To achieve the look, white blackface performers used a mixture of grease and burnt cork to color the skin to an unnaturally dark hue. The transformation was completed by putting red greasepaint around the mouth to accentuate the lips and adorning a curly black wig and tattered clothing. The practice of blackface is most closely associated with blackface minstrelsy, a popular form of entertainment in the late 18th and early 19th centuries.

There are multiple viewpoints concerning the emergence of this entertainment form. Some point to folk and ritual sources (i.e., folk characters and traditions such as charivari and carnival). Others argue that the racial and ethnic heterogeneity of urban centers offered opportunities for people to co-opt elements of various cultures with which they came into contact. Although the origins of blackface continue to be debated, many view Thomas Dartmouth Rice as the original purveyor of blackface entertainment in the United States. Rice and others experienced success as one-man acts, but the formation of groups such as the Virginia Minstrels moved blackface minstrelsy into mainstream culture.

Starting in the 1840s, blackface became an increasingly carnivalesque form of entertainment and was increasingly viewed as an authentic representation of Southern plantation slave culture. Within minstrel shows, blacks were presented as both needing and longing for slavery through a number of stock characters. "Zip Coon," a free black man, represented blacks' inability to handle the responsibility of freedom. He attempted to appear dignified by mimicking the upper-class mannerisms and dress, but his malapropisms always exposed his incompetence. "Jim Crow," a slow-thinking, carefree plantation slave, and "Mammy," a loyal house slave, expressed contentment working for benevolent masters within the slave system.

Contemporary theory on minstrelsy can be separated into three distinct perspectives. The first perspective uncritically characterizes blackface as an outcome of cultural borrowing. The second perspective argues that instead of reflecting black culture, the content of blackface performances expressed the generally racist attitudes and beliefs of white audiences. At its height, purveyors and consumers of blackface minstrelsy sided with one of the two previously mentioned perspectives. On one hand, it was celebrated as a cultural form and viewed

Al Jolson performs in blackface in the 1927 motion picture, *The Jazz Singer*. (Library of Congress)

as an authentic American contribution to theater. On the other hand, blackface minstrelsy was criticized as a form of racial domination that appropriated black culture for economic and racist purposes. Frederick Douglass, for instance, expressed his disdain for the form in the abolitionist paper *The North Star*. Of late, the two perspectives have synthesized to emphasize the conservative and radical complexity of blackface performances. Eric Lott (1995), for example, points to "an unsteady but continual oscillation between fascination with 'blackness' and fearful ridicule of it" (227), which was used to demarcate the differences between the races while simultaneously allowing whites to engage with black culture.

Since the 1800s, the visibility of blackface has varied but has always remained part of American culture. Contemporarily, the appropriateness of blackface remains highly contested, and nearly annually, an instance of whites dressing in blackface appears in the U.S. national media. Reaction to a 2012 skit performed in blackface at a New York high school pep rally, for instance, was extremely polarized. Those who defended the skit dismissed any racist intentions and maintained that the students were unaware of the historical significance of blackface. Those who were critical of the skit argued that such performances were inappropriate in this day and age and suggested that the continuation of such skits were indicative of the continued significance of antiblack racism and unfriendly environment for nonwhite students.

Sheena Kaori Gardner and Matthew W. Hughey

Further Reading:

Johnson, Stephen. "Introduction: The Persistence of Blackface and the Minstrel Tradition." In *Burnt Cork: Traditions and Legacies of Blackface Minstrelsy*, edited by Stephen Johnson, 1–17. Amherst: University of Massachusetts Press, 2012.

Lott, Eric. *Love & Theft: Blackface Minstrelsy and the American Working Class*. New York: Oxford University Press, 1995.

Paskman, Dailey, and Sigmund Spaeth. *"Gentlemen, Be Seated!" A Parade of the Old-Time Minstrels*. Garden City, NY: Doubleday, Doran, 1928.

Saxton, Alexander. "Blackface Minstrelsy and Jacksonian Ideology." *American Quarterly* 27 (1975): 3–28.

Blaming-the-Victim Argument

Explanations of socioeconomic problems among blacks and other disadvantaged minority groups have focused either on minority members' cultural deficiencies, such as lack of motivation and work ethic or family instability, or on racial discrimination and other social barriers encountered by minority members. In the 1950s and early 1960s, cultural explanations focusing on minority members' cultural deficiencies were popular. But since the late 1960s, structural explanations emphasizing racial discrimination and industrial structure have gradually replaced cultural explanations.

Whether they are scholars or policymakers, conservatives have often provided cultural explanations to blame minority groups for their socioeconomic problems. For example, Charles Murray (1984) argued that a ghetto family that depended on welfare programs was more likely to bear children who lacked motivation and a work ethic and that therefore ending welfare programs was the solution to the problem of ghetto poverty. This argument intended to blame the victims—poor families in the inner city—for their economic problems. But some liberals who did not intend to blame the victims have sometimes provided cultural explanations for minority groups' economic problems. For example, in his 1965 report on black families, *The Negro Family: The Case for National Action*, cabinet member Daniel Patrick Moynihan argued that the instability of African American families was the main cause of their poverty and that, therefore, the government should take action to help stabilize black families. Moynihan was a staunch liberal and wanted to eliminate poverty in the black community. However, because he focused on blacks' family instability rather than their social barriers as the main cause of poverty, his cultural argument had the effect of blaming the victims: inner-city African American residents.

Because of their conservative implications, cultural explanations are not popular in social-science discourses. Since culture and structure mutually influence each other, motivations and a work ethic do influence the attitudes and behavior of minority members. But even those social scientists who consider cultural mechanisms important for minority members' socioeconomic adjustments are careful not to emphasize cultural variables in their reports, because they often lose their argument when their facts are correct but they are "politically incorrect."

Sandra L. Barnes

See also

Culture of Poverty

Further Reading:

Mead, Lawrence. *The New Politics of Poverty: The Nonworking Poor in America*. New York: Basic Books, 1992.

Moynihan, Daniel Patrick. *The Negro Family: The Case for National Action*. Washington, DC: Office of Policy Planning and Research, U.S. Department of Labor, 1965.

Murray, Charles. *Losing Ground: American Social Policy, 1950–1980*. New York: Basic Books, 1984.

Blanqueamiento

Blanqueamiento (or whitening) is the ideological and material process and practice of whitening or distancing Latin Americans from blackness, in other words, of "becoming white." In recent times, *blanqueamiento* is used to refer to the practice of people that marry someone of a lighter skin color in order to achieve higher social status and also mitigate or hide the African heritage in their offspring. *Blanqueamiento* is thus understood as a process by which one eliminates most of the African heritage and becomes white. In many ways, *blanqueamiento* is ideologically opposed to the notion of embracing *mestizaje*, which refers to a biological and cultural blending of different race in one person or culture.

The practice of whitening often occurs in three ways: intergenerational marriage (when a black person marries a person with lighter skin color and the offspring is considered white), social whitening (a black person increases social class and status and is considered white), and cultural whitening (a person is born indigenous, then appropriates the dominant culture and is considered white). The outcome of the practice of *blanqueamiento* depends on the fluidity of racial boundaries and categories in Latin America.

The ideology of *blanqueamiento* was used during the colonial era by the elites in Latin America to boost immigration from Europe and to slowly transform the native population into a predominantly white European context. Latin American cultures reinforce *blanqueamiento* by representing their heritage as a "mix of ethnic roots" that are arranged in an ethnic hierarchy. This racial structure is quite apparent in Puerto Rican culture, whereby they represent their racial-cultural heritage by way of three ethnicities: Spanish, Taino (Indigenous), and African. The Spanish cultural traits, like Catholicism, the Spanish language, and traditions like the "Three Kings Day," are seen as the dominant or core part of the culture. In Cuba, *blanqueamiento* was promoted during the 19th century by the elites to resolve what they call "the Cuban race problem"; by encouraging whitening, the nation explicitly and implicitly advocated a European culture as an important fixture of the racialized nationalist project in Cuba at the time. In the early 20th century, census data all throughout Latin American countries showed a rapid increase by those who identified as "white." These trends were tied to the *blanqueamiento* process sought out by elites who, through a belief in scientific racism and eugenics, promoted whitening as a way of "improving" the stock of their nation.

Blanqueamiento labors to reproduce the racial social hierarchy. In an ethnographic study conducted in Colombia, non-black status was associated with upward social mobility; the successful blacks were seen to be dependent on non-blacks. Hence, being whiter is generally associated with being better educated, having more money, power, and upward mobility . Many scholars argue that *blanqueamiento* has failed as an instrument of upward social mobility. The process of *reindigenizacion* (becoming indigenous again) has been recently observed in Colombia as a reaction to *blanqueamiento*.

Bianca Gonzalez Sobrino and Matthew W. Hughey

Further Reading:

Chaves, Margarita, and Marta Zambrano. "From Blanqueamiento to Reindigenzacion: Paradoxes of Mestizaje and Multiculturalism in Contemporary Colombia." *Revista Europea de Estudios Latinoamericanos y del Caribe* 80 (2006): 5–23.

Godreau, Isar P., Mariolga Reyes Cruz, Mariluz Franco Ortiz, and Sherry Cuadrado. "The Lessons of Slavery: Discourses of Slavery, Mestizaje, and Blanqueamiento in an Elementary School in Puerto Rico." *American Ethnologist* 35, no. 1 (2008): 115–35.

Golash-Boza, Tanya. "Does Whitening Happen? Distinguishing between Race and Color Labels in an African-Descended Community in Peru." *Social Problems* 57 no. 1 (2010): 138–56.

Guevara, Gema R. "Inexacting Whiteness: Blanqueamiento as a Gender-Specific Trope in the Nineteenth Century." *Cuban Studies* 36 (2005): 105–28.

Loveman, Mara. "The U.S. Census and the Contested Rules of Racial Classification in Early Twentieth-Century Puerto Rico." *Caribbean Studies* 35, no. 2 (2007): 79–113.

Wade, Peter. *Race and Ethnicity in Latin America.* London: Pluto Press, 2010.

Blepharoplasty

Blepharoplasty, or cosmetic eyelid surgery, is a procedure that removes or repositions excess tissue to change the appearance of either the upper or lower eyelid. Because this procedure is mostly commonly performed on individuals of select East Asian descent, and occurring particularly in Taiwan, South Korea, and other rapidly Westernizing nations, the impact of Eurocentric standards of racial beauty and aesthetics related to cosmetic surgery should be considered. The ongoing conversation on the practice is polarized by two dominant interpretations: (1) a nonracial expression of individual identity and choice (Davis 1994) or (2) a coercive and damaging practice that emerges from uneven racial and social relations (Gilman 2000; Kaw 1993).

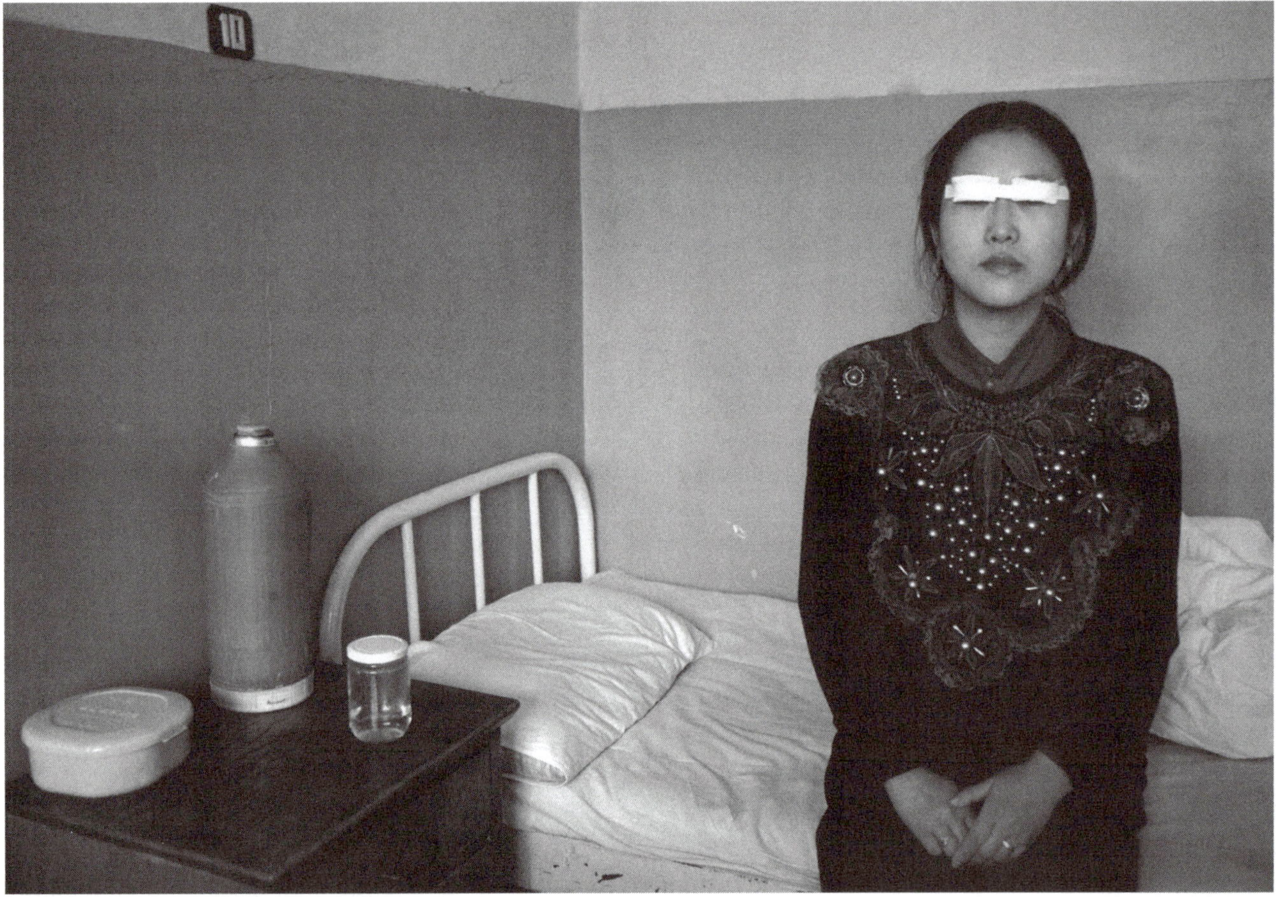

Woman recovering in a clinic after having had her eyelids operated on (blepharoplasty). The surgery removes the folds in the eyelids and makes the eyes look round like those of Western women. (Bettmann/Corbis)

In the former, Kathy Davis's *Reshaping the Female Body* (1994) is a highly cited work that challenges the long-standing feminist critique of cosmetic surgery as a practice that sustains hegemonic beauty standards. Davis's dissatisfaction with the feminist critique increased as she spoke with women who had cosmetic surgery. She argues that women make complicated decisions, and their decision to have cosmetic surgery is irreducible to being a "cultural dupe" of patriarchal or Eurocentric ideology. Although Davis recognizes that cosmetic surgery can serve oppressive interests, she argues that the surgery should be understood as a personal choice that enhances women's lives by delivering a sense of normalcy. Gagne and McGaughey (2002) take a more moderate approach, arguing that women exercise agency but must do so within the confines of a hegemonic beauty standard.

The second body of scholarly literature on the topic positions blepharoplasty within the larger practice of "ethnic modification surgery," such as African American or Jewish rhinoplasty ("nose jobs") whose aim is to reduce the presence or salience of "racial" or "ethnic" markers toward phenotypes associated with Anglo conformity. The animating theme of this perspective draws attention to how supposedly aesthetic or "common sense" beauty standards are not "natural," but are rather the arbitrary products of social interactions and institutions and are historically embedded in particular regimes of asymmetrical racial and ethnic relations (Kaw 1993).

For example, Gilman (2000) finds a correlation between the rise of cosmetic surgery and the emergence of racial sciences. As early as the 1600s, naturalists, philosophers, and early social scientists began to categorize racial groups.

French physician François Bernier (1620–1688), Swedish botanist Carolus Linnaeus (1707–1778), German physician Johan Blumenbach (1752–1840), and French naturalist Georges Cuvier (1769–1832) each developed a racial typology that categorized people into groups ranging in size from three to five based on features such as skin color, lip size and shape, hair texture, skull angle, and smell. Racial sciences constructed a value-laden continuum that situated "superior" whites at one end and "inferior" blacks at the other. Because particular physical characteristics were associated with negative personality traits, cosmetic surgery emerged as an option for those who wanted to alter or erase the stigma associated with a particular racial or ethnic phenotype (Gilman 2000).

In modern times, Eugenia Kaw (1993) found a gendered dynamic to this racialized practice; Kaw discovered that women's decision to undergo blepharoplasty was influenced by a racialized desire to evade the socially constructed undesirability of the epicanthic eye fold common amongst certain Asian populations. Despite female patients' claims that their reasons for undergoing surgery were related to racial teasing, feelings of social alienation, and hopes for better economic mobility, many refused any admission they are pursuing a white or Eurocentric appearance. Moreover, surgeries often resulted in women appearing closer to a media- and culturally defined standard of white feminine ideals.

On a whole, social scientific evidence and theory indicate that surgeries like blepharoplasty are not reducible to aesthetic or individual choices that exist outside of the indelibly racialized and gendered social and historical context, given the unidirectional trend toward Anglo-European features. Given that the body remains a crucial site for the marking of ethnic and racial belonging, such "modification" surgeries that target potent phenotypical features like eye folds also serve as mechanisms that reproduce the supposed deviance and otherness of nonwhite populations.

Sheena Kaori Gardner and Matthew W. Hughey

See also

Beauty Standards; Cosmetics; Skin Lightening

Further Reading:

Davis, Kathy. *Reshaping the Female Body: The Dilemma of Cosmetic Surgery*. New York: Routledge, 1994.

Gagne, Patricia, and Deanna McGaughey. "Designing Women: Cultural Hegemony and the Exercise of Power among Women Who Have Undergone Elective Mammoplasty." *Gender and Society* 16 (2002): 814–38.

Gilman, Sander L. *Making the Body Beautiful: A Cultural History of Aesthetic Surgery*. Princeton, NJ: Princeton University Press, 2000.

Kaw, Eugenia. "Medicalization of Racial Features: Asian American Women and Cosmetic Surgery." *Medical Anthropology Quarterly* 7 (1993): 74–89.

Blockbusting

Blockbusting is defined by the Department of Housing and Urban Development as the practice of persuading owners to sell or rent housing, based on information or perceptions related to the residency of members of the protected classes, for a profit. Strategies used in blockbusting include the real estate agent inducing whites to sell their homes in a particular neighborhood by suggesting that an influx of black home buyers are soon approaching. Blockbusting was realized as a major concern and issue throughout the United States during the 1950s and beyond. The U.S. Congress recognized blockbusting as a problem used by many real estate agents and enacted the Fair Housing Act of 1968 of the Civil Rights Act of 1968, Title VII, as a policy prohibiting blockbusting.

The objective of the blockbuster was to profit from home sales by purchasing homes from white homeowners and then reselling the homes to black buyers. Real estate agents and landlords developed and engaged in various blockbusting campaigns and activities to achieve profits. Activities included sending cards to white homeowners strongly advising them to sell before the neighborhood changed to an all-black neighborhood, refusing to show homes to white families, and showing black families many homes in the same all-white neighborhood. The blockbuster's objective was to make a profit by purchasing a house below fair market value from the frightened white homeowner and then reselling the house to an eager black buyer at a price significantly above fair market value to achieve a huge profit as a result of the transaction accomplished through exploitation, fear, and victimization. Real estate agents encouraged the belief and the view that neighborhoods that were all black and racially mixed were inferior to all-white homogenous neighborhoods.

In *Broadmore Improvement Association, Inc. v. Stan Weber & Associates, Inc.*, the Court of Appeals for the Fifth Circuit granted standing to a nonprofit corporation composed mainly of residents of a particular New Orleans neighborhood dedicated to preserving its integrated character. Under section 812 of the Fair Housing Act, the corporation sued a realtor allegedly engaged in blockbusting with the intended effect of steering blacks to the neighborhood and whites from the neighborhood. The court noted that residents of the target area and the affected municipality have, in light of Gladstone, standing under Title VIII of the Civil Rights Act of 1968.

Chicago's west side neighborhood of Lawndale is significant to the history of blockbusting and provides a prime example of blockbusting during 1940–1960. Roger Biles (1998) provides several historical incidents of self-reported blockbusting by real estate agents. Real estate agents engaging in blockbusting claimed to have a "green light" and declared "open season" on sales to black homebuyers. Real estate agents reportedly stated, "We don't care if the whites run all the way to Hong Kong as long as they run," and "It's good business for us when they're frightened" (Biles 1998). Real estate agents strongly suggested and encouraged residents to sell their homes and leave the neighborhood quickly, many times provoking violence to erupt within the neighborhood. Biles (1998) refers to these real estate agents as the "panic-peddlers" who would go into white neighborhoods and purchase homes at bargain prices and then significantly increase and inflate the price of the homes to sell to black homebuyers. In urban areas, landlords divided apartment buildings and single-family houses into very small housing units and eagerly sold these properties to black homebuyers at overcharged prices. Additionally, real estate agents lured homebuyers into making low down payments on homes only to later pay large monthly payments while accruing negative equity in the home.

Blockbusting is an illegal activity, and homebuyers are protected under the Fair Housing Act of 1968. Blockbusting consists of activities that involve the practice of persuading owners to sell or rent housing for a profit and includes strategies where the real estate agent may induce whites to sell their homes in a particular neighborhood. The real estate agent accomplishes this by suggesting that the arrival of black homebuyers are soon approaching and will cause the neighborhood to socially change. Many individuals and companies benefitted from supporting and reinforcing racial discrimination in the housing market by capitalizing on the housing needs of black home buyers and exploiting the racial fears of white home owners in an attempt to cause neighborhoods to drastically and quickly change their racial make-up as an unethical means of profit and economic gain.

Sonja V. Harry

See also
White Flight

Further Reading:

"Benign Steering and Benign Quotas: The Validity of Race-Conscious Government Policies to Promote Residential Integration." *Harvard Law Review* 93 no. 5 (1980): 938–65. Academic Search Complete, EBSCOhost (accessed November 11, 2013).

Biles, Roger. "Race and Housing in Chicago." *Journal of the Illinois State Historical Society (1998)* 94 no. 1 (2001): 31–38. http://dig.lib.niu.edu/ISHS/ishs-2001spring/ishs-2001spring031.pdf.

Galster, George, and Godfrey, Erin. "By Words and Deeds." *Journal of the American Planning Association* 71 no. 3 (2005): 251–68. Academic Search Complete, EBSCOhost (accessed November 11, 2012).

Gotham, Kevin Fox. "Beyond Invasion and Succession: School Segregation, Real Estate Blockbusting, and the Political Economy of Neighborhood Racial Transition." *City & Community* 1 no. 1 (2002): 83–111. DOI: 10.1111/1540-6040.00009.

Haber, Gary M. "Gladstone Realtors v. Village of Bellwood: Expanding Standing Under the Fair Housing Act." *Boston College Environmental Affairs Law Review* 8 (1980): 783–819. http://lawdigitalcommons.bc.edu/ealr/vol8/iss4/4.

Orser, Edward W. "Secondhand Suburbs: Black Pioneers in Baltimore's Edmondson Village, 1955–1980." *Journal of Urban History* 16 (1990): 227–62. DOI:10.1177/009614429001600301.

U.S. Department of Housing and Urban Development. "Fair Housing and Equal Opportunity—Violation Examples." *HUD.GOV*. Accessed December 2012. http://portal.hud.gov/hudportal/HUD?src=/program_offices/comm_planning/affordablehousing/training/web/crosscutting/equalaccess/fheoviolation).

Blood Quantum

Blood quantum is a term used to describe the degree of ancestry an individual holds as a member of a particular racial or ethnic group (e.g., one-eighth Apache tribe or one-quarter Navaho nation). Blood quantum has almost exclusively been applied to Native Americans and has been a key feature of Native American identity, politics, and tribal membership governance in the United States.

Blood quantum law, the earliest example dating as far back as 1705 (Spruhan 2006), describes legislation that historically determined how mixed-ancestry persons could be classified as Native American. Originally, the law served to limit the rights of those with more than half Native American ancestry. In the 19th and 20th centuries the U.S. government widely applied blood quantum definitions of tribal membership in order to regulate treaties and payment to tribal members for benefits or land cessations. The concept of blood quantum became most widely applied after the Indian Reorganization Act of 1934 (Spruhan 2006). For the purposes of the act, those deemed "Indian" included persons of one-half or more Indian blood. Governments used this categorization to determine who was eligible for financial and other benefits under treaties and land sales.

Compared to other ethnic and racial groups in the United States, Native Americans are unique in their formal relationships with the federal government. For example, in 2012, the Bureau of Indian Affairs recognized 566 tribal entities as eligible for funding and services. However, there are significant differences in how blood quantum and Indianness is defined by tribal and federal governments. In an empirical study of 322 current and historical tribal constitutions, Gover (2008) found that measures and concepts of blood quantum are specific to particular tribes, whereas federal policy tends to adopt a "pan-tribal" concept of Indian blood quantum without tribe-specific considerations. Although in more recent years, with increased tribal autonomy and self-determination policy, the federal government has limited its use of blood quantum rules as criteria for program eligibility, the concept of blood quantum persists in social, political, and personal contexts.

Blood quantum is not without controversy. Many tribes include blood quantum rules as *one* criteria for tribal citizenship despite reduced pressure on them to do so. However, while some Native Americans see the appeal in and embrace the logic and terminology of blood quantum, many find it offensive. The idea is contentious largely because the federal government has historically used blood quantum to racially classify and identify Native Americans. Another key criticism and implication surrounding the concept includes concern about distinctions between legal and biological definitions. Some critics object to the idea of mixed-bloodedness because the notion is seen as central to biological definitions of race that risk upholding objective genetic differences between groups of people. Scholars hold that this false assumption continues to be used to diminish categories of people (Garroutte 2003). Further, biological determinations of identity can be used to challenge the legitimacy of Indian identity claims, where such inquiries are often not made of other racial and ethnic groups. For example, Sturm (2002) explains that unlike other underrepresented groups, proof of one's tribal affiliation is required of Native American applicants for affirmative action. On one level, this difference in treatment recognizes the federal government's understanding of Native American self-government. On another level, it reflects a reaction to a Native American multiracial population that may be seen to challenge long understood cultural and racial boundaries (Sturm 2002). As Garroutte (2003) and others explain, blood quantum has allowed some Indians to be seen as "really real" or quintessential Indians, while others are understood as Indian in lesser degrees.

Other concerns contend that biological support of Indianness may signal stronger claims on identity. As a result, those who physically appear "less" Native American may be subject to additional scrutiny, including proof of one's blood quantum. Other criticisms include concerns that reliance on biological definitions can serve to limit the numbers of Native Americans and, consequently, limit government obligations to these groups. Issues of blood quantum (and perceptions of skin color) also raise tensions among groups looking to validate belonging. As Perdue (2005) argues, blood quantum can be used to both privilege and discredit individuals and thus risks creating a divide within Native communities. Another major criticism holds that blood quanta depends on the idea that interracial mixing will eventually lead to Indian extinction.

The idea of biology and identity is further complicated when contrasted with ideas of the one drop rule, as the biological definitions applied to Native Americans has differed significantly from those applied to blacks and other racial groups. Unlike the one drop rule, Native Americans must generally establish high blood quanta to validate their racial identity claims, regardless of their own identity or opinion. Whereas African Americans have historically required only traces of "black blood" to be considered African American, Native Americans must formally provide strong supporting evidence of Indian blood in order to be granted membership in that racial group.

As debates about blood quantum continue, questions persist. The impact of racial ideologies on Native American identity politics needs ongoing examination, particularly how race operates to both exclude and include individuals within tribal communities. Conflicting understandings of Native American identity and belonging continue to pose challenges as Native Americans and government bodies seek to determine the criteria for deciding who is Indian (Sturm 2002). These questions are of the utmost importance, particularly in our increasingly multicultural and multiracial society in which questions of identity remain a key site of personal, social, and political contestation.

LEANNE TAYLOR

See also

Hypodescent (One Drop Rule); Multiracial Identity; Race

Further Reading:

Bureau of Indian Affairs, Interior. Federal Register, vol. 77, no. 155, Friday August 10, 2012, notices. http://www.loc.gov/catdir/cpso/biaind.pdf (cited December 2, 2012).

Ellinghous, Katherine. "The Benefits of Being Indian: Blood Quanta, Intermarriage, and Allotment Policy on the White Earth Reservation, 1889–1920." *Frontiers: A Journal of Women Studies* 29, no. 2–3 (2008): 81–105.

Garroutte, Eva Maria. *Real Indians: Identity and the Survival of Native America.* Berkeley: University of California Press, 2003.

Gover, K. "Genealogy as Continuity: Explaining the Growing Tribal Preference for Descent Rules in Membership Governance in the United States." *American Indian Law Review* 33, no. 1 (2008): 243–309.

Meyer, Melissa L. "American Indian Blood Quantum Requirements: Blood Is Thicker Than Family." In *Over the Edge: Remapping the American West,* edited by Valerie J. Matsumoto and Blake Allmendiger. Berkeley: University of California Press, 1999.

Perdue, Theda. *Mixed Blood Indians: Racial Construction in the Early South.* Athens: University of Georgia Press, 2005.

Spruhan, P. "A Legal History of Blood Quantum in Federal Indian Law to 1935." *South Dakota Law Review* 51, no. 1 (2006).

Sturm, Circe. *Blood Politics: Race, Culture, and Identity in the Cherokee Nation of Oklahoma.* Berkeley: University of California Press, 2002.

Wilson, Terry, P. "Blood Quantum: Native American Mixed Bloods." In *Racially Mixed People in America,* edited by Maria P. P. Root. Newbury Park, CA: Sage Press, 1992.

Bloody Sunday

No event called more attention to the civil rights movement than the 65-mile march from Selma to the Alabama state capitol in Montgomery on March 21, 1965. What started out small and local grew into one of the most significant civil disobedience landmarks of the time and was a historical turning point in the voting rights struggle. However, the historic Selma-to-Montgomery Voting Rights March is the result of two previous demonstration attempts, particularly the march now known as Bloody Sunday.

On March 7, 600 college students, community protesters, and grassroots leaders from the Student Nonviolent Coordinating Committee (SNCC) and the Southern Christian Leadership Conference (SCLC) assembled to protest, among other things, the killing of Jimmie Lee Jackson. As the marchers walked toward the Edmund Pettus Bridge on the outskirts of Selma, they were intercepted by Alabama state troopers who attacked them with tear gas, whips, and clubs. This event was captured by cameras, and TV stations interrupted programming to show clips of the violence. In one instance, a station was showing a documentary on Nazi war crimes, *Judgment at Nuremberg.* Viewers were shocked when they realized that the images from Selma were not part of the film. Often regarded as the nova of the civil rights movement, the events in Selma helped usher in the Voting Rights Act of 1965 five months later. The passage of the act reshaped civil rights legislation in the nation by eliminating literacy tests, poll taxes, and other roadblocks, and finally opened the doors to black participation in the electoral process.

The journey from Bloody Sunday to the passage of the Voting Rights Act actually began in early 1965 when civil rights groups like the SNCC and the SCLC began focusing their attention on voting registration issues in Selma, an area that had the lowest voter registration record in the Black Belt. Less than two months after receiving the Nobel Peace Prize, Martin Luther King, Jr., along with 250 marchers, was arrested on February 1, 1965, during a peaceful voting rights demonstration in Selma. While in jail, King wrote the letter that was eventually titled "Civil Right No. 1—The Right to Vote." Although less well known than his famous "Letter from a Birmingham Jail," this letter from a Selma jail calls attention to the horrific measures used to prevent black voter registration and details his demands for immediate legislative action. The jailing of Dr. King in February led to several small local protests.

The killing of Jimmie Lee Jackson, a 26-year-old black participant at one of these protests in Marion, Alabama, motivated workers to organize a march from Selma to Montgomery. Jackson, his mother, and grandfather were participating in a peaceful voting rights demonstration on February 18. State troopers attacked the marchers and both Jackson's mother and grandfather were clubbed. Jackson, who was shot in the stomach by a trooper as he attempted to aid his mother, was arrested and charged with assault and battery before being hospitalized. Jackson's death a few days later stimulated renewed mass protests, and in early March, the SCLC announced plans to hold the Selma-to-Montgomery protest march.

On the afternoon of Sunday, March 7, some 600 marchers assembled under the leadership of Hosea Williams of the SCLC and John Lewis and Robert Mants of the SNCC. Although still a key figure in the voting rights efforts in Selma, Dr. King was not present at the march this day. As they proceeded toward the Edmund Pettus Bridge, the marchers encountered a combination of deputies and state troopers led by Sheriff Jim Clark and Maj. John Cloud. Cloud told the protesters to leave, but when they refused, they were attacked by police using billy clubs. Sen. John Lewis, who was a college student at the time, would later recall in his autobiography *Walking with the Wind: A Memoir of the Movement* how the marchers bowed in a prayerful manner as the troopers, many on their horses, attacked them with tear gas, whips, and clubs. Protesters' ribs and limbs were broken and many were hospitalized. Lewis's skull was fractured as a result of the attacks.

Upon his return to Selma, Dr. King led a symbolic march to the bridge on March 9. This march was also stopped short as troopers pushed protesters back with the threat of jail. National Association for the Advancement of Colored People Legal Defense Fund lawyers petitioned the court for protection to hold a full-scale march from Selma to Montgomery. Federal District Court Judge Frank M. Johnson Jr. ruled in favor of the demonstrators, noting that "the right to petition one's government for the redress of grievances may be exercised in large group" (*Williams v. Wallace*, 240 F.Supp.100, M.D. Ala. 1965) and this included the right to march along public highways.

By March 21, three weeks after the first attempt, approximately 4,000 protesters left Selma for Montgomery once again. Although there were incidences of violence during and after the march, notably the killing of Viola Luizzo by the Ku Klux Klan, the march was deemed successful. By the time they reached Montgomery on March 25, more than 25,000 people were present as Dr. King handed a petition demanding voting rights for African Americans to Gov. George Wallace.

Although Bloody Sunday called the nation's attention to the violence in the South, it is also the key event that impressed upon Congress the urgency for a new bill to protect the rights of African Americans as guaranteed by the Constitution. Less than five months after the last of the three marches, under pressure from President Lyndon Johnson's White House, Congress passed the Voting Rights Act of 1965, which aimed to redress white resistance to black democratic participation. The Voting Rights Act sought to eliminate the various legal and cultural tactics administered by state governments, particularly in the Black Belt region where SNCC and SCLC workers devoted much of their efforts.

Dara N. Byrne

See also

Documents: Atlanta (Georgia) Riot of 1967; Disenfranchisement; Race Riots in America; Rape as Provocation for Lynching. Documents: Report on the Memphis Riots of May 1866 (1866); Account of the Riots in East St. Louis, Illinois (1917); A Southern Black Woman's Letter Regarding the Recent Riots in Chicago and Washington (1919); The Cook County Coroner's Report Regarding the 1919 Chicago Race Riots (1920); The Final Report of the Grand Jury on the Tulsa Race Riot (June 25, 1921); Testimony from *Laney v. United States* (1923); The Governor's Commission Report on the Watts Riots (1965); Cyrus R. Vance's Report on the Riots in Detroit (1967); The Reports of the Oklahoma Commission to Study the Tulsa Race Riot of 1921 (2000–2001); Draft Report: 1898 Wilmington Race Riot Commission (2005)

Further Reading:

Black Issues in Higher Education, and Dara N. Byrne, eds. *The Unfinished Agenda of the Selma–Montgomery Voting Rights March*. Hoboken, NJ: John Wiley & Sons, 2005.

Carson, Clayborne. *In Struggle: SNCC and the Black Awakening of the 1960s*. Cambridge, MA: Harvard University Press, 1995.
King, Martin Luther, Jr. "Civil Right No. 1—The Right to Vote." *New York Times Magazine*, March 14, 1965, 26–27, 94–95.
Lewis, John. *Walking with the Wind: A Memoir of the Movement*. New York: Simon & Schuster, 1998.

Blues

The blues emerged in the rural segregated South, and particularly in the Mississippi Delta, in the early years of the 20th century. African American blues pioneers such as Henry Sloan (1870–?), "Blind" Lemon Jefferson (1893–1929), and Charley Patton (1891–1934) developed a raw interpretive style that contrasted sharply with the compositional structures of ensemble playing featured in contemporaneous traveling shows. Performers could collaborate, but the performance featured a singer, self-accompanied on guitar, or in more urban venues, on piano. A few professional traveling musicians like Gertrude "Ma" Rainey (1886–1939) and W. C. Handy (1873–1958) quickly incorporated and adapted the style for ensemble performance, but retained the harmonic structure of the blues and, importantly, the individual voice of the lyric.

Blues developed out of a musical tradition that included the work songs of antebellum slavery, but blues is by no means a continuation of that tradition. Metrically, the work songs follow the rhythms of labor; the subject of the songs is often quite literally the work at hand. Blues, in contrast, utilized a distinctive 12-bar pattern, often with a simple verse pattern in which the first line of lyrics repeats in the second line and a third line concludes. Musically, the blues employed a scale with flatted thirds and sevenths, although in vocal and instrumental performance, there were extraordinary and subtle variations. The subject matter of blues is the individual, alone or in relationships. It is the individual at leisure—loving, fighting, drinking, crying—not at work.

Likewise, blues music draws upon the call-and-response traditions of African American spirituals, but has little use for the spiritual content. Occasionally, God might be called upon, but not to bring salvation—spiritual or worldly—but simply to witness the trials of the individual suffering. Nor is there a parallel in African American spirituals to the boast of Robert Johnson (1911–1938) of a personal encounter with the devil in "Cross Road Blues" or "Me and the Devil Blues."

The early blues musicians of Mississippi and Southern states to the west would have been identified as "songsters," and their repertoire also included popular dance tunes and ballads. Charley Patton was such a versatile and prolific musician that when he recorded for the Paramount label in 1929, several recordings were released pseudonymously so that he would not so dominate the catalog that year. His two-part "Prayer of Death," a more traditional spiritual, was released under the name "Elder J. J. Hadley." Even so, his distinctive vocalizations and complex guitar playing mark the rise of a new style of music. Most blues musicians learned from one another, playing in "jook" joints or informal dances in all-black sections of rural communities. Others took to street corners, working individually or in small groups for tips, learning techniques and songs from one another. In addition to Paramount, the Okey record company recorded a number of early blues artists, and these recordings, released as "race records" and intended for sale primarily in African American communities, further expanded the market for the new music and attracted other musicians to the style. These early recordings were particularly important in the careers of female artists, who, unless they were employed full time as musicians in traveling shows, were less likely than their male counterparts to reach wide audiences.

More important even than the musical innovation was the radical individualism of the blues. The feelings and experiences of an individual blues composer were in themselves significant and offered a challenge to the racist underpinnings of the Southern social order in the early decades of the 20th century. The racial hierarchy of the Jim Crow South precludes the individual case. Exceptions were outlaws, and extraordinary measures were available to guarantee their elision. The blues singer, in contrast, expressed feelings that mattered to a person and, by expressing the worst of them, could undermine the stereotype of the African American content with his or her lot. The artist also expressed an autonomy that challenged racial strictures. A man with the "walkin' blues" asserted the right to go anywhere he wanted. A female artist could assert her sexual independence. Even songs about fighting and killing asserted a right to one's own black body that would have been unachievable a half-century earlier.

Blind Lemon Jefferson (1897–1930), American country bluesman, singer, and guitarist, 1925. (Hulton Archive/Getty Images)

Recent scholars have criticized blues artists for avoiding important social issues, for creating complaint songs rather than protest songs. W. C. Handy, often described as the "Father of the Blues" for his popular success in composing music based on blues patterns, generally avoided controversy both in his lyrics and in his professional life. But his most famous composition, "St. Louis Blues," opens with the line, "I hate to see that evenin' sun go down." The song is the lament of a woman abandoned by her man, but Handy in his autobiography offered another context: "More than once during my travels in the North and South I had passed through towns with signs saying, 'Nigger don't let the sun go down on you here'" (Handy 1941: 86). Handy also reported that he left the South for good after an experience in Memphis. A lynch mob had murdered a young man named Tom Smith, putting out his eyes with hot irons and burning his body. The killers tossed the skull into a crowd of African Americans that had gathered at the square on Beale Street, which subsequently would be named for Handy. "They'd look for me on Beale Street, up and down the river, along the Yellow Dog and the Peavine, but I would not be there," he wrote. "Somebody else would have to play" (Handy 1941: 178).

In a region where African Americans could face lengthy jail time for minor or fictional offenses, blues artists often sang of life behind bars. The narrator of an Alger "Texas" Alexander (1900–1954) song complains that he is falsely accused of murder and forgery even though he can neither read nor write (Oliver 2006: 107). Another Texan, Sam "Lightnin'" Hopkins (1912–1982), who had firsthand experience in the matter, addresses his jailer in one song, asking vainly for a key to his cell (Oliver 2006: 108).

Mississippi's infamous state penitentiary, Parchman Farm, housed at least two important bluesmen. Musicologist Alan Lomax (1915–2002) recorded inmates there in 1939, including Booker T. Washington "Bukka" White (1909–1977), composer of "Parchman Farm Blues." In "Country Farm Blues," Edward James "Son" House Jr. (1902–1988) recalled an experience that echoed the cruelties of slavery. Arbitrary and harsh treatment were so common as to hardly merit comment, but House warned listeners that any who were unlucky enough to find themselves at Parchman Farm likely would endure whippings that would scar them long after their release (Evans, Komara, and Spottswood 2001).

Blues artists could not afford to address openly the most egregious injustices that Southern society offered, at least not in a venue that might include a white audience. In the Jim Crow South, a singer who sang about lynching likely would be lynched. With cautious producers, recorded blues were even less likely to venture a critique of the social order. But there are cases of allusion, such as a variation of a traditional blues lyric "Hesitating Blues," recalled by blues artist Sammy Price (1908–1992). Price reported that following a lynching in Robinsonville, Texas, near the town of Waco, people began singing a new version of the song with a verse that threatens a labor boycott in response to the mob's actions. There is even a subtle revision of the "hesitation" of the original song, suggesting a threat to the white establishment. The promise to "get you" in the original no longer has an apparent romantic connotation, but now promises something more revolutionary. The contextual change would be evident only to an audience familiar with the lynching and sympathetic to the possibility of an African American's violent response.

The critique of white-on-black violence was coded, but even with recorded music, a change of color in the lyrics could make the message plain. Erreal "Little Brother" Montgomery (1906–1985) recorded "The First Time I Met You" in 1936. The only characters in the song are the narrator and "Mr. Blues." An inattentive audience might hear Mr. Blues as a personification of the singer's feelings, but in Montgomery's song, the character's actions betray another allusion. The blues, and then Mr. Blues particularly, chase the narrator though the woods. They chase him into his home and harm him. The narrator ends the song begging Mr. Blues not to murder him. A black audience would know that every African American in the South was obliged to address every white adult male as "Mister." This is not just a singer trying to shake off a depressive gloom. It is a black man confronted with the real dangers of a white mob.

Other artists sang about tragic events that affected black communities in particular. Songs that highlighted the suffering of African Americans during the flooding of the Mississippi River in 1927 rarely dealt explicitly with racism, but the unequal treatment of black victims in the floods would have been a part of an audience's response to those songs. Sippie Wallace's (née Beulah Thomas, 1898–1986) "Flood Blues," Bessie Smith's (1894–1937) "Backwater Blues," and Charley Patton's "High Water Everywhere" catalogued the sufferings of folks whose homes were destroyed when the levees failed. Black audiences knew that black men were conscripted at gunpoint for relief work, and that mob violence against African Americans increased following the floods. Patton's "High Water Everywhere," recorded in 1929, pointedly observed that the homes of African Americans were most likely to be in the flood plain. The hill country, safe from the floodwaters, was off limits to African Americans.

Blues musicians accompanied, physically and musically, the Great Migration of African Americans out of the rural South to the cities of the North in the decades including the two World Wars. On occasion, the farewell critique of the Jim Crow South was explicit, as in the case of Charles "Cow Cow" Davenport's (1894–1955) 1929 recording, "Jim Crow Blues," about leaving the Jim Crow South for Chicago. Other artists were more cautious. In "L&N Blues," Clara Smith (1894–1935) sang in 1925 about going the other direction, but she makes the point that in returning to the South, she will have to relinquish her Pullman berth for less comfortable accommodations.

In Northern cities, particularly in Chicago, blues artists extended their craft and found a wider audience. Blues records were advertised prominently in the *Chicago Defender*, the nation's premier African American newspaper. There was also a greater opportunity for employment for blues artists, both as musicians and as laborers. With urban life came changes in the music, although the radical, subversive individualism that characterized its earliest formulations remained at its core. Exchanging their acoustic guitars for electric, a new generation of blues artists reached a wider audience than their rural predecessors. Muddy Waters (né McKinley Morganfield, 1913–1983), a migrant from Mississippi, became an internationally acclaimed star, although many of his first white fans were young musicians in England rather than in his home country. The urban music scene that finally embraced blues music in the decades following World War II was by no means color blind, but it was a far cry from the music's roots in Jim Crow Mississippi.

James Ivy

See also

Rhythm and Blues; Rock and Roll

Further Reading:

Davis, Angela Y. *Blues Legacies and Black Feminism: Gertrude "Ma" Rainey, Bessie Smith, and Billie Holiday*. New York: Random House, 1998.

Evans, David, Edward Komara, and Dick Spottswood. Liner notes to *Screamin' and Hollerin' the Blues: The World of Charley Patton*. 6-CD boxed set. Revenant, 2001.

Gussow, Adam. *Seems Like Murder Here: Southern Violence and the Blues Tradition*. Chicago: University of Chicago Press, 2002.

Handy, W. C. *Father of the Blues: An Autobiography*. New York: Macmillan, 1941. Reprint, New York: Da Capo Press, 1985.

Oakley, Giles. *The Devil's Music: A History of the Blues*. New York: Da Capo Press, 1997.

Oliver, Paul. *The Meaning of the Blues*. New York: Collier, 1960.

Oliver, Paul. *Broadcasting the Blues*. New York: Routledge, 2006.

Palmer, Robert. *Deep Blues*. New York: Viking Press, 1981.

Blumenbach, Johann (1752–1840)

The German physiologist Johann Blumenbach greatly expanded upon the study of humanity's place in natural history. He is known as one of the first to bring a scientific method to anthropology, a discipline that had hitherto been mostly a speculative pursuit of philosophers and humanists. As one of the preeminent professors at Gottingen University in Germany, Blumenbach can be seen as a transitional figure in the professionalization of anthropology and its establishment as an academic discipline. In his first major work on human variation, *On the Natural Variety of Mankind* (1776), Blumenbach used comparative anatomy to document what he labeled as the five races of the human species. Blumenbach's five races were defined by geography and skin color: white Caucasian, yellow Mongolian, brown Malayan, black Ethiopian, and red American. While there have been many other definitions of race, Blumenbach's five races would dominate racial thinking for generations. Like many of the most prominent Enlightenment-era scientists, Blumenbach's thinking challenged religious convention but was also circumscribed by it.

According to the theological doctrine of the day, God had created Adam and Eve as white, a view that was challenged as Europeans encountered human physical diversity during their exploration of the world in the 18th century. One theory for the presence of human diversity, known as polygenism, argued that racial differences were so great that they must have been created by God. This departed from strict biblical accounts by arguing that the different races must have been created at the same time, but in different parts of the world. Thus the polygenists proceeded from the assumption that whites must be set apart from all other races by definition. Blumenbach belonged to a different camp. The monogenists argued that there had been one act of creation and that original race was white; however, all other races derived from that one over time. This departed from the doctrine of the "fixity of species" or the belief that all living things were created by God in their modern form, precluding morphological change over time.

Blumenbach argued that the different races' skin colors were the result of environmental conditions and diet. The black skin of Africans is the result of exposure to tropical sun, for example. This is known as degeneration theory: racialized difference is understood as stemming from a fall from grace because God's original creation was the white race. If racial differences were the result of environmental conditions like Blumenbach thought, then race must be mutable and could change over time. Therefore behavioral characteristics could not be linked to biological race as Linnaeus agued. There was a racial hierarchy, but it had slowly emerged over time as natural environmental forces had worked upon human populations.

Blumenbach and his predecessor, Linnaeus, are foundational to our understanding of scientific racism. Their research set precedents that were long lasting and far reaching. Both scientists proceeded under the assumption that race is an objectively existing, naturally occurring property of human populations and it could therefore be documented and analyzed with biology. As authors both men published renowned texts that were translated into many languages, disseminating their knowledge around the world. They established race as a valid scientific category, lending the authority of science to racial classifications and reinforcing the notion that racial difference is real and natural.

Matthew D. Thompson

See also

Biological Racism; Linnaeus, Carolus; Racial Taxonomy

Further Reading:

Banton, Michael. *Racial Theories*. Cambridge: Cambridge University Press, 1987.

Boas, Noel T., and Alan J. Almquist. *Essentials of Biological Anthropology*. Upper Saddle River, NJ: Prentice Hall, 1999.

Stanton, William. *The Leopard's Spots: Scientific Attitudes towards Race in America, 1815–59*. Chicago: University of Chicago Press, 1960.

Boat/Jet People

Boat people is a pejorative used to describe refugees who use common boats (such as fishing vessels) or handmade rafts to seek asylum abroad. A less-common (but still derogatory) term, *jet people*, describes refugees or migrants arriving by air transportation, often in chartered or private planes. In the United States, the term *boat people* is often affiliated with Cubans and Haitians entering the United States to seek asylum since the 1960s and 1970s. It is also associated with Vietnamese fleeing Vietnam following the collapse of Saigon. The term *jet people* more generally attaches to refugees and migrants from around the world utilizing air transportation to move across the globe, and can be attributed partly

Vietnamese refugees are rescued by the USS *Blue Ridge* in May 1984 after eight days aboard a tiny craft. Fleeing their homeland on crowded fishing boats and makeshift vessels, Vietnamese refugees became an ever-visible reminder of the Vietnam War for decades after the fall of Saigon in April 1975. (Defense Visual Information Center)

to globalization and the proliferation of air travel. Refugees often take extreme risks travelling by boats and rafts (and, to a lesser extent, planes), leading to many deaths. However, the practice remains common today.

The term *boat people* has been attached to several historical waves of refugees following crises and conflicts. One common example is refugees fleeing Cuba in the 1960s and 1970s. Perhaps the most famous incidence is the Mariel Boatlift (April 15–October 31, 1980) in which approximately 125,000 Cuban refugees (called *Marielitos*) fled for the United States in crude boats not intended for open waters. Most were allowed to remain as refugees in the United States. Until 1995, the United States also accepted Cuban refugees rescued at sea and seeking asylum. However, the so-called Wet Foot, Dry Foot policy restricted the opportunity to seek asylum to those who physically step on U.S. soil. Since the 1970s, Haitians have also attempted to obtain refugee status in the United States, travelling by water to Florida's coast. Similar to Cubans, after 1995, Haitian refugees arriving by boat often were intercepted at sea and returned to Haiti without receiving the chance to request asylum. In both cases, return policies place an additional pressure to arrive at their destination quickly, creating new risks by attempting to travel lightly and with few supplies.

The term *boat people* is also often linked to Vietnamese, Cambodian, and Laotian refugees fleeing the nation following the fall of Saigon, the economic collapse created by the Vietnam conflict, and the later war between Cambodia, China, and Vietnam. As the North Vietnamese government took control of the southern portion of the nation, South Vietnamese intellectuals and associates of the fallen government fled by boat to escape persecution and forced assignment into reeducation camps. Between 1975 and 1992, approximately 2 million people fled Vietnam by boat. Once on open waters, refugees hoped to be picked up by passing boats (rather than Thai pirates) or land in neighboring nations and then seek asylum abroad. Unlike Cubans and Haitians who travelled directly to their desired destination, Vietnamese used boats to travel to faraway nations by using intermediaries.

Unauthorized migration by boat is relatively dangerous. Refugees seeking asylum via water typically travel shorter distances, such as from Cuba to Florida. However, refugees using boats often employ vessels not intended for open waters, such as small fishing vessels or rafts. These vessels are frequently overcrowded, undersupplied for an extended stay at sea, and lacking in safety equipment. As a result, deaths at sea are quite common. National polices (such as the Cuba–United States Wet Foot–Dry Foot Policy) have attempted to mitigate the instances of fatalities while a small debate over who is responsible for those dying at sea begins.

Utilizing air travel allows refugees to look to faraway nations that may offer asylum or for migrants simply looking for viable migration routes into their destination. For landlocked nations or nations lacking open borders, migrating by jet is one option. As it is fairly difficult to travel by air without documentation (such as a passport), refugees may

Wet Foot–Dry Foot Policy

Following the Cuban Adjustment Act of 1966, Cubans physically present in the United States for two years (and later, one year) could apply for permanent residency. At the time, the United States also admitted Cubans found at sea as refugees. A 1995 agreement between Cuba and the Clinton administration attempted to normalize migration between the two nations and reduce the dangers of boat migration. The United States stopped directly admitting refugees caught at sea. Instead, the United States only admitted Cubans who managed to make it onto dry land, hence the term *wet foot–dry foot.*

elect to charter private planes or sneak onto planes on the runway. For example, private planes have become a new, costly possibility for Latinos entering the United States. *Coyotes* (individuals or businesses that transport migrants without authorization into the United States for a fee) have turned to chartered planes as one outlet for their services. Coyotes can minimize some risks in that they have familiarity with unauthorized migration, but create new risks in their motives for profits over the safety of their passengers. Migrants making the trip alone and attempting to stow away on airplanes are sometimes killed by freezing to death in wheel wells or falling during the flight. However, those able to book legitimate passage to their destination by plane may elect to simply overstay their visa and remain without authorization.

Today, migrating by boat and plane still remains a current phenomenon around the world and a viable but risky option for those seeking asylum and escape from their home nations. Cuban refugees (called *balseros*) continue to seek asylum in the United States, travelling by means of simple rafts. Jet skis have also now been employed to cover the distance between Cuba and Florida. Others have emigrated from Tunisia to Italy by boat, and Libya to Malta using simple boats to cross short distances. As the prevalence and coverage of air transport grows, planes also remain a useful route entering both faraway and neighboring nations.

James Maples

See also

Derogatory Terms

Further Reading:

Gibbings, Beth. "Remembering the SIEV X: Who Cares for the Bodies of the Stateless, Lost at Sea?" *Public Historian* 32, no.1 (2010): 13–30.

Milanes, Cecilia Rodriguez. *Marielitos, Balseros and Other Exiles.* New York: Ig Publishing, 2009.

Mitchel, Christopher. "U. S. Policy toward Haitian Boat People, 1972–93." *Annals of the American Academy of Political and Social Science* 534 (1994): 69–80.

Zhou, Min, and Carl L. Bankston III. *Growing Up American: How Vietnamese Children Adapt to Life in the United States.* New York: Russell Sage Foundation, 1999.

Boldt Decision (1974)

Better known as the Boldt Decision, *United States. v. Washington* (1974) marked the legal turning point in the Northwest Native American fishing rights controversy. In Phase I (1974), U.S. District Judge George Boldt decreed that the treaty tribes' reserved right to fish "in common" entitled them to 50 percent of the harvestable salmon entering their "usual and accustomed places." He also held that the tribes could regulate their share of the fishery, but non-Native protests and state resistance obstructed his ruling until the U.S. Supreme Court affirmed it in 1979. In Phase II (1980), Boldt's successor ruled that the tribes had rights to hatchery fish and to protection of the salmon from environmental degradation. Although many problems remain unresolved, the Boldt Decision set an enduring standard for allocation and helped revive the moribund tribal fishing economy in the Pacific Northwest.

The case was the culmination of more than a century of conflict and litigation over off-reservation fishing rights. In 1854–1855, the Native Americans of Puget Sound had signed five treaties that ceded most of their aboriginal territory but explicitly reserved "the right of taking fish at all usual and accustomed places, in common with the citizens of the Territory." Although federal officials assumed that indigenous peoples would eventually abandon their subsistence practices and assimilate into American society, tribal representatives believed that their fishing rights had been guaranteed in perpetuity. They would not have signed the treaties without such promises, and they did not anticipate future restrictions on their rights.

By the early 20th century, however, non-Native commercial fishing and habitat destruction had decimated salmon populations, leading Washington State to impose regulations on tribal fishing in ceded territory. State officials argued that Native Americans should obey the same restrictions as non-Natives, even though those rules often discriminated against indigenous peoples, violated their treaty rights, and undermined both their economic self-sufficiency and cultural traditions. Six fishing rights cases reached the U.S. Supreme Court prior to 1974. The Court upheld the treaties every time, but it also refused to preclude state regulation of tribal fishing rights. Consequently, Washington State continued to harass Native American fishers despite the fact that, by the late 1960s, their share of the salmon harvest had fallen to less than 5 percent. Tribal activists such as Hank Adams, Robert Satiacum, and Billy Frank Jr. responded with "fish-ins" to challenge state law and provoke a test case. Following a series of violent police raids that attracted national media attention, the federal government finally agreed to pursue legal action on behalf of 14 treaty tribes.

Judge Boldt hoped that *United States v. Washington* would settle the matter once and for all. Considering both contemporary dictionary definitions and Native American understanding of the treaties, he construed the words "in common" to mean that the treaty tribes had a right to half of the allowable harvest. In addition, he held that the treaty tribes could regulate off-reservation fishing by their members, whereas the state could only regulate them for "reasonable and necessary" conservation purposes. Although his decision built on existing precedents, it shocked many non-Natives and triggered waves of protest, including extensive outlaw fishing and numerous countersuits. Washington State also appealed and refused to enforce the ruling until the Supreme Court affirmed it in 1979.

The controversy did not end there. In 1980, shortly after Boldt's retirement, Judge William Orrick heard Phase II of the case. He ruled that the tribal share included hatchery fish and that the treaties implied the right to have salmon habitat protected from environmental threats. Two years later, however, a circuit court review overturned his opinion on the latter issue. The tribes continue to press for environmental protection, but they face strong opposition from regional politicians and business interests as well as lingering intertribal differences over allocation. Even so, the Boldt Decision helped to revitalize their fishing economies and gave them a meaningful role in the management of Northwest salmon fisheries.

Andrew H. Fisher

See also

Bureau of Indian Affairs; Native Americans, Conquest of; Native Americans, Forced Relocation of

Further Reading:

Clow, Richmond L., and Imre Sutton., eds. *Trusteeship in Change: Toward Tribal Autonomy in Resource Management*. Boulder: University Press of Colorado, 2001.

Cohen, Fay G. *Treaties on Trial: The Continuing Controversy over Northwest Indian Fishing Rights*. Seattle: University of Washington Press, 1986.

Wunder, John R. *Native Americans and the Law: Contemporary and Historical Perspectives on American Indian Rights, Freedoms, and Sovereignty*. New York: Garland, 1996.

Bolling v. Sharpe (1954)

Bolling v. Sharpe was one of several racial segregation cases of public schools decided on May 17, 1954. Issued the same day as *Brown v. Board of Education*, the U.S. Supreme Court outlawed racial segregation in the public schools of Washington, D.C. It ruled that racial segregation was inherently unequal and violated the constitutional rights of African American students. Like *Brown*, *Bolling v. Sharpe* signified federal judiciary protection of African Americans' access to integrated schools and equal educational facilities.

When the Consolidated Parents Group from the Anacostia section of Washington petitioned the Board of Education of the District of Columbia to open John Phillip Sousa Junior High as an integrated school in 1949, the school board rejected their petition and allowed only whites to enroll. On September 11, 1950, the Consolidated Parents Group, a minister and community leader named Gardner Bishop, and activist Nicholas Stabile attempted to enter 11 African Americans students to the junior high school. When the school's principal blocked them, Sarah Bolling and two other parents filed a suit against C. Melvin Sharpe, president of the Board of Education of the District of Columbia, to permit the African American students admittance to the school. The case was named after Bolling's son, one of the 11 African American students, Spottswood Thomas Bolling Jr.

In 1951, the District Court of Washington, D.C., dismissed the complaint based on the previous ruling in *Carr v. Corning* (1950) that segregated schools were constitutional in Washington. A year later, the U.S. Supreme Court decided to hear the case because it presented significant constitutional issues. James Nabrit, a law professor at Howard University, represented the parents and argued that school segregation was completely unconstitutional. He further challenged the Board of Education to show any reasonable basis for school segregation solely on race or color. George Edward Chalmers Hayes joined Nabrit as legal counsel in the latter part of 1952, when *Bolling v. Sharpe* became one of the five U.S. Supreme Court cases of segregation in public schools. Four of the cases—*Brown v. Board of Education*, *Briggs v. Elliott*, *Davis v. Prince Edward County School Board*, and *Gebhart v. Belton*—were consolidated, but *Bolling* remained separate since the District of Columbia is not a state.

The U.S. Supreme Court unanimously decided that racial discrimination in the public schools of Washington, D.C., denied African Americans due process of law as provided in the Fifth Amendment. When writing the majority opinion, Chief Justice Earl Warren found that the due process clause of the Fifth Amendment must be extended to include equal protection as in the Equal Protection Clause of the Fourteenth Amendment. Unlike in the *Brown* decision, the Fourteenth Amendment could not directly apply to *Bolling* because it had been adopted to protect individuals at the state and local level. Since Washington, D.C., is not a state, Warren adapted the Fourteenth Amendment's Equal Protection Clause into the Fifth Amendment because it applied to the federal government's authority over the area. With the Fifth Amendment's guarantee of "liberty" to African American students, racial segregation in the Washington, D.C., public schools was declared unconstitutional.

Dorsia Smith Silva

See also

Bates, Daisy; *Brown v. Board of Education*; *Brown v. Board of Education* Legal Groundwork; Desegregation; Segregation. Document: *Brown v. Board of Education* (May 1954)

Further Reading:

Currie, David P. *The Constitution in the Supreme Court: The Second Century, 1888–1986*. Chicago: University of Chicago Press, 1990.

Irons, Peter. *Jim Crow's Children: The Broken Promise of the Brown Decision*. New York: Penguin, 2004.

National Park Service. *Bolling v. Sharpe* [Online, May 2000]. *Brown v. Board of Education* National Historic Web Site. http://www.nps.gov/archive/brvb/pages/bolling.htm.

"Bombingham"

"Bombingham" was the nickname given to the city of Birmingham, Alabama, as a consequence of the domestic terrorism, consisting of more than 50 dynamite bombings that occurred between 1947 and 1965. Bombings began at the homes of blacks who moved to the fringes of white neighborhoods and eventually expanded to include prointegrationist white activists and civil rights leadership and recognized movement centers, such as the historic 16th Street Baptist Church.

Known as the worst city for antiblack racism, Birmingham in the civil rights movement era was the site of escalating conflict between the city's whites against steadily increasing numbers of rural black immigrants drawn by the promise of jobs in the coal mines and steel mills. African American Birminghamians began legal and protest challenges to racial segregation laws in the 1940s, focusing on housing segregation.

Between the late 1940s and late 1950s, the likely undercount of the white Birmingham press acknowledged 22 dynamite bombings and four arson burnings. Between 1957 and 1963, a number of bombings occurred, including a cluster of unsolved bombings around the court-ordered integrated black enclave in a North Smithfield neighborhood that earned it the nickname Dynamite Hill.

In 1956, Birmingham had over 350,000 residents (nearly 40 percent black), and 400 African American churches, some of which founded the Alabama Human Rights Commission (AHRC), led by Bethel Baptist Church's Rev. Fred Shuttlesworth (whose house was bombed twice). A coalition between the AHRC and the Southern Christian Leadership Conference undertook a signature moment in the movement, culminating with the confrontation with Public Safety Commissioner T. Eugene "Bull" Connor during the "children's marches" on May 2–6, 1963.

Revs. King and Shuttlesworth and Ralph Abernathy announced a "truce" between the city and the movement that included desegregation, job opportunities, better communication, and release of all protestors. The next Saturday, bombs exploded at the A. D. King house, the First Baptist Church of Ensley Parsonage, and at the A. G. Gaston Motel, sparking violent black retaliation and the federalization of the Alabama National Guard by President John F. Kennedy. At a mass meeting at the Sixth Avenue Baptist Church on May 13, Dr. King referred to the city as "Bombingham."

When the first two African American children to desegregate Birmingham's public schools enrolled on September 4, Ku Klux Klan elements responded by bombing Attorney Arthur Shores's home on Center Street, in the Smithfield/Dynamite Hill neighborhood, for the second time in three weeks. Ten days later occurred the most memorable of the Klan's Birmingham bombings, that of the 16th Street Baptist Church, which killed four girls—Cynthia Wesley, Carol Denise McNair, Addie Mae Collins, and Carole Robertson. In May 2001 and 2002, respectively, Klansmen Thomas Blanton and Bobby Frank Cherry were convicted of these bombings.

Gregory E. Carr

See also

Black Church Arsons; Civil Rights Movement; Connor, "Bull"; Desegregation; Segregation

Further Reading:

Birmingham Historical Society. *A Walk to Freedom: The Reverend Fred Shuttlesworth and the Alabama Christian Movement for Human Rights, 1956–1964*. Birmingham, AL: Birmingham Historical Society, 1998.

Eskew, Glenn T. *But for Birmingham: The Local and National Movements in the Civil Rights Struggle*. Chapel Hill: University of North Carolina Press, 1997.

Boston (Massachusetts) Riots of 1975 and 1976

From 1974 to 1976, the court-ordered busing of students to achieve school desegregation led to sporadic outbreaks of violence in Boston's schools and in the city's largely segregated neighborhoods. Although Boston was by no means the only American city to undertake a plan of school desegregation, the forced busing of students from some of the city's most impoverished and racially segregated neighborhoods led to an unprecedented level of violence and turmoil in the city's streets and classrooms and made national headlines.

The reasons for the rioting were many and were bound up with the unique history and development of Boston's tightly knit ethnic neighborhoods as well as with the economic changes brought about by the city's rapid growth and development in the 1950s and 1960s. The black migration to Boston during World War I was much smaller than it was in other cities. The historically small black population of Boston began to grow in the post–World War II era when more African Americans migrated to the city in search of jobs and improved political and economic opportunities. Unlike other immigrants, however, notably Irish-Americans, blacks were not able to secure the government jobs that occupied a large percentage of the city's workforce. In the 1970s, black workers earned only about two-thirds of what their white counterparts did. A legacy of redlining and discriminatory lending practices prevented blacks from moving into areas such as Hyde Park and West Roxbury where many working-class people owned their own homes. Blacks were also kept out of poorer white working-class neighborhoods, such as South Boston, Charlestown, and East Boston. As gentrification set in and African Americans were pushed out of the historically black neighborhoods of the South End and lower Roxbury, ghettos began to emerge in the areas surrounding Roxbury, Mattapan, and North Dorchester. The schools in these neighborhoods were inadequate and lacked basic resources. At the same time, Boston underwent many structural changes in the name of urban renewal as entire neighborhoods were demolished to make way for the city's expansion. The white working-class victims of the city's transformation responded by electing leaders who would defend the neighborhoods at all costs, including the right to retain their own neighborhood schools.

In the face of municipal power and the federal court, antibusing extremists resorted to violence to protest against school desegregation. The tension created violence in the streets and erupted into almost daily fights in the hallways and classrooms of Boston's public schools. The installation of a police presence in the hallways of South Boston High as well as the use of metal detectors kept a lid on most tensions.

However, hostile crowds gathered outside the school almost daily. In response, Judge Arthur Garrity, architect of the original Boston school desegregation plan, issued a judicial order in September 1975 that prohibited groups of three or more persons from gathering within 100 yards of the school. For the first time since the first turbulent year of busing, South Boston High opened its doors with the presence of 500 state troopers, an occupying force that would remain there for the next three years. Fights broke out on an almost daily basis. Altercations arose between students, and even teachers were pulled into the fray.

Troopers wearing riot helmets and carrying batons were forced to intervene. At Hyde Park High, on January 9, 1975, the second day back to school after the winter break, a fistfight in the first floor corridor erupted into a series of confrontations that spilled out into the streets of Hyde Park, causing police to rush to the scene. Police arrested 15 students, 13 of whom were black, and classes were suspended after the third period. One female black student was charged with assault and battery for allegedly kicking a policeman, while the other 14 were charged with disorderly conduct.

Calm lasted for about a month but ended abruptly when fighting broke out once again on February 12 and lasted for three days. Although no major disturbances occurred in the schools during the months of March and April 1975, hostilities erupted on April 7 at a political forum in Quincy where Sen. Ted Kennedy was giving a speech. Kennedy's address was interrupted by a rowdy antibusing delegation that peppered the senator with insults, jeers, and name calling. Kennedy, once the pride of Boston's Irish community, had paid dearly for his support of busing. In this instance, he was chased to his car, which had already been vandalized by thugs. Kennedy had to be whisked away by police to the train station, where the crowd hurled stones at the departing train. On May 3, a skirmish in South Boston involving local youths and members of the Progressive Labor Party (PLP) on a march against racism resulted in the arrest of eight people and at least 10 injuries. Police estimated that 250 persons, nearly all of whom were from out of state, attempted to march from Dorchester to South Boston to the home of Boston city councilwoman Louise Day Hicks, an ardent defender and prominent leader of the antibusing cause. Boston Police superintendent-in-chief Joseph M. Jordan said the violence along the route was initially provoked by the PLP's strike team when they encountered South Boston youths. About 100 persons, believed to be South Boston neighborhood residents, returned to the parade route with baseball bats, hockey sticks, and rocks in an attempt to disrupt the march as it passed Columbia Stadium in South Boston.

The PLP riot sparked another melee at Hyde Park High School that lasted for two days on May 7 and 8, when a black student reportedly waved a flag bearing the PLP symbol. On May 9, an angry crowd at South Boston High threatened to throw projectiles at black students attempting to exit the school. Leaders of the antibusing movement used tactics borrowed from the civil rights movement when the group Restore Our Alienated Rights (ROAR) staged a sleep-in at Boston mayor Kevin H. White's penthouse suite in the Sheraton Boston Hotel to protest his failure to place the issue of forced busing before the 43rd session of the U.S. Conference of Mayors, then meeting in Boston. ROAR members also demonstrated on June 8 in front of the home of *Boston Globe* publisher John J. Taylor, for what they perceived as the newspaper's pro-busing slant. On June 21, ROAR members picketed the *Boston Globe* plant in Dorchester.

As summer began and the 1974–1975 school year drew to a close, the violence seemed to peter out until an incident involving some out-of-town blacks, unaware of the invisible lines separating the black and white neighborhoods of Boston, plunged the city into violence once again on July 27. The unwelcome black visitors were threatened by hundreds of white bathers who taunted and insulted them as they unknowingly attempted to swim at Carson Beach, located in the heart of South Boston. They were forced to flee on foot after their rental car was destroyed and two of them were injured by crowds of angry whites who gave chase for several blocks. As the hot summer wore on, several other skirmishes filled Boston's newspapers, and hopes for an incident-free opening to the 1975–1976 school year were not high.

With the start of the school year, the so-called Phase II plan of busing, which called for an increase of the total population of bused students from 19,000 to 24,000, went into effect. The plan rearranged school assignments, increased the number of schools, and expanded busing into other white working-class neighborhoods. The plan excluded East Boston with its limited access through the two tunnels that connected it to the rest of Boston. It did include Charlestown, which would now bring blacks into the neighborhood while white students would be sent to schools in Roxbury. Organizers and antibusing leaders quickly moved into action in preparation for the new school year, holding an antibusing rally of more than 10,000 people in Boston's City Hall Plaza the night before the school year was to begin. That same evening, several South Boston toughs attacked a building that housed National Guard troops. Rocks and bottles were thrown at the guardsmen. Later some 300 youths clashed violently with police in front of South Boston High.

When school opened the next day, attendance was down, with only 58.6 percent of students attending. At Charlestown High, only 314 students out of 883 enrolled showed up for class. While antibusing leaders made good on their threats to boycott the schools, the first day of classes was relatively quiet with only one school bus being stoned as it traveled from Roxbury to South Boston. On Friday, October 24, police arrested 15 students at South Boston High for fighting. Judge Garrity responded by holding hearings on the escalating violence in the schools. On the table was the idea of closing South Boston High altogether. On December 9, an order was issued that put South Boston High into federal receivership and Headmaster William Reid out of a job. The headquarters of the Boston National Association for the Advancement of Colored People (NAACP), the oldest chapter in the nation, was firebombed that night in retaliation for the order. On December 12, a large crowd of antibusing advocates tried to break into South Boston High and vandalize it. Some succeeded and were arrested as they scattered leaflets.

Violence broke out at Hyde Park High on January 21, 1976. Thirteen hundred black and white students fought each other throughout Hyde Park High. Although East Boston High was not a bused school, fighting also plagued that institution while residents held a demonstration to block a plan that would have made East Boston a magnet school the following year. As the antibusing leadership split on tactics, creating divisions within the movement that would ultimately spell its downfall, the month of April 1976 saw some of the worst violence yet. On April 5, Theodore Landsmark, a black lawyer and executive director of the Boston Contractors' Association, was on his way to a meeting at City Hall when he was intercepted by a delegation of South Boston and Charlestown High students who were leaving the city council chamber after having aired their views on busing. As Landsmark crossed through the plaza, he was accosted by the marchers, struck several times in the side and back, and belted by the staff of an American flag. A *Boston Herald American* photographer snapped a picture of one of the students attempting to stab Landsmark with the flag. The picture earned a Pulitzer Prize and appeared in newspapers across the country, etching the hatred and bigotry that Boston was now becoming known for in people's memories.

Later that month on April 20, Richard Poleet, a 34-year-old man from Boston's Jamaica Plain neighborhood, was brutally beaten by black youths in Roxbury. Poleet's car was stoned at a red light and collided with another vehicle. He was then pulled from his vehicle and received several blows to the head and face and had his skull crushed with rocks. He was rushed to the hospital where he slipped into a coma and eventually died. Many antibusing leaders claimed the attack was in response to the Landsmark beating and spoke out against it. On April 28, a bomb threat evacuated Hyde Park High, resulting in a melee between motorists and pedestrians who were being harassed by students as they passed the building. When the white students stoned some of the black students, a full-fledged riot began, which was only put down with the help of a large police unit.

Racial fights continued to take place in the schools through the end of the 1975–1976 school year. By opening day of the 1976–1977 school year, which was year three of busing, things were relatively calm in the schools. The newspapers reported rock-throwing incidents in Charlestown, South Boston, and other neighborhoods, but compared to the preceding years, the antibusing crusade appeared to be running out of steam. Empty gestures on the part of President Gerald Ford and the refusal of the U.S. Supreme Court to hear further appeals on the issue of busing represented a major setback for antibusing forces. Although their leaders issued warnings about continued violence and promised to never give up the fight, the antibusing forces had failed to stop busing through legal or extralegal means. By the end of the 1976–1977 school year, the antibusing riots had all but ended.

Zebulon V. Miletsky

See also

Desegregation; Race Riots in America. Documents: The Report on the Memphis Riots of May 1866 (July 25, 1866); Account of the Riots in East St. Louis, Illinois (July 1917); The Cook County Coroner's Report Regarding the 1919 Chicago Race Riots (1919); A Southern Black Woman's Letter Regarding the Recent Riots in Chicago and Washington (November 1919); The Final Report of the Grand Jury on the Tulsa Race Riot (June 25, 1921); Testimony from *Laney v. United States* Describing Events during the Washington, D.C., Riot of July 1919 (December 3, 1923); The Governor's Commission Report on the Watts Riots (December 1965); Cyrus R. Vance's Report on the Riots in Detroit (July-August 1967); The Reports of the Oklahoma Commission to Study the Tulsa Race Riot of 1921 (2000-2001); The Draft Report of the 1898 Wilmington Race Riot Commission (December 2005)

Further Reading:

Formisano, Ronald. *Boston Against Busing: Race, Class and Ethnicity in the 1960s and 1970s*. Chapel Hill: University of North Carolina, 1991.

Tager, Jack. *Boston Riots: Three Centuries of Social Violence*. Boston: Northeastern University Press, 2001.

Bracero Program

On July 23, 1942, Mexico and the United States signed an agreement to bring Mexican men north for agricultural work. This joint labor program, adopted under Public Law 45 and later extended and revised under Public Law 78, emerged from a push from growers who claimed an imminent scarcity of laborers as more farmhands enlisted in the armed forces or found better-paying jobs in urban industry. While originally expected to last the duration of World War II, the Mexican-U.S. Program of the Loan of Laborers would last for 22 years. Over its duration, the Bracero Program, as this regulated migration was informally termed, would offer nearly 4.5 million contracts to almost 2 million Mexican men, most of whom migrated after the war.

Mexico's principal interest was who would officially employ braceros. To avoid problems earlier migrants had faced when recruited during World War I, Mexico would only consider an agreement in which the U.S. government acted as the employer and where both governments administered the program and investigate claims of abuse. This condition prevailed for all but a brief period (1948–1951), when growers were braceros' employers. Complaints surged and as Mexico's negotiating strength rose with the start of the Korean War, the United States was again forced to be the employer of record with the revision of the labor program under Public Law 78.

The agreement guaranteed (on paper) that migrants would live in sanitary housing, have access to medical care, and be paid the prevailing wage for the crop they picked—protections far stronger than those accorded U.S. domestic farm workers. Mexico also sought to control the location of the reception centers, where the processing of braceros took place, arguing for their placement in the interior of the country and not near the border. For Mexico, which lost this condition over time, the issue was both cost and control over migration; cost, in that Mexico paid men's transportation and board to reception centers, where the United States took over; and control over migration, in that it wanted to prevent both undocumented migration and the mass exodus from farm jobs in northern Mexico, where labor was scarce and lower paid.

The agreement also required that growers demonstrate that they could not attract U.S. workers before they became eligible for Mexican farmhands (again, at least on paper). Over time these requirements effectively depressed wages and worked against farm labor unionization because growers, especially large growers, mobilized into associations and thus were able to act collectively, set salaries below what they would have needed to pay to attract domestic workers, and use the presence of these workers to undercut collective resolve.

In addition, Mexico foreclosed—at least at the outset—laborers going to Texas, citing discrimination against people of Mexican descent. And although the U.S. government set the number needed, Mexico retained control to allocate bracero slots and reduce the number of men selected. That Mexico never adjusted this number suggests that it recognized that it could not restrain men from going and reasoned that men garnered more protections from the program than by migrating outside it. The agreement also stipulated that braceros—only men—would come for a limited amount of time, set according to the needs of growers.

Lastly, Mexico mandated that 10 percent of workers' wages be held in escrow, to be made available when

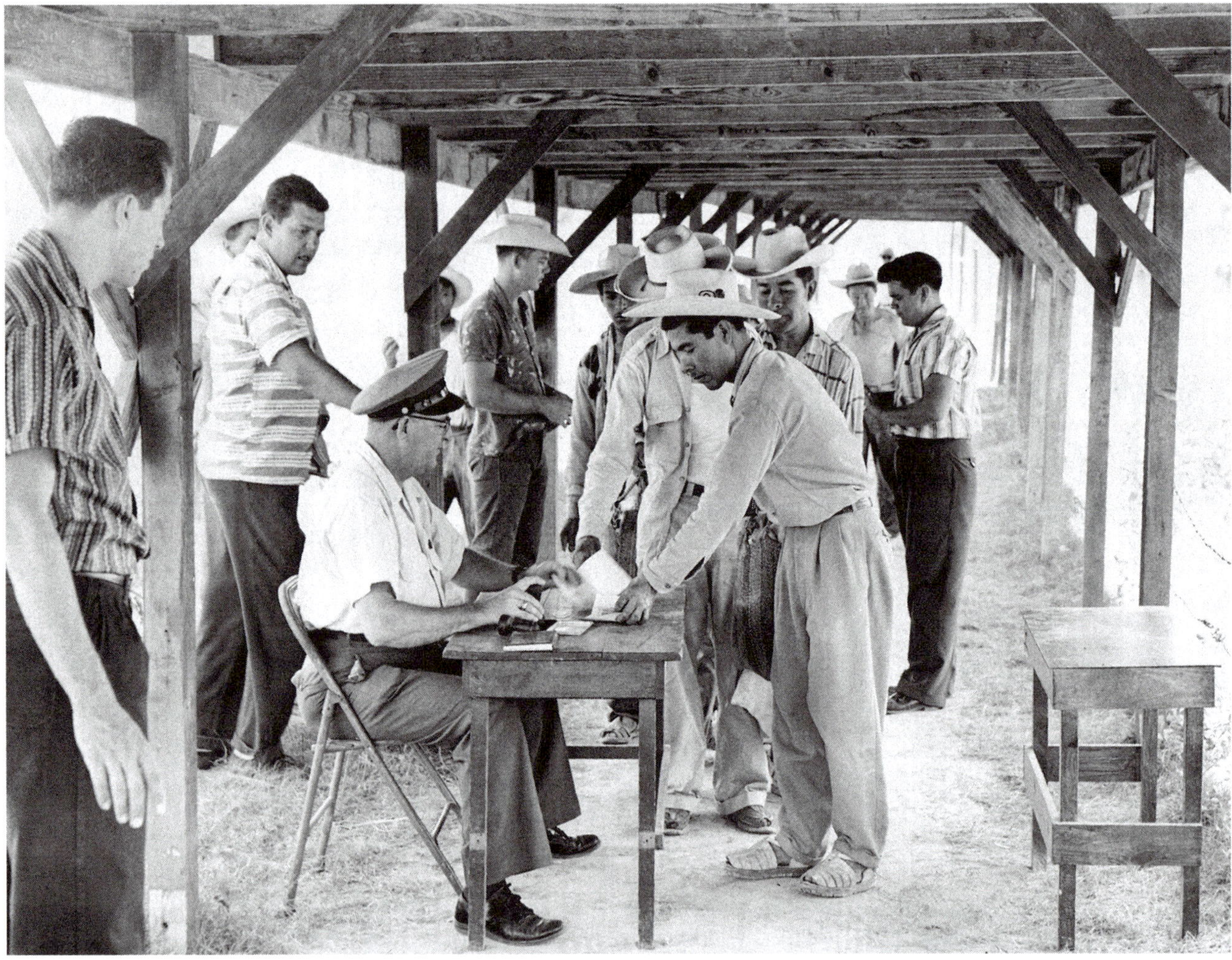

Mexican farm workers are shown being registered in the Bracero program at the labor center at Hidalgo, Texas, June 18, 1959. (AP Photo)

migrants returned home. This provision increased the likelihood that men would return home and would do with some money, unlike previous migrations. This money (deducted during 1942–1948) would be put to good use on tractors and other equipment on Mexican farms. The government was so invested in this aspect of the agreement that it halted negotiations at one point during World War II when the United States, with so-called limitation orders restricting the civilian production of farm equipment, refused to include it in the agreement. Most workers, however, never received these funds and many were not aware of them.

While growers lobbied for a formal program without any governmental control and while migrants were deported for union activity, two important things had changed. First, President Franklin D. Roosevelt's Good Neighbor policy required that he (outwardly) treat Mexico as a sovereign country, changing the dynamics of negotiation and the clout that Mexico brought to the bargaining table. Second, in 1938, President Lázaro Cárdenas stood up to the Roosevelt administration and nationalized the oil fields, some held by U.S. companies. He claimed sovereignty over its territory and subsoil, and refused to bow to U.S. pressure. While from the beginning Mexico tried to compensate companies, these companies felt that this compensation, calculated according to how oil companies had listed their assets and income on Mexican tax rolls, was insufficient. The result was a general boycott on Mexican oil, ignored by Japan, Germany, and Italy, and a U.S. refusal to settle the dispute. It was finally resolved when U.S. involvement in World War II sought to shore up hemispheric allies and access to Mexican oil and other products.

In the end, the United States got most of what it wanted from the program: a World War II ally, increased imports of Mexican silver and grains, and the rationalized temporary employment of laborers for agricultural work. Mexico received respect and an international partnership in accordance with a new set of foreign policy relationships and objectives. When the program was terminated in 1964, a move pushed for by the United States, Mexico instituted the Border Industrialization Program, under which *maquiladoras*—assembly plants using imported materials and domestic labor—were set up just south of the U.S.-Mexican border. These plants, now owned by Koreans, Japanese, Americans, and others, were to industrialize Mexico using former bracero labor. In actuality, the preferred worker for maquiladora jobs is and has generally been a young Mexican woman, seen as more docile and controllable, and less likely to engage in union activity.

Since the program's end, braceros have struggled to recoup the 10 percent of their salaries withheld. They captured international attention when they filed a lawsuit in the early 2000s in California federal court. The case was thrown out, but the pressure still yielded results. Mexican president Vicente Fox called for small payments to be made to former braceros or their descendents for monies lost.

Alma Alvarez-Smith

See also
H-2A Visa; Labor Unions; Migrant Workers

Further Reading:

Calavita, Kitty. *Inside the State: The Bracero Program, Immigration, and the I.N.S.* New York: Routledge, 1992.

Cohen, Deborah. "From Peasant to Worker: Migration, Masculinity, and the Making of Mexican Workers in the US." *International Labor and Working Class History* 69 (2006): 81–103.

Galarza, Ernesto. *Merchants of Labor: The Mexican Bracero Story.* Charlotte, NC: McNally and Loftin, 1964.

Lytle Hernández, Kelly. "The Crimes and Consequences of Illegal Immigration: A Cross-Border Examination of Operation Wetback, 1943–1954." *Western Historical Quarterly* 37 (Winter 2006): 421–44.

Scruggs, Otey. *Braceros, "Wetbacks," and the Farm Labor Problem: A History of Mexican Agricultural Labor in the United States, 1942–1954.* New York: Garland Publishers, 1988.

Brooklyn Dodgers

The Brooklyn Dodgers, a major league baseball team formerly in Brooklyn, New York, integrated major league baseball on April 15, 1947, when Jackie Robinson, the first African American in baseball since the 19th century, took the field. The Dodgers were not the first team in Brooklyn, but the club established in 1883 became the historic Dodgers franchise. After several name changes and participation in different leagues, the team in Brooklyn joined the National League in 1890. In 1913, the team changed its name to the Dodgers, a shortening of the nickname Trolley Dodger, and moved into Ebbets Field, where they would play until 1957. The Dodgers were the heart of the city, and later borough, of Brooklyn. In 1958, the Brooklyn Dodgers moved to California and became the Los Angeles Dodgers.

Like the rest of major league baseball in the first part of the 20th century, the Dodgers supported baseball's color line. Since the 1880s, team owners participated in a "gentleman's agreement" and did not hire African Americans or other players or color in any capacity. First the major leagues, and then the minor leagues followed this unwritten rule. This policy forced several African American players off teams in the 19th century. Individuals tried to challenge the color line, but did so without success until Branch Rickey and Jackie Robinson. Wesley Branch Rickey was born December 20, 1881, in Portsmouth, Ohio. Branch Rickey, as he was known, graduated with a BA from Ohio Wesleyan University and a law degree from the University of Michigan. Rickey played baseball in college and professionally in the minor leagues. He also coached before moving into management. Richey worked as an executive for major league baseball teams and established an extensive minor league farm system while working for the St. Louis Cardinals, an innovation copied by other teams. In 1942, Rickey became the president and general manager of the Brooklyn Dodgers. In 1950, Rickey moved to the Pittsburgh Pirates, where he ended his career in baseball.

Jack Roosevelt Robinson was born in Cairo, Georgia, on January 31, 1919. When he was a child, his mother moved the family to Pasadena, California. Robinson attended Pasadena City College and transferred to the University of California, Los Angeles, where he lettered in four sports. In 1942, the Army drafted Robinson. After completing Officer Candidate School at Fort Riley, Kansas, the Army commissioned

Robinson as a second lieutenant and transferred him to Fort Hood, Texas. In November 1944, Robinson received an honorable discharge from the Army. The discharge came after a court martial in which Robinson went to trial on a charge of insubordination after refusing to move to the back of a bus on base. He was found not guilty. In 1945, Robinson played a season for the Kansas City Monarchs, a Negro League team.

On May 7, 1945, Dodgers General Manager Branch Rickey announced a plan to create the Brooklyn Brown Dodgers, a team in the United States League, a new Negro League. Rickey sent scout Clyde Sukeforth to evaluate Jackie Robinson and wanted to meet with him. On August 28, 1945, Rickey and Robinson met in New York City. The Brown Dodgers served as a distraction from Rickey's plan to integrate the Brooklyn Dodgers. Rickey signed Robinson to a contract of $600 a month with a $3,500 signing bonus. On October 23, 1945, Rickey held a press conference announcing the signing of Jack Roosevelt Robinson to a Dodger contract. For the 1946 season, Rickey sent Jackie Robinson to the Montreal Royals, the Dodgers AAA-level minor league affiliate. The Dodgers also signed pitcher John Wright, who accompanied Robinson to Montreal so he would not have to room alone. Robinson and Wright reported to Florida for spring training in 1946. Segregation laws, the reaction of teammates, and injury made spring training a difficult one for Robinson and Wright.

Robinson debuted as a Dodger on April 15, 1947, and integrated major league baseball. Robinson faced taunts and threats from fans, his own teammates, players, coaches, and managers from other teams. To aid in the success of the experiment, Robinson had agreed to Rickey's request not to respond to critics in any way for the first three years. In 1947, the members of the Baseball Writers Association of American voted Robinson rookie of the year. John Wright, having returned to baseball in the Negro Leagues, did not leave Robinson alone for long, as other black players joined the Dodger system in subsequent years. Roy Campanella and Don Newcombe, who played on the Nashua Dodgers in Nashua, New Hampshire, in 1946, moved up to Brooklyn in 1948 and 1949. In subsequent years, dozens of players followed Robinson onto major league rosters. Some teams were slow to integrate, however, and it took until 1959 for all 16 major league teams to sign and field players of color.

Both Rickey and Robinson were elected to the Baseball Hall of Fame. Robinson was elected in 1962 as a second baseman and Rickey, posthumously, in 1967 as an executive/pioneer. Rickey died in 1965. Robinson died in October 24, 1972, 10 days after speaking at the World Series. The Dodgers retired Robinson's number 42 in 1972. In 1997, to honor the 50th anniversary of the integration of baseball, all of major league baseball retired Jackie Robinson's number, the only number to receive such an honor.

Amy Essington

See also

Robinson, Jackie; Sports and Racism

Further Reading:

Lowenfish, Lee. *Branch Rickey: Baseball's Ferocious Gentleman.* Lincoln: University of Nebraska Press, 2007.

Stout, Glenn, and Richard A. Johnson. *120 Years of Dodgers Baseball.* New York: Houghton Mifflin, 2004.

Tygiel, Jules. *Baseball's Great Experiment.* New York: Oxford University Press, 1997.

Brown, H. Rap (b. 1943)

Hubert Gerold Brown, who as a civil rights activist during the 1960s was known as H. Rap Brown, is also an African American writer, Muslim cleric, and former member of the Student Nonviolent Coordinating Committee (SNCC). Brown was born in Baton Rouge, Louisiana, on October 4, 1943, the son of Eddie C. and Thelma Warren Brown. In 1962, Brown left Southern University in Baton Rouge to devote his life to the struggle for civil rights. He moved to Washington, D.C., where he worked in an antipoverty program and as a librarian for the U.S. Department of Agriculture before becoming a member of the Nonviolent Action Group (NAG), a local SNCC affiliate at Howard University. In 1964, he volunteered for the Mississippi Summer Project (see the entry Freedom Summer [Mississippi] of 1964).

In 1965, Brown returned to Washington to become chairperson for NAG, and in 1966 he became the SNCC project director in Alabama. In May 1967, he succeeded Stokely Carmichael as national director of the SNCC. On July 24, 1967, Brown achieved lasting notoriety by delivering a speech in Cambridge, Maryland, in which he urged his listeners "to

H. Rap Brown, national chairperson of the Student Nonviolent Coordinating Committee (SNCC) and a leader in the Black Power movement, during a press conference on July 27, 1967. Brown was shot and wounded in 1967 after delivering a fiery speech about the cause. The Black Power movement was an attempt by militant African Americans to establish their own political, cultural, and social institutions independent of white society. (Library of Congress)

meet violence with violence," and declared to them that "If this town don't come around, this town should be burned down" (Carson and Hamburger 1997: 11A). Within hours, Cambridge was in flames and Brown was charged with arson and inciting a riot. From that night forward, he was associated with the infamous slogan "Burn, Baby, Burn!" and by 1968, when he joined the Black Panther Party, had completely abandoned the belief in nonviolence advocated by SNCC. His autobiographical political memoir, *Die, Nigger, Die!* which was published in 1969, reflected the extremist views for which he had become famous. Imprisoned several times between 1967 and 1970, Brown appeared on the Federal Bureau of Investigation (FBI) Ten Most Wanted List after avoiding trial on charges of inciting a riot and taking a gun across state lines. He was wounded during a shoot-out with New York City police in 1971, subsequently convicted of robbery, and incarcerated in Attica Prison until 1976.

In 1972, while in prison, Brown converted to orthodox Islam and changed his name to Jamil (beautiful) Abdullah (servant of God) al-Amin (the trustworthy). When he was paroled in 1976, al-Amin made a *hajj*, or pilgrimage, to Mecca, the birthplace of Muhammad and the most sacred Islamic site. After returning from Mecca, al-Amin moved to Atlanta, Georgia, where his brother was director of the Voter Education Project. Between 1976 and 1993, he had little public exposure and no recorded encounters with the authorities. He operated the Community Store, a grocery he opened in one of Atlanta's impoverished areas, and started the Community Mosque in one of Atlanta's African American neighborhoods. In 1993, following the bombing of the World Trade Center, al-Amin was interrogated by the police. In 1995, he was arrested and accused of a shooting, but the charges were later dropped. Five years later, on March 16, 2000, two Fulton County deputies, both African American, were shot near the Community Mosque. One deputy died and the other suffered serious injuries. Al-Amin was charged with the crime and on March 9, 2002, was found guilty of the shootings and sentenced to life in prison.

John G. Hall

See also

Black Power; Congress of Racial Equality (CORE); Student Nonviolent Coordinating Committee

Further Reading:

Al-Amin, Jamil. *Revolution by the Book: (The Rap Is Live).* Beltsville, MD: Writers' Inc. International, 1993.

Brown, H. Rap. *Die, Nigger, Die!: A Political Autobiography*. New York: Dial Press, 1969.

Carson, Clayborne, and Tom Hamburger. "The Cambridge Convergence: How a Night in Maryland 30 Years Ago Changed the Nation's Course of Racial Politics." *Minneapolis Star Tribune*, July 28, 1997, 11A.

Forman, James. *The Making of Black Revolutionaries*. New York: Macmillan Publishing Company, 1972.

Thelwell, Ekwueme Michael. "H. Rap Brown/Jamil Al-Amin: A Profoundly American Story." *The Nation*. March 18, 2002. http://www.thenation.com/doc/20020318/thelwell.

Brown v. Board of Education (1954)

Brown v. Topeka, Kansas Board of Education, 347 U.S. 483, was decided by the U.S. Supreme Court in 1954. Two years earlier, *Brown* along with four other companion cases—*Belton v. Gebhardt (Bulah v. Gebhardt),* Delaware; *Bolling v. Sharpe,* 347 U.S. 497, D.C.; *Briggs v. Elliott,* South Carolina; *Davis v. Prince Edwards County School Board,* Virginia—were filed by the National Association for the Advancement of Colored People (NAACP) attorneys—Thurgood Marshall, Robert Carter, Jack Greenberg, Charles Bledsoe, Charles Scott, John Scott, and James Nabrit—on behalf of plaintiffs challenging the legality of de jure or state-mandated racial segregation of black and white children in public schools.

By 1949, at least 17 states—Alabama, Arkansas, Connecticut, Florida, Georgia, Kentucky, Louisiana, Massachusetts, Mississippi, Missouri, North Carolina, Oklahoma, Rhode Island, South Carolina, Tennessee, Texas, and West Virginia—and the District of Columbia had enacted laws requiring the racial segregation of public school children. Four other states—Arizona, Kansas, New Mexico, and Wyoming—provided for a local option in determining whether to segregate public education. Wyoming was the only state that did not exercise this option.

In Delaware (*Belton/Bulah*), a 1935 state law required that "[t]he schools provided shall be of two kinds; those for white children and those for colored children. The schools for white children shall be free for all white children between the ages of six and twenty-one years, inclusive; and the schools for colored children shall be free to all colored children between the ages of six and twenty-one years, inclusive. . . . The State Board of Education shall establish schools for children of people called Moors or Indians." This dual system of public education was contested because of the inferior conditions of the black schools.

In *Bolling,* the Court concluded that

> the Equal Protection Clause of the Fourteenth Amendment prohibits the states from maintaining racially segregated public schools. [Note: *Bolling* was decided on the same day as *Brown.*] The legal problem in the District of Columbia is somewhat different however. The Fifth Amendment, which is applicable in the District of Columbia, does not contain an equal protection clause as does the Fourteenth Amendment which applies only to the states. But the concepts of equal protection and due process, both stemming from our American ideal of fairness, are not mutually exclusive. The 'equal protection of the laws" is a more explicit safeguard of prohibited unfairness than "due process of law," and, therefore, we do not imply that the two are always interchangeable phrases. But, as this Court has recognized, discrimination may be so unjustifiable as to violative of due process. . . . In view of our decision that the Constitution prohibits the states from maintaining racially segregated public schools, it would be unthinkable that the same Constitution would impose a lesser duty on the Federal Government. We hold that racial segregation in the public schools of the District of Columbia is a denial of the due process of law guaranteed by the *Fifth* [emphasis added] Amendment to the Constitution. For the reasons set out in *Brown v. Board of Education,* this case will be restored to the docket for reargument on Questions 4 and 5 previously propounded by the Court.

Article 11, Section 7 of South Carolina's 1895 constitution required racial segregation of its public schools. According to the language of this article, "[s]eparate schools shall be provided for children of the white and colored races, and no child of either race shall ever be permitted to attend a school provided for children of the other race." Similarly, Section 5377 of the 1942 Code of Laws of South Carolina made it "unlawful for pupils of one race to attend the schools provided by boards of trustees for persons of another race." The emphasis in the *Briggs* case was on inequities—facilities, transportation, and teachers' salaries—that existed between white and black public schools.

Even though *Davis* was one of *Brown*'s companion cases, this case differed from the other cases in that the *Davis* challenge was initiated by a 1951 student protest against the disparities that existed between white and black public schools in the state of Virginia. The NAACP later joined the students to challenge various disparities.

The *Brown* plaintiffs brought suit to enjoin "a Kansas statute [Kan. Gen. Stat. 72-1724 (1949)] which permit[ted], but d[id] not require, cities of more than 15,000 population to maintain separate school facilities for Negro and white students." This case was brought on behalf of 20 black children who were denied admissions to public schools reserved for white children.

Brown was not the first legal challenge to racially segregated public education for white and black children. It is instead the most successful and well-known challenge to this form of segregation because of the final decree of the U.S. Supreme Court. The earliest challenge to segregated public schools dates back to 1849 in *Robert v. the City of Boston,* 59 Mass. 198. In fact, the *Brown* Court noted that "the [application of the separate-but-equal] doctrine apparently originated in *Roberts v. City of Boston,* 59 Mass. 198, 206 (1850), upholding school segregation against attack as being violative of a state constitutional guarantee of equality. [As a result], [s]egregation in Boston public schools was [not] eliminated [until] 1855."

Between 1881 and 1950, many lawsuits were filed challenging the constitutionality of racially segregated public schools. These lawsuits were as follows:

1881 *Elijah Tinnon v. The Board of Education of Ottawa, KS* (26 Kan. 1)
1891 *Knox v. The Board of Education of Independence, KS* (45 Kan. 152)
1903 *Reynolds v. The Board of Education of Topeka, KS* (66 Kan. 672)
1906 *Richardson v. The Board of Education of Topeka, KS* (72 Kan. 629)
1906 *Cartwright v. The Board of Education of Coffeyville, KS* (73 Kan. 32)
1907 *Rowles v. The Board of Education of Wichita, KS* (76 Kan. 361)
1908 *Williams v. The Board of Education of Parsons* (79 Kan. 202)
1916 *Woodridge v. The Board of Education of Galena, KS* (98 Kan. 397)
1949 *Webb v. School District No. 90, South Park Johnson County* (167 Kan. 395).

There were also challenges to racial segregation in higher education (*Berea College v. Commonwealth of Kentucky*).

Since this decision, there have been two other *Brown* decisions—*Brown* II, 349 U.S. 294 (1955), and *Brown* III, 84 F.R.D. 383 (D. Kan. 1979). In *Brown* II, the court ruled that "the cases are remanded to the District Courts to take such proceedings and enter such orders and decrees consistent with this opinion as are necessary and proper to admit to pubic schools on a racially nondiscriminatory basis *with all deliberate speed* (emphasis added) the parties of these cases." *Brown* III was brought by attorneys requesting that the courts revisit *Brown* I and *Brown* II to determine whether Kansas's public schools had been desegregated. The U.S. Supreme Court denied the appellants a writ of certiorari and remanded the case for implementation of the 10th Circuit's ruling on behalf of the *Brown* III plaintiffs. Years later, magnet schools were built in an effort to eliminate the remaining vestiges of segregation in the public schools of Topeka.

What distinguished *Brown* from previous attempts to integrate public education was the role played by the NAACP in working with community activists and parents in order to initiate class action lawsuits in specific localities. Beginning in the 1920s and specifically under the leadership of Walter White, the NAACP began developing a strategy to challenge the constitutionality of legally mandated racial segregation. In the 1930s, Charles Hamilton Houston replaced White and later became director of counsel for the NAACP. It was Houston's experience with Jim Crow laws during his military service that served as an impetus in his attack on segregation. Thus, the NAACP viewed *Brown* as the first of many steps toward the goal of integrating every aspect of American society.

Brown reached the Court in 1951 but was not argued until December 9, 1952. Rather than providing a ruling in 1952, the Court scheduled reargument of the case. This reargument was scheduled for December 8, 1953. In preparation for reargument, the justices asked the lawyers to consider five specific questions. Three of these questions focused upon the applicability or lack thereof of the 14th Amendment to the issue of racial segregation, and two questions focused upon the procedures and timetable for possible integration of public education. The attorneys were asked to address the following questions:

1. What evidence is there that the Congress which submitted and the State legislatures and conventions which ratified the Fourteenth Amendment contemplated or did not contemplate, understood or did not understand, that it would abolish segregation in public schools?
2. If neither the Congress in submitting nor the States in ratifying the Fourteenth Amendment understood

that compliance with it would require the immediate abolition of segregation in public schools, was it nevertheless the understanding of the framers of the Amendment:

   (a) that future Congresses might, in the exercise of their power under section 5 of the Amendment, abolish such segregation, or
   (b) that it would be within the judicial power, in light of future conditions, to construe the Amendment as abolishing such segregation of its own force?

3. On the assumption that the answers to questions 2(a) and (b) do not dispose of the issue, is it within the judicial power, in construing the Amendment, to abolish segregation in public schools?
4. Assuming it is decided that segregation in public schools violates the Fourteenth Amendment:
   (a) would a decree necessarily follow providing that, within the limits set by normal geographical school districting, Negro children should forthwith be admitted to schools of their choice, or
   (b) may this Court, in the exercise of its equity powers, permit an effective gradual adjustment to be brought about from existing segregated systems not based on color distinctions?
5. On the assumption on which questions 4(a) and (b) are based, and assuming further that this Court will exercise its equity powers to the end described in question 4(b),
   (a) should this court formulate detailed decrees in these cases;
   (b) if so, what specific issues should the decrees reach;
   (c) should this Court appoint a special master to hear evidence with a view to recommending specific terms for such decrees;
   (d) should this Court remand to the courts of first instance with directions to frame decrees in these cases, and if so what general directions should the decrees of this Court include and what procedures should the courts of first instance follow in arriving at the specific terms of more detailed decrees?

Prior to the reargument of *Brown*, Chief Justice Fred Vinson died and was replaced by Earl Warren. Warren eventually persuaded fellow justices of the importance of rendering a unanimous decision in the *Brown* case. On May 17, 1954, the Court issued a unanimous decision on behalf of the *Brown* plaintiffs.

When presenting their arguments in *Brown*, the attorneys relied upon the doll experiment of Professor Kenneth B. Clark and Mamie Clark to support their inferiority complex thesis. Professor Clark found that black children were consistently more likely to prefer a white doll to a black one, which they classified as "bad" or "looking bad." The attorneys successfully employed the contention relied upon by attorney Robert Carter in *Westminster School District of Orange County v. Mendez*, 161 F.2d 774 (Ninth Circuit 1947), to convince the court that racially segregated public schools resulted in black children feeling inferior to their white counterparts and experiencing psychological harm. In agreement, the court stated:

> To separate them from others of similar age and qualifications solely because of their race generates a feeling of inferiority as to their status in the community that may affect their hearts and minds in a way unlikely ever to be undone. The effect of this separation on their educational opportunities was well stated by a finding in the Kansas case by a court which nevertheless felt compelled to rule against the Negro plaintiffs: "[s]egregation of white and colored children in public schools has a detrimental effect upon the colored children. The impact is greater when it has the sanction of the law, for the policy of separating the races is usually interpreted as denoting the inferiority of the negro group. A sense of inferiority affects the motivation of a child to learn. Segregation with the sanction of law, therefore, has a tendency to [retard] the educational and mental development of negro children and to deprive them of some of the benefits they would receive in a racial[ly] integrated school system."

In addition to their emphasis upon an inferiority complex thesis, the *Brown* attorneys challenged the "separate but equal" doctrine established in *Plessy v. Ferguson*, 163 U.S. 537 (1896). This strategy forced the court to determine whether black and white public schools were in fact equal

Excerpt from *Brown v. Board of Education* (1954)

Segregation of white and Negro children in the public schools of a State solely on the basis of race, pursuant to state laws permitting or requiring such segregation, denies to Negro children the equal protection of the laws guaranteed by the Fourteenth Amendment—even though the physical facilities and other "tangible" factors of white and Negro schools may be equal.

(a) The history of the Fourteenth Amendment is inconclusive as to its intended effect on public education.
(b) The question presented in these cases must be determined, not on the basis of conditions existing when the Fourteenth Amendment was adopted, but in the light of the full development of public education and its present place in American life throughout the Nation.
(c) Where a State has undertaken to provide an opportunity for an education in its public schools, such an opportunity is a right which must be made available to all on equal terms.
(d) Segregation of children in public schools solely on the basis of race deprives children of the minority group of equal educational opportunities, even though the physical facilities and other "tangible" factors may be equal.
(e) The "separate but equal" doctrine adopted in *Plessy v. Ferguson* has no place in the field of public education.
(f) The cases are restored to the docket for further argument on specified questions relating to the forms of the decrees.

under the 14th Amendment and allowed plaintiffs' attorneys the opportunity to address the relevance of the 14th Amendment to the case.

Interestingly, the court's interpretation of the 14th Amendment in *Brown* differed considerably from its interpretation of this amendment in *Plessy*. Unlike the *Plessy* court's application of the separate-but-equal doctrine, the *Brown* court opined that

> In approaching this problem, we cannot turn the clock back to 1868, when the Amendment was adopted, or even to 1896, when *Plessy v. Ferguson* was written. We must consider public education in the light of its full development and its present place in American life throughout the Nation. Only in this way can it be determined if segregation in public schools deprives these plaintiffs of the equal protection of the laws. Today, education is perhaps the most important function of state and local governments. Compulsory school attendance laws and the great expenditures for education both demonstrate our recognition of the importance of education to our democratic society. It is required in the performance of our most basic public responsibilities, even service in the armed forces. It is the very foundation of good citizenship. Today it is a principal instrument in awakening the child to cultural values, in preparing him for later professional training, and in helping him to adjust normally to his environment. In these days, it is doubtful that any child may reasonably be expected to succeed in life if he is denied the opportunity of an education. Such an opportunity, where the state has undertaken to provide it, is a right which must be made available to all on equal terms. We come then to the question presented: Does segregation of children in public schools solely on the basis of race, even though the physical facilities and other "tangible" factors may be equal, deprive the children of the minority group of equal educational opportunities? We believe that it does.

Therefore, the *Brown* court concluded "that in the field of public education the doctrine of 'separate-but-equal' has no place. Separate educational facilities are inherently unequal. Therefore, we hold that the plaintiffs and others similarly situated for whom the actions have been brought are, by reason of the segregation complained of, deprived of the equal protection of the laws guaranteed by the Fourteenth Amendment."

Even though the court ruled that the "segregation of children in public schools solely on the basis of race . . .

deprive[s] the children of the minority group of equal educational opportunities," it failed to order states to immediately desegregate public schools. Instead, the court once again asked *Brown* attorneys to address questions focusing on the implementation of his desegregation order. Of course, the attorneys argued that the integration of public schools should occur immediately rather than in "gradual adjustments" or increments. Therefore, in 1955, the court issued a directive in *Brown* II requiring lower federal courts to "enter such orders and decrees consistent with [its] opinion as are necessary and proper to admit to public schools on a racially nondiscriminatory basis *with all deliberate speed* (emphasis added) the parties of these cases (*Brown* I).

White segregationists used the court's "with all deliberate speed" phrase as a loophole in their efforts to delay the implementation of *Brown*. As a result, in many localities, integration of public schools did not occur until many years after the *Brown* decision. Despite obstacles—the infamous actions of Gov. Orval Faubus of Arkansas, enactment of school closing laws, repeal of compulsory attendance and student placement statues, "freedom of choice" student plans, and passage of anti-NAACP laws—encountered in the implementation of the *Brown* ruling, the significance of this decision cannot be exaggerated.

This ruling had a far-reaching impact on civil rights in the United States and led to the eventual dismantling of Jim Crow laws throughout the United States. The Supreme Court's declaration in *Brown* that the separate-but-equal doctrine adopted in *Plessy* did not apply to the field of public education resulted in efforts to eliminate all forms of segregation—the initial and ultimate goal of the NAACP. As a result, post-*Brown* attention has focused on segregated housing, public accommodations, public transportation, voting, and employment.

Olethia Davis

See also

Brown v. Board of Education Legal Groundwork; Educational Achievement Gap; Hypersegregation; *Savage Inequalities*

Further Reading:

Brown v. Board of Education of Topeka, Kansas, 347 U.S. 483 (1954).

Brown v. Board of Education of Topeka, Kansas, 349 U.S. 294 (1955).

Ogletree, Charles J., Jr. *All Deliberate Speed: Reflections on the First Half Century of Brown v. Board of Education*. New York: W. W. Norton, 2004.

Patterson, James T. Brown v. Board of Education: *A Civil Rights Milestone and Its Troubled Legacy*. New York: Oxford University Press, 2001.

Plessy v. Ferguson, 163 U.S. 537 (1896).

Brown v. Board of Education Legal Groundwork

In a series of Supreme Court decisions that paved the way for black students to pursue graduate degrees at state universities, lawyers working for the National Association for the Advancement of Colored People (NAACP) laid the groundwork for extinguishing the legal basis for Jim Crow segregation in other public arenas. The architect of the NAACP's legal strategy was Charles Hamilton Houston, who has since become known as the "Man Who Killed Jim Crow." Houston, a graduate of Harvard Law School, eventually became dean of the Howard University Law School. Houston trained a significant portion of the nation's black lawyers during the middle of the 20th century.

Houston considered the U.S. Supreme Court's "separate but equal" doctrine, established in *Plessy v. Ferguson* (1896), to be the legal foundation of Jim Crow. Houston's strategy was to undermine incrementally this doctrine in a series of lawsuits brought by NAACP lawyers beginning in the 1930s, and culminating in 1954 with *Brown v. Board of Education*. Houston aimed to demonstrate that "separate but equal" doctrine led to inequality, and thus violated the Fourteenth Amendment right to equal protection under the law. Houston's primary target was segregation in the American education system.

One of the NAACP's first significant victories was *Pearson v. Murray* (Md. 1936). Donald Gaines Murray, a black graduate of Amherst College, was denied admission to the University of Maryland Law School. Future U.S. Supreme Court Justice Thurgood Marshall served as Murray's attorney. Marshall had also been denied admission to the same school years before, and had instead obtained his law degree from Howard University.

Maryland argued that it could meet the requirements of "separate but equal" doctrine by providing scholarships for black students to fund their graduate education at out-of-state schools. The trial court held that the legislature's appropriation for the scholarship fund was obviously inadequate to support the population of black law students in Maryland. Nor could black students study Maryland law and court procedures at out-of-state law schools. The state appealed the case to Maryland's highest court, which affirmed the lower court's ruling in favor of Murray. The court required the University of Maryland Law School to admit black students. Because the NAACP prevailed in Maryland's Supreme Court, thus ending the litigation, the court's judgment was not binding outside of Maryland.

In 1938, the U.S. Supreme Court decided *Missouri ex rel. Gaines v. Canada*. Lloyd Gaines, a black student represented by the NAACP, complained that Missouri had no grounds to exclude him from the state university's law school, because Missouri provided no alternative state law school for him to attend. He argued that this condition thus violated his Fourteenth Amendment right to equal protection. The Court agreed, and held that states that provide a public legal education to white students must also make a comparable education available to black students as well. However, this did not end segregation nationwide. The decision permitted states to continue to maintain segregated graduate schools by creating additional law or medical schools for blacks. Thus states could avoid Fourteenth Amendment challenges by fulfilling the requirements established by *Plessy*'s "separate but equal" doctrine.

Ada Lois Sipuel, a black student, applied to the School of Law at the University of Oklahoma, and was turned down on the basis of race. Oklahoma had no alternative state-funded law school that admitted blacks. In *Sipuel v. Oklahoma State Regents* (1948), the U.S. Supreme Court held that in such circumstances, states must admit black applicants to white law schools. Thus the Court upheld and extended *Gaines.*

With *Gaines* and *Sipuel*, Houston and the NAACP legal team had successfully established that black students had an equal right to a legal education at state universities. Their next challenge was to overturn the "separate but equal" doctrine that segregated white and black law students into separate schools. They came close to accomplishing this by winning *Sweatt v. Painter* (1950). Herman Sweatt, a black mail carrier, applied to the University of Texas Law School and was denied admission on the grounds that the Texas constitution prohibited racially integrated public education. There were no other law schools in Texas that admitted black students. Thus Texas was in violation of the rule set in *Gaines* and *Sipuel.*

The Texas trial court attempted an end run. The court set aside the case for six months, to give the state time to create a law school for blacks (which eventually developed into what today is Texas Southern University). Sweatt complained that the makeshift facility—a few rooms staffed by underqualified teachers—was clearly unequal compared with the University of Texas Law School.

The Supreme Court agreed with Sweatt, and overturned the lower court in 1950. The Supreme Court held that if a state establishes separate black schools, they must be "substantially equal" to the comparable white schools. The Court held that the new black law school was clearly inferior on objective criteria. It also held that intangible factors must also be considered, such as the graduates' isolation from the broader population of future lawyers. These intangibles were a component of the new doctrine of substantive equality, along with the objective criteria used to evaluate schools. Thus, in *Sweatt*, the principle of "separate but equal" was seriously undermined. The Court now held states to the "equal" part of the rule, which states had been evading for decades. As a result, segregation was effectively eliminated with regard to higher education at state law schools, because funding two fully equal law schools made segregation too expensive to be practical, and because the intangible aspects of substantive equality were nearly impossible to re-create in a segregated system of graduate education.

The Supreme Court heard another significant case in Oklahoma the same year, in *McLaurin v. Oklahoma State Regents for Higher Education* (1950). A retired black professor, George McLaurin, had successfully sued the University of Oklahoma for admission into the school's PhD program in education, after the university denied his admission on the basis of race. Because Oklahoma had no other state-funded graduate school in education, the court forced the university to admit McLaurin. The university reluctantly complied, but relegated McLaurin to segregated facilities within the university. He was required to sit at a designated desk in an anteroom next to his classroom, and was not permitted to sit in the classroom itself. He was given another designated desk on the mezzanine in the library, and was not permitted to study on the main floor. In the school cafeteria, he was forced to sit at a designated table and eat at a separate time from the white students.

The U.S. Supreme Court held that such restrictions violated McLaurin's Fourteenth Amendment rights under the equal protection clause, because they prevented McLaurin from interacting with other students in a meaningful fashion, thereby impinging on his education. Thus the Court overturned segregation within the facilities at state universities, and established the principle that students of different races must be treated equally.

The cases discussed in this article were at the core of the NAACP's attack on Jim Crow. While the NAACP attacked segregation in other cases outside the arena of graduate education, the education cases incrementally undermined the "separate but equal" doctrine. Education cases in general were highly symbolic, in that the issue of segregation in public schools tended to inflame emotions among Southern whites more so than any other aspect of Jim Crow, save interracial sex and marriage. The cases outlined in this article created the groundwork for the *Brown v. Board of Education* decision. By establishing the necessary precedents for *Brown* at the graduate school level, the NAACP lawyers prepared the way for the Supreme Court to drive the final nail into the coffin of the "separate but equal" doctrine in *Brown*.

Thomas Brown

See also

Brown v. Board of Education

Further Reading:

Kluger, Richard. *Simple Justice: The History of Brown v. Board of Education and Black America's Struggle for Equality*. New York: Knopf, 2004.

McNeil, Genna Rae. *Groundwork: Charles Hamilton Houston and the Struggle for Civil Rights*. Philadelphia: University of Pennsylvania Press, 1983.

Brownsville (Texas) Incident of 1906

The Brownsville incident refers to a racial event that occurred in 1906 in Brownsville, Texas, between black soldiers and white townspeople. The incident involved members of the U.S. Army's all-black 25th Infantry who were stationed at nearby Fort Brown. These were the Buffalo Soldiers, a segregated unit. When a local white bartender was killed and a white police official injured on the evening of August 12, 1906, Brownsville townspeople accused the Buffalo Soldiers at Fort Brown, and a lengthy investigation ensued. Although 167 of the soldiers received a dishonorable discharge for the crime, it is widely agreed today that they were innocent and that evidence was planted against them.

Companies B, C, and D of the U.S. Army's all-black 25th Infantry were deployed to Fort Brown, just outside of Brownsville, in the summer of 1906. Even before they arrived, there was lingering apprehension among the troops about the entire Texas assignment. Chaplain Theophilus G. Steward, the only black officer among the troops, recalled that the only time he had suffered verbal assaults from a U.S. soldier was at Fort Riley, Kansas. The soldier was from Texas. Steward wrote one of his superiors, telling him of his concern about the deployment to Fort Brown. Steward's fears turned out to be justified.

During the first decade of the 20th century, tensions were rising between blacks and whites, in various places all over the country. In this environment, race riots were becoming more frequent. They erupted in New York City in 1900; Springfield, Ohio, in 1904; Atlanta, Georgia, in 1906; and Greensburg, Indiana, in 1906. The Brownsville incident occurred at a chaotic time for race relations in the country.

On July 25, 1906, the 25th Infantry entered Brownsville, a town of about 6,000 residents at the time. The custom officials harassed and treated them roughly. Business owners and townspeople met them with either stony silence or taunts, racial slurs, or other hostile gestures. The 25th Infantry knew right away that the new community was not going to be a friendly place. This was quite demoralizing to the black troops for they had served with distinction and honor in previous assignments. The troops were banned from entering many of the predominantly white establishments in Brownsville, including all three of the white bars on the main street in the town. Already, it was clear there was a strong racial prejudice in Brownsville against the black troops.

On August 12, 1906, about a week after the servicemen arrived in Brownsville, a white woman in the town claimed that she had been assaulted by one of them. The possibility that this could have happened and that the person responsible was one of the black soldiers infuriated many in the

DISHONORABLY DISCHARGED

After the 25th Infantry garrison in Texas refused to identify 12 African American soldiers involved in a 1906 shooting with white Brownsville residents, all 167 black soldiers were dishonorably discharged under the orders of President Theodore Roosevelt. Despite the criticism that followed, the decision remained in effect until 1972, when the army changed the record to reflect honorable discharges. (Library of Congress)

town. The soldiers were equally offended at the accusation. Recognizing the potential for trouble, Maj. Charles W. Penrose consulted with Mayor Frederick Combe before declaring an 8:00 P.M. town curfew the next day, hoping to prevent trouble. But around midnight on August 13, Brownsville was engulfed in a wild disturbance that included a shooting spree. The result was the death of Frank Natus, a local bartender; the injury of police official M. Y. Dominguez, who lost an arm; and other lesser injuries. The incident was over in approximately 10 minutes. It was very dark outside. Visibility was limited. Yet, there were 22 eyewitnesses who later came forward with testimony. Eight identified the attackers as blacks. The implication, of course, was that the attackers were black soldiers. At the barracks, the soldiers were summoned outside. The gun racks were opened and all of the guns were retrieved. According to Dorsie Willis, the last survivor of the Brownsville incident, all of the soldiers' rifles were inspected and none were found to have been recently used. The soldiers complied with a command for them to sign sworn statements denying any knowledge of who had done the shooting.

The white commanders at Fort Brown gave an official statement corroborating that the black soldiers were in their barracks. Officers and a sentry reported hearing rifle shots outside of Fort Brown while the soldiers were in their barracks sleeping. Nevertheless, some whites in Brownsville insisted that they found Springfield rifle clips on the scene of the disturbance. Black soldiers replied that the rifle clips must have been planted and that the entire affair was a setup against them. They claimed no knowledge of the incident. At that time, some of the military officers began doubting the black soldiers. For reasons not completely clear, the investigators accepted the version given by the white townspeople. Several civilian and military investigations were held. A citizens' committee demanded that the troops be removed. Maj. Augustus P. Bloxsom, an official in the army's Southwestern Division, demanded that the soldiers tell who among them was responsible. They were threatened that a refusal would mean being uncooperative. Again, the men denied knowing anything about the incident.

On August 17, 1906, a letter was sent from John Bartlett, Brownsville's county judge, to Samuel Willis Tucker Lanham, the governor of Texas, describing a city in grave danger from the black infantrymen. Bartlett insisted that after a full investigation, a citizen committee in Brownsville had found that the black soldiers from Fort Brown attacked the city as part of a premeditated plot. He further stated that the townspeople in Brownsville had since lived in constant fear of another attack from the soldiers. Bartlett expressed his wish that the black soldiers be removed from Fort Brown and replaced with white soldiers.

William Jesse McDonald, a captain in the Texas Rangers and a person with the reputation of being tough, identified 12 black soldiers as having knowledge of the conspiracy. Yet, a Cameron County grand jury refused to indict the men.

Inspector Gen. Ernest R. Garlington charged all of the soldiers in the 25th Infantry with a conspiracy of silence. The U.S. State Department demanded that the soldiers name the alleged perpetrators. Once again, each and every soldier denied, unequivocally, any knowledge of the incident in Brownsville.

In November, President Theodore Roosevelt, with the consent and support of Secretary of War William H. Taft, issued a dishonorable discharge for each of the 167 black soldiers in the 25th Infantry. Among those discharged by President Roosevelt were two men who had served in the distinguished Bicycle Corps. They were Pvt. John Cook and Sgt. Mingo Sanders. At the time of the Roosevelt dismissal of the entire division, Brig. Gen. A. S. Burt gallantly defended Sergeant Sanders, who had been sleeping at the time of the shooting. Yet, despite many strong commendations and an excellent service record including an outstanding record of fighting in Cuba and the Philippines, he too was a victim of President Roosevelt's decision to expel all of the 25th Infantry from the U.S. military. Sergeant Sanders had less than a year before his retirement.

After a few days of political posturing connected with the 1906 elections, President Roosevelt announced his decision. His decision made sure that the soldiers would not receive any military benefits. There was no trial. There was no due process. President Roosevelt, in a harangue, said that some of those soldiers were butchers who should be hung. There was much outspoken opposition to this act of injustice. Despite many voices raised in opposition to Roosevelt's decision, including objections from Booker T. Washington and Mary Church Terrell, the president of the National Association of Colored Women, the discharge stood.

A *New York Times* editorial at the time wrote of being astonished that there was no evidence gathered that proved a conspiracy on the part of the troops. The entire proceeding had been predicated on the assumptions of the officers who made the inquiry and assumed that those who did not take part in the incident at Brownsville must know the culprits.

At the 1908 meeting of the Niagara movement, the forerunner of the National Association for the Advancement of Colored People (NAACP), W. E. B. Du Bois, along with other leaders, sent a letter to the *Oberlin Tribune* referencing the matter. The letter was published on September 4, 1908. It called for voters to remember the Brownsville affair and the "sin" that Roosevelt had committed in regard to his discharge of the black soldiers involved.

Eventually, a U.S. Senate committee investigated the Brownsville incident. In March 1908, the majority report from that committee upheld Roosevelt's decision. However, President Roosevelt's action in this matter was seen by many as a travesty of justice, giving rise to the establishment of two civil rights organizations: the NAACP and the National Urban League. This, along with similar political missteps by members of the Republican Party, contributed to the massive exodus of blacks away from the Republicans.

Senator Foraker is acknowledged as the key person in Congress to keep the issue of the Brownsville soldiers alive. He gave speeches about it and wrote extensively about it. He broke with Roosevelt over it. He chided his fellow politician from Ohio, William Taft, about it. From his seat on the Senate's Military Affairs Committee, he conducted related hearings. Penrose and Capt. Edgar A. Macklin, the officer of the day during the Brownsville incident, were finally cleared through courts martial, even as the hearings were held.

In light of the conflicting nature of the reports from the senatorial committee, the Roosevelt administration in 1910 relented by appointing a group of retired army officers known as the Court of Military Inquiry to review applications from the dismissed black soldiers for reconsideration of their military status. Inexplicably, only about 80 of the men were interviewed and 14 were approved for reenlistment. Eleven chose to do so. The rest of the 156 black soldiers from the Brownsville incident never dressed in an official U.S. military uniform again. Almost as a footnote, on the last day of President Roosevelt's term in office, he signed a bill that would allow the soldiers of the 25th Infantry to reenlist. This gesture proved to be too little, too late.

By 1910, Senator Foraker had lost his reelection bid amidst what many believed were bogus charges designed to disgrace him. Roosevelt had been succeeded as president by Taft. The issue surrounding the soldiers of the 25th Infantry ceased to be heard and remained dormant for more than half a century.

Finally, in 1972, John Downing Weaver, a respected writer, published a book entitled *The Brownsville Raid*, in which he wrote with great detail and compelling research about the grave injustice that the men in the 25th Infantry had suffered. He concluded that the black soldiers had been innocent. This was revealed at the height of the modern civil rights era. Largely due to Weaver's book, Brownsville became an embarrassment to the army and to the U.S. government. With this new information along with the urging of Rep. Augustus Hawkins, a black Democrat from California, the infamous decision of 1906 was voided. The Buffalo Soldiers of the 25th Infantry were exonerated and reinstated by President Richard Nixon. By this time, only two survivors of the Brownsville incident were found by Rep. Hawkins: Edward Warfield of California and Dorsie Willis of Minnesota.

After tireless work by author John Weaver, Rep. Augustus Hawkins, Sen. Hubert Humphrey, and other sympathizers, a compensation bill was passed in Congress. The army dispatched Maj. Gen. DeWitt Smith to present the compensation to Dorsie Willis. At a ceremony in Minneapolis on January 10, 1974, the major general on behalf of the government presented Willis with a $25,000 check.

On August 29, 1977, Willis, the last black soldier from the Brownsville incident, was laid to rest in Fort Snelling, Minnesota, with full military honors. He maintained his innocence to the end. He was 91 years old.

Betty Nyangoni

See also

Documents: Report on the Memphis Riots of May 1866 (1866); Account of the Riots in East St. Louis, Illinois (1917); A Southern Black Woman's Letter Regarding the Recent Riots in Chicago and Washington (1919); The Cook County Coroner's Report Regarding the 1919 Chicago Race Riots (1920); The Final Report of the Grand Jury on the Tulsa Race Riot (June 25, 1921); Testimony from *Laney v. United States* (1923); The Governor's Commission Report on the Watts Riots (1965); Cyrus R. Vance's Report on the Riots in Detroit (1967); The Reports of the Oklahoma Commission to Study the Tulsa Race Riot of 1921 (2000–2001); Draft Report: 1898 Wilmington Race Riot Commission (2005)

Further Reading:

Bartlett, John, to Hon. S. W. T. Lanham. Brownsville, Texas, August 17, 1906. Texas State Library & Archives Commission.

Bergman, Peter M. *The Chronological History of the Negro in America*. New York: Harper and Row, 1969.

Brown, Richard Maxwell. *Strain of Violence: Historical Studies of American Violence and Vigilantism*. New York: Oxford University Press, 1975.

"Denounced Republicans: Leaders of the Niagara Movement Succeed in Carrying Resolutions, Convention Was at a Dead-Lock at Morning Session—Many from Out of Town." *Oberlin Tribune*, September 4, 1908. http://www.oberlin.edu/external/EOG/Niagara%20Movement/niagaramain.htm.

Lane, Ann J. *The Brownsville Affair: National Crisis and Black Reaction*. New York: National University Publications, Kennikat Press, 1971.

Weaver, John D. *The Brownsville Raid*. College Station: Texas A&M Press, 1970.

Weaver, John D. *The Senator and the Sharecropper's Son: Exoneration of the Brownsville Soldiers*. College Station: Texas A&M University Press, 1997.

Buchanan v. Warley (1917)

Buchanan v. Warley was a unanimous U.S. Supreme Court decision that prohibited racial segregation in residential areas. By upholding the rights of African Americans and whites to sell residential property to each other, the case marked the first exception to segregation laws permitted under *Plessy v. Ferguson* (1896). Lauded as ensuring the personal and property rights of African Americans, the *Buchanan* decision is considered as the legal precursor to the renowned case prohibiting segregation in public schools, *Brown v. Board of Education* (1954).

In 1914, the city of Louisville, Kentucky, enacted a state law that prohibited African Americans and whites from residing in areas where members of another race were the majority. Charles H. Buchanan, a white real estate agent, sued William Warley in 1916 for breach of contract. Warley, the president of the Louisville chapter of the National Association for the Advancement of Colored People (NAACP) and an African American purchaser, stated that their contact was void because the Louisville ordinance prevented him from buying the home. He refused to pay the full price for the property and withheld $100 from the $250 amount. Since Warley could not use the property as a residence, he further claimed that the ordinance prevented him from benefitting from the property's full value.

After the Kentucky Court of Appeals upheld the Louisville ordinance, Warley appealed the decision, and the case moved to the U.S. Supreme Court in 1916. Represented by Moorfield Storey, the first president of the NAACP, Warley finally prevailed. Storey argued that the ordinance denied the legal rights of African Americans, had adverse social consequences for African Americans and whites, and prohibited landowners the right to sell their property to whomever they wanted. In 1917, the Supreme Court unanimously found that the Louisville ordinance violated the Fourteenth Amendment because this law entitles African Americans to have property without state discriminatory practices based on race. The decision, written by Justice William Rufus Day, also stated that race as a motive for the Louisville ordinance was insufficient to make the law constitutional, and laws cannot deny rights protected by the Constitution. The Court separated its decision in *Buchanan v. Warley* from its previous ruling of legalizing racial segregation in *Plessy v. Ferguson* and *Berea College v. Kentucky* (1908) by finding these cases equitably apply the separate but equal provision of the Fourteenth Amendment.

While *Buchanan v. Warley* prevented many cities from limiting black migration in residential areas and placing fixed boundaries on black neighborhoods, the case was faulted for drawing too much attention to upholding property rights rather than the equal protection of human rights. The case also promoted buyers and sellers of property to have private restrictive covenants, which effectively created residential segregation by race and did not legally violate the Equal Protection Clause of the Fourteenth Amendment. Even with these criticisms, the *Buchanan* decision garnered awareness to the fundamental rights of African Americans set forth in the Fourteenth Amendment. Most importantly, the case signaled the emergence of the protection of the liberties and rights of African Americans by the U.S. Supreme Court.

Dorsia Smith Silva

See also

American Apartheid; Hypersegregation; Racial Steering; Residential Segregation

Further Reading:

About, Inc. *Buchanan v. Warley* African American History Web site http://afroamhistory.about.com/library/blbuchanan_v_warley.htm (accessed June 9, 2008).

Fairclough, Adam. *Better Day Coming: Blacks and Equality, 1890–2000*. New York: Penguin, 2002.

Klarman, Michael J. *From Jim Crow to Civil Rights: The Supreme Court and the Struggle for Racial Equality*. New York: Oxford University Press, 2004.

Bureau of Indian Affairs (BIA)

Before the American Revolution, Native Americans benefited somewhat from protections afforded them through treaties made with the English. With the prospect of a war becoming more and more likely, in 1775, the Second Continental Congress established the Department of Indian Affairs, whose objective was to obtain treaties and to ensure tribal neutrality during the upcoming war. The department was separated into a northern, central, and southern division. Subsequent to the war, the U.S. War Department was officially formed, with one of its major responsibilities being Indian relations. Most politicians in the late 1700s and early 1800s retained the idea that Indian and American cultures were essentially incompatible; however, they did have faith in the fact that natives had the skills necessary to adapt and fit in to American culture. Congress passed four Trade and Intercourse Acts, which dealt entirely with Indian affairs. These four laws instituted a factory system in which trade goods were provided at a fair price so that the Indians would be able to trade easily with Americans, and thus become further assimilated into American culture.

President Thomas Jefferson (1801–1809) realized that the factory system was not an enduring solution because some Indian tribes were unwilling to stop hunting and gathering, and thus he felt that they would never be truly civilized. For this reason, in 1822, the factory system was terminated. Without the approval of Congress, John C. Calhoun, the secretary of war, established the Bureau of Indian Affairs (BIA) in 1824. This action took the War Department out of almost all responsibilities for daily issues concerning Indian affairs, while still maintaining all its authority. Calhoun made past superintendent of Indian Affairs Thomas McKenney chief of this new office. McKenney and his two assistants took over the job of passing vouchers for expenditures, apportioning funds for civilizing Indians, settling disagreements between natives and white settlers over land, and dealing with all correspondence related to Indian affairs that had previously been directed to the War Department.

McKenney quickly realized that in order to be successful in carrying out his new responsibilities, he would have to have the power to enforce the actions of the BIA. On March 31, 1826, he brought a bill to Congress to establish an Office of Indian Affairs that was completely independent from the secretary of war. This bill would make the Office of Indian Affairs an official body that would have the ability to take action on its own, while still serving under the secretary of war. The bill failed to pass through Congress twice, and it was not until 1931 that the BIA was legitimately created as an entity unto itself.

The creation of an independent BIA was expected to streamline the handling of Indian policy. The belief that Indians could be absorbed into white culture was abandoned, and a new idea was adopted to force the tribes off their land. In 1825, this removal policy was formally placed into the hands of the BIA, and by the 1830s, it was implemented. A determined effort from the BIA and the U.S. government led to vast numbers of Indians being forced off their lands and pushed further west. The consequences were particularly devastating in the Southeast, where many tribes were moved hundreds of miles moved to their new homes. The most infamous event concerning these removals dealt with the Cherokee Indians.

Traditionally located in present-day Virginia and West Virginia, Kentucky, Tennessee, western North Carolina, South Carolina, northern Georgia, and northeastern Alabama, the Cherokee were a considerable tribe thriving as hunter-gathers. The Cherokee had not attempted to assimilate into white American civilization. They had their own written language, their own newspapers, and had even adopted their own constitution. In an effort to resolve their problems legally, the Cherokee brought their case to the U.S. Supreme Court where, in an unprecedented decision, they were awarded ownership of their ancestral lands. Chief Justice John Marshall concluded that the Cherokee were "a domestic dependent nation and that Georgia State law had not applied to them." The vast majority of the nation, however, did not share the opinion held by the Supreme Court. Non-Indian sympathizers, such as President Andrew Jackson, declined to enforce any of the court's rulings. The Cherokee were forced to move from their land, often at American gunpoint, and thousands died in the process. The 1,000-mile march west became known as the Trail of Tears because the ancient Indian way of life was completely wiped out in the process of moving the Cherokee.

The BIA also participated in ethnic cleansing. The demand for more land by white settlers soon focused the government's attention to the West, where the recently displaced Indians were now settled. The BIA worked directly with the government to spread diseases, wipe out the buffalo population, and kill countless numbers of women and children. The Native Americans found themselves feeling hopeless and thought that fair treatment should be given to them by the BIA. However, the BIA did not act in response to their cries for help, but instead set out to eradicate Indian culture altogether.

John C. Calhoun, Secretary of War (1817–1827). Calhoun established the Bureau of Indian Affairs in 1824 and ratified 38 treaties with Indian tribes. (Perry-Castaneda Library)

In 1849, Congress moved the Bureau of Indian Affairs into the Department of the Interior, and by 1867, the BIA became more and more involved with the affairs of the Indians. The BIA had become the governmental body officiating over all of the Indian territories, and it took full authority in assaulting their way of life. The agency did not allow Indians to speak any language but English, and banned all Indian religious ceremonies. It also outlawed any kind of Indian government. The biggest prejudices that were a result of the BIA were felt by Indian children. These young Indians were abused physically, emotionally, and spiritually in boarding schools that attempted to make them ashamed of who they were at a young age. The malicious treatment of Indians and the indignity they endured caused suicide, alcoholism, and depression to become normal characteristics of Indian societies.

The BIA had acceded to the will of the people in the devastation of the Native Americans' way of life. It would not be until the early 20th century that the federal government began to realize the dreadfulness of their actions in attempting to destroy Indian culture, and to protect it. The BIA changed into an institution dedicated to helping and advancing the Indian cause. When the Meriam Report was published in 1938, for the first time the shortcomings of the services provided to the reservations were recognized. This report started an era in which the BIA and the government worked hard to improve Indian life socially, economically, and psychologically. By 1960, the BIA expanded to embrace forestry, agriculture extension service, range management, and land acquisition in an endeavor to improve the Indian's plight. The federal government later incorporated the education of Indian children into the Department of Health, Education, and Welfare (now the Department of Health and Human Services and the Department of Education).

Throughout the 1970s, Congress continued to pass laws that helped improve the situation of Native Americans. Included in these are the Self-Determination Act, the Health Care Improvement Act, and the Indian Child Welfare Act. Today, the BIA is making an effort to modify its stance from one of management of tribes to one of aid and support to tribes. One of the most vital facets of the modern BIA is that of its over 10,000 employees, 95 percent are Native American. In September 2003, the head of the BIA publicly expressed regret for the agency's "legacy of racism and inhumanity." It was perceived by all as admission of past misdeeds and a commitment to a better future. The final words of this act of contrition articulated the aspirations and expectations of the BIA and Native Americans in years to come: "The Bureau of Indian Affairs was born in 1824 in a time of war on Indian people. May it live in the year 2000 and beyond as an instrument of their prosperity."

Arthur Holst

See also

Dawes Act; Indian Claims Commissions; Indian Reservations. Document: The Dawes Act (1887)

Further Reading:

"Alcohol and the Indian Fur Trade." http://www.thefurtrapper.com/indian.htm (accessed November 4, 2004).

"American Indian Movement, North American Indigenous Peoples." http://reference.allrefer.com/encyclopedia/A/AmerIndMov.html (accessed November 5, 2004).

Bureau of Indian Affairs, U.S. Government. http://reference.allrefer.com/encylopedia/I/IndianAf.html (accessed November 4, 2004).

"Bureau of Indian Affairs Apologizes." http://www.ouachitalk.com/apologizes.htm (accessed November 5, 2004).

Henson, C. L. "From War to Self Determination: A History of the Bureau of Indian Affairs. http://www.americansc.org.uk/Online/indians.htm (accessed November 5, 2004).

"Trail of Broken Treaties Caravan." http://siouxme.com/lodge/treaties.html (accessed November 4, 2004);

"The Trail Where They Cried: *nu na hi du na tlo hi lu i.*" http://www.powersource.com/cocinc/history/trail.htm (accessed November 4, 2004).

Busing

Since the late 1960s, the term *busing* has implied the forced assignment of students to schools outside of their community for the purpose of racial integration in education. In the 1954 *Brown v. Board of Education*, the U.S. Supreme Court ruled that separate schools for black and white students were unequal and unconstitutional. This landmark decision forced politicians and educators to integrate their school system. But it was not until 1971, after civil rights leaders and educators won other lawsuits that forced school districts to integrate their schools, that local districts began to implement busing programs. The theory behind busing was that black children would be exposed to white culture and also benefit from the same educational resources that whites enjoyed. By bringing together white and black children, society would ultimately benefit, because the races would be exposed to each other's culture and they would also become more tolerant of their differences. In its 1967 report, entitled *Racial Isolation in the Public Schools*, the U.S. Commission on Civil Rights argued that black children could not obtain a proper education if they were exposed only to substandard education in predominantly minority schools.

As a result of the court order to integrate urban school systems whose minority population was over 50 percent, Cleveland, Boston, Yonkers, Buffalo, and other cities began to bus their children to schools that were predominantly white, or made arrangements with their local school boards to implement some form of desegregation. Many civil rights organizations, such as the Urban League, National Association for the Advancement of Colored People, and American Civil Liberties Union supported busing, while many white parents who were forced to adopt busing vehemently protested the policy. In 1974, when the courts ordered the Boston school system to implement busing, white parents organized marches, protests, and boycotts to prevent the busing of their children to predominantly black schools.

Busing, which civil rights leaders advocated as the ideal solution to achieve racial equality in education, was a failure in many communities because of white flight from the urban areas and inadequate government funding of school districts. Whites who did not agree with busing decided to remove their children from the public school system, or they moved to neighborhoods that had few black residents and thus the issue of busing was not even addressed. Moreover, politicians and civic leaders who were against busing initiated court actions to prevent it from taking place in their communities. The lawsuits delayed school integration in several communities because by the time a decision was reached, there was no longer a diverse student body to allow it to take place.

Four decades after the court decision to desegregate public schools through busing, school districts in the major cities of the United States are more segregated than ever. In 1976, when the Cleveland school district was ordered to bus its black school children to predominantly white schools, there were 128,000 students attending the public school system, and 57 percent of them were African Americans. Today, the public school system has fewer than 77,000 children, and 70 percent of them are African Americans (Ravitch 2000).

Those opposed to busing have argued that the forced mixing of children through court-ordered busing has been a failure and that it is now time for the U.S. government and local school boards to do away with it. They have argued that the inability of black school children to learn has little to do with segregation but is related instead to their low socioeconomic conditions, the small amount of resources that are given to the schools they attend, and the unwillingness of parents to support the education of their children. School districts that were originally forced to bus their students are now asking the courts to release them from the busing program and to allow them to experiment with new programs to improve the educational performance of their districts. So far, courts seem willing to allow many districts to experiment with new programs.

Francois Pierre-Louis

See also

Desegregation; Education and African Americans; Educational Achievement Gap; *Savage Inequalities*

Further Reading:

Dentler, Robert A., and Marvin B. Scott. *Schools on Trial: An Inside Account of the Boston Desegregation Case*. Cambridge, MA: Abt Books, 1981.

Ravitch, Diane. "School Reform: Past, Present, and Future." *Case Western Reserve Law Review* 51, no. 2 (Winter 2000).

C

California Ballot Proposition 187 (1994)

Proposition 187 was a ballot initiative passed by California voters on November 9, 1994. While largely invalidated by court decisions over the succeeding five years, Proposition 187 is nonetheless widely regarded as a watershed in the national consideration of immigration. Its requirement that the providers of public services verify the legal status of those who use the services, report violators to state and federal agencies, and ultimately deny services would have created an immigration monitoring system far more pervasive than any previously existing system.

Proposition 187 required the creation of a state system that would verify the legal status of those seeking public education, nonemergency medical care, and social services—denying benefits to those who were not citizens, legal permanent residents, or legal temporary visitors. Composed of 10 sections, the four that addressed social services, health care, and education were the core of the proposition. Much of the public debate and consequent litigation of the proposition hinged on the particulars of these sections, especially their requirement that social service providers report those they suspected to be illegally resident, including the parents of children enrolled in the public schools, even if those children were themselves U.S. citizens.

Proposition 187 was supported by 59 percent of voters and, according to exit polls, a majority of the whites, Asian Americans, and African Americans who voted. Only Latino voters opposed the measure, with a 69 percent negative vote. White Californians were disproportionately represented at the polls. Seventy-five to 80 percent of those who voted were white, while the state's population is 57 percent white. Only eight California counties—all in the San Francisco Bay Area—failed to support the measure.

Initial reaction to the measure was swift. The day after its passage, suits were filed in state and federal courts by immigrant rights groups arguing that the law violated both the California state constitution and U.S. Constitution. Simultaneously, Gov. Pete Wilson ordered implementation of Section 6 by barring state-reimbursed prenatal services and nursing home care of undocumented immigrants. Within a few days, the courts had enjoined implementation of almost all sections of the proposition pending a court decision.

The suits filed by immigrant rights groups contended, first, that the proposition was in conflict with the Supreme Court rulings establishing the primacy of the federal government in the establishment of immigration policy, second, that it would deny due process, and, third, that it violated the equal protection clause of the Fourteenth Amendment. Each of these arguments was illustrated in the major complaint, *Gregorio T. v. Wilson*. Gregorio T. was a seven-year-old receiving Medicaid for treatment of encephalitis, and in their brief the plaintiffs argued:

> Proposition 187 creates a state immigration enforcement mechanism separate from the *Immigration and Naturalization Service* (INS) and employing standards different from those required under federal law.... States have no power to regulate immigration or the incidents thereof [primacy of the federal government in the establishment of immigration law].... The initiative... violates due process by cutting off benefits without a hearing on mere "suspicion" by any one of tens of thousands of untrained state employees [due process]. It denies equal protection of the laws by creating classes and subclasses of *aliens* without any rational basis, and by encouraging rampant discrimination against persons who appear or sound foreign [equal protection].

In defense of the proposition, California's attorney general argued that the measure assisted, rather than supplanted, federal immigration laws, that due process issues would be resolved in the regulations that would be developed to implement the proposition, and that the equal protection clause of the Fourteenth Amendment covered citizens but not undocumented immigrants.

Less than a month after its passage, a federal judge barred implementation of the verification provisions until the constitutionality of the proposition was affirmed by the courts. A year later, in November 1995, U.S. district judge Mariana Pfaelzer (presiding over a consolidated case of five of the challenges) issued a partial ruling that the ban on elementary and high school education for undocumented immigrants was unconstitutional because it violated a 1982 Supreme Court ruling, *Plyler v. Doe*, that guaranteed public education to all children irrespective of their legal status. In her final ruling on the cases in 1997, Pfaelzer concluded that Proposition 187 "is not constitutional on its face," because it presumed that a state could regulate immigration, which is the exclusive domain of the federal government. Judge Pfaelzer did let stand Section 2 of the proposition, which barred "the manufacture, distribution, or sale of false citizenship or resident alien documents." This section applied only to documents that would "conceal the true citizenship or resident alien status of another person" and not to documents used for other purposes, for example, by teenagers to buy alcohol.

Ironically, Proposition 187 was itself the catalyst for the 1996 welfare reform act. Thus, supporters of Proposition 187 argued that it was illogical for the Court to throw out the very initiative that had sparked welfare reform. While President Bill Clinton had opposed the proposition in his 1996 reelection campaign, he had also promised that the federal government would do more to help states deal with the costs of illegal immigration. The 1996 welfare reform was in some ways even more broadly cast than Proposition 187. Most significantly, it denied nonemergency health care and public benefits (such as disability benefits and food stamps) to many categories of those legally admitted to the country, not just to undocumented immigrants. Still, the welfare reform package did not bar undocumented immigrants from public primary and secondary education, nor did it require that officials be informed of suspected undocumented immigrants.

That three years passed before Judge Pfaelzer issued her ruling raised considerable criticism from the proposition's backers, since during that period Proposition 187 could neither be implemented nor moved to the next level of judicial review. The delay prompted consideration of court reform by the U.S. Congress, which has proposed legislation requiring that federal challenges to state initiatives be heard by a panel of three judges (rather than one) and that courts complete their review within a year.

Karen E. Rosenblum

See also

California Ballot Proposition 209 (1996); California Ballot Proposition 54 (2002); Immigration and Customs Enforcement (ICE); Unauthorized Immigration

Further Reading:

Armbruster, Ralph, Kim Geron, and Edna Bonacich. "The Assault on California's Latino Immigrants: The Politics of Proposition 187." *International Journal of Urban and Regional Research* 19 (1995): 655–63.

Zavella, Patricia. "The Tables Are Turned: Immigration, Poverty, and Social Conflict in California Communities." In *Immigrants Out: The New Nativism and the Anti-Immigrant Impulse in the United States*, edited by Juan F. Perea, 131–61. New York: New York University Press, 1996.

California Ballot Proposition 209 (1996)

Initiated by two California State University professors, Glynn Custred and Thomas Wood, both of whom are self-described "angry white men," the 1996 Proposition 209 (the California Civil Rights Initiative) was the first ballot measure in the nation that sought to repeal affirmative action in public employment, public education, or public contracting. However, its real intent was disguised in neutral language, as shown in the following key paragraph: "The state shall not discriminate against, or grant preferential treatment to, any individual or group on the basis of race, sex, color, ethnicity, or national origin in the operation of public employment, public education, or public contracting."

Proposition 209 was passed by California voters on November 5, 1996, with 54 percent of the vote. Upon its passage, some anti–Proposition 209 groups immediately filed law suits. They contended that Proposition 209 contradicts federal civil rights laws, and that it violates the U.S. Constitution's equal-protection clause because it singles out women and minorities, making it more difficult for them to win passage of laws and policies that benefit them. After almost one year of legal battles, on November 3, 1997, the U.S. Supreme Court rejected, without comments, the appeal of the American Civil Liberties Union, clearing the way for the full enforcement of the nation's first across-the-board abolition of affirmative action in state and local government.

Proposition 209 has generated ripple effects across the nation. Other states and cities have initiated similar measures. Efforts were also made to push through Congress a bill to end affirmative action in public hiring and contracts. The latest Supreme Court rulings on lawsuits against the University of Michigan and its law school in admission policies virtually invalidate part of Proposition 209.

Philip Yang

California Ballot Proposition 54 (2002)

California Proposition 54, also called the Racial Privacy Initiative (RPI), or the "California Ballot Initiative to Ban Racial Data" was created in 2002 by Ward Connerly, the black University of California regent who had supported Proposition 209, a successful 1996 measure that abolished affirmative action in state-run agencies and educational institutions. Proposition 54 called for a ban on the use and production of racially coded data across a spectrum of state and municipal agencies. Both supporters and critics agreed that, if passed, the initiative would have a tremendous impact on how race relations were recorded, viewed, and interpreted in the future. Although controversial, the proposition was overshadowed by California's gubernatorial recall election, which resulted in the ouster of Governor Gray Davis and his replacement by actor Arnold Schwarzenegger. Appearing on the same ballot as the recall, Proposition 54 was defeated on October 7, 2003, receiving only 36 percent of the vote.

Connerly viewed Proposition 54 as an important step toward a truly color-blind society. He claimed that since 1996 state and local institutions had continued to collect and use racial data, which were used to side-step the anti-affirmative-action mandates of Proposition 209. Connerly envisioned Proposition 54 as a way of responding to these "violations" of the earlier measure. The RPI would have prevented state and municipal agencies from classifying people according to race, ethnicity, or national origin. It would have effectively barred the use and collection of racially coded data in public education, municipal social services, public contracting, and employment. Certain exceptions were allowed under the RPI's provisions, including data for medical research or data needed to meet federally mandated requirements. Some institutions would have been affected by both the ban and its exemptions. For example, the state Department of Education would have been required by federal conditions to continue tracking the performance of students from certain racial groups in some subjects (such as mathematics and language arts) but would have been banned under the RPI from doing so in other subjects (such as science or history). Approval of any exemptions from the RPI would have required a two-thirds majority in the state legislature.

Supporters of Proposition 54 argued that the multiracial character of California, where whites make up less than 50 percent of the population, made race-based classification increasingly anachronistic. A growing number of interracial marriages further muddied the clear racial divisions upon which data had hitherto been based. Continuing to collect racially coded data, according to supporters of the measure, would be time-consuming, costly, and ultimately misleading. A reliance on racial statistics could also mask the presence of other crucial factors that determine hiring practices, admissions practices, and the rewarding of government contracts. Proponents argued that the principles behind Proposition 54 thus reflected the shift in society toward an increasingly multiracial and color-blind outlook. They believed it was the duty of the government and its attendant institutions to reflect and legitimize this trend.

Critics argued that the "information ban" on racial data would have a pernicious effect on race relations and negatively impact the lives of countless people. In areas such as education, employment, and public health in particular, the absence of racial statistics would prevent the development of programs and policies specifically targeted toward vulnerable minority populations. Without racially coded data, litigation to combat racial discrimination would be impossible. Also, researchers and policymakers would be unable to track the changing economic and social conditions of various minority groups over time.

The heart of the opposition's argument was the principle that race is the fundamental marker and determinant of inequality in society. Opponents believed that race continues to affect the quality of education, the likelihood of exposure to environmental hazards or of contracting certain medical conditions, and an individual's ability to access fair housing and employment. Opponents argued that by "hiding" the role of race, Proposition 54 only provided the framework for further racial and ethnic discrimination. Although many people believed that passage of the proposition would cause other states to follow California's lead, defeat of the measure has at least temporarily cooled the issue.

Rebekah Lee

Further Reading:

Coalition for an Informed California. http://www.defeat54.org.

El Nasser, Haya. "California Candidates Seize Prop 54 Issue." *USA Today*. September 8, 2003. http://www.usatoday.com/news/politicselections/state2003-09-07-prop54-usat_x.htm.

Rossomondo, John. "California Initiative Seeks to End Racial Classifications." *Cybercast New Service*. December 31, 2001. http://www.conservativenews.org/politics/ archive/200112/POL20011231a.html.

Sanders, Jim. "Racial Battle Line Drawn." *Sacramento Bee*. August 10, 2003.

Carmichael, Stokely (1941–1998)

Stokely Standiford Churchill Carmichael was born on June 29, 1941, in Port of Spain, Trinidad, to Adolphus and Mabel Charles Carmichael. His parents immigrated to the United States when he was three years old, leaving him in the care of his maternal grandmother, Cecilia Harris Carmichael. When Cecilia Carmichael died in 1952, he joined his parents in New York. After graduating from junior high school in 1956, Carmichael enrolled in the highly selective Bronx High School of Science. At Bronx High, he befriended several members of the Young Communist League (YCL) and began attending their study groups and rallies. His exposure to European radical writing and revolutionary theory sharpened his emerging political interests. He never officially joined the YCL, however, because of its hostility toward organized religion (he and his family were active members of the Anglican Church) and its general disinterest in the condition of people of African descent. His association with the YCL did, however, bring him into contact with radical black socialist Bayard Rustin, who introduced him to civil rights protest.

In 1960, Carmichael enrolled in Howard University in Washington, D.C. The pre-med major learned as much outside of the classroom through his affiliation with the campus-based Nonviolent Action Group (NAG), as he did in the classroom from the more progressive members of Howard's faculty, including historian Rayford Logan and poet Sterling Brown. Significantly, Carmichael's association with NAG put him on the front lines of the Southern civil rights movement. It introduced him to the Deep South in the summer of 1961 as a freedom rider; his reward for participating in the Freedom Rides was 49 days in Mississippi's infamous Parchman Penitentiary. It steered him to Cambridge, Maryland, where he experienced his first protracted organizing campaign and the satisfaction that accompanied working with local people. Additionally, it linked him to the Student Nonviolent Coordinating Committee (SNCC), which led him back to Mississippi where, by his own admission, his real political education took place.

During the summers of 1962 and 1963, Carmichael worked as an SNCC field secretary in Greenwood, Mississippi, where he honed his skills as a grassroots organizer. In 1964, after graduating from Howard, he returned to Mississippi and joined the SNCC full time, serving as project director for the Second Congressional District of the Mississippi Freedom Democratic Party (MFDP), which covered most of the Mississippi Delta. The MFDP's inability to unseat Mississippi's pro-segregation delegates at the 1964 Democratic National Convention convinced Carmichael that working with Democrats was pointless. From then on, he sought to organize Southern blacks into independent, grassroots political parties.

In January 1965, Carmichael left Mississippi for Selma, Alabama, where he sought to apply the organizing lessons that he had learned in the Magnolia State. After strategic and philosophical differences between SNCC field secretaries and Southern Christian Leadership Conference (SCLC) organizers led the SNCC to withdraw from the Selma voting rights campaign, Carmichael led a team of SNCC workers into neighboring Lowndes County. During the next twelve months, he spearheaded the SNCC's Lowndes County Project, overseeing the development of the Lowndes County Freedom Organization, a countywide, independent third party that fielded a full slate of local black candidates in the November 1966 general election in a bid to gain control of the county courthouse. Carmichael's success in Lowndes prompted veteran SNCC organizers to elect him chairman in May 1966; he replaced John Lewis, who had fallen out of step with the organization's more political approach to change.

As chairman, Carmichael sought to spread the SNCC's new political program, which centered on developing grassroots independent political parties. A desire to showcase the new program led Carmichael back to Mississippi in June 1966 to take part in James Meredith's March against Fear. By participating in the protest, Carmichael sought to reestablish a foothold in Mississippi and to advance the SNCC's new program within the national movement. The high point of the demonstration came on June 16 when Carmichael, speaking at a rally in Greenwood, introduced the nation to Black Power.

The whirlwind of controversy that enveloped Carmichael following his call for Black Power forced him to spend much of the remainder of his tenure as the SNCC's chairman explaining the ideology to a disbelieving white public. In 1967, he and political scientist Charles V. Hamilton coauthored *Black Power: The Politics of Liberation*, which detailed the origin and meaning of the controversial slogan.

Stokely Carmichael, an effective leader of the Student Nonviolent Coordinating Committee (SNCC), brought the concept of Black Power into the U.S. civil rights struggle. In 1967, Carmichael, an advocate of militancy rather than nonviolent cooperation, broke with the SNCC and joined the more radical Black Panthers. (Library of Congress)

In May 1967, Carmichael opted not to seek reelection as chairman of the SNCC, choosing instead to organize local people in Washington, D.C. His call for Black Power, however, had made him a celebrity in revolutionary circles, and very soon he was holding court with Fidel Castro in Cuba, Ho Chi Minh in Vietnam, and FLN (Front de Libération Nationale) freedom fighters in Algeria. It was at this time that former Ghanaian president Kwame Nkrumah, living in exile in Guinea, invited Carmichael to become his political secretary. Carmichael accepted the invitation, but not before returning to the United States and being drafted by the Black Panther Party (BPP) for Self-Defense as a field marshal; BPP leaders later elevated him to prime minister. Conflicting leadership styles and decision-making practices quickly led Carmichael to disassociate himself from the BPP. In late 1968, he and his wife Miriam Makeba, the famed South African singer, joined Nkrumah in Sekou Toure's Guinea. Once there, he changed his name to Kwame Ture—in a tribute to the two African statesmen who had embraced him as their intellectual and political heir—and began working through the All-African People's Revolutionary Party to bring about an African-inspired, transnational, socialist revolution.

Conakry, Guinea, served as Ture's base of operations for the next 30 years. During this time, he made frequent trips back to the United States for speaking engagements. In 1995, he was diagnosed with late-stage prostate cancer. His terminal illness prompted him to pen his posthumously published autobiography *Ready for Revolution: The Life and Struggles of Stokely Carmichael (Kwame Ture)*. On November 15, 1998, a frail-bodied but strong-spirited Carmichael died of cancer at his home in Guinea.

Hasan K. Jeffries

See also

Black Panther Party (BPP) ; Civil Rights Movement; Freedom Rides; Southern Christian Leadership Council (SCLC)

Further Reading:

Carmichael, Stokely, with Ekwueme Michael Thelwell. *Ready for Revolution: The Life and Struggles of Stokely Carmichael (Kwame Ture)*. New York: Scribner, 2003.

Carver, George Washington (1864–1943)

George Washington Carver was an African American botanical researcher and educator born into slavery in Missouri. He was owned by a German American immigrant, but when Carver was just a young child, he was kidnapped together with his mother and his sisters by Confederate night raiders. When his owner found them, only George was still alive, although this is a much disputed version of what really happened. After the abolition of slavery, Carver and his brother were raised by his former owner and his wife as if they were their own children. The master's family taught him to read and write and encouraged him in his intellectual vocation.

After a failed attempt to enter Highland University in Kansas, where he was rejected because of his color once his application had already made it through, Carver entered Simpson College in Iowa. In 1891, he went to Iowa State University (then called Iowa State Agricultural College) and became its first African American student. Carver was praised by his teachers. He excelled in his major areas, botany and bacteriology. At the time, Iowa State Agricultural College had several prestigious professors who later would become advisers to U.S. presidents. Some of Carver's outstanding professors were James G. Wilson and Henry C. Wallace. Seeing his potential, Joseph Budd and Louis Pammel persuaded him to stay at Iowa State Agricultural College to pursue a master's degree. Upon finishing it, Carver received several job offers and accepted Booker T. Washington's invitation to lead the Agricultural Department at Tuskegee Institute, Alabama. He entered the institution in 1896 and would remain there until his death in 1943. He served the institute for 47 years, although his stay was not always a peaceful one. Carver threatened to resign several times and was resented by some members of the faculty because of certain privileges he enjoyed. When Carver arrived at Tuskegee in 1896, the institution had limited means, but that was not an obstacle for him. Carver constructed much of his equipment using junk material and everyday objects.

Carver traveled throughout the South showing farmers how to improve their techniques and giving them advice. He and his students spent most of their weekends demonstrating to farmers how to manage their farms, prepare foods, and rotate crops. This initiative became known as the Agriculture Movable School. Carver also wrote agricultural pamphlets (such as *Twenty-Nine Ways to Cook Cowpeas*, *Ten Choice Wild Vegetables*, and *One Hundred and Five Ways of Preparing the Peanut for Human Consumption*) and regularly published a newspaper column entitled "Professor Carver's Advice."

One of Carver's most famous accomplishments was his study and promotion of peanuts as an alternative crop to cotton. In the aftermath of the American Civil War, the Southern soil was exhausted because of cotton monoculture. Carver proposed peanuts and sweet potatoes both as a source of food for farmers and as a way to regenerate the soil. Carver succeeded in producing more than 300 products out of peanuts, such as metal polish, shampoo, sauces, and washing powder.

During his life, Carver received many recognitions for his work. He was appointed to the British Royal Society of Arts in 1916; he received the Thomas A. Edison award, the Spingarn Medal from the National Association for the

Advancement of Colored People (1923), the Franklin D. Roosevelt Medal for Outstanding Contribution to Southern Agriculture in 1939, among others. Carver was also active in the eradication of illiteracy among blacks and whites and toured the South with the Commission on Interracial Cooperation from 1923 to 1933.

Carver continued to receive honors after his death. In 1977, he entered the Hall of Fame for Great Americans, and in 1990, he was added to the National Inventors Hall of Fame. Carver died in 1943 after complications resulting from a bad fall down a flight of stairs. He was buried next to Booker T. Washington.

LAURA GIMENO-PAHISSA

See also
Washington, Booker T.

Further Reading:

Gyant, LaVerne. "Contributors to Adult Education: Booker T. Washington, George Washington Carver, Alain L. Locke and Ambrose Caliver." *Journal of Black Studies* 19, no. 1 (1988): 97–110.

Mackintosh, B. "George Washington Carver: The Making of a Myth." *Journal of Southern History* 42, no. 4 (1976): 507–28.

Casinos

Casinos have become a pervasive part of the public image of contemporary Native Americans. Since the 1970s, casinos and other gaming operations have become a source of income and development on many Native American reservations. Common misperceptions of the nature of Indian gaming include the myth of the "rich Indian," and as "getting back at the white man." "Indian gaming" is defined by federal law as gaming (casinos, bingo halls, and other gaming operations) conducted by an "Indian tribe" on "Indian lands," meaning a federally recognized tribal government conducting gaming operations on federal reservation lands or on trust lands. Indian casinos have also been a source of suspicion for non-Natives who do not understand why Native Americans are "allowed" to have casinos when other groups are not.

The main difference between tribal gaming and commercial gambling is that tribal gaming is conducted by tribal governments for the main purpose of benefiting tribal members. Reservations and reservation casinos are both founded on the concept of tribal sovereignty. The development of casinos and other gaming on Native American reservations was a result of legal decisions regarding the sovereignty of tribal governments. *Bryan vs. Itasca County* was the 1976 Supreme Court case in which it was decided that states did not have the authority to tax Indians living on Indian lands, neither did it have the right to regulate the activities of Indians living on Indian lands.

The U.S. Constitution states that the federal government has jurisdiction over Indian reservations, but in 1953, Congress passed Public Law 280 giving criminal jurisdiction to certain states. After several other court cases over the years, the Indian Gaming Regulatory Act of 1988 (IGRA) was passed to address confusion about state and federal jurisdiction over Indian gaming. The act declared that Indian tribes have the right to regulate gaming activity on Indian lands if that gaming activity is not specifically prohibited by federal law, and if the gaming is conducted within a state that does not prohibit that gaming activity. The IGRA established the National Indian Gaming Commission (NIGC) as a regulatory body. The stated goals of the NIGC are: (1) promoting tribal economic development, self-sufficiency, and strong tribal governments; (2) maintaining the integrity of the Indian gaming industry; and (3) ensuring that tribes are the primary beneficiaries of their gaming activities. The Indian Gaming Working Group (IGWG) was created in 2004 by the Federal Bureau of Investigations (FBI) and NIGC to address criminal violations in Indian gaming.

According to Darian-Smith (2004), for many Native Americans gambling does not have the same moral meaning as it does in mainstream Western societies. Rather than being seen as being associated with deviance and immorality, Native American communities tend to view gaming behavior as an important way to learn lessons about winning and losing. Devoid of the moral connotations, casinos and other gaming facilities are mainly viewed as a means to an economic end. However, because of the mainstream view of gambling with its negative connotations, Indian gaming is an opportunity for some to connect general negative associations with gambling to older stereotypes of the "savage" Indian who lacks self-control and discipline. A high-profile case, the Pequot tribe of Connecticut, sealed the stereotype of the "rich casino Indian" in the imaginations of many non-Native American. This stereotype has led to depictions of the mystical but shrewd Indian casino businessman in mainstream media (Light and Rand 2005).

In 2000, the median household income for Native Americans was 25 percent lower than that of the entire U.S. population, and Indians living on reservation have lower income levels and higher unemployment and poverty than those who do not (Reagan and Gitter 2007). For tribes that operate casinos and other gaming businesses, the revenue gambling activities generates can be a tremendous help to tribe members. Economist Robin Anderson found that Native Americans living on gaming reservations with large or medium casinos gained an average 7.4 percent increase in per capita income compared to those living on nongaming reservations, as well as a reduction in family and child poverty rates. Living on reservations with smaller casinos was not associated with improvements in well-being. Per capita income is affected by gaming in a number of ways including an increase in wages paid to individuals, employment rates, and cash transfers from the tribe to members from gaming revenue (Reagan and Gitter 2007).

Despite these gains in economic well-being for members of some tribes, only about a quarter of all recognized tribes operate gaming ventures, and casinos are not universally accepted or successful among all nations. For tribes, the geographic isolation of tribal lands from metropolitan areas and from potential customers have made economic success difficult if not impossible. There are also many tribal leaders and members who do not fully approve of gaming as an economic strategy, and would prefer to use the profits from gaming to develop other economic activities (Darian-Smith 2004). As the 21st century unfolds, the fate of the well-being of Native American communities may well rest on the success of gaming and its ability to spur diverse economic development.

Renee S. Alston

See also
Tribal Sovereignty

Further Reading:

Anderson, Robin J., "Tribal Casino Impacts on American Indians Well-Being: Evidence from Reservation-Level Census Data." *Contemporary Economic Policy* (2011).

Darian-Smith, Eve. *New Capitalists: Law, Politics, and Identity Surrounding Casino Gaming on Native American Land.* Belmont, CA: Wadsworth, 2004.

Light, Stephen A., and Kathryn R. L. Rand. *Indian Gaming and Tribal Sovereignty: The Casino Compromise.* Lawrence: University Press of Kansas, 2005.

National Indian Gaming Association. http://www.indiangaming.org/.

Reagan, Patricia B., and Robert. J. Gitter. "Is Gaming the Optimal Strategy? The Impact of Gaming Facilities on the Income and Employment of American Indians." *Economics Letters* 95 (2007): 428–32 .

Castration

Castration is the removal of testicles. This process was one of a myriad of brutal ways in which whites inflicted violence upon blacks from slavery to the early 20th century. Unlike other forms of racial violence such as burning, rioting, and beatings, castration was a distinctly male phenomenon in which white men were the attackers and black men were the victims. In fact, more black men than any other racial group were castrated as a form of punishment for numerous reasons, of which alleged crimes against white women were the most common.

In America, castration was first inflicted upon black men during slavery times. The first known African slaves in America arrived at Jamestown in 1619. During the colonial period, castration was made into law to punish slaves accused of crimes such as running away, stealing, striking a white person, and rape. This law also applied to free blacks. White men, even if accused of raping a white woman, were rarely castrated.

Castration was also used as a form of punishment in the antebellum South, although severe whippings were more common. Capital punishment was extremely rare and was generally reserved for slaves who participated in uprisings. White slave owners often showed reluctance in castrating black slaves, because they depended upon black men to produce offspring. In fact, black male slaves were prized for this ability and were even referred to as studs, stallions, and bucks. Surprisingly, blacks were also rarely punished when accused of rape by white women as such women were often from the poorer classes. Such accusations were sometimes legitimate, and sometimes made up to punish a black man who spurned a woman's advances or to cover up an illicit relationship with, or an actual rape committed by, a white man. Affluent whites, who dominated the social, economic, and political life in the South, looked down on any group in any class lower than their own and considered poor white women promiscuous and immoral.

Nonetheless, there were incidences where castration was performed on black slaves in the South who exhibited aggressive tendencies. In this way, slaves were treated in the same manner as their slave owners' animals.

White violence against blacks intensified in the wake of the Civil War. White vigilante organizations, which had previously targeted whites, roamed about the South randomly attacking blacks and castrating some. Frequently, whites created rumors about black attacks to justify their cruelty. They also targeted any person who advocated black empowerment, suffrage, equality, and civil rights. Antiblack violence subsided briefly during Reconstruction, only to be resuscitated by racist whites looking to regain their social, economic, and political power in the South.

Between 1882 and 1930, antiblack violence, including lynching and rioting, was rampant. Although a number of black men were indiscriminately castrated, living through the horror and humiliation, many more were murdered following the procedure. Castration, along with other mutilations and beatings, was often performed during the agonizing hours preceding the actual lynching. Whites frequently tortured their victims for two or more hours in the presence of a frenzied crowd of men, women, and children. Some black men were made to eat parts of their own testicles. Whites frequently cut the genitals up and distributed the pieces among the crowd. Generally, each lynching was different: some people were lynched with a rope and burned, others were dismembered. Sometimes, the body was left to dangle from a tree located near a black community as a warning for blacks to submit to white supremacy.

The black victims of these crimes were not the rapists that whites usually claimed them to be. The accusation of rape or other crimes was frequently based on the fallacy that blacks were prone to crime and that extralegal violence was a viable response. Philip Dray explains how white Southerners in the 1900s supported articles in the *Atlanta Georgian* that discussed "the restoration of such antebellum punishments as branding and castration to curb black crimes that led to lynchings" and even suggested "that rather than apply such punishments only to convicted felons, all black men should be immediately castrated, and that black women might also be 'unsexed' so they could not give birth to any more rapists" (Dray 2002: 144–45). In reality, murder, not rape, was the actual cause for the majority of lynchings. Rape was simply the constructed justification to commit violence against blacks. William F. Pinar describes this phenomenon as a type of "white-male fantasy" conceived to relieve the latent desires of white males.

Scholars give ample explanations of these "latent desires." Dr. Frances Cress Welsing asserts that, historically, white men have targeted the male sex organ because of the fear of the supposed contamination and extermination of the white race. Others emphasize the role that envy, fueled by stereotypes originating before slavery of the black man's large penis and sexual prowess, plays. Pinar and Trudier Harris suggest that castration, with its ritualistic ogling, touching, and subsequent hoarding of the penis, is homoerotic in nature.

Still others assert that by castrating blacks, whites were destroying the ultimate symbol of male power. Pinar makes reference to Harris's work when he states that "lynchings represented the final stage of an emasculation process that white men conducted every day by word and deed, a culmination of a psychosexual war on black men. Black men were not allowed to forget that they were commodities, bodies not citizens, objects not men" (Pinar 2001: 58).

Gladys L. Knight

See also

Lynching; Masculinity, Black and White; Rape as Provocation for Lynching; Slavery

Further Reading:

Dray, Phillip. *At the Hands of Persons Unknown: The Lynching of Black America*. New York: Random House, 2002.

Harris, Trudier. *Exorcising Blackness: Historical and Literary Lynching and Burning Rituals*. Bloomington: Indiana University Press, 1984.

Jordan, Winthrop D. *The White Man's Burden: Historical Origins of Racism in the United States.* New York: Oxford University Press, 1974.
Markovitz, Jonathan. *Legacies of Lynching: Racial Violence and Memory.* Minneapolis: University of Minnesota Press, 2004.
Pinar, William F. *The Gender of Racial Politics and Violence in America: Lynching, Prison Rape, & the Crisis of Masculinity.* New York: Peter Lang, 2001.

Castro, Sal (1933–2013)

Social studies teacher Sal Castro played an important role in the historic East Los Angeles blowouts of 1968, in which thousands of students in predominantly Latino schools walked out of their classrooms to protest educational inequalities in the Los Angeles Unified School District.

Salvador Castro was the American-born son of undocumented immigrant parents. Born in the Boyle Heights neighborhood of Los Angeles on October 25, 1933, he accompanied them in their repatriation to Mexico in the 1930s and later came back to the United States. After returning to the United States, he was drafted into the Army and served in the Korean conflict. When he completed his military service, he attended Los Angeles City College and went on to major in business at California State University Los Angeles (CSULA), graduating in 1961. He also earned a credential to teach high school in California. He became active in the Democratic Party during his college years, serving as a cochair of the campus's Viva Kennedy club, and later took part in the Mexican American Political Association. While pursuing graduate studies at CSULA, he organized meetings of Mexican American college students and educational activists that resulted in the formation of the Mexican American Youth Leadership Conference in 1963.

After college, Castro obtained a position teaching at Belmont High School, where he began to spark social change by encouraging Mexican Americans to run for student government. The students caused an uproar and were disciplined after delivering their campaign speeches in Spanish at a school assembly. When Castro spoke up in their behalf, he was transferred to Lincoln High School, where he continued to help students push school board administrators for fair treatment. As a teacher, Castro came to the conclusion that Mexican American students needed to take steps for their own educational rights. The concept of the student walkout was his approach to solving the problem.

Castro leaped into the media spotlight in March 1968 when thousands of Los Angeles high school students walked out of the classroom. Active in picketing, sit-ins, and demonstrations, he quickly became the symbol as well as the leader of the walkout. Among the protesters' demands were access to bilingual education, a revised curriculum that included ethnic studies, and improved facilities. Along with 12 others (many of whom were Brown Berets), Castro was indicted in June by a Los Angeles grand jury on charges of felonious conspiracy. He was convicted. Two years later, on appeal, the charges were found unconstitutional and dropped, but Castro was barred from teaching for five years and continued to be harassed.

In 1973, after stints as a substitute teacher, he found himself back at Belmont, where he taught until his retirement in 2004. In 2006, the story of the walkouts was told in the HBO film *Walkout*, in which Castro was played by Michael Peña. Since 2009, he had also actively worked on lobbying the White House to formally recognize the students involved in the walkouts as an important part of civil rights history. He continued to advocate for educational reforms until his death on April 15, 2013, after a long struggle with cancer.

Matt Meier and Margo Gutierrez

See also
Chicano Movement

Further Reading

Muñoz, Carlos, Jr. *Youth, Identity, Power: The Chicano Movement.* New York: Verso, 1990.
Palacios, Arturo, ed. *Mexican American Directory.* Washington, DC: Executive Systems Corp., 1969.

Cesare Lombroso Theory

Cesare Lombroso (1835–1909) was an Italian physician often cited as the founder of criminological positivism, which in the Lombrosian sense refers to the study of crime and its causation rooted in the theories and methods of the natural sciences. To this end, Lombroso can be seen as one of the first thinkers to reject the assumptions of the 'classical

Cesare Lombroso (1835–1909) theorized that criminal behavior was innate rather than learned, and manifested itself through physical defects. (Library of Congress)

school' and those such as Cesare Beccaria (1738–1794), who focused on the free will and agency of the individuals making up society. Lombroso and early positive social scientists such as August Comte (1798–1857) believed that systematic scientific observation would provide objective knowledge of the forces that shaped individuals and society, not unlike the immutable laws of cause and effect that govern the natural world. Building upon these ideas, Lombroso sought to develop a "science of criminality" and ways to diagnose an individual's propensity to crime through biological characteristics, specifically physical anomalies or what he called stigmata.

Serving as a physician in the Italian army in the late 1850s, Lombroso undertook a meticulous study of the various disorders of some 3,000 soldiers under his care. Around the same time, he also studied inmates of the prison at Turin. In both instances, Lombroso documented and catalogued the physiology of his subjects, particularly convicted felons, hoping to identify physical distinctions linking biology to criminality. Both studies provided the foundation for his biologically deterministic theory of the "born criminal," introduced in his most influential work, *Criminal Man* (1876).

Performing an autopsy on a notorious criminal, Giuseppe Villella, Lombroso purportedly noticed similarities between Villella's skull and the inmates that he had studied at Turin. From this observation, Lombroso began to theorize that criminals were, in fact, atavistic throwbacks or "devolved" subhumans that had inherited traits from a "less-civilized" period in human history. This assertion delivered Lombroso to the belief that these characteristics or "stigmata" would allow professionals to identify and thus cordon "born criminals" from normal law-abiding citizens. Chief among Lombroso's stigmata were craniometric abnormalities such as the depth and the set of the eyes, slope and width of the forehead, and dimensions of the jaw. Lombroso's craniometric theories gave rise to the science of phrenology that, for a time, was among the most widely accepted and practiced anthropometric methods.

Lombroso was a tremendous influence on his contemporaries, Guglielmo Ferrero (1871–1942) and Enrico Ferri (1856–1929), who helped develop his early observations and apply them to a wide range of criminal classifications such as "alcoholics" and "hysterics" and most notably women in *The Female Offender* (1903). By mid-century Lombrosian criminal anthropometry fell from favor because of obvious homologies with Nazi eugenics and the Holocaust. Yet Lombroso's

Lombroso's Modern Legacy

Lombroso's concern with data collection, systematic evidence, and physical characteristics have left an indelible mark on criminal justice and its institutions. For instance, most policing and criminal justice agencies maintain extensive archives of photos or "mug shots" of criminals, fingerprints, and, increasingly, DNA. These scientific observations are used to identify victims, include or exclude criminal suspects, and track offenders across various social spaces. More recently, facial recognition and identification systems have been used to monitor and secure railway and subway stations and airports following a number of high-profile attacks.

influence, particularly on criminology, is impossible to deny. In particular, the influence of Lombrosian criminological positivism is readily apparent in the work of important criminologists such as Eleanor and Sheldon Glueck and their famous study of *500 Criminal Careers*.

The positivist approach, which Lombroso helped pioneer, is arguably the dominant paradigm in criminology today. New developments in biological and biosocial criminology, along with psychological and social psychological theories continue to attempt to locate crime's cause within the contours of the human body, functions of the mind, and double helix. To this end, Lombrosian theory continues in earnest.

Travis Linnemann and Danielle Dirks

See also

Prison-Industrial Complex; Sentencing Disparities

Further Reading:

Bradley, Kate. "Cesare Lombroso (1835–1909)." In *Fifty Key Thinkers in Criminology*, edited by Keith Hayward, Shadd Maruna, and Jayne Mooney. New York: Routledge, 2009.

Finn, Jonathan. *Capturing the Criminal Image: From Mug Shot to Surveillance Society*. Minneapolis: University of Minnesota Press, 2009.

Lombroso, Cesare. *Criminal Man*. Durham, NC: Duke University Press Books, 2006 [1876].

Morrison, Wayne. "Lombroso and the Birth of Criminological Positivism: Scientific Mastery or Cultural Artifice." In *Cultural Criminology Unleashed*, edited by Jeff Ferrell, Keith Hayward, Wayne Morrison, and Mike Presdee, 67–80. London: Glasshouse Press, 2004.

Rafter, Nicole. "The Murderous Dutch Fiddler Criminology, History and the Problem of Phrenology." *Theoretical Criminology* 9, no. 1 (2005): 65–96.

Rafter, Nicole. "HJ Eysenck in Fagin's Kitchen: The Return to Biological Theory in 20th-century Criminology." *History of the Human Sciences* 19, no. 4 (2006): 37–56.

Rafter, Nicole. *The Origins of Criminology: A Reader*. New York: Routledge, 2009.

Chain Migration

Chain migration describes the utilization of migrant networks between two locations that ease and encourage repeated migration from one location to the other. Chain migration is constructed around two spatial locations: sending communities and receiving communities. Workers migrate from the sending community to a corresponding receiving community repeatedly, creating a metaphorical chain linking the two locations. Early migrants moving to the receiving community experience difficulty as they etch out a new life in a strange place. However, later migrants from the sending community can access social capital (actual and virtual resources) by utilizing contacts with earlier migrants from the same sending community. Social capital helps reduce the economic and psychological costs of migration, further encouraging migration between the two locations. The movement of migrants, information, and money between sending and receiving communities can also dramatically alter both communities over time, a process described as the *cumulative causation of migration*.

Migration is generally considered an expensive and laborious process to undertake. For example, migrating requires learning much new information about one's destination, such as job opportunities, housing, language, shopping, culture, and transportation. Initial migrants to a particular place have little or no help waiting for them when they arrive, and may have little usable information about the place in which they arrive. For these persons, the costs of migration are very high. They must learn about their new home through trial and experience. However, over time, these individuals gain knowledge about the area that can benefit future potential migrants. They can also help support potential migrants by providing access to resources like jobs, and may share this information in communication with family and friends back home.

Having access to contacts already living and working in a potential destination can reduce the costs of migration for potential migrants. It makes moving to that destination (compared to a random destination) more desirable and, simply put, less scary. As a result, additional migrants may make the move to their contacts' destination. As each wave of migrants from one community arrives in another, it further simplifies the migration process for future potential migrants. Over time, this can foster chain migration, a metaphorical chain of migrants linking a sending community (home to potential migrants) and a receiving community (newly home to earlier migrants from the sending community).

The collective knowledge and experiences of early migrants can be considered social capital. Social capital consists of resources (both actual and virtual) that belong to a particular group and its members, and it can be used to facilitate action. Social capital can take multiple forms for migrants. For instance, it may be information about a great job opportunity and an introduction to the person in charge of hiring. It may be information about housing, such as a place to share with other new migrants, or even a short-term stay on a couch while looking for permanent housing. Social capital includes income from contacts to help cover the costs of migration. It can also take unexpected forms, such as information about private transportation to grocery stores once a week or information on finding cultural goods in a strange city.

Chain migration is related to the *cumulative causation of migration*, the idea that each subsequent act of migration between two locations readjusts social order at both locations. Each act of migration changes the context that encourages (or discourages) migration from the sending community to the receiving community. Successful migration networks can eventually create a moment where the costs of migration are very low and cannot effectively be reduced further by additional migration. The availability of potential migrants in the sending community also eventually dwindles, leading to a decrease in migration between the two points. Remittances are another way migration changes the context in sending and receiving communities.

Remittances primarily consist of sending wealth back home as a source of income. Remittances are often part of a greater migration strategy, with workers going to the receiving community with the hopes of sending home income to family members. Remittances may then be invested in the sending community, inadvertently creating changes in the local economic structure. For example, remittances may be used to invest in agricultural mechanization to improve yields, efficiency, and output in farming communities. However, utilizing machinery also has the effect of decreasing the amount of unskilled labor required, potentially creating higher unemployment in the sending community. This, in turn, creates a greater need to send workers to the receiving community, but may eventually outstrip the value of working in that area by oversaturating the labor market. Thus, each act of migration theoretically behaves as if in a feedback loop.

James Maples

See also

Anchor Baby; Arizona Senate Bill 1070; Diversities, Ethnic and Racial

Remittances and Remittance Corridors

The United States and Mexico represent an important *remittance corridor*: a steady remittance pathway from one country to another. Approximately $22 billion moved through this corridor in 2010, making it one of the largest remittance corridors by volume. Remittances are an important form of economic activity in receiving nations, sometimes accounting for high percentages of the receiving nation's GDP. For example, remittance corridors between the United States and Honduras, El Salvador, and Haiti account for approximately 15 percent of each nation's GDP in 2010. The United States also links to other remittance corridors in India, China, Philippines, and Vietnam. Remittances from the United States to other nations have steadily grown since the 1990s. Recent U.S. legislation requiring the tracking of money transfers (including remittances) has also greatly improved the data on remittances. Remittances are generally fairly stable, although they are still subject to fluctuations in the labor market (such as high unemployment) and political events like the Arab Spring. Remittances across the globe totaled approximately $372 billion in 2011.

Further Reading:

Massey, Douglas S., Jorge Durand, and Nolan J. Malone. *Beyond Smoke and Mirrors: Mexican Immigration in an Era of Economic Integration*. New York: Russell Sage Foundation, 2002.

Massey, Douglas S. and Magaly R. Sanchez. *Brokered Boundaries: Creating Immigrant Identity in Anti-Immigrant Times*. New York: Russell Sage Foundation, 2010.

Sassen, Saskia. *Guests and Aliens*. New York: New Press, 2000.

Thompson, Gabriel. *There's No Jose Here: Following the Hidden Lives of Mexican Immigrants*. New York: Nation Books, 2006.

Charleston (South Carolina) Riot of 1919

In Charleston, South Carolina, on the night of May 10, 1919, a black man allegedly pushed Roscoe Coleman, a Navy sailor, off the sidewalk. Other sailors and civilians gave chase. Both sides threw bricks, bottles, and stones until someone fired four shots into the air. Immediately after the incident, rumors circulated that a sailor had been "shot by a Negro" ("Six Men Killed" 1919: 1). Later that night, a mob of sailors stole rifles from two local gun clubs and started shooting, targeting black people indiscriminately. They robbed and vandalized black-owned businesses. The rioting spread to other parts of the city, until about 3:00 A.M., when Mayor Tristram T. Hyde requested detachments of marines from the Navy Yard to assist in restoring order. As a result of the riot, five white men and 18 black men were injured, and three black men—William Brown, Isaac Doctor, and James Talbot—were killed.

The report of the subsequent Navy investigation found that sailors Ralph Stone, George W. Biggs, Roscoe Coleman, Robert Morton, and white civilian Charleston resident Alexander Lanneau started the riot, and found Jacob Cohen and George T. Holliday jointly responsible for the death of Isaac Doctor. The report explicitly stated that the property damage and the injuries to the black men were caused by mobs made up of sailors. Cohen and Holliday were each sentenced to a year on Parris Island.

JAN VOOGD

See also

Race Riots in America; Red Summer Race Riots of 1919. Documents: The Report on the Memphis Riots of May 1866 (July 25, 1866); Account of the Riots in East St. Louis, Illinois (July 1917); The Cook County Coroner's Report Regarding the 1919 Chicago Race Riots (1919); A Southern Black Woman's Letter Regarding the Recent Riots in Chicago and Washington (November 1919); The Final Report of the Grand Jury on the Tulsa Race Riot (June 25, 1921); Testimony from *Laney v. United States* Describing Events during the Washington, D.C., Riot of July 1919 (December 3, 1923); The Governor's Commission Report on the Watts Riots (December 1965); Cyrus R. Vance's Report on the Riots in Detroit (July-August 1967); The Reports of the Oklahoma Commission to Study the Tulsa Race Riot of 1921 (2000-2001); The Draft Report of the 1898 Wilmington Race Riot Commission (December 2005)

Further Reading:

Headquarters Sixth Naval District, U.S. Navy Yard, Charleston, SC. JFM/MWM. *Charleston, S.C., Record of Proceedings of a Court of Inquiry Convened at the Navy Yard, Charleston, S.C., by Order of the Commandant, Sixth Naval Dist.* National Archives and Records Administration, Record Group 80, 26283–2588: 2, 4.

"Six Men Killed in Race Battle at Charleston." *Atlanta Constitution*, May 11, 1919, 1.

Williams, Lee E., II. "The Charleston, South Carolina, Riot of 1919." In *Southern Miscellany: Essays in History in Honor of Glover Moore*. Jackson: University Press of Mississippi, 1981.

Chattanooga (Tennessee) Riot of 1906

One of several racially charged riots during the early 1900s, the Chattanooga, Tennessee, riot of 1906 reflected growing social tension between whites and blacks in the United States. As lynching spread throughout Southern and Northern states, African Americans increasingly sought to defend themselves against white assault. The Chattanooga riot of 1906 reflected growing discontent among blacks concerning lynching. The uprising also led to a U.S. Supreme Court ruling that set precedence for due process and prisoners' rights.

In 1900, Chattanooga, Tennessee, was a bustling industrial city. The city boasted several large manufacturing companies and was a significant national transportation hub. Despite Jim Crow laws and other segregationist policies, blacks made modest economic gains. Social gains were slow in coming. Protesting segregation on the Chattanooga bus line, in 1905 African Americans organized a successful boycott of the segregated transit system and formed a black transportation system. Fueled by the passionate writings of activists like Monroe Trotter, Ida B. Wells-Barnett, and W.E.B. Du Bois, blacks increasingly challenged the sociopolitical system established by whites.

Improved conditions in the African American community threatened the established social order in America. As blacks increasingly refused to passively accept lowly social status, whites feared the loss of power and privilege regained following Reconstruction. Responding to the writings from the black press concerning crime reduction, white newspapers circulated rumors of an impending African American crime wave. Although few reports were actually verified, whites continued to view the black community with contempt and distrust. Blacks continued to seek economic and social gains.

Finally, the tension erupted on January 23, 1906. A white woman, Nevada Taylor, allegedly was attacked as she left work. Reportedly attacked from behind, she did not see her attacker. The sheriff, Joseph Shipp, launched an investigation. Based on an anonymous tip, Shipp arrested 23-year-old African American Edward Johnson. Upon hearing the news of an arrest, a white lynch mob formed. Johnson escaped the initial uprising, and the militia was called in to maintain order. Several months later, he returned to Chattanooga under court-ordered protection. On March 19, while awaiting his appeal, an angry mob broke into the jail, removed, and lynched Johnson. Although the militia had orders to protect Johnson, neither sheriff nor deputies alerted them to the lynching.

Angered that Sheriff Shipp stood by without informing the militia while the mob lynched Johnson, the African American community retaliated. Blacks rioted in downtown Chattanooga, throwing objects at whites and police. Businesses were destroyed, and there were injuries on both sides. The court also responded to Johnson's lynching. After the militia quelled rioting, investigators quickly gathered information on participants and witnesses to the lynching. This investigation illustrated the importance of due process in the judicial system. On May 24, 1909, in the *United States v. Shipp*, the court decided that Joseph Shipp and his deputies violated due process and were in contempt of court. The Chattanooga riot of 1906 tentatively restored African Americans' faith in the federal government and judicial system. Continued turbulence throughout the country would ultimately challenge this faith.

Janice E. Fowler

See also

New Orleans (Louisiana) Riot of 1866; Race Riots in America. Documents: The Report on the Memphis Riots of May 1866 (July 25, 1866); Account of the Riots in East St. Louis, Illinois (July 1917); The Cook County Coroner's Report Regarding the 1919 Chicago Race Riots (1919); A Southern Black Woman's Letter Regarding the Recent Riots in Chicago and Washington (November 1919); The Final Report of the Grand Jury on the Tulsa Race Riot (June 25, 1921); Testimony from *Laney v. United States* Describing Events during the Washington, D.C., Riot of July 1919 (December 3, 1923); The Governor's Commission Report on the Watts Riots (December 1965); Cyrus R. Vance's Report on the Riots in Detroit (July-August 1967); The Reports of the Oklahoma Commission to Study the Tulsa Race Riot of 1921 (2000-2001); The Draft Report of the 1898 Wilmington Race Riot Commission (December 2005)

Further Reading:

Collins, Winfield. *The Truth About Lynching and the Negro in the South*. New York: Neale Publishing Company, 1918.

Dray, Philip. *The Hands of Persons Unknown*. New York: Random House, 2002.

Hale, Grace Elizabeth. *Making Whiteness: The Culture of Segregation in the South, 1890–1940*. New York: Pantheon Books, 1998.

Chávez, César (1927–1993)

César Chávez was a social activist and union organizer whose struggle for the human dignity of workers in harvest agriculture made him a world-recognized Mexican American leader and a national metaphor for equality, humanity, and social justice. Both as a symbol and as an individual he was an energizing force bringing to the attention of all Americans the many injustices suffered by farm workers. Because of his leadership and dedication, powerful agribusiness interests were forced to face issues of social responsibility, decent wages, humane work and housing conditions, and pesticide abuse.

César Estrada Chávez was born on March 31, 1927, on a small farm homesteaded in 1909 by his Mexican grandfather Cesario near Yuma, Arizona. He was the second child of Juana Estrada and Librado Chávez, who eked out a precarious living on the farm. When the Great Depression of the 1930s occurred, the Chávez family, like thousands of other Americans, lost their land because they could not pay their taxes. Piling their meager possessions in their old Studebaker, they joined the long procession heading for California.

Chávez grew up following the harvests in California and Arizona. At best, his home was a tarpaper-covered shack in a farm labor camp and at worst, a tent, the Studebaker, or shelter under some overpass. Chávez and his brothers endured, but they learned little in school. By his own count, Chávez attended at least 30 schools before he dropped out in the seventh grade. He could scarcely read and write.

In the summer of 1952, there occurred an event that changed Chávez's life. Through a local priest, Rev. Donald McDonnell, he became acquainted with Fred Ross Sr., an organizer for the Community Service Organization (CSO). The CSO taught people how to solve their own problems.

Although skeptical at first, Chávez quickly joined the CSO as an unpaid volunteer, working in voter registration. By observing Ross carefully, he learned techniques of recruiting and organizing, holding meetings, and creating power among the powerless. At the same time, with help from his wife he began to read and study in order to improve his poor education and thereby become a more effective organizer.

By 1958, Chávez was a director in the CSO. During the next few years he became increasingly convinced that the organization had strayed from its earlier goal of mobilizing the very poor. Because workers in agriculture were among the poorest, he believed that the CSO should concentrate its efforts among them. The CSO board of directors disagreed. When his proposal to organize a farm workers' union was again voted down in 1962, Chávez resigned from the organization and moved to Delano in California's Central Valley. Here he began to build his National Farm Workers Association (NFWA). Helped by Fred Ross, Dolores Huerta, and others, Chávez spent 16 to 18 hours a day, seven days a week, talking to workers about the need for organization. In three years he enrolled some 1,700 families in the union and had achieved some minor successes.

On September 16, 1965, the NFWA voted to join some 800 Filipino grape workers in their strike for higher wages and better working and living conditions. Realizing that his fledgling union with its $100 treasury was far from ready and would need all the help it could get, Chávez sought and obtained support from the student movement, from civil rights and church groups, as well as from established unions and national leaders. He also converted *La Huelga* ("The Strike") from a mere labor dispute to a civil rights crusade—*La Causa* ("The Cause"). He strongly stressed its moral basis and dramatized it by making the Virgin of Guadalupe its unofficial symbol along with the black eagle; by organizing a long march from Delano to the state capital, Sacramento; by undertaking a 25-day fast to reaffirm his commitment to nonviolence; and by declaring a nationwide grape boycott that soon spread overseas.

At the end of the march to Sacramento in April 1966, Chávez's United Farm Workers Organizing Committee, as the union was now known, won contracts from 11 major wine grape companies, but growers of table grapes held out. Even with a conscience-stirring national and international boycott of California table grapes, it took Chávez until 1970 to bring them to the bargaining table. In July, with the help of the Catholic Bishops Committee on Farm Labor, three-year contracts were drawn up with 26 growers; the five-year strike had ended in success. Unfortunately, the United Farm Workers (UFW) sorely lacked a professional staff needed to successfully implement the contracts.

When the three-year UFW contracts expired, 59 California grape growers signed with the Teamsters Union. Meanwhile Chávez attempted to organize workers in the Salinas Valley lettuce fields, but encountered the Teamsters union there and failed after eight years of boycott. In announcing the boycott's end, Chávez declared it had served its purpose of calling attention to the workers' plight.

In spite of Chávez's continued vigorous leadership and the union's wide range of services to its members, UFW membership began to decline in the second half of the 1970s. By the end of the decade Chávez's union had shrunk to about 20 percent of the 90,000 to 100,000 California farm workers earlier enrolled. The promise of the 1975 state Agricultural Labor Relations Act, which provided statutory support for secret ballot union elections, was quickly sabotaged by the legislature's control of its funding. Two years later Chávez's leadership suffered another blow when a serious internal UFW split resulted in the loss of some of the union's most experienced organizers and staff. On top of this, by the 1980s unionism generally was running into hard times all over the country.

To counter rising antiunion sentiment and to recapture the dream of the 1960s, in the early 1980s Chávez turned to expanded objectives and new tactics such as mass mailings with computerized lists. Among his goals was the reduction of excessive use of pesticides; in 1984 he initiated a new grape boycott because of pesticide abuse. In July 1988, Chávez went on his third fast to publicize the boycott and to bring the pesticide issue dramatically to the attention of the American people. His 36-day fast left him greatly weakened physically.

The grip that Chávez held over the imagination of so many idealists of the 1960s and 1970s had also weakened. The Delano grape strike was a remarkable personal victory, but by the 1990s it seemed to many to be largely symbolic in its benefits. There was some criticism, even by friends and family, of his absolute and personal domination of the UFW. By the beginning of the 1990s the union had perhaps 20,000 members and about 100 contracts; statewide its influence appeared marginal. The grape boycott was still in place, but few consumers seemed aware of it. However, Chávez still had a devoted following.

Chávez died unexpectedly in his sleep on April 23, 1993, while in Arizona testifying in a UFW court case. He is the recipient of many awards and honors in recognition of his work on behalf of farm workers. In 1976, there was some talk of Chávez being a possible candidate for a Nobel Prize. In November 1990, Mexican president Carlos Salinas de Gortari conferred on him the highest award Mexico can give to a foreigner, the Aguila Azteca. One year later, U.S. president Bill Clinton honored Chávez with the nation's highest civilian award, the Presidential Medal of Freedom. At the end of March 1995, after a two-decade campaign by Mexican Americans and others, New Haven Middle School in Union City, California, was formally renamed César Chávez Middle School; several other public schools, parks, streets, and buildings across the United States are named after him. Furthermore, Chávez's birthday, March 31, is commemorated as a state holiday in California.

On October 8, 2012, at a ceremony in Keene, California, President Barack Obama formally dedicated the César Chávez National Monument at La Paz, which was designated as a National Historic Landmark. Chávez lived at La Paz in the final two decades of his life and is buried there; the site also served as the headquarters of the United Farm Workers beginning in the 1970s.

Matt Meier

See also

Chicano Movement; United Farm Workers

Further Reading:

Goodwin, David. *César Chávez: Hope for the People*. New York: Fawcett Columbine, 1991.

Griswold del Castillo, Richard, and Richard Garcia. *César Chávez: A Triumph of Spirit*. Norman: University of Oklahoma Press, 1995.

Levy, Jacques E. *César Chávez: Autobiography of La Causa*. New York: W. W. Norton, 1974.

London, Joan, and Henry Anderson. *So Shall Ye Reap: The Story of César Chávez and the Farmworkers Movement*. New York: Thomas Y. Crowell Co., 1971.

Pitrone, Jean M. *Chávez: Man of the Migrants*. New York: Pyramid Communications, 1972.

Chester and Philadelphia (Pennsylvania) Riots of 1918

On July 25, 1918, a race riot began in Chester, Pennsylvania, after four black men allegedly murdered a 21-year-old white man on his porch. What initiated the clash is unclear. However, like most racial conflicts of the era, the superficial cause for the Chester riots—the murder—was brought about during the localized fusion of white intolerance, black resentment, racism, segregation, migration, and economics. By the end of the riot, which lasted three days, five people—three blacks and two whites—died from their injuries, and more than 60 people were arrested. Under the auspices of similar social, economic, and housing circumstances, a few miles away and a few days later, a riot broke out in South Philadelphia when a black woman fired two shots into a crowd of whites gathered outside of her new home near Washington Avenue to protest her moving into the predominantly Italian neighborhood. When the three-day riot ceased on July 29, 1918, the results were similar to the Chester riots of 1918: three blacks and two white police officers were dead. Specific details of the race riots in Chester and Philadelphia, Pennsylvania, are limited to newspaper clippings and narrative accounts; however, the root causes for the riots are well documented.

At the end of Reconstruction (1865–1877), blacks in the South lived under Jim Crow de facto laws that demanded segregation across the board and social subjugation and economic oppression of blacks. By 1890, intermittent trickles of blacks in the South, many of them former slaves and their progenies, began moving North in search of relief from such conditions. In the years prior to American entrance into World War I, blacks remaining in the South were encouraged to also come North, not only in letters sent from family members who had already migrated, but also by the black media. The North, it was argued, was ripe with industrial jobs and offered social freedom. Believing that migration would release them from the fetters of a slavelike existence in the South, thousands of blacks began migrating to Northern states. With its steel mills, coal mines, shipyards, slaughter houses, and railroad construction jobs, Philadelphia and small cities south of the city, such as Chester, became magnets for blacks from Georgia, North and South Carolina, Maryland, and Delaware. Once in the Philadelphia and Pittsburgh metropolises, however, the new migrants experienced circumstances similar to what they believed had been left in the South. In Philadelphia, Pittsburgh, and Chester, black workers were invited to work at less than a living wage; membership in the union and access to benefits were unavailable to them. Additionally, the migrants realized that they would remain socially and educationally segregated from whites. Moreover, many migrants lived in impoverished, overcrowded conditions, and most remained poor and landless.

Across the North, whites, xenophobic and anxious because of the war, were suspicious of outsiders. Additionally, blue collar workers feared that the cheap labor provided by newly transplanted blacks would undercut the likelihood of earning a living wage. Poverty, overcrowded housing, growing unemployment, and the willingness of blacks to work for wages lower than whites were accustomed to accept intensified the probability of clashes between whites and blacks in the 1910s. All of these factors were exacerbated by the propensity of whites to exact violent attacks against blacks, who, having knowledge of widespread lynching and beatings, were eventually encouraged to strike back. In acts of self-defense, blacks responded to white attacks, and neighborhoods in the North erupted in protest and violence throughout July and August in 1918.

The level of antiblack activities in Philadelphia and its surrounding suburbs in the 1910s through the 1940s is historically documented. For example, Coatesville, a small town located in Chester County, housed active members of the Ku Klux Klan, which reached a membership of 200,000 living in Pennsylvania by 1920. Like that in other American towns and cities, Klan activity included voter intimidation, attempts to quell black labor movements and unionization, and lynchings. The 1911 murder of Zachariah Walker serves to demonstrate the volatile mixture of race, black migration, and labor economics.

During an alleged robbery, Walker, a Virginian working in Coatesville as a laborer at the local steel mill, shot and killed Edgar Rice, a white security guard. Under police guard, Walker was taken to Coatesville's hospital after attempting suicide, from where he was dragged into the street still attached to his bed. Once kidnapped by a large white mob, Walker was burned alive.

The Chester and Philadelphia riots were not isolated incidents, but rather parts of a larger, growing problem in American cities. In the early years after World War I ended, racial clashes across the nation were not unique events. In major cities all over the United States, not less than 15 riots broke out between 1917 and 1923. These racially charged acts of violence were not ignored in the black or white communities; nor were they overlooked by politicians. From Harlem renaissance writer Claude McKay, to political activist Marcus Garvey, to the Ku Klux Klan, the riots, their causes, and results, became an important part of American racial discourse.

Ellesia Ann Blaque

See also

Black Self-Defense; Great Migration; Jim Crow Laws; Race Riots in America. Documents: The Report on the Memphis Riots of May 1866 (July 25, 1866); Account of the Riots in East St. Louis, Illinois (July 1917); The Cook County Coroner's Report Regarding the 1919 Chicago Race Riots (1919); A Southern Black Woman's Letter Regarding the Recent Riots in Chicago and Washington (November 1919); The Final Report of the Grand Jury on the Tulsa Race Riot (June 25, 1921); Testimony from *Laney v. United States* Describing Events during the Washington, D.C., Riot of July 1919 (December 3, 1923); The Governor's Commission Report on the Watts Riots (December 1965); Cyrus R. Vance's Report on the Riots in Detroit (July-August 1967); The Reports of the Oklahoma Commission to Study the Tulsa Race Riot of 1921 (2000-2001); The Draft Report of the 1898 Wilmington Race Riot Commission (December 2005)

Further Reading:

Boskin, Joseph, ed. *Urban Racial Violence*, 2nd ed. Los Angeles: Glencoe, 1976.

Trotter, Joe W., Jr., and Eric Ledell Smith. *African Americans in Pennsylvania: Shifting Historical Perspectives*. State College: Penn State University Press, 1997.

Chicago Commission on Race Relations

Illinois Gov. Frank O. Lowden appointed the Chicago Commission on Race Relations to study the Chicago Riot of 1919, and make recommendations to avoid future riots. Twelve commissioners and an extensive staff studied the riot, and the context from which the riot sprung, beginning in December 1919. The commission's full report, *The Negro in Chicago: A Study of Race Relations and a Race Riot*, was first published in 1922. The policy recommendations of the commission—equal access to education and public facilities, ending real estate discrimination, reforming the city's police force—did not lead to new city ordinances or state laws. However, the commission's report both directly refuted a wide variety of claims about race and racism, and influenced a generation of black sociologists.

Two public requests for a scientific study of the riot were issued even as Chicagoans still fought in the streets in July 1919. Both requests urged Lowden to appoint a biracial commission for the study. Several of Chicago's most prominent African American leaders agreed to serve, including *Chicago Defender* publisher Robert S. Abbott Jr., Provident Hospital president George Cleveland Hall, and Olivet Baptist Church's Rev. Lacey K. Williams. Crucially, this group included men who had defended African Americans' right to armed self-defense, and who had insisted that whites, not blacks, initiated racial violence in Chicago to enforce racial stratification. These voices would prove critical, as the commission's white members were at best racial "moderates," such as Sears, Roebuck and Co. president Julius Rosenwald and Chicago National Association for the Advancement of Colored People head Edward O. Brown, who tended to view both blacks and whites as responsible for the riot, and argued against special measures to defend African Americans accused of riot crimes. Indeed, early in the commission's work, a heated discussion erupted between the white and black commissioners regarding the race of the commission's executive secretary. Ultimately, the commission chose Graham R. Taylor, a white man, for the position. But it was Assistant Executive Secretary Charles S. Johnson—then a graduate student at the University of Chicago's renowned sociology program, and a pioneering black sociologist—who provided the program for the commission's work. Johnson and the commission turned a searching eye toward the history of discrimination and violence black Chicagoans experienced as a means of defending and vindicating black Chicago from its critics and assailants.

In contrast to the predominant narratives of race riots, the commission's report identified African Americans as victims both of racism and racial violence, rather than instigators and perpetrators of the riot. African American self-defense was highlighted, while other violent acts committed by blacks were pointedly described as retaliation for white attacks. *The Negro in Chicago* related personal narratives of African American men, arrested and beaten by police for defending themselves, as illustrations of a more systematic miscarriage of justice on the part of Chicago police. Although roughly two-thirds of those shot, beaten, and stabbed during the riot were black, the report showed that African Americans made up two-thirds of those arrested, indicted, and convicted for riot crimes. Moreover, African Americans suffered the vast majority of property damage during the riot.

But *The Negro in Chicago* went the farthest beyond existing debates in its studies of Chicago's "Black Belt" and the Great Migration. Refusing to connect the mere presence of African Americans to the racism they were subjected to, the report exposed a wide field of responses to the migration on the part of business owners, factory supervisors, labor unions, political leaders, police, social workers, and ordinary Chicagoans. Rather than the inevitable result of a dramatic increase of Chicago's black population, the commission argued that the increased racial tensions that caused the riot were instead the product of whites'—and to some extent, African Americans'—acceptance and perpetuation of racial stereotypes originating in the crisis of Reconstruction. Moreover, the report argued, the consequences of the migration itself disproved the assumptions and prejudices, which led to the riot. African Americans showed themselves perfectly able to adapt to industrial, as opposed to agricultural, labor; to join labor unions that did not discriminate; to take advantage of the North's far superior opportunities for public education and recreation; to share public spaces with whites who did not forcibly bar them; and to create a strong and vibrant community that provided for its own institutional and spiritual needs. Only where whites attempted to impose segregation or otherwise discriminate against African Americans did racial tension result, and even this, the commission argued, manifested itself primarily in white racism against blacks. Ultimately, the commission concluded, racism was an irrational response of whites, which only impeded the city's economic progress, social stability, and political efficiency.

Subsequent analysis of the commission's report has faulted it for downplaying the significance of conflicts over unionization, and more broadly for assigning causation to ideology rather than economic and political interests. The commission clearly failed to see the ways in which, for example, labor markets kept divided by race could keep wages for all workers low and unions weak. At the same time, the report not only dispelled a myriad of powerful myths about African Americans but also provided a powerful counterexample to the racist pseudo-science that dominated the public sphere in the World War I era. Johnson's work with the commission influenced many other black sociologists, including E. Franklin Frazier, St. Clair Drake, and Horace Cayton.

JONATHAN S. COIT

See also

Chicago (Illinois) Riot of 1919; Race Riots in America. Documents: The Report on the Memphis Riots of May 1866 (July 25, 1866); Account of the Riots in East St. Louis, Illinois (July 1917); The Cook County Coroner's Report Regarding the 1919 Chicago Race Riots (1919); A Southern Black Woman's Letter Regarding the Recent Riots in Chicago and Washington (November 1919); The Final Report of the Grand Jury on the Tulsa Race Riot (June 25, 1921); Testimony from *Laney v. United States* Describing Events during the Washington, D.C., Riot of July 1919 (December 3, 1923); The Governor's Commission Report on the Watts Riots (December 1965); Cyrus R. Vance's Report on the Riots in Detroit (July-August 1967); The Reports of the Oklahoma Commission to Study the Tulsa Race Riot of 1921 (2000-2001); The Draft Report of the 1898 Wilmington Race Riot Commission (December 2005)

Further Reading:

Waskow, Arthur I. *From Race Riot to Sit-In: 1919 and the 1960s.* Garden City, NY: Anchor Books, 1967.

Chicago (Illinois) Riot of 1919

The killing of a 14-year-old African American male, Eugene Williams, on July 27, 1919, precipitated the riot that raged for five days, left approximately 38 dead, 537 injured, and about 1,000 homeless due to property damage. On this unusually hot day, Williams and four friends decided to raft between Lake Michigan's 25th Street beach, claimed by African Americans, and the 29th Street beach, claimed by whites. The teens drifted across the invisible line of demarcation that separated the races' beaches when a white man began to throw rocks at them, one of which hit Williams on the forehead. By the time one of the teens summoned help from the 25th Street beach, Williams drowned.

Then the four surviving teens, accompanied by black police officers, went to the 29th Street beach and identified the white man who had thrown the rock. The white officer on duty, Daniel Callahan, would not arrest the man and prevented the black police officers from arresting him. Williams's death and the lack of police action ignited the city's factions already fraught with racial tension. In addition to Williams's death, multiple other causative factors are attributed to the violent outbreak, including increased African American migration from the rural South (see Great Migration, The); the conflict between stockyard owners and labor unions; gangs; the emergence of the New Negro, a name applied to the more vocal and participant post–World War I African American male; police inefficiency and political power struggles in Chicago; and the role played by both white and black publications.

Officer Callahan's refusal to arrest the alleged perpetrator of Williams's death and obstruction of his arrest by another officer, followed by the arrest of a black man against whom a white person filed a complaint, were symptomatic of a much larger problem in the unequal treatment of blacks and whites by law enforcement. As word spread of the black youth's death and of police favoritism, more blacks came to the beach, the site of an incident earlier in the day when black couples came to the beach but were thwarted by rock-hurling whites. The races clashed once again, hitting each other with rocks, until a black man, James Crawford, fired a gun, which resulted in the injury of a police officer. Crawford was then shot and killed by a black police officer. The much-studied riot gained in velocity from this point.

Although Williams's death was the event that set the out-of-control violence into motion, the racial tension had festered for two to three years in Chicago. A major contributing condition to the release of anger was the mass migration of Southern, rural blacks, beginning in 1916, to Chicago. For example, during 1917–1919, more than 50,000

White children cheer outside an African American residence that they have set on fire, Chicago, summer of 1919. The police arrived soon afterward. (Bettmann/Corbis)

African Americans moved to an area in Chicago called the Black Belt, located on the city's south side between 12th and 57th Streets and Wentworth Avenue and Cottage Grove Avenue. The area, already strained for housing, became overcrowded. From 1910 to 1920 the enclave's population rose from 34,335 to 92,501. Most of the homes, built pre-1902, were in disrepair and did not have inside toilet facilities, yet the rents were higher than in other parts of the city, the traditionally white sections. The Black Belt was abutted by Irish and Polish neighborhoods, two groups of immigrants especially hostile to the black migrants, as all three groups competed for jobs during the recession that followed World War I. Southern blacks who had been in Chicago and had become economically stable left the Black Belt for white neighborhoods, which also increased racial tension, as evidenced by bombings of African American–owned homes in white neighborhoods, bombings of realtors' offices that sold the homes, and altercations between the races over the use of public spaces, such as parks and beaches. The Black Belt was hemmed in with little room for expansion, except to the Hyde Park and Kenwood areas to the south, also rundown areas. The Black Belt became a breeding ground for disease due to overcrowding, poor living conditions, and, hence, discontent.

The migration also brought a clash of values and lifestyles between the rural and the urban. The *Chicago Defender*, a militantly political African American newspaper edited by Robert S. Abbott, had a circulation that reached into the South, as well as other parts of the country. The Chicago Urban League was founded in 1915 as an affiliate of the National League on Urban Conditions among Negroes to promote the adjustment of African Americans to city life and to promote equal job opportunities. Both the *Defender* and the league viewed part of their mission as acclimatizing new arrivals to city ways. Both disseminated rules of conduct to new arrivals, such as do not allow your children to run barefoot in the streets, bathe and change your clothes after work, do not appear on the streets in ragged clothes, do not loiter, and do not be loud in public. The "Old Settlers," as they were called, African Americans who established themselves before the mass migration, did not welcome the newcomers with open arms either, as they feared the loss of their own status, both socially and economically. Some, in fact, accused the migrants of bringing discrimination to Chicago.

World War I increased job opportunities in Chicago's meat packing plants at a time when the labor force decreased due to the lack of immigrants from belligerent nations participating in the war, and due to decreased immigration from other European countries involved in the war. The labor shortage increased even more when the United States entered the war. Available jobs during this time period rose from 8,000 to 17,000. The packing plants looked to the South for labor and promised higher wages and more opportunity than workers could get if they stayed in the oppressive South. Although the meat packers hired the largest number of migrants, job opportunities with International Harvester and Sears, Roebuck and Co. mail order opened. When the war ended, so did the abundance of jobs. War contracts were lost, 400,000 service men returned home in search of jobs, and the country experienced a recession, which led to job competition, especially between the Irish and the African Americans.

Although the post-riot study drafted by the Chicago Commission on Race Relations, *The Negro in Chicago: A Study of Race Relations and a Race Riot*, declares labor relations a minor cause of the riot, others, especially historians, do not agree. African Americans had been resistant to unionization, especially in the stockyards. From 1894 to the riot in 1919, black and white laborers conflicted. During the strike of 1894, when packing and slaughterhouse workers walked in sympathy with Eugene V. Debs's American Railway Union, blacks were hired to replace them. Known as scabs, this practice occurred in other industries, such as coal, and in other locations. The unions did not alleviate the tension as they tended toward exclusion. The Amalgamated Meat Cutters and Butcher Workers formed in 1901, but was only open to skilled labor, thereby excluding many immigrant blacks. When a massive strike occurred in 1904, strikebreakers, reportedly black, helped to keep the strike going for 10 weeks. The strikebreakers were confined to the plant for their own safety. The situation became so tense that the union leaders asked Booker T. Washington to come to Chicago to encourage blacks not to act as strikebreakers. He refused. There were sporadic outbreaks of violence. Another strike in 1905, a teamsters strike, solidified the image of the African American as scab in the minds of unions and of union white workers. Attributed to this strike are 20 deaths and hundreds of injuries.

The situation favored the employers; it was not so favorable for unions, or the unionized workers, white or black. Violent acts against blacks happened throughout the city during the teamster strike. Eleven years later during the Pullman strike in 1916, African Americans once again were used to replace striking workers. With the power scabs afforded employers, unions made an effort to organize the African American workers, and the packing industry became the focus of their efforts as it employed the greatest number. The unions, especially the Chicago Federation of Labor (CFL), accused the packinghouses of bringing workers from the South as a means of thwarting unionization. The voice of the CFL was *The New Majority*, a union publication. In a city noted for more strikes than any other U.S. city except New York, the unions instituted a major membership drive that added fuel to an already nearly explosive fire.

African Americans resisted unionization, in spite of efforts by the unions, especially in June and July 1919. Immediately before the riot erupted, approximately 250,000 workers were either on strike, threatened to strike, or were locked out. Labor and industry battled. It should be noted that most of the unions did not have black members. Eleven unions in Chicago excluded blacks; others restricted membership. Unions that did extend membership frequently fostered segregation. One cannot deny the effect walkouts in the stockyards had on increasing racial tension in June 1919, as whites viewed blacks as the employers' pawns against them and said that they would not work unless blacks were fired or forced to join the union.

In addition to the struggle for power between unions and industry, which affected blacks' place in Chicago society, a struggle existed between immigrants, namely, the Irish, and the migrants. Organized gangs that had been in existence for years, ironically many of which were supported by the political machine, promoted segregation by the use of violence. The gangs of young thugs identified themselves as "athletic clubs." The Chicago Commission on Race Relations asserted in their report that "but for them [gangs] it is doubtful if the riot would have gone beyond the first clash" (11). The gangs, composed mostly of young white men ages 16–22, many of Irish descent, came from the stockyard area. They sported names such as the Canaryville Bunch, the Alyards, the Dirty Dozen, and the Hamburgers. But most agree that Ragen's Colts, named after their sponsor, Cook County commissioner Frank Ragen, was the most feared. In addition to the sponsorship of athletic clubs by those who held political office, gang members frequently had relatives in law enforcement and boasted of the protection this tie afforded them. Before the riot, gangs victimized blacks with drive-by shootings and beatings. On June 21, 1919, not long before the riot erupted, two blacks were murdered by gangs. The gangs seized the moment after the 29th Street beach confrontation on July 27 by attacking at least 27 blacks; some were beaten; some were shot. Ragen's Colts took the credit. Urban warfare raged as blacks armed themselves with bricks, knives, and guns to protect themselves within the Black Belt, as they feared invasion by the gangs. The gangs, on the other hand, waited for black stockyard workers to exit from the plant the day after the riot began. As the workers exited they were attacked by gang members armed with clubs, pipes, and hammers. Those who got away from the mob by jumping on streetcars were not safe. The roving gangs, cheered on by crowds, overtook them at other locations and beat to death those they caught. As is often the case during times of mob rule, innocent people are killed, as was the case in Chicago. Both blacks and whites lost their lives just by being in the wrong place at the wrong time. The rumor mill ran full throttle reporting killings, some true, some not, which added more tension to both sides.

From this point until August 2, the riot gained momentum. Black mobs and white mobs caused senseless injuries, death, and property destruction. The Chicago riot distinguishes itself from other riots, such as the East St. Louis riot of 1917, because it was not confined to the heavily populated African American section of the city, as was usual in other riots. In fact, it is estimated that 41 percent of the clashes took place in predominantly white neighborhoods.

The willingness of Chicago African Americans to fight back and off their turf is said to be a result in part of the World War I experience and its liberating effect. Men who fought for the United States gained a voice, a voice that was supported by African American intellectuals, such as W.E.B. Du Bois, founder of the National Association for the Advancement of Colored People and editor of its journal *The Crisis*; poets, such as Claude McKay; and newspaper editors, such as Robert S. Abbott. The "New Negro," as he was called, was encouraged to believe in self and his race and was urged to demand the guarantees to citizens granted by the U.S. Constitution. The New Negro also made it quite clear that physical aggression no longer would be tolerated; it would be met with an equally aggressive defense of life and property. The new outspokenness served to increase fear of retribution in whites and, hence, the tension between the races. Whites accused blacks, docile no longer, of being puppets of the Bolsheviks, as the Red Scare also proliferated throughout the nation in 1919. Ironically the major publications by African Americans denounced bolshevism.

In Chicago, the New Negro had gained a political voice and, with it, power, which also increased racial tension during 1919. Chicago politics were corrupt. For a vote, politicians would grant, for example, a blind eye to illegal activities in the Black Belt. In 1915, the black vote gave William Hale Thompson, a Republican, a wide majority in the mayoral race, much to the dismay of other Chicagoans who thought him to be unqualified for the position and an antipapist, which was especially vile to the Irish-Catholic population. After his victory, Thompson appointed African Americans to political posts, another strike against him. Politics, therefore, deepened the chasm between blacks and the immigrant groups, which were overwhelmingly comprised of Democrats. Thompson supported black and tan cabarets, saloons, and places of dance—targets for the reformers. In 1918, the city council voted to shut down the cabarets because they believed them to be hotbeds of vice. They ultimately were allowed to stay open, but they were not allowed to serve alcohol, which hurt the economy of the Black Belt. Thompson lifted the ban on alcohol before the 1919 election, a move to secure the much-needed black vote. Political discord also played a role in allowing the riot to rage before Thompson declared martial law and called in troops. Gov. Frank Lowden and Mayor Thompson, at one time supportive of each other politically, had a falling out during World War I when Thompson declared neutrality in the war, which Lowden viewed as anti-American. Other rifts occurred, which ultimately led to the hesitation of each to stop the riot by using troops. Thompson delayed requesting troops; Lowden refused to dispatch the troops without the request. It was not until the third day, at which time 80 percent of Chicago's police force was situated in or near the Black Belt, a positioning that left other parts of the city unprotected, that Thompson requested troops. But even though 3,500 arrived, they remained at the armory. The city at this point was all but shut down due to violence, yet Thompson and Lowden continued to stall. It wasn't until the employers and police officers put pressure on the mayor, and the threat of total destruction of the Black Belt after Ragen's Colts set more than 37 fires, that Thompson finally acted and asked the troops to be put on the streets. The violence greatly decreased once the troops hit the streets, yet blacks still refused to return to work due to the danger. By August 6, the stockyard owners finally convinced their black workers that it was safe to return, and they did so escorted and protected by 1,500 policemen, militia, and special and regular deputies. When they returned, 10,000 white workers walked off the job and, later in the week, called for a meeting in order to call for a strike. August 8, when troops withdrew, is considered to be the conclusion of the riot.

Publications, both African American and Caucasian, played a role in the increasing racial tension that preceded the riot. As has been noted by various scholars, Robert S. Abbott's editorials in the *Defender*, Carl Sandburg's articles for the *Chicago Daily News*, and the *New Majority*, a CFL publication, each with its own agenda yet each promoting an identity for a specific group, not only helped to bring the increasing racial tension to the public's eye, but also, in some instances, fueled the fire. Abbott's paper, with a large circulation both in Chicago as well as in the South, carried articles, for example, about the stockyard gangs' ties to law enforcement. Sandburg, the reporter and poet, was commissioned in 1919 by the *Chicago Daily News* to investigate the increasing racial tensions in Chicago. Some believe his articles perpetuated the stereotype of the rural blacks moving to the city bringing with them values nonconducive to assimilation and as a group in constant battle with the Irish for place. Sandburg did identify two major factors that contributed to the riot: inadequate housing and competition for employment. The *New Majority* used its voice against the employers whose businesses they wanted to unionize by claiming the employers encouraged rural blacks to come to undermine unionization and for cheap labor. The audience was white, blue-collar workers, who ultimately blamed the situation on the black workers.

Martin Luther King, Jr. said, "A riot is the language of the unheard" (King 1963). In Chicago, on an unusually hot summer day, a young man's lost life demanded a voice and received it in an undesirable way—more violence. Factions, ironically with the same goals—life, liberty, and the pursuit of happiness—took to the streets to be heard. A confluence of factors—increased African American migration from the rural South, conflicts between stockyard owners and unions, gangs and police inefficiency, the emergence of the New Negro, political corruption and warring, and publications that gave direction and voice to different factions—occurred on July 27, 1919, and set into motion a riot.

Claudia M. Stolz

See also

Race Riots in America. Documents: The Report on the Memphis Riots of May 1866 (July 25, 1866); Account of the Riots in East St. Louis, Illinois (July 1917); The Cook County Coroner's Report Regarding the 1919 Chicago Race Riots (1919); A Southern Black Woman's Letter Regarding the Recent Riots in Chicago and Washington (November 1919); The Final Report of the Grand Jury on the Tulsa Race Riot (June 25, 1921); Testimony from *Laney v. United States* Describing Events during the Washington, D.C., Riot of July 1919 (December 3, 1923); The Governor's Commission Report on the Watts Riots (December 1965); Cyrus R. Vance's Report on the Riots in Detroit (July-August 1967); The Reports of the Oklahoma Commission to Study the Tulsa Race Riot of 1921 (2000-2001); The Draft Report of the 1898 Wilmington Race Riot Commission (December 2005)

Further Reading:

Chicago Commission on Race Relations. *The Negro in Chicago: A Study of Race Relations and a Race Riot.* Chicago: University of Chicago Press, 1922.

Doreski, C.K. "Chicago, Race, and the Rhetoric of the 1919 Riot." *Prospects* 18 (1993): 293–309.

"Gangs and the 1919 Chicago Race Riot." http://www.uic.edu/orgs/kbc/ganghistory/Industrial%20Era/Riotbegins.html.

King, Martin Luther, Jr. "Address at Birmingham, Alabama." Speech, December 31, 1963.

Sandburg, Carl. *The Chicago Race Riots.* New York: Harcourt, Brace, and Howe, 1919.

Tuttle, William M., Jr. *Race Riot: Chicago in the Red Summer of 1919.* New York: Atheneum, 1970.

Waskow, Arthur I. *From Race Riot to Sit-In, 1919 and the 1960s: A Study in the Connections between Conflict and Violence.* Gloucester, MA: Peter Smith, 1975.

Chicana Feminism

The foundation of contemporary Latina feminism is a deliberate and collective response to both the surge of feminist consciousness in mainstream society and the civil rights movements of the turbulent and transformative 1960s and 1970s. While civil rights movements were inspired and led by ethnic minorities, Latina feminists recognized that leadership roles were dominantly filled by men who viewed Latinas and other women of color as allies in the social struggle against racism and discrimination but who too often failed to recognize women as social and political equals. Even as they fought alongside Latinos toward the objective of attaining legal rights and cultural recognition, Latina feminists rejected the gender subordination they experienced. As Latinas recognized that the civil rights actions and philosophies of their communities failed to address their rights as women, they turned to the feminist movement but found that the central issues, leadership, and actions of the 1960s and 1970s feminist movement were dominantly directed by and for white women. Latina feminists discovered that the feminist movement indeed attended to gender inequality and sexism, but for the most part, it failed to address the complexity of their experiences as women experiencing not only gender-based discrimination but also racism and, in many cases, discrimination based on socioeconomic status and even immigration status. Thus, like their Latino allies, Latina feminists refused to allow their racial and ethnic diversity to be obliterated through the concept of the U.S. melting pot, yet they also resisted the privileging of sexism and gender identity as disconnected from race, social class, and sexual orientation that traditionally served, and at times continues to serve, as the foundation of mainstream feminism.

Born of commitment to multiple loyalties—to ethnic and racial communities and to women—Latina feminism consistently attends to the intersections between race, class, ethnicity, sexuality, and gender to deconstruct both monolithic cultural nationalism and mainstream feminism. Two foundational examples are the 1980 "Chicanas in the National Landscape" issue of *Frontiers: A Journal of Women Studies*, the first ever monograph on Latinas published by and for an international distribution journal, and Cherríe Moraga's and Gloria Anzaldúa's jointly edited collection *This Bridge Called My Back: Writings by Radical Women of Color* (1981). Anzaldúa's edited collection *Making Face, Making Soul/Haciendo Caras* (1990) is a second collection of such testimony in the form of personal narrative, poetry, and essay. In these collections and others, Latina feminists challenge readers to think about the interconnectedness of racism, sexism, and homophobia, not only in contemporary mainstream society but in ethnic communities and movements as well. Through their writing and activism, Latina feminists expand the potential of all social movements striving for human rights. Differentiating feminist issues of the private sphere (consequences of standards of feminine beauty, division of labor within the household) and the sphere of public policy issues like affirmative action and voter education, for example, Latina feminists integrate this distinction into their activism in ways that benefit women as well as Latino communities.

As it is distinct from its counterparts—mainstream feminism and cultural nationalism—Latina feminism is heterogeneous, shifting to accommodate the diversity of Chicana, Puerto Rican, Cuban, and Central and South American feminists living in the United States. Latina feminists are diverse in age, national origin, education, socioeconomic class, language, and sexual orientation, among other factors. Also, many Latina feminists do not claim a single nationality or cultural background; writers Sandra Benitez and Aurora

Levins Morales stand as representatives of this group. Similarly, a growing population of Latina/os learn English as a first language, and Spanish-speaking Latinos vary in degree and range of bilingualism. Also, the Spanish utilized by Latina feminists varies by region and national background as well as by the continual innovation of language produced through the intersection of Spanish and English in the English-dominant United States.

In addition to the wide in-group diversity of Latina feminists, the breadth of Latina feminism is enhanced by strong alliances with other feminists, both in the United States and in Latin America, to bring attention to women's issues. Using organizations such as the Women of Color Resource Center, the Johns Hopkins University Center for Health and Gender Equity (CHANGE), and the anti-*femicidio* (femicide) network formed to respond to the mass killings of women along the Juarez–El Paso border, Latinas have helped bridge cultural differences to promote peace and justice. Because they are committed to the rights and recognition of their cultural communities, Latina feminists are dedicated to social activism, not as abstract or theoretical but grounded in the material circumstances of its advocates.

The heritage of contemporary Latina feminism is steeped with women who were feminists and social activists before contemporary definitions of feminism were formed. Historical forerunners of contemporary Latina activists include María Mercedes Barbudo, a Puerto Rican woman jailed in 1824 for active resistance against the Spanish colonizers; *soldaderas*, who fought alongside men in the Mexican Revolution of 1910; Teresa Urrea (1873–1906), a *curandera* (healer) known as La Santa de Cabora whose grassroots popularity led Mexican dictator Porfirio Diaz to deport her to Arizona for treason; and Emma Tenayuca, a famous labor activist and strike leader in Texas in the 1930s. These women exemplified the ideals of feminist activism; more recently, Dolores Huerta, Chicana co-organizer of the United Farm Workers, is a civil rights era example of principle put into grassroots sociopolitical action.

Drawing upon this rich history of community-centered activism, the most pressing issues Latina feminists address are the material conditions of their communities. Having fought for human rights in home nations such as El Salvador, Nicaragua, and Cuba, many Latinas continue to politically mobilize in their U.S. communities. Political marches and public demonstrations continue to be central to Latina feminist activism, as Latina feminists seek to improve conditions including unemployment rates, poverty, inadequate educational systems, poor health care and education, inadequate child care, and underserved reproductive rights. Since feminists are composed both of recent immigrants and longstanding residents of the United States, many also concern themselves with the citizenship and human rights of Latin American immigrants, a concern that also helps solidify international alliances between Latinas and women in Latin American countries. Antonia Pantoja, founder of the Puerto Rican Association for Community Affairs, was a visionary who worked toward a strong community, especially through leadership development for youth. Important unionizing activity as modeled by women like Huerta and Tenayuca is continued by women like Esperanza Martell, who helped organize the Latin Women's Collective in New York City and who focuses particularly on health issues. As Latinas politically mobilize to bring about positive change, they seek and encourage political empowerment for themselves, for the individuals they interact with, and for the communities to which they belong. Dominantly working class and race conscious, Latina feminists maintain strong connections and commitments to their families, their communities of origin, and Latin American women internationally.

Latina feminism's strong and crucial facet of social activism is complemented by the equally strong and crucial facet of art and scholarship. In practice, social activism inspires Latina creativity and defines much Latina art. Latina feminists in the visual arts as well as scholars and writers have felt largely silenced or ignored by white feminists and by a broader patriarchal and ethnocentric society. Many Latina feminist writers and artists seek to reclaim voices of U.S. Latina experience that have been omitted from history, community and local political impact, and cultural representation. They use their art to show the inequalities of privilege and power that perpetuate the marginal status of Latinas in the United States. Latina artists often struggle with questions of aesthetics and politics, how to combine agency and creative expression. Thus, the notion of liminality, of being in between worlds, is central to Latina artistic vision. For example, Latina feminists, especially artists, are very conscious of multiple audiences and have sought to negotiate these audiences—white women and men, Latinos and other

Latinas—in the linguistic composition of their works, sometimes translating Spanish terms or traditions into English and sometimes demanding that audiences view and interpret according to their unique vantage points, even when it may mean not reaching all audiences fully.

As Latina feminists establish their own artistic traditions through rich innovations in form, style, and content, and by enmeshing narrative, poetry, and public performance, as well as giving voice to their own complex sociological positions, other Latinas respond by interpreting Latina productivity in new ways. Additionally, Latina feminist scholars, while still a minority on campuses across the United States, are paving the way for a rising population of feminist-conscious students as they are also helping to reshape curriculum and to foster interdisciplinary bonds between women's studies, Latin American studies, Latina/o studies, and related global studies areas. As hosts and presenters of academic conferences, which provide space for dialogue, and as scholars who articulate the force of Latina feminism, Latina academics are also helping mobilize international alliances of idea and activism. Together, Latina artists and scholars have formed their own associations like Mujeres Activas en Letras y Cambio Social (Activist Women in Letters and Social Change) and work to establish productive relationships between professional Latinas and their communities through workshops and other projects. Inclusive and not elitist, Latina feminists do not privilege abstract academic theory over lived experience, political organizing, and artistic production.

Challenges for this generation of Latina feminists include educating young Latinas of the relevance of feminism to their lives, as many Latinas still find themselves in the double bind of feeling torn between mainstream consumerist values or dominant feminism and dissenting communities and identities of race and ethnicity. Latina feminists still must battle the hazards of tokenism, being treated as a representative for what more empowered individuals see as a homogenized community. They must also continue to confront the sustained relegation of their experiences to invisibility or unimportance as well as to avow the necessity and vitality of Latina feminism against the prominent assertion that social transformation has eradicated racism, sexism, heterosexism, and socioeconomic in equality.

R. Joyce Zamora Lausch and Cordelia Chávez Candelaria

See also

Chicano Movement

Further Reading:

Aparicio, Frances R., and Susana Chávez-Silverman. *Tropicalizations: Transcultural Representations of Latinidad.* Hanover, NH: University Press of New England [for] Dartmouth College, 1997.

Candelaria, Cordelia. "Constructing a Chicana-Identified 'Wild Zone' of Critical Theory." In *Feminisms: An Anthology of Literary Theory and Criticism*, edited by Diane P. Herndl. New Brunswick, NJ: Rutgers University Press, 1997.

Sandoval, Chela. "U.S. Third World Feminism: The Theory and Method of Oppositional Consciousness in the Postmodern World." *Genders* 10 (1991): 1–24.

Chicano Movement

The Chicano civil rights movement, commonly known as *el movimiento* ("the movement") or *la causa* ("the cause"), is the name given to the radical social justice activism within the Mexican American community beginning in the late 1960s and ending in the early 1980s. During this period, various organizations and individuals throughout North America struggled for self-determination, equal rights, and economic equality.

Most historians point to the National Chicano Youth Liberation Conference held in March 1969 as the moment when the various factions of the Chicano movement coalesced from regional and local sectors into a national alliance. This conference was hosted by the Denver-based Crusade for Justice, a civil rights organization headed by activist and boxing champion Rodolfo "Corky" Gonzales. Although the Chicano movement did not begin until the late 1960s, a period when anticolonial and anticapitalist movements were emerging on a global scale, its activist efforts built on previous experiences of resistance dating back many decades and even centuries. Accordingly, Chicano resistance to oppression began at least with the 1848 signing of the Treaty of Guadalupe Hidalgo. It was this document signed to end the Mexican-American War that transformed the northern frontiers of Mexico to the southern-most borderlands of the United States. In many ways, a unique Chicano community and identity

Chicano Student Walkouts

Influenced in part by a worldwide climate of youthful unrest and protest, by the leadership of the Brown Berets, and particularly by teacher Sal Castro, thousands of Chicano students walked out of East Los Angeles high schools in March 1968, asserting that they were being ignored and their educational rights abused. The walkouts set in motion a chain of similar protests in urban centers all over the West and Midwest, but especially in Texas, Colorado, Arizona, and New Mexico as well as elsewhere in California. The students protested overcrowding, poor educational facilities, racist and poorly trained teachers, an inadequate curriculum, and a dropout rate of over 50 percent. They demanded more Chicano teachers, counselors, and administrators as well as courses in the Mexican American experience and Mexican culture.

The high school "blowouts" led to comparable actions by Chicano college and university students who, by demonstrations, sit-ins, and abstention from graduation ceremonies, emphasized their demands for Chicano faculty, courses, departments, and administrators as well as for the admission of more Chicano students. The reasonableness of their demands combined with unthinking oppressive reaction from school officials and considerable police brutality to rally most Chicano community organizations behind the students and their leaders. Later a dozen of the militant leaders of the Los Angeles walkouts were arrested for criminal conspiracy; on appeal the charge was held unconstitutional and then dropped.

Although Chicano efforts for educational change were diffused because of differences over goals and absence of a central organization, by 1970 the student walkouts had achieved a degree of success. They were less successful in Arizona and least successful in New Mexico. The student walkouts formed the opening act in the Chicano movement. Since the early 1970s the walkout technique has been used sporadically by Chicano students to push school administrators toward greater awareness of their cavalier disregard of the students' educational rights and to persuade them to give serious consideration to the students' educational grievances.

was created practically overnight when Mexican nationals became "American citizens."

During the 1930s, Mexican American-ness was used as a way to produce a U.S.-centered social space for Mexicans whose citizenship belonged to the United States. This period came to a head in the 1940s when Mexican American World War II veterans returned to the United States from combat in Europe to face rampant segregation, particularly in Texas. With their homecoming, Mexican American soldiers expected to be treated with the respect and esteem they deserved as veterans of the U.S. armed forces. Instead, such veterans as Macario García faced the same segregated realities they had confronted before their military service.

In response to the needs of Latino veterans, the American GI Forum (AGIF) was an organization that strove for equal rights of Mexican Americans through a variety of campaigns, including antidiscrimination lawsuits, voter registration, and college scholarship competitions. The GI Bill gave many working-class enlistees access to higher education and served as a leveling device for blacks, Latinos, and working-class whites within a traditionally racist and classist civil society. Concurrent with the activism of the AGIF were the foundation and expansion of other Latino social justice organizations throughout the country.

One such organization was the Community Service Organization (CSO). The CSO was formed by Saul Alinsky in 1947. It applied union-organizing tactics to civic Mexican American issues in California. In the late 1940s, Fred Ross, a community planner and activist, was sent to Los Angeles to organize Chicano residents and was introduced to a young organizer named César Chávez. Working closely with Ross, Chávez organized more than 20 CSO chapters across California.

In 1962, Chávez met resistance from CSO leaders, who mainly focused on urban issues, about the prospects of working more closely with labor unions in more rural areas. In turn, Chávez resigned from his CSO appointment, closed the Los Angeles office where he had been working, and relocated to Delano in California's Central Valley. Along with fellow organizers Gilbert Padilla and Dolores Huerta, Chávez convened the first conference of the National Farm Workers Association (NFWA) that fall in Fresno, California. The first

NFWA-supported strike occurred in 1965 when workers on a McFarland, California, farm aligned with the union to ensure higher wages and rectify on-the-job problems.

In September 1965, the predominately Chicano NFWA joined the picket line with Filipino organizer Larry Itliong and Agricultural Workers Organizing Committee (AWOC) grape workers in the Delano grape strike. This strike, lasting five years, put tremendous economic pressure on the union and projected "the fight in the field" into the national consciousness. Through the direct action of farm workers and students alike, the support of activist solidarity, the production of community-based art, and international media coverage, the farm worker struggle was on the lips of workers and politicians alike. As this long-term strike persisted, the AWOC and NFWA merged to form the American Federation of Labor and Congress of Industrial Organizations (AFL-CIO)–affiliated United Farm Workers of America (UFW). The UFW, although not a "Chicano" organization, would become one of the hallmarks of the Chicano Movement.

In October 1967, Reies López Tijerina, an evangelical priest and leader of the Alianza de Pueblos Libres, called young Chicano activists to a summit in Albuquerque, New Mexico. It was here that fellow activist José Angel Gutiérrez, a *movimiento* leader associated with the Mexican American Youth Organization (MAYO) in Texas, argued that Chicanos should use the term "*la raza*" to self-identify, as "Chicano" had not gained widespread usage at that point. During the mid-1960s, Chicano student and youth organizations existed throughout the country, with solidarity networks across Mexico. These organizations included MAYO; United Mexican American Students in California and New Mexico; various chapters of the Mexican American Student Confederation also in California; and the Chicano Coordinating Council on Higher Education. These organizations also existed in barrios and colonias with large Latino populations in other parts of the country, particularly in Chicago, Michigan, and Washington state. When these organizations came together at the 1969 National Chicano Youth Liberation Conference in Denver, the diverse organizing principles of the various Chicano factions were centralized. While the movement maintained a commitment to the "national" identity and struggles of the Chicano community, it formed a network in alliance with international anticolonial struggles in Latin America, Asia, and Africa. By doing so, Chicano activists were not producing a cookie-cutter structure for the movement but instead created a network in which autonomous organizations could interact and work together. In northern New Mexico, Chicana feminists such as Betita Martínez and Enriqueta Longeaux y Vásquez produced *El Grito del Norte*, a newspaper in solidarity with the land grant struggle. This publication countered the assumptions that the Chicano movement was a male-dominated space.

Within a month of the Denver symposium, California students and university professors organized a summit at the University of California, Santa Barbara. It was here that activists wrote the seminal document El Plan de Santa Bárbara. This manifesto brought together all Chicano student groups under the name MEChA (El Movimiento Estudiantil Chicano de Aztlán). Although an acronym, the organization's name MEChA serves as a double-signifier in that *mecha* is also the Spanish word for "match." These young activists envisioned themselves not as the vanguards of *Chicanismo*, but rather as agitators who would ignite the flames of resistance. Collectively, these organizers saw Aztlán, the metaphorical homeland of the Aztecs, as the birthright of Mexican American peoples.

In the end, the Chicano movement changed the everyday reality of Mexican Americans through activism and confrontation of white privilege. However, as many historians have pointed out, the movement was crippled by the prevalence of *machismo* and homophobia. Even with these caveats, the Chicano movement cemented Latinos into the fabric of U.S. society.

Dylan A.T. Milner

See also

Chávez, César; National Chicano Moratorium

Further Reading:

Moraga, Cherríe, and Gloria Anzaldúa, eds. *This Bridge Called My Back: Writings by Radical Women of Color*. Watertown, MA: Persephone Press, 1981.

Muñoz, Carlos. *Youth, Identity, Power: The Chicano Movement*. New York: Verso, 1989.

Rosales, F. Arturo. *Chicano! The History of the Mexican American Civil Rights Movement*. Houston: Arte Público Press, 1997.

Vigil, Ernesto B. *The Crusade for Justice: Chicano Militancy and the Government War on Dissent*. Madison: University of Wisconsin Press, 1999.

Chinese Exclusion Act of 1882

A culmination of years of efforts to exclude Chinese economically and legally, the Chinese Exclusion Act of 1882 made it illegal for Chinese laborers to enter the United States and denied naturalized citizenship to Chinese people already in the country. Initially in place for 10 years, the act was extended in 1892 as the Geary Act and made permanent in 1902. The Chinese Exclusion Act marked the beginning of efforts to restrict all immigration to the United States, which was finally codified in the National Origins Act of 1924 and only repealed in 1943 in deference to China's role as a U.S. ally in World War II. It stands as the first and only federal law to attempt to limit immigration of a particular national-origin group.

Anti-Chinese Sentiment and Early Attempts at Exclusion

Chinese immigrants first arrived in California in 1849 to participate in the Gold Rush, and they soon entered the agricultural sector and, later, railroad construction. Initially welcomed as cheap and cooperative labor, Chinese immigrants quickly drew the ire of white immigrant laborers, who considered these "coolies" to be a threat to their jobs and wages. California's 19th-century economy fluctuated wildly from boom to bust, and Chinese workers became an easy scapegoat for white workers' economic woes. Anti-Chinese sentiments spread quickly, as did acts of anti-Chinese violence, including riots, beatings, and lynchings.

California's politicians exploited nativist sentiment to attract the votes of white workers and enacted a series of laws designed to exclude the Chinese from full participation in California society and preserve California for "Americans." The Foreign Miners License Tax (1852) targeted the expanding Chinese population by levying a monthly tax of $20 on every foreign miner who did not desire to become a citizen. Precluded from citizenship by a 1790 U.S. federal law, Chinese miners fell under the tax until its repeal by the federal Civil Rights Act of 1870. In *People v. Hall* (1854) the California Supreme Court ruled that both American-born and immigrant Chinese could not testify for or against whites in court. In 1855, California imposed a landing tax of $50 per person for transporting persons of Chinese origin or descent into the state. The 1862 California law entitled "To Protect Free White Labor against Competition with Chinese Coolie Labor, and to Discourage the Immigration of the Chinese into the State of California," established a monthly tax of $2.50 on Chinese residents of California unless they operated a business or were licensed to work in a mine or agriculture. The 1875 Page Law prohibited the entry of Chinese prostitutes. Its concomitant interrogations and examinations intimidated and discouraged many potential women immigrants, leading to a 68 percent decline in Chinese women arrivals between 1876 and 1882, compared with the previous seven-year period.

Anti-Chinese sentiment was not limited to the U.S. West Coast. East Coast missionaries, merchants, and diplomats often disparaged the Chinese as godless, dishonest, and uncouth. When, after the opening of the transcontinental railroad in 1867, Calvin T. Sampson recruited 75 Chinese workers from California to break the strike at his shoe factory in Adams, Massachusetts, other manufacturers soon followed suit, and anti-Chinese sentiment spread quickly among white East Coast workers. As a result, when California politicians sought to enact anti-Chinese legislation on a national level, their efforts found a receptive audience. In a nation evenly divided between Republicans and Democrats, the threat of Chinese workers became a useful rallying cry for getting out the vote.

An initial attempt to enact Chinese exclusion on a federal level in 1879 passed both houses of Congress. President Rutherford B. Hayes vetoed the act, however, charging that it was an abrogation of the 1869 Burlingame-Seward Treaty. That treaty, while primarily serving to allow U.S. industry to recruit Chinese laborers, had also recognized the right of migration between China and the United States, marking a sea change in China's restrictive policies on trade and migration. To overcome President Hayes's objections, a new treaty allowing the United States to regulate Chinese immigration was negotiated in 1880 and signed into law in 1881. In 1882 the U.S. Congress passed the Chinese Exclusion Act again, and this time President Chester Arthur signed it into law.

The Act and Its Extensions

The passage of the 1882 Chinese Exclusion Act initiated a series of increasingly narrow federal laws designed to exclude Chinese immigrants and institute national origins as the criterion for restricting immigration and controlling the ethnic and racial composition of the U.S. population, a trajectory that culminated in the passage of the National Origins Act of 1924. The Chinese Exclusion Act, initially enacted for 10 years, denied entry to Chinese laborers while providing exceptions for Chinese merchants, diplomats, teachers, students, and tourists. Later laws placed additional limits on Chinese immigrants already settled in the United States. In an 1884 Supreme Court case, a Chinese laborer residing in the United States returned to China and married. Upon returning together to the United States, the wife was denied admission. In its decision, the court ruled that Chinese women who married laborers were assigned their husbands' status upon marriage and so were prohibited admission. The 1888 Scott Act expanded exclusion to all Chinese except merchants. In addition, the Scott Act prohibited Chinese laborers who left the United States to return and canceled the reentry permits of those who had left previously and not yet returned to the United States, leaving more than 20,000 Chinese stranded outside the United States, often separated from families and property. The 1894 modifications to the Scott Act allowed laborers with wives, children, or $1,000 in assets in the United States to return. The Geary Act of 1892 extended the Chinese Exclusion Act for 10 more years and required Chinese laborers in the United States to obtain a certificate of residence. Failure to register within one year could be punished by deportation. In 1902, Congress extended the Chinese Exclusion Act indefinitely.

Gentlemen's Agreement of 1908

With the formal exclusion of Chinese immigration through the Chinese Exclusion Act of 1882, the anti-Asian sentiment in America turned to the Japanese as the 20th century began. For example, the San Francisco school board attempted to exclude Japanese children from public schools. President Theodore Roosevelt pressured San Francisco officials to back down from the resolution and negotiated with the Japanese government to prohibit Japanese immigration to the United States instead. In the 1907–1908 negotiations, Roosevelt persuaded the Japanese government to accept the infamous Gentlemen's Agreement, whereby no immigration passport would be issued by the Japanese government to anyone except immediate families of Japanese workers already living in the United States.

Unlike Chinese immigrants, Japanese workers in the United States were allowed to bring their brides. Through this and other exceptions, the number of Japanese immigrants continued to grow, albeit at a slower pace than before: between 1908 and 1924, more than 120,000 arrived at Pacific Coast ports and another 48,000 entered the Hawaiian Island. In spite of this increase, both the 1882 Chinese Exclusion Act and the Gentlemen's Agreement were effective in curbing immigration from East Asia. Plantation owners in Hawaii turned instead to the Philippines to fill their labor demand. The National Origins Act of 1924 closed off immigration from Japan.

SHIN KIM AND KWANG CHUNG KIM

Impact on the Chinese Community in the United States

The passage of the Chinese Exclusion Act and subsequent efforts to strengthen and extend its provisions had a profound impact on the Chinese community in America. In the succeeding years the Chinese population contracted dramatically as fewer immigrants were able to enter the United States and those who left were unable to return. The severe restrictions on the immigration of women, coupled with the pattern of young men migrating alone, led to the emergence of a largely bachelor society unable to reproduce itself. While the 1880 census recorded 105,465 Chinese and the 1890 census, 107,488, by 1900 the number had dropped to 89,863 and by 1920, to 61,639. The impact on communities in China as well should not be underestimated, as men who had gone abroad were unable to return for visits without losing their right to reentry, and their wives were left in China, effectively becoming widows.

Faced with rising anti-Chinese sentiment and the need to rely on Chinese compatriots for protection, social networks, and economic support, Chinatowns began to emerge in the urban centers of the West Coast. Forced to retreat into their own cultural and economic colonies, in the late 1800s and early decades of the 20th century, Chinese immigrants and their children converged on urban areas and shifted their employment niches from gold mining, agriculture, and

United States v. Thind (1923)

United States v. Thind was argued before the Supreme Court of the United States in the winter of 1923. At issue were whether a "high-caste Hindu of full Indian blood" qualified as a white person and whether the Immigration Act of 1917 disqualified Hindus from citizenship who would have been eligible before the passage of that law. The case also aimed to clarify a question left unanswered in *Ozawa v. United States* (1922), which was what the boundaries of whiteness were. The applicant for citizenship in this case claimed that he was white on the basis of his northern Indian Aryan/Caucasian background. The Court came to the conclusion that Aryan was a linguistic rather than a racial category and that Caucasian is a category too broad to be used in determining race. The Court followed this determination by stating that Indians, on the basis of their physical characteristics, which are distinct from those of Europeans, could not be contained within the group delineated as "free white persons eligible for citizenship." Additionally, the Court made the point that Congress would not have wanted to render a class of people eligible for citizenship who were not considered eligible for immigration (no Asian was able to immigrate at this time). The Court was careful to make the point that they were not suggesting racial superiority or inferiority, merely racial difference—and that this difference was sufficient to disallow citizenship.

The consequence of this decision was that only individuals considered to be of European or African descent were allowed to become citizens of the United States. Citizenship brings with it not only the right to vote and hold elected office but freedom from certain kinds of political and criminal persecution. Additionally, at the time that this case was argued, immigrants not eligible for citizenship were not allowed to own property or engage in certain occupations. This case, therefore, relegated Asian Americans to a subservient position in U.S. society, regardless of their education or income, until legislation began to repeal its effects, starting in 1943 when Chinese Americans were granted the right of naturalization. Filipinos and South Asians gained naturalization rights in 1946, but Japanese and Korean Americans had to wait until 1952.

MIKAILA MARIEL LEMONIK ARTHUR

railroad construction to laundries, restaurants, and light manufacturing, including garment factories. Chinatowns also began to attract white tourists, drawn to their images as exotic and foreign places.

Resistance to Exclusion

Escalating efforts by the U.S. government to prohibit Chinese immigration were met by increasingly creative efforts to circumvent those laws. The smuggling of Chinese workers across the Canadian-U.S. and Mexican-U.S. borders became a lucrative business for Chinese Americans and whites. But Chinese immigration to the United States, including laborers, continued, with entrants falling under the categories of merchant, student, teacher, diplomat, and tourist. Noncitizen laundrymen, laborers, and restaurant owners sought to represent themselves as "paper merchants" by buying shares in a merchant's company or by bribing a merchant to list them as a partner. Once recognized as a "merchant," Chinese immigrants were permitted to bring families to the United States under provisions of the Chinese Exclusion Act.

Statutes allowing citizens to bring wives and children to the United States led to the development of a "paper son" strategy. Children of citizens were automatically citizens of the United States even if born abroad. Children fathered by Chinese Americans during a visit to China, for example, automatically became U.S. citizens and could enter the country. Many wives and children entered the United States legitimately under these provisions. Others entered as paper sons: men returning to the United States from visits to China would claim to have fathered a child while there, and they could then sell this "slot" to a family in China that desired to send their son to America. Entry for these children, either legitimate or paper, was not automatic. As Ellis Island became symbolic of European immigrants' entry into the United States through New York Harbor, Angel Island became symbolic of Chinese immigrants' entry through San Francisco Harbor. At Angel Island, Chinese immigrants were detained and examined to prove their identity. If unsuccessful, they would be deported immediately. In preparation for these interrogations, families prepared extensive coaching books filled with minute details of their home life. The hopeful immigrant would memorize the information, sometimes 200 pages long, and toss the book into the harbor before arriving in San Francisco. The use of paper-son slots expanded dramatically after April 18, 1906, when an earthquake struck San Francisco. The resulting fires destroyed all municipal records, including birth records. Afterward, many Chinese men claimed to have been born in San Francisco, a claim that could not be contradicted. As U.S.-born citizens, they then availed themselves of the right to bring wives and children to the United States. It is uncertain how many Chinese men falsely claimed U.S. citizenship, but with the extreme imbalance of men to women at the time, by some estimates every Chinese woman living in San Francisco would have had to bear 800 children to account for all the men who claimed after the earthquake that they had been born in San Francisco.

Repeal of the Chinese Exclusion Act, and Its Aftermath

The Chinese Exclusion Act was repealed in 1943, in deference to China's role as a U.S. ally against Japan in World War II. After its repeal, Chinese immigration fell under the guidelines of the 1924 National Origins Act until its replacement in 1965. Under the national-origins provisions, Chinese were awarded an annual immigration quota of 105. For the 10 years that followed, however, only an average of 59 Chinese immigrants entered the United States. The repeal of the Chinese Exclusion Act also extended to Chinese immigrants the right to become naturalized citizens, and many then sought to reunite with their families. Chinese immigration to the United States after World War II was also bolstered by the War Brides Act and by refugee provisions available for Chinese fleeing communist China, often through Hong Kong. But true parity in immigration matters and the end of Chinese exclusion did not occur until 1965, with the passage of the Immigrant and Nationalities Act, which awarded an equal immigrant quota of 20,000 to each country outside the Western Hemisphere. Since 1965, Chinese immigration to the United States has grown steadily, and the Chinese American community has increased both in numbers and diversity in origin.

Kenneth J. Guest

See also

National Origins Act of 1924

Further Reading:

Hsu, Madeline. *Dreaming of Gold, Dreaming of Home: Transnationalism and Migration between the United States and South China, 1882–1943*. Stanford, CA: Stanford University Press, 2000.

Kitano, Harry H. L., and Roger Daniels. *Asian Americans: Emerging Minorities*. Englewood Cilffs, NJ: Prentice Hall, 1988.

Salyer, Lucy E. *Laws Harsh as Tigers: Chinese Immigrants and the Shaping of Modern Immigration Law*. Chapel Hill: University of North Carolina Press, 1995.

Takaki, Ronald. *Strangers from a Different Shore: A History of Asian Americans*. Boston: Back Bay Books, 1998.

Christian Identity Hate Groups

Christian identity is a religious ideology that is popular in right-wing political circles. Adherents hold both anti-Semitic views and antigovernment views (ADL 2012: 1). Despite limited numbers of followers, their ideology has influenced literally all other antigovernment groups and white supremacist groups that are active in the United States (Dobratz and Shanks Meile 1997: 4), and members of the movement have been linked with a variety of hate crimes and domestic terrorist activities. The Anti-Defamation League estimates that there are somewhere between 25,000 and 50,000 members of the Christian Identity Movement in the United States (ADL 2012: 4).

The origins of the current Christian Identity Movement can be found in the 19th century British Israelism doctrines developed in England. British Israelism is the belief that modern Europeans were biologically descended from the 10 lost tribes of Israel, that Anglo-Saxons are God's chosen people, and that it is their divine destiny to dominate and colonize the world (ADL 2012: 1; Dobratz and Shanks-Meile 1997: 74). The ideas of British Israelism were transplanted to the United States by Charles A. L. Totten, who was a military science instructor at Yale University in the late 1800s; Howard Rand, who established American outposts of British Israelism across the United States and distributed literature on British Israelism through his Anglo-Saxon Federation; and

The Phineas Priesthood

"Perhaps the most chilling manifestation of Identity terrorism can be found in the concept of the Phineas Priesthood, set forth by Richard Kelly Hoskins in his 1990 book Vigilantes of Christendom. The Priesthood is based on the concept of the obscure Biblical character Phinehas, an Israelite who used a spear to slay a 'race-mixing' fellow Israelite and the Midianite woman with whom he had sex. Hoskins conjured up the idea of an elite class of 'Phineas Priests,' self-anointed warriors who would use extreme measures to attack race-mixers, gays, or abortionists, among other targets. Over the years, some have committed crimes using the Phineas Priest label, including a group of about eight who committed bombings and bank robberies in the Spokane, Washington, area in 1996 (four of whom were caught and sentenced to lengthy prison terms)" (Anti-Defamation League 2012).

William Cameron, a Ford Motor Company executive, who published articles in *The Dearborn Independent* that combined the ideas of British Israelism with anti-Semitism and with the help of the influential Henry Ford helped link the ideas of British Israelism with the political right in the United States (ADL 2012: 2; Barkun 1994: 48, 74–75).

It was during this time period that a distinctly new group emerged and split from British Israelism. This group was known as the Christian Identity Movement (ADL 2012: 3). The Christian Identity Movement combined the ideas of British Israelism, demonic anti-Semitism, and political extremism. After the Christian Identity Movement was established, a preacher by the name of Wesley Smith became the single most important figure in the spread of this ideology in the United States (Barkun 1994: 61). He founded a church in California in the 1940s and also held a daily radio broadcast to spread his Christian Identity beliefs. In 1957 he changed the name of his church to the Church of Jesus Christ Christian to forward his notion that Jesus was not a Jew. During the 1970s and 1980s the Christian Identity Movement underwent another transformation under the influence of Wesley Smith's associate William Potter Gale. Gale was influential in bringing a militant aspect to the Christian Identity Movement. Today there are numerous Christian Identity Churches nationwide that promulgate the core beliefs of the Christian Identity Movement (SPLC 2012: 1).

There are two core beliefs associated with the Christian Identity Movement. The first is the belief in white supremacy. This belief is heavily influenced by the original ideas of British Israelism in that Christian Identity adherents believe that white Europeans are the descendants of the 10 lost tribes of Israel, that the Aryan people represent God's chosen people while Jews are the satanic offspring of Eve and the serpent, and other nonwhites are subhuman "mud people" (ADL 2012, 2). They argue that individuals of white European descent have displayed historic superiority over other races in science, technology, philanthropy, and economic organization. This superiority is not a result of their natural endowments but is instead a result of their stricter following of the biblical teachings. Christian identity followers believe that it is their mission to be the light of the world showing the misguided the true way (Swain and Nieli 2003: 205). The second core belief is millennialism. Adherents are convinced that the present world's problems are a result of disobedience to divine law, and as a result, a day of reckoning is forthcoming (Dobratz and Shank-Meile 1997: 77). They believe that the end of the world is coming and that this Armageddon will represent a cleansing process in which they will play a pivotal role. According to Christian Identity theology, during Armageddon the Jews will try to destroy the white race during a war, but after the final battle God will recognize the Aryan people as his chosen people (F.B.I. 1999: 5).

In the late 1980s the Southern Poverty Law Center estimated that there were 38 different Christian Identity groups active in the United States. Since the 1980s Christian Identity groups have been counted in the "other" category on their hate group watch list because the movement is now underground (SPLC 1989: 26). The movement gained significant followers in the 1990s following the Ruby Ridge and Waco standoffs. The movement is strongest in the Pacific Northwest and Midwest in the United States, but it can be found in every U.S. region as well as in Canada, Ireland, Great Britain, Australia, and South Africa (ADL 2012, 4–5).

Virginia R. Beard

See also

Hate Groups in America

Further Reading:

Anti-Defamation League (ADL). "Christian Identity," http://www.adl.org/learn/ext_us/Christian_Identity.asp?xpicked=4&item=Christian_ID (cited December 20, 2012).

Barkun, Michael. *Religion and the Racist Right: The Origins of the Christian Identity Movement*. Chapel Hill: University of North Carolina Press, 1994.

Dobratz, Betty A. and Stephanie L. Shanks-Meile. *White Power, White Pride!: The White Separatist Movement in the United States*. New York: Twayne Publishers, 1997.

"F.B.I. Records: The Vault. Christian Identity Movement." http://vault.fbi.gov/Christian%20Identity%20Movement%20/Christian%20Identity%20Movement%20Part%201%20of%201/view (cited December 15, 2012).

Southern Poverty Law Center (SPLC). "Active Christian Identity Churches," http://www.splcenter.org/get-informed/intelligence-files/ideology/christian-identity/active_hate_groups (cited December 20, 2012).

Southern Poverty Law Center (SPLC). "Christian Identity," http://www.splcenter.org/get-informed/intelligence-files/ideology/christian-identity (cited December 20, 2012).

Swain, Carol M. and Russ Nieli. *Contemporary Voices of White Nationalism in America*. New York: Cambridge University Press, 2003.

Cincinnati (Ohio) Riots of 1967 and 1968

Like many other American cities, such as Los Angeles and Detroit, Cincinnati was torn by racial violence in the mid-1960s (see Long Hot Summer Riots, 1965–1967). In June 1967, Cincinnati's minority neighborhoods, which had long suffered from racism, police brutality, and economic decline, experienced a devastating riot that had to be suppressed by the Ohio National Guard, and that left one dead and hundreds in custody. Less than a year later, in April 1968, the city again experienced racial violence, this time sparked by the murder of Dr. Martin Luther King, Jr.

Cincinnati had a long history of racial violence. In March 1884, serious disorders accompanied the attempt by a white mob to lynch William Berner, a German American, and his black accomplice, Joseph Palmer, who were accused of killing Berner's employer (see Lynching). White Cincinnatians, angry that Berner was convicted of manslaughter, not murder, attempted to storm the jail and seize the two men. When this failed, the mob returned the next evening and burned the courthouse to the ground, compelling the governor to call out the militia. Fifty-six people died and more than 200 were wounded before order could be restored. Palmer was eventually hanged.

Racially motivated violence exploded again in the city in 1929, when a young black man sitting in a restaurant got into a verbal altercation with two police officers. The officers followed the man out into the street, where shots were fired, killing the black man. The police claimed that he had attacked them with a knife; however, the publisher of *The Union*, Cincinnati's African American newspaper, charged that the murder was an act of naked racism.

By 1940, blacks made up 12.2 percent of the city's population. Although World War II–related jobs in the industrial sector were plentiful and blacks made some economic gains, they were, for the most part, confined to blue collar jobs and denied membership in unions. Blacks also still had difficulty obtaining service jobs and promotions, while schools, housing, and health care was still substandard in black communities. Sporadic racial incidents flared up during the war years. In June 1941, a race riot was barely avoided after a dispute between a white grocery store owner and a black customer. In the summer of 1944, a group of about 100 white men and boys stoned a house in Mount Adams where two black families lived. A white neighbor who tried to intervene was hung in effigy. Moreover, there were numerous incidents of racial profiling and harassment of African Americans by white police officers.

By the 1960s, housing segregation was especially bad in Cincinnati, which, like other Northern cities, struggled with a loss of population, white flight to the suburbs, and a declining manufacturing base. Moreover, Northern segregation was just as pernicious as its Southern counterpart. Cincinnati had its own Jim Crow stories—theaters, bowling alleys, libraries, and amusement venues remained defiantly segregated. The famous Coney Island amusement park, dance hall, and swimming pool was not integrated until 1961, after almost 10 years of work by the National Association for the Advancement of Colored People, the Cincinnati Committee on Human Rights, and local volunteers.

As the civil rights movement spread into the North in the 1960s, Cincinnati found itself the target of demonstrations by blacks frustrated at the slow pace of integration, the lack of jobs, substandard housing and schools, and continued police harassment. On June 11, 1967, Peter Frake, a black man, began a protest against the death sentence his cousin, Posteal Laskey, received after he was convicted of killing Barbara Bowman, a white woman. After incidents of vandalism, more than a dozen blacks were arrested, and the next day received the maximum sentence for that crime, which angered the black community. Within 24 hours, a full-scale riot erupted as blacks set fires, stoned businesses, and fought with police. A curfew was instituted and Ohio Gov. James Rhodes called out the Ohio National Guard, which received orders from the adjutant general to shoot to kill. By June 15, when the riot had been contained, one person was dead, 404 people had been arrested, and the city had suffered over $2 million in property damage. In the aftermath, the police chief of Cincinnati stated that he was proud of the state of race relations in the city.

Ironically, Dr. Martin Luther King, Jr. had visited Zion Baptist Church in Avondale on June 12. Calling it midnight in the social order of America, King had urged blacks and whites to work together to right the social wrongs so pervasive in the United States. He spoke of the racial segregation he had experienced as a boy growing up in the South and how he had never let it segregate his mind, imploring blacks in Cincinnati to follow his example.

Several days later, a white Republican state representative introduced a bill in the Ohio House to better define martial law and limit the amount of civil and criminal damages for which government entities would be liable. Civil libertarians protested against the bill, but Carl Stokes, a black Democratic representative from Cleveland, endorsed it, adding that it should be amended to clarify the governor's authority to call out the National Guard.

Like other large Northern cities in which riots broke out in the 1960s, Cincinnati lacked black representation in politics, business, and other policy-making bodies, and its minority communities suffered from chronic unemployment and underemployment, inadequate housing, police harassment, a racist justice system, poor educational facilities, and inadequate federal programs designed to alleviate poverty and injustice.

In April 1968, Dr. King was assassinated in Memphis (see King, Martin Luther, Jr.). On April 6, a memorial service organized by several Cincinnati-area pastors was held at a local cathedral. Although there were a few sporadic instances of vandalism, violence, and arson, the city remained calm for the most part. On April 8, a Black Monday memorial was held at a local recreation center. Blacks were encouraged to boycott schools and jobs, thereby opting out of participation in white society, which was held responsible for King's death. More than 1,500 blacks heard a speech by an officer of the Congress of Racial Equality, who blamed white Americans for King's death and urged blacks to retaliate. Still, the crowd was orderly when it left the meeting and spilled out into the street. Somewhere on the street there occurred the accidental shooting of a black woman by her husband. By the time the crowd heard of the incident, it had morphed into a shooting of a black woman by a white police officer, and a full-scale riot erupted. By the time the police had restored order a few days later, two people were dead and hundreds were under arrest. Property damage was estimated at $3 million.

After the 1968 disorders, race relations in Cincinnati remained strained. Blacks remained at the bottom of the socioeconomic ladder, and distrust between whites and blacks was high. Sporadic racial violence, boycotts, and incidents of police brutality continued. As recently as 2001, new race riots erupted in response to the shooting of a black teenager by a white police officer. In August 2001, the Cincinnati Museum Center presented *Unrest in Cincinnati: Voices in Our Community*, an exhibit chronicling the city's history of civil disorders. One of the most telling sections was the timeline of actions taken to improve race relations in Cincinnati. It stopped in 1972.

Marilyn K. Howard

See also

Cincinnati (Ohio) Riots of 2001; Race Riots in America. Documents: The Report on the Memphis Riots of May 1866 (July 25, 1866); Account of the Riots in East St. Louis, Illinois (July 1917); The Cook County Coroner's Report Regarding the 1919 Chicago Race Riots (1919); A Southern Black Woman's Letter Regarding the Recent Riots in Chicago and Washington (November 1919); The Final Report of the Grand Jury on the Tulsa Race Riot (June 25, 1921); Testimony from *Laney v. United States* Describing Events during the Washington, D.C., Riot of July 1919 (December 3, 1923); The Governor's Commission Report on the Watts Riots (December 1965); Cyrus R. Vance's Report on the Riots in Detroit (July-August 1967);

The Reports of the Oklahoma Commission to Study the Tulsa Race Riot of 1921 (2000-2001); The Draft Report of the 1898 Wilmington Race Riot Commission (December 2005)

Further Reading:

Cayton, Andrew R. L. *Ohio: This History of a People*. Columbus: Ohio State University Press, 2002.

Gerber, David A. *Black Ohio and the Color Line 1860–1915*. Urbana: University of Illinois Press, 1976.

Koehler, Lyle. *Cincinnati's Black Peoples: A Chronology and Bibliography*. Cincinnati: University of Cincinnati, 1986.

Miller, Zane L., and Bruce Tucker. *Changing Plans for America's Inner Cities: Cincinnati's Over-the-Rhine and Twentieth-Century Urbanism*. Columbus: Ohio State University Press, 1998.

Quillin, Frank U. *The Color Line in Ohio: A History of Race Prejudice in a Typical Northern State*. Ann Arbor, MI: George Wahr, 1913.

Report of the National Advisory Commission on Civil Disorders. Washington, DC: U.S. Government Printing Office, 1968.

Cincinnati (Ohio) Riot of 2001

On April 10, 2001, three days after a black teenager was slain by a white police officer, serious rioting erupted in downtown Cincinnati, Ohio. Coming on the heels of a series of high-profile cases involving allegations of police brutality and racial profiling leveled at the Cincinnati Police Department (CPD) by African Americans, the shooting precipitated the worst episodes of racial violence to hit Cincinnati since the late 1960s (see Cincinnati [Ohio] Riots of 1967 and 1968). Although the disorder resulted in no deaths, the physical damage to downtown businesses and the long-term damage to the city's economy were enormous. The riots also aggravated racial tensions, especially between the police department and Cincinnati's minority communities.

In the early morning of April 7, 2001, Officer Steven Roach shot and killed 19-year-old Timothy Thomas as he fled from police down a dark alley. The pursuing officers were attempting to execute an arrest warrant that had been issued against Thomas for 14 outstanding charges, all of which were nonviolent misdemeanors. Roach had joined a pursuit already in progress when he suddenly encountered Thomas as the fleeing youth came around a corner. Believing that Thomas was reaching for a weapon, Roach, who claimed that he was unaware of the nonviolent nature of Thomas's alleged offenses and that Thomas ignored an order to stop, fired his gun with deadly result. A later investigation concluded that Thomas had not been reaching for a gun, but had instead been trying to pull up his pants, which, according to the prevailing style, were loose and baggy. Thomas was the 15th young black man to die in a confrontation with Cincinnati police, or while in police custody, since 1995. During the same period, no white suspects had died in similar circumstances.

The Thomas shooting occurred less than six months after two other black men had died while in the custody of Cincinnati police officers. Roger Owensby Jr. died on November 7, 2000, allegedly of asphyxiation from a police chokehold, and Jeffrey Irons died the next day, also while scuffling with police. The officers accused of causing Owensby's death were brought to trial in January 2001, but, despite charges that a fellow officer who gave testimony at each trial committed perjury, one officer was acquitted and the other was not retried after his case ended in a mistrial. Frustrated by this result, a group of citizens filed a federal lawsuit in March 2001 on behalf of all the families of black men who had died in police custody since 1995; these cases were combined with other pending civil suits against the CPD, including that of Bomani Tyehimba, a black businessman who claimed that in 1999, during the course of a routine traffic stop, Cincinnati police officers illegally ordered him from his car and then handcuffed and beat him at gunpoint.

In light of these earlier cases, the Thomas shooting precipitated a strong and immediate reaction from the city's African American community. On April 9, a group of about 200 black protestors, including Thomas's mother, Angela Leisure, invaded the city council chamber in the midst of a public meeting. Demanding an immediate accounting of Thomas's death and the punishment of Roach, the protestors carried signs saying "Stop Killing Us or Else" and "Wear Seat Belt or Be Executed," the latter a reference to one of the misdemeanors changed against Thomas. When told that the CPD had not completed its investigation and was not yet ready to make a report, the protestors insulted and berated council members, vandalized the interior and exterior of city hall, and then marched to police headquarters, where they lowered the American flag and then raised it again upside down. After issuing several warnings, the police finally

National Association for the Advancement of Colored People (NAACP) president Kweisi Mfume (right) shows a spent shotgun cartridge to residents during a tour of Cincinnati, Ohio, on April 12, 2001. Mfume came to Cincinnati to ask local residents to stop the violent protests over the fatal shooting of an African American youth by white policemen. (AP/Wide World Photos)

dispersed the demonstrators around midnight by using beanbag bullets, tear gas, and pepper spray.

On the evening of the next day, April 10, serious rioting erupted in downtown Cincinnati, where crowds of young blacks set fires and looted and vandalized businesses. Although these disorders sparked riots in other Cincinnati neighborhoods, the most serious damage was reported downtown. Some gunshots were fired and a few people were injured, although none seriously. The disorders ended in the early morning hours, and many downtown businesses resumed normal operations on the next day. However, darkness brought a renewal of the rioting and the infliction of more extensive damage on downtown businesses, many of which did not open on April 12, both because of damage sustained and because neither customers nor employees were willing to venture downtown. After a third night of disorders, Mayor Charlie Luken's declaration of a citywide curfew and the coming of a cold rain finally ended the riots. Damage estimates for the three nights of violence were put at $3.6 million.

After Thomas's funeral on April 14, a crowd of about 2,000 began an impromptu, but peaceful, march of protest toward downtown. Wary of further disorders, the police injured several marchers by firing beanbag bullets and other nonlethal projectiles into the crowd. Although the police claimed that they had strictly followed their departmental use-of-force policy in firing on the marchers, eyewitnesses declared that the officers simply opened fire indiscriminately on the protestors without giving any warning. Angered by the police reaction to the peaceful protest of April 14, groups involved in the Owensby case organized a boycott of downtown businesses, and African American entertainers scheduled to appear in Cincinnati, such as Bill Cosby, Whoopi Goldberg, and Smokey Robinson, cancelled their performances. Within a year, the boycott was estimated to have deprived the Cincinnati economy of more than $10 million.

In September 2001, Officer Roach was tried for negligent homicide. The decision to waive a trial and have the case decided by the judge was widely criticized as an attempt by the CPD to dictate the outcome of the trial. When Roach was eventually acquitted, new disorders erupted, but they were brief and caused little damage. An internal police investigation of the Thomas shooting, issued after Roach had left the CPD to join a local suburban police force, concluded that the officer had lied in his official report, had not followed department procedures for handling a firearm, and had not given Thomas sufficient time to respond to his demands. The police chief thereafter suggested that if Roach were still with the CPD, he would be fired for these violations.

In 2002, the federal lawsuit filed on behalf of Tyehimba and others in the month before Thomas's death resulted in the signing of a collaborative agreement, whereby the city agreed to undertake a series of initiatives to improve police service to minority communities. The agreement, which had been encouraged by a critical report of the CPD issued by the U.S. Department of Justice, provided for a revision of the CPD's use-of-force policies, the creation of an independent citizen panel to hear complaints against the police, and the formation of a community focus group to recommend community-oriented policing policies. As a result of this more stringent scrutiny, CPD officers began an unofficial work slowdown to demonstrate their dissatisfaction with what they believed was the city administration's failure to support the department. Because this slowdown coincided with an increase in violent crime in the downtown area, it, along with the economic boycott, is considered one of the most serious consequences of the 2001 riots.

John A. Wagner

See also

Cincinnati (Ohio) Riots of 1967 and 1968; Race Riots in America. Documents: The Report on the Memphis Riots of May 1866 (July 25, 1866); Account of the Riots in East St. Louis, Illinois (July 1917); The Cook County Coroner's Report Regarding the 1919 Chicago Race Riots (1919); A Southern Black Woman's Letter Regarding the Recent Riots in Chicago and Washington (November 1919); The Final Report of the Grand Jury on the Tulsa Race Riot (June 25, 1921); Testimony from *Laney v. United States* Describing Events during the Washington, D.C., Riot of July 1919 (December 3, 1923); The Governor's Commission Report on the Watts Riots (December 1965); Cyrus R. Vance's Report on the Riots in Detroit (July-August 1967); The Reports of the Oklahoma Commission to Study the Tulsa Race Riot of 1921 (2000-2001); The Draft Report of the 1898 Wilmington Race Riot Commission (December 2005)

Further Reading:

Various articles describing the riot and its aftermath can be found on the Web sites of the *Cincinnati Enquirer* (http://www.enquirer.com) and *Cincinnati Post* (http://www.cincypost.cm) newspapers.

Cinema in the Jim Crow Era

Films depicting the era of Jim Crow or produced during its time tended to reinforce white supremacy until a more nuanced portrait began to emerge following the victories of the modern civil rights movement.

For all of its pioneering impact in graphic realism and establishing cinema as a competitive choice for entertainment, *The Birth of a Nation* (1915) attested to a virulent racism and its hold upon the former Confederacy. This silent epic chronicled the evolution of two families (one Northern and one Southern) from their cordiality in the antebellum years through the maelstrom of the Civil War and the onset of Reconstruction. Relying upon an exaggerated portrayal of corruption and ineptitude among Reconstruction officials as well as depredations against white women by blacks, the film treated the formation of the Ku Klux Klan as a reasonable response. White supporters of reform in the South appeared merely as craven opportunists willing to make any alliance that secured power. The film's only suggestion of evenhandedness was found in the brutality of white Southerners punishing blacks. President Woodrow Wilson, a proponent of segregation, enjoyed the production during a private screening at the White House. Despite temporary successes by the National Association for the Advancement of Colored People (NAACP) in banning the film in some metropolitan areas, director D. W. Griffith helped cement a façade of the genteel Old South united in a quixotic pursuit of the "Lost Cause."

Following *The Birth of a Nation*, the cinematography of the South remained mired in the plantation myth as the sole motif around which to shape a production. The plantation was often depicted as a bucolic refuge from the clamor, filth, and degradation of urban life. This agrarian world appeared run by noble landowners and worked by docile slaves. Such fabled portrayals paralleled the lack of serious scholarship on the region's turbulent political, social, and economic conditions.

The early cinematic forays into Southern life were shallow in their portrayal of blacks and romantic to the point of being maudlin. A partial explanation lies with the impact of the Great Depression, fostering a desire for escapism and nostalgia. *Hearts in Dixie* (1929) was Hollywood's first all-black feature film with its sketches of African American life. But the fawning Stepin Fetchit rendered the plotline surreal and reflected a society still preoccupied with a hierarchy of race. The film culminated in a grandson being shipped North for schooling so as not to end up like his lazy, ignorant father. *So Red the Rose* (1934) bombed at the box office due to its blatant pro-Confederate bias, as exemplified by slaves exhorting Southern troops to battle. Thanks in part to this debacle, studios began rejecting Civil War projects, such as the eventual hit *Gone With the Wind* (1939). The romanticization of the small-town South was evident in *Steamboat 'Round the Bend* (1935) starring Will Rogers, with Stepin Fetchit adding comedy relief. *The Littlest Rebel* (1935), designed primarily to showcase child star Shirley Temple, promoted the imagery of blacks as idiotic, slavish Sambos. Such productions left no room for a textured examination of Southern culture, as the Civil War seemed little more than the product of harmless miscommunication.

Stepin Fetchit built one of the most contradictory, controversial, and successful careers in entertainment history. A master of physical comedy, he managed to become a millionaire during the Great Depression of the 1930s, playing the unmotivated, dim-witted "coon" that has rankled African Americans ever since. Yet, the black community has gradually recognized him as an innovator, paving the way for other actors of color.

Born Lincoln Perry, he briefly wrote for a newspaper before developing a two-man vaudeville act for white audiences featuring a character known as "The Laziest Man in the World." As he ventured into solo performances, his soon-to-be infamous stage name stuck. Despite the widespread belief that this moniker formed a contraction for "step and fetch it" in the spirit of the subservient "Tom" persona (from *Uncle Tom's Cabin* by Harriet Beecher Stowe), Perry linked the name to a racehorse. Scholars have differentiated the Stepin Fetchit character from a "Tom" by noting its more rebellious characteristics as a "coon," that is, a black who feigns slothfulness and ignorance to resist white repression and disrupt economic activities. Integral to the "coon" persona was speaking in apparent gibberish that blacks appreciated as insults aimed at the pretensions of white society. Many whites accepted Stepin Fetchit as a mainstream characterization of African Americans. Yet, he found a way to turn the situation to his advantage. In a case of life imitating art, Perry grew adept at adopting the "coon" persona when auditioning for roles while imitating the Stepin Fetchit character during rehearsals. If he found particular lines offensive, he would omit or mumble them so as to discourage their survival in the script. He succeeded in frustrating paternalistic whites by confirming their low expectations. As segregationists consolidated their post-Reconstruction gains, entertainment offered one of the few avenues for blacks to wage this subtle form of rebellion. Even in *Steamboat 'Round the Bend*, Stepin Fetchit maintained a screen presence on a par with Rogers. Wasting his fortune by the late 1940s, Perry no longer could land roles in "white" cinema. Boxer Muhammad Ali took up his cause in the 1960s and added him to his entourage. Perry joined the Nation of Islam that promoted the black nationalism of the era. Because of the visceral reactions of many black viewers to Stepin Fetchit's seemingly degrading roles, his appearances have often been excised from films, even if doing so created plot confusion. But in *Amazing Grace* (1974), Perry made his final showing with a scene and soundtrack that acknowledged the contributions made by his often-overlooked generation of African Americans.

Based upon Margaret Mitchell's sweeping novel of the Civil War, *Gone With the Wind* emerged as an international hit and the most popular film of the South ever produced. Scarlett O'Hara (played by the British actress Vivien Leigh) had to decide between the dashing, scandalous Rhett Butler (Clark Gable) and the faithful, aristocratic Ashley Wilkes against the backdrop of a war that would consume her Georgia plantation. Ultimately abandoned by Butler and unfulfilled by Wilkes, Scarlett grew to accept that the antebellum South could be no more. Integral to the plot was a celebration of the land that numerous Americans still down on their luck could appreciate.

The mobilization of resources necessary for a global war on fascism created opportunities for black empowerment and weakened white supremacy in the South. Proud of their military service and contributions to defense production, African Americans were poised to assume leadership roles in a burgeoning civil rights movement. President Harry S. Truman, in a modest attempt to reorient the Democratic Party with its powerful Southern wing, desegregated the Armed Forces in 1948 and banned discrimination in federal employment.

Hollywood responded slowly but steadily to a changing national mood on race. Although the most obvious caricatures disappeared from post–World War II films, a dearth of positive black roles was evident. In the 1950s and 1960s, most black characters were limited to productions in which race figured prominently in the plot. Films that featured primarily black actors were designed solely for black audiences. Only gradually were "color-blind" parts, such as black policemen and professionals, created for movies without a racial focus. Over time three categories emerged for films with African American stars or costars: mainstream productions, serious films with the potential for "crossover" appeal, and projects aimed at resonating solely with black popular culture.

Despite a trend towards progress, *Song of the South* (1946) enraged the black community, as the normally astute Disney Company employed James Baskett as Uncle Remus to amuse and enlighten a young white boy. In the eyes of many African Americans, the "Tom" stereotype had been resurrected. The film, based on Joel Chandler Harris's folk tales, was designed to recapture an earthiness and dignity amidst the impoverished.

Stimulated in part by revulsion over the Holocaust, the postwar period saw the rise of "social problem" films that confronted questions of race among other contested issues. *Intruder in the Dust* (1949), adapted from William Faulkner's novel, showed an African American veteran (Lucas Beauchamp) returning home to Mississippi only to be accused of murdering a white man. An unlikely alliance composed of a white teenager, his African American friend, the white boy's lawyer uncle, and an elderly white spinster proved Beauchamp's innocence and spared him a lynching.

For much of the 1950s, the ideological fixation with anticommunism engendered by the Korean War and McCarthyism militated against racially based films and the awarding of key roles to African Americans. But films on the South contributed to a growing trend towards probing the darker side of human nature to include portrayals of a violent lust for power, explicit sex, and moral decay.

In the wake of the civil rights triumphs of the 1960s, a series of films on the South proved more honest in their portrayal of white excesses, even if sometimes promoting stereotypes of their own. The earliest of these productions reflected the genre of "blaxploitation" that cast slaves as inveterate plotters in the spirit of the Nat Turner rebellion and whites as sexual predators with no redeeming qualities or conflicted emotions. This era marked the appearance of the strapping "buck" as the dominant characterization of black men by whites. This persona served as an embodiment of lingering anxiety over racial and sexual aggression. Michael Caine starred in *Hurry Sundown* (1967) as a soulless Southerner so hell bent on purchasing his cousin's farms that he provoked a mob of whites into destroying a dam that flooded nearby farms, including one that belonged to his wife's feeble, African American nurse. The film was notable for its employment of a largely black cast.

A predominantly black production with a more sophisticated treatment of Southern life was *Black Like Me* (1964), starring James Whitmore as a Texas journalist who went undercover with darkened skin to get the scoop on life for blacks. Despite unconvincing special effects, the film displayed the virtually unrelenting hostility of Southern whites as Whitmore found himself incredibly moved by the smallest degree of kindness. Although the production dodged many of the thornier questions of race relations in America, *Guess Who's Coming to Dinner* (1967) highlighted the ascension to mainstream status of Sidney Poitier. He played a world-renowned surgeon residing in Switzerland whose betrothal to a middle-class, white woman threw both families into an uproar. With the couple planning to live overseas, all of the pressing racial issues of the time were completely irrelevant to the story, for which Poitier took a good deal of criticism from the black community for accepting only saintly roles.

Yet that same year, Poitier contributed to the Best Picture Oscar for *In the Heat of the Night*. He played a Philadelphia homicide detective wrongfully arrested for murder by a prototypical sheriff (Rod Steiger) while visiting Mississippi. Much to the consternation of both men, they were ordered to collaborate in identifying the killer. The two solved the crime while gradually learning to understand and respect one another.

As a concurrent trend, other productions presented the harmless stereotype of the Southern "good ol' boy" content with fast cars, moonshine, and outwitting hapless police officers. In *Thunder Road* (1958) Robert Mitchum's character, Lucas Doolin, rejoined the family's bootlegging business after service in the Korean War.

Based on a novel by Harper Lee, *To Kill a Mockingbird* (1963) reflected the maturation of the white South beyond its segregationist past. Gregory Peck played a lawyer (Atticus Finch) almost singlehandedly defying racism in a small Southern town by defending an African American accused of raping a white girl. Although he lost the case and his client was killed in an "escape" attempt, Finch won the respect of local blacks. Peck won an Academy Award in this portrayal of a rural community in the Great Depression making its painfully slow transition to racial equality.

By the early 1970s, Hollywood retreated from civil rights projects as the movement splintered and a white backlash grew evident in electoral politics. With the exceptions of *The Man* (1972) and *The Klansman* (1974), television would lead the way with progressive advocacy until the 1980s.

Mississippi Burning (1988) provided a powerful account of the circumstances surrounding the disappearance of three civil rights volunteers (one black, two white) participating in the Mississippi Summer Project in 1964, whose bodies were eventually found in Neshoba County. But the film's focus on two FBI agents, played by high-profile actors Gene Hackman and Willem Dafoe, relegated the contributions of black activists to obscurity.

Ghosts of Mississippi (1997) traced the long-overdue justice provided to the family of slain NAACP leader Medgar Evers, through the conviction of his white supremacist killer. But the film avoided any serious treatment of the racial conflicts of the early 1960s by focusing on the retrial decades later.

Jeffrey D. Bass

See also

Blackface; Magical Negro Films; Narrowcasting; White Savior Films

Further Reading:

Campbell, Edward, Jr. *The Celluloid South: Hollywood and the Southern Myth*. Knoxville: University of Tennessee Press, 1981.

Heider, Karl. *Images of the South: Constructing a Regional Culture on Film and Video*. Athens: University of Georgia Press, 1993.

Kirby, Jack. *Media-Made Dixie: The South in the American Imagination*. Athens: University of Georgia Press, 1986.

Smith, Stephen. *Myth, Media, and the Southern Mind*. Fayetteville: University of Arkansas Press, 1985.

Civil Rights Act of 1875

The Civil Rights Act of 1875 could have been a step forward in attempting to ensure that all U.S. citizens would be able to use public accommodations without discrimination. This legislation was controversial for its granting of a fuller place in American society for African Americans. The first part of the Act stated:

> That all persons within the jurisdiction of the United States shall be entitled to the full and equal enjoyment of the accommodations, advantages, facilities, and privileges of inns, public conveyances on land or water, theaters, and other places of public amusement; subject only to the conditions and limitations established by law, and applicable alike to citizens of every race and color, regardless of any previous condition of servitude.

However ambitious and noble the aims of the law may have been, there was minimal enforcement of the Act after its passage. This was especially true after the withdrawal of federal troops from the South and the collapse of Reconstruction. Moreover, the lack of enforcement of the law was indicative of the deep historical chasm over race and rights that had come to a head in the Civil War and that did not disappear in the post–Civil War period.

This division in American politics was represented in the debates and negotiations of earlier versions of the Civil Rights Act of 1875. Senator Charles Sumner of Massachusetts, a leader of the Radical Republicans, had originally proposed a bill to protect the rights of African Americans in public settings of all kinds, including schools and churches, in 1870. That bill faced considerable opposition from less radical Republicans who feared the loss of political power in Congress. The bill also found substantive opposition from Southern senators and representatives who disagreed with the bill's wide-sweeping integrationist policy. As such, the bill was not taken up by the House of Representatives at that time even in a watered-down form. Sumner reintroduced the bill in 1873, which was voted for by the Senate after Sumner's death in 1874. The House of Representatives took it up and passed it in a form that dropped the sections that would have made segregation in education illegal. The actions by Congress were that of a lame-duck legislature that had lost control over the House of Representatives in part because of Republican support for the bill and other Reconstruction efforts. Yet, the legislative victory of the Civil Rights Act of 1875 was a hollow one without effective enforcement in the regions of the country most plagued with racial prejudice and institutionalized injustice.

There was occasional and inconsistent enforcement of the law, but even when citations and penalties were issued, they were often challenged in court. Five such cases arose in which African Americans did not receive the same treatment as other persons by private entities, including theaters, hotels, and other facilities. Those businesses appealed the enforcement of the law on the constitutional ground that Congress could not pass a law that would control their private business decisions. Although Congress had passed the Civil Rights Act of 1875 to enforce the Fourteenth Amendment's equal protection clause and specifically to prevent the kind of discrimination that was apparent in these cases, the U.S. Supreme Court sided with business owners and held that Congress's power did not reach into the world of discrimination in private business.

The lone dissenter was Justice John Marshall Harlan, who found the case to be an end run around the congressional intent of the law and the Fourteenth Amendment. Further, he saw the case as a matter of a poorly written law, in that the legal basis cited by the majority implied that states had no interaction or regulatory interest in business, when in fact they did have such an interest through the issuing of permits and licenses for business establishments. Therefore, claiming that the Fourteenth Amendment only had bearing on state action and had no bearing on private business action was fallacious. At the time of the decision, there was little public outrage, but in succeeding generations, the words of Justice Harlan resonated as a marker of another missed opportunity for the advancement of social and political equality in the United States.

Aaron Cooley

See also

Civil Rights Act of 1957; Civil Rights Act of 1964; Civil Rights Act of 1968; Dawes Act (1887). Document: The Civil Rights Act of 1964

Further Reading:

Franklin, John Hope. "The Enforcement of the Civil Rights Act of 1875." *Prologue: The Journal of the National Archives* 6, no. 4 (1974): 225–35.

Klarman, Michael. *From Jim Crow to Civil Rights: The Supreme Court and the Struggle for Racial Equality*. New York: Oxford University Press, 2004.

Civil Rights Act of 1957

The Civil Rights Act of 1957 was the first civil rights legislation enacted by the federal government since Reconstruction. The act was the product of liberal senators who, combined with the endorsement of President Harry Truman during the presidential election campaign of 1948, pushed for a civil rights bill. The idea was to get a law that guaranteed general civil rights to African American citizens including guarantees against discrimination in housing, public transportation, restaurants, hotels, etc. The growing desire for such a bill reflected growing disenchantment in both the black community and the community at large with the segregated nature of American society. World War II fought, at least rhetorically, against the racist policies of the Nazis, but seemed to ignore the status of blacks at home. This befuddled many citizens and angered a growing number of blacks. Many of those who had fought in the war emerged only to be second-class citizens. In addition, on the strength of the GI Bill, many attained college degrees, only to still be relegated to the lower ends of society—socially, economically, and politically.

Despite these pushes, almost all Southern senators and congressmen vehemently opposed such a bill that would, in essence, shatter Southern segregated society. Early forms of the bill, pushed by Northern members of Congress, included a voting rights bill and gave authority to the federal court system to become involved. In many ways, it was the fear of federal intervention, via the courts, that bothered Southerners the most.

Despite strenuous objections, by the late 1950s, many Southern senators, in an attempt to stave off major reform, were willing to allow a weak version of the proposed bills. A weak bill, they reasoned, could be manipulated and emasculated so that the much-feared change would not really take place. It would also maintain their power in the Senate. Others, such as Lyndon Johnson, the Democratic senator from Texas who had aspirations on the White House, were not willing to risk their political careers, despite their personal feelings to the contrary of a strong bill. Johnson pushed the bill by arguing to each side what they wanted to hear: To liberals it was the best they could get; to Southern Democrats it was as weak as could be.

Two key events paved the way for the passage of the bill. First, a provision that would have allowed the U.S. Department of Justice to sue for the enforcement of school desegregation was removed. Second, an amendment was included that guaranteed that state officials who were accused of violating court orders on voting rights had the right to a jury trial. The argument was that such an amendment nullified the voting rights provision, because what Southern jury would return convictions against state officials in black voting rights cases? At the last minute the amendments were secured, much to the chagrin of people like Richard Nixon, who decried the compromise.

The bill was greeted with mixed emotions by both the black and white communities, with some black leaders debating whether they should urge President Dwight Eisenhower to veto the bill because of its weakened form and diluted message. The Civil Rights Act of 1957 was largely ineffective in its enforcement and its scope. Three years after its enactment, fewer blacks were voting in the South. If its importance is to be noted for anything, it is that it was the first piece of civil rights legislation in 82 years. It created the authority for establishing a civil rights office in the Department of Justice, even if at is inception the office had fewer than 10 lawyers. Finally, it laid the groundwork for ensuing legislation in the 1960s.

Gary Gershman

See also

Civil Rights Act of 1964; Civil Rights Act of 1968. Document: The Civil Rights Act of 1964

Further Reading:

Branch, Taylor. *Parting the Waters.* New York: Simon and Schuster, 1988.

Caro, Robert. *Master of the Senate.* New York: Alfred A. Knopf, 2002.

Lawson, Steven F., and Charles Payne. *Debating the Civil Rights Movement: 1945–1968.* New York: Rowman and Littlefield, 1998.

Morris, Aldon D. *Origins of the Civil Rights Movement.* New York: Free Press, 1984.

Winquist, Thomas R. "Civil Rights Legislation—The Civil Rights Act of 1957." *Michigan Law Review* 56 (1958): 619–30.

Civil Rights Act of 1964

The Civil Rights Act of 1964 changed the social, economic, and political status of African Americans in the United States. The impact of the law was extensive and far reaching. It was not the first civil rights act. The Civil Rights Act of 1957 emerged during the Eisenhower administration. President Dwight Eisenhower did not demonstrate a lot of public support for the civil rights movement; he believed that social change must come from within individuals and not through legislation. However, he advanced the Civil Rights Act of 1957, which provided for African Americans to exercise their right to vote. Also, it called for a new division in the U.S. Department of Justice to monitor civil rights violations.

By no means was there unanimous support for the act. Publicly, President Eisenhower announced that he did not understand parts of it. Two different points of view about the act were expressed by two respected voices in the African American community. Dr. Ralph Bunche declared that he would rather not have any law than have the Civil Rights Act of 1957, which he thought was too weak. But Bayard Rustin

Civil Rights Act of 1991

From 1989 to 1991, the U.S. Supreme Court handed down decisions that undermined the protection granted by federal civil rights legislations. A case in point is four 5–4 decisions delivered in June 1989: *Lorance v. AT&T Technologies, Martin v. Wilks, Patterson v. McLean Credit Union*, and *Wards Cove Packing Co. v. Antonio*. By interpreting affirmative action narrowly, the Supreme Court restricted the rights of individuals to protect themselves from employment discrimination and shifted the burden of proof from employers to employees in these cases.

Civil rights advocates lobbied Congress to enact measures that would overturn the court rulings, arguing that the court had undermined the intent of federal civil rights and equal employment legislation. In October 1990, Congress approved a bill that was designed to reverse the court rulings and strengthen provisions of the 1964 Civil Rights Act. President George H. W. Bush vetoed the legislation, stating that it would encourage hiring quotas. In 1991, after months of negotiation, the U.S. Congress passed a bill that provided additional remedies to deter harassment and intentional discrimination. On November 21, 1991, President Bush signed the Civil Rights Act of 1991 into a law. Even though the act had mixed signals on the affirmative action and group rights, one of its widely anticipated consequences was an increase in employment discrimination litigation.

Shin Kim and Kwang Chung Kim

prophetically welcomed the act for what it represented. He saw it as the first civil rights legislation in 82 years, which was only the first piece of legislation on which subsequent, related legislation would be built.

After the 1957 Civil Rights Act, President Eisenhower introduced another bill, much to the displeasure of many Southern politicians in Congress. This was the Civil Rights Act of 1960. Both political parties were aware of the potential that the increased black vote would have in the political arena.

The bill introduced penalties to be levied on anyone who obstructed blacks from voting or registering to vote. It also provided for a Civil Rights Commission. Again, there were some who viewed this as being too little, too late. But it did build on the Civil Rights Act of 1957, as Rustin had predicted. Indeed this led to future landmark civil rights legislation, including the Civil Rights Act of 1964.

When President John F. Kennedy was given the report from the Civil Rights Commission, which grew out of the Civil Rights Act of 1960, he took action. Even though President Kennedy had opposed Eisenhower's Civil Rights Act of 1957, his reason was that he did not want to be on the wrong side of the Democratic Party's movers and shakers, who were against the act, since he too anticipated running for president in the future. Heretofore, Kennedy's record on civil rights had been lukewarm. But the Civil Rights Commission report was very compelling in its documentation of the glaring disparities between life for African Americans compared to that of other Americans. Kennedy made it clear that civil rights would be on his agenda from that point on.

After the assassination of President Kennedy in 1963, President Lyndon B. Johnson embraced the need for a stronger civil rights act. He believed that President Kennedy was moving in that direction when he was killed. So, he would honor Kennedy's memory, using the national climate of sympathy and goodwill that prevailed over the country immediately after the assassination, to advance a cause in which he, too believed. It fit with President Johnson's vision of the "Great Society." Also, African Americans were becoming more militant and aggressive in their demands for more equality and opportunities in mainstream American life.

As a long-time, savvy political operative in Congress, President Johnson knew how to get legislation passed. With help from some congressional allies such as Sen. Everett Dirkson, a Republican from Illinois and Sen. Hubert Humphrey, a Democrat from Minnesota, he was successful. On July 2, 1964, President Johnson signed the Civil Rights Act of 1964 into law. The ceremony took place only five hours after the House of Representatives passed it.

The Civil Rights Act of 1964 did the following:

- Prohibited discrimination on the basis of race, color, religion, or national origin in public places such as restaurants, cafeterias, lunchrooms, soda fountains, movies, concert halls, and other similar public places;
- Mandated the creation of the Equal Employment Opportunity Commission (EEOC);
- Mandated that federal funding would not be given to segregated schools; and
- Required that any company seeking federal business must have a pro–civil rights policy.

After signing the law, he immediately shook hands with Dr. Martin Luther King, Jr. in a symbol of victory. Roy Wilkins, secretary of the National Association for the Advancement of Colored People, described the new law as "the Magna Carta of human rights" ("On This Day" 2006).

The 1964 Civil Rights Act served as the precursor to the Voting Rights Act of 1965, which banned literacy tests and poll taxes; the Civil Rights Act of 1968, which outlawed discrimination in the selling and renting of housing, and the Civil Rights Act of 1991, which allowed lawsuits against employers if their hiring had a "disparate impact" (U.S. Congress 1991) on women and minorities.

Betty Nyangoni

See also

Civil Rights Act of 1875; Civil Rights Act of 1957; Civil Rights Act of 1968

Further Reading:

Cathcart, David A., Leon Friedman, Merrick T. Rossein, Mark Snyderman, and Steven H. Steinglass. *The Civil Rights Act of 1991*. Philadelphia: American Law Institute–American Bar Association, Committee on Continuing Professional Education, 1993.

Goodwin, Doris Kearns. *Lyndon Johnson and the American Dream*. New York: St. Martin's Press, 1991.

Kotz, Nick. *Judgment Days: Lyndon Baines Johnson, Martin Luther King, Jr. and the Laws That Changed America*. New York: Houghton Mifflin, 2005.

"On This Day: 1964: President Johnson Signs Civil Rights Bill." *BBC News*, July 2, 2006. http://news.bbc.co.uk/onthisday/hi/dates/stories/july/2/newsid_3787000/3787809.stm.

U.S. Congress. House of Representatives. *Civil Rights Act of 1991*. 102nd Cong., 1st sess., January 3, 1991.

Whalen, Barbara, and Charles Whalen. *The Longest Debate: A Legislative History of the 1964 Civil Rights Act*. Cabin John, MD: Seven Locks Press, 1991.

Civil Rights Act of 1968

The Civil Rights Act of 1968 is also known as the Housing Rights Act or Fair Housing Act of 1968. In the act, Congress expanded the scope and protections of Executive Order 11063, and together with the U.S. Supreme Court's 1968 decision in *Jones v. Alfred H. Mayer Co.* (which held that §1982 of the Civil Rights Act of 1866 protected racial minorities from discrimination in private as well as public housing), outlawed for the first time private as well as public discrimination in housing. It was the final part of what can be seen as a triumvirate of civil rights legislation—the first two parts being the Civil Rights Act of 1964 and the Voting Rights Act of 1965.

Similar to the previous two acts, which had been passed in the aftermath of the John F. Kennedy assassination and the violence in Selma, Alabama, the Civil Rights Act of 1968 came into being in the wake of the Martin Luther King, Jr. assassination (see King, Martin Luther, Jr.). However, unlike the other two acts, which were the product of protest and agitation by the Southern Christian Leadership Conference and the Student Nonviolent Coordinating Committee at Birmingham and Selma, this final piece of legislation resulted from the work of Clarence Mitchell Jr., the Washington director of the National Association for the Advancement of Colored People.

Originally designed as a means to protect civil rights workers, as the bill wound its way through Congress it was amended to prevent discrimination in the housing market. The key to its passage through the Senate was the support of Sen. Everett Dirksen of Illinois. Before he publicly came out in support of the bill, three cloture votes on a filibuster managed by Southern senators failed to get the required two-thirds majority. However, with Dirksen in the lead, the filibuster was defeated, and the bill moved forward.

By 1968, growing violence across the United States (see Long Hot Summer Riots, 1965–1967), the accompanying negative reaction to these race riots, as well as the Black Power movement, a slipping economy, and rising crime rates, made people less enamored with civil rights legislation. The House of Representatives reflected this growing conservatism and, unlike the act four years earlier, passage of this measure stalled in the House. Most people expected the House to emasculate the bill with various amendments, which would then be passed by both houses.

However, just as the stalled legislation in Congress had received a jumpstart in 1964 from the assassination of President Kennedy, and the collective grief of the nation was used by President Lyndon Johnson to push the Civil Rights Act through a deadlocked Congress, the national shock and sorrow over the assassination of Martin Luther King, Jr. swung the momentum in Congress. The day after King's funeral, the House Rules Committee voted to send the housing rights bill directly to the House floor. By limiting debate and not allowing any amendments, passage was secured. The King assassination made it politically inexpedient for members of the House to tamper with the bill, and they passed the strong Senate version rapidly on April 10, 1968, by a vote of 229 to 195. President Johnson signed the Civil Rights Act of 1968 into law the next day.

The Fair Housing Act of 1968 made unlawful all practices and transactions that would deny housing to anyone based on race, color, religion, or national origin. The act established legal mechanisms to prevent discrimination in housing. The structure included government at all levels, from federal to local, and established a system of judicial review. In short, the law provided for "aggrieved persons" to file complaints with the U.S. Department of Housing and Urban Development (HUD). Under the dictates of the act, HUD was required to investigate the allegation. However, strong enforcement mechanisms were not available to HUD or the U.S. Department of Justice (DOJ). HUD was limited to mediating disputes and the DOJ could only file suits to remedy what were thought to be established patterns of discrimination.

As a result of these and other shortcomings, the law came under regular criticism. It also exempted large numbers of houses. For example, individual sales, not including a broker or other agent, were not covered. Other situations also escaped coverage under the act. Accommodations by private clubs, noncommercial housing operated by religious groups, rental housing in which the owner lived, and housing containing four or fewer units were exempt.

The act's impact was debated the moment it was passed. Many critics argue over its effectiveness. Some note that the act has had a wide-ranging impact and resulted in breaking down neighborhood racial barriers culminating in integrated neighborhoods throughout the country. Others argue that the prevalence of single-race communities throughout the United States and the failure to truly break down racial barriers testifies to its ineffectiveness. Since its passage it has been amended and now prohibits discrimination in the sale, rental, and financing of dwellings, and in other housing-related transactions, based on race, color, national origin, religion, sex, familial status (including children under the age of 18 living with parents or legal custodians, pregnant women, and people securing custody of children under the age of 18), and handicap (disability).

Gary Gershman

See also

Civil Rights Act of 1957; Civil Rights Act of 1968. Document: The Civil Rights Act of 1964

Further Reading:

Chandler, James P. "Fair Housing Laws: A Critique." *Hastings Law Journal* 24 (1973): 159–205.

Kanter, Arlene S. "A Home of One's Own: The Fair Housing Amendments Act of 1988 and Housing Discrimination against People with Mental Disabilities." *American University Law Review* 43 (1994): 925–94.

Kushner, James A. "The Fair Housing Amendments Act of 1988: The Second Generation of Fair Housing." *Vanderbilt Law Review* 42 (1989): 1049–106.

Schwemm, Robert G. *Housing Discrimination: Law and Litigation*. New York: C. Boardman, 1990.

Civil Rights Movement

Lasting for more than a century, the Civil Rights Movement is the ongoing attempt by African Americans and their allies to secure the freedoms promised to them after Emancipation at the end of the Civil War in 1865. The movement was initially aimed chiefly at removing several

Excerpts from *Sweatt v. Painter* (1950)

Petitioner was denied admission to the state-supported University of Texas Law School, solely because he is a Negro and state law forbids the admission of Negroes to that Law School. He was offered, but he refused, enrollment in a separate law school newly established by the State for Negroes. The University of Texas Law School has 16 full-time and three part-time professors, 850 students, a library of 65,000 volumes, a law review, moot court facilities, scholarship funds, an Order of the Coif affiliation, many distinguished alumni, and much tradition and prestige. The separate law school for Negroes has five full-time professors, 23 students, a library of 16,500 volumes, a practice court, a legal aid association and one alumnus admitted to the Texas Bar; but it excludes from its student body members of racial groups which number 85% of the population of the State and which include most of the lawyers, witnesses, jurors, judges, and other officials with whom petitioner would deal as a member of the Texas Bar. Held: The legal education offered petitioner is not substantially equal to that which he would receive if admitted to the University of Texas Law School; and the Equal Protection Clause of the Fourteenth Amendment requires that he be admitted to the University of Texas Law School.

W. J. Durham and Thurgood Marshall argued the cause for petitioner. With them on the brief were Robert L. Carter, William R. Ming, Jr., James M. Nabrit and Franklin H. Williams.

Price Daniel, Attorney General of Texas, and Joe R. Greenhill, First Assistant Attorney General, argued the cause for respondents. With them on the brief was E. Jacobson, Assistant Attorney General.

MR. CHIEF JUSTICE VINSON delivered the opinion of the Court. [excerpt]

The University of Texas Law School, from which petitioner was excluded, was staffed by a faculty of sixteen full-time and three part-time professors, some of whom are nationally recognized authorities in their field. Its student body numbered 850. The library contained over 65,000 volumes. Among the other facilities available to the students were a law review, moot court facilities, scholarship funds, and Order of the Coif affiliation. The school's alumni occupy the most distinguished positions in the private practice of the law and in the public life of the State. It may properly be considered one of the nation's ranking law schools.

The law school for Negroes which was to have opened in February, 1947, would have had no independent faculty or library. The teaching was to be carried on by four members of the University of Texas Law School faculty, who were to maintain their offices at the University of Texas while teaching at both institutions. Few of the 10,000 volumes ordered for the library had arrived; or was there any full-time librarian. The school lacked accreditation.

Since the trial of this case, respondents report the opening of a law school at the Texas State University for Negroes. It is apparently on the road to full accreditation. It has a faculty of five full-time professors; a student body of 23; a library of some 16,500 volumes serviced by a full-time staff; a practice court and legal aid association; and one alumnus who has become a member of the Texas Bar.

Whether the University of Texas Law School is compared with the original or the new law school for Negroes, we cannot find substantial equality in the educational opportunities offered white and Negro law students by the State. In terms of number of the faculty, variety of courses and opportunity for specialization, size of the student body, scope of the library, availability of law review and similar activities, the University of Texas Law School is superior. What is more important, the University of Texas Law School possesses to a far greater degree those qualities which are incapable of objective measurement but which make for greatness in a law school. Such qualities, to name but a few, include reputation of the faculty, experience of the administration, position and influence of the alumni, standing in the community, traditions and prestige. It is difficult to believe that one who had a free choice between these law schools would consider the question close.

Moreover, although the law is a highly learned profession, we are well aware that it is an intensely practical one. The law school, the proving ground for legal learning and practice, cannot be effective in isolation from the individuals and institutions with which the law interacts. Few students and no one who has practiced law would choose to study in an academic vacuum, removed from the interplay of ideas and the exchange of views with which the law is concerned. The law school to which Texas is willing to admit petitioner excludes from its student body members of the racial groups which number 85% of the population of the State and include most of the lawyers, witnesses, jurors, judges and other officials with whom petitioner will inevitably be dealing when he becomes a member of the Texas Bar. With such a substantial and significant segment of society excluded, we cannot conclude that the education offered petitioner is substantially equal to that which he would receive if admitted to the University of Texas Law School.

It may be argued that excluding petitioner from that school is no different from excluding white students from the new law school. This contention overlooks realities. It is unlikely that a member of a group so decisively in the majority, attending a school with rich traditions and prestige which only a history of consistently maintained excellence could command, would claim that the opportunities afforded him for legal education were unequal to those held open to petitioner. That such a claim, if made, would be dishonored by the State, is no answer. "Equal protection of the laws is not achieved through indiscriminate imposition of inequalities."

concrete obstacles posed by white supremacy—including the barriers of segregation and disenfranchisement, discrimination in various spheres of life, and the ongoing threat of racial violence. Activists were successful in achieving many of their most tangible goals. Important legislation in the mid-1960s outlawed segregation and granted federal protection to black voters. However, many argue that racial differences still exist in American society, particularly in the economic realm, where many blacks remain disproportionately impoverished. Many also point to the fact that African Americans are underrepresented in many areas of American life, including the political arena, but overrepresented, for example, in the prison population as evidence that unequal treatment still exists. Those who accept this point of view would argue that the civil rights movement is still ongoing until greater equality has been achieved.

At the end of the Civil War and during the Reconstruction period following the war, blacks and whites, Northerners and Southerners, struggled to define what the outcome of the war should mean for the defeated South and also what emancipation should signify for the newly freed people. Above all else, the former slaves desired their own land. Like many other 19th-century Americans, they craved the self-sufficiency that an agrarian lifestyle seemed to offer. Despite some very tentative experiments with land redistribution, opposition to this proposal was severe, and the vast majority of the former slaves found themselves working as employees rather than yeoman farmers as they had desired.

Even though substantial economic reforms of this kind were deemed impractical, members of the Republican Party advocated for black rights in the political and social realm. Passed in relatively short succession, the Thirteenth, Fourteenth, and Fifteenth amendments to the U.S. Constitution freed the slaves, granted the status of citizen to the freed people, and guaranteed the right to vote for black men. (Black women were not technically enfranchised until the 20th century, along with white women.)

African Americans eagerly seized upon the freedoms promised to them as they struggled to rebuild lives for themselves. They searched for family members from whom they had been separated, set about building institutions such as schools and churches, and participated wholeheartedly in the political process. This unique historical moment was short-lived, however. By 1877, white Southerners had regained control of the governments of every former Confederate state and quickly and systematically set about returning blacks to a state that resembled slavery as nearly as possible in the post-Emancipation era.

In the 1890s, legislation was passed in every Southern state mandating segregation in public facilities, particularly streetcars. With *Plessy v. Ferguson* in 1896, the U.S. Supreme Court vouched for the constitutionality of these laws, enshrining the notorious "separate but equal doctrine" into American legal tradition. Separate accommodations were legal as long as the respective facilities were equal, according to this doctrine. Sadly, most Southern states were much more devoted to ensuring that the former stipulation was met rather than the latter. Facilities for blacks, ranging from restrooms to public schools, were chronically underfunded and generally inferior to those available to whites.

White Southerners also began to search for ingenious ways to deprive blacks of their constitutionally guaranteed right to vote. Many had been frightened away from the polls due to the terrorist tactics of organizations such as the Ku Klux Klan and their allies. During the 1890s, disenfranchisement legislation such as literacy tests and poll tax laws further reduced the number of blacks casting ballots. In some regions, such as the state of Mississippi, a viable black electorate was almost completely eliminated. During this era, violence against blacks, including frequent lynchings, was socially acceptable and used as a form of social control to prevent blacks from reasserting demands for protection of their civil rights.

In this hostile climate, African Americans struggled to find ways to successfully protest. They were increasingly confined to a separate social sphere, mired in poverty, and barred from the ballot box. Any overt attempt to fight against these inequalities might result in violent attacks on the black community, or more subtle but no less coercive attacks on their livelihood through the loss of employment.

One of the most prominent black leaders to arise during this period was Booker T. Washington. Washington was born a slave but overcame great personal obstacles not only to gain an education but also to found the Tuskegee Institute, a school for blacks in Alabama. Washington's first students literally built the campus brick by brick. The Tuskegee curriculum emphasized vocational skills rather than a liberal arts education because Washington sought, above all else, to be practical. He gave a famous speech in Atlanta in 1895, which became known as the Atlanta Compromise, where he urged blacks to abandon the fight for civic equality for the time being and instead to concentrate on economic advancement. The speech was well received by both blacks and whites. Although some black intellectuals were frustrated at Washington's seeming willingness to forsake civil rights issues, others believed his strategy was a practical one in the unremittingly hostile racial climate of the early 20th century.

Black women, too, sought opportunities to uplift the black community without directly attacking Southern white supremacy. Many clubs sprang up throughout the nation, which aimed to help the must vulnerable members of the community and to promote middle-class values on topics ranging from hygiene to child care. Some black women also promoted the cause of temperance. In 1895, the National Association of Colored Women was founded and adopted as their slogan the phrase "Lifting as We Climb." One hope implicit in that motto was that aid to black community was but one phase on a larger road to the restoration of black civil rights.

In 1909, an interracial group of activists concerned about the abysmal state of race relations gathered to form the nation's oldest civil rights organization, the National Association for the Advancement of Colored People (NAACP). Most of the early members of the group were white, but prominent African Americans including the great intellectual W. E. B. Du Bois and the crusading journalist Ida B. Wells-Barnett were among the founders. The organization quickly established an office in New York City and branches around the country.

Du Bois created the official magazine of the organization, *The Crisis*. In addition to critiquing the racial climate in the country, the journal also published the works of many prominent black writers, including Harlem Renaissance luminaries Langston Hughes and Countee Cullen. Du Bois strongly believed that art could be used as a political tool in the struggle for civil rights, both by demonstrating the quality of African American creative and intellectual work and by dramatizing the plight of those reduced to second-class citizenship.

One of the earliest goals of the NAACP, which was ultimately never met, was to secure legislation to make lynching a federal crime. Although such a bill was never passed, the organization helped decrease the number of incidences of lynching in the South by documenting them and by educating the public about the horrors of racial violence.

The NAACP employed a variety of tactics to agitate for social and political equality, and these activities signaled a growing African American militancy that continued to accelerate in the coming years. However, the organization became most famous for using the legal system to achieve their goals and to wage countless battles against discriminatory practices.

Many Americans, black and white, became politically mobilized during the desperate years of the Great Depression. Labor organizations grew in size and in militancy as workers sought to protect their rights. Left-leaning political

Flag-bearing demonstrators march from Selma to Montgomery, Alabama, in the historic March 1965 voting rights protest. The march led directly to the 1965 Voting Rights Act, which outlawed Southern states' attempts to prevent African Americans from voting. (Library of Congress)

groups, including Communists and Socialists, increased their membership as suffering Americans began to suspect that capitalism had failed them. In 1934, white and black sharecroppers in Arkansas collaborated in a rare showing of interracial solidarity, forming the Southern Tenant Farmers' Union to advocate for fair treatment by Southern planters.

Most blacks did not get swept into the realm of radical politics, but the vast majority did change their political affiliation during these years. Democratic President Franklin D. Roosevelt's New Deal programs were designed to promote greater government intervention in the inner workings of the economy and to provide direct relief for the needy. Roosevelt demonstrated at most a tepid concern for the welfare of black citizens, and discrimination was banned in many government programs. Inevitably, blacks continued to receive unequal treatment, including being paid lower wages, receiving fewer relief dollars than their white counterparts, and finding themselves excluded from some government initiatives altogether. Nonetheless, the African American electorate shifted its alliance away from the Republican Party, which had been their first political ally in the fight for civil rights.

Although most blacks were barred from voting in the South, Northern blacks emerged as an important group able to occasionally swing elections and gain concessions from politicians. African Americans capitalized on their growing political clout, and an unprecedented number received government appointments, working in various New Deal and cabinet offices. Prominent blacks such as Mary McLeod Bethune and Ralph Bunche advised the Roosevelt administration on issues involving their community, becoming known as the "Black Cabinet" and foreshadowing the greater role that blacks would play in Democratic Party politics in the coming years.

As the United States mobilized to enter World War II, African Americans participated in the war effort in a variety of ways, and these patriotic activities made many even more reluctant to accept their role as second-class citizens. Many blacks left the rural South and migrated to cities and to other regions of the country to work in defense industries. Although they still grappled with differential treatment, blacks also sampled greater racial tolerance and earned higher wages than had been possible in the agricultural South.

Furthermore, blacks composed one-eighth of the U.S. armed forces. Although they were disproportionately relegated to noncombat positions, many engaged in warfare. Some, like the Tuskegee Airmen, received a degree of fame. Many blacks were angered at being asked to fight against fascism abroad, while tyrannical conditions also existed at home. Many soldiers self-consciously fought a Double V campaign, seeking to promote democracy and freedom abroad and in the United States. A. Philip Randolph, head of the Brotherhood of Sleeping Car Porters, a black labor union, urged President Roosevelt to end discrimination in defense industry jobs. He ingeniously threatened to organize a march on Washington in protest should the president refuse. Roosevelt was eager to avoid a mass demonstration and thus in 1941 issued Executive Order 8802, which outlawed discrimination in defense industries and set up a government agency to investigate allegations of inequitable pay. This action demonstrated to African Americans that the executive branch of the federal government, though hardly an outspoken champion of black rights, could be coerced into aiding in the cause of liberation. In 1948, President Harry S. Truman responded to continued pressure from Randolph and others and issued Executive Order 9981, which ended segregation in the U.S. military.

Meanwhile, membership in the NAACP surged during the war years. During the 1940s, the organization claimed nearly 400,000 members. Enthusiasm for the cause of civil rights was bolstered by an important victory with the 1944 Supreme Court decision in *Smith v. Allwright*, which put an end to the all-white Democratic Party primary. This decision gave Southern blacks greater access to the political process than they had had since Reconstruction and encouraged many to attempt to register and vote. White Southerners responded violently to this new black militancy, beating blacks who were wearing their military uniforms and, in several documented cases, shooting black veterans who attempted to vote. However, despite this strenuous opposition, the most dramatic phase of the civil rights movement was about to be launched.

Beginning in the mid-1930s, the NAACP legal department, under the leadership of Charles Hamilton Houston, began waging an intense battle to force Southern states to improve public education for blacks and to end segregation in schooling altogether. Strategists determined that an assault on education at the graduate level would be more palatable to the courts and to the public at large, so they began their attempt to dismantle segregation at that level, winning an important victory in 1950 with *Sweatt v. Painter*. Heman Sweatt had been denied admission to the law school at the University of Texas. Forced to comply with the *Plessy* decision, which mandated separate but equal accommodations, the state created a makeshift black law school. Undaunted, Sweatt continued to pursue his case. Although the court stopped short of overturning the *Plessy* verdict, the unanimous ruling agreed that Sweatt had been denied equal access to education and effectively outlawed segregation at the graduate level.

The *Sweatt* decision foreshadowed the monumental *Brown v. Board of Education* ruling (1954), which struck down the doctrine of separate but equal, declaring segregation in the school system illegal and providing a legal foundation for the burgeoning civil rights movement. A follow up decision in 1955, which has become known as *Brown* II, mandated that desegregation should progress "with all deliberate speed."

In most instances, Southern states balked at this order, using every tactic at their disposal to halt or delay integration. In 1956, 101 congressmen from the South signed a "Southern Manifesto," which declared the *Brown* decision an abuse of federal power and articulated their intention to thwart the court's ruling. In 1957, Little Rock became the first large Southern city to take the court's edict seriously by quickly designing a plan for token integration of the city's school system. Local whites even rebelled at the thought of nine, hand-selected black students entering a high school populated by nearly 2,000 whites. In response to public sentiment, Gov. Orval Faubus called out the National Guard to prevent integration and backed down only when President

Dwight D. Eisenhower called out federal troops to enforce the *Brown* ruling.

Although some communities integrated peacefully to avoid becoming a public spectacle, massive resistance did not end there and manifested itself even at the university level. In 1962, federal marshals escorted James Meredith to his first day of classes at the University of Mississippi. In what has been called the "Battle of Ole Miss," more than 3,000 whites rioted in protest. The next year, Alabama's governor George Wallace physically blocked the door of the state's university to prevent two black students from entering.

Despite this resistance, African Americans persevered in their campaign to open the schools. Brave students, ranging from youngsters in elementary school to middle-aged adults returning to school, endured campaigns of physical and verbal abuse and continued to assert their right to equal access to education, inspiring African Americans throughout the South to fight for open access in other areas of life as well.

One of the most fateful events of the civil rights movement occurred on December 1, 1955, when Rosa Parks, an assistant tailor and civil rights worker, refused to give up her seat to a white passenger on a city bus in Montgomery, Alabama. Parks was sitting in the first row of the section of the bus designated for blacks, but the bus was full and the driver ordered her to relinquish her seat to a white passenger who was standing. Weary of the continual burden of racial discrimination, Parks bravely remained seated until she was ejected from the bus and taken to jail.

Although this was not a premeditated action on Parks's part, it was not a completely spontaneous one, either. Blacks had been protesting segregation on public transportation ever since laws mandating separate seating began to appear in the 1890s. The Women's Political Council (WPC) had been protesting conditions on city buses for more than a decade before Parks's courageous stand. Prior to her arrest, Parks was already engaged in the struggle for civil rights, having worked as a secretary for the local branch of the NAACP and having already received training in nonviolent resistance at Highlander Folk School in Tennessee.

Quickly after Parks's arrest, members of the local NAACP and the WPC began mobilizing. Jo Ann Robinson, leader of the WPC, mimeographed and distributed flyers calling for a one-day boycott of the bus system. The black community responded so enthusiastically that the boycott was extended indefinitely. Despite ongoing reprisals from the white community, the black citizens of Montgomery persevered and were rewarded for their efforts when the Supreme Court declared segregated seating on public transportation unconstitutional in 1956.

The success of the protestors in Montgomery helped jump-start other civil rights activities throughout the South. It also catapulted Martin Luther King, Jr., the charismatic young minister of Dexter Street Baptist Church, into the national spotlight. Local residents elected him to serve as a leader of the newly formed civil rights group the Montgomery Improvement Association and to help spearhead the protest.

It soon became clear to King and to those who admired him that the young pastor had found his calling. He and a group of black ministers founded the Southern Christian Leadership Conference (SCLC) in 1957. King was elected leader of the new organization, which was dedicated to spreading the freedom struggle throughout the South. King was an eloquent speaker who inspired masses of people with his intellect and his unfailing belief in the power of nonviolent resistance and of Christian love. He quickly became one of the most visible faces in the movement, appearing on the cover of *Time* magazine as its "Man of the Year" in 1963 and being awarded the Nobel Prize for Peace in 1964.

This fame came at a high personal price, and King had a grueling schedule as he traversed the South, giving speeches, leading marches, and spending time in jail. The SCLC was a key player in one of the most notorious civil rights battlegrounds, Birmingham in 1963. At the invitation of minister and local activist Fred Shuttlesworth, the SCLC came to Birmingham in 1963 and helped organize sit-ins, demonstrations, and a boycott of local businesses. Although the city was granted an injunction forbidding protest activities, King defied the court order and was arrested and put into jail, where he penned his famous "Letter from Birmingham Jail." He defended civil disobedience and the righteousness of his cause and implored local ministers to join him in the struggle. Despite King's eloquence, the city resisted the protestors' demands, spraying teenage and school-aged protestors with fire hoses and attacking them with police dogs.

Due in large part to the presence of the media and an outraged public, local officials ultimately conceded to many of

Eyes on the Prize

Eyes on the Prize: America's Civil Rights Years (1954–1964) and *Eyes on the Prize II: America at the Racial Crossroads (1965–1985)* is a 14-part original documentary series that chronicles the civil rights movement from 1954 to 1985 developed by executive producer Henry Hampton (1940–1998) and narrated by civil rights leader Julian Bond. Produced by Blackside Incorporated, the award-winning series originally aired as an *American Experience* television presentation on the Public Broadcasting Service (PBS) network in 1987. Part II initially aired in 1990 on PBS. Bringing the documentary to fruition was a struggle, as Hampton often described the difficulties he experienced in obtaining funding for the project. *Eyes on the Prize* is recognized for its historical contribution to the film documentation of the civil rights movement since it provides accounts by several key figures in the movement. The series received numerous prestigious awards, including the Television Critics Association Award, the George Foster Peabody Award, the Alfred I. duPont–Columbia award, the International Documentary Association award, and an Academy Award nomination for Best Documentary, Features. In addition, it won the Black Independent Producers Award, several Emmy Awards for best TV Documentary, the National Association of Black Journalists award, and others.

Part I, *Eyes on the Prize: America's Civil Rights Years (1954–1964),* features six programs. *Eyes on the Prize II: America at the Racial Crossroads (1965–1985)* completed the series. The two parts of the documentary have companion books, *Eyes on the Prize: America's Civil Rights Years 1954–1965* and *The Eyes on the Prize Civil Rights Reader: Documents, Speeches, and Firsthand Accounts from the Black Freedom Struggle, 1954–1990.*

Carol Adams-Means

the protestors' demands. However, in one of the most gruesome displays of white resistance, the Ku Klux Klan bombed the Sixteenth Street Baptist Church on September 15, 1963, killing four young African American girls and demonstrating that the struggle had not yet been won.

Although King was certainly the best known individual civil rights leader, his organization, the SCLC, and the venerable NAACP were by no means the only civil rights organizations active in the South. For example, the Congress of Racial Equality (CORE) organized an interracial "Freedom Ride" in order to test the 1960 Supreme Court decision in *Boynton v. Virginia*, which declared that segregation in bus terminals, waiting rooms, restaurants, rest rooms, and other interstate travel facilities was unconstitutional. Unsurprisingly, the riders were met with violence as they traveled through the South, and Attorney General Robert F. Kennedy was forced to intercede to ensure the safety of the riders.

CORE also was active organizing local blacks in the rural South, training them in the art of nonviolent social protest. This was an approach also favored by the youthful members of the Student Nonviolent Coordinating Committee (SNCC). The SNCC was founded in 1960 and was directly inspired by a sit-in at a whites-only lunch counter at Woolworth's in Greensboro, North Carolina, earlier that same year. Four college students refused to leave until they were served and sustained the protest for several weeks, inspiring similar actions throughout the South. Capitalizing on the enthusiasm of these student protestors, then executive director of the SCLC, Ella Baker, called for a meeting of young people at Shaw University in Raleigh, North Carolina.

Baker advised the students to form their own organization rather than to channel their energies into existing civil rights groups. Although the young people admired King, some resisted the idea of hierarchical leadership, favoring instead a more democratic, group-centered organization. Headquartered in Atlanta, the group eventually established several smaller field offices in Alabama, Georgia, Arkansas, and Mississippi. Unlike King and the SCLC, which came into towns for relatively brief periods to stage demonstrations and then left, SNCC members actually relocated to the communities they sought to serve. Many lived communally in what became known as Freedom Houses. The SNCC's best known project was located in Mississippi, widely to be considered one of the most segregated and dangerous states. Volunteers operated Freedom Schools, where they tried to enhance the educational opportunities available to black children. They staged demonstrations and launched voter registration drives. In one of their most ambitious moves, SNCC and other activists working in the state created the Mississippi Freedom Democratic Party and elected their own slate of delegates whom they attempted to have seated at the 1964 Democratic Convention in place of the all-white Democrats from Mississippi.

Another ambitious SNCC initiative, the brainchild of legendary organizer Bob Moses, was the Mississippi Freedom Summer. In 1964, nearly 1,000 volunteers, the majority Northern, white college students, streamed into Mississippi to aid in a voter registration drive. During that tumultuous summer, at least 85 civil rights workers were beaten, 35 were shot at, and 4 were killed. Seventy black homes, businesses, and churches were bombed or burned, and at least 1,000 people were arrested. The presence of so many upper-middle-class white students in the Deep South proved titillating to the media, which covered their activities enthusiastically and won greater empathy for the cause of African American civil rights in the process.

Slowly, President John F. Kennedy began to believe that civil rights legislation was inevitable. Activists wished to seize on that sentiment from the president and to shore up widespread congressional support for such a bill, so they revived A. Philip Randolph's proposal from the 1940s to stage a massive march on Washington to demand support for the movement. Kennedy, like Roosevelt before him, was initially against the demonstration, but black leaders remained undaunted and eventually secured Kennedy's reluctant approval. On August 28, 1963, approximately 250,000 people gathered by the Washington Monument to show their support for the movement. The day featured speeches by John Lewis of the SNCC and Martin Luther King, Jr. among others, and music by musicians ranging from Mahalia Jackson to Joan Baez. As stirring as the rally was, it alone was not enough to ensure passage of civil rights legislation.

Kennedy, to the shock of the nation, was assassinated in Dallas, Texas, on November 22, 1963. His successor, Lyndon B. Johnson, drew on his tremendous skills as a politician to appeal to the sympathies of a nation in mourning. He urged Congress to pass the Civil Rights Act of 1964 in honor of the slain leader. Signed into law on July 2, 1964, the bill outlawed discrimination in public facilities and employment and authorized the federal government to enforce school integration. One of the major goals of the movement had been achieved.

The issue of voting rights remained unresolved, however. Demonstrators, including King and many SCLC members, planned a march from Selma to Montgomery, Alabama, in 1965. On March 7, 1965, more than 500 protestors began their journey only to be brutally beaten by the policemen on horseback as the tried to cross the Edmund Pettis Bridge in an assault that the media began referring to as "Bloody Sunday." Once again, Johnson seized on the national mood, convincing an outraged public to support the Voting Rights Act of 1965, which authorized the federal government to oversee voter registration in the South, effectively restoring the franchise to the regions' black citizens.

Thus by 1965, civil rights activists had achieved two of their most tangible goals. Voting rights and been restored to African Americans, and segregation was ended. Life for black Southerners changed dramatically and almost immediately. However, blacks living in other regions of the country, who were victims of a more subtle kind of racism than that practiced in the South, saw little or no change in their living conditions or in their access to opportunities. In 1965, outraged black residents of Los Angeles responded violently to the arrest of a resident of their neighborhood. Releasing pent-up frustration about police brutality and other forms of discrimination, residents of the Watts section of the city rioted for five days. Thirty-four people were killed, 1,000 were wounded, and $200 million worth of property was destroyed. Racial unrest of a similar nature erupted throughout the country after the assassination of Martin Luther King, Jr. in 1968.

Many activists began to realize that the important civil rights legislation of the 1960s removed only the most outward vestiges of discrimination and did not even began to solve more systemic problems such as access to opportunities, and, perhaps most importantly, did not tackle the problem of poverty, which many began to see as a civil rights issue. Furthermore, although desegregation was one of the most cherished goals of the struggle, many protestors became weary of being threatened and beaten and wondered if being integrated into such a society was really a worthy goal. Many attempted to solve these dilemmas by continuing to organize and by expanding their protest activities to include antipoverty programs and a variety of other causes, including opposition to the Vietnam War.

Others began to, in some sense, turn inward and to focus on new ways to empower the black community. Some of this sentiment is captured in the phrase, "Black Power," which was popularized by SNCC members Stokely Carmichael and Willie Ricks beginning in 1966. Many advocates of the Black Power position advocated black economic and political independence as a means to combat existing racism. Many drew their inspiration from the slain former Nation of Islam leader Malcolm X, who had always held an ambivalent attitude toward the goals of the mainstream civil rights organizers. Groups such as the Black Panther Party, founded in Oakland, California, in 1966, sought various ways to protect, educate, and serve their communities. For example, they developed free breakfast programs for needy children and attempted to guard individuals from police brutality. Cultural nationalism too became a part of the Black Power platform, as individuals began making choices in hairstyle, clothing, and music that emphasized their African origins. Many artists attempted to develop and nurture a unique black aesthetic.

The first hundred years of the civil rights movement did not end all inequalities between white and black citizens, but black activism did impact nearly every facet of American life. Various groups including women, Native Americans, homosexuals, Latinos, and Asian Americans seized on lessons learned from the black freedom struggle, channeling these insights into organizations and protest movements of their own.

Jennifer Jensen Wallach

See also

Black Panther Party (BPP); King, Martin Luther, Jr. Little Rock Nine; Malcolm X; Montgomery Bus Boycott

Further Reading:

Branch, Taylor. *Parting the Waters: America in the King Years, 1954–63*. New York: Simon and Schuster, 1988.

Branch, Taylor. *Pillar of Fire: America in the King Years, 1963–65*. New York: Simon and Schuster, 1998.

Branch, Taylor. *At Canaan's Edge: America in the King Years, 1965–1968*. New York: Simon and Schuster, 2006.

Carson, Clayborne. *In Struggle: SNCC and the Black Awakening of the 1960s*. Cambridge, MA: Harvard University Press, 1995.

Carson, Clayborne, et al. *The Eyes on the Prize Civil Rights Reader: Documents, Speeches, and Firsthand Accounts from the Black Freedom Struggle, 1954–1990*. New York: Penguin Books, 1987.

Eyes on the Prize: The Civil Rights Movement 1954–1985. A Special Presentation of the American Experience. http://www.pbs.org/wgbh/amex/eyesontheprize/ (accessed August 4, 2007).

Garrow, David. *Bearing the Cross: Martin Luther King, Jr. and the Southern Christian Leadership Conference*. New York: William Marrow, 1986.

Sullivan, Patricia. *Days of Hope: Race and Democracy in the New Deal Era*. Chapel Hill: University of North Carolina Press, 1996.

Williams, Juan. *Eyes on the Prize: America's Civil Rights Years 1954–1965*. New York: Penguin Books, 1987.

Civilian Conservation Corps

In an attempt to ease the devastating levels of joblessness during the Great Depression, President Franklin D. Roosevelt proposed a series of legislative acts to Congress. One of these acts, the Emergency Conservation Work Act, passed by Congress in 1933, formed the Civilian Conservation Corps (CCC). The Department of Labor recruited young people to the CCC to be employed on public works projects, primarily in rural areas. These work projects varied across the country but mainly focused upon erosion control, forestry, flood control, recreation, wildlife, transportation, and structural improvement. Initially only single, physically fit unemployed males between the ages of 18 and 25 whose fathers were on relief were accepted into the CCC. These young men could enlist for a six-month period and reenlist for up to two years. They would work 40 hours each week at $30 per week, with most of that wage sent home to family or held in escrow for the enlistee until leaving the CCC. In addition to providing jobs, an underlying reason for the CCC was to give young men in urban areas something to occupy them to keep them out of trouble, such as turning to crime or radicalism in response to the Depression. Courses were also offered, ranging from basic literacy and vocational skills to college-level courses. Later in 1934, young women were recruited in small numbers, and by 1935, the age range was expanded to between 17 and 28. A series of residential camps were created in each state, as well as the territories of Alaska, Hawaii, Puerto Rico, and the Virgin Islands, to house the CCC members. These camps, which eventually numbered 4,500, were under the control of the War Department and run in a quasi-military manner. During its existence, approximately 3 million men and 8,500 women served in the CCC.

The act that established the CCC forbade discrimination based upon race. All enrollees received the same pay and benefits. Black membership was set proportional to their population at 10 percent, and they could not serve in camps outside their home state. Approximately 250,000 African Americans and 80,000 Native Americans served during the life of the program. The CCC camps were integrated until July 1935, when the War Department reversed the policy, claiming complaints from locals around the camps. In addition to these complaints, there was also violence within some integrated camps between various ethnic and racial groups. Also, many administrators of the army and CCC held racist views. Neither of these realities was used as a public reason for segregation. There were at least 150 all-black camps, and although most Native Americans enrollees did not live in camps (instead living and working around their home reservations), there was at least one separate camp for Native Americans, Camp Marquette in Michigan; there they lived on the camp and worked in the area near the camp.

Civil rights activists, such as NAACP leader Thomas Griffith, complained about the Jim Crow policy, yet CCC director Robert Fechner replied that segregation was not discrimination. Quite a few others in FDR's administration vehemently disagreed, like Harold Ickes. Jim Crow also impacted minorities in that many states ignored highly qualified applicants in preference of white applicants. African Americans were also overlooked for supervisory positions within the CCC. In September 1935, President Roosevelt ordered Fechner to appoint a few more African Americans at CCC camps on National Park Service properties. Fechner ignored the order and leaked Roosevelt's mandate to some prominent white Southern Congressmen. In the culminating uproar, Roosevelt revoked the demand. A more welcoming approach to minorities did not exist until 1941, when recruitment was more encouraged because of dropping enrollment among whites, due to their taking jobs in the developing wartime industry. With the rapid mobilization toward war, by 1942, the CCC program ended.

JULIEANNA FROST

See also

Works Projects Administration (WPA)

Further Reading:

Cole, Olen. *The African American Experience in the Civilian Conservation Corps*. Gainesville: University of Florida Press, 1999.

Hill, Edwin. *In the Shadow of the Mountain: The Spirit of the CCC*. Pullman: Washington State University Press, 1990.

Clansman, The

Published in 1905, Thomas Dixon, Jr.'s *The Clansman* was penned as a reaction to what Dixon perceived to be Harriet Beecher Stowe's overly sentimental portrayal of African Americans in *Uncle Tom's Cabin* (1852). Convinced that American society had been duped by Stowe's romantic rendering of the character of Uncle Tom, Dixon endeavored to "set the record straight" (Snow, 1980) according to his own racist beliefs. Subtitled *An Historical Romance of the Ku Klux Klan*, *The Clansman* offers a romantic rendering of its own. The novel opens with a fated encounter between a beautiful young Northern woman and a wounded Confederate soldier slated for execution. Determined to save the soldier's life, the woman, who is the daughter of the radical leader of Congress, Austin Stoneman, appeals to President Abraham Lincoln for clemency. But as Elsie Stoneman endeavors to save the life of one Southerner, her father plots the ruination of the entire South.

Dissatisfied with President Lincoln's postwar plans to first enfranchise and then exile African Americans to the tropics, Stoneman uses Lincoln's assassination as a catalyst for his own Reconstruction scheme. Under the apparent spell of his mulatto housekeeper, Stoneman works swiftly to try to pass an act that will reduce the conquered provinces of the South to African American rule. When the bill is vetoed by Lincoln's successor, President Andrew Johnson, Stoneman tries to have Johnson impeached. Unsuccessful in his efforts, an ailing Stoneman heads south with the intention of single-handedly destroying the former "slaveholding oligarchy" (Dixon, 1905: 192). With the aid of his mulatto henchman, Silas Lynch, Stoneman realizes his vision of African American rule, as former masters and mistresses are forced to submit to the will of those they once enslaved.

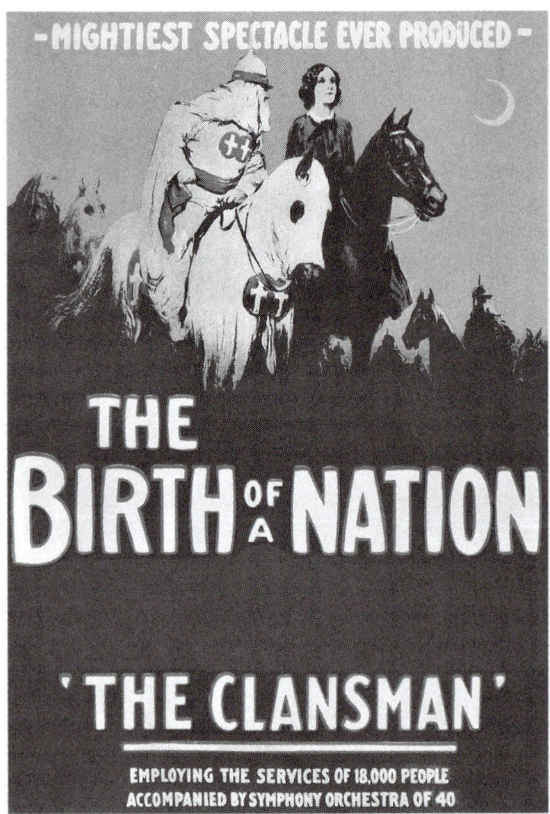

Birth of a Nation poster highlighting the fact that the film was based on Thomas Dixon, Jr.'s *The Clansman*. (Getty Images)

When the figurative rape of the South culminates in the literal ravishing of an innocent Southern belle at the hands of a former slave, the Ku Klux Klan (KKK) are summoned to avenge the girl and protect the maidenhood of the South. Threatened with the loss of his only son to the regime he empowered, Stoneman finally recognizes the error of his ways.

With its inauspicious representations of African Americans and its noble depictions of the KKK, *The Clansman* perpetuated racial discrimination at a formidable rate. Given the social and historical landscapes from which *The Clansman* emanated, Dixon's motives were undoubtedly political. By depicting the African American male as a sadistic brute and spoiler of white women, Dixon hoped to incense the white community. In a discussion of *The Clansman* in his autobiography, *A Man Called White* (1948), Walter White, executive secretary of the National Association for the Advancement of Colored People, examined the impact of Dixon's hate-mongering. During the Atlanta (Georgia) Riot of 1906, writes White, the city was a tinder box lit by anti–African American sentiment (1948: 8). According to White, this fire was fuelled by the release of D. W. Griffith's *The Birth of a Nation* (1915), the anti–African American film based on Dixon's *The Clansman*. The fact that the KKK grew from a few thousand members to more than 100,000 within the same year as the film's release reveals just how big a role these works played in the Klan's revival. The myths perpetuated by Dixon's fiction and Griffith's dramatization of the same advocated the continued exploitation and oppression of African Americans.

Alex Ambrozic

See also

Birth of a Nation, The; Films and Racial Stereotypes; Ku Klux Klan (KKK)

Further Reading:

Dixon, Thomas, Jr. *The Clansman: An Historical Romance of the Ku Klux Klan*. New York: Doubleday, Page & Company, 1905.

Franke, Astrid. *Keys to Controversies: Stereotypes in Modern American Novels*. New York: St. Martin's Press, 1999.

Slide, Anthony. *American Racist: The Life and Films of Thomas Dixon*. Lexington: University Press of Kentucky, 2004.

Snow, Richard F. "American Characters: Thomas Dixon." *American Heritage Magazine* 31, no. 6 (October/November 1980). http://www.americanheritage.com/articles/magazine/ah/1980/6/1980_6_80.shtml.

White, Walter. *A Man Called White: The Autobiography of Walter White*. New York: Viking Press, 1948.

Clark Doll Study

During the 1940s, Kenneth and Mamie Clark, two black psychologists of the time, conducted a number of experiments using dolls that tested African American children's sense of self. The Clarks, as well as others before them, believed that racial segregation was inherently damaging to the psyche of black children and created feelings of inferiority. Using data from the doll experiments, Kenneth Clark testified in *Briggs v. Elliot* (1952), one of the cases that later comprised the *Brown v. Board of Education* (1954) case, that black children, from an early age, accept negative stereotypes of their own group. His testimony, as well as others who believed in the dismantling of segregation, paved the way for the end of de jure (segregation by law) segregation.

Concerned with racial awareness, or the consciousness of belonging to a specific racial group, the Clarks conducted a number of doll studies to test racial identification and racial preferences of black children (Clark and Clark 1947). One of the studies conducted consisted of 253 black children, ages three to seven, from segregated and integrated nursery and public schools in Arkansas. In each experiment, participants were given four dolls, and the only characteristic they differed on was skin color. Two of the dolls had brown skin and black hair, while the other two dolls had white skin and blonde hair. The children were asked eight questions that assessed racial differences, racial self-identification, and racial preference.

In regards to racial differences, when children were asked to give the interviewer the doll that looked like them, over 90 percent of respondents gave the interviewer the appropriate doll (white or brown doll). However, when the participants were asked to choose the doll that looked like them, 33 percent of black children identified with the white doll, while the remaining 66 percent of children identified with the brown doll. Thus, even though children were able to perceive racial differences, not all children self-identified as black, although society labeled them as such.

When asked about racial preferences, roughly two-thirds of black children specified that they liked the white doll the "best," would rather play with the white doll, or that the white doll was the "nice doll." Further, almost 60 percent of participants stated that the black doll "looks bad." According to Clark, due to the experience of school segregation black children believed they were inferior to whites, which had damaging consequences to the psyche.

While Clark provided integral testimony paving the way for the end of racial segregation, there were many critics of their work. In 1952, when Clark testified in the *Brigss v. Elliot* trial, he gathered data from schools in Clarendon County, South Carolina, where the case was initiated. In this doll study, 16 children, ages six to nine, were shown drawings of brown and white dolls. Similar to the Arkansas study, black children were more likely to associate positive feelings towards the white doll. However, scholars were critical of his methods, specifically of the terms used (nice/bad), the use of drawings and not dolls, and the number of children in the Clarendon County experiment (Patterson 2001). Critics also questioned whether school segregation, not discrimination or poverty, caused feelings of inferiority. Last, in a doll study conducted in Massachusetts, black children in integrated schools were more likely to like the white doll than black children in segregated schools, thus creating a hole in his theory.

Since the 1960s, civil rights leaders, among others, have advocated for the protection of all-black schools. While segregated schools face a lot of obstacles, segregated schools can be successful, especially when a relationship exists between the community and the school (Siddle-Walker 1996). Similar to the doll experiment in Massachusetts, research has highlighted how black students in predominantly black schools have higher self-esteem compared to black students in predominantly white schools, while other scholars have shown no positive relationship between school desegregation and self-esteem among blacks.

Kenneth Clark

Kenneth Clark, an educator, psychologist, civil rights advocate, and author, was born on July 24, 1914, in Panama and raised in a Harlem ghetto. He attended Howard University in Washington, D.C., where he earned his bachelor's and master's degree. In 1940, he continued his studies at Columbia University in New York, where he became the first black to receive a PhD in psychology. In 1942, he began a career at the City College of New York, and retired as a distinguished professor in 1975. Along with his wife, Dr. Mamie Clark, he created the Northside Center for Child Development in 1946, which provided assistance to Harlem children. In 1964, Clark founded the Harlem Youth Opportunities Unlimited, which was devoted to helping black youth overcome the obstacles of living in the ghetto. Through the creation of organizations, representation on the New York State Board of Regents, and scholarly work, Kenneth Clark devoted his life to improving the educational and occupational opportunities for black youth. He passed away in 2005.

In 2005, Kiri Davis, a 16-year-old filmmaker from New York, re-created the Clarks' doll experiments. In her documentary, *A Girl Like Me*, Davis highlights how 15 of the 21 black children interviewed viewed the black doll as bad. Although school segregation is no longer legal, Davis re-created the studies to show how whites are valued more in society, specifically in regards to beauty, and how this hurts black children's self-esteem. However, Robin Bernstein, an associate professor at Harvard University, argues that the tests were scientifically flawed and do not demonstrate black self-hatred (Proulx 2011). She argues that the historical cultural portrayal of black and white dolls was very different (white dolls were cherished, black dolls were abused) and it was this difference that influenced children's decisions to choose the white doll as better, not self-hatred.

While the doll studies beginning in the 1940s have been criticized for their lack of methodical criteria, studies have shown that children as young as four and five years old still experience the effects of living in a society where racial stereotypes of what is or is not good, bad, pretty, or ugly still exist.

Bobette Otto

See also

Desegregation; Intelligence Testing; Segregation

Further Reading:

Clark, Kenneth B. *Dark Ghetto: Dilemmas of Social Power*. Middletown, CT: Wesleyan University Press, 1989.

Clark, Kenneth B., and Mamie P. Clark. "Racial Identification and Preference in Negro Children." In *Readings in Social Psychology*, edited by Eleanor E. Maccoley, Theodore M. Newcomb, and Eugene L. Hartley, 602–11. New York: Halt, Rinehart, and Winston, 1947.

Davis, Kiri. *A Girl Like Me*. 2007. https://www.youtube.com/watch?v=YWyI77Yh1Gg.

Klein, Woody, ed. *Toward Humanity and Justice: The Writings of Kenneth B. Clark Scholar of the 1954 Brown v. Board of Education Decision*. Westport, CT: Praeger, 2004.

Patterson, James P. *Brown v. Board of Education: A Civil Rights Milestone and its Troubled Legacy*. Oxford: Oxford University Press, 2001.

Proulx, Michael G. "Professor Revisits Clark Doll Tests." *Harvard Crimson*. December 1, 2011. http://www.thecrimson.com/article/2011/12/1/clark-dolls-research-media/.

Siddle-Walker, Vanessa. *Their Highest Potential: An African American School Community in the Segregated South*. Chapel Hill: University of North Carolina Press, 1996.

Cleaver, Eldridge (1935–1998)

A 1960s Black Panther Party (BPP) activist, essayist, and fugitive, Eldridge Cleaver was a symbol of black rebellion and an advocate of revolutionary violence to win power for black Americans. A self-taught writer, he is best known for the publication of his prison essays, *Soul on Ice* (1968). The book is infamous for its admission of his rape of several white women, which he defended as "insurrectionary acts." The philosophical foundation of the Black Power movement, the book became a best-seller, its searing social analysis resonating with the rebelliousness of the times.

Leroy Eldridge Cleaver was born on August 31, 1935, in Wabbaseka, Arkansas. His family moved repeatedly; as a teenager he was sent to reform school for petty crimes. In 1957, he was convicted of assault with intent to murder and was sentenced to 14 years in prison. There, he began reading extensively and was particularly influenced by Malcolm X, Frantz Fanon, and Sigmund Freud. He wrote his series of essays and became senior editor of the radical magazine *Ramparts*, which helped wage a legal campaign on his behalf.

He was paroled in 1966 and married Kathleen Neal on December 27, 1967. Cleaver joined the BPP as minister of information, or press agent. Cleaver is responsible for creating the Panthers' famous icon, the photograph in which Huey Newton sits in a wicker chair, a rifle in one hand and an African spear in the other.

In 1968, Cleaver ran for U.S. president on the ticket of the Peace and Freedom Party, founded in 1967 in opposition to the Vietnam War. Although a convicted felon, Cleaver carried nearly 37,000 votes. On April 6, 1968, Cleaver and seven other BPP members were involved in a two-hour shoot-out with Oakland, California, police. Although the incident was described as an instance of police brutality, Cleaver later revealed in an interview that he had staged the confrontation with police in the wake of the Martin Luther King, Jr. murder.

Cleaver was arrested but jumped bail in November 1968, fleeing to a series of dictatorships offering him protection. Cleaver first lived under guard in Havana, until 1969, when mutual distrust developed between Cleaver and the Cubans. He then moved to Algiers, where his son, Maceo, named for black Cuban general Antonio Maceo, was born. While in North Korea in 1970, his second child, Joju Younghi (Korean for "young heroine"), was born.

Eldridge Cleaver led a life of transformations: youthful years of crime and imprisonment; a decade as a famous African American activist and writer; a period of exile; and recent years as an outspoken and conservative Christian. (Library of Congress)

His 1978 book, *Soul on Fire*, offers details about the training camp for revolutionaries he organized in Algeria under the protection of that government, with financing from the North Vietnamese government. Cleaver's group also ran a stolen car ring out of Europe. But mutual dissatisfaction between Cleaver's criminal friends and the Algerian government led to a series of gunfights, and Cleaver, unable to control his protégées, fled for his life, hiding in France.

From Paris, Cleaver made several unsuccessful appeals for asylum. In 1973, Kathleen Neal Cleaver returned to the United States to try to arrange her husband's return as a parolee on bail and to raise a defense fund to cover legal fees. In 1974, the French government granted legal residency to the Cleavers. While in France, he underwent a mystical religious experience, deciding to return to the United States to preach the Christian gospel.

In the United States in 1975, he told reporters that he believed he would be treated fairly by the American judicial system. Renouncing his former radicalism, he became a born-again Christian, embracing conservative political causes, including anticommunism, attributing his changed politics to his experiences in communist countries during his years in exile. (On the basis of his religious and political conversions, he was freed on bail, then served only a few months' prison time and community service.)

He began a period of religious experimentation, attempting social transformation through spirituality. He ran Cleaver Crusade for Christ. He developed a plan to combine Christianity and Islam, called *Christlam*. He advocated the religious ideas of Sun Myung Moon; and he later became involved with Mormonism. As a political conservative, he unsuccessfully ran for the 1986 Republican nomination to the U.S. Senate from California.

He and his wife divorced in 1985. During this period, Cleaver became addicted to crack cocaine and endured a series of drug-related arrests. In 1994, after a cocaine-related assault, he kicked his addiction and returned to his belief in Christianity. At the time of his death, Cleaver was working as a diversity consultant for the University of La Verne, California. On May 1, 1998, Cleaver died at the age of 62 in Pomona, California. His family requested that the hospital not reveal the cause of his death. He is interred in Mountain View Cemetery, Altadena, California, and is survived by his daughter, Joju Younghi Cleaver; his son, Maceo Cleaver; and his former wife, Kathleen Neal Cleaver.

VALERIE BEGLEY

See also

Black Panther Party (BPP)

Further Reading:

Barnes, Bart. "Eldridge Cleaver, Author and Black Panther Leader, Dies." *Washington Post*, May 2, 1998, D06. http://www.washingtonpost.com/wp-srv/politics/campaigns/junkie/links/cleaver.htm.

Cleaver, Eldridge. *Eldridge Cleaver Is Free*. New York: Random House, 1969.

As Ministry of Information for the BPP, Cleaver published a number of pamphlets, including *On the Ideology of the Black Panther Party* (1969); *Revolution in the White Mother Country and National Liberation in the Black Colony: An Analysis and*

Assessment of the Political Dynamics in the White Mother (1968); and *Credo for Rioters and Looters* (1969).
Cleaver, Eldridge. *On the Ideology of the Black Panther Party*. Pamphlet, 1969.
Cleaver, Eldridge. *Eldridge Cleaver: Post-Prison Writings and Speeches*. Edited and with an appraisal by Robert Scheer. New York: Random House, 1969.
Gates, Henry Louis, Jr. "Interview: Eldridge Cleaver." *PBS Frontline*, February 1998. http://www.pbs.org/wgbh/pages/frontline/shows/race/interviews/ecleaver.html.
Horowitz, David. "Eldridge Cleaver's Last Gift." *FrontPageMagazine.com*, May 3, 1998.

Cleveland (Ohio) Riot of 1966

The Cleveland, Ohio, Riot of 1966 occurred in the Hough, one of the nation's most economically depressed African American communities. The civil unrest began on Monday, July 18, and continued for several days until the National Guard and local police combined forces to bring an end to the protests, looting, burning, and violence. In the wake of the riot, four people were dead, many others were injured, and area businesses and homeowners had suffered more than $1 million in property damage. Although some written accounts charged that the riot was started by communists and Black Nationalist instigators, many others concluded that deteriorating housing stock, overcrowded living conditions, high unemployment, and the lack of city services, among other things, added to the level of frustration for Hough's African American residents and eventually sparked the violence and fanned the flames of discontent. Hough came to symbolize everything that could go wrong when city leaders failed to address legitimate concerns about discrimination and social ills and the challenges faced by those who dared travel the long and difficult road to rebuilding a riot-torn community.

Numerous government-sponsored and scholarly studies document the problems leading up to the explosion of violence in Hough. On the eve of the Hough riot, the community had already been identified as an area deserving of special attention based on a number of social indicators. Median family income in Hough, for example, declined from $4,637 in 1960 to $4,050 in 1965. The comparison income figures for all families in the city were $5,935 in 1960 and $6,895 in 1965. Not only did Hough residents lose ground in the income category, similar losses also occurred in the workforce. In 1965, Hough's 15 percent unemployment rate was more than double the 7.1 percent rate for the city.

In addition to these disparities, racial segregation in the city's housing market and schools had long been a concern for government and grassroots leaders alike. Throughout most of the 20th century, Cleveland remained one of the nation's most segregated cities, with the lion's share of the city's African American population concentrated on the east side of the city. Even as many barriers to social integration began to fall during the decade of the 1960s, residential segregation and overcrowding in Hough became more entrenched. By 1960, the percent of housing reported as crowded in Hough was more than double the rate for the city.

Since the era of the Great Depression, similar concerns had also been expressed about conditions in the public schools serving African American students. When school officials tried to relieve overcrowding in Hough by busing African American students to an underutilized building in Murray Hill in 1965, residents in the largely Italian-American community responded with what has been referred to as the Murray Hill Riot. Given these and other conditions in Hough, it is not surprising that in the 1960s civil rights advocates and others described the community as one of the nation's worst ghetto communities, in terms of the poverty, vice, crime, and inadequate social services there.

The incident cited most often as the initial spark for the rioting occurred at the Seventy-Niner, a popular white-owned bar located at the intersection of East 79th Street and Hough Avenue, the symbolic heart of the community. Newspaper accounts suggest that an African American woman entered the establishment to solicit donations for the children of a deceased prostitute. A verbal disagreement ensued between the white owner and the woman, who eventually left the establishment. Later that day, an African American man reportedly made a take-out purchase of a bottled alcoholic beverage and then requested a container of ice water. When his request was refused, he also exchanged angry words with the white owner. After he left the bar, a handwritten sign was posted on the establishment's door: "No water for Niggers."

When a crowd of angry patrons and neighborhood residents gathered outside the bar, the owners called the police. When the armed policemen arrived, the violence erupted at this point of confrontation.

Looting and burning of area businesses; confrontations among police, firemen, and rock-throwing youths; and sniper fire characterized the first day of rioting. Although the majority of those arrested for participation in the riot were teens, many adults participated in the riot. A 26-year-old African American mother of three was the first person to die in the rioting. Caught in the crossfire between police and snipers, she was shot in the head as she stood in the window of an apartment building.

On July 19, Cleveland's mayor, Ralph Locher, a white male who was accused by many local African Americans of being out of touch with the needs of Hough's African American residents, requested and received backup from Gov. James Rhodes, who ordered the National Guard to report for duty and help restore order in Hough. Between July 19 and July 31, when the last troops were withdrawn, approximately 2,000 guardsmen patrolled Hough with rifles and bayonets, guarding buildings, directing traffic, and riding escort with local police and fire units. In the wake of the rioting, four people were dead, dozens were injured, and widespread property destruction had displaced residents and business owners alike.

Although a grand jury report suggested that communists and radical militants had instigated the riot, scholars, African American community leaders, and reports from undercover policemen agreed that no conclusive evidence was found linking the riot with any organized group. There was abundant evidence, however, suggesting that the rioting could be directly linked to existing social conditions and the benign neglect of Hough at all levels of government; a fact that would be reiterated later in the Kerner Commission Report.

In the decades since the rioting, grassroots leaders, longtime Hough resident and Cleveland City Council representative Fannie Louis, and private investors have joined forces to lead efforts to rebuild Hough. Several new housing developments, including one at East 79th Street and Hough Avenue, the flashpoint for the rioting, are partially responsible for the many new housing units built in Hough since 1966. Interestingly enough, the building of many upscale houses and mansions in Hough was made possible by the availability of land due to the property destruction during the rioting and generous tax incentives in recent years.

Even with these new units, Hough is a long way from replacing the number of units. Census information obtained from the Northern Ohio Data and Information Service at Cleveland State University suggests that Hough had 22,954 housing units in 1960, but it only had 8,409 units in 2000. Hough's population in 2000 was 16,294, a far cry from the 1960 population figure of 76,738. Income levels in Hough remain low. In 2000, the median family income in Hough was $13,630, while the comparable figure for the city of Cleveland was $30,286. It appears, then, that this once riot-torn community has yet to address some of the issues that led to the rioting two generations ago.

REGENNIA N. WILLIAMS

See also

Black Nationalism; Long Hot Summer Riots (1965–1967); Race Riots in America. Documents: The Report on the Memphis Riots of May 1866 (July 25, 1866); Account of the Riots in East St. Louis, Illinois (July 1917); The Cook County Coroner's Report Regarding the 1919 Chicago Race Riots (1919); A Southern Black Woman's Letter Regarding the Recent Riots in Chicago and Washington (November 1919); The Final Report of the Grand Jury on the Tulsa Race Riot (June 25, 1921); Testimony from *Laney v. United States* Describing Events during the Washington, D.C., Riot of July 1919 (December 3, 1923); The Governor's Commission Report on the Watts Riots (December 1965); Cyrus R. Vance's Report on the Riots in Detroit (July-August 1967); The Reports of the Oklahoma Commission to Study the Tulsa Race Riot of 1921 (2000-2001); The Draft Report of the 1898 Wilmington Race Riot Commission (December 2005)

Further Reading:

Cho, Yong Hyo. "City Politics and Racial Polarization: Bloc Voting in Cleveland Elections." *Journal of Black Studies* 4 (June 1974): 396–417.

Kerner, Otto. *Report of the National Advisory Commission on Civil Disorders.* New York: Elsevier-North Holland, 1968.

Lackritz, Marc E. "The Hough Riots of 1966." Senior thesis, Princeton University, 1968. E-book available at Cleveland State University, Library Special Collections, http://web.ulib.csuohio.edu/hough/.

Richan, Willard C. *Racial Isolation in the Cleveland Schools.* Cleveland: Case Western Reserve University, 1967.

Stokes, Carl B. *Promises of Power: Then and Now.* Cleveland: Friends of Carl B. Stokes, 1989.

Upton, James N. "The Politics of Urban Violence: Critiques and Proposals." *Journal of Black Studies* 15 (March 1985): 243–58.
Williams, Walter. "Cleveland's Crisis Ghetto: Causes and Complaints." In *Ghetto Revolts*, edited by P. H. Rossi. New Brunswick, NJ: Transaction Books, 1973.

Cobell v. Salazar (2009)

The agreement reached in *Cobell v. Salazar* (2009) marked the largest government class-action settlement in U.S. history. In 1996, Elouise Cobell from the Blackfeet Nation, along with the Native American Rights Fund, led a class-action lawsuit to recover millions of dollars of leases and royalties supposed to be held in trust by the Bureau of Indian Affairs (BIA) and paid out to individuals. The lawsuit lasted 13 years, and on December 7, 2009, Cobell accepted a settlement of $1.4 billion dollars.

Beginning in 1887, through the General Allotment Act (sometimes known after its primary congressional sponsor, Sen. Henry Dawes), Native Americans were designated as owners of individual lands, going against communal traditions that were thousands of years old. These lands were managed by the BIA, part of the Department of the Interior. In theory, like other owners of resources, the Native land owners were supposed to be paid royalties through the BIA and Treasury Department, through accounts called "Individual Indian Monies."

More than a century later, when Cobell filed a lawsuit to allow Indians' access to their money, she had only the slightest inkling of the financial morass she had discovered. While working as an accountant on the Montana Blackfeet reservation during the 1990s, Cobell began to inquire into the management of bank accounts managed "in trust" by the federal government. First estimates of mismanaged funds ranged from $2 billion to $4 billion—a lot of money, surely, but a pittance compared to the $176 billion that was estimated 10 years later. Cobell rented a four-room office in Browning, Montana, and, by 2005, had funded her legal challenge with about $12 million in grant money. By 2006, the Individual Indian Monies (IIM) mess had become the stuff of political and legal legend; nine years after the case was first filed, it employed more than 100 lawyers on the payrolls of the Interior and Treasury departments.

Before Cobell's challenge, many IIM accountholders had been wary of confronting the system because the BIA could (and sometimes did) declare them incompetent to handle their own money. The U.S. Treasury holds the accounts in trust for Native Americans, as wards of the government. "Trust" is also the legal rubric under which the BIA (or other agencies of the Interior Department) first became bankers for Native American communities. The handlers of Native Americans in the War Department, Interior Department, and the BIA have always had available to them two versions of reality: one is the official ideology of "trust" and "guardianship." In the other reality, the federal agencies that had lost and abused Native Americans' funds were empowered, by their interpretation of the law, to decide whether Native individuals were competent to handle their own money.

With broad Native American support, the Department of Interior hired Paul Homan, a former director of Riggs Bank and an expert at cleaning up failing private financial institutions, as Special Trustee for Native Americans. Homan, having taken stock of the situation, later quit. Day by day, piece by piece, the IIM inquiries were producing evidence of poor record keeping. The BIA had never established an accounts receivable system, so its bankers never knew how much money they were handling at any given time. More than $50 million had not been paid to individual Native Americans because the BIA had lost track of them, or because they had not left forwarding addresses. Roughly 21,000 accounts listed the names of people who were dead. Large numbers of records were stored in cardboard boxes in leaky warehouses, destroying them.

About $695 million in Native funds had been sent to the wrong Native group, tribe, or nation. Some of the funds never were sent at all. Some funds had been posted to the wrong accounts. One property record valued three garden-variety chain saws at $99 million each. During 1996, $17 million in trust fund money simply vanished due to sloppy bookkeeping. Exhumation of the BIA's financial record keeping came to resemble an archaeological dig. Asbestos had contaminated some of the financial records, and other records had been paved over by a parking lot.

In 1996, Cobell finally became fed up with government inaction after Attorney General Janet Reno reneged on a promise to look into the money-funds mess. With Cobell, the Native American Rights Fund announced the class-action suit on behalf of the 300,000 (later 500,000) holders of IIM accounts. Attorneys pointed to people such as Bernice Skunk Cap, an elderly Blackfeet, who lost her cabin to fire in 1994. Planning to build a new home, Skunk Cap applied to the BIA for $2,400 from her IIM account, but was told she could have only $1,000 of it. She was forced to move into a nursing home.

The chief judge in the case, Royce C. Lamberth, a Republican appointee, possessed a keen knowledge of bureaucratic politics and an ability to read and comprehend vast amounts of information. On December 21, 1999, Lamberth, who was overseeing the case in the Washington, D.C. Federal District Court, issued his first (Phase One) opinion (the case is divided into two phases). The 126-page opinion stated that the government had boldly violated its trust responsibilities to Native Americans. He called the IIM issue the "most egregious misconduct by the federal government."

In a major victory for the plaintiffs, Lamberth ruled September 29, 2004, that all sales and transfers of Native-owned land by the Department of the Interior's Bureau of Indian Affairs must include a detailed, court-approved notification of landowners' rights as trust beneficiaries and class members. For the first time in history, individual Native American landowners would be informed of their rights as trust beneficiaries and class members before the sale of their lands.

On June 20, 2005, several prominent Native American leaders, including Cobell, convened in Washington to announce principles for legislation that they said could settle the case. Most significantly, they said they would settle the case for $27.5 billion. The government refused the offer.

By 2008, the case was dragging on, with the Native accountholders having received nothing. The U.S. government showed little inclination to solve the money-funds problem. Instead, the Department of the Interior's small army of attorneys went to federal appeals court and removed Lamberth from the case, arguing that he was biased in favor of the plaintiffs. The appeals court agreed.

Late in 2009, the Obama administration submitted to Congress a plan to pay $1.4 billion to the plaintiffs in Cobell's lawsuit, as well as an additional $2 billion to repurchase land, ending the 13-year-old lawsuit. Under the settlement, most of the plaintiffs would get $1,000, with some who suffered larger losses receiving more. On December 8, 2010, President Barack Obama signed the Claims Resolution Act of 2010, part of which approved the settlement of *Cobell v. Salazar* and authorized $3.4 billion in funds for Native claimants.

Bruce Johansen

See also

Native Americans, Conquest of; Native Americans, Forced Relocation of

Further Reading:

Cobell, Elouise. "Indians Not Being Told Truth." *Daily Oklahoman* [Oklahoma City], April 22, 2005, n.p.

Johansen, Bruce E. "The BIA as Banker: 'Trust' Is Hard When Billions Disappear." *Native Americas* 14, no. 1 (Spring 1997): 14–23.

Johansen, Bruce E. "The Trust Fund Mess: Where Has All the Money Gone?" *Native Americas* 21 (Fall/Winter 2004): 26–33.

Washburn, Wilcomb E. *The Assault on Indian Tribalism: The General Allotment (Dawes Act) of 1887*. Malabar, FL: Krieger, 1986.

Code of the Street

The "code of the street" was introduced by sociologist and ethnographer Elijah Anderson in his 1999 work of the same name. It is a set of informal rules governing public social interaction in low-income, inner-city neighborhoods based in demanding respect, and often enforced with violence or the threat of violence. This code is presented in contrast with the code of civility Anderson identifies as the rules governing public social interaction in the public spaces of middle-class, mainstream neighborhoods. *Code of the Street: Decency, Violence, and the Moral Life of the Inner City* is based on time Anderson spent studying inner-city communities in Philadelphia, Pennsylvania. Widely read in sociology, criminology, and urban studies, the book introduces the concept of the code of the street and details its components, making the case that the code is applicable in low-income, inner-city

Cool Pose

According to Richard Majors and Janet Mancini Billson, authors of *Cool Pose: The Dilemmas of Black Manhood in America*, the cool pose is a set of language, mannerisms, gestures, and movements common among young inner-city blacks that communicate an exaggerated or ritualized version of masculinity. The ultimate goal of the cool pose is to appear in control of one's self and surroundings. Majors and Billson describe cool pose as a way to combat oppression, communicating strength and confidence to the dominant culture, despite minority status. Cool pose includes a fearless, stylish way of walking, an aloof facial expression, wearing flashy clothes, like expensive sneakers and loose clothing, as well as particular gestures and a way of talking. Although cool pose provides dignity and confidence to those who embody it, whites often misinterpret it, reading the aloof, unflappable demeanor as irresponsibility.

neighborhoods. Anderson examines the ways the code influences violence, drugs and street crime, intimate relationships, and child bearing and child rearing. *Code of the Street* features the typologies of the Decent Daddy and the Black Inner-City Grandmother in order to detail the implications of the code on inner-city life.

As a foundation for the code of the street theory, Anderson presents two categories of inner-city residents: those from decent families and those from street families. The categorical labels can be applied to individuals and families; however, families can and often do contain members of both orientations.

Street-oriented people and families behave and approach the world without deference to mainstream values and social norms. Street families can be seen as representing stereotypical characterizations of inner-city poor. Violent, inconsiderate of others, including intimate partners and children, street-oriented people demonstrate irresponsibility in many aspects of life. In the late 1980s and throughout the 1990s there was widespread concern about violence in urban areas, especially among inner-city youth. Discussions about the underclass and the culture of poverty thesis were also in progress at this time, necessarily informing Anderson's research. The code of the street has a strong connection to oppositional culture theory.

Anderson's treatment of decent families in the book was a timely and important contribution to combatting generalizations of inner-city residents. By presenting decent families and individuals, he provides an alternative to ideas of inner-city residents as members of the behavioral underclass, like welfare queens, drug-dealers and gang members. Grounded in black inner-city youth culture, the code of the street is adapted by community members of all ages as a means of navigating the complex and often threatening environment of public space. Street-oriented people also do not necessarily conform to underclass image. Anderson describes the code of the street as a distinctive, collective reality created by patterns of criminal violence specifically in inner-city neighborhoods. He argues that it is not the product or goal of any individual's action, but the fabric of everyday life, impacting routines, educational orientations, familial relations, and neighboring.

The code of the street originated with street-oriented people, but is enacted by neighborhood residents from both orientations as it became the primary way of interacting in the public spaces of the neighborhood as a result of the constant threat of violence and negative interaction while unemployment and underemployment enhanced the lure of street life. The uncertainty created by drug culture and street crime in public spaces causes otherwise nonviolent individuals to the threat of victimization. Violence, and the threat of violence, and retribution undergird the code of the streets, enforcing its tenets and ensuring its perpetuation. Decent and street individuals alike use a form of self-presentation in public spaces that engenders confidence and suggests that they will defend themselves if challenged. Majors and Billson (1992) call this street persona a "cool pose." Children from decent families practice code-switching, alternating between the street code in public social interaction and the civility code at home and with other decent individuals.

The code of the street was an extremely important theoretical development in sociology, urban studies, and criminology, influencing many further studies and inciting important debates. It continues to be parsed, expanded, and applied in various situations, especially as it pertains to the criminal justice system. For example, Brookman, Copes, and Hochstetler (2011) investigated how inmates incarcerated for violent offenses in the United Kingdom use the code of the street in their narratives of specific violent events, finding that they portray themselves as being respectable according to the code. Stewart, Schreck, and Simon (2006) challenged Anderson's theory, finding no support for the idea that adopting the code of the street is an effective manner of avoiding or reducing victimization. Rather, they found that using the street code actually increases the risk of victimization, even beyond the risk associated with living in a dangerous neighborhood. Code of the street has been appropriated in a number of ways, by academics, policy makers, and others. It remains a topic of inquiry in the social sciences as researchers continue to investigate the realities of urban black life.

Renee S. Alston

See also

Oppositional Culture; Underclass (Ghetto Poor); Welfare Queens

Further Reading:

Anderson, Elijah. *Code of the Street: Decency, Violence, and the Moral Life of the Inner City*. New York: W. W. Norton, 1999.

Brookman, Fiona, Heith Copes, and Andy Hochstetler. "Street Codes as Formula Stories: How Inmates Recount Violence." *Journal of Contemporary Ethnography* 40, no. 4 (2011): 397–424.

Majors, Richard, and Janet Mancini Billson. *Cool Pose: The Dilemmas of Black Manhood in America*. New York: Lexington Books, 1992.

Stewart, Eric A., Christopher J. Schreck, and Ronald L. Simons. "'I Ain't Gonna Let No One Disrespect Me': Does the Code of the Street Reduce or Increase Violent Victimization among African American Adolescents?" *Journal of Research in Crime and Delinquency* 43, no. 4 (2006): 427–58.

COINTELPRO (Counter Intelligence Program)

COINTELPRO is an acronym for Counter Intelligence Program, a Federal Bureau of Investigation (FBI) program designed to investigate, disrupt, and neutralize dissident domestic organizations. COINTELPRO formally started in 1956 to investigate foreign spies operating within the U.S. Communist Party. By the time COINTELPRO officially ended in 1971, its targets included the Socialist Workers Party (SWP), the Ku Klux Klan, black civil rights organizations, Puerto Rican nationalists, Native American organizations, and the New Left/antiwar movements. Post-Watergate congressional hearings revealed that the FBI opened more than 500,000 files on more than 1 million Americans during the COINTELPRO era.

From the standpoint of being a domestic program aimed at neutralizing individuals and organizations with views that were unpopular to the U. S. government, COINTELPRO-like activities effectively began with the FBI's General Intelligence Division (GID). J. Edgar Hoover directed the GID from its inception in 1917. In the 1920s, Hoover developed counterintelligence methods to neutralize workers' unions, communists, and anarchists during the Palmer Raids. Subsequently, the Red Scare of the 1940s and 1950s motivated Congress to pass the Smith Act and the McCarran Internal Security Act, which subjected subversives to formal government scrutiny. By 1956, when COINTELPRO formally began, the legislative landscape as well as public anxieties about the looming, or perceived, threat of communism gave unprecedented power and autonomy to the FBI. In addition, after over 30 years of Hoover's self-described, micromanaging control, the FBI had become somewhat of a monolith, reflecting Hoover's broad interpretation of threats to the state and clandestine means of neutralizing those who opposed the status quo.

COINTELPRO-CPUSA was the first COINTELPRO initiative. Acting on classified memoranda that revealed the Soviet Union was funneling spies through the U.S. Communist Party, the FBI launched COINTELPRO to disrupt domestic communism. COINTELPRO-CPUSA was the first observed period in which the FBI used dirty tricks. Operation Hoodwink, for example, was a dirty trick that involved sending bogus communiqués to Mafia families, warning them that the Communist Party's activities on the New York waterfront would marginalize their profits. The Mafia retaliated with violence against the Communist Party.

COINTELPRO effectively defused the Communist Party, but continued to operate long after the party's demise. In 1960, COINTELPRO was expanded to include non–Communist Party members who sympathized with the movement. By 1961, individuals advocating Puerto Rican independence and the SWP were COINTELPRO targets. When COINTELPRO became subject to congressional hearings in the mid-1970s, operatives revealed that the FBI established over 2,218 separate COINTELPRO actions between 1956 and 1971. Among the more extensive programs were COINTELPRO-New Left, COINTELPRO-AIM (American Indian Movement), and COINTELPRO-Black Nationalist-Hate Groups.

COINTELPRO used a variety of tactics to keep watch on and hamper the activities of targeted groups. Eavesdropping involved secret surveillance of organizations and individuals with wiretaps, burglaries, and the surreptitious opening of mail. Post-Watergate congressional hearings revealed that the FBI installed more than 2,000 telephone taps and 700 bugs and opened over 57,000 pieces of mail. Bogus mail included fabricated correspondence between members of targeted groups, or between two or more targeted groups, designed to instigate tensions, occasionally leading to violence among group members. Black propaganda publications were fabricated, circulated on behalf of targeted organizations or individuals, and designed to misrepresent their positions and discredit them to the public.

Harassment involved repeatedly arresting targeted individuals, on spurious and bogus charges. Often, the goal was not to convict, but to temporarily suppress leadership and tarnish the reputations of the organization. Infiltrators and agents provocateurs were planted within the targeted organizations to either provide information to the FBI about the organizations' operations or to provoke between-group or within-group tensions. When organizations became aware of the presence of infiltrators within the ranks, the agents would bad-jacket bona fide members by accusing them of being FBI informants.

Other tactics included the fabrication of evidence, withholding exculpatory evidence, intimidating witnesses, and other measures designed to prosecute key members of targeted organizations. The FBI has also been implicated in the deaths of key members of targeted organizations through the use of such tactics as inciting shootouts between organizations and local police departments and using infiltrators and provocateurs.

COINTELPRO-SWP was initiated in 1961, largely because of philosophical similarities between the SWP and the Communist Party. However, covert surveillance activities of the SWP were documented at least 20 years before COINTELPRO was initiated, and as many as five years after COINTELPRO officially dissolved. FBI informants operating within the SWP focused on monitoring and neutralizing SWP influence on the Vietnam War antiwar movement, the civil rights movement, and groups opposing U.S. foreign policy. Efforts were also made through COINTELPRO activities to raise public skepticism of the SWP or, in the FBI's own words, to "alert the public to the fact that the SWP is not just another socialist group but follows the revolutionary principles of Marx, Lenin, and Engels" (Churchill and Vander Wall, 2002: 49–50).

The federal civil rights case *Socialist Workers Party v. Attorney General* documented that the FBI amassed 10 million pages of surveillance records on the SWP through illegal means. The FBI paid an estimated 1,600 informants $1,680,592 and used 20,000 days of wiretaps to undercut the SWP's influence on mainstream Americans.

COINTELPRO-Black Nationalist-Hate Groups began in 1967. According to FBI files, the purpose of the operation was "to expose, disrupt, misdirect, discredit, or otherwise neutralize the activities of black nationalist, hate-type organizations and groupings, their leadership, spokesmen, membership, and supporters, and to counter their propensity for violence and civil disorder" (Davis, 1992: 44). The original memoranda delivered to 23 FBI field offices identified the Southern Christian Leadership Conference, the Student Nonviolent Coordinating Committee, the Revolutionary Action Movement, the Deacons for Defense and Justice, the Congress of Racial Equality, and the Nation of Islam as primary targets. Individuals listed included Stokely Carmichael, H. Rap Brown, Elijah Muhammad, and Maxwell Stanford.

Within a year of its inception, COINTELPRO-Black Nationalist-Hate Groups was expanded to 41 field offices, and the scope, according to the memoranda, was to (1) prevent the coalition of militant black nationalist groups; (2) prevent the rise of a black messiah; (3) neutralize black nationalist groups before they became violent; (4) prevent groups from achieving respectability among the "responsible Negro community" and the white community; and (5) prevent the groups from recruiting young people (Davis, 1992: 44).

Martin Luther King, Jr., in particular, was subjected to an intense and relentless campaign to marginalize his effectiveness as a civil rights leader. The FBI maintained surveillance on Dr. King's home telephone, Southern Christian Leadership Conference headquarters, and the homes and offices of Dr. King's advisers. When all attempts to find evidence of

Dr. King engaging in illegal or subversive activities failed, the FBI focused their attention on his personal life. According to the FBI's domestic intelligence division chief, the agency sought to spur a separation between Dr. King and his wife to damage King's credibility. An FBI official described Dr. King's famous "I Have a Dream" speech as a "demagogic speech," and called Dr. King, "the most dangerous Negro of the future in this Nation" (U.S. Senate, "Political Abuse," 1976). FBI files also revealed preparations being made to seek a more acceptable person "to assume the role of leadership of the Negro people when King has been completely discredited" (U.S. Senate, "Political Abuse," 1976). Although the Black Panther Party (BPP) was not included in the first two memoranda, by November 1968, a letter to selected field offices ordered "imaginative and hard-hitting counterintelligence measures aimed at crippling the BPP" (Churchill and Vander Wall, 2002: 124–25). In January 1969, the program against the BPP was expanded to become one of the most extensive COINTELPRO initiatives on record.

In one of the final COINTELPRO-Black Nationalist-Hate Groups operations, the FBI recruited local police officers to conduct a raid on the Republic of New Africa (RNA) headquarters in Jackson, Mississippi. In the ensuing gun battle, an FBI agent was wounded and a Jackson police officer was killed. Dr. Imari Obadele, RNA president, was arrested and detained in federal prison for five years.

COINTELPRO-New Left, started in October 1968 largely in response to the antiwar movement among young Americans and a rise in student demonstrations across the United States. According to FBI memoranda, the purpose of COINTELPRO-New Left was to "expose, disrupt, and otherwise neutralize" (Churchill and Vander Wall, 2002: 165–66) the activities of New Left organizations, their leadership, and supporters. Under COINTELPRO-New Left, police brutality against student demonstrations was justified. Specific efforts were initiated to increase campus administrators' tolerance and acceptance of student injuries resulting from demonstrations, riots, and other confrontations with police officers.

According to COINTELPRO-New Left files, the FBI initiated formal tactics designed to depict the New Left movement as sexually promiscuous youth with proclivities for substance abuse. Tactics included having members arrested on drug charges and using cartoons, photographs, and anonymous letters to mock the New Left agenda.

On March 8, 1971, a group called the Citizens Commission to Investigate the FBI broke into a small FBI office in Media, Pennsylvania, and stole hundreds of classified documents. The stolen documents detailed the widespread surveillance of thousands of individuals and organizations. The Citizens Commission to Investigate the FBI photocopied the files and circulated them to legislators and the media. By April 1971, Sen. Edward Kennedy called for Hoover's resignation, which led to Hoover dismantling COINTELPRO amid enormous public scrutiny.

Carl Stern, an NBC newsperson, noticed the word "COINTELPRO" at the top of one of the documents, but did not find out the meaning until after Hoover died in 1972. Between 1973 and 1976, Stern used the Freedom of Information Act to sue the FBI, an effort that resulted in the disclosure of COINTELPRO operations.

The mid-1970s post-Watergate congressional hearings further exposed the abuses of the COINTELPRO period. The testimony led President Jimmy Carter to issue an executive order to tighten investigative guidelines and protect civil liberties. However, in the 1980s, when President Ronald Reagan reignited the Cold War, he loosened post-Watergate restrictions on the FBI and pardoned former bureau officials convicted of COINTELPRO-related crimes.

Ivory Toldson

See also

Black Nationalism; Hate Groups in America; Police Brutality

Further Reading:

Churchill, Ward, and Jim Vander Wall. *The COINTELPRO Papers: Documents from the FBI's Secret Wars against Dissent in the United States.* Boston: South End Press, 2002.

Davis, James Kirkpatrick. *Spying on America: The FBI's Domestic Counterintelligence Program.* New York: Praeger, 1992.

FBI. *COINTELPRO—Black Nationalist Hate Groups.* 1967.

U.S. Congress. *House Committee on Internal Security Hearings on Domestic Intelligence Operations for Internal Security Purposes.* 93rd Cong., 2d sess., 1974.

U.S. Senate, Select Committee to Study Government Operations. "COINTELPRO: The FBI's Covert Action Programs Against American Citizens." *Supplementary Detailed Staff Reports on Intelligence Activities and the Rights of Americans: Book III, Final Report,* April 23 (under authority of the order of April 14), 1976. http://www.icdc.com/~paulwolf/cointelpro/churchfinalreportIIIa.htm.

U.S. Senate, Select Committee to Study Government Operations. "COINTELPRO: The FBI's Covert Action Program to Destroy the Black Panther Party." *Supplementary Detailed Staff Reports on Intelligence Activities and the Rights of Americans: Book III, Final Report*, April 23 (under authority of the order of April 14), 1976. http://www.icdc.com/~paulwolf/cointelpro/churchfinalreportIIIc.htm.

U.S. Senate, Select Committee to Study Government Operations. "Political Abuse of Intelligence Information." *Intelligence Activities and the Rights of Americans: Book II, Final Report*, April 26 (legislative day, April 14), 1976. http://www.icdc.com/~paulwolf/cointelpro/churchfinalreportIIce.htm.

Wolf, Paul, Noam Chomsky, and Howard Zinn. *COINTELPRO*. Presented to U.N. High Commissioner for Human Rights, 2001.

Cold War

One feature of American standing in the Cold War was the argument that democratic capitalism represented a better world order than Soviet-style communism. Racism and Jim Crow undercut that claim. American leaders found it difficult to attack Soviet injustices and demand equality and the rule of law worldwide when African Americans endured systematic segregation throughout much of the nation. Facing Soviet propaganda that declaimed such hypocrisy, and fearful it would alter the status of the Cold War enabling the Soviets to lure African, Asian, and Middle Eastern states into their orbit, American politicians made halting efforts against Jim Crow and racial inequality. The Cold War thus acted as one factor influencing politicians to support domestic racial reform. At the same time, the Cold War limited the framework of those reforms. The focus for politicians was as much diplomatic as domestic, so symbolism that undercut Soviet rhetoric often was favored over substantive reforms that actually attacked segregation. Over the course of two decades, the Cold War thus both constrained and encouraged the fight against Jim Crow.

The impact of domestic racial issues on the global scene arose during World War II, when the Germans and Japanese made note of racial conflict in America. The segregation of the U.S. Army, violence at Southern encampments between African American soldiers and local whites, and the internment of Japanese Americans all served as fodder for the Axis. The Japanese and Germans used these issues as propaganda designed to destroy the morale of African American soldiers. Those propaganda efforts had little impact on the battlefield, but when the soldiers returned from overseas, many began to demand the democracy at home for which they had fought abroad. Most Southern states determined to prevent such a domestic revolution, and reinforced the already entrenched system of Jim Crow.

The Soviet Union, the nation's new enemy, readily picked up on the domestic racism and growing desire of African Americans to oppose it, and used both as propaganda against the United States. The administration of President Harry S. Truman quickly realized the danger of such propaganda. In 1946, Secretary of State Dean Acheson issued a study of the damage domestic racism had on American diplomacy. In 1947, Truman's Presidential Committee on Civil Rights issued a report entitled *To Secure These Rights*, in which it argued that the nation needed to address civil rights issues not simply because discrimination was morally wrong, but because of the damage done to foreign relations.

Truman agreed with these assessments and, in public speeches, continually stressed the need for civil rights reform as a part of the nation's Cold War struggle. While he occasionally invoked morality, Truman consistently placed civil rights within the international arena. That placement proved especially prophetic when dignitaries from developing countries visiting the United States encountered American-style racism. In 1947, Mahatma Gandhi's physician was barred from a restaurant. In November of that year Haiti's Secretary of Agriculture François Georges traveled to Georgia for a conference. Although he had a reservation, the hotel refused to allow him to room or to dine with his fellow conference attendees. Georges returned to Haiti rather than endure the indignity. The foreign press railed against such outrages, and the nation's moral standing sank.

African American leaders viewed such treatment, and the mingling of civil rights with diplomacy, as an opportunity. In 1947, W.E.B. Du Bois authored a document entitled *An Appeal to the World*, which the National Association for the Advancement of Colored People (NAACP) issued to the United Nations (UN). In it, Du Bois argued that Mississippi, not the Soviet Union, threatened the United States, and that Theodore Bilbo (former governor and U.S. senator from Mississippi) and John Rankin (U.S. congressman from Mississippi) were greater dangers than Stalin. When additional

African Americans spoke out, the State Department revoked their passports and worked with host countries to cancel international appearances. Thus, Paul Robeson, Richard Wright, James Baldwin, and Josephine Baker faced harassment and interruptions in their careers as a result of their efforts to protest a Jim Crow America.

Fearful that this domestic unrest and the furor over the treatment of diplomats would aid the Soviets, the Truman administration issued a rebuttal to Du Bois's essay and sent African American leader and executive secretary of the Council on African Affairs Max Yergen on an international goodwill tour. Truman also appointed the first African American ambassador when he stationed Edward Dudley in Liberia. When such efforts failed to improve the nation's image abroad, Truman made more substantive attempts to help African Americans. In 1948, he desegregated the military, and in the years leading up to the *Brown v. Board of Education* Supreme Court decision, his Justice Department filed numerous amicus curiae briefs that pointed out the negative impact segregation had on the nation's ability to wage the Cold War.

Despite these achievements, in 1949, the American ambassador to the Soviet Union noted that the Soviet press continued to pound away on the topics of segregation, racial violence, and the lack of social equality. The continuation of this racial injustice, the Soviets explained, proved that the U.S. Constitution did not guarantee liberty, but rather enabled capitalists to exploit racial divisions for their own economic gain. Faced with such enduring criticism, in 1950 Massachusetts Senator Henry Cabot Lodge Jr. dubbed racism America's diplomatic Achilles' heel.

In 1951, the United States Information Agency (USIA) created a pamphlet for American ambassadors designed to help them depict American race relations in a positive manner. Entitled *The Negro in American Life*, this work portrayed the nation's racial history as one of redemption. The pamphlet did not hide the legacy of racial strife, but rather depicted it openly as a means of showing how far the nation had advanced. It also made clear that only the openness of American society allowed for such a frank depiction of the nation's past. The pamphlet thus created an overly optimistic picture of race relations that served to offset the overly negative image created by Soviet propaganda.

The outbreak of the Korean War made the claim of racial improvement difficult to sustain. During the war, the Soviets continued to denounce the United States for its segregation, and rhetorically asked how the nation could force black soldiers to fight for the freedom of foreigners when they had no freedom at home. Domestic events helped prove this point, as in July 1951, when 3,000 people rioted to prevent the integration of a Cicero, Illinois, neighborhood. By this point, ordinary Americans realized the damage such events had on diplomacy, and one citizen wrote to the *New York Times* to suggest that every rioter deserved an Order of Lenin for the harm they caused the nation.

The Truman administration responded to these wartime developments with a new propaganda campaign that moved a step beyond the USIA report. The Voice of America (VOA), American diplomats, and federal writings admitted that the task of racial reconciliation was not complete and that segregation remained, but tried to depict the racial issue as a sectional problem, not an American one. Racism, in other words, was not a deeply held American ideal, but rather a Southern flaw that could be corrected. As a part of this new campaign, Nobel Peace Prize winner Ralph Bunche and Edith Sampson, a member of the American delegation to the UN, travelled abroad extensively to sell the concept and shore up the nation's image.

The Truman administration thus sought to undercut Soviet propaganda with a few well-placed reforms and a mass of counterpropaganda. President Dwight D. Eisenhower had a similar path in mind when he succeeded Truman in 1953. Eisenhower had little interest in civil rights and actually testified against desegregating the military. At the same time, he understood the damage racism inflicted on America's international image and recognized the need for at least symbolic improvements. Thus, between 1953 and 1955, the president desegregated the public areas and schools in Washington, D.C. Although a step forward, Eisenhower took it for the image desegregation provided rather than for larger moral or ethical principles.

The same was true when the U.S. Supreme Court issued the *Brown v. Board of Education* decision in May 1954. The Eisenhower administration quickly used it to counter Soviet propaganda. The VOA announced the decision in 34 languages worldwide, implied that it had ended segregation forever, and suggested that race relations thereafter would be perfect. The *Brown* decision did not end racial strife in America, however, and the Soviets continued to pummel the nation with propaganda that focused on the white backlash known as "massive resistance."

While American diplomats pointed to the *Brown* decision and the peaceful settlement of the 1955 Montgomery Bus Boycott as evidence that the political system was working to end Jim Crow, the refusal of Southern states to desegregate and the continuing racial discord remained problematic. The Emmett Till case, in particular, created a powerfully negative international reaction and served as evidence of the nation's dilemma. NAACP chairman Channing Tobias understood as much when he claimed the Till jury deserved a Soviet medal for its role in undercutting the nation's standing. A year later, in 1956, the failure of Autherine Lucy to integrate the University of Alabama provided additional fodder for communist propaganda as yet more evidence of "massive resistance."

The most problematic development during the Eisenhower administration emerged in 1957 with the Little Rock Nine crisis. The Soviets quickly broadcast news of the violence surrounding the effort of the nine African American children to integrate Central High School. The Soviet paper *Pravda* carried a headline declaring "Troops advance against children!" while *Izvestia* described the event as a "tragedy" that displayed the "façade" of American democracy. The Soviets also mockingly included Little Rock in the itinerary of cities over which Sputnik orbited. The mass coverage led the American magazine *Confidential* to suggest mockingly that Arkansas governor Orval Faubus was a communist agent, since his actions had provided the Soviets with such a useful Cold War tool.

This international outrage was one of the reasons Eisenhower, who was loath to intervene, finally did so. In his September 24, 1957, speech on the crisis, he made specific note of the damage events in Little Rock had on the nation's standing and the use being made of them by the communists. Once Eisenhower sent in federal troops, he ordered diplomats to explain the crisis as an aberration that was being attended to by the full power of the federal government. They were to present Little Rock within the context of continued gains for African Americans and as a part of the ongoing struggle for racial equality, a struggle supported by the Eisenhower administration. The Soviets were unconvinced, however, and Radio Moscow presciently noted that the president and American diplomats seemed more interested in the international impact of Little Rock than with the underlying causes of the crisis.

Beyond these domestic issues, Eisenhower faced an additional diplomatic reality that forced him to confront American racism. Soviet Premier Nikita Khrushchev sought to extend communist influence into the nonaligned world and, by the late 1950s, was using Jim Crow to woo African, Asian, and Middle Eastern nations to the communist fold. In 1957, Illinois Senator Paul Douglas responded to this Soviet effort by explaining that not only was every riot, bombing, and racial clash immoral and antithetical to the nation's founding, but each crisis assisted Khrushchev in his effort to broaden the Soviet sphere of influence. Douglas was not alone, and the fear that the nonaligned world might accept communist guidance because of American racism permeated the nation.

In spite of that fear, Eisenhower did little to affect civil rights and left a festering domestic and diplomatic situation for President John F. Kennedy. The new president considered the need to win the Cold War as his primary mission, but he also understood that the Soviets would continue to use racial unrest in their effort to win support in the colored community of the world. Kennedy thus determined to control and moderate the civil rights movement so it did not interfere with his diplomacy. Proof of this came when he backed down from a campaign pledge to desegregate the National Guard. Faced with a crisis in Berlin in 1961, Kennedy refused to order integration, and explained that he could not risk a "social revolution" in the military while he was on the brink of nuclear war with the Soviet Union.

The violence surrounding the Freedom Rides of 1961 further threatened his control. Kennedy was upset with the rides because he was on the verge of a summit meeting with Soviet leader Khrushchev in Vienna. Kennedy feared that his already weakened position, due to the Bay of Pigs fiasco, would be weakened further by the violence in Anniston and Birmingham, Alabama. When the rides continued into Mississippi, the Kennedy administration convinced Senator James Eastland to find a peaceful solution by warning of the dangers of sending a weak, young president to the Vienna summit. Mississippi officials acquiesced to Kennedy's wishes and arrested the riders without violence, thus allowing Kennedy to meet Khrushchev without this millstone around his neck. The damage had already been done, however, as Soviet papers played up the Freedom Rides as further proof that racial violence was a way of life in America.

In 1962, Kennedy faced another threat with the effort of James Meredith to integrate the University of Mississippi. In his address to the nation in the midst of the crisis, Kennedy appealed to the citizens of Mississippi for calm by noting that the eyes of the world were on them. When his appeal failed and he was forced to send in federal marshals, Kennedy, like Eisenhower before him, wanted to display to the world that the federal government would go to great lengths to enforce the law of the land. Kennedy thus hoped to control the story so that the enforcement of federal authority would overwhelm the images of racial violence. After the fact, administration officials believed they had achieved this goal, and claimed that during the ensuing Cuban Missile Crisis, several African nations had refused to allow Soviet planes to refuel on their territory due to Kennedy's handling of events in Mississippi.

Events closer to Washington caused Kennedy further concerns, however, and laid the foundation for a potentially more damaging international spectacle. With the explosion of independence movements in Africa in the early 1960s, large numbers of African diplomats appeared in Washington, D.C., as ambassadors, and in New York City as representatives to the United Nations. Many of those diplomats experienced great difficulty finding acceptable accommodations in the D.C. area, and the White House soon learned that only eight of 200 apartments available for rent in the capital were open to blacks. As Kennedy feared, the Soviets exploited the issue by offering to rent apartments for African ambassadors who might otherwise have been refused. At the same time, many African diplomats faced the humiliation of being denied service at hotels and restaurants on Route 40 between Washington and New York City. The problem came to a head in June 1961 when Ambassador Adam Malik Sow of Chad was denied service and then physically abused at a Howard Johnson's along Route 40. Fearing the Soviet Union again would exploit this treatment to win the support of African nations, Kennedy searched for a solution. He first angrily asked why African ambassadors simply did not fly from Washington to New York to avoid the problem. More usefully, he created a Special Protocol Service Section of the State Department. Led by Pedro Sanjuan, the section's goal was to convince restaurant and hotel owners along the route to desegregate. Sanjaun visited every restaurant on Route 40, but after nine months, fewer than half of the 70 restaurants had complied. Only in January 1963 did Maryland pass a law forcing desegregation of public accommodations, thus alleviating the problem.

Violence in Alabama, however, soon subsumed this accomplishment. In response to the Southern Christian Leadership Conference's effort to demonstrate in Birmingham, Sheriff "Bull" Connor called out attack dogs and water hoses and arrested thousands of peaceful demonstrators. The images offered the Soviets yet another propaganda tool. According to USIA studies, Soviet radio spent one-fifth of its news coverage in late April and early May 1963 on the violence in Alabama. Not only did Birmingham offer the Soviets an opportunity, it also potentially threatened America's standing in Africa. In May 1963, leaders of the various African states met in Addis Ababa, Ethiopia, to create a series of resolutions setting a framework for the continent's standing in the world. On the second day of the conference Ugandan prime minister Milton Obote issued an open letter to President Kennedy protesting the treatment of blacks in Alabama. He tied the treatment of African Americans to imperialism and colonialism, and portrayed the American civil rights struggle as part of the larger worldwide battle for the rights of people of color. Many in the Kennedy administration feared this letter would lead African nations to break relations with the United States and potentially turn to the Soviets. No such break occurred, but the fear once again reinforced the connection between civil rights and the Cold War.

Realizing that his government simply had been reactive to events that threatened the nation's standing, in the summer of 1963, Kennedy became proactive and began work on a civil rights bill. In trying to sell the bill to Congress, the administration noted that the Soviets continued to use racial issues in the global struggle and that passage of the bill would provide a diplomatic benefit. As Congress debated the bill, the March on Washington occurred. Kennedy knew this march posed dangers, but also offered a propaganda opportunity. If the march was peaceful, it would offer further proof of the strength of the American system, which allowed people the free expression of their opinions. When the march did go off peacefully, Kennedy encouraged diplomats to compare the United States, where the government allowed protest, with the Soviets, who brutally crushed all dissent. The problem was that the civil rights bill remained tied up in Congress, and only days after the march, a bomb explosion at a Birmingham church killed four black girls. Although Kennedy met with Martin Luther King, Jr. and issued a statement denouncing the attack, the violence and the failure to achieve civil rights legislation again demonstrated that the struggle against Jim Crow was not over.

For Kennedy, the struggle was more about the Cold War than about moral integrity, yet his administration oversaw a number of civil rights victories. After the Kennedy assassination, Lyndon B. Johnson carried on and expanded his predecessor's policies. He also carried on the practice of viewing civil rights through the prism of diplomacy. That view helped Johnson exploit the landmark Civil Rights Act of 1964. Soviet papers covered the congressional debate over the act, and noted the Southern intransigence with glee. Once the act passed, however, the Johnson administration used it against the Soviets as evidence of the nation's racial progress.

Tragically, events soon threatened to subsume that progress once again. The June 1964 murders of Freedom Summer activists Andrew Goodman, James Chaney, and Michael Schwerner in Neshoba County, Mississippi, drew massive international coverage. More trouble erupted in July, when racial violence exploded in New York City. For a decade, American efforts to counter Soviet propaganda had explained racism as a regional problem. The riot, which began after a white police officer shot a black teenager in Harlem, proved the fallacy of that claim. To make things worse, civil rights activists sent a letter to the UN asking it to bring the issue of violence before the Security Council and suggesting the use of UN peacekeeping forces in Mississippi. At the same time, Malcolm X appealed to the international community to pressure the United States toward racial reform. The USIA tried to depict the violence and the African American protest to it within the context of continued racial progress, but the world was skeptical.

The spasm of racial confrontation continued in March 1965 in Selma, Alabama. Surprisingly, the violence at the Edmund Pettis Bridge received only minimal worldwide coverage. USIA studies contended that the reasons were the passage of the Civil Rights Act of 1964 and Johnson's open and uncompromising promise to bring civil rights to the nation. According to a USIA report, earlier foreign editorials had condemned the United States for allowing racial violence to occur. By 1965, however, the international community condemned the violence, but not the United States. As a result, instead of seeing Selma as a symptom of national pathology, the world purview was that it was the final spasm of white racism. In other words, racial strife no longer threatened the nation's standing. Instead, the international community acknowledged the American position that the federal government supported equality, that racism was an aberration not part of mainstream society, and that democracy was the system best suited to facilitate racial reconciliation. Even the Soviets accepted this changed paradigm. The passage of the Voting Rights Act in 1965 offered the United States another opportunity to enhance this new worldview, but only five days after Johnson signed the bill into law, more racial violence erupted with the Watts riots and the onset of the "long, hot summers." Despite the urban chaos, the new paradigm held. The connection between domestic racial issues and international affairs thus had diminished considerably, despite the obvious fact that serious racial problems remained. In 1966, the USIA explained that this diminished reaction did not mean the world had changed its view on how the nation treated African Americans. Most people worldwide continued to hold a negative impression of the nation's racial issues. What had changed was that this impression no longer affected the overall image of the United States. Racism had become a blot, rather than the defining national characteristic.

Proof that the nexus between the Cold War and Jim Crow had collapsed for good was more evident by 1968. The assassination of Martin Luther King, Jr. and the ensuing violence received wide international coverage, with the Soviet press contending that the nation was on the verge of civil war. The focus of the foreign press, including the Soviets, however, was on the issue of violence in America, not race. The same was true with international coverage of the Vietnam War. Unlike the coverage of the Korean War, by 1968 the foreign focus on the war in Vietnam was the nation's militarism rather than the disproportionally high number of African American soldiers who saw combat or the fact that the United States was once again fighting a people of color.

This changed international perspective, combined with détente and the thawing of the Cold War under Nixon, gave the federal government less incentive to push for racial reform. At the same time, the major legal issues had been addressed, and the goal became implementation. Struggles over how to implement racial equality found little international interest, and by the end of the 1960s, the world abided by American claims of racial improvement.

Although the impact of the Cold War on the struggle against Jim Crow waned by the late 1960s, during the previous 20 years the two issues were linked intimately. The need to address foreign criticism served as one powerful factor in pushing the federal government to support civil rights reform. Once that criticism waned, however, federal support for change diminished as well. The Cold War thus helped instigate the campaign to end American segregation, but it also helped constrain the depth and breadth of that campaign according to diplomatic needs.

GREGORY S. TAYLOR

See also
Communist Party

Further Reading:

Borstelmann, Thomas. *The Cold War and the Color Line: American Race Relations in the Global Arena*. Cambridge, MA: Harvard University Press, 2001.

Bryant, Nick. *The Bystander: John F. Kennedy and the Struggle for Black Equality*. New York: Basic Books, 2006.

Dudziak, Mary. *Cold War Civil Rights: Race and the Image of American Democracy*. Princeton, NJ: Princeton University Press, 2000.

Mann, Robert. *The Walls of Jericho: Lyndon Johnson, Hubert Humphrey, Richard Russell, and the Struggle for Civil Rights*. New York: Harcourt Brace, 1996.

Nichols, David. *A Matter of Justice: Eisenhower and the Beginning of the Civil Rights Revolution*. New York: Simon and Schuster, 2007.

College Admission, Discrimination in

Higher education is now and has long been a gateway to opportunity in the United States. However, access to this gateway has been constrained by many waves of discriminatory action at colleges and universities throughout the centuries, on the basis of socioeconomic status, religion, and gender as well as race. The earliest colleges all required a test of Christian religious faith for admission. The first not to require such a test was Brown University, founded in 1766. For many years, significant income was required to pay tuition costs at most colleges and universities unless an individual student was sponsored by a philanthropist. Individual colleges did not institute financial-aid systems until just before the 20th century, and mass financial aid was only made possible by the GI Bill in the 1940s. Women were denied formal education at the level of men's colleges until at least 1814, when Emma Willard opened the Middlebury Female Seminary in Connecticut.

The first integrated college to officially and knowingly admit African American students, Oberlin College, did so in the early 1850s, though undoubtedly African American students had graduated from colleges by passing as white. This method became the impetus for admission of African American students to other colleges and universities as the schools saw individual students achieve academic success and graduate, and decided to open their doors to a few, selected others. Cheyney University, in Pennsylvania, founded in 1837, was the first institution of higher education founded specifically for the education of blacks. It was not an easy path to integration. The early African American students admitted were held to extremely high standards and few were admitted. Universities also began admitting small numbers of Asian and Latino/a students, at first as international students. Later, students of these racial backgrounds who had grown up in the United States were admitted to college, but they were often still treated as foreigners.

Later, as increasing numbers of Southern and Eastern European immigrants, including large numbers of Jews and Catholics, entered the United States, many universities and colleges instituted quota systems to ensure that their student bodies would remain primarily "white" and Christian. Specific percentage limits, ranging from 20 percent at Columbia in the early 1940s to 6 percent at Dartmouth in 1934, capped the number of Jewish students who would be admitted, regardless of their qualifications. Even after these systems were abolished, quota systems on the basis of geography (often specifically limiting the number of students who could be admitted from the New York metropolitan area) continued to discriminate against the ethnic groups concentrated in that area, especially Jews. Methods for determining the Jewish origin of applicants included requiring the attachment of photographs to the application, specific questions concerning race and religion, interviews, and restricted scholarships.

Affirmative Action, University of Michigan Ruling on (2003)

In the first ruling on affirmative action in university admission decisions in 25 years, the U.S. Supreme Court ruled on June 23, 2003, that race can be used in university admission procedures to achieve racial diversity in college classrooms. But the narrowly divided court also ruled that factoring race into admission decisions must be "narrowly tailored" to harm as few people as possible.

The University of Michigan faced two different but parallel lawsuits. One is *Grutter v. Bollinger*, involving the university's law school and Barbara Grutter. Grutter, a white woman who applied for the law school and was rejected, later found that there were African Americans and ethnic minorities who were admitted with admission scores lower than her own. She felt it to be an illegal discrimination and sued. She won the first round in U.S. District Court but lost in the Sixth Circuit Court of Appeals. The Supreme Court upheld the decision by a vote of 5–4. Justice Sandra Day O'Connor, who cast the deciding vote, acknowledged that the United States still needs affirmative action but hoped the days were numbered.

In the other case, *Gratz v. Bollinger*, the 6–3 majority ruled that the points system violated equal protection provisions of the Constitution. The University of Michigan had an affirmative action policy in undergraduate admissions that automatically awarded 20 points, one-fifth of the points needed to guarantee admission, to every single "underrepresented minority" applicant, based solely on race. The Court decided that the policy was "not narrowly tailored" to achieve the interest in educational diversity. Chief Justice William Rehnquist, representing the majority opinion, declared that while race can be used as a factor in admission decisions, it must not be a "deciding factor."

Dong-Ho Cho

The U.S. Congress passed Title VI of the 1964 Civil Rights Act, barring federal funding of universities and colleges that discriminate on the basis of race. As almost all colleges and universities receive some federal funding, including at a minimum student financial aid or faculty research grants, this sort of discrimination is illegal. Other, more subtle forms of racial discrimination can continue; for instance, making it easier for students who have relatives who attended the college before it was racially integrated to be admitted or preferentially admitting students who have been involved in specific extracurricular activities that are primarily engaged in by white students (such as the game of squash), as well as the geographical quota systems already discussed. Additionally, many universities and colleges rely significantly on the SAT and similar tests in their admission processes. ETS statistics show that there is a clear racial gap in scores on the SATs, which put African Americans at a disadvantage.

A new debate over discrimination in admissions has arisen more recently. In the wake of the civil rights legislation and movement of the 1950s and 1960s, many universities and colleges instituted policies that have come to be known as affirmative action. These policies vary: explicit quota systems ensuring that a certain percentage of students of color will be admitted; processes whereby students of color receive some additional points in the scoring of their application; lowering test-score thresholds; and considering past racial disadvantage are a few examples. They are described as a way to make up for the legacy of past discrimination and resulted in significant increases in African American and Latino/a students at many colleges and universities. They have, however, been the source of significant controversy for decades. For instance, some white students have claimed that affirmative action policies constitute reverse racism against white students, who are being supplanted by underqualified students of color, though most affirmative action policies only admit students who meet some minimum qualifications to which all students are held. Some public universities have recently been forced to abandon their affirmative action policies, which has led to precipitous declines in the number of students of color, especially African Americans.

Asian American students have been left in a marginal position with respect to affirmative action: in some colleges and universities they are considered to be in the same group as African Americans and Latino/as as beneficiaries of

Regents of the University of California v. Bakke (1978)

The decision in the 1978 U.S. Supreme Court case *Regents of the University of California v. Bakke* represented the first time that the Court upheld the concept of affirmative action and its goal of remedying past discrimination against members of minority groups and women. When Allan Bakke's application to the University of California, Davis, Medical School was denied a second time, Bakke, a white man, charged that he had been passed over in favor of less-qualified African American applicants. Claiming he was a victim of reverse discrimination, Bakke argued that the decision to deny him admission was based solely on his race, since his academic credentials were better than some African Americans who were admitted to the UC Davis Medical School. Bakke filed a suit against the Regents of University of California, claiming that his constitutional right to equal protection under the Fourteenth Amendment had been violated.

During the 1970s, the UC Davis Medical School employed a dual admissions process: a regular admissions program in which applicants with a grade-point average of 2.5 or lower on a scale of 4 were automatically rejected, and a special admissions program to increase the representation among the student body of minorities and other "disadvantaged" groups. Special-admissions applicants did not need to have maintained a 2.5 GPA. Of the 100 spaces available in each class, 16 were reserved for special-admissions applicants. The Court ruled by 5–4 that the use of quotas in affirmative action programs was unconstitutional and, hence, not permissible. As a result, Bakke was admitted to the medical school, and he graduated in 1992. However, writing the decision of a closely divided Supreme Court, Justice Lewis F. Powell (who died in August 1998) also held that race, along with other factors, could be used as a "plus" factor in admissions decisions. Interestingly, in a subsequent law suit filed against the University of Michigan in 2003, the U.S. Supreme Court offered a similar ruling that rejected the university's undergraduate admission system based on a quota for minority students but accepted its use of race as one criterion for admission to the law school.

Tarry Hum

programs aimed at all students of color, while other colleges and universities see the growing numbers of Asian American students as a reason to remove them from affirmative action programs. However, Asian Americans do not benefit from the removal of affirmative action programs in the way whites do. Preferences for legacy students (students whose parents or grandparents have attended the school) and certain types of extracurricular activities are a hardship for Asian American applicants. Additionally, emphasis on outstanding English skills can be a challenge for immigrant students and the children of immigrants. All of these factors resulted in several high-profile cases in the 1980s of Asian American students accusing universities of having anti-Asian American quota systems similar to those experienced by Jews in the early part of the 20th century.

Mikaila Mariel Lemonik Arthur

See also

Affirmative Action; *Berea College v. Kentucky* (1908); Education and African Americans; Educational Achievement Gap; Ethnic Retention and School Performance; UC Berkeley Bake Sale

Further Reading:

Synott, Marcia Graham. *The Half-Opened Door: Discrimination and College Admissions at Harvard, Yale, and Princeton.* Westport, CT: Greenwood Press, 1979.

Takagi, Dana Y. *The Retreat from Race: Asian-American Admissions and Racial Politics.* New Brunswick, NJ: Rutgers University Press, 1992.

Wechsler, Harold S. *The Qualified Student: A History of Selective College Admission in America.* New York: John Wiley, 1977.

Color-Blind Racism

In 1963, Martin Luther King, Jr., gave his now famous "I Have a Dream" speech, which predicts that one day people will not be judged based on skin color. As the overt racism of the 1960s has faded, many have turned to King's speech as a foundation for color-blind principles—to not acknowledge or "see" race. Furthermore, some believe that any policies that address race, such as affirmative action or

Covert versus Overt Discrimination

Overt discrimination, sometimes called "old-fashioned" discrimination, refers to public or private conscious attitudes and behaviors intended to harm or damage a person or a group of people of color or to define people of color as inferior to whites and therefore less entitled to society's benefits. The discrimination typical of the Jim Crow era, such as lynchings, the use of racial epithets, the enforcement of laws designed to prevent minorities from voting, and terrorist acts by white supremacist organizations, represents discrimination as most individuals understand it. These acts, which constitute overt discrimination, have come to define what discrimination is.

By contrast, covert discrimination is hidden and much less public than overt discrimination. Examples of covert discrimination include cultural and religious marginalization, color-blind racism, and tokenism. Covert discrimination, a form of modern racism, is often not recognized by members of the majority group as being discriminatory. It is disguised with language that downplays the clearly racial aspects of the discrimination, and it is rationalized by invocation of or reliance on nonracial explanations more acceptable in the broader society. The existence of covert discrimination is therefore more difficult to prove than are acts of overt racism. In contemporary society, covert discrimination is more commonplace.

KHYATI JOSHI

integration efforts, are inherently bad because they take race into account and therefore violate color-blind ideals. The problem with this logic is that race continues to be a central organizing principle of society, and raced-based inequalities persist. Thus, color-blind racism uses race-neutral rhetoric to defend white privilege, explain the racial hierarchy, and expunge whites from any responsibility to address racial inequality, all while making whites appear to be rational and nondiscriminatory.

Many theorists of race have used a version of the theory of color-blind racism in order to analyze and understand how contemporary racism operates. Anderson (2010) explains that people with strong color-blind attitudes place more blame on the individual, are less likely to support affirmative action, and have an increased fear of minorities. Forman (1997) states that people who espouse color-blind principles are likely to believe that the United States is a racial meritocracy, do not care about or notice race, believe racialized patterns of inequality are outcomes of individual or group-level deficiencies, and do not think anything systematic should be implemented to address racialized patterns of inequality. Gallagher (2003) also describes color-blind racism as the strategy used to emphasize individual merit while simultaneously ignoring structural conditions that benefit whites and disenfranchise blacks. In addition, Gallagher argues that race is consumed as a cultural marker (fashion, food, festivals) so that in a "postracial" era, race can be benignly consumed but not discussed. Bonilla-Silva (2010) defines color-blind racism by four "frames" (set ways of viewing and filtering information): abstract liberalism, naturalization, cultural racism, and minimization of racism. These four frames are used in complex combinations to justify white privilege and abdicate responsibility for racial inequality. In general, color-blind racism can be identified by how whites use principles of equality, individualism, merit, and equal opportunity to defend their position while simultaneously dismissing any claims of racial discrimination that people of color experience. Examples of color-blind racism include a belief in equal opportunity, which is available to everyone as long as one works hard enough; a belief that whatever "privileges" whites have are a consequence of hard work; a belief that slavery (and racism) was a long time ago so no one living today can be held accountable; and a belief that not paying attention to race is a more egalitarian way to live. These views could, potentially, be viewed as accurate and fair and not racist if it were not for the institutional discrimination that maintains wealth, education, residence, and employment gaps among whites and nonwhites.

Whites' attitudes after the civil rights movement have changed from overt discrimination, such as "Blacks should be segregated from whites," to covert discrimination, such as "Blacks don't work hard enough to do well." Since President Obama's election and the successes of black celebrities like Oprah and Jay-Z, it is increasingly difficult for some to understand how racism continues to be a barrier to upward mobility for people of color. Color-blind racism greatly aids in deconstructing this seeming paradox since it helps in understanding how: (a) the focus on achieving a race-neutral society prevents people from seeing and understanding racism; and (b) contemporary racism is difficult to see, understand, and legally combat. During Jim Crow racism, segregation was clearly observable and therefore could be countered in the court system; however, when people make claims to racism today they are criticized for "playing the race card." Thus, on the one side are those who claim that racism is in the past and talking about race is what actually keeps "the race problem" alive, while those on the other side argue that color-blind racism is the new way that the racial hierarchy is maintained.

Due to the covert and complex nature of color-blind racism and great opposition to discussing race, it is difficult to address contemporary racial discrimination. Via color-blind logic, many whites are (eagerly) ridding themselves of any culpability or responsibility while also appearing to have racial morality. The seductive logic of color-blind racism is particularly insidious and dangerous as a racial caste can emerge due to people's unwillingness to recognize racial discrimination or talk about race.

Hephzibah Strmic-Pawl

See also

Ideological Racism; Laissez-Faire Racism; Racism; Symbolic Racism; Systemic Racism

Further Reading:

Anderson, Kristin J. *Benign Bigotry: The Psychology of Subtle Prejudice.* Cambridge: Cambridge University Press, 2010.

Blake, John. "Are Whites Racially Oppressed?" *CNN U.S.* Last modified March 4, 2011. http://www.cnn.com/2010/US/12/21/white.persecution/index.html.

Bonilla-Silva, Eduardo. *Racism without Racists: Color-Blind Racism & Racial Inequality in Contemporary America*, 3rd ed. New York: Rowman & Littlefield Publishers, 2010.

Forman, Tyrone A. "Color-Blind Racism and Racial Indifference: The Role of Racial Apathy in Facilitating Enduring Inequalities." In *The Changing Terrain of Race and Ethnicity*, edited by Maria Krysan and Amanda E. Lewis, 43–66. New York: Russell Sage Foundation, 1997.

Gallagher, Charles. "Color-Blind Privilege: The Social and Political Functions of Erasing the Color Line in Post Race America." *Race, Gender & Class* 10 (2003): 1–17.

Omi, Michael, and Howard Winant. *Racial Formation in the United States: From the 1960s to the 1990s.* New York: Routledge, 1991.

Colored Farmers' Alliance (CFA)

The Colored Farmers' Alliance (CFA) was one of the largest black organizations in American history, with a membership of about 1 million—though this number is in dispute and difficult to verify. Indeed, one leading scholar argues that the number was probably close to 250,000. However, it does appear that the membership peaked from about 800,000 to 1,200,000 members. Evidence on the CFA is fragmentary at best, but it is clear that it had a large and active membership and a strong cadre of leaders who organized the black community in an attempt to improve the lot of African American farmers at the end of the 19th century, during a period of economic stagnation in the rural South. The CFA preached self-help and cooperation. The CFA existed from the late 1880s into the 1890s. The CFA was an independent organization connected to the Southern Farmers' Alliance—with a separate leadership and dues-paying members. Reflecting the times and the racism of whites, the two organizations did not formally unite with one another; rather, they would meet in separate conventions. However, the organizations would cooperate on economic matters—to help farmers, black and white. In addition, at the national level there was a great deal of communication and planning between the various groups.

The CFA formed in Texas in 1886, and its rank-and-file members were African Americans in the South who farmed their own land or more commonly were sharecroppers and tenants. The foundation of the CFA came at a farm in Lovelady in Houston County, Texas. The CFA quickly spread outwards across the South and, more often than not, it followed the rapid expansion of the Southern Alliance across Dixie. The CFA focused its recruiting and organizing activities in rural areas, such as the Black Belt, but exchanges also existed in Southern cities such as New Orleans, Mobile, Charleston, and Norfolk. The alliance emphasized both economic and political education for farmers at a time when farmers faced deteriorating conditions, such as rising freight costs, rising interest rates, the crop lien, declining prices for cash crops such as cotton, and debt peonage. These problems affected all small farmers, but African Americans faced even greater problems—fewer African Americans owned land, and those who did often had the poorest land. The overwhelming majority of black farmers either rented poor-quality farms at high prices or worked as sharecroppers. If this was not bad enough, to compound these problems, African Americans had to deal with racial injustices, discrimination in the prices of goods and availability of credit, and white hostility to success. Advocating "producerism"—that is, that the producer deserves the fruit of his or her work—the alliance quickly found an attentive audience and a massive following for its mission to improve the lives of the common farmer. The alliance was the last (and largest) in a long line of farming organizations in the second half of the 19th century, including the Grange and the Agricultural Wheel.

Traveling lecturers in the CFA educated black farmers on the need for economic cooperation to alleviate the worst effects of the farm crisis. For example, buying in bulk to offset high freight rates, using fertilizers and practicing modern farming techniques, as well as building exchanges where farmers could buy products at reduced costs, were all remedies advocated by the CFA. Indeed, in exchanges black and white farmers often cooperated with one another. The exchanges often failed, due to lack of money and poor planning, but the cooperative element installed a movement culture based on producerism that ultimately radicalized many farmers into independent political action. By early 1888, the CFA was so large that it needed to procure a federal charter, and after a convention at Lovelady, the Colored Farmers' National Alliance and Cooperative Union were born.

Not surprising, perhaps, the CFA also quickly entered the political realm. Although it began as a nonpartisan organization, the CFA voted and campaigned for politicians who were sensitive to the needs of farmers and who promised to effect change. At this time, the Bourbon Democrats largely ignored the pleas of small farmers and paid even less attention to the plight of black farmers. Still, the CFA educated and organized African Americans to use their votes effectively and strategically.

The success of the CFA in the Southern states reflected the nature of local politics and conditions on the ground as well as the activism of local leaders. For example, North Carolina witnessed a strong CFA due in part to the foundational work of the Knights of Labor and the indefatigable leadership of Walter Patillo. Patillo was a black Baptist minister from Granville County who quickly rose to position of lecturer and secretary of the North Carolina CFA with close associations with leading white Alliance leaders, such as state president Elias Carr. Patillo worked very hard to educate black farmers and organize them in local cooperatives and also in politics. It is highly probable that other such leaders and close relationships existed in other states in the South.

Reflecting the racism of the times, the national leader of the CFA was Richard M. Humphrey, a notable white Texas farmer. He was originally from South Carolina, but by the mid-1880s, he was a leading member of the alliance in Texas—he was present at the founding of the CFA in Lovelady in 1886. Humphrey was a Confederate veteran and Baptist preacher who built a career as an ally with black congregations in East Texas. Humphrey had a long history of political activism, running as a congressional Union Labor candidate in Texas. Although Humphrey was the titular head of the CFA, it appears that much of the local leadership held the power to effect change and increase membership. As the CFA grew, it absorbed other black farming groups including, in 1890, the Consolidated Alliance led by Andrew J. Carothers, another white leader from Texas.

Many white members of the Southern Farmers' Alliance held negative views of African Americans—most white Southerners at this time were racist and believed in the inferiority of blacks. In addition, many did not believe in black leadership and feared a return to black power and the days of Reconstruction. As a result, in several states, such as Alabama, Virginia, and North Carolina, the state leadership of the CFA was white. But in other states, such as Georgia, Louisiana, and Mississippi, the CFA leadership was black. For example, Frank Davis, the black leader of the CFA in Alabama, was well respected and held some power. Most of the local leaders within all the Southern states were African American, and they worked to organize black farmers as best they could.

In each state, the CFA organized suballiances at the local level. Although evidence at the local level is sparse, it does appear that the CFA followed the same organizational structure of the white alliance—it was a secret fraternal organization that welcomed women, met regularly, discussed issues facing farmers, and welcomed traveling alliance lecturers. The suballiances across the South organized local cooperatives and exchanges and attempted to improve the lot of the local farmers. However, perhaps in part to avoid white violence or reprisals, most of the local CFA activities were covert. Many cooperatives failed in economic terms, but they provided leadership opportunities in the black community and fostered a movement culture that aided in the politicization of the Black Belt in the 1890s.

As the CFA rapidly expanded in size and scope by the end of the 1880s, it faced increased hostility from entrenched Democrats who were both unsympathetic to the plight of farmers and opposed to African Americans. Economic and political unions between organized labor and farmers were ridiculed by Democrats. In some locations, Democrats attacked and even killed CFA leaders. The Mississippi Delta witnessed one such terrible incident. In addition, Republicans also opposed the formation of the alliance because they worried that the CFA would weaken the GOP in elections—this was a justified fear. Thus it appears that in Alabama, North Carolina, South Carolina, Texas, and Virginia, black Republican leaders stymied the CFA at every turn.

In late 1891, as conditions for black farmers worsened, particularly in the cotton economy, the CFA debated supporting a cotton pickers strike. The CFA's national leader, R. M. Humphrey, believed a strike across the South was the only way to improve pay and conditions for black farmers, and so he worked with other CFA members to organize the Texas CFA to strike. These developments were kept from the white Southern Farmers' Alliance. However, the strike was poorly planned and executed, and occurred only in a few isolated places in Texas, South Carolina, and Arkansas. The CFA did not have the funds to mount a strike, and the merchants were too powerful. Violence also followed; for example, in Texas, 15 strikers were killed. The planned strike outraged the Southern white leadership of the alliance, and they refused to back any attempts at striking. In Georgia, for example, the alliance opposed the strike. The strike was a complete failure. The strike debacle exacerbated internal problems within the CFA, and by the end of 1891, the organization was in terminal decline.

As the alliance moved towards political insurgency in 1892—culminating in the formation of the People's Party—the CFA and its members faced a choice: either support the Populists or remain within the Republican Party. The CFA's leader, Humphrey, supported the People's Party and urged African American members to join the nascent party. From the evidence, it seems that in many locations, African Americans voted or campaigned for the Populists in 1892; for example, John B. Rayner became a black Populist leader in Texas, while in North Carolina, Walter Patillo supported the Populists. However, a larger number of African Americans stayed with the party of Lincoln. Even if many black members of the CFA supported the Populists' economic and political platform, they could not abandon the Republican Party.

Following the formation of the People's Party, the alliance witnessed a period of rapid decline, due in part to the internal divisions within the alliance, the fallout over outright political action, and the worsening economic situation facing farmers across the South. The CFA mirrored this decline. Indeed by 1892, the CFA was an empty shell, with little or no power. Black farmers now faced worsening economic conditions as rates of tenancy and sharecropping increased and foreclosures and debt peonage abounded. As the 1890s continued, African Americans faced political disfranchisement and Jim Crow. The Colored Farmers' Alliance was no more. By the end of the 1890s, the numbers of African Americans owning farms decreased, and many began to move to cities in the South, move out West to look for work, and later many began the Great Migration northwards as industrialization and urbanization took a hold of the United States. The heyday of black farming was over.

For a brief time, African Americans worked together in the CFA and achieved some notable victories, but these successes proved short lived. The CFA was the largest black organization in the history of the United States, and from the evidence, it is clear that it helped to organize black farmers to cooperate with one another and to alleviate some of the problems facing agrarians.

James M. Beeby

See also

Labor Unions; Segregation, Rural; Southern Tenant Farmers Union (STFU)

Further Reading:

Gaither, Gerald. *Blacks and the Populist Revolt: Ballots and Bigotry in the New South.* Tuscaloosa: University of Alabama Press, 1977.

Goodwyn, Lawrence. *Democratic Promise: The Populist Movement in America.* New York: Oxford University Press, 1976.

Holmes, William F. "The Demise of the Colored Farmers' Alliance." *Journal of Southern History* 41 (1975): 187–200.

McMath, Robert. *Populist Vanguard: A History of the Southern Farmers' Alliance.* Chapel Hill: University of North Carolina Press, 1975.

Combahee River Collective (CRC)

The Combahee River Collective (CRC) was one of the most important black feminist organizations in African diaspora history. Formerly known as the Boston chapter of the National Black Feminist Organization (NBFO), the CRC issued one of the most publicly recognized position papers on the intersections of race, class, gender, and sexual orientation in 1977. The CRC broke new ground in the development of other black feminist organizations and is important because it was one of the first nationally recognized grassroots organizations that sought to address the simultaneity of oppressions that affect black women's lives.

Named after the South Carolina river where Harriet Tubman mounted a military campaign to free 750 enslaved Africans during the Civil War, thereby positioning Tubman as one of black feminism's predecessors, the CRC wanted other organizations (especially white feminist and black liberationist) to understand that the tradition of black feminism had a long history that did not just start in 1974.

Black women's troubled relationships with different movements, including women's suffrage, feminist movements, the civil rights movement, Black Nationalism, the Black Panthers, and the Student Nonviolent Coordinating Committee, had situated them within a matrix of such domination as male privilege, patriarchy, racism, classism, and heterosexism, often relegating their concerns to the periphery of the black and women's communities as well as the larger society. As a result, when black women participated in black and feminist liberation movements, they often had to confront sexism and racism. Black feminist theory and the black feminist movement grew out of, and in response to, this phenomenon. It has been one of the only movements that has historically made an effort to complicate the ways in which people look at, analyze, and discuss black women's lives and oppression. Most black feminist scholars and activists argue that black feminism had its roots in historical resistance to oppression, such as the women's movements and black liberation struggles. Although this is true, most of the recognized black feminist resistance struggles became visible only after 1970. Most of the invisibility and silencing around the black feminist movement had to do with black women's relationship with the political and academic canons. Either black women simply did not have access to them, or their struggles were prevented from airing on television, being documented, or being covered in newspapers.

The CRC felt that there had always been a black feminist presence in literature, academia, and the larger society. At the same time, the CRC also recognized that black feminism had been silenced and rendered invisible by the highly androcentric civil rights and black liberation movements and the white-dominated women's suffrage and white feminist movements. Consequently, three members of the CRC—Barbara Smith, Beverly Smith, and Demita Frazier—took it upon themselves to issue a statement outlining their philosophy, activities, and agenda. In April 1977, the Black Feminist Statement was published as a manifesto that articulated, for the first time in history, the genesis and evolution of black feminist theory and praxis, the specific political agenda of the organization, the myths surrounding black and other women of color's apprehension in aligning themselves with the black feminist movement, and the CRC brief history as a chapter of the NBFO.

Believing in the simultaneity of oppressions (race, class, gender, and sexual orientation), the CRC urged theoreticians, academics, activists, and other organizations to investigate black women's individual lives as a means to understand their collective political commitments. More specifically, the CRC believed that all black women were linked together by their personal relationships with the political institutions that sought to oppress them. The CRC contended that other mass movements and organizations had never developed a collective political agenda or personal commitment to black women's liberation. Therefore, in their Black Feminist Statement, the CRC candidly argued that in order for the United States or the black community to take black women's lives seriously, they had to examine the ways in which black women's lives were shaped around and within the oppressive forces of racism, sexism, heterosexism, and classism. In addition, the CRC also clearly outlined that the audience of their Black Feminist Statement was to be black women, rather than white feminists or black male activists. The CRC felt that black women had spent entirely too much wasted energy addressing their oppressors' (white men, white women, and black men) agendas and needs. The CRC also urged black women to develop a critical, feminist consciousness and begin a dialogue that directly addressed their experiences and connected them to a larger political system. They also urged black women and men to have respect for one another's ideas and agendas and contended that the reason other organizations had failed in their agendas was that they focused on only one type of liberation.

The CRC's Black Feminist Statement, as well as the organization's activism, helped many communities across the African diaspora to engage in a dialogue with one another about the ways in which racism, sexism, heterosexism, and classism affected their personal lives.

Kaila Adia Story

See also

Black Nationalism; Black Panther Party (BPP); Student Nonviolent Coordinating Committee

Further Reading:

Cole, Johnnetta Betsch, and Beverly Guy-Sheftall. *Gender Talk: The Struggle for Women's Equality in African American Communities.* New York: Johnson, 2003.

Collins, Patricia Hill. *Fighting Words: Black Women and the Search for Justice.* Minneapolis: University of Minnesota Press, 1998.

Giddings, Paula. *When and Where I Enter: The Impact of Black Women on Sex and Race in America.* New York: HarperCollins, 1984.

Guy-Sheftall, Beverly, ed. *Words of Fire: An Anthology of African American Feminist Thought.* New York: New Press, 1995.

Hull, Gloria T., Patricia Bell Scott, and Barbara Smith, eds. *All the Women Are White, All the Blacks Are Men, But Some of Us Are Brave.* New York: Feminist Press, 1981.

Mankiller, Wilma, Gwendolyn Mink, Marysa Navarro, Barbara Smith, and Gloria Steinem, eds. *Reader's Companion to U.S. Women's History.* New York: Houghton Mifflin, 1998.

Commemoration Movement

Commemoration movements have arisen to acknowledge racial violence that occurred throughout U.S. history. Rather than ignoring or denying these events, the commemoration movement forces these events into public view. "These responses have taken various forms, including calls for slavery reparations, projects to memorialize lynching victims, re-prosecutions of civil-rights era 'cold case' murders, state-issued apologies for slavery and inaction on lynching, efforts to change school curricula to incorporate more information on white terrorism after the fall of slavery, and more" (Ghoshal 2010: 5).

Commemoration movements, as noted above, can include a variety of actions. While some activists seek retrial and conviction of perpetrators of racial violence, others focus on memorializing those who were victims of violence. Ghoshal provides just a few examples of these movements that do not focus on specific individuals but on the violence against many. "Other projects not around specific incidents of violence, but closely related, include the 'Without Sanctuary' traveling exhibit of lynching postcards and memorabilia that has traveled the country for the past decade, drawing hundreds of thousands of visitors, Alabama's Birmingham Pledge, which allows signatories to commit to rejecting racism, Richmond's Hope in the Cities, an effort aimed at racial reconciliation, the re-enactment of a slave auction in Virginia in the 1990s, the U.S. Senate apology for inaction on lynching, and efforts by Brown and Emory Universities to investigate benefits they gained from slavery" (Ghoshal 2010: 26). As Ghoshal points out, these movements are not about convictions or compensation for victims, but instead "all of these efforts emphasize symbolic or cultural change" (Ghoshal 2010: 26).

In Waco, Texas, some are attempting to start a commemoration movement of lynching victim "Jesse Washington, a 17-year-old black farmhand railroaded to a conviction in the murder and rape of a white woman in Waco on May 15, 1916. He was snatched from court and mutilated and burned alive outside City Hall before some 15,000 spectators—half of Waco's population at the time—and a photographer alerted in advance to shoot pictures. Afterward the charred corpse was dragged through the streets and hung from a telephone pole" (*New York Times* News Service 2005). The photograph of Washington has been circulated in local churches, and there have been discussions by some local activists to erect a formal memorial, which would join memorials in the city commemorating the death of the Branch Davidians and victims of a 1953 tornado. However, it has been difficult to finalize the memorial due to a lack of support by some residents in the city. Many residents in the town are unaware that this event even occurred, making the commemoration even more important.

There have also been commemoration events around the more well-known lynching of Emmett Till. "On August 28, 1955, 14-year-old Emmett Till was kidnapped in the middle of the night from his uncle's home near Money, Mississippi, by at least two men, one from LeFlore and one from Tallahatchie County, Mississippi. Till, a black youth from Chicago visiting family in Mississippi, was later murdered, and his body thrown into the Tallahatchie River. He had been accused of whistling at a white woman in Money. His badly beaten body was found days later in Tallahatchie County, Mississippi. The Grand Jury meeting in Sumner, Mississippi, indicted Roy Bryant and J. W. Milam for the crime of murder. These two men were then tried on this charge and were acquitted by an all-white, all-male jury after a deliberation of just over an hour" (Emmett Till Memorial Commission). The Emmett Till Memorial Commission of Tallahatchie County has initiated several events and memorials to recognize and remember this horrific part of U.S. history. There is a civil rights driving tour, a memorial event, and a series of markers that demarcate various locations related to the murder of Till. In Chicago, "nearly 150 people showed up to participate in the 'Hands Across Emmett Till Road' commemoration," which included a march across a bridge named for Till and the displaying of a sign on the bridge.

Commemoration movements are not confined to only events that happened in the South. In Duluth, Minnesota, a commemoration event occurred in 2003 remembering the lynching of "Elmer Jackson, Elias Clayton and Isaac McGhie, three young black men who were lynched in Duluth in 1920 while a mob of 10,000 looked on" (*New York Times* 2003). Thousands of people from around the area attended the event, which included a memorial and speakers. All of these events attempt to reveal what happened in the past in order to honor victims and acknowledge this horrible period of history. "These projects reckoning with past violence have attempted to bring honor to lynching and riot victims who met inglorious fates a century ago, sought to inspire young African Americans to set high aspirations by documenting how much worse racial oppression was several generations ago, and attempted to educate whites about past racial terrorism" (Ghoshal 2010: 26).

Kathrin A. Parks

See also
Emmett Till Murder; Juneteenth Celebration

Further Reading:

"Background." Emmett Till Memorial Commission Tallahatchie County, Mississippi. http://www.etmctallahatchie.com/.
"Emmett Till's Story." Emmett Till Legacy Foundation. http://www.emmetttilllegacyfoundation.com/emmett-story.php.
Ghoshal, Raj Andrew. "Remembering Racial Violence: Memory Movements and the Resurgence of Traumatic Pasts." PhD diss., University of North Carolina at Chapel Hill, 2010.
Lesley Chin. "Remembering Emmett Till; Emmett Till Memorial Bridge Sign Unveiled." *Chicago Citizen*, August 31, 2005.
New York Times News Service. "City Still Coping with Fury over 1916 Lynching." *Baltimore Sun*, May 01, 2005. http://articles.baltimoresun.com/2005-05-01/news/0505010133_1_waco-lynching-white-hands.
New York Times. "A Lynching Memorial Unveiled in Duluth." December 5, 2003. http://www.nytimes.com/2003/12/05/opinion/a-lynching-memorial-unveiled-in-duluth.html.

Confederate Flag Controversy

For over a decade, various debates have revolved around the symbolism associated with the Confederate battle flag, also known as the "Southern Cross." Many people in the South see the Confederate battle flag as a symbol of Southern heritage and Southern pride. According to Gerald Webster and Jonathan Leib, for example, many White Southerners view the confederate battle flag as "emblematic of the honor and integrity of the struggle for Southern independence as embodied in the myth of the 'Lost Cause'" (2008: 169). The Lost Cause refers to an interpretation of the U.S. Civil War from a Confederate perspective. This perspective emphasizes how Confederate soldiers fought valiantly for a "noble cause" that involved defending Southern sovereignty and a Christian identity against Union forces that represented a Godless and tyrannical government. Therefore, drawing from this interpretation of history, many White Southerners understand the Confederate battle flag as "symbolic of the bravery and sacrifice of their ancestors during the Civil War" (Webster and Leib 2008: 169).

In stark contrast, many other people from the South (and other parts of the United States) understand the Confederate battle flag as a shameful reminder of slavery and the South's military and political efforts to defend this institution. Furthermore, African Americans in particular often associate this flag with the Jim Crow system, as well as the physical and symbolic racial violence inflicted on black people during the myriad of attempts by the Ku Klux Klan and other racist organizations (who often displayed the Confederate battle flag) to oppose racial desegregation and racial equality in the name of defending "Southern heritage." In short, from this latter perspective, the Confederate battle flag is little more than a symbol of white supremacy and black subordination. Those who lionize this flag are thus romanticizing an era and political culture that normalized intolerance and racial oppression.

In 2000, the Confederate battle flag controversy took center stage in South Carolina. On April 12, 2000, the legislature of this state passed a bill to remove the Confederate battle flag from the top of the State House dome, where it had been placed by an all-White South Carolina legislature in 1962. This bill was passed in response to protests and an economic boycott issued by the National Association for the Advancement of Colored People (NAACP) against the state of South Carolina. However, the Confederate battle flag was not removed but rather transferred from the top of the State Capitol dome to the front of the State Capitol, next to a monument that honors fallen Confederate soldiers. Because the flag was never entirely removed, the NAACP maintains an official economic boycott of the State of South Carolina.

The state of Georgia has also been a site of controversy regarding the Confederate battle flag. In 1956, two years after the U.S. Supreme Court ruling to desegregate public schools in *Brown v. Board of Education*, the state flag of Georgia was redesigned to incorporate the Confederate battle flag. During the 1990s, the NAACP and other civil rights groups organized a series of protests, urging the Georgia legislature to remove the Confederate battle flag from its state flag. Spurred by these protests, Georgia governor Roy Barnes led a successful effort to change the Georgia State flag in 2001. Although the Confederate battle flag was not entirely removed, it was displayed far less prominently in the new flag of Georgia. Partly in response to Barnes's efforts to minimize the Confederate battle flag's prominence within the Georgia state flag, angry white voters turned out in record numbers to vote the governor out of office in 2002 (Gettleman 2002). However, in 2003, partly as a way to avoid the ongoing controversy associated with the Confederate battle flag, the flag of Georgia was once again redesigned and modeled after the first national flag of the Confederate States of America, also known as the "Stars and Bars."

A similar controversy associated with the confederate battle flag took place in Mississippi. Since 1894, Mississippi's state flag has prominently displayed the Confederate battle flag. Although the adoption of this flag had actually been repealed by the state legislature in 1906, the state flag remained in use, mostly on the basis of tradition (i.e., unbeknownst to many, the state had no "official" flag). The "unofficial" status of Mississippi's state flag was brought into the public limelight in 1993, when the Mississippi Supreme Court reviewed a lawsuit filed by the NAACP against the state's use of the Confederate battle flag. In 2000, the then governor of that state, Ronnie Musgrove, issued an executive order to make the state flag official. After further controversy, voters in Mississippi were given the opportunity to vote on whether or not the Confederate battle flag should be part of the state flag. A majority of Mississippians voted to retain the Confederate battle flag within the state flag by a margin of 2:1 (CNN Politics 2001).

The National Collegiate Athletic Association (NCAA) has also been involved in the Confederate battle flag controversy. For over a decade, the NCAA has banned staging championship games in states that display the Confederate battle flag. Although exceptions to this policy have been made, the ban remains official. As stated in the 2013–2014 NCAA championship bid specification booklet, "No predetermined session of an NCAA championship may be conducted in a state where the Confederate flag is flown" (NCAA, Championship Bid Specification: 3).

In recent years, many people have expressed as desire to reclaim and redefine the Confederate battle flag as a symbol of state sovereignty and rejection of "big government." Many of these people want to downplay the flag's link to slavery and claim that many other flags (including the U.S. flag) are tainted with the abuses of slavery. Yet the symbolic connection this flag has with slavery and white supremacy remains strong in the minds of millions of Americans. As a result, the Confederate battle flag remains, and will likely remain, a divisive symbol.

Luigi Esposito

See also

Neo-Confederate Movement

Further Reading:

CNN Politics. "Mississippi Votes 2–1 to Keep Existing Flag." 2001. Accessed November 19, 2012. http://articles.cnn.com/2001-04-17/politics/mississippi.flag.02_1_confederate-battle-state-flag-new-flag?_s=PM:ALLPOLITICS.

Gettleman, Jeffrey. "The 2002 Elections: Georgia; an Old Battle Flag Helps Bring Down a Governor." *New York Times*, February 7, 2002. Accessed November 14, 2012. http://www.nytimes.com/2002/11/07/us/the-2002-elections-georgia-an-old-battle-flag-helps-bring-down-a-governor.html?ref=royebarnes.

National Collegiate Athletic Association. "NCAA 2013–2014 Championship Bid Specification." Accessed November 19, 2012. http://fs.ncaa.org/Docs/championships/Bid%20Information/2012/General+Bid+Specifications+6.14.12.pdf).

Webster, Gerald, and Jonathan I. Leib. "Fighting for the Lost Cause: The Confederate Battle Flag and Neo-Confederacy." In *Neo-Confederacy: A Critical Introduction*, edited by Euan Hague, Edward H. Sebesta, and Heidi Beirich, 169–201. Austin: University of Texas Press, 2008.

Congress of Racial Equality (CORE)

During the spring of 1942, the Congress of Racial Equality (CORE), initially called the Committee of Racial Equality, was founded by a group of blacks and whites on the campus of the University of Chicago. James L. Farmer Jr., Bernice Fisher, Joe Guinn, George House, Homer Jack, Bayard Rustin, and James R. Robinson are credited with the establishment of CORE. The initial leaders of CORE were George Houser, a white student, and James Farmer, the Race Relations Secretary for the Fellowship of Reconciliation (FOR).

Many of CORE members were also members of FOR, its parent organization founded in 1914. Like CORE, FOR was a pacifist organization concerned with promoting justice with nonviolent civil resistance based upon the philosophical teachings of Mahatma Gandhi. Consequently, CORE members embraced such nonviolent disobedience techniques as sit-ins, picketing, jail-ins, and freedom rides to fight Jim Crow laws.

The earlier membership of CORE consisted mainly of white college students from the Midwest. To date, "[m]embership in CORE is open to anyone who believes that 'all people are created equal' and is willing to work towards the ultimate goal of true equality throughout the world." Therefore, CORE's mission remains "to bring about equality for all people regardless of race, creed, sex, age, disability, sexual orientation, religion or ethnic background." In pursuing its aim, CORE seeks to identify and expose acts of discrimination in the public and private sectors of society.

CORE's mission statement continues, "CORE is the third oldest and one of the 'Big Four' civil rights groups in the United States. From the protests against 'Jim Crow' laws of the 40s through the 'Sit-ins' of the 50s, the 'Freedom Rides' of the 60s, the cries of 'Self-Determination' in the 70s, 'Equal Opportunity' in the 80s, community development in the 90s, to the current demand for equal access to information, CORE has championed true equality. As the 'shock troops' and pioneers of the civil rights movement, CORE has paved the way for the nation to follow" (CORE official Web site).

CORE began organizing sit-ins in 1942 to protest segregated public accommodations. Their first sit-in occurred at a coffee shop in Chicago. These sit-ins were the first such nonviolent resistance activities in the United States. Based upon the success of this technique, CORE is credited with desegregation of public accommodations in cities in many Northern and border states. It was this success that resulted in CORE turning its attention to the segregated South.

In 1947, George Houser and Bayard Rustin organized a two-week Greyhound and Trailways bus journey, referred to as the Journey of Reconciliation, to the South in order to test the U.S. Supreme Court's *Morgan v. Commonwealth of Virginia*, 328 U.S. 373 (1946), ruling that forbade racial segregation of bus passengers engaged in interstate travel. In 1944, 10 years before the arrest of Rosa Parks and the Montgomery Bus Boycott, Irene Morgan, a resident of Baltimore, Maryland, was arrested and incarcerated in Virginia for resisting arrest and refusing to give up her seat on a Greyhound bus to a white person.

CORE sent a team of eight white and eight black men on the Journey of Reconciliation through the states of North

Carolina, Kentucky, Tennessee, and Virginia. Members of the team were Louis Adams, Dennis Banks, Joseph Felmet, George Houser, Homer Jack, Andrew Johnson, Conrad Lynn, Wallace Nelson, James Peck, Worth Randle, Igal Roodenko, Bayard Rustin, Eugene Stanley, William Worthy, and Nathan Wright. The members were arrested several times for violating state-imposed Jim Crow bus statutes. Despite the members' arrest, the Journey of Reconciliation marked the beginning of an arduous national campaign against racial segregation.

After the *Brown v. Board of Education* ruling, CORE began focusing on segregated public accommodations in the Deep South by engaging in similar nonviolent disobedience tactics as those used in Northern cities. CORE also launched several voter registration drives for black Southerners. CORE member Bayard Rustin served as an adviser to Martin Luther King, Jr. during the Montgomery Bus Boycott.

In response to Southern resistance, CORE organized student sit-ins in 1960 and provided assistance to college students throughout the country in their attempts to challenge racial segregation. These sit-ins successfully ended racial segregation of restaurants and lunch counters in some Southern cities. CORE also targeted other segregated public facilities such as parks, beaches, transportation, swimming pools, theaters, libraries, churches, and museums.

On May 4, 1961, CORE and the Student Nonviolent Coordinating Committee (SNCC) organized Freedom Rides throughout the Deep South. These Freedom Rides were similar to the Journey of Reconciliation. The Freedom Rides tested the *Boynton v. Virginia*, 364 U.S. 454 (1960), ruling that extended the *Morgan* decision to bus terminals used in interstate bus service. The original participants were six whites and seven blacks who rode buses from Washington, D.C., to New Orleans, Louisiana. Over a thousand people participated in these rides. Despite violent attacks and incarcerations, CORE maintained its overall mission and continued to grow as an organization. Additionally, the Freedom Rides were viewed as having some measure of success because the Interstate Commerce Commission passed new regulations to desegregate bus terminals.

In 1963, CORE played an instrumental role in the March on Washington and in President John F. Kennedy's Voter Education Project. One year later, CORE, in collaboration with the SNCC and the National Association for the Advancement of Colored People (NAACP), organized the Freedom Summer campaign in Mississippi. The purpose of this campaign was to increase black voter registration and to promote civic literacy in Mississippi. CORE, the SNCC, and the NAACP formed the Mississippi Freedom Party and established 30 Freedom Schools in order to teach civic education.

The participants of Freedom Summer experienced a rash of violence. In fact, three members of CORE—James Chaney, Andrew Goodman, and Michael Schwerner—were killed. Ironically, their deaths resulted in Freedom Summer receiving national publicity. Hence, one year later, President Lyndon B. Johnson requested passage of his Voting Rights Act. Despite opposition, in 1965, the Voting Rights Act was successfully passed.

By the mid-1960s, as CORE began opening chapters in the North and West, it experienced both an ideological and membership shift. During this time period, CORE membership became increasingly black and its ideology shifted more toward "Black Power." The ideological change was welcomed by the new national director Floyd McKissick, even though it alienated some of CORE's previous allies.

In 1968, Roy Innis became the national director of CORE. Innis restructured the organization and improved its financing health. He also promoted what was considered a less radical approach than McKissick and involved the organization in black economic development and community self-determination efforts—Black Nationalism.

Olethia Davis

See also

Black Nationalism; March on Washington of 1963; March on Washington Movement; Student Nonviolent Coordinating Committee

Further Reading:

Arsenault, Raymond. "'You Don't Have to Ride Jim Crow': CORE and the 1947 Journey of Reconciliation." In *Before Brown: Civil Rights and White Backlash in the Modern South*, ed. Glenn Feldman, 21–67. Tuscaloosa: University of Alabama Press, 2004;

Bell, Inge P. *CORE and the Strategy of Non-Violence*. New York: Random House, 1968;

CORE Official Web site. http://www.core-online.org.

Meier, August, and Elliott Rudwick. *CORE: A Study of the Civil Rights Movement 1942–1968*. New York: Oxford University Press, 1973.

Connor, "Bull" (1897–1973)

Theophilus Eugene "Bull" Connor was a longtime police commissioner of Birmingham, Alabama, who supported segregation. Connor was born on July 11, 1897, in Selma, Alabama. While he enjoyed popular support among Birmingham's white voters, he was not well known outside of the city. This changed in May 1963, when he ordered the use of fire hoses and police dogs to deter citizens who were protesting the condition of civil rights for African Americans in Birmingham. This display of violence catapulted the nation's attention to the civil rights movement at a time when the movement was in need of political support.

The confrontation in Birmingham was in stark contrast to the movement's previous stage in Albany, Georgia. Connor's tough stand against integration was in contrast to that of the local Georgia sheriff Laurie Pritchett, who, for the sake of expedience, allowed demonstrators to protest without incident. Connor was very much a product of his environment. Having been raised in Alabama's Black Belt region, strict social segregation of black and white citizens was a way of life. Many white citizens in Birmingham held similar beliefs, although many were not considered to be members of higher socioeconomic status. These citizens gave Connor a political base that supported a longtime career in public service, including six terms as police commissioner.

Segregation was the law of the land as far as many white citizens of Birmingham were concerned. In his inaugural remarks in 1957, upon winning the post of Commissioner of Public Safety, Connor publicly stated he would protect segregation by any legal means. This was reflected in many aspects of daily life in Birmingham. The city was often described as the most segregated large city in the nation. For example, in 1960, it was the only city with at least 50,000 citizens with an all-white police force. When federal courts ordered public parks and golf courses in Birmingham to integrate, Connor had them closed rather than face an end to segregated facilities.

While Connor will be remembered primarily for his role of violence against civil rights marchers in May 1963, he will also be remembered for things he did not do. Primarily, he seldom took action against individuals who perpetuated violence against African Americans in Birmingham, especially those who were involved with the civil rights movement. Connor could be counted on to look the other way when violence was taken against black citizens in Birmingham. One of the most notorious moments was allowing an attack by members of the Ku Klux Klan against Freedom Riders as the bus stopped in Birmingham.

After serving two terms as president of the Alabama Public Service Commission, Connor suffered a severe stroke and died March 11, 1973.

James Newman

See also

Civil Rights Movement; Police Brutality; Segregation

Further Reading:

McWhorter, Diane. *Carry Me Home.* New York: Simon and Schuster, 2001.

Nunnelley, William A. *Bull Connor.* Tuscaloosa: University of Alabama Press, 1991.

Conyers, John, Jr. (b. 1929)

African American John Conyers Jr. served as a congressional representative for the State of Michigan, playing a key role in pushing civil rights legislation and advocating for African Americans and other people of color at the national level. Throughout his long career in public service, Conyers established himself as a prominent Washington politician, characterized by his support of legislation to alleviate the socioeconomic plight of the disadvantaged.

Conyers was born on May 16, 1929, in Detroit to John and Lucille Conyers. His father worked on the Chrysler Corporation assembly line and was actively involved with the union, serving on the board of the United Automobile Workers (UAW). Conyers attended public schools in Detroit and began working on the Lincoln-Mercury assembly line when he graduated from high school. He joined the union and was named education director of UAW Local 900.

At age 21, Conyers enrolled at Wayne State University in Detroit. However, in August of 1950, his National Guard unit, which he had joined in 1948, was called to active duty and Conyers had to leave school. During his four years with the Guard, he attended officer training school and attained the rank of second lieutenant, serving a year in Korea during the Korean War. When he was discharged from active duty in the army in 1954, he continued in the National Guard until 1957 but also returned to school at Wayne State University, graduating in 1957 and immediately entering Wayne State's law school. After he received his law degree the following year, Conyers began practicing in his own firm, Conyers, Bell, and Townsend.

Although he was busy with his law practice, Conyers was also becoming interested in politics and accepted the position of legislative assistant to John Dingell, who was then a state representative in Michigan. Conyers served as general counsel for the Detroit Trade Union Leadership Council, a position his father had previously occupied. In 1961, after leaving his position with Dingell, he was appointed a referee with the Michigan Workmen's Compensation Department. In 1963, he was appointed by President John F. Kennedy to the National Lawyers Committee for Civil Rights.

In 1964, Conyers decided to run for Congress in Michigan's First Congressional District. He drew upon his union contacts and the political base he had been building to challenge a crowded field of contenders in the Democratic primary, winning by a mere 45 votes over his nearest competitor. In the general election, he faced Republican Robert Blackwell in a predominantly Democratic district, winning by a wide margin and becoming the youngest member of the U.S. House of Representatives.

When Conyers was sworn into Congress in 1965, the civil rights movement was at its height. Backed by the National Association for the Advancement of Colored People, as well as by lobbyists with an interest in minority rights, Conyers was able to obtain an appointment on the powerful House Judiciary Committee. Although President Lyndon B. Johnson was pursuing the Vietnam War with congressional approval, Conyers spoke out against it and advocated for peace. A vocal supporter of civil rights, Conyers cosponsored the Voting Rights Act of 1965, as well as Johnson's Medicare program. As such, with his record in the House, Conyers had no difficulty winning reelection in 1966.

During his second term, Conyers was named the sole African American on the investigating committee looking into the activities of Adam Clayton Powell Jr. While others spoke of ousting Powell from his seat in the House entirely, Conyers spoke in his favor. Conyers felt that the harsh censure of Powell passed by the House was a blow against African Americans. He again defended Powell in 1969, although Powell had called him a traitor for serving on the original investigating committee in 1967.

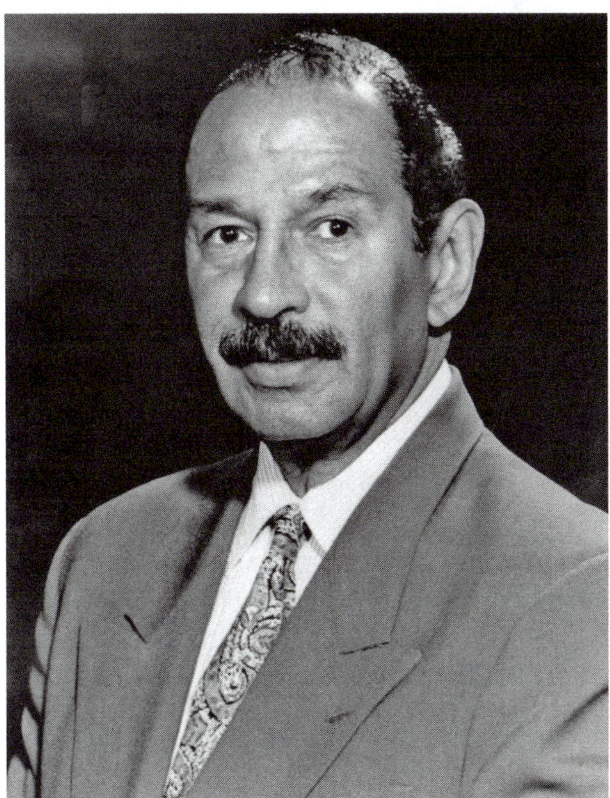

John Conyers Jr. has served in the U.S. House of Representatives since 1965. A Democrat and native of Detroit, Conyers represents Michigan's 14th District. (U.S. House of Representatives)

Conyers has actively shaped public policy, writing legislation such as the Racial Justice Act, Voter Registration Reform Act, Martin Luther King, Jr. Holiday Bill, and Public Safety Officers Benefits Bill. And in 1970, he was one of the founding members of the Congressional Black Caucus, formed to promote minority interests in Congress. With his reelection in 1994, he became the first African American to serve as the Democratic leader of the House Committee on the Judiciary, where, in 1998, he was a leading voice against the impeachment of President Bill Clinton.

Following the 2003 U.S. invasion of Iraq, Conyers became a staunch critic of President George W. Bush and his administration's policies, especially those regarding intelligence gathering, allegations over the use of torture, and suspected voter fraud in the 2004 presidential election. In 2005, Conyers and other members of Congress wrote an inquiry to the White House regarding the alleged Downing Street Memorandum, which described a secret 2002 agreement between Britain and the United States to attack Iraq. Moreover, that same year, Conyers' report *What Went Wrong in Ohio: The Conyers Report on the 2004 Presidential Election*, which discussed allegations of disenfranchisement and tampering of voting machines perpetrated by voting officials, was published. In 2006, Conyers released his report of *The Constitution in Crisis: The Downing Street Minutes and Deception, Manipulation, Torture, Retributions and Cover-ups in the Iraq War*, where he documents his allegations against the Bush administration's handling of the Iraq War.

As of 2010, Conyers continues to serve as congressional representative for Michigan's 14th District, which had been part of the First District prior to its redistricting in 1993.

James Haskins

Further Reading:

Clay, William L. *Just Permanent Interests: Black Americans in Congress, 1870–1991*. New York: Amistad Press, 1992.
Estell, Kenneth. *African America: Celebrating 400 Years of Achievement*. Detroit: Visible Ink Press, 1994.
Maurine, Christopher. *America's Black Congressmen*. New York: Crowell, 1971.

Coolie

Coolie refers to a popular stereotype of Chinese working as cheap labor in mines, agriculture, and railroad construction in the 19th-century United States. Originally, the term referred to a system of indentured labor established by the British in the 19th century to recruit primarily Indian and Chinese workers for plantations in Asia, Africa, and Latin America. With the end of the African slave trade and the abolition of slavery at home, the British shipped tens of thousands of Chinese coolies—often war prisoners, kidnapping victims, and debtors coerced into service—from southern China to Latin America, particularly Cuba and Peru, between 1845 and 1874, to work on plantations and in mines. Their transportation recalls the African slave ships, which were replete with death, disease, starvation, riots, murders, and mutinies. Recruiters delivered workers in this Chinese "pig trade" with signed contracts for terms of service that were then sold to the highest bidder upon arrival.

Most Chinese arriving in the United States in the 19th century, however, were not indentured laborers; they bought tickets on credit, repaying the fare with labor after arrival. The creditors' control of migrants after arrival, though, left many believing the credit-ticket arrangement varied from the coolie trade only in that the Chinese willingly participated in their subjugation. An American law prohibited coolies or indentured workers. But the image of slave-like living and working conditions, combined with the perceived threat to the jobs and wages of the American white working class, became a rallying cry for white American workers and formed the base of the economic argument for Chinese exclusion later in the 19th century.

Kenneth J. Guest

See also

Chinese Exclusion Act of 1882; Racism; Stereotype

Further Reading:

June, Moon-Ho. *Coolies and Cane: Race, Labor, and Sugar in the Age of Emancipation*. Baltimore: Johns Hopkins University Press, 2006.
Kwong, Peter. *Forbidden Workers: Illegal Chinese Immigrants and American Labor*. New York: New Press, 1997.
Light, Ivan, and Steven J. Gold. *Ethnic Economics*. San Diego: Academic Press, 2000.
Ong, Paul. *Beyond Asian American Poverty: Community Economic Development Policies and Strategies*. Los Angeles: Leadership Education for Asian Pacifics, 1993.
Parreñas, Rhacel Salazar. *Servants of Globalization: Women, Migration, and Domestic Work*. Stanford, CA: Stanford University Press, 2001.

Cooper, Anna Julia (1858–1964)

Anna Julia Cooper was an African American educator, essayist, orator, and activist. She dedicated her life to improving opportunities for black women in employment and education, refuting stereotypes about their promiscuity and laziness, arguing for the vote, and exposing the economic and political reasons for the widespread lynching of African Americans. Her book of essays, entitled *A Voice from the South, by a Black Woman of the South* (1892), anticipates 20th-century feminism by discussing class and race issues that divided African American women and other women of color from white women, and by describing the reasons why women deserved more equitable treatment in their homes and communities than society currently offered them. Her contribution during the Jim Crow era rests in how she kept African American women's lives at the forefront of discussions of race relations and social justice, and in how she modeled ways that privileged African American women could guide the less advantaged of their race. In an era when the voices of African American male leaders such as Alexander Crummell and W.E.B. Du Bois dominated discussions of racial progress, Cooper's writings and speeches expressed value for the opinions of intellectual African American women like herself, and she denounced the double standard within the race that praised and supported the accomplishments of black male leaders yet ignored or devalued how black women leaders were effecting positive changes for their people.

Cooper shared the mixed-race heritage that is often recounted in biographies of black Americans born in bondage. Hannah Stanley Haywood, her mother, was a slave in Raleigh, North Carolina, and her father, most likely Fabius J. Haywood, the son of a prominent lawyer, was her mother's white master. She had two older brothers, Andrew and Rufus. In 1877 she married George A. C. Cooper, a Bahamian who was studying for the Episcopal ministry, but he died two years later. She had met George at St. Augustine's Normal School and Collegiate Institute, a teacher training school in Raleigh, where she had enrolled at the age of nine and distinguished herself for excelling in the math and science courses normally reserved for men. After graduation and before her marriage, she had taught at St. Augustine's. She entered Oberlin College in 1880, where she continued to pursue the so-called Gentleman's Courses, to earn a BA in math in 1884 and an MA in the same subject one year later.

Following brief stints at Wilberforce University and St. Augustine's to teach classical languages, math, and German, in 1887 she was hired by the elite M Street High School in Washington, D.C. (later renamed Dunbar High School), the only African American high school in the city. From 1901 to 1906, she served as principal of M Street, at a time when it was rare for formerly married women to remain in the profession, and for any woman to become a high school principal. Cooper defied the racism and sexism of the Board of Education by offering students advanced college prep courses instead of giving them only vocational training, before she finally was asked to resign. She returned to M Street as a Latin teacher in 1910, and 15 years later, she earned a PhD in history from the University of Paris-Sorbonne.

Both on the public and private levels, Cooper dedicated her energies to confronting those who practiced racism and sexism and creating opportunities to ensure the advancement of her people. For example, in 1902, she cofounded the Colored Settlement House in Washington, D.C., which she would manage well into the 1930s. The first of its kind in the city, the house offered summer camps for children, daycare programs, and other social services. Since the white YWCA would not admit African American women, in 1905 she was instrumental in cofounding the nation's first all-black YWCA, the Phillis Wheatley YWCA, in the District of Columbia. Characteristically critical of racism among white feminists, Cooper participated in a protest against the omission of black women speakers from the World's Congress of Representative Women at the 1893 Chicago Columbian Exposition. Her outspokenness resulted in the organizers of the Congress inviting six African American women, herself among them, as speakers. On a personal note, in 1915, she adopted and raised her younger brother Andrew's five grandchildren when they became orphaned. Another instance of where the lines between her community activism and her family life blurred was in her establishment in 1930 of the Hannah Stanley Opportunity School in honor of her mother, for black adults with learning disabilities. She ran the school concurrently while serving from 1930 to 1940 as president of Frelinghuysen University, a night and weekend school for African American adults.

Cooper's adult years coincided with a period in late 19th-century American history called race uplift, which emphasized the obligation of middle- and upper-class African Americans to help improve the lives of their poorer and more ignorant brothers and sisters. Yet, uplift was more than a nationalist, self-help movement. During Jim Crow, it also meant to shift the attitudes of whites who thought that blacks, especially the descendants of slaves, were unworthy and incapable of assuming the full privileges and responsibilities of citizenship. Cooper's contribution to race uplift was to recommend that black families and communities could focus on such goals as gaining an education, pursuing thrift and hard work, and putting Christian beliefs into practice in order to attain material success and social acceptance.

Cooper also seized the moment to criticize problems within the race that held African Americans back from full parity within American society. For example, in her essay in *A Voice from the South* called "The Higher Education of Women," she spoke out for recognition of what she called "the feminine factor," the calming and loving influence that women contributed to humanity, and against the prejudice in black communities that made many distrust whether college education for women was worthwhile. Another attitude adjustment that she thought both blacks and whites would benefit from was to reject collectively the stereotype of black women, especially poor Southerners, as promiscuous and hypersexual. This perception, which had been used to rationalize the rape and sexual abuse of black women in slavery, had been resurrected during the post-Reconstruction years to defend Jim Crow policies and to justify racial violence targeting black women. Scholars like Cooper understood that this stereotype had little basis in the realities of impoverished black women's lives as wives and mothers, and that instead it was a form of social control and intimidation. In her 1886 speech to a group of black Episcopal ministers, "Womanhood a Vital Element in the Regeneration and Progress of a Race," Cooper called upon African American men to shield poor black women from such slurs upon their reputations and to lift them out of the poverty and ignorance that made them vulnerable to such accusations.

Cooper's feminism was also dominated by her interest in places where the concerns of white women and women of color overlapped, and her conviction that by working together they could eradicate oppressions they shared in common. In public, she criticized white club women and suffragists for recognizing the oppression black women experienced, yet remaining complicit in that oppression by keeping their groups segregated, spreading stereotypes, and marginalizing black women in their campaign to attain the vote. In "What Are We Worth?" from *A Voice from the South*, she applauded social efforts to alleviate poverty and illiteracy among "'our working girls'" but scornfully questioned why Northern white women and other reformers usually assumed that such women were white. In "Woman Versus the Indian," also from her book, she singled out the provincialism of Southern white women for scrutiny. She chastised a Kentucky women's group called Wimodaughsis (an acronym for "Wives, Mothers, Daughters, and Sisters") for refusing to admit a black teacher, and she challenged respectable Southern white women to be more proactive in eliminating racism by influencing white men to extend civil treatment to black women on public conveyances and in public facilities.

Barbara McCaskill

See also

Civil Rights Movement; *Cooper v. Aaron* (1958)

Further Reading:

Cooper, Anna Julia. *A Voice from the South. By a Black Women of the South*. Xenia: Aldine Printing House, 1892. Accessed August 2007. http://docsouth.unc.edu/church/cooper/menu.html.

Epstein, Barack, Nima Khomassi, and Gabrielle Ben-Eli. "Anna Julia Cooper." Accessed June 12, 2008. http://www.gwu.edu/~e73afram/be-nk-gbe.html.

Glass, Kathy L. *Courting Communities: Black Female Nationalism and Syncre-Nationalism n the Nineteenth-Century North*. New York: Routledge, 2006.

May, Vivian M. *Anna Julia Cooper, Visionary Black Feminist*. New York: Routledge, 2007.

McCaskill, Barbara. "Anna Julia Cooper, Pauline Elizabeth Hopkins, and the African American Feminization of Du Bois's Discourse." In *The Souls of Black Folk: One Hundred Years Later*, edited by Dolan Hubbard, 70–84. Columbia: University of Missouri Press, 2002.

Waters, Kristin, and Carol B. Conaway, eds. *Black Women's Intellectual Traditions: Speaking Their Minds*. Burlington: University of Vermont Press, 2007.

Cooper v. Aaron (1958)

Cooper v. Aaron was a significant U.S. Supreme Court decision during the tumultuous period of school integration efforts in the United States in the mid-20th century. In *Cooper v. Aaron*, the Supreme Court ruled unanimously on September 12, 1958, for integration to proceed immediately at Little Rock Central High School in Arkansas. Following the landmark *Brown v. Board of Education* decision in 1954, whereby the Court officially denounced the institution of "separate but equal" facilities in public education and called for desegregation in public schools, this case placed itself in the middle of a period of racial upheaval in the Little Rock school system, the state of Arkansas, and nationally as well.

In the year before the *Cooper v. Aaron* ruling, the Little Rock school board voted to admit African American students to Central High School beginning in the fall of 1957 in compliance with the *Brown* decision. A select group of nine African American students, sponsored by the National Association for the Advancement of Colored People (NAACP) and who came to be known as the "Little Rock Nine," enrolled under the new desegregation plan. Immediately before the students could begin the fall term in September, Arkansas governor Orval Faubus ordered the Arkansas National Guard to prevent the entrance of the nine students, claiming that public disturbances and violence would prove too great a disruption to the school and to other students. Although the students were eventually allowed to attend school, the year at Central High following this initial refusal of entry was marked by widespread tensions throughout the community. Beyond confrontations involving the nine African American students with other white classmates, civic strife was rampant as segregationist "citizens' councils" clashed with antisegregation demonstrators including "The Council of Church Women" and NAACP supporters. Gov. Faubus's refusal to obey the school board's decision prompted President Dwight D. Eisenhower to federalize Arkansas's entire national guard and reluctantly order the U.S. Army's 101st Airborne Division into Little Rock to protect the students' entry. At the end of the school year, Little Rock school officials asked for a delay on implementing desegregation from the federal district court. U.S. District Judge Harry Lemley granted the delay until January 1961.

The NAACP appealed this decision, and in August 1958, the Eighth U.S. Circuit Court of Appeals in St. Louis reversed the delayed integration order. Following this decision, the Supreme Court, for only the fifth time in four decades that the high court was to meet in an off season, took up the Little Rock desegregation case in an extraordinary session. In September 1958, in *Cooper v. Aaron*, the Court affirmed in a six-paragraph decision the judgment of the Court of Appeals and ruled unanimously for integration to proceed immediately at Central High School. The ruling cited that under the equal protection clause of the Fourteenth Amendment, no state can withhold constitutional rights from its citizens, even in the face of the chaos and violence ensuing from the situation in Little Rock. Importantly, this decision stated that governors and state legislatures must uphold U.S. Supreme Court decisions, as dictated by the supremacy clause of the Constitution.

In Little Rock, the governor and school board remained embroiled in the process of desegregation in public schools. Immediately after *Cooper v. Aaron*, and in an effort to prevent desegregation at any cost, Gov. Faubus, along with almost unanimous support from the legislature, signed into law six segregationist bills that allowed for the temporary closing of all schools within the Little Rock school district. This sentiment was confirmed by the community, as 72 percent of citizens casting ballots in a special Little Rock School District election on September 27, 1958, voted against racial integration and to shut down all public schools in favor of private schools that could more effectively prevent biracial education. Responding two days after, the U.S. Supreme Court issued a clarifying opinion on *Cooper v. Aaron* that reaffirmed its ruling in *Brown* as "the supreme law of the land" and attempted to define as illegal "evasive schemes for segregation" such as those promoted in Little Rock.

Cooper v. Aaron was an important step in the enforcement of the *Brown v. Board of Education* decision, and as a polarizing event that contributed significantly to race relations, it garnered national and international attention in the establishment of, and debates over, civil rights in the United States.

William A. Morgan

See also

Brown v. Board of Education Legal Groundwork; *Brown v. Board of Education* (1954); Desegregation; School Segregation. Document: *Brown v. Board of Education* (May 1954)

Further Reading:

Aldridge, Delores P. "Litigation and Education of Blacks: A Look at the U.S. Supreme Court." In "Desegregation in the 1970s: A Candid Discussion." *Journal of Negro Education* 47, no. 1 (Winter 1978): 96–112.

Cooper v. Aaron, 358 U.S. 1 (1958).

Library of Congress. "With an Even Hand: *Brown v. Board* at Fifty" (Online, accessed July 2007). Online exhibition, http://www.loc.gov/exhibits/brown/ (accessed July 2007).

Wilkinson, J. Harvie, III. "The Supreme Court and Southern School Desegregation, 1955–1970: A History and Analysis." *Virginia Law Review* 64, no. 4 (May 1978): 485–559.

Cosby, Bill (b. 1937)

It is ironic that the legendary African American actor, comic, and musician—Dr. William H. "Bill" Cosby—would have his own entry in an encyclopedia on racism, but such inclusion is understandable given remarks he made on May 17, 2004, at a NAACP event celebrating the 50th anniversary of *Brown v. Board of Education*.

Cosby was born in 1937 and grew up in a housing project in Philadelphia. Cosby credits his paternal grandfather for teaching him how to be a story-teller and a comedian. Cosby dropped out of Temple University in the early 1960s for a shot at a career in stand-up comedy. He got his break in 1964 as co-star in the TV show *I Spy*, and became one of the first African Americans to break through the color line on television. In 1974 Cosby became spokesperson for Jell-O pudding pops, evincing a charm and charisma that appealed to people of all races. Cosby's first major television project was *Fat Albert and the Cosby Kids*, which ran through the 1970s and 1980s. His most successful venture was *The Cosby Show*, which aired from 1984 to 1992, won multiple Emmy Awards, and made Cosby an icon of American fatherhood.

Cosby has always been political. In the 1980s he helped organize the 20th anniversary of the 1963 March on Washington, and he was also a leading voice against apartheid in South Africa. Cosby won the Presidential Medal of Freedom in 2002, the Mark Twain Prize for American Humor in 2009, and was inducted in the Grammy Hall of Fame in 2012. On his television career, he comments, "I did what I did carefully, putting myself in a position to teach with that TV set."

On May 17, 2004, Cosby gave a speech to the NAACP that argued that "the lower economic and lower middle economic people" in the black community were making a travesty of civil rights accomplishments such as the *Brown* decision. They "are not holding their end in this deal," Cosby said (American Rhetoric). Cosby offered much tough love for the black community, restating—in his own inimitable way—much of what is known (and also criticized) in social science circles as the "culture of poverty thesis," which suggests that impoverished groups often establish cultural patterns and behaviors at odds with larger society and which can be inimical to social advancement. Cosby's speech covered a range of social concerns impacting African Americans, including low expectations and lax moral standards, illiteracy, negligent parenting, gun violence, teen pregnancy and promiscuity, lack of ambition, the limits of religion, Afro-centric names, body piercing, Ebonics, attitudes of victimization, and prison.

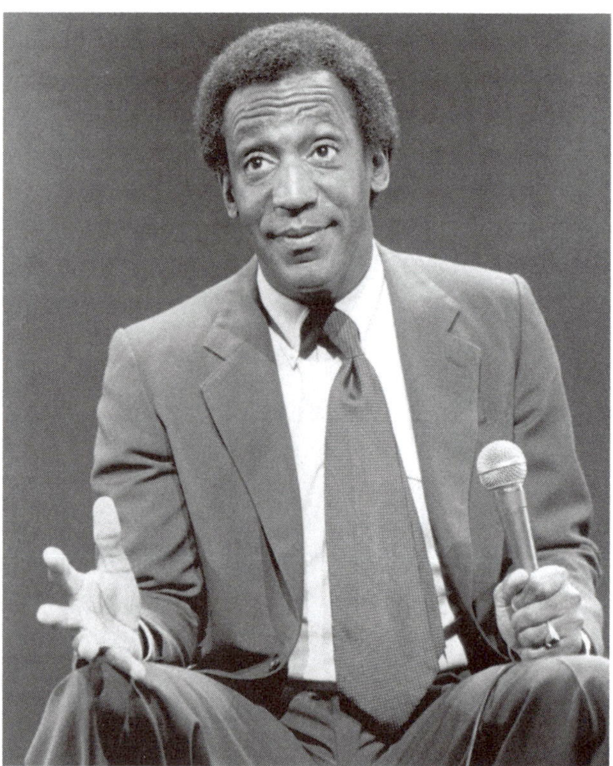

Bill Cosby remains one of the most influential comedians in American entertainment history. (Twentieth Century Fox Classics/Photofest.)

Cosby delivered his speech to much laughter and immediate applause. African American luminaries such as Cornel West and Cory Booker publically praised him for his remarks. Much of the media congratulated Cosby on his candor. An editorial in *USA Today* argued that "destructive personal habits and low education expectations are crippling young black Americans, especially men. [Cosby] is just the voice America needs to break through the silence." Yet the positive reviews were not universal. Some took issue with Cosby airing the black community's dirty laundry in public and suggested his remarks played into the hands of white racism. Critics such as Michael Eric Dyson accused Cosby of having lost his mind by blaming the poor for conditions over which they have little control. He said Cosby should "pick on someone in his own class. If he had come out swinging at Condi Rice or Colin Powell, they could defend themselves. But he's beating up on poor black people, the most vulnerable people in this nation. And why jump on them?" Dyson admits that, "taken in one sense, a lot of what he said we can agree with." Dyson's beef is that "Cosby never acknowledges that most poor blacks don't have a choice about these things."

Cosby has been unrepentant. He has called his words, "blunt, but not harsh" and refers to his critics as "intellectual panhandlers." He says: "You've got these idiots [who] say, 'Bill, you're picking on the poor.' . . . Well, so did Jesus." In 2006, Cosby embarked on a 20-city U.S tour, "A Call Out with Bill Cosby," in which he followed up on the themes of the NAACP speech and which laid the foundation of a book published the next year with Alvin Poussaint.

In recent years, Cosby has weathered multiple accusations of sexual assault with little apparent damage to his reputation, while remaining a strong advocate for social change. He has worked to create socially conscious hip-hop music, as an alternative to what he sees as the regressive, misogynistic, and violent nature of much of the genre. He is still occasionally at odds with majority opinion in the African American community. He suggested in the wake of the 2012 shooting of Trayvon Martin, for example, that ineffective gun laws, more so than racism, were the main factor in the tragedy. Cosby is still performing stand-up and working with the Discovery Channel on a *Brown Hornet* show about the quixotic superhero of the same name from *Fat Albert and the Cosby Kids*. He remains a fierce critic of U.S. society and culture.

Daniel M. Harrison

See also

Television and Racial Stereotypes; Trayvon Martin Case

Further Reading:

American Rhetoric. "Speech to the NAACP on the 50th Anniversary of *Brown v. Board of Education*," http://www.americanrhetoric.com/speeches/billcosbypoundcakespeech.htm (accessed February 4, 2013).

Cosby, Bill and Alvin F. Poussaint. *Come on People: On the Path from Victims to Victors*. Nashville, TN: Thomas Nelson, 2007.

Deggans, Eric. "Cosby's Chuckles Mask a Message." *St. Petersburg Times*, March 21, 2010.

Dyson, Michael Eric. *Is Bill Cosby Right? Or Has the Black Middle Class Lost Its Mind*. New York: Basic Civitas Books, 2005.

Farhi, Paul. "Bill Cosby's Gift of Gab." *Washington Post*, October 26, 2009.

Soloman, Deborah. "Bill Cosby's Not Funny." *New York Times*. March 27, 2005.

USA Today. "Funnyman's Serious Message." May 22, 2006.

Weekend Australian. "Cosby to Blacks: Take Responsibility." May 3, 2008.

Cosmetics

The role that cosmetics played in African American life in the era of Jim Crow owed much to slaves' interactions with beauty culture prior to the Civil War. While enslavement dramatically limited the ability of men and women to engage in any extensive physical adornment, both sexes practiced some forms of cosmetic enhancement using what limited materials were available. Using a blend of traditional African beauty techniques and new practices developed in the Americas, enslaved men and women applied homemade beauty products and special hairstyling techniques to augment their appearances. In a system designed to negate the individuality and personal freedom of the enslaved, such attention to personal grooming could serve as a means of reasserting one's identity and control over the body.

Some slaves had more extensive experience with beauty culture and cosmetic enhancement, however. Both enslaved and free blacks were sometimes employed as beauticians, hairdressers, and barbers for well-off whites. For some free blacks, such employment could be fairly lucrative. In an environment in which there were few well-paying jobs for African Americans, a number of black stylists and beauticians were able to use their earnings to buy others out of slavery or to establish organizations for African Americans that would become central to black communities after Emancipation.

Given the importance of cosmetics and beauty preparations to enslaved African Americans, it is not surprising that Emancipation brought a dramatic increase in African Americans' participation in beauty culture. This was particularly true for black women. While white standards of physical appearance held the physical attributes of both black men and women in low regard, black women had been especially marked by this discourse, and thereby were refused any social claim to beauty or femininity. As African American women's access to cosmetics and other personal care items expanded, the ability to care for and control one's appearance quickly became a central feature of the way African American women created and defined their new identities as free women.

Prior to the late 19th century, most cosmetics for most American women were home preparations or the products of very local manufacturers. In the years leading up to the 20th century, however, national changes in production and consumption helped to establish the development of a large-scale cosmetics industry. Despite the relatively limited purchasing power of African Americans, early cosmetics companies recognized the desire of black women to participate in beauty culture. Encouraged by customer demand, black migration to urban areas in the North and South, and the growth of a black middle class, 19th-century cosmetics companies developed and marketed products for African American consumers.

While most of these companies were white-owned, some African Americans who had been employed in the beauty industry prior to Emancipation were able to use their skills to establish black-owned cosmetics companies. Regardless of business ownership, however, cosmetics produced for black consumers were largely similar. Early commercially produced beauty products for African Americans relied on a racial discourse that continued to regard black physical attributes as ugly or pathological, and linked these features to African Americans' low socioeconomic status and political disenfranchisement. Rather than being designed to enhance natural features, these products promised to help black men and women achieve an appearance that mimicked white standards of beauty, particularly by lightening dark skin and straightening kinky or curly hair.

The early 20th century saw a further expansion of the African American cosmetics and beauty industries, which was part of a larger general development of black-owned businesses and African American entrepreneurship. As African Americans continued to migrate to urban centers in the North and South, the formalized segregation of Jim Crow and informal racial segregation in the North encouraged the growth of black communities. These communities often supported black-owned businesses created to cater solely to an African American base of customers. The growing number of black-owned businesses was accompanied by a continued growth of the black middle class.

Many African American leaders promoted this type of entrepreneurship and community building as a means of improving the conditions of life in America for blacks. African American activist Booker T. Washington was among this group, and in 1900, Washington founded the National Negro Business League to promote African American entrepreneurship and support black-owned businesses. As a result of the support of Washington and others, the success and number of black-owned cosmetics companies rose dramatically in the first few decades of the 20th century. Along with this expansion came increased economic opportunity for African Americans and the foundation for a growing movement for African American social justice and black identity.

Anthony Overton, a child born into slavery in 1865, was one of the first very successful African American cosmetics manufacturers. After a number of disappointments in other professions, Overton founded the Overton Hygienic Manufacturing Company in 1898. The popularity of this company's products led to the Overton line's establishment as the first black-owned line of products to be sold in F. W. Woolworth's, a popular national chain store. Like many black business owners in the cosmetics industry and other trades, Overton used his success to contribute to African American organizations and institutions. Additionally, the Overton Hygienic Manufacturing Company only hired black employees, and Overton personally helped to finance *Half-Century* magazine, an African American publication that helped to promote black women's associations.

While Overton was one of the earliest success stories in the African American cosmetics industries, this field soon came to be dominated by African American women, who proved to be uniquely adept at identifying and responding to the complicated physical anxieties and social meanings of cosmetics shared by other black women. One of the early female large-scale manufacturers of cosmetics for black women was Annie Turnbo Malone, who began her career in 1900 marketing a formula to promote hair growth, but whose business expanded to become Poro, an international company with customers in the United States, Africa, South America, and the Caribbean.

One of Malone's biggest competitors was a former employee, Madam C. J. Walker, who was born Sarah Breedlove to former slaves in Louisiana in 1867. Walker's early life was a difficult one. Like Malone, Walker was orphaned as a young child. Unlike Malone, Walker's life was marked by physical abuse, intense poverty, and very limited education. Like many African American women with few appealing economic choices, Walker was attracted to a career in the African American beauty industry, and began working for Poro as a sales representative in 1903. Within three years, Walker had founded Madam C. J. Walker Preparations, which, like Poro, sold facial treatments, powders, and other cosmetic treatments created for and marketed exclusively to African American women.

As black women became influential manufacturers of African American beauty products, and as African American engagement with social justice issues increased, the nature of cosmetics for black consumers began to change. While hair products and treatments continued to be a cornerstone of African American beauty culture, both Walker and Malone refused to include hair-straightening products in their cosmetics lines, choosing instead to focus on the manufacture of products designed to care for and enhance the natural beauty of African American hair.

Other notable cosmetics companies founded by African American women include the Apex Beauty System, founded in 1920 by Sarah Spencer, which later made Spencer one of the first African American millionaires in America. Madame N. A. Franklin expanded a 1915 beauty salon into a chain of salons and, eventually, one of the first major lines of cosmetics to include face powders intended to flatter, rather than lighten, darker skin tones.

Like Overton, many African American women who founded cosmetics companies used their success as a sociopolitical tool, using their sometimes substantial wealth to contribute financially to African American activist organizations. In 1917, Walker founded the Madam C. J. Walker Hair Culturists Union of America. That same year, Malone founded Poro College, a school for aspiring African American beauticians. Spencer likewise founded beauty schools in the United States and in international locations. In addition to providing support for African American stylists and beauticians, these institutions also acted as important sites of black consciousness and activism. Agents of the Madam C. J. Walker Hair Culturists Union of America staged letter-writing and petition campaigns to protest lynching and demand a presidential response to race riots in East St. Louis, while Poro College temporarily housed the National Negro Business League.

In addition to active support of black racial issues, manufacturers and distributors of cosmetics for African Americans provided economic opportunities that were not available elsewhere. While relatively few blacks were able to become successful founders of their own cosmetics company, a great many African Americans, women in particular, were able to find employment in such companies, which provided a much-desired alternative to the grueling, low-paying agricultural and domestic work that most black workers faced.

Despite the employment opportunities that careers in the cosmetics industry offered to African Americans, and the potential that cosmetics offered black women for reclaimed femininity and self-actualization, many African Americans from all socioeconomic classes were troubled by black beauty culture. Some of these concerns were similar to those shared by entrepreneurs like Walker and Malone, as the continued market popularity of skin-lightening creams and hair-straightening treatments struck many black Americans as a troubling sign of continued racism in physical culture and a lack of pride in African American identity among consumers.

Other critics of African American beauty culture feared that, in the process of using personal adornment to forge their identities, black women risked neglecting internal personal development in the form of education, social activism, and moral development. Furthermore, while the economic hardships of the Great Depression forced many black-owned businesses to close, black consumption of cosmetics and beauty aids dipped only slightly, causing many African Americans to worry that the funds of black communities were being misspent.

Despite the concerns of critics of the African American cosmetics industry, the popularity of black beauty culture only increased into the latter half of the 20th century, as did the power and status of African American stylists and cosmetologists within black communities. Much of this power and status was derived from the relative economic freedom these careers bestowed. While most African Americans relied on whites for employment or customers, beauticians, cosmetologists, and hairdressers remained one of the few categories of business owners catering exclusively to a black clientele. As such, these individuals were able to participate in civil rights activities and the growing civil rights movement without fear of economic retribution. As a result of this freedom, beauty shops and salons became popular public spaces within which black activists could organize, recruit, and hold meetings. Staging such activities worked to the benefit of visitors to salons and beauty shops as well, as it allowed black activists to mask their engagement with the civil rights movement as the mundane, seemingly apolitical act of personal grooming.

As black communities and the African American beauty industry became increasingly activist and political, many symbols of African American beauty and black femininity changed or took on new meanings. The most dramatic change that occurred within the cosmetics and beauty industry during this era centered on hair treatments, one of the industry's most important products. Despite the objections of many early 20th-century African Americans and some black manufacturers of cosmetics, the popularity of straightened hair for black women only increased throughout the 1940s, becoming a standard marker of black female beauty and feminine respectability by the 1950s.

In the years following 1960, with the growth of the civil rights movement, some black men and women, particularly young and educated black men and women, rejected hair-straightening treatments, choosing instead to wear their hair as it grew naturally, in a style that became known as the Afro. For those who wore it, the Afro served as a political statement and an assertion of black pride and beauty that extended beyond activism and became part of one's physical appearance. Like generations of African Americans before them, those who adopted the Afro used personal adornment as a means of creating a sociopolitical identity to make a statement about black personhood in America. While this look initially required little assistance from cosmetics companies or salons, it was not long before a market arose to provide products and services designed to enhance the appearance and upkeep of the Afro hairstyle.

SKYLAR HARRIS

See also

Cosmetic Surgery; Passing; Skin Lightening

Further Reading:

Banks, Ingrid. *Hair Matters: Beauty, Power, and Black Women's Consciousness.* New York: New York University Press, 2000.

Blackwelder, Julia Kirk. *Styling Jim Crow: African American Beauty Training During Segregation.* College Station: Texas A&M University Press, 2003.

Bundles, A'Leila. *On Her Own Ground: The Life and Times of Madame C. J. Walker.* New York: Scribners, 2001.

Craig, Maxine Leeds. *Ain't I a Beauty Queen: Black Women, Beauty, and the Politics of Race.* New York: Oxford University Press, 2002.

Peiss, Kathy. *Hope in a Jar: The Making of America's Beauty Culture.* New York: Metropolitan Books, 1998.

Walker, Susannah. *Style & Status: Selling Beauty to African American Women, 1920–1975.* Lexington: University Press of Kentucky, 2007.

Costigan-Wagner Anti-Lynching Bill

The Costigan-Wagner Anti-Lynching Bill was an important and controversial bill calling for the federal government to take an active role in ending lynching in the United States. Senators Edward Costigan of Colorado and Robert Wagner of New York introduced the bill into Congress on January 4, 1934. Under the bill, any state officer who failed to exercise diligence in protecting a person under their care from a lynch mob or who neglected to arrest persons involved in a lynching could themselves be subject to federal imprisonment for five years and a $5,000 fine. The Costigan-Wagner Bill received support from several members of Congress; however, the bill never passed. Southern opposition managed to defeat it in 1934, 1935, 1937, 1938, and 1940.

The Costigan-Wagner Anti-Lynching Bill was not the first anti-lynching bill proposed and failed in Congress. The history of failed attempts to pass a federal anti-lynching law goes back to the 1890s, when racist Southerners took control of the Democratic Party and redeemed the South. Southern redemption came at the high cost of black lives. Blacks were lynched in record numbers by whites, many for crimes they did not commit. Lynching became a tool used by racist white Southerners to scare the South's black population into submission, while opening the door to several new laws that infringed on their legal rights. These new laws, known as the Jim Crow laws, created an atmosphere of segregation, discrimination, and disfranchisement.

Racism in the South became so oppressive that blacks began to migrate to the North. The Northern migration of blacks between 1914 and 1950 is known as the Great Migration. During this period, over 1 million blacks migrated to the North in hopes of escaping the Jim Crow South. As a result, racial tensions rose in the North. In the summer of 1919, the racial tensions in the North turned violent with several race riots. These race riots dispelled any notion that racism and violence were uniquely Southern problems. Blacks soon realized that racism and violence could be found in most parts of the nation.

In the midst of all of this racial violence, a campaign to end lynching across the United States began. The campaign was led by black women who called themselves the Anti-Lynching Crusaders. The goal of the Anti-Lynching Crusaders was to raise money to support the passage of an anti-lynching bill introduced into Congress in 1918 by Congressman Leonidas Dyer of Missouri. On January 26, 1922, the Dyer Bill made history. It became the first anti-lynching bill to pass the House of Representatives. However, the bill never made it through the Senate. In 1923, the Dyer Bill was reintroduced into Congress. Once again, the bill was defeated in the Senate.

By 1930, the anti-lynching campaign picked up again when the National Association for the Advancement of Colored People (NAACP) announced it would lead a national campaign to end lynching across the United States. The NAACP enlisted the help of two U.S. senators, Edward Costigan of Colorado and Robert Wagner of New York. The two senators agreed to draft and introduce a new anti-lynching bill in Congress. The Costigan-Wagner Anti-Lynching Bill would punish any law officer who did not protect a person from being lynched.

At the time that the Costigan-Wagner Anti-Lynching Bill was being introduced in Congress, America was experiencing the worst economic depression in its history and embarking on a presidential election. In 1932, Franklin D. Roosevelt became president of the United States. In 1933, he initiated a series of programs, called the New Deal, to end the economic hardships of the Great Depression. The president geared the New Deal programs to big business, agriculture, and labor. During this time, Roosevelt did not try to pass any legislation regarding race relations in the United States because he was fearful that white Southern Democrats would not support his New Deal programs. Thus, the president did not support the Costigan-Wagner Anti-Lynching Bill. The bill was introduced in Congress several times, but without the support of the president, it never passed.

SHARLENE SINEGAL DECUIR

See also

Anti-Lynching Legislation; Lynching

Further Reading:

Sitkoff, Harvard. *A New Deal for Blacks: The Emergence of Civil Rights as a National Issue: The Depression Decade.* New York: Oxford University Press, 1978.

Zangrando, Robert L. *The NAACP Crusade Against Lynching, 1909–1950.* Philadelphia: Temple University Press, 1980.

Crack versus Cocaine

Two forms of cocaine, powder and crack, have been treated very differently by the criminal justice system in the United States, ultimately leading to a disproportionate number of African Americans being incarcerated on narcotics charges. African Americans are statistically more likely to use crack than powder cocaine, and American laws treat possession of crack as a more serious offense than powder cocaine. Thus, the crack vs. cocaine debate has come to stand for the idea that in the United States, the legal system itself is at least partly responsible for the overrepresentation of blacks in prisons.

There are several key differences between crack and powder cocaine. Cocaine is derived from the coca plant, which is grown primarily in the Andes. Crack is produced by heating powder cocaine and mixing it with baking soda or ammonia to produce small crystals. Pure powder cocaine is snorted, bringing it to the nasal passages to produce feelings of euphoria. Crack cocaine is usually smoked and is known for giving a faster high. Crack is much cheaper to buy than powder cocaine.

There are also key differences in the way the American legal system has treated crack versus powder cocaine. In 1986, the Anti–Drug Abuse Act stipulated that possessors of five grams of crack—an amount equal to about two sugar packets—would receive a mandatory five-year sentence. Surprisingly, a similar penalty was meted out to those found

ACLU Statement on the Fair Sentencing Act (FSA), June 21, 2012

The FSA was passed to "correct the problems with the Anti–Drug Abuse Act of 1986, which created an unfair sentencing scheme that unequally punished comparable offenses involving crack and powder cocaine—two forms of the same drug—and resulted in racially biased sentencing. To remedy the fact that the 100:1 ratio was without penological or scientific justification, and that it resulted in black defendants suffering significantly harsher penalties than white defendants, Congress passed the FSA and reduced the ratio from 100:1 to 18:1. . . . the only truly fair and empirically sound ratio would be 1:1." (ACLU)

guilty of possessing *500* grams of powder cocaine. The chemical structure of both substances is the same, whereas their treatment in the legal system is very different.

Narcotics laws, created as part of the "War on Drugs" that began with President Richard Nixon in the 1970s, mandate minimum sentences for drug offenses. When an individual is found guilty of illegal behavior in the area of narcotics, judges have no discretion in sentencing. Thus, the disparity in sentencing for offenses in crack versus powder cocaine possession means that those found guilty of crack possession are treated much more harshly than those with powder cocaine. Since blacks are statistically more likely to use crack than powder cocaine, these minimum sentence requirements have had a strong negative effect on this population. There are many examples of the harsh consequences of these narcotics policies for black Americans. For example, a 25-year-old mother of four, with welfare her only source of income and no criminal record, mailed a package containing crack for a dealer. She received $47.40 for the transaction. The judge reluctantly sentenced her to the mandatory 10-year sentence for such an infraction. If she had been paid for mailing powdered cocaine, her punishment would have been only three years.

The laws treating possession of crack as the more serious offense are at least partially responsible for the overrepresentation of African Americans in prisons. Although more whites and Latinos use crack than do blacks, blacks are more likely to be found guilty of violating the laws against crack. Some studies indicate that black crack users are more likely to be arrested than any other category of drug users. Once a person is convicted of a crack-related crime, their lives will be negatively altered even after release. Since those found guilty of such crimes are more likely to be black, the inequalities in narcotics punishments help to perpetuate racial inequalities.

The differential treatment of the two forms of cocaine has been justified by some policy makers on grounds that suggest racial stereotyping. Compared to powder cocaine, crack was alleged to create antisocial, violent, and criminal behavior, supposedly contributing to the deterioration of urban neighborhoods. Although there is no concrete evidence to support such assertions, alarmists have claimed crack could spread from poor black neighborhoods into white communities.

The media has been responsible for reinforcing these racist images surrounding crack cocaine. According to sociologists Craig Reinarman and Harry G. Levine, in the late 1980s and into the early 1990s, American politicians and news media outlets regularly promoted stories of an "epidemic" of drug use, especially of crack cocaine. One notable allegation was that "crack babies" were being born to irresponsible pregnant women. There is no evidence, however, that crack is more harmful to a developing fetus than is powder cocaine, or that there has been an "epidemic" of crack over powder cocaine use in the United States among pregnant women or any other population.

Although the American legal system has been unrelenting in its war against crack cocaine, it is arguable that U.S. foreign policy actually helped create the crack trade. During the Reagan administration in the 1980s the CIA supported the Contras, a paramilitary group in Nicaragua and Honduras that was trying to overthrow the progressive Sandinista government. When Congress forbade direct aid to the Contras because of their atrocious war strategies, the Contras turned to cocaine trafficking, working with the Colombian Medellín Cartel. Some of that cocaine found its way to Los Angeles, where an enterprising narcotics dealer named Rick Ross found that large profits could be made by transforming an expensive drug into a much cheaper one: crack. A market for crack then developed in African American and Latino communities where life is difficult and this drug-induced escape could be achieved relatively cheaply. Selling crack also offered employment opportunities for those otherwise shut out of the job market. Those on the lowest rungs of this enterprise—blacks—are most likely to be imprisoned.

There have been attempts to rectify the disparity between the legal system's treatment of crack versus powder cocaine. The U.S. Sentencing Commission is a bipartisan body that makes recommendations to Congress and the federal courts on sentencing guidelines. In 1995 the commission unsuccessfully recommended equal sentencing for the two forms of cocaine. U.S. Sentencing Commission chairman Richard P. Conaboy testified that the commission was troubled by the disparity in penalties between crack and powder cocaine, and that they believed those penalties had a disproportionately greater negative impact on minorities. Many judges have also opposed the mandatory minimums and the differences in punishment for the two types of cocaine. During his 2008 campaign, Barack Obama said publicly that he believed the disparity should end.

There have been some reforms, although the impact has been relatively minor. In 2010 the Fair Sentencing Act reduced the amount of crack that would lead to a mandatory sentence. The ratio to powder cocaine became 18 to 1, instead of 100 to 1, and a few states ended mandatory minimums. Nevertheless, many would argue that there is still an unjustifiable disparity in the legal penalties for crack versus powder cocaine; a disparity that has contributed significantly to the disproportionately high imprisonment of blacks.

Barbara Chasin

Further Reading:

ACLU. http://www.aclu.org/blog/criminal-law-reform/aclu-lens-supreme-court-rules-fairer-sentencesapply-more-drug-cases (accessed November 19, 2012).

Bourgois, Philippe. *In Search of Respect: Selling Crack in El Barrio.* Second ed. New York: Cambridge University Press, 1996.

"House I Live In: New Documentary Exposes Economic, Moral Failure of U.S. War on Drugs." *Democracy Now.* http://www.democracynow.org/2012/1/31/the_house_i_live_in_new. January 31, 2012.

Mauer, Marc. *Race to Incarcerate,* 2d ed. New York: New Press, 2006.

McCoy, Alfred W. *The Politics of Heroin: CIA Complicity in the Global Drug Trade.* Chicago: Lawrence Hill Books, 1991.

National Drug Strategy Network. "Newsbriefs: House Holds Hearings on Crack/Powder Cocaine Sentencing Disparity." http://www.ndsn.org/sept95/crack.html. September 1995.

Reinerman, Craig, and Harry G. Levine. "Crack in Context: America's Latest Demon Drug." In *Crack in America: Demon Drugs and Social Justice,* edited by Craig Reinarman and Harry G. Levine. Berkeley: University of California Press, 1997.

Craniometry

A subdiscipline of anthropometry, the study of the human body for use in anthropological classification and comparison, craniometry is the practice of the measurement of various features of the human face and cranium in order to classify subjects according to race, sex, and body type. Craniometry, and the related practice of phrenology and other positivistic pseudo-scientific methods, entered the burgeoning fields of criminology and penology with the writings and early work of Franz Josef Gall, Johan Gaspar Spurzheim, Eliza W. Farnham, and Cesare Lombroso.

While the practice of assigning social characteristics to physical traits had been a folk-practice in numerous cultures, physiognomy, or reading the outward physical appearance as an indicator or predictor of social behavior, did not emerge in its own right until the early writings of Swiss poet and cleric Johann Caspar Lavater. Lavater, who in 1878 wrote in *Essays in Physiognomy,* "It is equally clear that intellectual life, or the powers of the understanding of the mind, make themselves most apparent in the circumference and form of the solid parts of the head, especially the forehead," is perhaps the first to advance early positivistic logics associating physical traits with psychological health, morality, and criminality.

Expanding upon these early physiognomic concepts, German physiologist Franz Josef Gall's practice of phrenology purported that human behavior, including emotions and cognitive ability, localized in certain parts of the brain and therefore could be estimated by reading the contours of the skull.

Though Gall and his student, Johann Gaspar Spurzheim, are credited with founding "bumpology" as it was later called, phrenology is perhaps best known in the field of criminology as discussed by Italian physician and psychiatrist Cesare Lombroso in his important work, *Criminal Man.* First published in 1876, *Criminal Man* outlined the Lombrosian theory of the born criminal (*delinquent nato*)—a morally defective and dangerous individual marked with various physical anomalies or stigmata. The first chapter of the first edition of *Criminal Man* details a thorough examination of 66 "criminal craniums" and notes various characteristics including the age and crimes of the individuals as well as the exact circumference of their skulls. Lombroso further identifies a number of other details including the distance between the ocular cavities, pattern of cranial sutures, prognathism or an "ape like" forward thrust of the lower face, as dominant characteristics in his sample and thus dominant predictors of criminality. Lombroso theorized that these stigmata, with cranial abnormalities chiefly among them, identified atavistic, or devolved, individuals biologically predisposed to antisocial and criminal behaviors. Along with other physical and social stigmata such as tattoos and jargon, Lombroso offered up a catalogue, or archive, of the characteristics of his atavistic criminal man and later criminal woman.

Craniometry and phrenology, like the balance of physiognomic methods, were dismissed as pseudo-sciences as the fields of medicine, psychiatry, and psychology advanced. However, the legacy of biological positivism entwined with early physiognomy and craniometry left an indelible mark on the social sciences and attendant social policies. For instance, Spurzheim, along with Charles Darwin, were among the first to suggest a eugenic solution to social problems such as drunkenness, crime, and poverty. Spurzheim suggested that craniometrics and other anthropometric stigmata be used to govern the laws of propagation with the hope that social maladies could be effectively bred out of society.

Though craniometry and phrenology have long been dismissed, they remain important contributors and the forebears of modern criminology, criminal jurisprudence, and penology. Today, some argue technological advances in genetics promise to resurrect the legacy of craniometry and its unfortunate eugenic connections. Critics of the burgeoning fields of biosocial criminology argue that the search for "criminal genes" is but an up-to-date, technological take on the craniometry and phrenology of old.

Travis Linnemann and Danielle Dirks

See also

Cesare Lombroso Theory

Further Reading:

Lavater, Johann Caspar. *Essays on Physiognomy*, trans. W. Teggs, 1878.

Lombroso, Cesare. *Criminal Man*. Durham, NC: Duke University Press, 2006 (1876).

Rafter, Nicole. "The Murderous Dutch Fiddler Criminology, History and the Problem of Phrenology." *Theoretical Criminology* 9 (2005): 65–96.

Rafter, Nicole. "HJ Eysenck in Fagin's Kitchen: The Return to Biological Theory in 20th-Century Criminology." *History of the Human Sciences* 19, no. 4 (2006): 37–56.

Rafter, Nicole. *The Origins of Criminology: A Reader*. New York: Routledge, 2009.

Crime and Race

The relationship between crime and race in the United States is a subject of intense and very contentious inquiry. The controversy begins with large disparities in crime counts between blacks and whites. Differing explanations for these disparities keep the argument going. Complicating this issue is the fact that black Americans tend to have a less favorable view of the criminal justice system, especially the police.

Two of the most well-known measures of crime in the United States are the Federal Bureau of Investigation's (FBI) Uniform Crime Reports (UCR) and the Bureau of Justice Statistics' National Crime Victimization Survey (NCVS). Since 1930, the UCR has provided official statistics collected from police agencies throughout the United States. Police agencies voluntarily submit statistics on the crimes that are reported to them and the arrests they make to the FBI, which then collates the data. In 2001, nearly 17,000 agencies participated, covering 92 percent of the total population. The NCVS, on the other hand, collects data through the use of a telephone survey conducted by the Bureau of the Census. A nationally representative sample of about 45,000 households and 94,000 persons are asked whether they have been victims of crime and, if so, the characteristics of that crime.

Both the UCR and the NCVS show similar trends regarding the race of offenders. Generally, the number of minorities identified as offenders is disproportionately high compared with their overall numbers in the population. As Ronald J. Berger et al. advise the NCVS, "Data are consistent with the UCR. The offenders in these types of crimes are disproportionately young, nonwhite, and male" (2001: 51). Even though both indicators show minorities as offenders

National Crime Victimization Survey (NCVS)

The National Crime Victimization Survey (NCVS) is an annual, nationally representative survey of 42,000 households meant to determine the frequency, characteristics, and consequences of various kinds of crimes in the United States. The results can be sorted and analyzed with regard to gender, race, age, and urbanization. The Bureau of Justice Statistics (BJS) has administered this survey since 1973. The data collected through this survey is available to researchers and has resulted in many published books and articles addressing crime, changes in crime rates over time, and the relationship between crime rates and race. Preliminary analyses of this survey are also published by the BJS, allowing those without advanced statistical training to gain access to the data and findings.

Since 1997, as part of this NCVS, the BJS and the FBI have been collecting data about hate crimes. These are the first significant data on hate crimes broken down by race available in the United States, and so the NCVS has been important both in terms of research and public policy with regard to these crimes. The numbers found in this survey have forced both academia and lawmakers to take note of hate crimes as a serious social problem. The study has also revealed such surprising findings as African Americans being disproportionately represented among those charged with hate crimes, particularly against whites.

MIKAILA MARIEL LEMONIK ARTHUR

in disproportionate numbers, there are well-known weaknesses with both measures, which means one must use extreme caution when interpreting these figures.

Arrest statistics for murder/nonnegligent manslaughter provide an example of how crime figures can be interpreted with respect to race. These figures indicate that blacks generally have high rates of arrest disproportionate with their numbers in the population. In 2001, blacks were the subject of arrest in 48.7 percent of the murders/nonnegligent manslaughters, and whites represented 48.4 percent of the arrests for those same crimes (Federal Bureau of Investigation 2001: 252). Since whites make up approximately 75 percent of the population and blacks about 12 percent of the population (based on 2000 census data for those reporting only one race), this means that blacks are overrepresented in this arrest category. One way to interpret this disparity is that it is because of overt discrimination by police in arresting more blacks. However, examining the characteristics of the offenders (based on victims' descriptions) for murder/nonnegligent manslaughter, approximately 48 percent of offenders are identified as white and 49 percent of offenders are identified as black (*Sourcebook of Criminal Justice Statistics, 2001* 2002: 314). These offender percentages closely reflect the arrest percentages, suggesting that interpretation of these statistics must be done cautiously, especially with respect to determining overt discrimination in the system.

Regarding race as a correlate of crime, today researchers essentially accept the paradigm that "although some of the racial differences observed in official statistics can be attributed to differential responses by the criminal justice system, criminologists generally agree that there are real differences in behavior as well. . . . However, . . . there has been a general reluctance 'to speak openly about the race and crime connection' and thus the theoretical mechanisms underlying the race-crime connection are not well understood" (South and Messner 2000: 87–88).

Even though the connections between race and crime are not fully known, explanations for this disparity are plentiful and have led to enormous debate. Some of the more notable arguments to explain the disparity center on poverty and disadvantage due to race; cultural phenomena, such as a subculture of violence; the neighborhood or area where minorities tend to live; family disruption; and similar causes. Multilevel analysis argues that there are many causes and that explanations can be found by looking at the individuals, the communities, and, some anecdotal work suggests, in discrimination rampant in the criminal justice system.

Regardless of these arguments, it is clear that there is a racial divide in trust of various aspects of the criminal justice system, especially the police. In a recent Gallup poll, 61 percent of whites expressed confidence in the police, compared to only 34 percent of blacks. Additionally, high-profile incidents of police brutality, such as in the Amadou Diallo, Abner Louima, Rodney King, and Patrick Dorismond cases, certainly leave an impression of discrimination, even though it may not be systemic.

Thus, the relationship between crime and race is not fully explored. Social scientists generally agree that there is a disparity between whites and blacks in crime statistics and in the response of the criminal justice system. The reasons for this disparity are the subject of continued scrutiny and debate.

John Eterno

See also

Criminal Justice System and Racial Discrimination; Domestic Violence; Felon Disenfranchisement; Furtive Movement; *Gonzales v. Abercrombie & Fitch Stores* (2003); Implicit Bias; Police Brutality; Prison Gangs; Prison-Industrial Complex; Prisons; Racial Disparities in Capital Punishment; Racial Profiling; Sentencing Disparities; Three Strikes Laws. Document: *Furman v. Georgia* (1972)

Further Reading:

Berger, Ronald J., Marvin D. Free Jr., and Patricia Searles. *Crime, Justice and Society: Criminology and the Sociological Imagination*. New York: McGraw-Hill, 2001.

Federal Bureau of Investigation. *Crime in the United States: Uniform Crime Reports*. Washington, DC: U.S. Government Printing Office, 2001.

Senna, Joseph J., and Larry J. Siegel. *Essentials of Criminal Justice*, 3rd ed. Belmont, CA: Wadsworth, 2001.

Sourcebook of Criminal Justice Statistics, 2001. Washington, DC: U.S. Government Printing Office, 2002.

South, Scott J., and Steven F. Messner. "Crime and Demography: Multiple Linkages, Reciprocal Relations." *Annual Review of Sociology* 26, no. 1 (2000): 83–106.

Criminal Justice System and Racial Discrimination

The criminal justice system encompasses policing, criminal-court processes, sentencing, incarceration, and additional supervision. In each of these areas, research has shown race to be a significant factor in outcome. Frequently, race interacts with economic status, leading many prominent social scientists to conclude that justice policies targeting low-income and otherwise disadvantaged communities are likely to have a more severe impact on African Americans than on people of other races. Census data demonstrates that a disproportionately high percentage of black and Latino households fall below the poverty line, and Justice Department statistics demonstrate that blacks and Latinos make up a disproportionately high percentage of defendants, inmates, probationers, and parolees. Justice Department data also demonstrates that a higher percentage of black defendants than white or Latino defendants are indigent.

According to the Bureau of Justice Statistics, 9 percent of all African Americans were under correctional supervision of some sort (incarcerated, or supervised by probation or parole) in 1997, while only 2 percent of whites and 1 percent of all other races combined were under correctional supervision. In many U.S. cities, young black men are taken out of their communities through incarceration at very high rates. Although research has shown that there are race-based inconsistencies in the application of sentences, including capital punishment, the federal courts have been equivocal in response. In *Gideon v. Wainwright* (1963) and then in *Miranda v. Arizona* (1966) the Supreme Court established, respectively, the right to an attorney and the right of suspects to be informed of their rights prior to questioning in police custody. Both of these decisions had the effect of increasing protections that had previously been lacking for low-income suspects and defendants. However, these two decisions rested firmly on principles of equality before the law regardless of financial resources, thereby protecting against explicit discrimination. The Court has not, however, supported protections against implicit discrimination based on race.

The War on Drugs initiated by the Reagan administration mandates sentences based on type and weight of drug. Sentences for crack cocaine, a less expensive form of cocaine used primarily by African Americans, are one hundred times more severe than sentences for cocaine in its powder form, which is more expensive and more prevalent than crack among white drug users. This disparity alone is responsible for a significant portion of the increase in incarceration of African Americans since 1980. Many activists argue that American drug laws are disproportionately targeting

Attorneys Barry Scheck (left) and Johnnie Cochran (right) flank their clients: Jarmaine Grant (second left), Keshon Moore (center), Danny Reyes (center right), and Rayshawn Brown at a press conference in New York on September 8, 1999. The four African American men were stopped on the New Jersey Turnpike in 1998 and shot by state troopers, which led to a criminal investigation of two state troopers and a statewide examination of racial profiling among the state police. (AP/Wide World Photos)

minorities and are discriminatory. Whether or not there was any discriminatory intent in the law, it is clear that American drug laws are affecting minorities and minority communities to a greater degree than they are affecting white communities. There is also evidence that blacks and Hispanics are sentenced to longer prison terms than are their white counterparts.

Race is also a factor in who is questioned and arrested for crimes. There has been considerable controversy over racial profiling, which is the practice of questioning people, most often black men, who are statistically more likely to have been involved in a crime. Critics of this practice argue that it constitutes racial harassment. The practice of police pulling over African American motorists has become so common that the "offense" has become informally known as a DWB—Driving While Black. After the terrorist attacks of September 11, 2001, racial profiling began to target men of Middle Eastern descent. Civil libertarian groups object to the practice of racial profiling because it violates the right to equal treatment under the law. Some law enforcement officials argue that it is an essential tool in combating crime and terrorism.

Robin Roger-Dillon

See also

Crime and Race; Felon Disenfranchisement; Marked; *New Jim Crow, The*; Prison Industrial Complex; Racial Disparities in Capital Punishment; Racial Profiling; Three Strikes Laws

Further Reading:

Beckett, Katherine, and Theodore Sasson. *The Politics of Injustice: Crime and Punishment in America*. Thousand Oaks, CA: Sage Publications, 2000.

Cole, David. *No Equal Justice: Race and Class in the American Criminal Justice System*. New York: New Press, 1999.

Kennedy, Randall. *Race, Crime and the Law*. New York: Pantheon, 1997.

Tonry, Michael. *Malign Neglect: Race, Crime, and Punishment in America*. New York: Oxford University Press, 1995.

Crusade for Justice (CFJ)

The Crusade for Justice (CFJ), for a short time, was the most successful organization in the Chicano movement.

Founded in Denver, Colorado, in 1966, the CFJ was led by poet Rodolfo "Corky" Gonzales, a former professional boxer, bail bondsman, Democratic Party leader, and major protagonist in Denver's War on Poverty. Gonzales had become disenchanted with mainstream politics and began protesting Denver's policy toward its impoverished Mexican American population. The name of the organization came from a 1966 speech in which Gonzales declared "that on this day a new crusade for justice has been born." The name stuck. In 1968, Gonzales and his group bought a building and named it the Center for the Crusade for Justice; it became a place where the Mexican American community could gather for a variety of services. It contained a 500-seat auditorium, a ballroom, a dining room, a kitchen, a Mexican gift shop, a gymnasium, a nursery, an art gallery, a library, and classrooms.

The CFJ became involved in educational reform in the late 1960s, seeking to end discrimination in the Denver Public Schools. In November 1968, the CFJ presented a list of demands at a school board meeting, and the following spring, Gonzales led a walkout at West Side High School, calling for the removal of a teacher who had made racist remarks in the classroom. The walkout lasted three days, during which riots broke out and several confrontations with the police ensued. The police jailed 25 protesters, including Gonzales.

The CFJ achieved prominence after Gonzales co-chaired, with Reis López Tijerina, the Mexican American contingent of the Poor People's March in the spring of 1968. The Poor People's March and efforts by blacks to gain civil rights and achieve self-sufficiency greatly impressed Gonzales, who then sought to achieve self-sufficiency for his community in Denver. The CFJ became so well-known that in 1969 it sponsored the National Chicano Youth Liberation Conference to bring together and unify Mexican American young people from around the country. The conference focused on cultural identity and social revolution, emphasizing ethnic nationalism and cultural pride. An estimated 1,500 youths attended, including young, artists, poets, and filmmakers such as Alurista and Jesús Treviño. During the conference, those in attendance drafted *El Plan Espiritual de Aztlán*, a manifesto that articulated the growing feelings of nationalism and desire for self-determination among the Mexican Americans of the Southwest. It also asserted the need for Mexican Americans to control their communities. In short, *El Plan* stressed the movement's commitment to developing justice and independence.

The group then took on the issue of police brutality and earned the enmity of Denver's law enforcement establishment—and with it constant police harassment. On March 17, 1973, Denver police clashed with CFJ members; in the fracas, a policeman and a Crusade member were wounded, and 20-year-old Louis Martínez was killed. This outbreak, which led to the almost complete dissolution of the CFJ, was indirectly provoked by incessant police vigilance regarding CFJ activities in Denver.

F. Arturo Rosales

See also

Chicano Movement; Gonzales, Corky

Further Reading:

Marín, Christine. *A Spokesman of the Mexican American Movement: Rodolfo "Corky" Gonzales and the Fight for Chicano Liberation, 1966–1972*. San Francisco: R and E Research Associates, 1977.

Meier, Matt, and Feliciano Rivera. *Dictionary of Mexican American History*. Westport, CT: Greenwood Press, 1981.

Cultural Genocide

Cultural genocide refers to the deliberate and systematic destruction of the cultural heritage, religion, language, and way of life of a group of people. Initial drafts of the 1948 United Nations Convention on Genocide included an explicit statement forbidding cultural genocide, as well as biological genocide (e.g., restricting births, sterilization, compulsory abortions, and segregation of sexes), and physical genocide (killing—whether quickly as in mass murder, or slowly as in economic deprivation). Examples of cultural genocide include the forcible transfer of children to another group, the forced and systematic exile of individuals representing the culture of a group, prohibition of the use of the national language (even in private), the systematic destruction of religious works or books printed in the national language (as well as prohibition of new publications), systematic destruction of historical or religious monuments or their diversion to alien uses, and destruction or dispersion of documents and objects of historical, artistic, or religious value and of objects used in religious worship.

The United States immediately resisted the 1948 UN proposal (the Genocide Convention on the Prevention and Punishment of Genocide) to prohibit cultural genocide because U.S. politicians were concerned that U.S. treatment of minorities would be in violation of such injunctions. As a result, the subsequent version of the convention has excluded any explicit mention of cultural genocide. In the United States, American Indians have historically suffered both physical and cultural genocide at the hands of the U.S. government. After the physical genocide of conquest, the remaining American Indians were subject to a cultural genocide in which their land was taken away; their icons were destroyed; their children were forcibly removed, taught to speak other languages, and worship other gods; and their religious practices were forbidden.

Tracy Chu

See also

American Eugenics Movement; Genocide

Further Reading:

Davidson, Lawrence. *Cultural Genocide*. New Brunswick, NJ: Rutgers University Press, 2012.

Tinker, George E. *Missionary Conquest: The Gospel and Native American Cultural Genocide*. Minneapolis: Fortress Press, 1993.

Cultural Racism

"Latinos don't care about American laws" or "Blacks are lazy and prefer welfare over work" are common sentiments of cultural racism. Cultural racism is denoted by wide, sweeping generalizations about racial groups and the cultural traits that society associates with them. When racial disparities are raised in conversation, such as educational or employment gaps, adherents to cultural racism blame the racial minority group for having a bad, dysfunctional culture as the cause of the racial disparity.

Democratic U.S. senator Daniel Patrick Moynihan, who wrote the 1965 report *The Negro Family: The Case for National Action*, a report analyzing dysfunctional black families, characterized by single mothers, out-of-wedlock births, and unemployment. (U.S. Senate)

Columbus Day Controversy

October 12 has been recognized in the United States as Columbus Day to exalt the Italian voyager Christopher Columbus and to celebrate his "discovery" of the "New World" in 1492. Many Italian Americans observe Columbus Day as a celebration of their ethnic heritage. Historically, it is believed that the first Columbus Day celebration took place in New York in 1792. In 1937, President Franklin D. Roosevelt reserved October 12 as a national holiday, and since 1971 it has been observed as a federal holiday.

However, in recent decades, the commemoration has been a source of social controversy and political division among ethnic and racial groups. The controversy revolves around demands by many Native American and other non-European communities to remove Columbus Day as a federal holiday because it has its origins in conquest, colonialism, and slavery. This has caused a persistent conflict between Native Americans, and Italian and other white Americans.

In response to this controversy, Native American and other minority leaders argue that the federal government should establish a holiday that recognizes Native Americans. As a result, since 2000, more than 20 states in the United States do not recognize Columbus Day as a national holiday, and some states, such as South Dakota and Delaware, have taken the matter one step further and changed Columbus Day to Native American Day. Critics of commemoration and celebrations of Columbus do not necessarily deny the historical contribution of his legacy, but they argue that the existing celebrations of a specific understanding of the legacy of Columbus justify stereotypes of Native Americans or other minority groups and the racist ideology toward them and thus contribute to the maintenance of existing social inequalities against them.

Nicholas Alexiou

Cultural racism has a long history in the United States. During plantation slavery, blacks were regularly depicted as hard-working, intuitive, and capable as a slave with good traits was more likely to sell and bring in a good price; however, after plantation slavery ended and freed blacks became potential employment competition, they were characterized as lazy, dishonest, and unreliable. Black culture became synonymous with a host of negative traits. Cultural racism, as recognized today, had one of its first popular inceptions in the 1965 report, *The Negro Family: The Case for National Action*, written by Senator Daniel Patrick Moynihan. In this report, Moynihan analyzes dysfunctional black families, characterized by single mothers, out-of-wedlock births, and unemployment. Moynihan recognizes that the legacy of slavery and racial discrimination greatly contributed to the problems of black families, but ultimately he places the onus of the blame on the pathology of black families. Moynihan challenges blacks to fix their culture, rather than holding society and the government accountable for ending discrimination and creating equal opportunity. Such cultural racism, typified by "blaming the victim" is emblematic of racism today. Eduardo Bonilla-Silva (2010) identifies cultural racism as one of the four frames of contemporary color-blind racism. Color-blind racism uses race-neutral logic and an emphasis on individualism to explain away racial disparities and white privilege without sounding racist. Thus, the frame of cultural racism helps them to achieve this end. For example, Bonilla-Silva asks whites if they agree with the sentiment that blacks don't do well because they lack motivation and work ethic. He finds that whites overwhelmingly agree with this sentiment and point to blacks' bad culture such as "Blacks want hand-outs," "Blacks don't have much ambition," "Blacks were raised in the projects," and/or "Black families don't have the same priorities as whites."

The frame of cultural racism does not belong only to color-blind whites; there are also social scientists both on the Right and the Left that invoke culture arguments to explain racial disparities. On the Right, Dinesh D'Souza, author of *The End of Racism*, is well known for citing nonwhite culture as the cause of racial minorities' downfall. Both in his book and in numerous other writings, he blames the low socioeconomic status of blacks on their bad culture. He argues that the United States has seen the end of racism and that any enduring discrimination is "rational discrimination" based on the easily observable bad values that blacks espouse; therefore, the solution to the race problem is for blacks to accept, learn, and strive for the (white) dominant values of society. On the Left, there are also some who invoke the culture thesis including David Harding, Orlando Patterson, and most famously, William Julius Wilson. Wilson and others argue that via restricted economic, social, and political options, a culture of an underclass grows that teaches and promotes bad behavior along with a lack of motivation to succeed. For example, black parents become resigned to their economic status and then do not properly encourage their children to work hard in school. In other words, these scholars argue that there is "more than just race" that leads to racial disparities, which in and of itself doesn't sound racist; however, cultural racism is invoked through the focus on how racial minorities reproduce a "bad culture" rather than focusing on how institutional racism is the foundational problem.

Cultural racism has a long historical legacy, is a common argument used by conservative thinkers, and is a part of the color-blind repertoire. However, cultural racism is also becoming acceptable by making a resurgence among more liberal scholars who argue that "political correctness" scares people away from discussing culture; such scholars are trying to resurrect culture as a topic of serious analysis. Others, however, maintain that this focus on culture largely detracts from the greater and more important conversation about institutional racism.

Hephzibah Strmic-Pawl

See also

Color-Blind Racism; *End of Racism, The*; Racism; Reverse Racism

Further Reading:

Bonilla-Silva, Eduardo. *Racism without Racists: Color-Blind Racism & Racial Inequality in Contemporary America*, 3rd ed. New York: Rowman & Littlefield Publishers, 2010.

D'Souza, Dinesh. *The End of Racism: Principles for a Multiracial Society*. New York: Free Press, 1995.

Moynihan, Daniel Patrick. "The Negro Family: The Case for National Action." United States Department of Labor, March 1965. Accessed December 5, 2012. http://www.dol.gov/oasam/programs/history/webid-meynihan.htm.

Steinberg, Stephen. "Poor Reason: Culture Still Doesn't Explain Poverty." *Boston Review*. January 13, 2011. Accessed December 5, 2012. http://www.bostonreview.net/BR36.1/steinberg.php.

Culture

Culture is especially an object of focus within the disciplines of anthropology and cultural sociology. It is often defined as the shared values, understandings, symbols, and practices of a group of people. According to Clifford Geertz, culture is "a historically transmitted pattern of meanings embodied in symbols" (1973: 89). The shared symbols are the means by which people "communicate, perpetuate, and develop their knowledge about and attitudes toward life" (Geertz 1973: 89). Unlike "ethnicity," it does not necessarily require a real or putative story involving shared origin. This distinctive feature of "culture" makes possible the assimilation of other groups into a culture, since they only need to participate actively in the activities or beliefs of a culture, depending on the definition used, in order to be a part of it.

In the United States, culture is frequently discussed in the context of immigration and racial/ethnic conflict between different cultural groups such as dominant culture, the understandings and symbols created and controlled by a powerful group, and an immigrant culture, the understandings and symbols of an immigrant group entering the sphere of the dominant culture. Milton Gordon, a theorist of assimilation, postulates that immigrant groups coming to North America are to be absorbed into the dominant core culture and host society by relinquishing their own cultures. In this assumption, culture revolves around meanings and practices, whereas society typically reflects the structure that exists in a group.

In anthropology, the notion of culture was developed out of its German cognate *Cultur* (later *Kultur*), which emphasizes a diversity of possibilities. In place of one generalizable notion of "culture" that applies to everyone, the world can be divided up into multiple cultures that guide meaning in that geographical region. This sense relates culture to the features of nearly any social group.

Franz Boas, a German-American anthropologist, was instrumental in forming the modern understanding of culture: a dynamic view depicting culture as evolving and transforming over time. He saw culture as contingent upon the particular historical events of a people, which developed temporally. With this principle, he helped move cultural anthropology toward cultural relativism, allowing it to explore the structure of a culture without evaluating its preferability.

Ruth Benedict, a student of Boas, offered a famous definition from 1943, inspired by Boas's teachings: "Culture is the sociological term for learned behaviour: behaviour which in man is not given at birth, which is not determined by his germ cells as is the behaviour of wasps or the social ants, but must be learned anew from grown people by each new generation. The degree to which human achievements are dependent on this kind of learned behaviour is man's great claim to superiority over all the rest of creation; he has been properly called 'the culture-bearing animal'" (Benedict 2000: 115).

Fredrik Barth also influenced the development of studies of culture in key ways. He has emphasized that individuals are not inextricably tied to a culture in the way many studies had treated them. Culture exists although those who are a part of it change over time, and some individuals may even identify with more than one culture. Culture in this sense is at least partially distinct from those participating in it, and the boundaries that delineate cultures are permeable, allowing for both the exchange of members as well as external influences.

Geertz adopted a framework from Weber that depicts meaning as a web-like structure. Social groups spin these webs themselves, which form a support structure for their interactions among themselves. Culture, then, is the webs themselves, and the study of culture is the analysis of the shared bonds of meaning created by a society to facilitate its own activity. Following Wittgenstein's view of language, Geertz argues that "culture is public, because meaning is" (1973: 12). Human groups have different modes of cognition, and their symbols are different as well. But symbols are expressions of social phenomena. They provide the elements that shape culture. In turn, culture is the context in which human life is experienced. In this account, it is a series of patterns comprised of symbols.

Alfred Louis Kroeber labeled culture "superorganic." According to this view, while culture may in some ways be a product of human society, the individuals that make up a society cannot be the object of an analysis of culture. Culture gains its own dynamic, working on a scale that goes beyond the individuals to the degree that culture ultimately produces or directs the individuals within it.

From the perspective of cultural sociology, meaning takes priority over structure as an object of analysis. This is because human making of meaning in socially located contexts is what defines culture. This is whether it takes place in institutions or not or within bounded groups or not. The object of study of cultural sociology is thus how the making of meaning occurs, how it varies, how it changes human behaviors and agency, and how it generates antagonism or cooperation.

Social scientists commonly approach the study of culture from a position of cultural relativism, though the approach is perhaps most common in anthropology where it was developed. Anthropologists like Kroeber argued that culture is sui generis, suggesting that it can only be understood per se and cannot be evaluated with a universal metric. Reactions to explicitly ethnocentric research about so-called primitive people during the 19th century, along with Social Darwinism, is what led to the rise of cultural relativism.

The cultural relativist view has caused some controversy, however. Some critics argue that it represents a disciplinary distaste for Western values, as evidenced by a desire to identify with and defend the values of indigenous groups and non-Western societies over the norms dominant in the homelands of academic practitioners. Others contend that cultural relativism provides a defense of practices that violate universal human rights as if they were integral to that culture. Such controversies arise especially regarding topics like genocide, female genital mutilation, and infanticide, among others.

Due to the vision of culture as continuously evolving, it remains a constant source of interest for social scientists, as in each society, each new era of culture presents new webs and strings of social meanings for social scientists to explore. Scholars appreciate culture as a dynamic process of social interaction that governs behaviors, and that can help explain why different groups clash in their behavior.

Kazuko Suzuki

See also

Culture of Poverty; Oppositional Culture

Further Reading:

Barth, Fredrik. *Process and Form in Social Life: Selected Essays of Fredrik Barth, Vol. I.* Boston: Routledge and Kegan Paul, 1981.

Barth, Fredrik, ed. *Ethnic Groups and Boundaries.* Boston: Little, Brown & Co, 1969.

Benedict, Ruth. "Race: What It Is Not." In *Theories of Race and Racism: A Reader*, edited by Les Back and John Solomos, 113–18. New York: Routledge, 2000.

Boas, Franz. *Race, Language, and Culture*. Chicago: University of Chicago Press, 1995 [1940].
Feagin, Joe R., and Clairece Booher Feagin. *Racial and Ethnic Relations*, ninth ed. Upper Saddle River, NJ: Prentice Hall, 2010.
Geertz, Clifford. *The Interpretation of Cultures*. New York: Basic Books, 1973.
Gordon, Milton. *Assimilation in American Life: The Role of Race, Religion, and National Origins*. Oxford: Oxford University Press, 1964.
Ritter, Malcolm. "You Insult Me, Sir: Lab Study Says Southern Men Take Insults Seriously." WRAL News. July 8, 1996. http://www.wral.com/news/local/story/149263/.
Rosenstein, Carole E. "How Cultural Heritage Organizations Serve Communities: Priorities, Strengths, and Challenges." *Nonprofits in Focus: Urban Institute Policy Briefs* 3 (October, 2006). Washington, DC: Urban Institute.
Walker, Tim. "Closing the Culture Gap." National Education Association. http://www.nea.org/home/43098.htm (accessed January 2, 2012).

Culture of Poverty

The culture of poverty thesis is a theoretical framework that has been used to explain the poverty of African Americans and other racial minority groups in the United States in terms of their cultural deficiencies. Culture can be broadly defined as the material and nonmaterial features of a group of people. Although few cultures exist in isolation, members of a cultural group have a similar ideology, behavior, norms, values, artifacts, and a shared set of experiences. The word *culture* is often used to distinguish groups based on characteristics such as race, ethnicity, religion, and national origin. The central feature of the culture of poverty thesis is that the poor share a common culture (i.e., attitudes, behavior, lifestyle, beliefs) that directly or indirectly perpetuates their impoverished conditions.

According to the thesis, because of dire economic conditions, the poor attempt to cope with feelings of hopelessness and despair that come with knowing that their chances for success in life are few. These adaptations include (1) a sense of resignation and passivity because of long-term poverty; (2) a present-time orientation because of pressures to survive day to day; (3) feelings of fatalism and powerlessness because of separation from the political process; (4) low aspirations from lack of opportunity; (5) feelings of inferiority because of society's contempt and aversion to the poor; and (6) an increased number of female heads of households due to lack of a male breadwinners and unstable families. Gaining popularity in the 1960s and early 1970s, the theoretical view was used to place the onus of escaping poverty on the poor.

Although various scholars and writers have espoused a culture of poverty thesis, anthropologist Oscar Lewis (1914–1970) is credited with having developed it. He performed research in impoverished Latin American barrios (neighborhoods), using participant observation and life-history analysis. According to Lewis, a culture of poverty had economic, psychological, and social features and was both an adaptation and reaction by the poor to their marginal position in a class-stratified society. Just as culture reflects a shared way of life, Lewis suggested, the poor he studied shared a common way of life that served as a coping mechanism but also perpetuated poverty. Thus, poverty created an environment that fostered more poverty. For persons who embraced a culture of poverty, it was difficult to exhibit attitudes and behavior that could help them escape poverty, and their condition became matter of fact. Lewis posited that the long-term self-perpetuating cycle of poverty also subsumed the children of the poor, who were socialized into this culture as well. Lewis suggested that economic changes in society as a whole would help the poor, as would involvement in trade-union movements and efforts to raise class-consciousness. Lewis's findings were published in *Five Families* (1959), *The Children of Sánchez* (1961), *La Vida* (1966), and *Anthropological Essays* (1970).

Daniel Patrick Moynihan's *The Negro Family: The Case for National Action* (1965) is quite possibly the most widely known example of the culture of poverty thesis applied to explain the poverty of a minority group in the United States. Moynihan suggested that poverty among blacks was primarily a result of black family instability evidenced by high divorce rates, female-headed households, out-of-wedlock births, and welfare dependency. Moynihan noted that the effects of slavery, racial discrimination, segregation, and poverty in urban cities made it difficult for many blacks to establish economically stable families, but that, for poor blacks to escape poverty, they must establish and maintain family stability. Moynihan concluded that social policy should be directed toward strengthening the black family.

Commissioned by President Lyndon B. Johnson, Moynihan's results were widely read and publicized, and influenced how the academia and the wider public viewed black families. The Moynihan report resulted in numerous studies on poverty among blacks that emphasized a culture of poverty as the main cause of poverty in the black community. The theoretical basis of many of these studies was a pathology model that correlated chronic socioeconomic problems with inherent individual character flaws among the poor. The pathology model suggested that the long-term effects of poverty are linked to historic economic inequities but are largely a result of poor personal choices among the poor that create economic, social, and cultural conditions that are difficult to escape.

In contrast to the culture of poverty thesis applied to blacks and Hispanics, the model-minority thesis has been associated with Asian Americans. Some scholars and the mainstream media have applauded Asian Americans for possessing a strong work ethic and stable families, emphasizing education, exhibiting delayed gratification, and responding to racism and discrimination in less confrontational ways. They have attributed the socioeconomic success of Asian Americans to these positive cultural traits that poor blacks and Hispanics are encouraged to emulate.

The Culture of Poverty and the Structure versus Individual Agency Discourse

The culture of poverty thesis can be positioned within the broader "structure versus agency" academic discourse, where structure and agency represent two ends of a polemic to explain social issues such as poverty. By focusing on the effects of structural constraints on poverty, the structural approach considers macrolevel dynamics, most of which are outside the control of the poor, as the primary reasons most poor remain so and the ranks of the poor are growing. Structural constraints often associated with urban poverty are (1) deindustrialization that resulted in demand shifts from manufacturing to service occupations, (2) globalization, (3) the increase in demand for technical workers, (4) racism and discrimination, (5) residential isolation, and (6) out-migration of businesses and jobs from urban areas to the suburbs. From this perspective, poverty is not inevitable and economic improvements can occur for members of disadvantaged minority groups through social policy and government intervention.

In contrast, the agency discourse assumes that persons have free will or a choice in matters that directly affect them. In an open socioeconomic mobility system such as that in the United States, it is commonly believed that everyone who is willing and able has an opportunity to succeed. Thus the individual's effort to improve his or her conditions is the most important determinant of socioeconomic position. When considering poverty, an agency-based premise would suggest that the poor are largely to blame for their impoverished state because they often exhibit aberrant attitudes and behavior. For example, a poor work ethic, failure to seek employment or to take jobs that are available, or lacking the skills and education to compete in society all represent personal choices that explain poverty. This position suggests that certain groups of poor people, such as widows and orphans, would be more worthy of assistance than others but that most of the poor would be considered undeserving of governmental assistance or help through other organized channels. The culture of poverty thesis is usually associated with agency-based explanations for poverty.

Oscar Lewis's culture of poverty has been applied beyond its original scope, focus, and context. Although Lewis's research focused on poor barrios in Latin American cities, the thesis has been largely applied to explain the experiences of residents in poor U.S. urban settings. The original research examined the experiences of persons of Hispanic descent; but the thesis is commonly associated with commentaries about poor African Americans and, to a somewhat lesser degree, Native Americans, Chicanos, and Puerto Ricans. Lewis's original work also recognized the effects of structural forces, but such factors are secondary in many current applications.

Empirical studies testing the culture of poverty thesis have yielded conflicting findings regarding the culture of poverty on the part of members of disadvantaged minority groups. Edward Banfield suggested that, among inner-city residents, continued experience of and exposure to poverty resulted in a culture that undermined expectations of achievement and personal initiative. Like Lewis, Banfield argued that the poor tended to exhibit a present-time orientation rather than

Poverty Rates and Racial Difference

Poverty occurs when an individual or group lacks socially acceptable amounts of money or material possessions to meet basic living needs. In the United States, poverty is determined based on the official poverty line formulated in 1964 by the Social Security Administration. This threshold reflects a set of rock-bottom allowances that includes a certain proportion of yearly costs for food. An individual is officially considered poor if his or her personal family income falls below this governmental standard. In 1975, the poverty line for a nonfarm family of four was $5,500. In 2002, the threshold for a family of four was approximately $18,556. Although the poverty line has been criticized for excluding in-kind government transfers in its income calculation and for strict income cut-offs, it is a commonly implemented threshold for comparing basic quality-of-life measures across various groups.

Poverty rates differ dramatically by racial/ethnic group, and these differentials have been consistent over many decades. In 2001, approximately 11.7 percent of the U.S. population lived in poverty, a significant decrease from 15.1 percent in 1993. Poverty rates for African Americans and Hispanics were 22.7 percent and 21.4 percent, respectively, in 2001, compared with 9.9 percent for whites and 10.2 percent for Asians and Pacific Islanders. In addition, poverty rates are highest for families headed by single women, especially Hispanic and African American women. In 2001, only 4.9 percent of married-couple families and 13.1 percent of male-headed families lived in poverty. By contrast, the rate was 26.4 percent for female-headed families, and rates for African American and Hispanic female-headed families exceeded 35 percent. Given the high incidence of poverty among female-headed families, it is not surprising that children are also disproportionately represented among the U.S. poor. Although children composed about 25.6 percent of the total population, about 35.7 percent of them lived in poverty. Increasingly, younger children are experiencing the most poverty, especially if they are part of single female–headed families. In 2001, about 18.2 percent of children under age six were living in poverty. However, about 48.9 percent of children younger than age six who lived in female-headed families were poor. Factors such as deindustrialization, racism, disparate marriage rates, housing discrimination and segregation, unemployment, and inadequate educational systems have contributed to continued racial differentials in poverty rates. The vast majority of poor racial/ethnic minorities live in urban areas.

SANDRA L. BARNES

attitudes and behavior associated with delayed gratification, planning for the future, working hard, and frugality. More recently, in *The New Politics of Poverty*, Lawrence M. Mead (1992) focused on the experience of the nonworking poor and argued that poverty is not a result of limited employment opportunities, but rather, a result of failure to work. Mead contended that the majority of poverty-stricken people are female heads of families and single adults. Reminiscent of Lewis's terminology, Mead associated their behavior with "a culture of poverty that discourages work" (24).

However, other empirical studies have demonstrated the invalidity of the culture of poverty thesis. Chandler Davidson and Charles M. Gaitz (1974) examined work ethic among poor African American, white, and Hispanic people. Their findings showed that members of these urban poor are just as willing to work as nonpoor persons. Moreover, the poor racial/ethnic minorities in the sample were found to be more work-oriented than their white counterparts. According to William Ryan (1974), unequal access and distribution of resources and wealth and a disparate opportunity structure explain continued poverty among the urban poor in the United States as compared to countries that emphasize economic equity. Macrolevel societal factors that foster economic instability, rather than individuals, are to blame for poverty. Furthermore, Ryan contended that low aspirations among the poor are a consequence, rather than a cause, of poverty. Rather than blame the victims, Ryan recommended policies to empower the poor economically and socially. Other studies, such as *Ain't No Makin' It* by Jay MacLeod (1995) and *No Shame in My Game: The Working Poor in the Inner City* by Katherine Newman (1999) also found the achievement-oriented attitude and strong work ethics among the poor and situated their experiences within a larger economic context.

Although Lewis's thesis was initially met with wide interest and support, it has been subjected to various criticisms, which can be summarized into the following three major categories. First, detractors have contended that the thesis is theoretically and methodologically limited because it emphasizes the individual initiative to escape poverty and other forms of disadvantage and minimizes possible negative effects of structural dynamics such as international and national economic changes that have reduced the number of high-paying manufacturing jobs. They suggest that failure to use a more comprehensive research approach has resulted in conservative policy implications.

Second, the culture of poverty thesis is believed to be overly simplistic in its presentation of who experiences poverty. Critics argue that it minimizes the existence of nonpoor African Americans and Hispanics and their hard work, ignores poor whites and Asians, and may reinforce racial stereotypes. For example, despite the model-minority thesis's positive depictions of Asian Americans, many Asian American scholars are critical of it because it oversimplifies the Asian American experience in the United States, based on inappropriate interracial and intraracial contrasts, and tends to ignore social problems faced by Asian Americans.

Third, because the thesis tends to question other factors that result in economic disadvantage, it may make it difficult to objectively study the problem of poverty and result in placing blame on the poor for their condition. Although Lewis did not totally blame the poor for their state, his work has been heavily cited by persons who hold the poor largely accountable for their circumstances. Moynihan's pathology model, the model-minority thesis, and related studies represent applications of the cultural explanation that were widely accepted as ways to describe minority experiences in the United States. Some of these frameworks continue to be used today.

Sandra L. Barnes

See also

Culture; Oppositional Culture

Further Reading:

Banfield, Edward. *The Unheavenly City Revisited*. Boston: Little, Brown, 1974.

Davidson, Chandler, and Charles M. Gaitz. "'Are the Poor Different?' A Comparison of Work Behavior and Attitudes Among the Urban Poor and Nonpoor." *Social Problems* 22 (1974): 229–45.

Lewis, Oscar. *The Children of Sanchez*. New York: Random House, 1961.

Lewis, Oscar. "The Culture of Poverty." *Scientific American* 115 (1966): 19–25.

Mead, Lawrence. *The New Politics of Poverty: The Nonworking Poor in America*. New York: Basic Books, 1992.

Moynihan, Daniel Patrick. *The Negro Family: The Case for National Action*. Washington, DC: Office of Policy Planning and Research, United States Department of Labor, 1965.

Ryan, William. *Blaming the Victim*. New York: Vintage Books, 1976.

Cumming v. Richmond County Board of Education (1899)

In 1899, *Cumming v. Richmond County Board of Education* was brought before the U.S. Supreme Court as a class action suit. The case authorized complete racial segregation of American public schools.

J. W. Cumming, James S. Harper, and John C. Ladeveze, the plaintiffs in the case, were all persons of color and were residents, taxpayers, and landowners in Georgia. They were suing on behalf of themselves and all others who would be affected by the case's outcome. The case was about a $45,000 tax that the Richmond County, Georgia, Board of Education had imposed to be used as provisions for the county's public and private schools. Cumming, Harper, and Ladeveze argued not in opposition to the tax, but that the tax money was being illegally appropriated for the benefit of the white population exclusively.

Under the law, the board was authorized to levy any such tax that supported a high school system for white students, but not one for black students. The petitioners argued that being taxpayers, landowners, and citizens entitled them and their children the same advantages as white citizens and their children. The Supreme Court's decision in the case stated that due to the fact that there were many more black children than white children in the area, the board was unable to provide everyone with an education. The court contended that the board's funds are so small compared to the child population that it could either sufficiently educate a handful of white students or no one at all.

In the end, the Supreme Court ruled that it had no authority to interpose in the decisions of the state courts. A few years prior to the Cumming case, the Supreme Court ruled in *Plessy v. Ferguson* (1896) that the constitutionality of racial segregation was validated under the "separate but equal" doctrine. Although this case did not deal directly with education, the impact of the decision carried over to the Cumming case. In *Cumming v. Richmond*, the court was content with the county's defense that it did not have the money to support a high school for black children.

Cumming v. Richmond was a landmark case in the struggle for equal rights in the 19th and 20th centuries. The case emphasized the lenience of the Supreme Court in defining what exactly was meant by "separate but equal." Separate but equal would continue to be the standard in U.S. law until it was superseded by the Supreme Court's decision *Brown v. Board of Education* (1954).

ARTHUR HOLST

See also

Brown v. Board of Education Legal Groundwork; *Brown v. Board of Education* (1954); *Cooper v. Aaron* (1958); Education and African Americans; School Segregation. Document: *Brown v. Board of Education* (May 1954)

Further Reading:

"*Cumming v. Board of Ed. of Richmond County*, 175 U.S. 528 (1899)." About.com, African-American History. http://afroamhistory.about.com/library/blcumming_v_richmond.htm (accessed May 8, 2007).

Cumming v. Board of Ed. of Richmond County, 175 U.S. 528. U.S. Supreme Court. http:caselaw.lp.findlaw.com/cgi-bin/getcase.pl?court=us&vol=175&vol+175&invol=528 (accessed April 19, 2007).

Lewis, Rudolph. "Up from Slavery: A Documentary History of Negro Education." *ChickenBones: A Journal*. http://www.nathanielturner.com/educationhistorynegro28.htm (accessed April 19, 2007).

"Segregation and the 'Separate but Equal' Doctrine." http://web.naesp.org/brown/1895.htm (accessed May 14, 2008).

Southern Education Foundation. "1895–1915: Separate & Unequal." May 3, 2007. http://www.southerneducation.org/1896.asp (Accessed May 14, 2008).

Taylor, Jared. "Brown v. Board: the Real Story," *American Renaissance*. http://www.amren.com/ar/2004/07/ (accessed May 14, 2008).

Cumulative Discrimination

Cumulative discrimination refers to the idea that intentional discrimination that occurs at one point in time in one domain can have detrimental impact on subsequent generations and/or in different domains. The important point is that discrimination is not just a single event.

Racial differences in home ownership and wealth provide a good example of how discrimination can affect subsequent generations. During the post–World War II period, the federal government provided programs that allowed white working- and middle-class families to buy their own homes. Mortgage programs through the Federal Housing Administration and Veteran's Administration made home ownership accessible to millions of Americans. For many of these families, home ownership was their first real asset.

Blacks, however, did not have access to these programs at the same rate as whites. The FHA encouraged banks not to give mortgages to purchase homes in poorer, inner-city areas where many blacks lived; this was called *redlining*. Restrictive covenants prevented blacks from buying homes in the newer suburban neighborhoods. Higher dishonorable discharge rates for blacks from the segregated World War II army made them ineligible for VA loans. Intentional discrimination, then, made it less likely for blacks than whites to buy a home, even if they could afford one.

Homeowners can pass their home equity wealth on to their children in the form of paying for college education, making down payments for their children's first home, and giving inheritance at the time of their death. Discriminatory housing policies, along with employment discrimination and Social Security policies that excluded agricultural and domestic workers, meant that blacks were less likely to own homes and were less able to pass this wealth onto their children. In other words, in the post–World War II baby-boomer generation, blacks had fewer assets than whites because of the housing discrimination that their parents experienced.

This still has an influence in the 21st century when examining racial differences in wealth. In 2007, for example, black households had only 10 percent of the wealth of white households. More important, even at the same income levels, whites have more wealth than blacks. Although some blacks can parlay a college education into a decent income, it is more difficult to acquire wealth. A substantial part of these racial differences in wealth differences can be traced back to the housing discrimination that existed in the 1940s and 1950s.

Cumulative discrimination against blacks and other people of color has a flip side—cumulative advantages to whites. In the 21st century, whites benefit from the privileges that their parents and grandparents received decades earlier. It doesn't matter if they, personally, are not perpetrators of discrimination.

Another aspect of cumulative discrimination is that negative treatment in one domain can have impacts in other domains. Housing discrimination, along with other factors, has resulted in blacks and Hispanics being disproportionately represented in poor inner city neighborhoods with concentrated poverty. Since most businesses have left the area, it is difficult to find jobs close to home. Since public transportation in many cities leaves much to be desired, it is difficult for blacks to get to jobs in suburban areas. Since many inner city areas are food deserts with no supermarkets, health can be negatively impacted. This is compounded by the lack of doctors. Local public schools tend to be older and more likely to appear on low academic achievement lists. Inner-city residents are more likely to be victims of crime and to be treated harshly by the criminal justice system. Clearly, discrimination is not a single, isolated act.

Skeptics may argue that there is some kind of "statute of limitations" on cumulative discrimination across generations. They assert that one should not still blame government policies from the 1940s and 1950s for current racial inequality. They argue that current equal housing laws mean that individual agency now determines success or failure.

Current racial differences in home ownership are striking. According to the U.S. Census Bureau, 74 percent of white, non-Hispanic householders own their own home in 2010 compared to 59 percent of Asians, 52 percent of Native Americans, 48 percent of Hispanics, and 45 percent of blacks. These inequalities have a variety of causes, including the lower family incomes that people of color tend to have. Yet, the history of housing discrimination and the cumulative impact across domains cannot be denied.

In spite of the equal housing laws that exist at all government levels, some studies have suggested that there is still discrimination on who gets mortgages. Banks have paid large settlements to resolve lawsuits alleging that blacks have disproportionately been directed to more expensive subprime mortgages during the Great Recession of 2007–2012. Melvin Oliver and Thomas Shapiro state: "The process of asset accumulation that began in the 1930s has become layered over and over by social and economic trends that magnify inequality over time and across generations (2006: 54)."

Fred L. Pincus

See also

Discrimination; Institutional Discrimination; Reverse Discrimination; Structural Discrimination

Further Reading:

Lipsitz, George. *The Possessive Investment in Whiteness: How White People Profit from Identity Politics*. Philadelphia: Temple University Press,1998.

National Research Council. *Measuring Racial Discrimination*. Washington, DC: National Academies Press, 2004.

Oliver, Melvin L., and Thomas Shapiro. *Black Wealth/White Wealth: A New Perspective on Racial Inequality, Tenth Anniversary Edition*. New York: Routledge, 2006.

D

Dahmer, Vernon (1908–1966)

Vernon Dahmer's advocacy for African American voting rights in Mississippi was vital to the development and success of the National Association for the Advancement of Colored People (NAACP) in the state in the 1960s. Born in 1908 in Forrest County, Mississippi, Dahmer (pronounced DAY-mer) rose to economic prominence after World War II in Hattiesburg, Mississippi. He employed his considerable resources to secure and safeguard voting rights for African Americans. An owner of several successful businesses in Hattiesburg, including a sawmill and grocery store, Dahmer personally registered blacks to vote and paid the two-dollar poll tax for African Americans too poor to afford the fee. Dahmer also led the Hattiesburg chapter of the NAACP, taking under his wing young men from NAACP and the Student Nonviolent Coordinating Committee and helping them set up their operations in Mississippi.

Dahmer always insisted that receipts be issued for payment of the poll tax. The receipts were part of a larger plan for reestablishing the franchise for African Americans in Mississippi. Until the Voting Rights Act of 1965 outlawed poll taxes and other disenfranchisement schemes, Mississippi required voters to provide a record of their paid poll taxes before they could register. A poll tax receipt automatically qualified voters, black and white, for registration. Some white registrars refused to accept the poll tax receipt, however. Dahmer's leadership in the NAACP branch in Hattiesburg allowed him to report the cases of illegal and discriminatory treatment to the Board of Elections, the main branch of the NAACP, and other civil rights organizations. Steadfast in this extremely dangerous activism, Dahmer's defense of African American political rights made him the target of death threats by terrorist groups and economic pressure from white business leaders in Hattiesburg.

In January 1966, the group of white men, led by Samuel Bowers, the Imperial Wizard of the Ku Klux Klan (KKK), firebombed Dahmer's house as he and his family slept inside. The attackers gathered with their weapons in the front yard of the house, cutting off one escape route of the family. Dahmer warded off the attackers and fired his shotgun from inside until his family broke down the back door and fled. He collapsed outside his burning house, his blackened skin hanging from his skeleton and his lungs badly seared. Dahmer's 10-year-old daughter, Bettie, also suffered severe burns. That evening at the hospital, Dahmer remained adamant that African Americans in Mississippi use their voting rights to end Jim Crow in Mississippi. Before succumbing to the irreversible damage to his lungs and skin, Vernon Dahmer's last words were, "People who don't vote are deadbeats on the state."

Smoke rises from the firebombed home of civil rights leader Vernon Dahmer on January 10, 1966, after an early morning attack in Hattiesburg, Mississippi. Dahmer died the next day from burn injuries. (Associated Press)

Fourteen men, including Samuel Bowers, were arrested for arson, murder, and conspiracy. All of the defendants had ties to the KKK or were members of the terrorist organization. Five defendants were convicted or pled guilty, and were given life sentences. They were set free after serving less than 10 years. The ringleader of the plot, Samuel Bowers, and his closest associates in the KKK, escaped prosecution for 30 years. Three of the 1968 trials against Bowers ended when the juries could not unanimously reach a verdict. Samuel Bowers returned to Laurel, Mississippi, and for several years, lived 30 miles away from the Dahmer family.

Spurred by Dahmer's widow, Ellie, the district attorney of Forest County, Mississippi, reopened the case against the leaders of the plot in the late 1990s. In 1998, three men were indicted in the bombing of Dahmer's home and the murder of Vernon Dahmer: Samuel Bowers, Charles Noble, and Deavours Nix, former members of the Klan. Nix died before trial, and in 1999, the jury could not reach a verdict in Noble's trial. Samuel Bowers had already served six years in the federal penitentiary for the 1964 murder of Andrew Goodman, Michael Schwerner, and James Earl Chaney, three activists in the voting registration drives in Mississippi. In 1998, after four mistrials a jury found Samuel Bowers guilty of firebombing Dahmer's house and of Dahmer's murder. Bowers died in prison in 2006. Vernon Dahmer Jr. said that his father spent his life working for the voting rights of African Americans in Mississippi, despite never having the opportunity to vote.

NIKKI BROWN

See also

National Association for the Advancement of Colored People (NAACP)

Further Reading:

Cohen, Adam. "The Widow and the Wizard." *Time*, May 18, 1998. http://www.time.com/time/ (accessed June 16, 2008).

Dahmer (Vernon F.) Collection. McCain Library and Archives, University of Southern Mississippi. http://www.lib.usm.edu/~archives/ (accessed December 2007).

Newsome, Melba. "Another Ghost of Mississippi Laid to Rest." *New Crisis*, November 1998. http://findarticles.com/p/articles/mi_qa3812/is_199811/ai_n8815983 (accessed June 16, 2008).

Payne, Charles. *I've Got the Light of Freedom: The Organizing Tradition and the Mississippi Freedom Struggle*. Berkeley: University of California Press, 1995.

Dawes Act (1887)

The Dawes Act, or General Allotment Act of 1887, was the most significant assimilation-oriented Indian legislation of the 19th century. Eastern reformers and Western congressional delegations promoted the law as a means of solving the "Indian Problem" of having surviving Native American cultures and tribal nations within the jurisdictional boundaries of the United States. The act contained provisions for allotting reservations into individual homesteads, granting citizenship to Native Americans, and selling surplus tribal lands to non-Indians. Along with educational programs, proponents of the bill hoped it would destroy Indian tribalism and culture, paving the way for eventual Native American integration into the larger American society.

The Lake Mohonk Conference of the "Friends of the Indians," a largely non-Indian group of Eastern philanthropists and legislators, was the driving force behind the Dawes Act. These well-intentioned reformers, led by educator Merrill E. Gates and Massachusetts senator Henry L. Dawes, believed the legislation would prove the magic tonic to turn nomadic tribal Indians into land-owning, "civilized" American citizens. The law culminated a century-long drive by Indian advocates to integrate native peoples into the American "Melting Pot." It was a clear reversal of previous federal removal and reservation policies that treated tribes as sovereign nations and segregated them from American society. As planned, land ownership would transform communally oriented Indians into individualistic, acquisitive Americans who would abandon indigenous cultures and come under U.S. law as full citizens. The legislation passed in 1887 because it harmonized the humanitarian goals of Eastern reformers with Western legislators' desire to open "unused" tribal lands to white settlers. Advocates proclaimed the Dawes Act the "Emancipation Proclamation" for Native Americans, hoping it would solve the "Indian Problem" once and for all by mainstreaming them and freeing them from the control of the federal government.

Although Henry L. Dawes's name adorns the 1887 legislation, Texas senator Richard Coke was the unsung originator and champion of the allotment idea. As passed by Congress, the law contained several interlocking provisions designed to assimilate Indian individuals and tribal nations. Revealing the paternalism common to the era, the act went into effect over the objections of the majority of Indian tribes, although the Five "Civilized" Tribes of Indian Territory and several smaller groups secured exemption from it. The Allotment Act gave the U.S. president authority to survey reservations into 160-acre homesteads for male heads of households, 80-acre plots for unmarried males over 18 years of age, and lesser tracts for orphaned boys. Under the treaty's provisions, certain tribes received different allotment sizes from what the general law provided. Under the Dawes Act, unallotted reservation lands were classified as "surplus" and sold to non-Indians, with the proceeds held in trust by the federal government for education and other civilizing programs for enrolled tribal members.

Advocates envisioned the rapid dissolution of tribal governments, entities reformers believed hindered Native American assimilation by coddling and controlling members. In the interim, however, legislators hoped to shield individuals from unscrupulous land speculators until they were ready for full citizenship. The law required a 25-year waiting period before allottees received full title and citizenship. During this period, the allotment was tax-exempt, held in trust by the U.S. Treasury Department. In the thinking of policy makers, Native Americans would not receive automatic citizenship. Rather, they would have to prove their ability to manage their financial affairs and take up civilized, Christian ways. Revealing the racial presumptions of lawmakers, when the Five "Civilized" Tribes later were brought within the allotment regimen, mixed-blood members of under one-half Indian blood were exempt from the trust provisions under the assumption they were competent to manage their affairs.

Excerpt from Dawes Act (1887)

An act to provide for the allotment of lands in severalty to Indians on the various reservations, and to extend the protection of the laws of the United States and the Territories over the Indians, and for other purposes.

Be it enacted by the Senate and House of Representatives of the United States of America in Congress assembled, That in all cases where any tribe or band of Indians has been, or shall hereafter be, located upon any reservation created for their use, either by treaty stipulation or by virtue of an act of Congress or executive order setting apart the same for their use, the President of the United States be, and he hereby is, authorized, whenever in his opinion any reservation or any part thereof of such Indians is advantageous for agricultural and grazing purposes, to cause said reservation, or any part thereof, to be surveyed, or resurveyed if necessary, and to allot the lands in said reservation in severalty to any Indian located thereon in quantities as follows:

To each head of a family, one-quarter of a section.
To each single person over eighteen years of age, one-eighth of a section.
To each orphan child under eighteen years of age, one-eighth of a section. and
To each other single person under eighteen years now living, or who may be born prior to the date of the order of the President directing an allotment of the lands embraced in any reservation, one-sixteenth of a section: *Provided,* That in case there is not sufficient land in any of said reservations to allot lands to each individual of the classes above named in quantities as above provided, the lands embraced in such reservation or reservations shall be allotted to each individual of each of said classes pro rata in accordance with the provisions of this act: *And provided further,* That where the treaty or act of Congress setting apart such reservation provides for the allotment of lands in severalty in quantities in excess of those herein provided, the President, in making allotments upon such reservation, shall allot the lands to each individual Indian belonging thereon in quantity as specified in such treaty or act: *And provided further,* That when the lands allotted are only valuable for grazing purposes, an additional allotment of such grazing lands, in quantities as above provided, shall be made to each individual.

Sec. 2. That all allotments set apart under the provisions of this act shall be selected by the Indians, heads of families selecting for their minor children, and the agents shall select for each orphan child, and in such manner as to embrace the improvements of the Indians making the selection. Where the improvements of two or more Indians have been made on the same legal subdivision of land, unless they shall otherwise agree, a provisional line may be run dividing said lands between them, and the amount to which each is entitled shall be equalized in the assignment of the remainder of the land to which they are entitled under this act: *Provided,* That if any one entitled to an allotment shall fail to make a selection within four years after the President shall direct that allotments may be made on a particular reservation, the Secretary of the Interior may direct the agent of such tribe or band, if such there be, and if there be no agent, then a special agent appointed for that purpose, to make a selection for such Indian, which election shall be allotted as in cases where selections are made by the Indians, and patents shall issue in like manner.

Full-bloods and other high-blood-quantum individuals remained under the control of federal bureaucrats, treated as incompetent minors under federal law.

The Dawes Act failed in its major goals save one: opening surplus reservation lands to non-Indian settlers. It did not bring about the disappearance of American Indian tribes or the full assimilation of Native Americans into the mainstream as individuals. The law's originators misjudged the readiness and willingness of most tribes to abandon centuries-old cultures. Western groups such as the Nez Percés and Jicarilla Apaches subverted the allotment policy, utilizing the law to strengthen tribal governments and protect their homelands. The Navajos and others with marginal lands avoided the breakup of their reservations. Despite these exceptions, as allotment proceeded on most reservations, desperate Indians sold their homesteads, lost them in tax foreclosures, or were defrauded by unscrupulous land agents. Rather than emancipating Indians from the control of federal officials, tribes lost two-thirds of their remaining estate (roughly 90 million acres of a previous total of 138 million acres), resulting in further dependency on the federal government and impoverishment of most indigenous societies. Those that did retain lands often found their allotments woefully inadequate to support family farming. Over time, heirs subdivided parcels into smaller and smaller sections that proved unproductive.

Although many supporters of the Dawes bill had good intentions, states used the tax-exempt status of Indian lands as an excuse to deny providing Indian schools, improving roads, and providing allottees access to local courts. Subsequent leasing provisions thwarted reformers' goals by allowing non-Indians access to allotted lands and natural resources. An amendment to the Dawes bill, the Burke Act of 1906, led to widespread competency hearings that lifted trust protections and tax exemptions from thousands of Indian allottees. With these changes to the original 1887 law, Native Americans routinely lost the very homesteads that reformers hoped would transform them into American citizens. Government mismanagement resulted in allottees receiving a paltry percentage of the revenue from resources derived from their former homelands.

By the turn of the 20th century, the humanitarian impulse behind the Dawes Act was all but forgotten. Paternal concern for Indian welfare transformed into a Western-oriented program aimed at wresting native lands from their indigenous owners. The law's optimistic goal of full assimilation was replaced by a pessimistic design to integrate the remaining Indians into the lowest rung of American society. The Dawes Act brought about one of the darkest eras for Native Americans. U.S. policy makers, however, later acknowledged the failure of the law, abrogating it and replacing the legislation with the landmark Indian Reorganization Act of 1934, a bill that ushered in the modern era of Indian tribalism and sovereignty.

Mark Edwin Miller

See also

Bureau of Indian Affairs; Native Americans, Conquest of; Native Americans, Forced Relocation of; Tribal Sovereignty.

Documents: Andrew Jackson: Indian Removal Message (1829); Indian Removal Act (1830); *Cherokee Nation v. Georgia* (1831)

Further Reading:

Carlson, Leonard A. *Indians, Bureaucrats, and Land: The Dawes Act and the Decline of Indian Farming*. Westport, CT: Greenwood Press, 1981.

Greenwald, Emily. *Reconfiguring the Reservation: The Nez Perces, Jicarilla Apaches, and the Dawes Act*. Albuquerque: University of New Mexico Press, 2002.

Hoxie, Frederick E. *A Final Promise: The Campaign to Assimilate the Indians, 1880–1920*. Lincoln: University of Nebraska Press, 1984.

Native American Document Project, http://www.csusm.edu/nadp/index.html (accessed July 25, 2008).

Washburn, Wilcomb E. *The Assault on Indian Tribalism: The General Allotment Law (Dawes Act) of 1887*. Philadelphia: J. B. Lippincott Company, 1975.

Day Laborers

Day laborers are employed on a short-term basis (usually a day or less, sometimes for extended periods) without the employer feeling obliged to offer future employment after the work is completed. Day labor work can offer a short-term supplement to unemployment, the opportunity to sell one's skills off the books (often for cash), or work opportunities where legal authorization is not necessarily required. With few exceptions, day labor jobs are part of the secondary labor market, a market consisting of unskilled, low-paying jobs that have few or no benefits. Workers connect with employers by waiting at particular street corners, utilizing staffing agencies, or using labor halls. Employers find day labors useful because day laborers can be used to cut costs and bypass U.S. labor laws. Due to the nature of their employment, day laborers are at a high risk for exploitation through wage theft and worksite injuries.

A common misperception of day laborers is one of male Latino construction and demolition workers gathering at a street corner for work. Day laborers actually run the gamut in terms of jobs, race and ethnicity, and gender. Day laborers can also be found in retail, home health care, car washes, manufacturing, dry-cleaning, plumbing, and even restaurants. Still, many day labor jobs entail undesirable work due

While the stereotype of day labor consists of Latino men working in construction, many workers turn to day labor as a supplement to their jobs. (iStockPhoto)

to dangerous conditions (such as building demolition) and/or high levels of physical labor (e.g., ditch digging). Most day labor jobs require few or no special skills, meaning that many unskilled workers may be competing for the same jobs.

Day laborers typically seek jobs at three locations: staffing agencies (sometimes called *labor pools*), street corners (*catch-out corners*), and nonprofit hiring halls (*worker centers*). Staffing agencies receive employment quotas from local employers and select workers from a pool of day laborers to fill these quotas. Agencies formalize the employment process (unlike street corners), and may require evidence of authorization to work. Agencies also take a portion of the worker's wage in exchange for linking employers and workers. Street corners allow potential employers to recruit labor informally. This allows the worker to potentially receive higher, untaxed wages, but puts workers at great risk of exploitation and wage theft. Nonprofit hiring halls provide the protective benefits of agencies but without the need for a profit margin. They also offer an enforceable labor contract that is designed to prevent wage theft or exploitation. This makes hiring halls desirable to day laborers where they are available and unattractive to exploitative employers. However, most day laborers are connected with employers through agencies and at the street corner given the rarity of hiring halls.

From an employer perspective, utilizing day laborers can be a cost-cutting measure. Day laborers fulfill the need for short-term secondary labor market workers in periods of growth without requiring investment in long-term labor, including the costs of recruiting and employee benefits. Day laborers may be utilized to skirt laws regarding hazardous

Working Under the Table

Work done *under the table* or *off the books* implies that the work is done without reporting it to government agencies. Frequent examples are private house workers and construction workers. Typically workers are paid in cash because this eliminates any paper trail between the employer and the employee (unlike a paycheck or pay stub). Working under the table is one form of tax evasion, as the money is not taxed as employment unless the worker elects to report it as such. It is unclear how many workers are employed each year off the books as few workers or employers are willing to admit to this activity in the Bureau of Labor Statistics' Current Employment Statistics payroll survey. As under the table work is not documented, it also allows for circumvention of labor laws, including minimum wage requirements and labor conditions. As a result, day labors working under the table often find themselves employed in unsafe or unhealthy work sites where employers could not typically put employees due to labor laws.

jobs, such as asbestos removal. Day laborers also offer employers the ability to minimize both responsibility for worker safety and liability in the event of injuries on the job site. This lack of attachment and reciprocity between worker and employer establishes the potential for exploitation.

In the absence of an enforceable contract, day laborers are at high risk for exploitation by employers. For example, day laborers are extraordinarily exposed to the dangers of being injured on the job. Exploitative employers may put workers in unsafe situations without adequate equipment or training, or fail to be forthcoming about the details of the job at the initial point of employment. Workers facing a dangerous work environment versus the loss of a job opportunity may elect to accept the risk over unemployment. If injured, day laborers are still eligible to file for worker's compensation. However, they face many practical hurdles in receiving assistance due to the nature of their employment.

Day laborers are also at elevated risk of wage theft. Employers may verbally promise a specific pay rate for a particular job but fail to keep their agreement after the work is completed. Workers may similarly experience wage theft in the form of shortened breaks, employers skipping required breaks altogether, or unauthorized deductions from day laborers' pay. Staffing agencies can also be seen as engaging in a form of wage theft. Staffing agencies negotiate with local employers to provide a set number of employees for a specific price per laborer per hour. The employers pay the staffing agency, not the worker, and the worker receives only a portion of the per hour fee (usually minimum wage).

Day laborers experience exploitation differently based on race, gender, and documentation status. For example, day laborers are stratified in terms of risk levels for wage theft. Women and minorities are at a higher risk of wage theft than white males. Day laborers who are undocumented also suffer exploitation in that they cannot report wage theft or risk filing complaints. Language barriers (specifically a worker's inability to speak fluent English) can also be used as a means of exploitation by employers. Still, day labor remains a viable form of employment in uncertain economic times.

James Maples

See also

H-2A Visa; Migrant Workers

Further Reading:

Reavis, Dick. *Catching Out: The Secret World of Day Laborers.* New York: Simon and Schuster, 2010.

Ross, Andrew. *Nice Work If You Can Get It: Life and Labor in Precarious Times.* New York: NYU Press, 2009.

Turner, Juno. "All in a Day's Work? Statutory and Other Failures of the Workers' Compensation Scheme as Applied to Street Corner Day Laborers." *Fordham Law Review* 74, no. 3 (2009): 1521–55.

De Jure and De Facto Segregation

Most books, discussions, and court decisions dealing with racial segregation draw a distinction between the two forms of segregation known as de jure and de facto. The distinction made between them, in most definitions, hinges on whether or not segregation is a state's or a local government's official and legal policy. De jure segregation occurs when a community or state makes and abides by laws that require separation of two or more races (in schools, public accommodations, seating arrangements, and so forth). People who practice racial integration in a society where de jure segregation principles are in force are liable to be arrested, fined, or jailed by the criminal justice system (or worse if caught and punished by vigilante groups that try to uphold the "color line"). In this situation, attempts to make legislative bodies rewrite the segregation laws, or to have the courts overturn them, are a central part of the antiracism movement. Much of the history of the U.S. civil rights movement's battle with "Jim Crow" laws involved that sort of struggle against de jure segregation.

In contrast, de facto segregation occurs when members of two or more races live and pursue their life activities apart from each other because of social customs, norms, preferences, choices, and power relations that are not dictated or required by law. This covers several situations. Members of different races may avoid one another out of mutual indifference, unfamiliarity, dislike, or fear. Or one racial group, typically one in a dominant position, may reject another's desire to be treated as equals and neither invite nor allow them into certain social circles or areas. The stronger or more assertive group may claim a particular beach or park as its turf and informally enforce a norm that excludes other races from using it. School board members might draw the attendance zone boundaries of a city's best high school in such a way that it excludes the streets or neighborhoods where members of a stigmatized racial group live. In each case of de facto segregation, the racial separation arises from traditions, choices, preferences and/or power relations rather than the requirements of law. Those who favor racial integration and oppose de facto segregation may not be arrested for breaking a law, but in the eyes of those who support segregation, they are deviants and often are subjected to verbal and physical abuse. Civil rights history includes many such instances.

The two most well known court decisions dealing with racial segregation focused on the de jure form. The U.S. Supreme Court's 1896 *Plessy v. Ferguson* decision upheld a Louisiana law that required train companies to have separate cars for whites and nonwhites and to enforce separate-race seating policies. The court stated that separate cars for each race had to be of equal quality to be legal, but it had no way of enforcing that requirement, and the whites who wanted to impose segregation had no interest in providing equal facilities for blacks. So the precedent of "separate and unequal" rather than "separate but equal" was rapidly extended to schools, stores, buses, parks, and other public areas throughout the South.

In the other case, *Brown v. Board of Education of Topeka* (1954), the Supreme Court ruled against de jure school segregation. It asserted that state laws requiring or permitting racial segregation are unconstitutional violations of the Fourteenth Amendment because the racially separate schools they create are inherently unequal. At that time, 17 Southern states had laws requiring racial segregation, and four others made it a local option. They were ordered to dismantle their segregated systems and establish integrated systems, but most of them stalled and resisted for many years. School systems that were racially segregated by de facto arrangements were not affected directly by the *Brown v. Board of Education* decision until other law suits challenged de facto segregation in the 1970s (e.g., *Keyes v. Denver School District no. 1*, 1973). These resulted in rulings to require busing or other efforts to desegregate schools if there is evidence that school officials intentionally try to maintain a segregated, unequal school system, for example, by gerrymandering attendance zones to keep racial minorities out of certain schools, by unequal school funding or teacher-assignment patterns, or through decisions to close certain schools closings and on the locations of new school construction. More recently, advances in school desegregation have slowed or even been reversed, largely by de facto causes that are difficult to alter (e.g., residential segregation, whites shifting from public to private schools).

CHARLES JARET

See also

American Apartheid; Cultural Racism; Institutional Racism; *New Jim Crow, The*; *Plessy v. Ferguson* (1896); Segregation. Document: *Plessy v. Ferguson* (1896)

Further Reading:

Goodman, Frank. "Some Reflections on the Supreme Court and School Desegregation." In *Race and Schooling in the City*, edited by Adam Yarmolinsky, Lance Liebman, and Corinne S. Schelling, 45–83. Cambridge, MA: Harvard University Press, 1981.

Stephan, Walter G., and Joe R. Feagin, eds. *School Desegregation: Past, Present, and Future*. New York: Plenum, 1980.

Declining Significance of Race, The

Published in 1978, William J. Wilson's *The Declining Significance of Race* generated an important polemic about race in America among diverse scholars. It was reviewed by a large number of academic and nonacademic publications and won prestigious academic prizes. Key parts of the polemic, namely the relative importance of race versus class, and the best policies to deal with the black underclass, are not completely settled today, and to this extent, the arguments set forth in *The Declining Significance of Race* are still relevant. The argument in the book, the debate it generated, and its legacy are considered here.

Wilson's central argument is clearly stated in the book's first sentence: "Race relations in America have undergone fundamental changes in recent years, so much that now the life chances of individual blacks have more to do with their economic class position than with their day-to-day encounters with whites." While, in his view, the history of race relations is characterized by slavery, segregation, exploitation of black labor by white economic elites, and actions of the white masses to eliminate competition, particularly economic competition, in the last half of the 20th century, "many of the traditional barriers have crumbled under the weight of the political, social, and economic changes of the civil rights era." To support his argument, Wilson made a historical analysis of the different race-relations systems in the United States. Each system was a combination of economic characteristics that included dominant production forms, economic groups generated by these forms, and their influence on or dominance of the political system. He distinguished three major periods.

The first period of racial-caste oppression began with slavery and lasted until the end of the Civil War. This system was based on a plantation economy, with a hegemonic, small slave-holding elite that controlled economic power and had great influence in the political life of the South. Economic relations in the plantation economy implied a simple division of labor in which slave owners and slaves were the major actors and there were few gradations in between. Because slaves performed tasks at lower costs than free whites, white free labor had few economic opportunities and resources and therefore lacked political and economic power. The polarity between slave owners and slaves, and the absence of a middle class and an influential working class, was not universal in the South, but it was the most representative pattern of the racial-caste oppression system. Social relations, in turn, followed paternalistic racial patterns that "reveal[ed] close symbiotic relationships marked by dominance and subservience, great social distance and little physical distance." The slaveholders' domination of Southern politics provided the basis for their influence on national politics.

The second period of class conflict and racial oppression started with the end of slavery and ended with the New Deal in the late 1930s. It was marked by the growth of industrialization based on manufacturing and by the presence of a more complex class structure that, significantly, included a white working class that competed with black labor. In the different economic and political contexts of the North and the South, the competition between white and black labor was critical in producing two outcomes: a split labor market in the North, in which the demise of slavery was followed by laws designed to curtail black economic competition, and Jim Crow segregation in the South, in which the demise of slavery threatened white labor to a greater extent than in the North. In both contexts, however, there was a combination of class competition between blacks and whites in the labor market, accompanied by racial oppression in the form of physical exclusion and segregation of blacks from public spaces in the South, and exclusion from entering occupations controlled by organized labor in the North. Wilson emphasized that these systems of race relations were erected with the interests of the white working class being taken into account. Free labor had to compete with slave labor, creating labor-market conflicts along racial lines.

The third period, this one of predominant class oppression and declining racial oppression, was characterized by modern industrialization and by two critical processes: mass migration of blacks from the South to Northern cities and an increasing geographic dispersion of business that had begun to move away from central cities. The timing of black migration, accompanied by an extensive concentration of blacks in the cities, had important consequences for the slow growth of their urban political power. Wilson argued that since migration took place only after 1940, blacks were already several decades behind the European whites who had migrated in the 1920s and earlier, and this belated entry left them without the sociopolitical influence that the cities had provided to other immigrant groups. Further, after the 1950s, economic shifts meant that business decentralized and moved out of the cities, while the industrial structure shifted from manufacturing to service jobs. This economic shift generated white-collar positions for skilled, educated workers, and low-paying, dead-end jobs that did not offer wages high enough to support a family. Thus, demographic and structural economic factors conjured the development of an economic chasm among blacks: a middle social class, and an underclass of largely unemployed or underemployed blacks.

A critical aspect of Wilson's argument was that educated (middle-class) blacks were beneficiaries of the increasing demand for skilled workers and of government civil rights laws that basically eliminated overt discrimination. He documented the growth of the middle class with statistics showing that an increasing number of blacks were employed in middle-class occupations. Conversely, he argued that uneducated blacks had higher rates of unemployment than educated blacks, and that the highest gap in unemployment between whites and nonwhites during the 1970s was with nonwhites who had less than 12 years of education. Marginality and redundancy created by modern industrial society affected all the poor, regardless of race, including whites, Native Americans, and Hispanic Americans. And, according to Wilson, the fact that one-third of the total black population was in the "underclass" in the 1970s reflected more than the legacy of past racial oppression. Drawing a logical implication from this argument, he argued that "the challenge of economic dislocation in modern industrial society calls for . . . programs . . . to attack inequality on a broad class front, policies that go beyond the limits of ethnic and racial discrimination."

The book caused a widespread controversy, and critics' responses were varied. Some critics claimed that the thesis of the book was true but that it did not really advance any new arguments and was poorly documented, whereas others focused on the lack of direct evidence to support the decline of the importance of race, claiming that the author's belief that an increase in the predictive power of one variable (class) necessitated a decrease in another (race) was a fallacy. However, the core of the controversy centered on three related points, the issue of race versus class in explaining the socioeconomic status of blacks, the particular role of race in explaining the black underclass, and the policy recommendations drawn from the book.

For Wilson, the very existence of a black middle class was proof that race as a sole criterion to allocate blacks in the economic structure was declining. This conclusion was logical from the standpoint of the author's conceptual apparatus: a racial system is one that, with the help of institutional sanctions, systematically uses race as the only or as the fundamental criterion to allocate blacks in the economic and social structure, and therefore, it is a system that precludes substantial economic differentiation of blacks. A class system, on the other hand, allocates people according to market resources (156). Wilson did not argue that racial discrimination had disappeared; he rather argued that it was less enveloping than before. While class factors were now operating in the economic sphere, race was displaced to the social and political spheres.

The role of the black middle class in the book's overall argument made it the subject of critics' comments. For example, Joe Feagin (1991), based on in-depth interviews with middle-class blacks, argued that they still encountered discrimination in different places, including workplace and educational sites, and particularly in public places, such as restaurants, stores, and motels. Feagin added that this discrimination in public places that existed in spite of the assumed protection of the civil rights laws contradicted Wilson's argument. And Stephen Steinberg (1988) pointed out that Wilson minimized the current importance of race, because although "class disabilities are real enough, . . . they are the byproduct of past racism, they are reinforced by present racism, and they constitute the basis for perpetuating racial divisions and . . . inequalities." Steinberg also noted the extraordinary dependence of middle-class blacks on government jobs, arguing that "without this public sector employment . . . much of the black middle class would not exist" (291). This dependence of the middle class on government jobs contradicted the argument that market mechanisms were responsible for its creation and were symptoms of the increasing importance of class. Other critics also pointed out that the black middle class was precarious and weak, very much subject to economic cycles, and that by calling attention to class differences, he was inviting the dismissal of the racial inequities prevalent in America.

Particularly controversial was the idea that the black underclass was the creation of market forces and not of racial discrimination. Wilson stressed that the lingering effects of past racism, mass migration, the existence of many young people among blacks, the movement of the middle class out of cities, and especially a mismatch between uneducated blacks and the skills that many service jobs required, contributed to the creation of a black underclass. Critics argued that contrary to Wilson's claims of a skills mismatch and implicitly of a lack of education among the poor, blacks were generally excluded from whole sectors of jobs, and from entry-level jobs with career ladders, such as waiters and cooks in full-service restaurants, and relegated to menial, low-paying and dead-end jobs. Others pointed out that blacks were excluded from construction jobs and that only black protest in the 1960s and government programs partially eliminated entry barriers.

Also disputed were the policy recommendations that followed from the book. Wilson (1978) recognized the multiple problems that afflicted underprivileged blacks and was not optimistic about the future: "Economic recovery is not likely to reverse the pattern of unemployment, underemployment, poverty, welfare, and female headed households," and "there are clear indications that the economic gap between the black underclass . . . and the higher-income blacks will very likely widen and solidify" (134). However, for him, the solution for the problems of the underclass resided in policies that should affect all poor Americans, not in programs specifically designed for blacks. These policy recommendations provoked an intense controversy, especially since affirmative action programs were, in the eyes of many critics, precarious, poorly implemented, and always under political attack. Critics argued that the elimination of the most urgent problems of the underclass required race-specific policies and a national commitment to eliminate ghettos. Diluting the solutions for the black underclass under a general economic program for all poor people would help blacks last and least.

Recent reappraisals of the book, as well as research on race, indicate that *The Declining Significance of Race* made durable contributions to black studies in particular and to ethnic studies more broadly. It acknowledged class divisions among blacks, criticizing the talk about blacks as a monolithic block in academic and political writings, and forced students of race to examine more carefully the interactions between race and class. One long-term result has been a growing methodological and conceptual sophistication in academic studies specifying and isolating the current role of race, especially for the underclass. Today, it is commonly accepted that the two dimensions do not exclude each other and that market and racial factors are both frequently present in, for example, employers' decisions about hiring.

Furthermore, Wilson's argument that affirmative action programs were helping mainly educated middle-class blacks, those who needed help least, induced a broader discussion about the limitations and advantages of government policies toward blacks. Yet, the debate about the benefits of and the need for such programs is far from settled.

Above all, Wilson's analysis of the underclass and the complex interconnected factors that perpetuate it has been a lasting contribution to the national debate about blacks and low-income communities. In *The Declining Significance of Race*, Wilson attributed the rise of the underclass to economic transformations, the rise of low-paid service jobs that drastically reduced the number of jobs paying wages sufficient to support a family, the geographic concentration of poor blacks, and the cumulative effects of these problems on black neighborhoods. Many subsequent studies have built on the dynamics of the underclass that Wilson set forth in *The Declining Significance of Race* and expanded on in his later books *The Truly Disadvantaged* and *When Work Disappears* (see, for example, Massey and Denton 1993).

Wilson's book was not the first to call attention to the impact of class on the socioeconomic status of blacks. And the debates it generated are certainly not settled, or at least not in a manner that makes the arguments of the book right or wrong. Yet, by making compelling arguments about largely underanalyzed issues, and by articulating central political and analytical concerns of both scholars and politicians at the time it was published, *The Declining Significance of Race* set forth the coordinates that guided scholarly research and political debate on race in America for many years.

Carmenza Gallo

Further Reading:

Bagley Masset, Cora. "The Precariousness of Social Class in Black America." *Contemporary Sociology* 9, no. 1 (1980): 16–19.

D'Amico, Ronald, and Nan L. Maxwell. "The Continuing Significance of Race in Minority Joblessness." *Social Forces* 73, no. 3 (1995): 969–91.
Feagin, Joe R. "The Continuing Significance of Race: Anti-Black Discrimination in Public Places." *American Sociological Review* 56 (February 1991): 101–16.
Jaret, Charles. *Contemporary Ethnic and Race Relations*. New York: HarperCollins, 1995.
Massey, Douglas S., and Nancy A. Denton. *American Apartheid: Segregation and the Making of the Underclass*. Cambridge, MA: Harvard University Press, 1993.
Pettigrew, Thomas F. "The Changing—Not Declining—Significance of Race." *Symposia on the Declining Significance of Race in Contemporary Sociology* 9, no. 1 (1980).
Sowell, Thomas. "On Race and Class in America." *Heritage Foundation Policy Review* 7 (1979).
Steinberg, Stephen. *The Ethnic Myth: Race, Ethnicity and Class in America*. Boston: Beacon Press, 1988.
Waldinger, Roger. *Still the Promised City? African Americans and New Immigrants in Postindustrial New York*. Cambridge, MA: Harvard University Press, 1996.
Wilson, William Julius. *The Declining Significance of Race: Blacks and Changing American Institutions*. Chicago: University of Chicago Press, 1978.
Wilson, William Julius. *The Truly Disadvantaged*. Chicago: University of Chicago Press, 1987.
Wilson, William Julius. *When Work Disappears*. New York: Random House, 1996.

Derogatory Terms

Anyone on the receiving end of racial or ethnic slurs such as *gook*, *spic*, *coolie*, and *nigger* can testify to the tremendous psychological and social impact of such words. Race-based derogatory terms are not a new phenomenon: they have complex historical and political origins.

Derogatory terms are words that label or mark an individual in a negative, often harmful way. In the context of race relations in the United States, derogatory terms slander the entire minority community. Because other categories of derogatory terms are usually based on singular, alterable aspects of a person (such as their ability or behavior), their negative effects can be somewhat tempered. However, race-based derogatory terms, because they label a person on the basis of unalterable physical characteristics (such as skin color), more completely mark, classify, and reduce the identity of the receiver. Furthermore, racial and ethnic labeling carries the threat of "other-ing," which can increase the alienation felt: those who use racial epithets reaffirm their position at the center of mainstream culture and power and cast the objects of these slurs as a deviant "other."

It is at this point useful to distinguish between stereotyping and using derogatory terms. A stereotype is a mental image one assigns to others. Ethnic or racial stereotypes are created when distinctive behavioral or physical characteristics of a group are chosen by members outside a particular group to signify them. Stereotypes operate to reinforce the preconceived beliefs of those using them and help sow the seeds of prejudice. A derogatory term is the verbal expression of a stereotype, rather than the stereotype itself. A derogatory term is given life through language, and as such, must be spoken or written to exist.

Because of this inherent connection to language, both the evolution and interpretation of derogatory terms are complicated. As the following history of racial derogatory terms suggests, determining which labels constitute a derogatory term is often highly subjective and affected by relations of power.

A given term may not be spoken with the same injurious intent with which it is received. Words can gain or lose their potency based on changing historical circumstance. As minority groups gain political voice and access to mainstream media and culture, they may choose to reappropriate words previously used against them. A derogatory term can thus metamorphose from a slur to a symbol of solidarity and power.

Derogatory terms have a complex history rooted in both social and political circumstances and shaped by those who use them and by those who are their objects. Some key dynamics emerge from the African American and Asian American historical experience.

Derogatory terms are not formed in a historical vacuum. They arise out of a particular set of social and economic conditions. For Asian Americans, the term *coolie* (*see* Coolie, for a fuller explanation) grew out of the context of Chinese immigration to the United States in the latter half of the 19th century. Whites perceived the Chinese as a "threat" to working-class solidarity, which was predicated on racial solidarity. Thus, the Chinese were marked as coolies, and their labor denigrated as coolie labor. This labeling reflected the larger exclusion of Chinese from the working class, especially from skilled labor.

As the historical context changed, so did the terms chosen to mark and degrade Asian Americans. The term *gook* gained popularity in the 1960s and 1970s. Its origins may be traced to the Korean War (1950–1953). *Megook* is the Korean word for "American," and GIs who heard the phrase mistakenly believed Koreans were referring to themselves "me (I am a) 'gook.'" *Gook* embodied the "invisible enemy" of the East and was used extensively by U.S. soldiers in the next major conflict in Asia: the Vietnam War. Back on home soil, the term helped single out Asian Americans of any ethnic origin—Korean, Vietnamese, Chinese—for opprobrium, and to equate Asian Americans to the same faceless enemies that fought, and in Vietnam, conquered, U.S. forces. Thus, *gook* can be seen as a term that found purchase in a destabilized, post-Vietnam world.

Racial resentment was shaped and channeled in different ways. Changing social and political landscapes created new racial discourses, from which new derogatory terms could develop. However, some derogatory terms have remained embedded in the racial lexicon and in public consciousness for a long time. The epithet *nigger* is one such word, and tracing its evolution can provide more clues as to how racial slurs find new meaning with time.

The origin of the term *nigger* can be traced to the word *negro*, the Latin origins of which denote the color black. The term *nigger* first appeared in the late 18th century in England, used by such literary notables as the poets Robert Burns and Lord Byron. From the 19th century, the term had been used in combination to refer to a wide variety of flora and fauna, suggesting more their color than any racial connotation: thus a "nigger" daisy, a "nigger fish," "nigger pea," and so forth. It is unclear precisely when or how *nigger* became derogatory, but the term had become recognized as a significant insult by the beginning of the 19th century.

As racialized slavery became increasingly coercive and oppressive, so also did the potency of the term *nigger*. This association with the darkest period of African American history continued to give the epithet a transcendent and deeply layered meaning and a particular venom. In the South during the segregation period between 1890 and 1954, the persistent usage of the term by anxious whites conveniently and effectively recalled blacks' previous position at the bottom of the social and economic ladder. However, as blacks continued to make headway into mainstream U.S. society and politics, any use of the word in public became progressively more unacceptable. The virtual absence, at least in public, of *nigger* from whites' vocabulary in the 21st century can thus be traced to effective political mobilization and African Americans' own changing socioeconomic position.

That said, the term has found a new lease on life in recent years. African Americans have appropriated the term for use amongst themselves—a subversive, if ironic, act of self-definition. First popularized in the 1970s by prominent black comedians such as Richard Pryor and increasingly an integral part of present-day hip-hop, rap, and street cultures, the use of the word *nigger* by African Americans has evolved to express affection, closeness, or a subtly joking familiarity. However, it is widely agreed that this new usage is confined strictly within the bounds of the black community. Only then can the term retain its noninflammatory quality. Tracing the evolution of the various meanings associated with the word amply shows how dramatically a given derogatory term's meanings can shift. Once a signifier of the deepest of racial prejudices, *nigger* has been given a second life by those who were once the object of its poison.

What is the significance of derogatory terms? At the heart of the debate is the issue of language. Language has become an increasingly important subject of study, particularly as postmodernist theories have encouraged scholars to view reality not as an objective occurrence, but constituted by subjective experience and relations of power. It is through language that humans conceive the world and express their place in it. Some argue that language is inherently political—that not only do words express our ideas, they have the ability to shape our ideas and experiences as well. In an unequal social order, therefore, language is able to serve the interests of the dominant class. Language can help entrench unequal social institutions and perpetuate an ideology of inferiority among the dominated class.

In this context, derogatory terms have important social and political implications. Derogatory terms express power differentials; however, through their utterance, racial epithets may also reinforce and perpetuate inequality. In this interpretation, the use of the word *nigger* up until the civil rights era did not just reflect underlying white prejudice, it actively helped to maintain a layered and coercive system of racial oppression.

Psychological impact is one mechanism through which derogatory terms may accomplish this end. Some argue that because race-related stigmatization is based on an unchanging aspect of one's being (their race), its harm is far more direct and personal than any other negative speech. Minority groups who repeatedly struggle with racial stigmatization develop low self-esteem and low expectations of success. Also, those who are frequently exposed to racial epithets may develop a hypersensitivity to issues of race and experience increased psychological and social stress levels, all of which further impede emotional, social, and economic well-being.

Some people believe that a derogatory term can never lose its harmful impact. Within the black community, debate continues as to the appropriateness of using the word *nigger*. Black intellectuals, musicians, and performers have weighed in on both sides (gunned-down rap star Tupac Shakur was said to have asserted that *nigga* stood for "Never Ignorant, Get Goals Accomplished," while comedian Bill Cosby stressed that the word could never lose its destructive potential).

For those who believe that derogatory terms exact a long-lasting and harmful toll on their victims and that racist speech perpetuates a larger social inequality, inaction is unthinkable. However, the extent to which all racial epithets need to be stamped out, and the steps by which they should be removed from public discourse, have been subjects of heated debate. At one end of the spectrum are the people who believe the eradication of words such as *nigger* from the public arena is the only solution. That would mean censoring literary classics such as *The Adventures of Huckleberry Finn*, which used the word repeatedly, and attempt to prevent its continued use under any circumstance.

Opponents of this view argue that eradicationists fail to see racial epithets in their historical context. For example, Mark Twain's use of the word *nigger* was not intentionally pejorative; he was attempting to accurately portray local use of the term. To erase it would deprive the novel of its historical relevance. Also, erasing the term *nigger* would deny legitimacy to the ways in which African Americans have reappropriated the word as a signifier of their own.

Critics of eradication further emphasize that an overzealous pursuit of elimination of all forms of hate speech may create a climate of intolerance and ignorance, precisely at odds with eradicationists' own goals. For example, in 1999, educator Ken Hardy was removed from his position at Jefferson Community College after using the word *nigger* in a class about taboo words. The same year, a white director of a Washington, D.C., municipal agency was forced to resign when he used the word *niggardly*, although the term has no etymological connection to *nigger* and the director had used it in the appropriate context. A University of Wisconsin professor who similarly used *niggardly* in a literature class provoked a campus protest. Thus, critics argue that heightened vigilance against racial epithets may yield unintended consequences: racial scapegoating and the creation of an environment that discourages open communication and debate.

Those who believe hate speech should be regulated as opposed to eliminated support a legal response to its use. "Regulationists" argue that the only effective, long-term solution can be effected through the courts. Several different avenues of action are possible. Some private institutions have developed speech codes, which may in the future become models for the public domain. For example, Stanford University in 1990 instituted a code that prohibits "harassment by personal vilification" and prevents verbal assault on the basis of race, color, handicap, religion, sexual orientation, or national and ethnic origin. Also, regulationists point out that some antidiscrimination statutes already exist that can be used to help monitor the use of derogatory terms and make provisions for appropriate action in cases of abuse. For example, the provisions of Title VII of the Civil Rights Act of 1964 were meant to prevent racial discrimination in employment. Black employees may cite repeated use of the term *nigger* by white colleagues as possible proof that the company has created a "racially hostile environment," grounds for action under Title VII.

A second means of redress is through tort law. Many jurisdictions already protect against what tort law terms as "the intentional infliction of emotional distress." Supporters of a tort law for racial slurs argue that the legal system does protect an individual's right to humane treatment, and therefore victims of hate speech should have recourse to legal action. Supporters contend that tort law would create an institutional arrangement in which discriminatory behaviors have no room to exist. Detractors argue that litigation would be expensive and time-consuming, it would be difficult to prove intent to cause emotional distress, and free speech may be threatened.

Finally, there are those who argue that both regulationists and eradicationists are missing the point. Focusing on derogatory terms detracts from the real mission at hand—to stamp out the racism that breeds them. W. E. B. Du Bois penned the following words in response to growing debate in the early 20th century within the black community about the political ramifications of racial labeling: "Names are only the conventional signs for identifying things. Things are the reality that counts. If a thing is despised, either because of ignorance or because it is despicable, you will not alter matters by changing its name." His words have a striking relevance in contemporary debates concerning derogatory terms. Supporters of Du Bois's viewpoint contend that the continual use of derogatory terms is but one manifestation of the racism that flows through American society and that only by stemming the flow of racism itself will discriminatory behavior, including the use of derogatory terms, cease.

Rebekah Lee

See also

Anchor Baby; Coolie; Cultural Racism; Magical Negro Films; Pimps and Hoes Parties; Stereotype; Welfare Queens

Further Reading:

Delgado, Richard. "Words That Wound: A Tort Action for Racial Insults, Epithets, and Name-Calling." *Harvard Civil Rights-Civil Liberties Law Review* 17 (1982).

Gates, Henry Louis, Jr. "War of Words: Critical Race Theory and the First Amendment." In *Speaking of Race, Speaking of Sex: Hate Speech, Civil Rights and Civil Liberties*, edited by Henry Louis Gates Jr. et al. New York: New York University Press, 1994.

Grant, Ruth W., and Marion Orr. "Language, Race and Politics: From 'Black' to 'African-American.'" In *Notable Selections in Race and Ethnicity*, 3rd ed., edited by David V. Baker. New York: McGraw-Hill, 2001.

Green, Jonathan. *Words Apart: The Language of Prejudice.* London: Kyle Cathie Publishing, 1996.

Kennedy, Randall. *Nigger: The Strange Career of a Troublesome Word.* New York: Vintage Books, 2003.

Kramarae, Chris, Muriel Schulz, and William O'Barr, eds. *Language and Power.* Beverly Hills, CA: Sage, 1984.

Desegregation

Desegregation is the legal process of ending racial segregation in public facilities and institutions. As a legal process, desegregation predates the landmark 1954 *Brown v. Board of Education* Supreme Court ruling that outlawed segregation in public schools and other areas. Local efforts to desegregate public facilities have been recorded as early as the 18th century. For example, in 1787, black parents petitioned the Massachusetts state legislature to allow their children to enroll in local public schools. These Bostonians made their case on the grounds that their young were being denied access to the very school that they, like their fellow white citizens, shared the tax burden of supporting. The request, although denied, was an augur of future struggles to desegregate public facilities in the United States and to extend the constitutional guarantee of equal protection of the law to all American citizens.

In 1865, Congress established the Bureau of Refugees, Freedmen, and Abandoned Lands, also known as the Freedmen's Bureau. A primary mission of the Freedmen's Bureau was to help newly freed slaves to become self-sufficient in all areas of American life. The establishment of the Freedman's Bureau was followed by the ratification of the Fourteenth Amendment in 1868. This amendment guarantees American citizenship and equal protection of the law to all persons born or naturalized in the United States; it is also the legal cornerstone of all desegregation policies, including those established to abolish segregation in public school systems, the armed forces, the workplace, and even in penitentiaries.

The desegregation of previously segregated public facilities presupposes some degree of their integration. Integration includes goals such as eradicating barriers to associations, creating equal opportunity for all, and forging an American culture that draws on diverse traditions. However, as a remedy primarily designed to abolish legal, or de jure, discrimination, desegregation policy cannot guarantee the conditions to facilitate the comparatively ambitious social goal of integration. Thus, many attempts to integrate public facilities have been met with resistance, and the history of racial desegregation in the United States is one marked by violence. Violent responses to racial desegregation have been most observable in schools and the workplace; in contrast, measures to desegregate the armed forces and the penal system have been met with more favorable results.

Racial Desegregation in the Armed Forces

One of the first federal acts to facilitate the desegregation of an American public institution occurred in 1862 when Congress passed a law permitting black men to enlist in the Union Army during the Civil War. Black leaders, such as Martin Delaney and Frederick Douglass, actively recruited black men for the military, and nearly 180,000 free black men and escaped slaves volunteered for service. However, these volunteers encountered resistance from white servicemen, who were more concerned about maintaining the Union than freeing slaves, and ambivalence from Congress, who left it up to the president to determine the duties of black volunteers. President Lincoln decided that black servicemen were to be used only as laborers and not as soldiers. Thus, although black volunteers desegregated the armed forces in the technical sense, they were confined to drudgery, a form of de facto segregation, and were routinely subjected to violence by their white Union comrades.

The U.S. armed forces remained largely segregated in this manner through the end of World War II. Opposition to the desegregation of the military came largely from representatives of many of the Southern states. For instance, in May 1948, Sen. Richard B. Russell, a Democrat from Georgia, attached an amendment to the selective services bill then being debated in Congress. This proposed attachment, which would have allowed new enlistees in the military the choice of serving in segregated units, was defeated both in committee in 1948, and once again in 1950, when the now Selective Services Law came up for reauthorization.

In July 1948, President Harry Truman signed Executive Order 9981, which authorized the desegregation of the armed forces. An executive order grants the president authority to bypass Congress to establish federal policy. By exercising his executive prerogative in issuing Executive Order 9981, President Truman avoided congressional opposition to his plan to desegregate the armed forces. The executive order, though, had a limited immediate impact on changing the composition of the U.S. military. However, during the Korean War, the American-led United Nations forces were met with staggering losses among U.S. white units, and ground commanders were compelled to accept black replacements. Black soldiers ably executed their responsibilities and, following the war, the Army High Command made the formal decision to desegregate the military in 1951, exactly three years to the day after Truman had issued Executive Order 9981. According to military historian Morris J. MacGregor Jr., for the most part, the desegregation of the armed forces resulted in "no increase in racial incidents, no breakdown of discipline, no uprising against integration by white soldiers or surrounding white communities, no backlash from segregationists in Congress, or major public denouncements of the new policy" (MacGregor 1981).

Since the 1950s, the military has assumed leadership in desegregation and integration efforts in the United States. In 2003, for instance, 29 former high-ranking officers and civilian leaders of the Army, Navy, Air Force, and Marine Corps, including military academy superintendents, former secretaries of defense, and current and former members of the U.S. Senate, signed a Military Amicus Brief that urged affirmative action in higher education. The brief, filed during the landmark *Grutter v. Bollinger* case in which the Supreme Court upheld affirmative action at the University of Michigan, argued that higher education was the source of entry-level military officers. According to former undersecretary of the U.S. Army Joe Reeder, signer and co-counsel of the Military Amicus Brief, "to lead our country's racially diverse enlisted men and women, our nation's fighting force requires a diverse office corps: affirmative action policies have helped our military build a top-quality officer corps that reflects America's diversity" (Greenberg Traurig 2003).

Desegregation and School Violence

In 1954, the Supreme Court rendered the landmark decision in *Brown v. Board of Education* to abolish segregation in public schools. *Brown* was sweeping in its mandate to reshape the racial landscape of American education and went beyond Executive Order 9981 to serve as a basis for the desegregation of other public facilities in the United States as well. The Supreme Court, though, did not provide clear guidelines to end de jure public school segregation, as captured in the imprecision of its order to proceed in the dismantling of segregated schools "with all deliberate speed" (Anti-Defamation League 2004). Thus, little dismantling of de jure segregation in public schools occurred during the decade after *Brown*.

Once black students finally began to desegregate previously all-white schools, they were often met with resistance. For example, in 1957, Gov. Orval Faubus mobilized troops

African American students Elizabeth Eckford (l) and Jefferson Thomas and others walk away from Central High School in Little Rock, Arkansas, after class, 1959. (Library of Congress)

from the Arkansas National Guard to prevent nine black students, known as the Little Rock Nine, from attending the previously all-white Little Rock Central High School. At one point, President Dwight Eisenhower told the governor to protect the students and to allow them to enter the school. However, Faubus defied the order and withdrew the National Guard. This left the Little Rock Nine to fend for itself against the mob, which encircled the school and prevented the group from entering. After trying for several days to persuade the Arkansas governor to abide by federal orders, President Eisenhower federalized the Arkansas National Guard and deployed the 101st Airborne Division to Little Rock to enforce *Brown*. A paratrooper was assigned to walk with each student to and from school and to remain with each student at school. However, white mobs were still able to physically assault the students and, in one incident, stabbed one and sprayed acid in her eyes. Despite attending school under such hostile conditions, eight of the Little Rock Nine eventually completed the term and one graduated at the end of the year.

Similarly, in September 1962, an attempt by James Meredith, a 28-year-old Air Force veteran, to desegregate the University of Mississippi was met with days of violence and rioting by white mobs. Escorted by federal officials, Meredith eventually enrolled and, transferring credit hours from a previous school, graduated within the year without further incident. Perhaps one of the more enduring symbols of the racial violence associated with early efforts to desegregate public schools is that of Ruby Bridges, the six-year-old who desegregated an all-white New Orleans elementary school in 1960. The young Bridges's resolve inspired the 1966 painting by Norman Rockwell titled *The Problem We All Live With.*

The painting depicts the little girl, elegantly attired in a white dress with a matching hair ribbon and shoes, and accompanied by federal marshals, as she fearlessly made her way to class past a tomato-splattered racial epithet sprawled on the side of the school building.

Despite the often-violent resistance to school desegregation, the constitutional impact of *Brown* has been enormous. For instance, the Supreme Court's ruling resulted in a dramatic increase in the number of desegregation suits filling lower court dockets. It also formed the legal basis for the civil rights acts of the early 1960s that resulted in the systematic dismantling of segregation in public school districts and other public facilities across the country from the late 1960s through the mid-1980s. However, *Brown*'s implications for Northern schools were even less clear than they were for those in the South and presented a different set of challenges to implementing desegregation policy. The early efforts to desegregate schools in the South occurred under conditions where white lawmakers coded segregation in policy (de jure); segregation in the North, however, was not written into law but rather existed as fact (de facto).

For example, in many cities in the Midwest, on the Pacific coast, and along the Eastern seaboard, housing patterns revealed segregated neighborhoods. Because children were assigned to neighborhood schools, the schools were segregated as a matter of fact, as opposed to a matter of law. However, plaintiffs in desegregation suits in these areas provided courts persuasive evidence that many white homeowners used public agencies, real estate agents, and civic leaders to maintain de facto segregation in their schools. Eventually, in 1973, in *Keyes v. School District of Denver*, the Court expanded *Brown* to also include the dismantling of de facto segregation in public schools, and by the early 1970s courts began to render rulings that enforced *Brown* throughout the North. Some court-ordered mandates unified entire metropolitan school districts and placed previously separate entities under the control of a centralized authority. More often than not, though, courts employed formulae to promote the interdistrict busing of black students to white schools and of white students to selective schools in predominantly black neighborhoods. In their attempt to desegregate Northern schools, black students typically were met with resistance and, at times, with violence not unlike that of their predecessors in the South.

For example, black students who attempted to desegregate schools in South Boston in the fall of 1974 were greeted by angry, violent mobs that threw rocks through the windows of the buses that carried them into the community; on one such occasion, nine young children were injured when shards of glass rained upon them. Efforts to desegregate Northern schools were eventually met with limited success. The net gains of the 1970s and 1980s, however, were reversed as a result of local efforts to thwart integration and of significant Supreme Court rulings such as *Milliken v. Bradley* (1974) that removed federal courts' powers to impose interdistrict remedies between cities and surrounding schools to desegregate city schools. As a consequence, public schools became increasingly resegregated during the 1990s and the early years of the 21st century. Jonathan Kozol, a prominent critic of educational inequality, observed that schools were more segregated in 2006 than they were any time since 1968. Along these lines, urban and fringe-city school districts were being populated by increasingly multicultural populations of students of color from working-class, poor, and immigrant families and more affluent suburban schools were being populated by homogeneous bodies of white students from middle-class families.

During this period, violence erupted in a number of urban schools as a result of interracial tensions between students from black, Latino, Asian American, and immigrant groups. For example, since 2000, conflicts were frequently reported between white and Asian American students in the San Francisco Bay area, between black and Latino students in Albuquerque, and between black and Bosnian students in St. Louis. In those truly desegregated school districts that remained, students were often resegregated via racially informed tracking systems. Racial tracking minimizes contact between students of different groups and may have accounted for fewer reports of race-based violence in these schools. In addition, racial disparities in the ways these schools meted out discipline may have also contributed to reduced rates of violence reported in desegregated schools. Although, in general, poor students were more likely to be disciplined than wealthy students, researchers have found that black students from the wealthiest families were suspended at almost the same rate as white students from the poorest families. Interestingly, a 2005 Yale University study found that, nationally, prekindergarten students are expelled three times as often as students in K–12 settings and, predictably, that black prekindergarten students were twice as likely to be expelled as their white and Latino preschool peers. Such disparities reduced the opportunity for students of different races to interact with one another and, thus, undermined both the spirit of integration and the goal of equal education intended by the landmark 1954 Supreme Court decision.

Desegregation and Violence in the Workplace

Although *Brown* did not achieve its primary goal to guarantee equal educational opportunity for all black children, it reasserted the equal protection clause of the Fourteenth Amendment and provided the impetus to cripple segregation in the broader society. For instance, the Civil Rights Act of 1964 included Title VII, which established the U.S. Equal Employment Opportunity Commission and gave it the mandate to stamp out workplace discrimination. However, like the campaign to desegregate schools, the drive to eliminate segregation in the workplace encountered resistance at every turn.

Riots engulfed American urban communities throughout the 1960s in partial response to the debilitating conditions in ghettos and the limited opportunities their residents had to change their lots (see Long Hot Summer Riots, 1965–1967). The 1965 Watts riot is perhaps most closely associated with the racial unrest that marked the period (see Los Angeles [California] Riot of 1965). However, it was only the first burst in a wave of riots to spread across the United States over the next few years, including those that engulfed Chicago, Tampa, Cincinnati, Atlanta, Newark, Detroit, and numerous smaller cities and communities. Various well-publicized studies were produced in the wake of these uprisings to offer explanations for Negro discontent, especially in light of the gains of the civil rights movement. The most notable of these studies was the 1968 Kerner Commission Report that President Lyndon B. Johnson commissioned in 1967. This report issued the now famous warning that the "nation is moving toward two societies" (Kerner Commission 1968), one white, one black. Altogether, the various reports pointed to a lack of job opportunities as being at the root of much of the racial unrest in American cities.

As previously suggested, desegregation presupposes some degree of integration, a social goal that cannot be achieved through legal means. In the workplace, white employees view the extension of job opportunities to minorities as a challenge to their own privilege and financial well-being. A 2001 Harvard University study of attitudes among residents in Boston and three other cities that sought to explain the coexistence of declining openly racist attitudes with persistent pro-segregationist attitudes, continued racial conflict, and opposition to affirmative action programs sheds light on the potential for desegregation policy to create hostile environments in workplaces. Among other findings, the author concluded that whiteness is experienced as a privilege, which leads members of the white working class to express a defensive sense of entitlement to jobs as well as to schools and neighborhoods.

Another significant study compiled hate crime statistics provided by law enforcement agencies and supplemented by hate incident reports from individuals, community groups, and media reports to examine racial incidents of violence in workplaces following the terrorist attacks in the United States on September 11, 2001. The study, "Backlash: When America Turned on Its Own," identified 243 race-based attacks against Asian Americans in the three-month period after the attacks. In contrast, racially motivated attacks against Asian Americans for a typical 12-month period previously numbered around 400, according to the report. Victims described in the report included a Sikh American from Mesa, Arizona, who was shot and killed by a gunman who yelled, "I stand for America all the way." The study reports that South Asian Americans, including Indian and Pakistani Americans, in general, suffered the brunt of the violence. However, of the group, Sikh American men have been singled out as targets because, according to the report, they are often mistakenly perceived to be Arab because many of them wear turbans and long beards. The vast majority of the incidents during the three-month period occurred in the first weeks after the attacks, with 27 percent occurring in schools and 29 percent taking place in the workplace.

In the 21st century, racial inequality and, thus, the potential for violence persist in the American workplace. Some of the inequality is attributable to deindustrialization, that is, the shift in the American economy from manufacture to service, which has resulted in the loss of jobs, especially in the public sector, that have historically employed the black working and middle class as well as other minorities and immigrant groups. In addition, technological advances have also compromised the work opportunities for these groups as automation and cyber technologies have proven themselves more profitable for employers than human beings. Grassroots conservatism, changing city demographics attributable to immigration, impoverished public policy, and diminished access to quality education also contribute to workplace inequalities. In addition, an uncertain U.S. economy contributes to social tensions and fosters potentially volatile conditions in the workplace as working-class Americans of all backgrounds compete for a diminishing pool of jobs.

Desegregation and Inmate Violence

As indicated above, economic changes in the United States from the late 1980s into the first decade of the 2000s have contributed to a reduced urban human workforce that largely impacts African Americans and other minority groups. The black unemployment rate in some cities, for instance, reached as high as 37 percent. Within the same period, the United States also experienced a dramatic increase in the number of incarcerated Americans. For instance, more Americans were incarcerated during a 15-year time spanning the mid-1980s through the 1990s than during the entire 50-year period before it. The swell in the prison population precipitated a prison-building boom and concurred with public policy investments in criminal justice that surpassed their investments in other areas of social spending, including education, food stamps, Aid to Families with Dependent Children, and Temporary Assistance for Needy Families.

At the end of 2004, the U.S. prison population stood at 2,135,901 and 1 out of every 138 Americans was incarcerated either in jail or prison. Black male inmates made up 41 percent of the U.S. prison population and Latino male inmates made up 19 percent. Eighty percent of the inmate population had been either charged with, or convicted of, nonviolent offenses; 15 percent were mentally ill, and the vast majority hailed from working-class and poor communities. The features particular, but not unique, to prison life (including overcrowding, the presence of gangs, diminished physical mobility, and reduced access to recreation and education) combined with the demographic make-up of the inmate population to create social tensions and to foster conditions for violence in U.S. penitentiaries.

Along these lines, prison officials reported an increase in race-based gang violence in penitentiaries across the United States since the 1990s. In 1996, for instance, the Hudson County Correctional Facility imposed a partial lockdown after an inmate was stabbed and three others were injured in a melee between members of the Latin Kings, a Latino gang, and the Five Percenters, a black gang. The outbreak followed a fight the previous week when another inmate was stabbed and four others were hurt. In 2002 in California, prisons reported that the vast majority of their nearly 7,000 incidents of assault and battery and seven deaths were race-based. In 2006, also in California, tensions erupted during several days of fighting between Latino and black inmates in the 21,000-inmate Los Angeles County jail system, leaving two prisoners dead and around 100 injured. Racial violence also occurred at centers throughout the California juvenile system as well. According to reports, violent incidents increased from 2,094 in 2003 to 2,352 in 2004, and to approximately 2,700 in 2005.

Some prisons have resorted to segregating inmates as a strategy to reduce race-based violence. For instance, until 2005, the California Department of Corrections (CDC) practiced blanket racial segregation in its reception centers where it housed inmates when they first arrived. These inmates were routinely kept with members of their own race at least for the first 60 days of their incarceration. The rationale for this unwritten policy was rooted in the view of prison officials that, given the prominence of inmates from race-based gangs, such measures were necessary to reduce the violence evident in the aforementioned accounts.

However, courts had long declared such measures unconstitutional. After the passage of the Civil Rights Act of 1964, for instance, not unlike other groups, inmates all over the country began filing complaints to assert their civil rights. In 1972, a black inmate named William Robert Eugene Battle filed a federal lawsuit, *Battle v. Anderson*, in the U.S. District Court in Muskogee, Oklahoma. Included among other violations, Battle's suit alleged racial segregation and discrimination in inmate housing, job assignments, and employment practices in the Oklahoma prison system, specifically at Oklahoma State Penitentiary. The federal court ruled in favor of the plaintiff and ordered, among other things, the reconfiguration of the racial composition of all housing units to approximate that of the inmate population as a whole.

Similarly, in 1995, California inmate Garrison Johnson began filing a series of complaints alleging that the CDC reception area violated his constitutional rights. Serving a sentence for murder, robbery, and assault since 1987, Johnson had been transferred between multiple CDC facilities. The CDC segregation policy, as indicated previously, was predicated on the assumption that prison violence was the result of the presence of different race-based gangs and thus grouped inmates according to racial groups to prevent the eruption of interracial violence. Thus, Johnson was segregated with other black inmates each time he changed facilities. However, Johnson was not a gang member and felt that he would be safer housed among members of other races where he did not face the pressure to join a gang or the violence he encountered when he refused to do so. Therefore, the CDC policy, he argued, violated the equal protection clause of the Fourteenth Amendment because it used race as a factor in determining housing assignments for the first 60 days of incarceration and, in doing so, placed him in harm's way. In January 2005, the Supreme Court agreed with the inmate and ruled in *Johnson v. California* that the CDC had to abandon its policy of assigning inmates to racially segregated cells upon arrival in new prisons, unless it could prove it has no race-neutral way to prevent interracial violence.

Only days before the Supreme Court's ruling, Sen. Gloria Romero, a democrat from Los Angeles, introduced Senate Bill 814 to abolish prison segregation in the CDC. A California Senate majority leader, Senator Romero pointed to a study of Texas prisons that indicated that only 5 percent of all incidents of violence involved racial motivations and, of those, only 1.2 percent were attributable to interracial violence. She further noted that the CDC had been unable to identify a single incident of interracial violence between cellmates, thus undermining its claim that segregation was necessary to stem the wave of prison riots. Senator Romero's bill was vetoed. Despite this effort, several California prisons continue to have a race-segregated prison system.

Garrett A. Duncan

See also

American Apartheid; Hypersegregation; *Plessy v. Ferguson* (1896); *Savage Inequalities;* School Segregation; Segregation. Document: *Plessy v. Ferguson* (1896)

Further Reading:

Anti-Defamation League. "Lesson 3: With All Deliberate Speed." *Exploring the Promise of Brown v. Board of Education 50 Years Later* (2004). http://www.adl.org/education/brown_2004/lesson3.asp.

Armor, David J. *Forced Justice: School Desegregation and the Law.* New York: Oxford University Press, 1995.

Greenberg Traurig, LLP. "Military Amicus Brief Cited in Supreme Court's Decision in the University of Michigan Case, *Grutter v. Bollinger.*" *GT Press Release,* June 27, 2003.

Kerner Commission. *Report of the National Advisory Commission on Civil Disorders.* Washington, DC: U.S. Government Printing Office, 1968.

Kozol, Jonathan. *The Shame of the Nation: The Restoration of Apartheid Schooling in America.* New York: Crown, 2005.

MacGregor, Morris J., Jr. *Integration of the Armed Forces, 1940–1965.* Washington, DC: Center of Military History, 1981.

Mauer, Marc. *Race to Incarcerate.* New York: New Press, 1999.

Wilson, William Julius. *When Work Disappears: The World of the New Urban Poor.* New York: Alfred A. Knopf, 1996.

Detroit (Michigan) Riot of 1943

The Detroit Riot of 1943 was by many accounts the most severe manifestation of urban unrest in America since the Chicago, Illinois, Riot of 1919 and the Tulsa, Oklahoma, Riot of 1921. At the conclusion of three days of rioting in Detroit, Michigan, in the summer of 1943, there were 34 confirmed deaths, 760 injured, and an estimated $2 million of property damage. The 1943 Detroit riot can be understood as part of a larger cycle of civil disorder that took place in several American cities during this time, including Harlem, New York; Los Angeles, California; and Beaumont, Texas. By 1943, wartime mobilization efforts had brought new waves of black and Hispanic migrants in contact with previous generations of white migrants and European immigrants in major cities across the United States. In Detroit, much of the conflict occurred between working-class white immigrants from Europe and black migrants from the rural South. Instigated largely by interpersonal violence between members of these groups who vied for space, jobs, and political power, the 1943 Detroit riot can be seen as a prime example of a communal riot.

The proximate cause of the 1943 Detroit riot, like the Chicago Riot of 1919, involved contested access to recreational space. The initial precipitating incident occurred when a scuffle ensued among black and white youths who were playing cards at Belle Isle, a sprawling public park located on the east side of Detroit. On June 20, 1943, throngs of people headed to Belle Isle seeking relief from the oppressive summer heat. Among the crowds was a small group of black teenagers who, a few days earlier, had been forcibly ejected from a privately owned amusement park by a group of white teenagers and white army recruits.

As a result of the incident at the amusement park, this group decided to walk nearly three miles to the public beach at Belle Isle, where they entered into a game of dice with some white youths. Accusations of cheating soon developed, and fighting broke out among the black and white youths. Other youths from both races began to join the fray, and skirmishes erupted elsewhere on the island. Toward the end of the day, as crowds filed out of the park, fighting broke out on the causeway connecting Belle Isle to the mainland. While black and white youths fought on the bridge and throughout the island, white mobs gathered on the mainland side, waiting to attack returning blacks. Later that evening, a black man who claimed to be a police officer jumped on stage at a black-owned nightclub and announced that a black lady and her baby had been thrown off the Belle Isle bridge and drowned in the Detroit River.

Meanwhile, at a white nightclub, a similar rumor circulated that a white woman and her baby had been thrown off the bridge. Another unsubstantiated story described how a group of blacks had slit a white sailor's throat and murdered his girlfriend. By dawn of the next day, mobs of white and black people had mobilized on their respective sides of Woodward Avenue, the dividing line between white and black communities, determined to exact revenge upon one another. White mobs, numbering in the hundreds, stopped streetcars, pulled black passengers off, and beat them. Black civilians who had strayed across the boundaries of their neighborhoods into white space were severely punished. In the black neighborhoods to the east of Woodward Avenue, black mobs retaliated by throwing rocks and bricks at passing vehicles driven by white motorists, and breaking into white-owned stores. Police soon found themselves overwhelmed and unable to contain the spreading violence.

Hostility between whites and blacks in Detroit had been building since World War I when black migrants first began to move northward in large numbers to take advantage of jobs in Detroit's booming defense and automotive industries. The black population in Detroit increased dramatically between 1910 and 1940. During the wartime years, from 1940 to 1950, the black population of Detroit nearly doubled, from 153,773 to 304,677, a gain of 98.1 percent. Black migrants were largely confined to a narrow strip of land just east of the central business district known as Paradise Valley or alternatively as Black Bottom for its tar-like soil. As more and more rural black migrants arrived, the population density of Black Bottom increased dramatically, and a housing shortage ensued.

Middle-class blacks who sought to move beyond the confines of Black Bottom often faced harassment and violence at the hands of white residents. However, by the 1940s, as a result of a renewed wave of black migration, some neighborhoods in Detroit were undergoing a rapid transition from white to black. During this time, white residents reacted violently to the movement of blacks into the newly constructed low-income black communities springing up in their midst. Fearing that their neighborhoods would be overrun by black migrants, whites in Detroit often turned to violence as a means of preserving racial boundaries.

Whites also resisted integration of their workplaces. Black migrants, despite being assigned to the dirtiest and lowest-paying jobs in the factories, were often viewed with suspicion as potential strikebreakers or scabs, who, given their willingness to work for less pay, would take the jobs of unionized white workers. White workers in the automobile and defense plants fought vigorously to exclude black workers from the more skilled, higher-paying positions. Racial animosity pervaded the workplace in Detroit and carried over to the neighborhoods where white workers lived, often leading to violent racial conflicts. This long-building tension between blacks and whites in Detroit formed the backdrop for the riots that broke out in 1943.

The Detroit police can be seen as contributing to the racial tensions at this time rather than alleviating them. By the early 1940s, the Detroit police found themselves vastly understaffed and unprepared to deal with widespread racial unrest in their city. They focused their efforts on restoring the informal geographic boundaries between white and black residents in the city, patrolling on the fringes of white and black neighborhoods where much of the violence was taking place. Rarely did they arrest white perpetrators of violence. In some cases, police officers stood idly by as white mobs assaulted black individuals. In other cases, police employed violence against suspected black looters. There is evidence that the police themselves were responsible for the majority of deaths among the all-black riot victims of 1943.

As the riots began on June 20, 1943, Detroit police massed on Woodward Avenue attempting to separate white and black mobs. However, violence spread elsewhere to the east and west. On the second day of the riots, it became clear that the Detroit police could not control the situation. Despite the fact that there was a formal protocol in place for the use of federal troops, which stated that army troops could be mobilized on an emergency basis without presidential approval, neither the mayor of Detroit nor the governor of Michigan seemed aware of the proper procedure for calling out the National Guard and Army. Neither wanted to declare martial law for fear of alienating their constituents. Nor were Army generals able to clearly explain the procedure for requesting federal troops. As a result, officials continued to debate semantics and points of protocol, delaying the entry of Army troops into Detroit. Finally, three days after the riots had started, the governor declared a state of emergency. Soon thereafter, federal military police entered the city. Once engaged, with bayonets drawn, the federal troops quickly dispersed the mobs gathered along Woodward Avenue and rounded up bands of roving whites operating in the black neighborhood of Paradise Valley. Within less than four hours, order had been restored. A presidential proclamation finally came in the waning hours of June 22, retroactively authorizing the use of federal troops in Detroit. The proclamation remained in place for the next six months in case racial violence was to flare up again.

Within a few weeks of the riot, it seemed that a sense of normalcy had returned to the city. Yet racial tensions continued to lurk under the surface and political officials continued to fear the possibility of future violence. The governor commissioned a study that mostly blamed the city's black population for the riot, suggesting that militant black leaders had incited violence by advocating for racial equality. Civil rights leaders, led by Thurgood Marshall of the National Association for the Advancement of Colored People Legal Defense Fund, issued their own report decrying the manner with which the police handled the riot and warning against future outbreaks if racial inequalities in employment, housing, and education were not addressed. Over the next decade following the riots, political officials set up several committees and commissions to try to address the racial conflicts in the city. However, often lacking adequate resources, these commissions were unable to redress the structural inequalities in Detroit that lay at the heart of the urban unrest.

Over the next two decades (1950–1970), white flight, combined with deindustrialization and disinvestment, further chipped away at Detroit's fragile social base. By the summer of 1967, indicative of the extent of white out-migration, blacks represented more than 40 percent of Detroit's population. By 1970, blacks had attained a residential majority in Detroit. Yet the political and economic status of black people in Detroit had changed little since the 1940s. African Americans in Detroit still lacked adequate political representation and economic opportunities. This would prove to be a recipe for disaster. In the summer of 1967, Detroit would erupt again in a racial rebellion that would impact the entire city for decades to come.

Max Herman

See also

Detroit (Michigan) Riot of 1967; Race Riots in America; White Flight. Documents: Report on the Memphis Riots of May 1866 (1866); Account of the Riots in East St. Louis, Illinois (1917); A Southern Black Woman's Letter Regarding the Recent Riots in Chicago and Washington (1919); The Cook County Coroner's Report Regarding the 1919 Chicago Race Riots (1920); The Final Report of the Grand Jury on the Tulsa Race Riot (June 25, 1921); Testimony from *Laney v. United States* (1923); The Governor's Commission Report on the Watts Riots (1965); Cyrus R. Vance's Report on the Riots in Detroit (1967); The Reports of the Oklahoma Commission to Study the Tulsa Race Riot of 1921 (2000–2001); Draft Report: 1898 Wilmington Race Riot Commission (2005)

Further Reading:

Capeci, Dominic J. *Race Relations in Wartime Detroit.* Philadelphia: Temple University Press, 1984.

Capeci, Dominic J., and Martha Wilkerson. *Layered Violence: The Detroit Rioters of 1943.* Jackson: University Press of Mississippi, 1991.

Herman, Max Arthur. *Fighting in the Streets: Ethnic Succession and Urban Unrest in 20th Century America.* New York: Peter Lang Publishers, 2005.

Platt, Anthony M. *The Politics of Riot Commission 1917–1970.* New York: Macmillan Publishing Company, 1971.

Shogan, Robert, and Tom Craig. *The Detroit Race Riot: A Study in Violence*. New York: Da Capo Press, 1964.
Sitkoff, Harvard. "The Detroit Race Riot of 1943." *Michigan History* 53 (Fall 1969): 183–206.
Sugrue, Thomas. *The Origins of the Urban Crisis*. Princeton, NJ: Princeton University Press, 1996.

Detroit (Michigan) Riot of 1967

The Detroit Riot of 1967 was not a race riot in the traditional sense of the term. Unlike the race riots that had taken place earlier in the 20th century in cities like East St. Louis (1917), Chicago (1919), Tulsa (1921), Harlem (1943), and Detroit (1943), the 1967 Detroit riot did not pit black and white civilians against one another in direct interpersonal combat. Rather, the 1967 riot was primarily a struggle between working-class African Americans (and some working-class whites) against the police, National Guard, and forces of the U.S. Army. At its conclusion, after five days of rioting, 43 people were dead, 1,189 were injured, and over 7,000 were arrested, making the 1967 Detroit riot the deadliest episode of urban unrest during the 1960s.

The Precipitating Incident

The precipitating incident for the 1967 Detroit riot was a police raid on an after-hours drinking establishment, locally referred to as a blind pig. Whereas legal bars closed around midnight, blind pigs stayed open all night. Often located in people's homes or, in the case of larger blind pigs, above business establishments, these informal bars catered to the entertainment needs of working-class Detroiters, providing them with a place to go after the 4:00 P.M. to midnight shift at local factories. In the early morning hours of July 23, 1967, Detroit police raided one such establishment located at 9125 12th Street, above the Economy Printing Shop. Such police raids were common at the time and usually resulted in a few symbolic arrests and a small fine for the proprietors. But this police raid on the blind pig at 12th and Clairmount would prove different. When police arrived, they expected a small crowd, but instead found the place packed with over 80 people celebrating the return of two soldiers from the Vietnam War. Unlike previous raids, where police arrested the owners and a few patrons, typically for possession of illegal drugs or firearms, the police attempted to arrest everyone on the premises. They called for backup, but it took nearly a half hour before the first transport van arrived and was loaded. During the interim, a crowd gathered outside the blind pig and began protesting the police presence.

As the police wagons departed, protestors began to hurl rocks and bricks at them. An empty bottle broke the rear window of a police transport van. Shortly after the police vans departed, a group of 10 to 12 men broke a plate glass window and began looting Jack's Esquire, a clothing store located on the corner of 12th and Clairmount. During this time, according to several eyewitnesses, there were no police in sight. After breaking into the clothing store, looters continued to break into other stores in succession along 12th Street. Despite attempts by the police to cordon off the area, within the next 24 hours, rioting began to spread throughout the city, from its epicenter on the city's northwest side, to the eastside and downtown.

Underlying Structural Conditions

The underlying structural conditions that helped give rise to the 1967 Detroit riot had been in existence for at least a decade prior to the eruption of hostilities. During the 1950s and early 1960s, a federally sponsored urban renewal program gutted the primarily black enclave on the eastside known as Black Bottom. Black Bottom, whose origins dated back to the 19th century, was a thriving black commercial and residential district, but was demolished to make way for the construction of a new interstate highway that would shuttle people quickly in and out of the downtown. In addition to its thriving mainstream businesses, Black Bottom was also a magnet for vice: unauthorized alcohol sales or production, gambling, and prostitution. Prior to the demolition of Black Bottom, a middle-class black neighborhood had emerged on the west side of the city, around 12th Street, in a formerly Jewish neighborhood. With the destruction of Black Bottom, a new working-class and poor element moved, bringing with it some of the same vices that had existed in Black Bottom. As a result of the demographic shift, tensions flared among the newcomers and those residents and merchants who were more established in the 12th Street area.

Detroit, as a city, was also undergoing demographic change. White residents were moving to the surrounding suburbs at an increasingly rapid pace. By 1967, Detroit's black population had increased from 30 to 40 percent of the city's population. By the end of the decade, Detroit would be a majority black city. Yet despite their increasing numbers, African Americans were underrepresented in city government. Although a new liberal mayor was elected with the support of black voters, nonetheless there were few black political officials, either elected or appointed, at the time. Blacks were particularly underrepresented on the city's police force, where they accounted for less than 5 percent of all police officers. Although the number of black teachers in Detroit's schools was closer to the proportion of blacks who were Detroit residents, Detroit schools were segregated along racial lines and black teachers complained of discrimination in promotion and disciplinary actions. At the same time as blacks students came to represent a larger portion of pupils, funding for public schooling was decreasing, and the schools were in the midst of a long decline. Taken together, this demographic change, coupled with political exclusion and lack of educational resources, all added fuel to the fire that would erupt in July 1967.

These structural inequalities, combined with the expectations engendered by the civil rights and anti–Vietnam War movements, helped give rise to militancy within Detroit's black community. Martin Luther King, Jr. led a massive march for civil rights along Woodward Boulevard in1963, just prior to the more famous March on Washington that year. In the years between July 1963 and July 1967, more radical civil rights spokesmen like Malcolm X, Stokely Carmichael, and H. Rap Brown visited Detroit regularly, engaging in fiery rhetoric that called for Black Power and black self-determination. Local militants like Rev. Albert Cleage, and the Henry brothers (Milton and Richard) sought to channel the frustrations of Detroit's inner-city black communities toward effecting political change. Their language stoked the embers of resentment emanating from the streets.

A great deal of resentment among people of Detroit was due to the constant presence of the police in the black community. The vice crimes unit known as *The Big Four* quickly established a reputation for brutality, routinely beating black youths, suspected drug dealers, and prostitutes, as they attempted so-called clean-up of the streets. In the five years preceding the riot, the police had been implicated in the shooting of several unarmed black civilians. In one high-profile case that took place in 1964, police officers brutally beat a prostitute whom they had detained after breaking up a dispute she had with a customer. In another case from 1965, a 15-year-old was beaten severely after officers arrested him for "disturbing the peace" (Fine 1989, 117). For many residents in the black communities of Detroit, such occurrences were all too common. This may explain how a routine police raid on a blind pig led to a melee between police and black citizens.

Initial Police Response

The initial police raid that sparked unrest in Detroit occurred at 3:45 A.M., on Sunday, July 23. Because it was a Sunday, the number of police on duty was less than it would have been on a weekday or Saturday night. By 5:10 A.M., a plainclothes police officer and a lieutenant sergeant who had just arrived on the scene reported the throwing of objects and breaking of windows. At 5:20 A.M., Police Commissioner Ray Girardin was notified of the disturbance and immediately called Mayor Jerome Cavanaugh. By 5:30 A.M., Girardin ordered eight scout cars with 17 men from outside the 10th Precinct to report for duty in the 10 Precinct (which included the 12th Street area). By 6:42 A.M., Girardin had mobilized 369 officers including 43 officers of the elite Tactical Mobile Unit.

At 7:50 A.M., police officers attempted a sweep of 12th Street but were unsuccessful due to a growing crowd of over 3,000 people. By 8:00 A.M., the total number of Detroit police officers mobilized for riot duty had increased to 1,004, with 364 committed to the riot area, which at that point was localized along 12th Street. Police then attempted to seal off the 12th Street-Clairmount area. Between 9:30 and 10:30 A.M., community leaders including U.S. Representative John Conyers sought to calm the crowd, but were rebuffed. Conyers stood on top of a police car, and used a bullhorn to address the crowd, but was shouted down. By 10:30 A.M., police reported widespread looting and several fires. When firefighters responded, they were hit with rocks and bottles. At this point, police officers shifted their efforts from cordoning off 12th Street to protecting firefighters. Looting then spread to surrounding thoroughfares such as Linwood and Dexter Boulevards. At 2:00 P.M., Mayor Cavanaugh held a meeting with political officials and community leaders at police headquarters. Shortly thereafter, Cavanaugh requested that the

Michigan State Police be sent immediately to Detroit. By 3:00 P.M., 300 state police had arrived at a local armory. Until this point, there were no reports of police using their weapons and no confirmed deaths due to riot activity.

The Riot Intensifies

By Sunday afternoon, the riots had spread beyond the 12th Street neighborhood to nearby neighborhoods on the west side of Detroit. Widespread looting of stores was followed by incidents of arson. Winds clocked at 20–25 miles per hour fanned the flames, spreading fires from the point of origin to adjacent businesses and residences. In one ironic incident, a fire set by an arsonist spread from rooftop to rooftop, eventually consuming the arsonist's own home. "Fire Chief Charles J. Quinlan estimated that at least two-thirds of the buildings were destroyed by spreading fires rather than fires set at the scene. Of the 683 structures involved, approximately one-third were residential, and in few, if any, of these was a fire set originally" (National Advisory Commission on Civil Disorders 1968, 92).

Sunday afternoon was also marked by the first known riot fatalities. Around 2:30 P.M., Krikor "George" Messerlian, a white merchant who owned a shoe repair shop, was beaten by a group of black youths while he attempted to defend his store with a ceremonial sword. His death was followed by that of Sharon George, a 23-year-old white woman who was hit by a bullet while riding in her husband's car. Later that evening, Walter Grzanka, a second-generation Polish immigrant, was shot while looting a grocery store, by the store's owner. Although the first three fatalities of the 1967 Detroit riot were whites, by the end of the riot, 33 of the 43 deaths attributed to the riots were blacks. Many of those deaths were attributed to the police and the National Guard, which arrived in Detroit during the early hours of Monday, July 24. By Monday morning, rioting had spread throughout the city, with looting and fires reported on both the west side and the east side. Despite the presence of 800 state police and 1,200 national guardsmen, the riot was still not under control. At 2:15 A.M., Mayor Cavanaugh alerted federal authorities to the seriousness of the situation and shortly thereafter a conference call took place between the mayor, Gov. Hugh Romney, and U.S. Attorney General Ramsey Clark. At this time, there was considerable debate among these men over whether federal troops should be sent to Detroit. Clark implied that to send federal troops, the governor would have to declare that a civil insurrection was in progress. The governor was reluctant to do so because of his fears that insurance companies would refuse to compensate people for losses due to civil insurrection. In the interim, President Lyndon Johnson sent his envoy, Cyrus Vance, to tour the area and report to him on whether federal troops were needed. Vance toured the city Monday afternoon, between 3:00 P.M. and 6:00 P.M., during a lull in the violence. Because he did not personally witness any looting or sniper fire, Vance related his opinion to the president that federal troops were not necessary. But during the evening, violence flared once more. Eventually, at 11:20 P.M., President Johnson agreed to send Army paratroopers to Detroit. During the evening, a number of incidents were reported that involved National Guard troops firing machine guns at buildings in pursuit of alleged snipers. Overnight, nine people lost their lives.

Federal Troops Arrive, Reports of Sniper Fire Increase

At 4:00 A.M., the first paratroopers of the 101st Airborne arrived in Detroit; among them were seasoned Vietnam veterans. These military troops, under Lieutenant General Throckmorton sought to engage the community in restoring order, help pick up garbage, and locate missing persons. Meanwhile, the National Guard and police continued to pursue suspected snipers, sometimes with disastrous consequences. In one particular case, the National Guard sent tanks to an apartment building where a sniper had been reported. Noticing a flash of light coming from the building, National Guard troops opened fire with .50-caliber machine guns. Inside the building, four-year-old Tanya Blanding was struck in the chest and subsequently died. Eyewitnesses and the police later established that the flash observed by the guardsmen was not that of a sniper's rifle but came from a match used by Tanya's uncle to light his cigarette.

Emboldened by the presence of the National Guard and Army troops, Detroit police rounded up suspected looters in large-scale street sweeps. By Monday evening, around 4,000 had been arrested, 1,000 of those arrested on Monday alone. The jails rapidly filled up, so prisoners were taken to a temporary holding cell in the parking garage of police headquarters where they were held incommunicado for the next 12 to 24 hours before being transferred to another temporary facility at the bathhouse on Belle Isle, an island park located in the Detroit River. Some former detainees refer to this facility as Bellecatraz. Prisoners were then put on buses where they waited to be arraigned by local judges. Many of these cases were dismissed due to lack of evidence.

During the daytime on Tuesday, July 26, over 500 reports of sniper fire were recorded. It is unclear how many of these incidents were due to actual sniper fire and how many could be attributed to crossfire between police and National Guard units. In response to these reports of sniper fire, police and National Guard troops initiated house-to-house searches. Another estimated 3,000 people were arrested over the next two days. In perhaps the most high-profile incident to take place during the riot, police officers, responding to reports of sniper fire, raided the Algiers Motel located on Woodward Avenue and Virginia Park, and shot three unarmed black teenagers who were enjoying the company of two white prostitutes. The police officers were later indicted for murder by a federal grand jury in 1968 but were acquitted by an all-white federal jury in 1970. Two of the three officers were reinstated to the police force in 1971. This case is the topic of *The Algiers Motel Incident*, a book by journalist John Hersey.

Aftermath

By Thursday, July 27, looting and sniping had ceased, and federal paratroopers were withdrawn from the city of Detroit. At the conclusion of five days of rioting, 43 people had been killed; 33 (79 percent) of the victims were black. According to the city assessor's office, over $22 million of property had been destroyed. This is a low estimate, as property damage estimates ranged from $22 to $500 million (National Advisory Commission on Civil Disorders 1968, 107). After the riot, white flight from Detroit accelerated, establishing Detroit as a majority black city. Demographic change was accompanied by a shift in political power. In 1973, Coleman Young was elected mayor of Detroit, a position he held for nearly 20 years. As the first black mayor of Detroit, Young sought to restore pride in the city, especially among its black residents, but the post-riot climate under Mayor Young was characterized by polarization between whites and blacks, suburbanites and city dwellers. These divisions persist in the present day.

Within the past three decades, Detroit has seen its population drop to under 1 million residents, from a peak of just over 2 million people in 1950. The city, while engaged in bold efforts for economic redevelopment, continues to suffer from persistent fiscal crises triggered by the erosion of its municipal tax base. The downtown is currently experiencing a renaissance fueled by the restoration of the Fox Theater, the construction of sports stadiums, and the relocation of General Motors' world headquarters to the Detroit riverfront. Yet much of the city remains in limbo, its houses abandoned and factories shuttered due to deindustrialization and global competition. The extent to which these problems of uneven development are a product of the riot is debatable (see Sugrue 1998). Nonetheless, Detroit continues to struggle with the stigma of the riots that took place in the summer of 1967.

Max Herman

See also

Detroit (Michigan) Riot of 1943; Race Riots in America. Documents: The Report on the Memphis Riots of May 1866 (July 25, 1866); Account of the Riots in East St. Louis, Illinois (July 1917); The Cook County Coroner's Report Regarding the 1919 Chicago Race Riots (1919); A Southern Black Woman's Letter Regarding the Recent Riots in Chicago and Washington (November 1919); The Final Report of the Grand Jury on the Tulsa Race Riot (June 25, 1921); Testimony from *Laney v. United States* Describing Events during the Washington, D.C., Riot of July 1919 (December 3, 1923); The Governor's Commission Report on the Watts Riots (December 1965); Cyrus R. Vance's Report on the Riots in Detroit (July-August 1967); The Reports of the Oklahoma Commission to Study the Tulsa Race Riot of 1921 (2000-2001); The Draft Report of the 1898 Wilmington Race Riot Commission (December 2005)

Further Reading:

Fine, Sidney. *Violence in the Model City.* Ann Arbor: University of Michigan Press, 1989.

Gordon, Leonard. *A City in Racial Crisis.* Dubuque, IA: Wm. C. Brown Publishers, 1971.

Herman, Max. *The Newark and Detroit "Riots" of 1967.* http://www.67riots.rutgers.edu.

Hersey, John. *The Algiers Motel Incident.* Baltimore: The Johns Hopkins University Press, 1997.

Locke, Hubert. *The Detroit Riot of 1967.* Detroit: Wayne State University Press, 1969.

National Advisory Commission on Civil Disorders. *Report of the National Advisory Commission on Civil Disorders.* New York: Bantam Books, 1968.

Sugrue, Thomas. *The Origins of the Urban Crisis.* Princeton,NJ: Princeton University Press, 1998.

Digital Divide

Large divisions exist between racial groups and their use and access to the Internet and other forms of communication technologies, despite the exponential expansion of technology use in the United States over the last several decades. In 2009, this division was evident as 73.3 percent of non-Latino whites, 54.5 percent of African Americans, and 52.8 percent of Latinos had the Internet at home (U.S. Census 2009). This division of access and use of the Internet and other communication technologies along racial lines—known as the racial "Digital Divide"—may have serious consequences for racial minority groups as information technology skills are becoming increasingly important in economic markets. These divisions may also be compounded by the fact that the Internet is expected to become an essential form of communications, commerce, and education in the 21st century. Future social advancement for racial minority groups are likely to depend on access to computers and all the technological tools they offer.

The "racial digital divide" represents the idea that access to and use of digital content is unequal across racial groups. The divide inside countries, such as the digital divide in the United States, refers to inequalities between individuals, households, businesses, and geographic areas at different socioeconomic and other demographic levels, while the "global digital divide" designates countries as the units of analysis and examines the divide between developing and developed countries on an international scale.

Scholars generally argue that the racial digital divide has progressed through two phases: (1) access and (2) computer

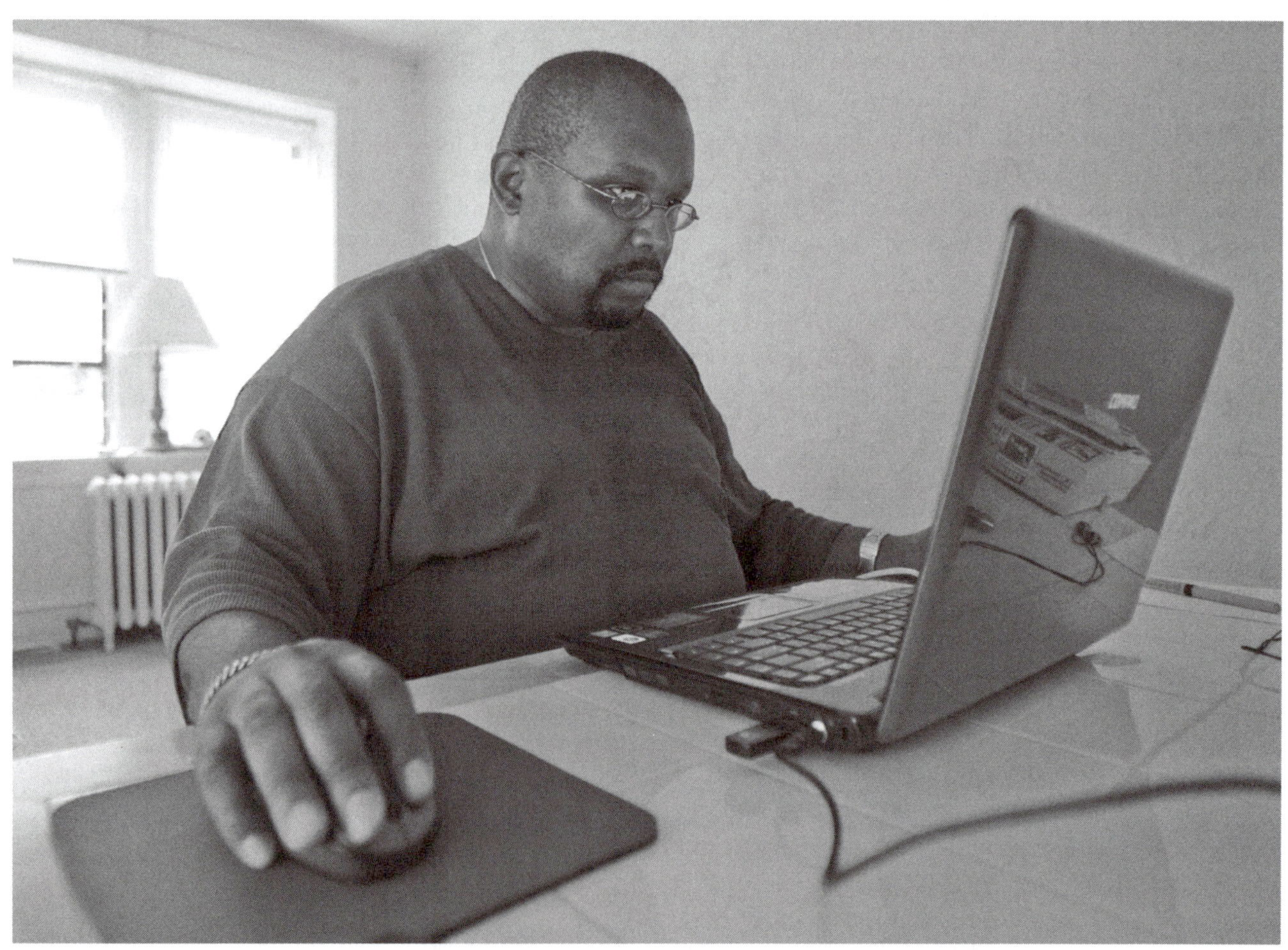

Hercules Jones surfs the Internet from his apartment in Philadelphia, August 10, 2007. Jones was among the first customers of the Digital Inclusion program designed for low-income residents. Officials are hoping that launching the world's largest citywide wireless network will help bridge the digital divide between Philadelphia's richest and poorest residents. (AP Photo/Matt Rourke)

use. In terms of access, often called the "first digital divide," empirical evidence reveals that racial minorities are less likely to own computers and are also less likely to have Internet access at home, when compared to whites (Attewell 2001). Equally problematic is the fact that from 1994 to 2000, the technology gap between blacks and whites widened, giving the impression that the divisions were not correcting over time (U.S. Department of Commerce 2000). Research on this digital divide has shown that, even where access to technology is available, many still cannot access the Internet due to racial and other social barriers (Norris 2001). The divide remains largely due to income and educational inequalities between and among racial groups.

Relating race and the digital divide to use, the "second digital divide," differences remain along racial lines that block entrance to valued social networks containing important, social resources (i.e., social capital) (Zhao and Elesh 2007). This occurs despite ubiquitous connectivity to the Internet, whether in public or at home. Access to valuable social resources (i.e., social capital) is mediated online, just as it is in the offline world. Individuals, based upon existing positions in offline social hierarchies, have differential access to valued network resources on the Internet. This suggests that those with similar types or amounts of social resources will "bunch" together and decide those to include and those to exclude. For example, in a study of an online network called *BlueSky*, researchers discovered that this seemingly open network consisted of professionals who had relatively homogenous backgrounds (Kendall 2002).

Despite the fact that information and communication technologies often attempt to foster openness, divisions continue to emerge that are largely based upon socially constructed ideas that exist in the offline world. Rather than being able to contact or interact with anyone from anywhere at anytime, people in the online world encounter various barriers that the Internet cannot overcome. The divisions that exists in regards to the first and second digital divides reflect and extend the institutionalized inequities that exist and persist in the offline world. Similar normative rules operating offline also regulate human contact online, allowing certain individuals and organizations to acquire a greater share of valued online resources because of their favored positions in the social hierarchy (Zhao and Elesh 2007).

The Global Impact of the Digital Divide

In addition to its within-nation influences, the *digital divide* has global effects and can be seen creating colonial-type inequality between countries throughout the world. In particular, the lack of technologies, such as the Internet, causes significant problems in struggling parts of the world. Poorer nations are often unable to afford initial startup costs to invest in technology access. This often puts these countries at a competitive and economic disadvantage and has serious impacts on the nation at many levels. They are often unable to carry out e-commerce and e-business, which puts companies located in these nations at a major disadvantage in the global market. Countries with limited or no Internet access and unable to teach children and students about these technologies, placing them at a disadvantage in the global economy by restricting access to the vast amount of information available on the Web.

As the empirical evidence shows, racial minorities have lower levels of access to information and communication technologies while also using information and communication technologies at a lower rate than whites. The gap between racial groups has been evident for some time; however, the divide seems to be narrowing as demographic changes occur in the United States, such as the notable increase in Latino populations (Livingston 2010). Nevertheless, social structural factors that restrict or allow access to these forms of technology are essential and must be considered. Education, employment, knowledge creation, and other social institutions facilitate differential access to technology, including the Internet. Without equal access in the "real world," divisions will continue to remain in the offline world. These divisions, despite the ubiquity of connectedness, will continue to determine how racial groups access and use the Internet.

James W. Love

See also

Internet Racism

Further Reading:

Attewell, Paul. "Comment: The First and Second Digital Divides." *Sociology of Education* 74, no. 3 (2001): 252–59.

Eubanks, Virginia. *Digital Dead End: Fighting for Social Justice in the Information Age*. Cambridge, MA: M.I.T. Press, 2011.
Jones, Steve, Camille Johnson-Yale, Sarah Millermaier, and Francisco Seoane Pérez. "U.S. College Students' Internet Use: Race, Gender and Digital Divides." *Journal of Computer-Mediated Communication* 14 (2009): 244–64.
Kendall, Lori. *Hanging Out in the Virtual Pub: Masculinities and Relationships Online*. Berkeley: University of California Press, 2002.
Livingston, Gretchen. *The Latino Digital Divide: The Native Born versus the Foreign Born*. Pew Research Center, 2010.
Norris, Pippa. *Digital Divide: Civic Engagement, Information Poverty, and the Internet Worldwide*. Cambridge: Cambridge University Press, 2001.
Straubhaar, Joseph, Jeremiah Spence, Zeynep Tufekci, and Roberta G. Lentz, eds. *Inequity in the Technopolis: Race, Class, Gender, and the Digital Divide in Austin*. Austin: University of Texas Press, 2012.
U.S. Bureau of the Census. *Computer and Internet Use in the United States: 2009*. Washington, DC: Government Printing Office, 2009.
U.S. Department of Commerce. *Falling Through the Net: Toward Digital Inclusion*. Washington, DC: Government Printing Office, 2000.
Zhao, Shanyang and David Elesh. "The Second Digital Divide: Unequal Access to Social Capital in the Online World." *International Review of Modern Sociology*, 33, no. 2 (2007): 171–92.

Discrimination

Discrimination can be defined as actions that deny equal treatment to persons perceived to be members of some social category or group. Discrimination often takes the form of prejudicial treatment and can lead to the exclusion of individuals or entire groups of people. Discrimination can happen between individuals, but there are also many instances of discrimination being carried out in larger social conventions such as traditions, political policies, and laws. Affirmative action has been used in some places to right the perceived wrongs of discrimination patterns. Discrimination can apply to a wide number of groups including women, gays and lesbians, the disabled, the elderly, etc.; however, perhaps one of the most prevalent forms in the United States is race and ethnic discrimination.

Discrimination Table

	Prejudiced	*Not Prejudiced*
Discriminates	Prejudiced Discriminator	Nonprejudiced Discriminator
Doesn't Discriminate	Prejudiced Nondiscriminator	Nonprejudiced Nondiscriminator

The unequal treatment that characterizes discriminatory practices can be distinguished from negative attitudes, which are referred to as *prejudice*. *Discrimination* refers to actions, not just attitudes. More than 50 years ago, sociologist Robert Merton introduced his 2 × 2 paradigm that differentiated individual attitudes from actions.

The prejudiced discriminator and the nonprejudiced nondiscriminator are easy to understand since their attitudes and actions are consistent. The more interesting cells are the prejudiced nondiscriminator, who may not discriminate because of fear of legal action or social ostracism, and the nonprejudiced discriminator, who may discriminate for financial gain rather than prejudice. The important point is that there is not necessarily a direct link between prejudice and discrimination. Since prejudice refers to attitudes while discrimination takes the form of direct action, one does not necessarily lead to the other.

The concept of denying equal treatment is actually more complex than it may first appear. Wanting to date, marry, or be friends with same-raced people (sometimes called *differential association*) does deny equal treatment to other-raced people since they cannot become part of someone's primary group. However, many social scientists would not describe this type of behavior as discrimination since it is a matter of personal preference in primary group relationships. Most social scientists would use the term *discrimination* to refer to actions denying equal treatment in areas like education, employment, housing, health care, etc. There are also laws against denying equal treatment in these areas, but there is long history of institutional discrimination in the United States that has prevented minority groups from having equal access to things like education and housing. Discrimination is deeply embedded in many social customs and attitudes, making it notoriously difficult to identify and prove. This has limited somewhat the effectiveness of many antidiscrimination laws.

The line between differential association and discrimination is not always clear. For example, college sororities and fraternities used to argue that they could keep out opposite-raced people because they were friendship groups who liked to associate with like-minded people. In the 1960s, college administrators and the courts began to define this behavior as discrimination because these institutions were part of the larger campus community where differential treatment because of race was illegal. Private country clubs can still legally exclude prospective members because of race and gender, although public country clubs cannot.

Discrimination also takes place at different levels. The Merton typology above refers to the actions of individuals, small groups, and small businesses. Both dominant and subordinate group members can be both perpetrators and victims of this individual-level discrimination. A black employer can refuse to employ a white person just as a white landlord can refuse to rent to a black person. However, the history of discrimination in the United States is one where minorities such as blacks and women have long been the victims of discriminatory practices. Affirmative action has been used in the United States to benefit these minority groups who have historically been underrepresented in areas of society such as higher education, politics, and business.

Large corporations and governments can also discriminate, and this practice is referred to as *institutional discrimination*. The apartheid system in South Africa prior to 1993 and legal segregation in the Southern United States before 1970 are both examples of institutional discrimination. In both these examples, government systems and laws were employed to restrict the opportunities and privileges of black minorities. Institutional discrimination is almost always carried out by the dominant group against the subordinate group because of the superior political and economic power of the dominant group.

Governments and large corporations can also have race-neutral policies that have a negative impact on subordinate groups. This is called *structural discrimination*. For example, the higher a family's income, the easier it is to get a home mortgage. Since blacks and Hispanics tend to have lower incomes than whites, they are less likely to qualify for mortgages. This is an example of structural discrimination even though there was no intent to discriminate on the basis of race. Structural discrimination is also almost always carried out by the dominant group against the subordinate group.

The debate over voter identification cards during the 2012 presidential election illustrates the debate about whether a particular policy constitutes institutional or structural discrimination. Supporters of voter ID cards, who tended to be Republicans, argued that even though black and Hispanic voters are more likely to have trouble getting these cards, the policy is color-blind in terms of intent; they simply want to prevent voter fraud. However, due to its differential impact

Adaptive Discrimination

Adaptive discrimination is a form of discrimination in which an individual acts in a discriminatory manner to conform to the prejudiced attitude of others, or the prejudiced attitude of the larger society. Although the person may not personally harbor any racial prejudice, he or she discriminates to "fit in" or adapt to society.

Adaptive discrimination is often seen as contrasting with overt discrimination, in which individuals discriminate based on their own prejudicial attitude. An example of adaptive discrimination would be a white landlord refusing to rent to an African American family because he or she feared that prejudiced white tenants might move out. On a macro level, adaptive discrimination can be caused by larger political mechanisms. For example, white British citizens who moved to South Africa during apartheid were compelled to accept a system of institutionalized racism that was completely alien to them. To adapt to white South African society, they had to accept and abide by discriminatory practices that were based in the racism of others. In his typology of people with a combination of prejudice and discrimination, Robert Merton referred to unprejudiced discriminators as "fair-weather liberals," and he called prejudiced nondiscriminators "timid bigots."

Tracy Chu

on minority voters versus white voters, many have identified this policy as structural discrimination. Opponents to voter ID card requirements, who tend to be liberal Democrats, argue that this is institutional discrimination because the *intention* behind the voter identification card is to reduce the turnout among black and Hispanic voters. This example illustrates that discriminatory practices are still very much a part of U.S. society, despite the passage of legislation designed to prevent and reverse it.

FRED L. PINCUS

See also

Cumulative Discrimination; Institutional Discrimination; Predatory Lending; Reverse Discrimination; Structural Discrimination

Further Reading:

Ehrlich, Howard J. 2009. *Hate Crimes and Ethnoviolence: The History, Current Affairs and Future of Discrimination in America*. Boulder, CO: Westview Press.

Merton, Robert. "Discrimination and the American Creed." In *Discrimination and National Welfare*, edited by R. M. MacIver, 99–126. New York: Institute for Religious and Social Studies, 1949.

National Research Council. 2004. *Measuring Racial Discrimination*. Washington, DC: National Academies Press.

Pincus, Fred L. 1996. "Discrimination Comes in Many Forms: Individual, Institutional and Structural." *American Behavioral Scientist* 40 (November/December): 15–21.

Disenfranchisement

Depriving African Americans the right to vote, or disenfranchisement, was a significant feature of Jim Crow politics for almost a century. It began in the late 19th century as a means to curtail the political advantages African Americans had gained during Reconstruction. After the Civil War, three constitutional amendments were ratified to ease the transition from slavery to freedom: the Thirteenth Amendment abolished slavery, the Fourteenth Amendment granted former slaves the right to citizenship, and the Fifteenth Amendment granted black men the right to vote. These three Reconstruction amendments were contested by the former Confederate states because African Americans were no longer under whites' control. This period of relative freedom and equality lasted for about a decade, until Southern states repealed all the Reconstruction Acts created by radical Republicans, the party once headed by Abraham Lincoln. By the mid-1870s, the Democratic Party had regained much of their former congressional power with the support of a new administration. White Southerners sought redemption for the loss of the Civil War, and their most pressing concern was, as one historian puts it, a "struggle for mastery" once again over African Americans.

In a move to return to the white supremacy status quo, disenfranchisement was a political process that took only a few decades to accomplish. The history of black suffrage began when the Fifteenth Amendment was ratified in 1870. Only a small percentage of free blacks, primarily in the North, had voting privileges prior to then. During Reconstruction, African Americans took full advantage of their voting rights by supporting Republican officials, particularly electing other blacks to office. High-ranking black Republicans during this period included state legislators, governors, and U.S. senators. Congressmen Robert Smalls from South Carolina and John Lynch from Mississippi as well as Louisiana governor P. B. S. Pinchback were among the many black politicians elected by black voters during the 1870s and early 1880s. Such victories were short-lived, as white Southerners began manipulating the elections in various ways. Black voters were often verbally harassed or physically assaulted to prevent them from casting their ballots or even reaching the polls. Violent threats and terror campaigns for voter intimidation usually occurred without legal intervention.

Some African Americans would refuse to be intimidated despite such warnings. If they did succeed at casting their votes, however, white election officials often destroyed these ballots. Black voters were usually unaware that their votes were not counted under such conditions. "Ballot box stuffing" was yet another deceptive tactic used to disenfranchise African Americans. This practice of "counting out" the intended votes of African Americans for an opposing candidate or using phony ballots against the candidate supported by a black majority were ways of "stealing" the vote. This second phase in the history of black suffrage was an age of "Redemption," when white Southerners schemed to regain political control of once Republican-dominated governments.

"Would Frighten White Women Voters with a 'Black Menace.'"

The article insists that by extending the right to vote to black women, an entire black menace will follow, bringing with it intermarriage and a coarsening of Southern culture.

In speaking before a democratic audience of Norfolk on Wednesday night, W. E. Cardwell, of Richmond, referring to the Negro vote as the "black menace," had the following to say:

"If the Democrats of Norfolk have not seen the handwriting on the wall, we of Richmond have. The paramount issue in the South is not the League of Nations, but the program that grows out of the new duties imposed upon women by universal suffrage. If the white women of the South don't know whether they are Democrats or not, it is high time they were learning, for the white women of the South will be the first to suffer humiliation if Democracy is defeated. And if the women don't hurry up and decide whether they prefer white or black supremacy, the Republicans will have the battle won before the women get through being advised as to what they are politically."

The old-time political bugaboo is not likely to have much effect upon the intelligent white women voters. They realize that the principle of everybody up and nobody down is likely to be more effective in solving the problems of the South than the old time principle of all white folks up and all Negroes down. It is the demagogue such as Cardwell who has kept the South in the mire of political and economical slavery throughout the past generations. By spending all their time trying to keep the Negro down the white men of the South have neglected the greatest opportunities for the South's advancement, hence, the North and West have outstripped it in progressiveness, commercial and political supremacy. The white women voters are in open defiance of the old self-seeking politician and declare they will vote for principles and not for parties.

The action of the lady members of the city Democratic committee who resigned rather than be gagged is evidence that the newly enfranchised white women are not going to follow blindly the worn-out political traditions of by-gone days.

Source: *Norfolk* [Virginia] *Journal Guide,* September 20, 1920.

White Democrats were determined to find other ways of effectively disenfranchising blacks that would prevent them from even registering to vote. They drew a fine distinction between having "the *ability* to vote at *elections*" and "the *right* to vote" at all. The latter option was a more permanent solution to the "race problem" attributed in part to black suffrage. All the political, social, and economic advancements African Americans had made in just a few years since slavery antagonized white supremacist ideas about natural social order. The rallying cry of "Negro domination" signaled the fears of white Southerners in regard to the power wielded by the black vote in support of the Republican Party. African Americans were never in control as white Southerners imagined, because segregation laws upheld white hegemony. Blacks were deemed social inferiors with little or no civil rights to protect. Yet, the idea of blacks ruling whites inspired a revolution. The specter of "Negro domination" could only be replaced by another political obsession, "white supremacy." Complete disenfranchisement resolved the ideological conflict of race by restoring white supremacy.

By the 1890s, Southern states began to deprive African Americans of their voting rights by creating stringent voting restrictions. Property qualifications were required in Alabama, Louisiana, Virginia, North Carolina, Mississippi, Georgia, and South Carolina; the registered voter had to own as much as $300 or more in real estate or personal assets. Poll taxes were imposed in Tennessee, Arkansas, Florida, Texas, and several other states with property qualifications. A third common voting restriction was an education qualification. Literacy tests were administered to prove if a potential voter was capable of understanding his rights. Often these tests included reading and interpreting passages from the U.S. Constitution. Sometimes the election officials would read an article or constitutional amendment and ask the applicant to explain the passages. Such practices were common in Mississippi, South Carolina, Louisiana, Alabama, North Carolina, and Virginia. Not all of the voting restrictions were effective in just eliminating black voters, but some whites could also be disenfranchised too. Therefore, "saving clauses" were often included in voting restriction proposals as loopholes for whites who would be otherwise disqualified by property, poll tax, and educational qualifications. The "grandfather clause" was intended as a nonracial requirement that nevertheless limited black suffrage; it stipulated that any son or descendent of a (Confederate) soldier or any one who had the right to vote prior to 1867 would then inherit his ancestral voting rights. This law of inheritance did not always prevent African Americans from voting, considering the documented participation of black soldiers in both the Union and Confederate armies during the Civil War. Nevertheless, the grandfather clause did eliminate a majority of black voters who were themselves descended from former slaves. Some African Americans just faltered under considerable pressures of disenfranchisement. They would not vote at all or would sell their votes altogether. These two forms are not technically forms of disenfranchisement, since the individual was not prevented from voting but instead chose not to do so. However, the employment qualification and character assessments were two notorious forms of voting restrictions found in Alabama. The black voter would have to prove that he had suitable employment and then that he was of "good character." Both qualifications were judged by a white election official and therefore subject to his discretion.

African Americans responded to the motives and means of disenfranchisement with their actions and words. In record numbers, they continued to vote despite the fraudulent election schemes. Less-educated blacks would sometimes be accompanied to the polls by others to ensure a fair chance at voting. Most African Americans believed that voting was a basic right of U.S. citizenship and were determined to maintain their civil rights at all costs, even to their personal safety. Writer Charles Chesnutt participated in the public debates about the second-class citizenship status being forced on African Americans. In his article, "The Disenfranchisement of the Negro" (1903), Chesnutt challenged the constitutionality of the various voting restrictions imposed in Southern states. He therefore criticized the federal government for being influenced by white Southerners: "Not only is the Negro taxed without representation in the [South], but he pays, through the tariff and internal revenue, a tax to a National government whose supreme judicial tribunal declares that it cannot, through the executive arm, enforce its own decrees, and, therefore, refuses to pass upon a question, squarely before it, involving a basic right of citizenship" (92). Chesnutt believed that the federal government could have taken action by using congressional regulations, under the Fourteenth Amendment, to prevent Southerners from "a district where voters [had] been disfranchised" from ever holding office. Thus, white Southerners' political power would be just as limited as disenfranchised African Americans. The black press also responded to voter manipulation by castigating the perpetrators. The *Richmond Planet* and *Southwestern Christian Advocate* (a Methodist paper in New Orleans), for example, featured editorials about black disenfranchisement that was occurring throughout the South. Between 1902 and 1905, the *Baltimore Afro-American Ledger* led a series of campaigns against the move to segregate public transportation, as an additional consequence of disenfranchisement. It circulated few successful petitions and organized boycotts that would allow blacks to retain at least an illusion of political power.

"Restoration," or the third phase in the history of black suffrage, was completed by the early 20th century. The black vote was eliminated by amendments to state constitutions. Southern states held conventions to revise their suffrage requirements that could circumvent federal election laws. The Democrats secured their political power through voting manipulation and intimidation. They had also manipulated public opinion against black suffrage as a challenge to white supremacy. Only when organizations such as the National Association for the Advancement of Colored People (NAACP) began to take action did white supremacists lose some footing. By the 1930s and 1940s, organized by the NAACP, black voter registration drives once again appeared as the modern civil rights movement began to take shape. Medgar Evers and other activists challenged the election of racist demagogues in Mississippi and Georgia. It was the black vote that secured the presidential election of Harry S. Truman in 1948. As evidenced in Truman's administration, civil rights legislation was reintroduced to the national public. African Americans staged massive protests against racial discrimination and segregation throughout the 1950s and 1960s. Militant opposition to racial oppression and support of voting rights was signaled by Malcolm X's speech "The

Ballot or the Bullet" (1964) to a gathering in Cleveland. Black disenfranchisement, one of the last vestiges of Jim Crow, would finally be overturned by the Voting Rights Act of 1965 when federal authorities would regulate voter registration and blacks could free access to the ballot.

Sherita L. Johnson

See also

Florida Effect; Jim Crow Laws; Voter ID Requirements; Voting and Race

Further Reading:

Chesnutt, Charles. "The Disenfranchisement of the Negro" [1903]. In *The Negro Problem*, edited by Bernard R. Boxill, 77–124. Amherst, NY: Humanity Books, 2003.

Gilman, Glenda Elizabeth. *Gender and Jim Crow: Women and the Politics of White Supremacy in North Carolina, 1896–1920.* Chapel Hill: University of North Carolina Press, 1996.

Perman, Michael. *Struggle for Mastery: Disenfranchisement in the South, 1888–1908.* Chapel Hill: University of North Carolina Press, 2001.

Wormser, Richard. *The Rise and Fall of Jim Crow.* New York: St. Martin's Griffin, 2003.

Disproportionality Index Scores

At nearly every stage of the criminal justice process, there is evidence of the overrepresentation of blacks and Hispanics, compared to their relative representation in the population as a whole. One specific arena of overrepresentation that has received significant scholarly attention and popular press coverage is traffic stops. African Americans and Hispanics consistently report being selectively targeted for routine traffic stops because of their membership in a racial or ethnic minority group, and large-scale studies of official police data and traffic patterns have lent support to these contentions.

Historically, anecdotal evidence, surveys, public opinion polls, and even the examination of arrest, sentencing, and prison data would suggest that minorities in the United States are disproportionately stopped by police. However, objectively measuring disproportionality has proven challenging, especially when analyzing disparity in traffic stops that results direct from racial profiling. Data on traffic stops generally comes from three sources: observation, citizen reports, or official police data. Direct observation studies of police stops, such as those initiated by Lamberth in New Jersey and Maryland (see Harris 1999), provide robust data, but observing traffic stops on a large scale, especially nationwide, is frequently cost prohibitive. In contrast, narratives and qualitative data provide compelling evidence of the interactive dimensions of traffic stops, their emotional character, and even disproportionality, but they do not capture the scope and magnitude of the social problem. Moreover, the public frequently dismisses qualitative data as isolated incidents or the result of "sour grapes" following a search or arrest.

Official data sources on traffic stops are limited as well, insofar as not all stops are recorded, and even when they are, key information may be omitted. If a citation or written warning is not issued following the stop, in some jurisdictions, the data on the vehicle, the driver, and the reason for stopping is not noted. Although data reporting has improved, and is now mandatory for federal officers, state and local data is not standardized. Technological innovations, such as dashboard cameras, and data collection forms that expedite the process of collecting information about individuals stopped by police offer more data on driver demographics, but a lack of nationwide legal mandates that force law enforcement officers at all levels to collect data on race and ethnicity hampers the analysis of the breadth of the disparity. Just half of all states in the United States have passed legislative mandates requiring state police to collect data on the race and ethnicity of the citizens they stop. The majority of the other states voluntarily collect data, but specific policies vary by municipality. As of 2012, four states do not collect any data on the race/ethnic composition of their traffic stops.

Notwithstanding the difficulties in collecting data, creating measurement tools to assess the degree to which blacks and Hispanics are targeted by police, or even disproportionately represented among traffic stops, has been equally problematic. In determining proportionality, knowledge of the driver pool from which potential motorists could be stopped is critical to the analysis. The data do show that Hispanics and blacks are stopped, searched, and arrested by police more frequently than their white counterparts. But, what does this mean? Disparate representation does not necessarily imply intent, nor does it signify overrepresentation if the population of drivers within a certain geographic area is stilted toward one demographic group. Responding to difficulties in measuring the risk of being stopped, a number of researchers have advanced the creation and use of a disproportionality index as one potential method for exposing disparity. The disproportionality index (DI) is created by dividing the proportion of traffic stops of minority group members by that group's proportional representation within the larger population (Rojek et al. 2004). However, determining the overall proportional representation or baseline can be problematic. Demographics of individuals operating motor vehicles in a community can differ from day to day, and week to week. Likewise, disagreement exists over whether to use census data of individuals over the age of 16 in the surrounding area, accident data, licensed vehicle owners, distribution of all traffic violators, or an officer's own citation pool as the most accurate way to assess racial composition of motorists in an immediate area. If only a small proportion of a community's members are minority, but the bulk of commuters within a stretch of roadway is disproportionally minority, then the analysis needs to reflect this aberration. Thus, the implications of which baseline group is used are far reaching in terms of uncovering the level of disparity.

According to Lippard and Dellinger (2011), the numerator of the DI score is calculated by dividing the percentage of traffic stops that were minority by the proportion of the driving population that is minority. The denominator is calculated by dividing the proportion of traffic stops involving white motorists by the overall proportion of drivers who are white. If the resulting score is over one, then there is evidence of overrepresentation, whereas if the score is less than one, it is evidence of a group's underrepresentation among traffic stops. A score of precisely one would indicate racial/ethnic equality in traffic stops.

When examining traffic stops by police, many studies of disproportionality using DI scores suggest higher rates of stops, searches, and arrests for Hispanics and blacks. For example, Lippard and Dellinger (2011) find black-white and Hispanic-white disproportionality among the majority of policing agencies they investigated, in some instances scores between six and seven. However, poststop disproportionality appears to be lower than is evident in the initial stop, such that the decision to search and arrest reflects less disproportionality than the initial decision to conduct a traffic stop.

The DI score itself merely reflects a prediction of the probability of being stopped by police, but does not suggest an underlying reason for the disproportionality, nor does it provide direct evidence of racial profiling. Evidence of racial profiling would presuppose officer knowledge of the race/ethnicity of the vehicle operator, along with substantiation of bias in decision making. This type of data, however, remains elusive. With improved data availability and a means of assessing disproportionality, as well as further research into the rationale behind stopping drivers with certain demographics, researchers continue to uncover the level and sources of disproportionate criminal justice system involvement at key stages of the decision-making process.

Danielle Lavin-Loucks

See also

Driving While Black, Stopping People for; Gates/Crowley Incident, The; Racial Profiling

Further Reading:

Harris, David A. "The Stories, the Statistics, and the Law: Why 'Driving While Black' Matters." *Minnesota Law Review* 84 (1999): 265–326.

Institute on Race and Justice at Northeastern University. *Racial Profiling Data Collection Resource Center*. http://www.racialprofilinganalysis.neu.edu/background/jurisdictions.php.

Lippard, Cameron D., and Amy Dellinger. "Driving While Non-White: Exploring Traffic Stops and Post-Stop Activities in North Carolina, 2005–2009." *Sociation Today* 9, no. 2 (2011). http://www.ncsociology.org/sociationtoday/v92/drive.htm.

Lundman, Richard. "Are Police-Reported Driving While Black Data a Valid Indicator of the Race and Ethnicity of the Traffic Law Violators Police Stop? A Negative Answer with Minor Qualifications." *Journal of Criminal Justice* 38 (2010): 77–87.

Rojek, Jeff, Richard Rosenfeld, and Scott Decker. "The Influence of Driver's Race on Traffic Stops in Missouri." *Police Quarterly* 7 (2004): 126–47.

Diversities, Ethnic and Racial

Much of the racial and ethnic diversity found in the United States today can be attributed to the liberalization of U.S. immigration brought about by the U.S. Immigration Act of 1965, also known as the Hart-Cellar Immigration Act. The enforcement of the liberalized immigration law, along with the U.S. government's military involvement in many countries in the world, has resulted in the influx of immigrants and refugees from Latin America, Asia, and the Caribbean Islands. Between 1970 and 2000, more than 20 million immigrants were admitted to the United States. The vast majority of them originated from Third World countries; Europeans made up less than 15 percent of the total number of immigrants during the period.

In 1970, non-Hispanic white Americans made up 87 percent of the U.S. population. African Americans made up the majority of racial minority members, and three Latino groups (Mexicans, Puerto Ricans, and Cubans) and some Asians in the West Coast composed the other racial minority groups. Thirty years later (in 2000), the proportion of white Americans decreased to only 70 percent. As immigrants are heavily concentrated in large metropolitan areas, white Americans in many cities have become numerically minority groups. In fact, according to 2000 census data, in 48 of the 100 largest cities in the United States, racial and ethnic "minorities" composed the majority of the population. The black population currently includes not only African Americans, but also a large number of Caribbean blacks (Jamaicans, Dominicans, Haitians, and Guyanese), Africans, and their children. The Latino population includes Colombians, Ecuadorians, Salvadorans, Brazilians, and Peruvians, as well as Mexicans, Puerto Ricans, and Cubans. Asian Americans include Indians, Pakistanis, Koreans, Vietnamese, and Filipinos, as well as Chinese and Japanese.

In addition to the influx of non-European immigrants in the post-1965 era, two other factors have made American cities far more culturally diverse now. One is the change in government's policy toward minority and immigrant groups, from Anglo conformity to cultural pluralism. In the early 20th century, the U.S. government enforced the assimilationist policy to make immigrants and their children give up their cultural traditions and acculturate to American society. By contrast, the government and public schools currently encourage immigrants and their children to preserve their cultural traditions. The government and schools gradually adopted this multicultural policy beginning in the late 1960s.

The other factor that has contributed to ethnic and cultural diversity in contemporary America is transnational ties facilitated by technological advances. Immigrants and their children can now watch television programs made in the home country in the form of videotapes or satellite broadcasting. Most immigrants in large American cities watch television programs in their native language more often than they watch American television programs. They can buy almost all grocery items in American cities that they can get in their home country, making it much easier for contemporary immigrants to eat ethnic food than earlier white immigrants at the end of the 19th century.

Khyati Joshi

See also

Black and Non-Black Hierarchy; Multiracial Identity; Panethnic Movements; Tri-racialization

Further Reading:

Farley, Reynolds. *The New American Reality: Who We Are, How We Got Here, Where We Are Going.* New York: Russell Sage Foundation, 1996.

Min, Pyong Gap, ed. *Mass Migration to the United States: Classical and Contemporary Periods.* Walnut Creek, CA: AltaMira, 2002.

Portes, Alejandro, and Ruben Rumbaut. *Immigrant America: A Portrait*, 2nd ed. Berkeley: University of California Press, 1996.

Dixiecrats

In 1948, a group of conservative Southern Democrats formed the States Rights Democratic Party to oppose the reelection of President Harry S. Truman because of his proposed civil rights program. Committed to the maintenance of white supremacy and Jim Crow segregation, party members were nicknamed "Dixiecrats" by North Carolina journalist Bill Weisner.

For over a decade, conservative Southern Democrats had increasingly felt alienated from their national party largely due to Franklin D. Roosevelt's New Deal reforms. As the Democratic organization recast itself as a progressive party committed to special interest politics, conservative Southerners became disenchanted with the liberal course of the Democratic Party. This sense of alienation reached a tipping point when Truman introduced a legislative package designed to improve the political and economic position of African Americans in the South. On February 2, 1948, the president sent a special message to Congress proposing a 10-point civil rights program, including an anti-lynching measure, abolition of the poll tax, a permanent fair employment practices committee, a Justice Department civil rights bureau, and the abolition of segregation in interstate commerce.

Truman's pronouncement came just before a scheduled meeting of the Southern Governors' Conference. Meeting in Tallahassee, Florida, the assembled state executives publicly deplored the president's proposals but refused to endorse Mississippi governor Fielding L. Wright's call for Southerners to bolt the Democratic Party. Although they refused to formally break with their party, the executives adopted a resolution proposed by South Carolina's Strom Thurmond to reconvene in 40 days if the party refused to abandon Truman's civil rights program.

Meanwhile, on May 10, 1,000 Southern Democrats met in Jackson, Mississippi, to force the national party to reject President Truman's civil rights program. Governors Wright, Thurmond, and Ben Laney of Arkansas dominated the proceedings, which called for the national party to reject Truman, nominate a presidential candidate who was committed to states' rights and white supremacy, and defeat any candidate who failed to refute civil rights. If these demands were not met, the conference agreed to reconvene in Birmingham, Alabama, after the Democratic convention to discuss additional resistance.

As a show of defiance, Gov. Fielding Wright led his fellow Mississippi delegates out of the convention hall vowing to nominate a states' rights candidate for president. Six thousand delegates convened in Birmingham on July 17 to offer a Southern alternative to Truman. Strom Thurmond was nominated to head the States' Rights presidential ticket, while Mississippi's Fielding Wright ran for vice president. Recognizing that they had little chance of winning the White House, instead Thurmond and the Dixiecrats hoped to prevent either Truman or the Republican nominee Thomas E. Dewey from garnering an electoral majority. This would then require members of the House of Representatives to decide who would become the next president of the United States. Southern support would be required in order for anyone to achieve a majority in the House, so the Dixiecrats believed they could force the presidential choice to abandon civil rights and therefore protect Jim Crow segregation in the South.

The Dixiecrats were far more of a reactionary protest movement than a formal political party, but nevertheless they dominated the Democratic Party machinery in Alabama, Mississippi, Louisiana, and South Carolina. As a result, Thurmond, rather than Truman, was listed on the ballot as the Democratic nominee in those states. This political sleight-of-hand undoubtedly contributed to the Dixiecrats winning a majority of votes in those four states. In addition to winning in Alabama, Mississippi, Louisiana, and South Carolina, Thurmond and Wright carried 12 counties in Georgia, three counties each in Arkansas and Florida, and two in Tennessee. However, they received only one-fifth of the popular vote, which was not enough to throw the election into the House of Representatives. Consequently, Truman defeated Thurmond in the rest of the South and easily won the presidential election.

In 1949, the Dixiecrats attempted to create a permanent organization, but they were unable to maintain unity as many returned to the Democratic fold, including Strom Thurmond. For those who could not abide rejoining their former affiliation, they turned to the conservative wing of the Republican Party. Welcomed with open arms, former Dixiecrats helped transform the GOP into a mirror image of the pre–New Deal Democratic Party. What was left of the organization limped along for a couple of years, but never became a viable third party.

Although the Dixiecrats failed to prevent Truman's reelection, conservative Southerners in Congress did succeed in blocking his civil rights program. In addition, the Dixiecrats' virulent defense of white supremacy emboldened white Southerners to oppose any federal legislation designed to dismantle Jim Crow segregation. Former Dixiecrats played conspicuous roles in white resistance to the struggle of African American Southerners to achieve social and political equality. Therefore, the Dixiecrats were an important factor in the white South's stubborn refusal to abandon the discriminatory customs and laws of Jim Crow segregation.

Wayne Dowdy

See also
Jim Crow Laws

Further Reading:

"Dixiecrats." In *Civil Rights in the United States*, 2 vols, edited by Waldo E. Martin Jr. and Patricia Sullivan. New York: Macmillan Reference USA, 2000. Reproduced in History Resource Center. Farmington Hills, MI: Gale Group. http://

galenet.galegroup.com/servlet/HistRC/ (accessed May 4, 2007).
Feldman, Glen. "Dixiecrats—The States' Rights Party, 1948." http://www.alabamamoments.state.al.us/sec54.html (accessed May 4, 2007).
Frederickson, Kari. *The Dixiecrat Revolt and the End of the Solid South*. Chapel Hill: University of North Carolina Press, 2001.
Haas, Edward F. "Dixiecrats." In *The Encyclopedia of Southern Culture*, edited by Charles Reagan Wilson and William Ferris. Chapel Hill: University of North Carolina Press, 1989.

Do the Right Thing

Do the Right Thing is Spike Lee's 1989 hit film. It was inspired by the December 20, 1986, racial incident that took place in the Italian-American Howard Beach neighborhood of Queens, New York. Three black men walked into a pizzeria in Bensonhurst after their car broke down on the highway. They asked to use the phone, and after being refused they sat down to eat. A group of Italian-Americans chased them out of the neighborhood with bats. One of the men got away, while the other two were beaten. Getting away from them, Michael Griffith wandered in a daze onto the highway, was struck by a car, and was killed. When the white men involved in the incident were acquitted, black citizens in New York were thrown into an uproar, and protest marches led by Rev. Al Sharpton were organized.

Following the trial, Lee wanted to make a movie that analyzed how racism affects not only the recipients but also those who engage in racist behavior. He also placed the action of his film on the hottest day of the year to illustrate how heat affects an already tense racial climate. He borrowed fixtures from the Howard Beach incident like the bats and the pizzeria. The movie covers a 24-hour period on the hottest day of the year in a predominantly black neighborhood

Director Spike Lee on the set of *Do The Right Thing*, 1989. (Photofest)

in Brooklyn. In this neighborhood, different racial groups coexist in a racially tense atmosphere. The main conflict of the film is between a black resident, Buggin' Out, and Sal, the Italian-American owner of the pizzeria he frequents. Buggin' Out wants to know why Sal has only Italian-American people on his restaurant's wall of fame when he has a predominantly black clientele. The climax of the film comes after Buggin' Out is unsuccessful at organizing a boycott of Sal's pizzeria and storms the pizzeria with his friend Radio Raheem, who was slighted by Sal earlier in the day for playing his radio too loud. A fight breaks out between Sal, his sons, Radio Raheem, and Buggin' Out when Sal destroys Radio Reheem's pride and joy, his radio. Police arrive on the scene and kill Radio Raheem in an act of police brutality that sends the community into an uproar. As the main character, Mookie, throws a garbage can into the window of the pizzeria, members of the community begin rioting and looting, and the pizzeria burns to the ground.

American media criticized this film for its representation of violence, which they saw as a call to action for American black youths. During the time the movie came out there was a firestorm raging in New York over the police department's use of excessive force and racial profiling in black communities. The media thought the movie would incite blacks to violence around the country since tensions were already running high, protests having already occurred over the Howard Beach and Bensonhurst incidents in the late 1980s. In both cases, the whites involved were acquitted. *Do the Right Thing* brought to the country's attention the racial tension that was occurring in urban areas across the United States. It also called attention to the racist practices of the police in black communities. There has been no evidence of violence or riots occurring in association with this film.

CATHERINE ANYASO

See also

Films and Racial Stereotypes; Hollywood and Minority Actors; White Savior Films

Further Reading:

Hardy, James Earl. *Spike Lee*. New York: Chelsea House Publishers, 1996.

Lee, Spike, with Kaleem Aftab. *That's My Story and I'm Sticking to It*. New York: W.W. Norton, 2005.

Lee, Spike, with Lisa Jones. *Do the Right Thing*. New York: Fireside, 1989.

Domestic Violence

In the wake of social mobilizations during the civil rights movement, the need to address violence on multiple levels became apparent—from the private to public spaces, as well as individual and institutional. Domestic violence was a hot topic for those concerned with gender and race issues. The U.S. Department of Justice defines domestic violence as "a pattern of abusive behavior in any relationship that is used by one partner to gain or maintain power and control over another intimate partner"; domestic violence may be physical, sexual, emotional, economical, or psychological actions or threats of actions against another person.

Women of color's responses to domestic violence occurred in everyday gathering places such as the kitchen table and day care centers, places where women began to share their stories and respond by helping one another. In the 1970s the movement shifted towards social service responses and the implementation of formal gathering spaces. The first women of color shelter opened to serve survivors of domestic violence—*La Casa de Las Madres*, in San Francisco—in 1976. In 1978 the National Coalition Against Domestic Violence, founded by lesbians, two spirited individuals, native women, women of color, and formerly battered, made the movement a national grassroots initiative. Central to national discussions included the need to fight sexism, racism, and homophobia in order to end domestic violence in the United States. Awareness-raising initiatives took place in the 1980s, coalitions were built, and the domestic violence movement was mainstreamed. And by 1994 the U.S. government passed the Violence Against Women Act (VAWA).

The intersectional identity for women of color is both gendered and raced, shaping how they are marginalized in domestic violence discourse, their experiences, and the responses of nongovernmental and governmental entities to domestic violence. The use of intersectionality, developed by Kimberle Crenshaw, is therefore essential and does not mean reducing all experiences to one unified experience; an intersectional analysis of domestic violence enables a deeper understanding of the structural context of violence and accounts for differences among individuals and collectives. Domestic violence in Asian American communities is underreported. In spite of the stereotype of the "Model Minority Myth," the 4 percent of the population that Asians constitute in the United States is overly represented in domestic violence–related homicides; between 1993 and 1997, 31 percent of women killed in domestic violence–related homicides were Asians. Barriers for the Asian American community include concerns about publicizing domestic violence due to pressure within the community and belief in family harmony, unique immigration experiences, multiple abusers (in-laws and partners), and communication barriers with the criminal justice system. In 2000 it was estimated that a little over 23 percent of Latinas experience intimate partner violence. Scholarly discussions of Latinas who survive domestic violence show that Latinas are more likely to return to their abusers more often than non-Latino white Women. The challenges of leaving abusers for Latinas include language barriers, low levels of education and income, and poor knowledge of existing services. Beth Richie illustrates that black women experience a diversity of forms of violence including sexual, physical, and emotional, and their abusers are their intimate partners, the community, state agencies, and a part of a larger pattern of abuses. For African Americans, the barriers of attempting to access services are due to systemic discriminatory treatment. African American women are stereotyped as strong, not needing services, physically capable of taking care of themselves, too loud, bringing on the abuse, or not looking enough like a victim of abuse.

Native communities have had a particularly challenging history of responding to domestic violence. Prior to European contact, domestic violence against women was rare due to the cultural values of respecting and upholding women. Rape and sexual assault of native women, colonization of native lands, assimilation programs, and economical and social enfranchisement of native people created vulnerabilities to domestic violence. U.S. federal restrictions of tribal law—including the Major Crimes Act (1885) that requires "major crimes" such as rape, sex abuse, aggravated assault, sexual violence on Indian land to be prosecuted by the U.S. federal government, and Public Law 280 (1953)—placed legal power over tribal jurisdiction into the hands of states. Further limitations were created through the Indian Civil Rights Act (1968) for tribal prosecutors of serious crimes. The barriers native women experience are due to policies, especially when survivors seek protections orders, divorces, child custody, or need support from the legal system.

Not only are people of color impacted by domestic violence, but also those who are identified as Lesbian, Gay, Bisexual, Transgender, Intersexed, and Queer (LGBTIQ) experience another layer of oppression in accessing resources due to sexuality. The National Coalition of Anti-Violence Programs found that violence towards the LGBTIQ community is increasing (Richie 2012). The political implications of homophobia have led to exclusionary practices against the LGBTIQ from receiving protections in states such as Delaware, Montana, and South Carolina. Social barriers include denial of shelter services to lesbians based on the assumption that their partner can infiltrate the shelter.

Since the 1960s social service responses from culturally aware organizations and entities, community, faith-based, and preventative, have increased, but the policy changes have been limited. In 2012 was the first time since 1994 that VAWA was not reauthorized. VAWA, historically a bipartisan policy came to a standstill due to tensions about resources for native people and tribal lands, immigrants, and the LGBTIQ community.

Annie Isabel Fukushima

See also

Anti-Miscegenation Laws; Down Low; Illegitimacy Rates; Lesbian, Gay, Bisexual, Transgender, Intersex, Queer, and Queer Questioning Community (LGBTQ); Mixed Race Relationships and the Media; Tripping Over the Color Line

Further Reading:

Bent-Goodley, Tricia B. "Domestic Violence in the African American Community: Moving Forward to End Abuse." In *The War Against Domestic Violence*, edited by Lee E. Ross, 15–26. Florida: Taylor and Francis Group, 2010.

Cahill, Sean, and Sarah Tobias. *Policy Issues Affecting Lesbian, Gay, Bisexual, and Transgender Families*. Ann Arbor: University of Michigan Press, 2010.

Crenshaw, Kimberle. "Mapping the Margins: Intersectionality, Identity Politics, and Violence Against Women of Color." *Stanford Law Review* 43, no. 6 (July 1991): 1241–99.

Dobash, Rebecca Emerson, and Russell P. Dobash, eds. *Rethinking Violence Against Women*. Thousand Oaks, CA: SAGE Publications, 1998.

Klevens, Joanne. "An Overview of Intimate Partner Violence Among Latinos." In *The War Against Domestic Violence*, edited by Lee E. Ross, 1–14. Florida: Taylor and Francis Group, 2010.

Office on Violence Against Women (OVW) and the National Center on Full Faith and Credit. *Violence Against Native*

Women: A Guide for Practitioner Action. Washington, DC: United States Department of Justice, Fall 2006.

Richie, Beth E. *Arrested Justice: Black Women, Violence, and America's Prison Nation*. New York: New York University Press, 2012.

Ross, Lee E., ed. *The War Against Domestic Violence*. Florida: Taylor and Francis Group, 2010.

The United States Department of Justice. *Domestic Violence*. http://www.ovw.usdoj.gov/domviolence.htm.

Xu, Qiang, and Allen Anderson. "Domestic Violence in Asian Cultures." In *The War Against Domestic Violence*, edited by Lee E. Ross 27–40. Florida: Taylor and Francis Group, 2010.

Domestic Work

Few trades within the American workforce were as difficult or possessed as little control over working conditions and wages as domestic work in the early 20th century. While the roots of domestic work stretched back to slavery in the antebellum South, it was in the decades after Reconstruction that household service carried a broad stigma for its low pay, poor working conditions, and lack of personal autonomy. Domestic work also demonstrated the social idiosyncrasies of Jim Crow. Black domestics were caught in the contradiction of what has been called "public segregation and private integration." White employers imposed a peculiar strain on black houseworkers by enforcing widely held beliefs about black inferiority on one hand, and relying on black women's labor to maintain households on the other. As domestic workers migrated into Northern urban communities, the nature and the conditions of domestic work improved substantively. By 1960, domestic workers had become some of the most loyal and steadfast members of the civil rights movement, as the elimination of institutionalized black subservience lent greater visibility and respect to the household labor of African American women.

1890 to World War I

Prior to 1890, most white families in the North and South preferred to employ white immigrant women as domestic workers. The federal government attempted to persuade white housewives to hire former slaves as domestic workers in the postbellum years. The influx of immigrants from England, Ireland, Germany, Russia, and Italy provided a steady stream of laborers. It was the tremendous growth in manufacturing in American cities in the 1870s and 1880s—garment making in New York, toolmaking in Pittsburgh, fabric processing in New England, meatpacking in Chicago—that drew female immigrants into other fields of work. Domestic work was not typically filled by native-born white women; if they worked outside the home, it was usually as office workers and clerks in department stores.

After 1900 and through the 1960s, domestic work was primarily associated with African American women. Over 40 percent of black women worked as domestics across the country, a job that was second only to agricultural work for its low pay and poor conditions. One significant problem in prewar domestic work was that "domestic" implied several different types of work—cooking, laundering, table serving, general serving, personal shopping, sewing, ironing, nursing, and child rearing. But the laborer received only one wage for the myriad forms she completed. Employers throughout the North and South discouraged labor unions, lending considerable autonomy to employers, who defined the terms and conditions of domestic labor. An anonymous black domestic in Georgia in 1912 compared her work to virtual slavery in an interview to the weekly New York *Independent* newspaper: "I frequently work from fourteen to sixteen hours a day. I am compelled by my contract, which is oral only, to sleep in the house. I am allowed to go home to my own children . . . only once in two weeks, every other Sunday afternoon—even then I'm not permitted to stay all night. . . . I am the slave, the body and soul of this family. And what do I get for this work—this lifetime bondage? The pitiful sum of ten dollars a month!"

The work was grueling, unpredictable, and sometimes dangerous, consigning domestic work near the bottom of the economic ladder. Prior to 1915, the most common complaint from domestic workers was the low pay. In some Southern states, workers earned as little as 50 cents per day. In a field that was largely unregulated and unstandardized, black domestics worked long hours in isolation, had little personal time, and were paid, on average, \$8 to \$10 per month across the United States—if, that is, they were paid on time. A significant problem reported by domestics was that employers often paid less than they promised or paid later than the agreed date. Finding good child care also perplexed black domestic workers with their own children, since day-care facilities for working women were scarce until the 1920s.

Families also expected black domestics to "sleep in," or live and work on the job, which diminished the domestics' personal time and space. Older and married domestics often resisted the constraints on their labor, because they had responsibilities to other family members and to their communities. But, older and married domestics were not hired as frequently as young, single women, who averaged about 70 percent of all domestics between 1900 and 1920. Older African American women were more likely to work as laundresses in the South, while younger African American women, if they had no children, were more likely to sleep or live in and undertake many more household responsibilities.

Sexual abuse and unwanted attention from members of the employing family were also dangerous hazards of domestic work. Sexual abuse and exploitation of domestic workers remained vastly un- or underreported. White husbands, fathers, and sons carried an enormous influence in the family and community, particularly the Southern communities. The working relationships between heads of households and servants were rarely questioned in public, which gave the employer the benefit of the doubt. Domestic workers and household servants who bore the children of white employers were not only cast out of the employing family, but they were also stigmatized within black communities for bearing biracial children out of wedlock.

1914–1918

Middle-class African American women, in organizations such as the National Association of Colored Women (NACW) and the Young Women's Christian Association (YWCA), attempted to professionalize domestic work after the turn of the century. Nannie Burroughs founded the National Training School for Women and Girls in 1909 to provide standardized classes and to unify domestic workers in a recognized community. Eva Bowles, the secretary of Colored Work for the YWCA, criticized white employers for bilking household servants out of promised wages or time off, which led to hostility and mistrust between black domestics and white families. Bowles stressed that white, middle-class housewives would have to impose on themselves a strict business model and change their attitude if the working relationship with domestic workers had any chance to improve. It was a shift in labor relations that white employers were reluctant to make prior to 1915.

The outbreak of World War I in Europe led to a significant shortage in European immigrant labor in the United States, which, in turn, led to a leap in the number of native-born white women and men entering manufacturing industries. Considerable improvement in working conditions for domestic workers materialized as these shifts brought labor shortages in service industries. With more workers in demand, domestics had greater control over wages, hours, and type of employment. During the war years, Southern domestics on average commanded raises from \$2.50 per week to \$10 per week. They also demanded that the terms of service be recorded in a written contract and that they would have to work no more than 10 hours per day, with breaks for lunch.

Black domestics in World War I also explored other labor markets. The Great Migration, the tremendous relocation of 500,000 African Americans from Southern states to Northern cities, affected domestic workers as well. More than a third of Atlanta's domestic workers had left their profession between 1900 and 1920, from 214 in 1900 to 136 in 1920; the cities of Nashville and Richmond experienced similar fall-offs in the number of available domestics after the war. Even New Orleans, the only Southern city with a thriving domestic workers' union, lost a substantial number of domestics, with 121 in 1920, down from 157 in 1900, a change of 23 percent. When African American women moved Northward in search of better jobs, they considered switching to industrial and manual labor, such as meat packing and tobacco processing. Most of the wartime employment found by black women offered higher pay than domestic service, but the work required extensive training and the working conditions were negligibly better. For women who chose to stay in domestic service, the increase in pay and living in a city with a higher standard were enticing options. Thus, after World War I and throughout the 1920s, domestic service in the North was dominated by Southern migrant women.

The Depression and World War II

The Great Depression brought about an economic catastrophe in the United States that left nearly one-quarter of Americans without gainful employment. For African Americans, the number of unemployed after 1931 was greater than 25 percent, and in some cities, like Detroit,

"Colored Maid Has Family Guessing" (1919)

This article illustrates the social and cultural gulf between African American domestic workers and their white employers.

Efforts at Friendliness Fail to Increase Her Vocabulary

Once more we are spending our evenings cooking dinners and washing dishes. We decided we would try taking our dinners out for a while and do without a maid, but soon every one began to tire of it and long for some home cooking. So I started out to lasso another girl for general housework.

Just why every response this time came from colored girls I do not know, unless they would rather go home at night so as to be with those of their own kind. But without exception it was the unmistakable drawl which greeted my "hello" over the telephone.

And they were much more respectful. Evidently there are a great many people who will not employ colored help, for invariably the first question was:

"Do you object to a colored girl?"

I did not object to a colored girl. I would be glad to get any kind of a girl, if she could cook and keep seven rooms clean.

I don't know why people object so strenuously to colored help. My experiences have been no worse with them than with white help. They are not so afraid of work and not so fearful that they might do something out of their regular line of work.

I had found out from experience that no girl could be depended upon to come and see you if she said she would, or to appear if you hired her. So I made a vow that I would tell every one to come and see me and hire every one to come the next morning and start to work.

I hired six girls that afternoon. Mother was aghast as she overheard me calmly telling the sixth one to come and start to work.

"What do you think I am going to have in the morning," demanded Mother. "A reception?"

"Don't worry, mother dear," I soothed her. "None of them will come and we will still be maidless."

But I was mistaken. One did come. And you can bet we treated her like a guest.

She was a young colored girl, very neat, with large eyes that looked at you with a baby stare. She had just come from St. Louis and brought a letter from her former employer stating that Lily had been in her service for a year, that she had trained her until she was a model servant.

Lily was tractable. She was in the house a whole day and in that time in spite of repeated efforts, all she would say was "Yes, ma'am," and "No, ma'am."

When you told Lily to carpet sweep the rugs, wipe up the floors and dust the rooms, Lily did it. She moved so quietly and systematically and with such a vacant look on her face that I felt as if she were an automaton. She was just as human as a vacuum cleaner, only she made less noise.

It was a slow process showing Lily where the more than one spoon went, that there was a difference between a meat fork and a salad fork, and that the water glass went on a certain dolly. She would look at you and smile. She was willing to understand, but lacked the ability.

I thought I would try to make friends with her. But I only appeared to confuse her.

Then I happened to think of a hat I had grown tired of and decided to try what a small gift would do toward melting the ice.

That night Lily went out with the hat done up in a piece of newspaper, hugged tight to her breast. I began to congratulate myself.

But that was the last we ever saw of Lily.

Source: Tuskegee Institute News Clipping File.

nearly 70 percent of African American women were unemployed. Across Northern cities, African American migrants found that their new jobs were not at all secure. Prior to the Depression, nearly 30 percent of African American women worked as farmers, and 36 percent worked as domestic workers. At the height of the Depression, 34 percent of African Americans had no means of financial support, with little prospect of finding relief.

Domestic work was among the hardest hit trades in the Depression. Middle- and working-class white women, who had shunned domestic work since the 1900 in favor of better-paying clerical and manufacturing employment, returned to domestic work during the Depression. In turn, African American women were pushed out of work, and left to find employment on a day-to-day basis or depend on their community or charities for relief. The labor phenomenon of the "slave market" appeared in Philadelphia, New York, Boston, and Chicago, all cities with growing populations of black migrant workers. In the slave market, groups of black women waited on street corners in downtown areas or their neighborhoods for a wealthy white woman to drive up and offer day labor. The desperate times gave the white employer the power to fix the terms of the labor—how much the domestic earned, how long she worked, and if she was allowed to go home after the work was completed. In most cases, the pay for day work only covered lunch or transportation. To cut costs, some household servants even lived in with their employers, a practice that had been abandoned in the North by 1920. The gains in personal autonomy and wages that domestic workers fought for after World War I and the 1920s had evaporated during the Depression.

The New Deal attempted to relieve the burden of most Americans in complete financial ruin. For the most part, however, the difficulties facing domestic workers went unresolved. Part of the problem was that many of the New Deal's most popular programs—the Federal Emergency Relief Administration, the Civilian Conservation Corps, the Agricultural Adjustment Act, and the Works Progress Administration—either did not address the service sector or were left to individual states to administer. Local officials usually had little interest in extending relief to poor blacks, who competed directly with out-of-work and poor whites for financial relief. The Social Security Act did not provide for pensions for farmers, domestics, or waitresses. Though African Americans voted to reelect President Franklin D. Roosevelt in 1936 and 1940, this was largely due to the popularity of Eleanor Roosevelt and the success of other New Deal programs that fought illiteracy and increased the number of college graduates.

World War II ushered in a return to greater control over working conditions and wages in domestic work. The demands on the defense industry boosted the need for defense workers. As in World War I, in World War II, white women moved into better-paying positions in defense work. The demand for household servants materialized again, and African American women returned to domestic work. African American women enjoyed other labor options at the outbreak of World War II; however, 64 percent of black women returned to domestic work in 1941. As wages rose and working conditions improved, African American women bargained heavily for even more autonomy, including a set number of working hours, days off, and the purchase of labor-saving devices.

Post–World War II

In the North and South, domestic work after World War II became much less stigmatized, isolated, and invisible. Though white working women were encouraged to return to housework after World War II, the demand for domestic workers remained steady in the late 1940s and 1950s. Many white women entered the "pink" collar trades as secretaries, teachers, nurses, and librarians, and they hired domestic workers to help maintain their households. Federal programs after World War II encouraged black women who were laid off from wartime factories to resume domestic work.

However, the difference between domestic service at the beginning of the 20th century and at its midpoint was that domestic work was a recognized professional trade. Though domestic workers still received few wage and pension benefits, the work itself was no longer hidden in the murky intersection between the public and private spheres. African American working women's experience as domestic workers cast a long shadow over their political and community activism, to such an extent that the postwar civil rights movement was directly informed by the legacy of domestic service. Furthermore, Jim Crow was under attack from several standpoints in the 1950s, facilitating an increase in opportunities to African American women to control their labor. Indeed, the rising visibility of domestic work coincided with the steady deterioration of Jim Crow. Though it is a profession overwhelmingly dominated by women of color, the stigma and lack of opportunity associated with domestic work, and by extension, all African American women's labor, continues to slowly evaporate.

Nikki Brown

See also

Day Laborers; Garment Workers; Migrant Workers

Further Reading:

Clark-Lewis, Elizabeth. *Living In, Living Out: African American Domestics in Washington, D.C., 1910–1940.* Washington, DC: Smithsonian Institution Press, 1994.

Haynes, Elizabeth Ross. "Negroes in Domestic Service In the United States." *Journal of Negro History* 4 (October 1923): 384–442.

Hine, Darlene Clark. *A Shining Thread of Hope: The History of Black Women in America.* New York: Broadway Books, 1998.

Hunter, Tera. *To 'Joy My Freedom: Southern Black Women's Lives and Labor after the Civil War.* Cambridge, MA: Harvard University Press, 1997.

Jones, Jacqueline. *Labor of Love, Labor of Sorrow: Black Women, Work, and Family from Slavery to the Present.* New York: Basic Books, 1985.

Don Imus Controversy

The Don Imus controversy refers to a racist comment the disc jockey and humorist Don Imus made on his radio program "Imus in the Morning" in 2007 and the subsequent backlash he received in the American press. The event is significant because Imus's radio show was one of the most widely listened to in the nation and Imus was one of the highest paid DJs at the time. Before the 2007 incident, Imus had a long history of making racist remarks on his radio show but had often justified them in the name of comedy. The press was divided over the controversy, alternately defending and vilifying Imus.

The Don Imus controversy began at 6:14 A.M. on April 4, 2007. The 66-year-old disc jockey and entertainer was hosting a radio program on CBS radio with a video simulcast on the cable news network MSNBC. "Imus in the Morning" was an eclectic mix of news, crude humor, shock-jock antics, and semiserious political analysis with hundreds of thousands of listeners and viewers. NBC's status as one of the nation's most respected news organizations gave Imus access to many notable politicians, journalists, commentators, and celebrities. Many former guests on the show were understandably chagrined when a one-minute clip of Imus's remarks about the Rutgers women's basketball team went viral. As transcribed from a 2007 YouTube clip of his radio show, Imus said, "So I watched the basketball game last night . . . between Rutgers and Tennessee. . . . That's some rough girls from Rutgers. Man, they got tattoos and . . ." At this point Imus was cut off by his long-time friend and the show's executive producer, Bernard McGuirk, who added, "Some hard core hos." Imus, now chuckling to himself, continued, "That's some nappy-headed hos there, I'm gonna tell you that now. . . . Man, that's some . . . ooh. . . . The girls from Tennessee they all look cute."

Statement by Rutgers Women's Basketball Coach C. Vivian Stringer

"I am deeply saddened and angered by Mr. Imus' statements regarding the members of the Rutgers women's basketball team. These talented, articulate young women put forth a great deal of hard work and effort this past season to reach the nation's grandest stage—the NCAA title game. Throughout the year, these gifted young ladies set an example for the nation that through hard work and perseverance, you can accomplish anything if you believe. Without a doubt, this past season was my most rewarding in 36 years of coaching. This young team fought through immeasurable odds to reach the highest pinnacle and play for the school's first national championship in a major sport. To serve as a joke of Mr. Imus in such an insensitive manner creates a wedge and makes light of the efforts of these classy individuals, both as women and as women of color. It is unfortunate Mr. Imus sought to tarnish Rutgers' spirit and success. Should we not, as adults, send a message of encouragement to young people to aspire to the highest levels as my team did this season?" (Associated Press 2013)

Rutgers University women's basketball coach C. Vivian Stringer speaks at a news conference on campus in Piscataway, New Jersey, 2007, in response to the racist and sexist on-air comments by shock-jock Don Imus. (Associated Press)

Video and audio clips of Imus's remarks instantly went rocketing through cyberspace. Imus was vilified in the press for his racist and insensitive remarks and his seeming remorselessness about the incident. *Ebony* magazine decried the incident, describing it as a public humiliation of a group of black women by a nationally syndicated white public figure. "In an April 2007 *Washington Post* commentary by Colbert I. King, then-presidential candidate Barack Obama is quoted as saying that "Imus fed into some of the worst stereotypes that [his] two daughters are having to deal with today in America."

This was not the first time Imus had been accused of being a racist. He had once referred to Gwen Ifill of PBS—arguably the most prominent female black journalist in America—as the "cleaning lady." There are also reports of him using the "n-word" frequently and unapologetically off the air, and the American Anti-Defamation League had been registering complaints of Imus's anti-Semitism for years. In a 2000 response to such allegations, Imus was noted as saying that while his program might be considered offensive, it was not racist, and that he did not care if people did not like his show.

Rutgers University and the NCAA were quick to condemn Imus, stating that it was unconscionable for a public radio host such as Imus to use his show to debase black Americans. On his Thursday show following the initial remarks, Imus tried to dismiss the utterance by referring to "some idiot comment meant to be amusing," as noted by Lisa de Moraes in the *Washington Post*. The next day, as noted in a YouTube video of Imus's apology, he expressed remorse for "an insensitive and ill-conceived remark we made the other morning referring to the Rutgers women's basketball team. It was completely inappropriate and we can understand why people were offended." It is clear that while Imus ultimately

Excerpt of Don Imus's Contextual Apology

"Do you want to know what people called me for supporting Harold Ford, Jr.? Do you want to know the mail I got that called me a 'n-lover' and—do you want to know what people said to me for the years that I played Bishop Patterson's sermons? People telling me, they didn't want to hear that—well, you can imagine. Do you know what people said to me when I booked the Blind Boys of Alabama here years ago, and they have been on fairly regularly ever since then? About what they said about them and about me having—about all of the African American musicians, over the years, who I have had on this program, and so on? Does that mean that it's okay for me to say what I said about these Rutgers women? I hope you don't think that, because I don't think that." (MSNBC 2013)

apologized, he did not initially see his remarks as offensive or derogatory.

Despite the public apology, the National Association of Black Journalists led the charge to terminate Imus, insisting that his apology came too little and too late. The Reverend Al Sharpton also threatened to lead mass protests against WFAN in New York if Imus was not fired within the week. The following Monday, Imus issued a longer, more contextual explanation for his remarks in which he discussed the sort of comedy on his show, his wife, his philanthropy, and his links to the black community. He ended his apology, as noted in an MSNB transcription of the April 2007 interview, by saying, "I'm sorry. . . . I'm embarrassed. . . . I did a bad thing." Imus was initially placed on suspension before being fired by MSNBC within the week. CBS followed suit the next day. Imus spent over four hours meeting with the Rutgers team and their family members delivering his apology in person.

Imus was off the air for about 18 months, but his career was not over. In 2008, "Imus in the Morning" was picked up by WABC, with Imus earning reportedly as much, if not more, money than he had under his previous contracts with CBS and MSNBC. In 2009, Imus told Fox News that meeting with the Rutgers basketball players was a "life-changing experience."

"Imus in the Morning" is now simulcast on the more conservative Fox Business Network. Bernard McGuirk—the man who uttered the "hos" reference in the first place—remains the show's executive producer. Since the Rutgers incident, Imus has generally managed to steer clear of racial controversies.

Daniel M. Harrison

Further Reading:

Associated Press. "NCAA, Rutgers Women's Coach Blast Imus," http://nbcsports.msnbc.com/id/17982146/ (accessed February 4, 2013).

Carr, David. "Networks Condemn Remarks By Imus." *New York Times*, April 7, 2007.

De Moraes, Lisa. "Sorry Excuses: MSNBC's Form Apology." *Washington Post*, April 7, 2007.

"Don Imus Apologizes for Remarks about Women's Basketball Team." http://www.youtube.com/watch?feature=player_detailpage&v=YLwGwraoCN8 (accessed February 4, 2013).

"Don Imus Calls Girls Basketball Team Nappy Headed Hoes." http://www.youtube.com/watch?v=ui1jPNDWArM (accessed February 4, 2013).

"Don Imus Comments on Rutgers Remarks." http://www.youtube.com/watch?v=kx9ON0tMs4E (accessed February 4, 2013).

Hinckley, David. "Foes Rip Imus in Times' Ad." *Daily News* (New York), May 11, 2000.

Hinckley, David. "Don Imus Back in Saddle." *Daily News* (New York), April 6, 2008.

King, Colbert I. "Standing Up to Imus." *Washington Post*, April 14, 2007.

MSNBC. "Transcript: Imus Puts Remarks into Context," http://www.msnbc.msn.com/id/18022596/ns/msnbc-imus_on_msnbc/t/transcript-imus-puts-remarks-context/#.UORcCuSxySp (accessed February 4, 2013).

New York Times. "Why Was Imus Fired? Just Do the Math," http://opinionator.blogs.nytimes.com/2007/04/22/imus-much-ado-about-nothing/ (cited February 4, 2013).

Rich, Frank. "Everybody Hates Don Imus." *New York Times*, April 15, 2007.

Samuels, Adrienne. "The Culture of Disrespect." *Ebony*, July, 2007.

"Don't Buy Where You Can't Work" Campaign

"Don't Buy Where You Can't Work" was an economic campaign developed in 1933 in Washington, D.C., by three men, John Aubrey Davis, Belford V. Lawson Jr., and M. Franklin

Thorne, of the New Negro Alliance. The campaign urged blacks not to buy merchandise from white-owned stores that did not employ blacks. By doing so, blacks would be able to use their economic strength to force white-owned businesses to hire black workers.

On Thursday, October 24, 1929, the United States experienced the worst economic disaster in its history. The day before, the stock market crashed, leaving much of the economy in chaos and Americans with an uncertain future. However, no future seemed certain to blacks, who before the Depression occupied the lowest socioeconomic status in the United States. By 1933, the Depression was at its worst. Poverty and unemployment soared as people constantly got laid off. Blacks suffered the most, because they got fired from traditionally black jobs in the service industries like porters, bellhops, bag boys, and waiters. These jobs were now reserved for whites.

The New Negro Alliance decided to do something about the high unemployment rate in the black community. The three founding members formed an alliance composed of black people organized for the mutual improvement of the community. The "Don't Buy Where You Can't Work" campaign was the tool that the alliance used to get their demands heard. The tactics used by the New Negro Alliance to enforce their "Don't Buy Where You Can't Work" campaign included picketing and boycotting of white-owned businesses. The campaign proved so powerful that it spread through several black communities in the United States, forcing white-owned businesses to hire blacks or lose their business.

Not all white-owned businesses complied with the demands of the campaign, and some businesses still refused to hire black workers. These businesses complained that the alliance had no right to boycott and picket businesses for whom no one in the alliance worked. In 1938, the Sanitary Grocery Company filed an injunction against the New Negro Alliance, arguing that the picketing and protesting of the grocery store by the alliance caused interference in the grocery store's ability to select employees. On March 2, 1938, the New Negro Alliance's lawyers, including Bedford Lawson, one of the New Negro Alliance founders, and Thurman L. Dodson, argued against the injunction. The case made it all the way to the U.S. Supreme Court. On March 28, 1938, the Supreme Court ruled that the alliance did in fact have the legal rights to picket and boycott a business regardless of whether anyone who picketed worked.

The "Don't Buy Where You Can't Work" campaign was a huge success. The campaign allowed white-owned businesses to feel the collective economic pressure of the black community. It also provided the basis of the *New Negro Alliance v Sanitary Grocery Company* lawsuit, which became a landmark case safeguarding the right to picket and boycott against discriminatory hiring practices.

Sharlene Sinegal DeCuir

See also

Civil Rights Movement

Further Reading:

Moreno, Paul D. *From Direct Action to Affirmative Action: Fair Employment Law and Policy in America. 1933–1972.* Baton Rouge: Louisiana State University Press, 1997.

Pacifico, Michele F. "'Don't Buy Where You Can't Work': The New Negro Alliance of Washington." *Washington History* 6, no. 1 (Spring–Summer 1994): 66–88.

Double V Campaign

As the United States entered World War II, much of black America was divided in its enthusiasm to sacrifice for a nation that treated African Americans as second-class citizens. It was only a generation earlier, during World War I, that W.E.B. Du Bois had urged African Americans to "close ranks" and support the war effort to, in President Woodrow Wilson's words, "make the world safe for democracy." While Du Bois initially believed that African American service in the war would prove to white America both their patriotism and their worthiness of equal citizenship, he, along with the rest of black America, was bitterly disappointed with the nation's response. Instead of earning acceptance and gratitude for the contributions of the 380,000 black men who served in the war, and the hundreds of thousands of African Americans who worked in war industries and bought war bonds back home, black America was instead met with unprecedented racial violence in the summer of 1919, an invigorated Ku Klux Klan, and a general unwillingness to pursue any change in the racial status quo.

Two decades later, black leaders were determined to be more aggressive in pushing the U.S. government to improve civil rights if it wanted black support for the war effort. In 1940, President Franklin D. Roosevelt appointed William Hastie as his "Aide on Negro Affairs" and promoted Benjamin O. Davis to brigadier general following pressure from both the National Association for the Advancement of Colored People and the Urban League. The next year, Roosevelt issued Executive Order 8802, outlawing discrimination in government and defense employment following A. Philip Randolph's threatened "March on Washington." Randolph and other black leaders also lobbied the president, unsuccessfully, for the end of segregation in the armed forces, but were successful in opening up opportunities in the service previously off-limits to African Americans, most notably the flight training program at Tuskegee, Alabama. The Marine Corps also accepted its first black recruits in 1942, and the army increased the number of African Americans admitted to officer training programs. Nonetheless, many black leaders, remembering the failure of the nation to reward black America for its service in World War I, were hesitant to urge African Americans to follow the flag in a war against fascist racism in Europe and Asia while fighting in a Jim Crow army and being denied many of the basic tenets of American democracy at home.

The black press, long the nation's watchdog for racial violence and an outspoken critic of the country's discriminatory policies, found itself in a delicate position with the entry of the United States into World War II following the bombing of Pearl Harbor. If it came out in support of the war effort, it risked not heeding the lessons of World War I by failing to pressure the United States to improve life for black Americans at a time when the nation needed them most; however, if it criticized the government at a time of war, it risked being labeled as unpatriotic and unsupportive of the tens of thousands of African American men and women who had already answered the call to service.

This dilemma was solved in January 1942 by James G. Thompson, a cafeteria worker at the Cessna Aircraft Corporation in Wichita, Kansas. In a letter to the editor of the *Pittsburgh Courier,* the nation's most widely circulated black newspaper, he wrote:

> Being an American of dark complexion . . . these questions flash through my mind: "Should I sacrifice my life to live half American?" . . . "Would it be demanding too much to demand full citizenship rights in exchange for the sacrificing of my life?" "Is the kind of America I know worth defending?"
>
> I suggest that while we keep defense and victory in the forefront that we don't lose sight of our fight for true democracy at home.
>
> The V for victory sign is being displayed prominently in all so-called democratic countries which are fighting for victory over aggression, slavery and tyranny. If this V sign means that to those now engaged in this great conflict, then let we colored Americans adopt the double VV for a double victory. The first V for victory over our enemies from without, the second V for victory over our enemies from within. For surely those who perpetrate these ugly prejudices here are seeking to destroy our democratic form of government just as surely as the Axis forces.

In response to Thompson's letter, the *Courier* instituted the "Double V" campaign, demanding a war to end fascism abroad and Jim Crow at home. Beginning with its February 7, 1942, edition (the first following Thompson's letter), the paper exposed the contradictions inherent in the country asking its black men and women to fight against Nazi racism abroad while being subjected to American racism at home, and demanded that African Americans serving their country abroad receive full citizenship rights when they returned. To promote this message, the paper adopted a design for its masthead. Under the word "Democracy," an eagle sat between two large letter Vs, one on top of the other, on a banner that said "Double Victory," while beneath the banner read "At Home—Abroad."

Over the coming weeks, the paper actively promoted the "Double V" campaign. *Courier* columnists wrote pieces prodding the black public to agitate for equality, while numerous letters and telegrams from readers voicing their support for the campaign were published. The *Courier* also began a weekly photo layout of people from around the nation smiling and making the "Double V" sign with their fingers. Soon, the photos began to include famous African

Americans who were supportive of the "Double V" campaign, such as Adam Clayton Powell and Marian Anderson, and even included some prominent whites, including Humphrey Bogart and Thomas Dewey, who flashed the "Double V" sign. "Double V" lapel pins were found on men's coats, women sported "Double V" hairdos, "Double V" posters were printed, and the *Courier* even began running a weekly "Double V Girl of the Week." Other African American newspapers picked up on the "Double V" campaign as well, giving it greater exposure and making it a nationwide effort. The *Courier*, like almost every other black newspaper in the nation, made it clear that it fully supported the war effort and encouraged all African Americans to do the same. Indeed, emphasizing patriotism was central to the "Double V" campaign, as the black press wanted to both promote the loyalty of black Americans to the United States while exposing the contradictions of asking people to fight for the preservation of freedom abroad when it was denied to them at home. The black press also regularly celebrated the achievements of African Americans in the service, which were almost universally overlooked by the mainstream white media.

Despite its unflappable support for the war effort, the "Double V" campaign disturbed members of the federal government, who believed it might undermine support for the war among African Americans. The U.S. military banned the *Pittsburgh Courier* and other black newspapers from base libraries, and even confiscated the papers from some newsboys. Most notably, Federal Bureau of Investigation director J. Edgar Hoover sought to indict black publishers for treason because of their support of the "Double V" campaign; his efforts were foiled, however, by the attorney general's office, which refused to pursue the indictments.

The *Courier* officially abandoned its "Double V" campaign in 1943, as photos and telegrams supporting the campaign began to dwindle, but the paper, along with most of the black press, continued to pursue the ideals of victory against fascism abroad and victory against racism at home throughout the war years. Despite its relatively short run, the impact of the "Double V" campaign in raising black consciousness to the contradictions of being asked to sacrifice for a nation in the name of freedom and democracy while being denied those benefits themselves was incalculable, and helped contribute to the resolve of African Americans to agitate for change in the postwar era.

Thomas J. Ward, Jr.

See also
World War II

Further Reading:

Buni, Andrew. *Robert L. Vann of the Pittsburgh Courier: Politics and Black Journalism*. Pittsburgh: University of Pittsburgh Press, 1974.

Eagles, Charles W. "Two Double V's: Jonathan Daniels, FDR, and Race Relations During World War II." *North Carolina Historical Review* 59, no. 3 (1982): 252–70.

Washburn, Patrick S. "The Pittsburgh Courier's Double V Campaign in 1942." *American Journalism* 3, no. 2 (1986): 73–86.

Washburn, Patrick S. *A Question of Sedition: The Federal Government's Investigation of the Black Press During World War II*. New York: Oxford University Press, 1986.

Down Low

"Down low" is a term commonly applied to any practice or activity kept secretive or at least discreet. It is commonly used as part of the phrasing, "Keep it on the down low" and is often abbreviated to "DL." Asking to "keep something on the DL" loosely translates to keeping some piece of information discreet. Down low has also largely been associated with sexual slang in the black community, referring to men who publicly identify as heterosexual but may have sex with men secretly. Although it may have originated as part of a black vernacular, "down low" is a phrase commonly used today, in reference to both sexual and nonsexual activities.

The origins of the term "down low" can be traced to black vernacular in the 1990s in which individuals asking one to "keep it on the DL" were asking for discretion. Recently, scholars have illustrated how the down low has come to represent overlapping issues of sexuality, race, and gender. However, "being on the down low" is still commonly assumed by many to refer to black men who engage in same-sex behavior while maintaining the perception of a heterosexual public life. Culturally, the term is connected to blackness, sex with men, secrecy, appearances of heterosexuality, and masculinity. The discourse in the 21st century around the concept of the down low has led to the term being associated not only with black men specifically, but also to deviant behavior linked to public health concerns. Thus, the term can be seen as at least partly responsible for linking blackness with notions of sexual deviancy.

There is a long history of black sexuality being marked as deviant. The social construction of black sexuality often relies on stereotypes of black men as hypersexual, uncontrollable, hypermasculine, and heterosexual. The rising rates of HIV/AIDS infections in African American communities has often been linked to black men who sleep with other black men, although there is no statistical evidence to back up this claim. While the sexual connotations of the term "down low" are frequently attributed to black sexuality specifically, there is no evidence to suggest that this behavior is race specific or that it explains HIV/AIDS disparities. However, the current racialization of who is assumed to be on the down low and the images that are connected to black sexuality continue to perpetuate racial stereotypes.

Examining a culture of being on the down low (i.e., heterosexually identifying men who sleep with other men in secret) enables a broader understanding of race and sexuality. Internet advertisements on such Web sites as Craigslist where men seek out men on the down low show that just as many white men post as do black men. Being on the down low can in fact be considered a separate sexual category in itself. Advertisements from men seeking other men on the down low show that the number one preference is for black men who are muscular and athletic, reaffirming the masculine nature of men on the down low, regardless of their race. Although just as many white men as black men seek men on the down low online, it is clear that the demand is for black racialized bodies.

The causes for men being on the down low have been situated in the context of homophobia. Cultural assumptions of black communities have led to interpretations that homophobia in these communities is due to black spirituality, which expects heterosexism and thus forces men to partake in double lives where they engage in sexual acts with other men only on the down low. However, scholarly examinations of black men on the down low are difficult, largely due to the stereotype that black men who engage in nonheterosexual sex do not fit into dominant narratives of black sexuality, thereby commonly labeling these men as "not black."

Several scholarly books and articles published in the 21st century have offered more nuanced interpretations of identity as it relates to being on the down low. Scholars have raised questions about who is allowed to name and identify as being on the down low, revealing that it is indeed a highly racialized and gendered term. Being on the down low is a relatively new area of discussion in race and sexuality studies that only fully manifested in the 21st century. Ultimately, however, it is clear that a practice of "being on the down low" is not new, is not limited exclusively to black communities, and encompasses a variety of genders.

Annie Isabel Fukushima

See also

Anti-Miscegenation Laws; Domestic Violence; Illegitimacy Rates; Lesbian, Gay, Bisexual, Transgender, Intersex, Queer, and Queer Questioning Community (LGBTQ); Mixed Race Relationships and the Media; Tripping over the Color Line

Further Reading:

Boykin, Keith. *Beyond the Down Low: Sex, Lies, and Denial in Black America.* New York: Carroll & Graf Publishers, 2004.

Ford, Chandra L., Kathryn D. Whetten, Susan A. Hall, Jay S. Kaufman, and Angela D. Thrasher. "Black Sexuality, Social Construction, and Research Targeting 'The Down Low' ('The DL')." *Annals of Epidemiology* 17, no. 3 (March 2007): 209–16.

Oprah Show. "A Secret Sex World: Living on the Down Low." http://www.oprah.com/oprahshow/A-Secret-Sex-World-Living-on-the-Down-Low.

Phillips, Layli. "Deconstructing 'Down Low' Discourse: The Politics of Sexuality, Gender, Race, AIDS, and Anxiety." *Journal of African American Studies* 9, no. 2 (Fall 2005): 3–15.

Robinson, Brandon Andrew, and Salvador Vidal-Ortiz. "Displacing the Dominant 'Down Low' Discourse: Deviance, Same-Sex Desire, and Craigslist.org." *Deviant Behavior* 34, no. 3 (March 2013): 224–41.

Downward Mobility

Social mobility refers to the likelihood of an individual to attain a different level of socioeconomic status than that of the family from which the individual originated. It is often used to describe upward mobility, or an improvement in socioeconomic status, but also can consist of downward mobility, or a reduction in socioeconomic status over time. Downward mobility, especially among the middle class, is a direct challenge to the dominant narrative of the American Dream. Americans firmly believe in the United States as a meritocratic society with ample opportunities to be successful. The idea that there are always opportunities available may cushion the blow of downward mobility.

Acs (2011) found that 38 percent of black men fall out of the middle class, compared to 21 percent of white men. However white, black, and Latina women are equally likely to drop out of the middle class. Sixty percent of whites were able to maintain their parents' occupational status. In the Great Recession, young families, African Americans, and the middle class experienced the most disproportionate loss, including mortgage delinquencies, home foreclosures, and personal bankruptcies, while the richest Americans, although they experienced the greatest absolute wealth loss, were cushioned against the detrimental impact of the crisis by their resources. Intragenerational social mobility of an individual through the life course has increasingly become a concern since the onset of the Great Recession as job security became perilous and even college-educated workers were unable to find or maintain work. Currently, children born into middle-income families have about an equal chance of upward mobility as downward mobility in adulthood; however, about 40 percent of those born into the bottom or top quintile of the income distribution will not experience any mobility.

This likelihood of upward mobility is likely to decrease in the future as a result of an unstable economy, but especially because of declining numbers of young people acquiring the advanced skills necessary to participate in the formal economy of the early 21st century. Retention and graduation rates for public high schools have been alarmingly low in the United States for a number of years. The rate of on-time graduation rates for public schools has been below 75 percent since the early 1990s, and the graduation rate for males is declining at a faster rate, which corresponds to the gender gap in college attendance. These trends are disturbing at face value, but even more so that the graduation rates for students of color are even more dismal, and the proportion of the population that identifies as nonwhite is growing. Acs (2011) finds that differences in average standardized test scores (the Armed Forces Qualification Test) are the most important observable difference accounting for the downward mobility gap between black and white men. These differences are very much linked to differences in educational backgrounds. People from educationally disadvantaged backgrounds are much more likely to perform poorly on standardized tests. Conversely, people raised in a middle-class home who obtain postsecondary education are less likely to be downwardly mobile.

Drug use as a teenager is associated with a precipitous drop in mobility among those who were in the middle class as a youth. Neighborhood context is quite influential in this respect. Black, Latino, and Native American youth are much more likely to be exposed to drugs and drug-users than are whites due to the neighborhood context typical for these groups. Black men experience downward mobility at nearly double the rate of white men; differences between black and white women were not statistically significant. This can be accounted for by the fact that women of different races experience downward mobility at greater rates than white men. This may be due to the number of women supporting children on their own, or this could have been a result of higher rates of divorce; they consistently show less downward mobility than black men.

Status reproduction of the black middle class is very important to consider because almost half of the children

The Great Recession

The Great Recession has become a common way of referring to the economic downturn that began at the end of 2007. While officially over as of 2009, the effects of the recession are still being seen. Commonly attributed to the housing market bubble of the early 2000s bursting, the downturn was primarily felt by the majority of Americans in job losses and foreclosures. The high foreclosure rates had a significant impact on homeownership, especially among blacks, Latinos, and Asians, as these groups mainly owned homes in boom markets that collapsed in the downturn. During the Great Recession, middle-class blacks reportedly lost more wealth at one time than at any other time in the history of the United States.

Economics of Discrimination

Discrimination in the labor market can take many forms and be measured by differential market outcomes, such as wages and earnings, occupational attainment, and employment levels. After holding such factors as education, work experience, and productivity constant, any wage and/or occupational differentials are evidence of racial discrimination. The economics of racial discrimination differentiate between premarket factors that may be an outcome of past discrimination, such as disparities in educational quality, aspirations, and child rearing, and discrimination in the labor market, although premarket factors may have consequences in the labor market. Labor-market discrimination occurs as a result of the valuation of ascriptive characteristics such as race, gender, physical handicap, religion, sexual preference, and ethnicity, which are unrelated to worker productivity.

There are two general explanations for labor-market discrimination, and each proposes different rationales. One explanation is based on personal prejudice. In his 1971 book *The Economics of Discrimination*, Gary S. Becker, the University of Chicago economist and 1992 Nobel Prize recipient, explained that employers, fellow employees, and customers may have a "taste" or personal preference to associate with workers of a given race or sex. Becker contends that employers, employees, and customers who discriminate are utility maximizers, because they are willing to forego profits and/or pay higher prices and wages to satisfy their discriminatory preferences, that is, prejudices. According to Becker, discrimination is economically irrational because it is not profit-maximizing behavior.

The second explanation, statistical discrimination, proposes that labor market discrimination may not necessarily be an outcome of personal prejudice but rather a lack of information about an individual's potential productivity. Because of imperfect information, employers resort to attributing information or statistics about the average performance of a group to individual members in making hiring decisions. Employers may use race and gender as predictors of worker productivity. If an employer perceives that, on average, blacks or women are unproductive workers, they will then use this information in individual hiring decisions.

Tarry Hum

born to middle-class blacks experience downward mobility as adults. Downward mobility has been a challenge for middle-class blacks for decades, and the economic impact of the Great Recession has made downward mobility much more of a mainstream experience, as large numbers of people became long-term unemployed, and many more perhaps became underemployed, accepting jobs far below their experience and skills in order to make ends meet. There is a possibility that such widespread downward mobility will shift attitudes toward public assistance over time, and create a different social policy landscape as a result.

Renee S. Alston

See also

Intergenerational Social Mobility; Laissez-Faire Racism; Meritocracy; Split-Labor Market Theory; *Wages of Whiteness, The*

Further Reading:

Acs, Gregory. "Downward Mobility from the Middle Class." *Pew Charitable Trusts*, 2011.

Beckeer, Gary S. *The Economics of Discrimination*, 2nd ed. Chicago: University of Chicago Press, 1971.

Lacy, Karyn R. "All's Fair? The Foreclosure Crisis and Middle-Class Black (In)Stability." *American Behavioral Scientist* 56, no. 11 (2012): 1565–80.

Sawhill, Isabell. "Are We Headed Toward a Permanently Divided Society?" Center of Children and Families at Brookings—CCF Brief #48. 2012. Washington, DC: Brookings.

http://www.pewtrusts.org/uploadedFiles/wwwpewtrustsorg/Reports/Economic_Mobility/Pew_PollProject_Final_SP.pdf

Driving While Black, Stopping People for

One area in which some police agencies and officers have admitted to abusing their authority is stopping cars solely because the driver and/or its occupants are black. That is, some police officers and, in fact, entire agencies conduct illegal stops, because they have no evidence of wrongdoing on the part of the driver or the occupants. In the United States, law enforcement does not have the power to stop a car or, for that matter, a person, merely because of the race or ethnicity of the driver and/or the occupants. Law enforcement must have, at a minimum, a level of proof called *reasonable suspicion*.

Various legal powers have been conferred upon police officers to allow them to enforce laws. These powers are written in what is called the *law of criminal procedure*. Officers, for example, have the power to arrest, write summonses, and forcibly stop people or cars. The law of criminal procedure, however, does not merely give officers power; it also places important limitations on that power. Officers may not, for example, forcibly stop just anyone they please; rather, police in the United States have the power to forcibly stop a person only if they *reasonably suspect* that individual has committed, is committing, or is about to commit a crime. Reasonable suspicion is defined as "the quantum of knowledge sufficient to induce an ordinarily prudent and cautious man under the circumstances to believe criminal activity is at hand" (Eterno 2003: 28). The U.S. Supreme Court, in the case *Terry v. Ohio* (392 U.S. 1 [1968]), and most state legislatures (e.g., New York State Criminal Procedure Law, §140.50) recognize that police have the power to conduct forcible stops. However, officers may stop the person only if he or she has reasonable suspicion to do so.

Law enforcement has tried to justify forcible stops of minorities by claiming that certain minority groups are more likely to engage in crime. That is, they try to use racial stereotypes rather than specific evidence to justify their actions. For example, a New Jersey chief of police troopers was fired in 1999 after he stated that "mostly minorities" were drug dealers (Harris 1999: 3). For the New Jersey State Police, there were not only statements but empirical studies indicating law enforcement's illegal behavior. One study showed that "although blacks and Latinos were 78 percent of persons stopped and searched on the southern portion of the Jersey Turnpike, police were twice as likely to discover evidence of illegal activity in cars driven by whites, relative to blacks, and whites were five times more likely to be in possession of drugs, guns or other illegal items relative to Latinos" (Wise 2003). Such studies show the fallacy of the officers' racial stereotyping. Because of these egregious illegal actions, the New Jersey State Police are under a consent decree and must stop conducting the illegal stops.

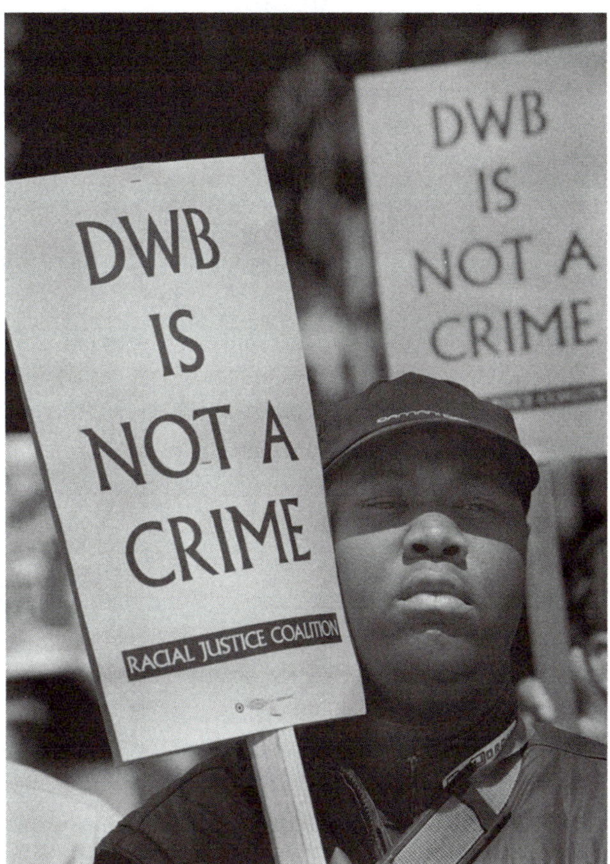

Lonnell McGhee of Oakland, California, listens to speakers at a rally against racial profiling at the state capitol in Sacramento, on April 27, 2000. Hundreds of others were there to show support for SB1389, the so-called DWB Bill, or Driving While Black/Brown Bill. (AP Photo/Steve Yeater)

These actions by police are sometimes termed *racial profiling*. The U.S. Department of Justice defines racial profiling as "any police-initiated action that relies on the race, ethnicity, or national origin rather than the behavior of an individual or information that leads the police to a particular individual who has been identified as being, or having been, engaged in criminal activity" (Ramirez, McDevitt, and Farrell 2000). In its essence, this means that law enforcement may use race in the case of specific descriptions but may not use racial stereotypes as a basis for an action.

With respect to car stops, a 1996 U.S. Supreme Court case, *Whren et al. v. United States* (517 U.S. 806), complicates the situation. In *Whren*, the Supreme Court ruled that a car could be stopped with probable cause for a violation. The concern with this case has to do with police using the probable cause from a traffic violation as a pretext to investigate other activity. As one scholar noted, "The average driver cannot go three blocks without violating some traffic regulation . . . [and] police will use the immense discretionary power *Whren* gives them mostly to stop African-Americans and Hispanics" (Harris 1999: 122–23). According to Justice Antonin Scalia, an unanimous Supreme Court decision directed that there was no alternative but to allow police the power to stop cars based on probable cause that a traffic infraction occurred. Even more liberal states such as New York are also adopting this rule. Interestingly, a recent study does indicate that police are conducting illegal car stops based on the driver's race, particularly black males (Lundman and Kaufman 2003). However, more study is needed to confirm those findings.

More recently, President George W. Bush adopted a new policy that essentially prohibits racial profiling by federal law-enforcement authorities. However, this policy further complicates matters by including an exception that allows agents to use race and ethnicity if there is a terrorist threat or something similar (Lichtblau 2003). Indeed, balancing civil liberties with the threat of crime and terrorism will be a major issue for the foreseeable future (see, e.g., Eterno 2003).

JOHN ETERNO

See also

Disproportionality Index Scores; Institutional Racism; Racial Profiling

Further Reading:

Eterno, John A. *Policing within the Law: A Case Study of the New York City Police Department.* Westport, CT: Praeger, 2003.

Harris, David A. "Driving while Black: Racial Profiling on Our Nation's Highways." *American Civil Liberties Union: Special Report.* June 1999.

Harris, David A. "'Driving while Black' and All Other Traffic Offenses: The Supreme Court and Pretextual Traffic Stops." In *Taking Sides: Clashing Views on Controversial Legal Issues*, 9th ed., edited by Ethan M. Katch and William Rose, 119–25. New York: McGraw Hill, 2000.

Lichtblau, Eric. "Bush Issues Racial Profiling Ban but Exempts Security Inquiries." *New York Times*, June 18, 2003, A1.

Lundman, Richard J., and Robert L. Kaufman. "Driving while Black: Effects of Race, Ethnicity, and Gender on Citizen Self-Reports of Traffic Stops and Police Actions." *Criminology* 41, no. 1 (2003): 195–220.

Ramirez, Deborah, Jack McDevitt, and Amy Farrell. *A Resource Guide on Racial Profiling Data Collection Systems.* Washington, DC: U.S. Department of Justice, 2000. See esp. p. 3.

Wise, Tim. "Racial Profiling and its Apologists." In *Annual Editions Criminal Justice 03/04*, 27th ed., edited by Joseph L. Victor and Joanne Naughton, 91–94. New York: McGraw Hill, 2003.

Du Bois, W.E.B. (1868–1963)

William Edward Burghardt Du Bois was an African American sociologist, historian, civil rights activist, writer, editor, and critic. Du Bois was a prominent intellectual and the most significant figure in the fight for racial equality in America during the first half of the 20th century. Through books, articles, and speeches, he tirelessly advanced the cause of the oppressed, not only for African Americans but also for all colored people in Africa, Asia, and Latin America. He is also considered the father of Pan-Africanism—a belief in the solidarity among Africans and diasporic blacks, as well as an anticolonial movement to unify all blacks in their struggle for civil and political liberty.

Du Bois was born in Great Barrington, a small town in western Massachusetts, on February 23, 1868. The child of Alfred and Mary Du Bois, he was valedictorian of his graduating class at—and the first black to graduate from—Great Barrington High School. Unable to attend Harvard University because of his financial strains, he attended Fisk University in Nashville, Tennessee, graduating as valedictorian with a BA in 1888. Living in the Deep South was an eye-opening experience for him. He witnessed the oppression of fellow blacks—in the forms of social segregation, Jim Crow cars, lynch law, and poverty—for the first time.

Scholarships allowed Du Bois to further his education at Harvard, where he earned a BA in philosophy (1890) and an MA in history (1891); his professors included such esteemed scholars as William James, George Santayana, and Josiah Royce. He then pursued a doctoral degree in history at Harvard, where he became the first African American to receive a PhD (1895). In 1892–1894, while still working on his doctorate, he was awarded a Slater Fund fellowship, which led him to study history and economics at the University of Berlin; he traveled throughout Europe during his stay there. Upon returning to the United States, Du Bois became a professor of Latin and Greek at Wilberforce University, a private African American institution in Ohio (1894–1896).

His doctoral thesis, *The Suppression of the African Slave-Trade to the United States of America, 1638–1870*, was published in 1896 as the first volume of the Harvard Historical Sketches series. It was the first sociological and historical study of the white enslavement of Africans in America. In the same year, Du Bois married Nina Gomer, a Wilberforce student with whom he would have two children: Burghardt, who died at age three, and Yolanda, who was briefly married to the black poet Countee Cullen.

After working as assistant instructor of sociology at the University of Pennsylvania in 1896–1897, Du Bois joined the faculty at Atlanta University in Georgia in 1897, where he served as professor of economics and history until 1910. During these years, he organized the university's conference series Studies of the Negro Problem, and edited the conference's annual *Publications*. His sociological study of African Americans, *The Philadelphia Negro: A Social Study*, came out in 1899. Developing out of his research at the University of Pennsylvania, it was the pioneering case study of an urban black community in the United States.

Du Bois was a leader of the first "Pan-African Conference" held in London in 1900. Designed to foster a feeling of unity among all blacks and discuss issues affecting their interests, this transatlantic meeting drew delegates from the United States, Ethiopia, Liberia, the Caribbean Islands, and West Africa. The Address to the Nations of the World by the Races Congress in London, 1900, was signed by four leaders of the conference: Alexander Walters, president; Henry B. Brown, vice-president; H. Sylvester Williams, general secretary; and W.E.B. Du Bois, chairman of the committee on the address.

The Souls of Black Folk: Essays and Sketches, Du Bois's most celebrated book, was published in 1903. Defining the problem of the 20th century as "the problem of the color line," he theorized in this work the double status—the status of conflicting identities—of African Americans: "One ever feels his twoness,—an American, a Negro; two warring souls, two thoughts, two unreconciled strivings; two warring ideals in one dark body, whose dogged strength alone keeps it from being torn asunder." The book also included Du Bois's open challenge to the American educator Booker T. Washington on how to advance American blacks. While Washington advocated racial accommodation, hard work, and education in improving the standing of blacks, Du Bois called for an unabated protest against racial injustice. Racial problems in America would be resolved only through "ceaseless agitation and insistent demand for equality" and through the "use of force of every sort: moral persuasion, propaganda, and where possible even physical resistance." He also emphasized the role of college-educated blacks in the civil rights struggle.

In July 1905, Du Bois, William Monroe Trotter, and 27 men founded the Niagara movement, an organization for young black intellectuals committed to ending racial prejudice, particularly in such areas as suffrage, freedom of speech and criticism, economic opportunity, education, courts, health, and employment. Their activities included lobbying against Jim Crow and sending protest letters to President Theodore Roosevelt following the Brownsville (Texas) Riot of 1906. The Niagara movement lasted until 1910, when the disagreement on whether whites should be admitted to the organization disrupted the unity of the members. Du Bois believed that they should; on February 12, 1909, he helped create the National Association for the Advancement of Colored People (NAACP), a new civil rights organization. It advocated nonviolence and legal actions as the means to achieve equal civil rights for all Americans in the matters of housing, employment, voting, schools, the courts, transportation, and recreation. The founding members included 60 black and white citizens; interestingly, Du Bois was the only black person on the organization's original board. The year 1909 also saw the publication of Du Bois's *John Brown: A Biography*, in which he defended the militant abolitionist martyr who led an attack on the armory at Harpers Ferry in 1859. In response to the accusation that he was a fanatic and traitor, Du Bois contended that Brown was "the man who of all Americans has perhaps come nearest to touching the real souls of black folk" (DuBois 1909).

In 1910, Du Bois left his faculty position at Atlanta University to serve as the NAACP's director of publicity and research full time; he also served as the editor of the monthly NAACP magazine, *The Crisis: A Record of the Darker Races*, for 25 years (1910–1934). The magazine covered many

Pan-African issues, recommending books on Africa, introducing conferences on African studies, and condemning the apartheid in South Africa. As editor of *The Crisis*, Du Bois also identified and promoted talented black writers and artists. He advocated cultural nationalism for fellow blacks, encouraging the development of African American writing that is both uniquely black and universally appealing. The 1926 Negro in Art symposium, for example, urged black artists to be more politically conscious.

In the early 1910s, Du Bois published three books: *The Quest of the Silver Fleece: A Novel* (1911), *The Star of Ethiopia* (1913), and *The Negro* (1915). Partly based on the ancient Greek story of the Golden Fleece, *The Quest of the Silver Fleece* was Du Bois's first work of fiction, set in Tooms County, Alabama. It traced the romantic relationship between Yankee-educated Bles Alwyn and Zora, the child of the swamp. As an economic novel, it has been compared to Frank Norris's *The Pit* and Upton Sinclair's *The Jungle*. *The Star of Ethiopia* was a theatrical production designed to promote African American history and civil rights. *The Negro*, in which the author considered race a social construct, was the earliest comprehensive historical examination of Africans and diasporic black peoples.

In 1919, Du Bois organized the first Pan-African Congress (PAC), held in Paris, France, to coincide with the Paris Peace Conference; it was part of the black transatlantic movement to represent the political and economic interests of blacks in Africa, the Caribbean Islands, and the Americas. (Du Bois was also the main organizer of the PAC in 1921, 1923, 1927, and 1945.) In 1920, he published *Darkwater: Voices from within the Veil*, which encompassed such genres as biographical essays, sketches, fiction, and lyrical poems. It addressed sociopolitical and economic issues relating to Africans from an anticolonial perspective. The author stressed the brotherhood of all men on the globe: they were different in appearances only; they were alike in their deep souls and in their potential for unlimited development. In the chapter "The Souls of White Folk," Du Bois explored what it meant to be white. According to the author, the idea of personal whiteness was a modern phenomenon that had not existed in ancient times; in their misguided racial arrogance, whites caused miserable pain for peoples of color—the Africans, Indians, Japanese, mongrel Mexicans, and mulatto South Americans. He drew a parallel between the white European oppression of Africans and the white American oppression of racial minorities. Although ancient societies such as the Roman Empire did have slaves, slavery as practiced in the United States was more severe in its violation of fundamental human rights. As a Pan-Africanist, Du Bois emphasized the need to free Africa from European colonialism and to restore self-rule on the continent.

Du Bois's next book, *The Gift of Black Folk: The Negroes in the Making of America* (1924), was based on the author's study of the many contributions blacks made toward the construction and progress of the United States. He started his book with a chapter on how black explorers were instrumental in the discovery of America. The succeeding chapters focused on other areas of contributions—black labor in making America a rich nation, black soldiers fighting in many wars (for the freedom of others, not for their own freedom), black civil rights struggles in democratizing the nation, black women in elevating the status of all women, black folk music in establishing itself as the sole American folk music, Negro art and literature in dealing with the American story of slavery, and the spirit of blacks in inspiring humility and forgiveness.

Growing increasingly militant, Du Bois quit the NAACP in 1934 because he was dissatisfied with the organization's conservative approach to the problems of racial segregation. He resumed his teaching at Atlanta University, where he chaired the sociology department from 1934 to 1944; he also edited the university's quarterly *Phylon* from 1940 to 1944. During this period, Du Bois published *Black Reconstruction: An Essay Toward a History of the Part Which Black Folk Played in the Attempt to Reconstruct Democracy in America, 1860–1880* (1935), an African American—and Marxist—analysis of the Reconstruction era; *Black Folk, Then and Now: An Essay in the History and Sociology of the Negro Race* (1939), a sociological study of the cultural and economic exploitations of African Negroes by slave traders; and *Dusk of Dawn: An Essay Toward an Autobiography of a Race Concept* (1940), in which the author explored the concept of race as the central issue of American democracy and of the world in the coming years.

In May 1942, Du Bois was investigated by the Federal Bureau of Investigation (FBI) for his left-wing and socialist activities. Two years later, he returned from Atlanta University to head the NAACP department of special research, a position he held until 1948. At the founding conference of the United Nations (1945), Du Bois represented the NAACP in San Francisco as associate consultant to the American delegation. The year 1945 also saw the publication of *Color and Democracy: Colonies and Peace*, in which Du Bois voiced his strong opposition to imperialism and advocated the independence of small nations. Two years later, he published *The World and Africa: An Inquiry into the Part Which Africa Has Played in World History*, in which he documented the way Africans contributed to the world and the way they had been enslaved by the colonial powers.

Irrevocably disillusioned with the conservative social positions of the NAACP and with the slow progress of race relations in America, Du Bois left the organization for the last time in 1948, embracing instead communism, which he considered the best ideology for Negroes. He chaired the Peace Information Center—a dissident organization in New York City—at the outbreak of the Korean War. In 1951, under the Foreign Agents Registration Act, Du Bois was indicted by a federal grand jury for being an unregistered agent for a foreign power, but he was later acquitted for lack of evidence. Du Bois also praised Joseph Stalin as a great man who was surpassed by few people in the 20th century, signed the Stockholm Peace Pledge (which condemned the use of nuclear weapons), visited Communist China during its Great Leap Forward era and was honored by Mao Zedong and Zhou Enlai, and received the 1959 International Lenin Peace Prize in the Soviet Union for "strengthening world peace" ("Philosopher" 1963).

Du Bois's later writings included *In Battle for Peace: The Story of My 83rd Birthday* (1952). Here the author reminisced about his arraignment and trial involving the Peace Information Center. *The Black Flame: A Trilogy* consisted of three novels—*The Ordeal of Mansart* (1957), *Mansart Builds a School* (1959), and *Worlds of Color* (1961). Written from an African American perspective, these works embodied Du Bois's increasingly radical ideology.

In the fall of 1961, at the age of 93, he officially joined the Communist Party. Later that year, he moved to Ghana as a special guest of President Kwame Nkrumah to serve as director of the *Encyclopedia Africana*, an ambitious government-sponsored project. In 1963, the United States government refused to reissue a new passport alleging his communist activities; he and his wife, Shirley Graham (whom he married in 1951, a year after the death of his first wife) renounced their American citizenship and became naturalized citizens of Ghana. Du Bois's health declined beginning in 1962; on August 27, 1963, he died in Accra, Ghana, at age 95—a day before Martin Luther King, Jr. delivered his monumental "I Have a Dream" civil rights speech in Washington, D.C. Du Bois was given a state funeral at Christianborg Castle in Accra and was buried outside the Castle; the *Encyclopedia Africana* remained unfinished at his death.

In his lifetime, Du Bois regularly contributed columns to such periodicals as the *Chicago Defender*, the *Pittsburgh Courier*, the *Atlantic Monthly*, the *New York Amsterdam News*, and the *San Francisco Chronicle*. His experimental creative works—such as the short story "The Coming of John" and the poem "The Song of the Smoke"—were included in the magazines he edited: *Moon Illustrated Weekly* (1905) and *Horizon* (1907–1910).

Du Bois received many honors and awards. In addition to the International Lenin Peace Prize, he received the Spingarn Medal from the NAACP, was made Knight Commander of the Liberian Humane Order of African Redemption, and by President Calvin Coolidge was conferred the rank of Minister Plenipotentiary and Envoy Extraordinary. Du Bois was the first African American to be elected to the National Institute of Arts and Letters and served as a lifetime member and fellow of the American Association for the Advancement of Science. Among the institutions of higher learning awarding him an honorary degree were Atlantic University, Charles University, Fisk University, Harvard University, Morgan State College, the University of Berlin, and Wilberforce University.

The Autobiography of W.E.B. Du Bois: A Soliloquy on Viewing My Life from the Last Decade of Its Final Century was brought out posthumously in 1968, and *The Correspondence of W.E.B. Du Bois* was published in three volumes in 1976. On January 31, 1992, the United States honored Du Bois by releasing a 29-cent stamp—the 15th in the Postal Service's annual Black Heritage Series. In 1994, the 28-story main library at the University of Massachusetts at Amherst was named as W.E.B. Du Bois Library; it offers services and resources in humanities and social sciences.

John J. Han

See also

Washington, Booker T.

Further Reading:

Byerman, Keith E. *Seizing the Word: History, Art, and Self in the Work of W.E.B. Du Bois*. Athens: University of Georgia Press, 1994.

Du Bois, W.E.B. *The Souls of Black Folk: Essays and Sketches*. Chicago: A. C. McClurg, 1903.

Du Bois, W.E.B. *John Brown*. Philadelphia: G.W. Jacobs, 1909.

Horne, Gerald. *Black and Red: W.E.B. Du Bois and the Afro-American Response to the Cold War, 1944–1963*. Albany: State University of New York Press, 1986.

Lewis, David Levering. *W.E.B. Du Bois—Biography of a Race, 1868–1919*. New York: H. Holt, 1993.

Lewis, David Levering. *W.E.B. Du Bois: The Fight for Equality and the American Century, 1919–1963*. New York: H. Holt, 2000.

Marable, Manning. *W.E.B. Du Bois: Black Radical Democrat*. Boston: Twayne, 1986.

Moore, Jack B. *W.E.B. Du Bois*. Boston: Twayne, 1981.

"Philosopher, Who Helped to Found N.A.A.C.P., Later Turned to Communism." *New York Times*, August 28, 1963: Obituary page.

Rampersad, Arnold. *The Art and Imagination of W.E.B. Du Bois*. Cambridge, MA: Harvard University Press, 1976.

Reed, Adolph L., Jr. *W.E.B. Du Bois and American Political Thought: Fabianism and the Color Line*. New York: Oxford University Press, 1997.

Rudwick, Elliott M. *W.E.B. Du Bois: Propagandist of the Negro Protest*, 2nd ed. Philadelphia: University of Pennsylvania Press, 1968.

Smith, Shawn Michelle. *Photography on the Color Line: W.E.B. Du Bois, Race, and Visual Culture*. Durham, NC: Duke University Press, 2004.

Dyer, Leonidas C. (1871–1952)

Leonidas C. Dyer was a white Republican politician who served in the U.S. Congress in the House of Representatives, notable for proposing anti-lynching legislation. While this attempt was ultimately unsuccessful, it was illustrative of how divisive the issue of lynching was in late 19th and early 20th century U.S. society, given the tense state of racial relations in the Jim Crow South as well as within Northern cities with growing African American populations.

Dyer was born on a farm in Warren City, Missouri, in June 11, 1871. Little is known about his early life, especially those forces that might account for the vociferous opposition to racial intolerance he displayed during his career in the U.S. Congress. Dyer attended Central Wesleyan College as an undergraduate. He subsequently studied law at the Washington University, and was admitted to the practice of law in 1893. Dyer also served in the U.S. military during the Spanish-American War.

Dyer was elected to the U.S. Congress in 1911 from a heavily African American district in St. Louis. This suggests that he was acquainted firsthand with the promises and perils of the Great Migration, that mass movement of African Americans from the rural South to the urban North during the Jim Crow era. Disenfranchisement, Jim Crow, unemployment, lynchings, and mob violence made life unbearable for African Americans in the South. African American migrants settled in the flourishing industrial cities of the North, among them St. Louis. Many of them found jobs in the factories that had been emptied of white men sent to serve in World War I. By the end of the war, about 500,000 African Americans had moved to the North.

The racial conflagrations so common in the South also migrated northward. In East St. Louis, public facilities, housing, and schools were segregated, creating a seething cauldron of racial tension. In April 1917, 470 black men were hired to replace whites striking against the Aluminum Ore Company. The strike was crushed and the men, members of the American Federation of Labor, blamed the African Americans who had been used as strikebreakers. At a meeting in May, the union demanded that the town be rid of African Americans. A riot ensued, and white mobs attacked blacks and destroyed buildings.

An uneasy truce was broken on July 1 when a carload of white men drove through East St. Louis firing guns. Two white plainclothes police officers followed; they were shot and killed by no doubt frightened and angry black residents. A full-scale riot erupted, and whites, joined by law enforcement officials, killed 35 blacks, many of them mutilated and their bodies thrown into the Mississippi River. African American homes and businesses were also destroyed.

Dyer was appalled not only by the violence in East St. Louis but by the increase in lynchings and the spread of mob violence. Decrying what he described as open contempt of the courts and the rule of law, he called for an end to mob violence and introduced an anti-lynching bill on April 1, 1918.

The Dyer Anti-Lynching Bill made participation in a lynch mob a federal crime. It also contained sections that would punish local, county, and state officials who failed to prevent lynchings. Finally, the bill allowed counties in which lynchings took place to be sued for damages. African American women were the first to document and protest the crime of lynching in the late 19th century. They, along with the National Association for the Advancement of Colored People, were instrumental in the bill's creation and its passage in the House. African American women mobilized citizens, lobbied government officials, donated and raised funds, and in 1922 formed the Anti-Lynching Crusaders, a group whose purpose it was to educate the public about the crime of lynching and work for its eradication.

Supporters of the Dyer Anti-Lynching Bill based that support in part on the equal protection clause of the Fourteenth Amendment. Opponents of the bill claimed its provisions violated the doctrine of states' rights as guaranteed in the Tenth Amendment. Moreover, they claimed that the protection of white women from sexual advances by black men made lynching a necessary evil. According to the bill's opponents, the threat of lynching was the only thing standing between the virtue of white women and sexually depraved black men.

Liberal Republicans took the lead in getting the bill through the House of Representatives. It passed on January 26, 1922; only 17 Republicans opposed it, and eight Northern or border state Democrats were convinced to support it. The bill moved on to the Republican-controlled Senate, where it was supported by Senate Majority Leader Henry Cabot Lodge. However, Lodge's colleague and nemesis, William Board, an Idaho Republican, opposed the bill and helped lead the opposition. Southern senators filibustered, and the bill went down to defeat. Dyer tried twice more during the decade to win passage of an anti-lynching law, but was unsuccessful.

Despite its failure to pass, the Dyer Anti-Lynching Bill did have a political impact. It brought the crime of lynching to the forefront of the political debate in the United States. Southern officials who had argued that lynching was a necessary tool in the fight to maintain the social order in the Jim Crow South were forced to ensure that violence against African Americans in the region was moderated. In 1918, there were 60 recorded lynchings of African American men; by 1922, that number dropped to 57. By the time the Costigan-Wagner Anti-Lynching Bill was introduced in 1934, the number of recorded lynchings had dropped to 15.

Dyer was defeated in the Franklin D. Roosevelt electoral landslide of 1932 and returned to the practice of law in St. Louis. Campaigns to return to the House in 1934 and 1936 were unsuccessful. He died in December 15, 1952.

Marilyn K. Howard

See also

Anti-Lynching Legislation; Lynching

Further Reading:

Brown, Mary Jane. "Advocates in the Age of Jazz: Women and the Campaign for the Dyer Anti-Lynching Bill." *Peace & Change* 28, no. 3 (July 2003): 378–419.

Gruening, Martha, Helen Boardman, and National Association for the Advancement of Colored People. *Thirty Years of Lynching in the United States 1889–1918*. New York: Negro Universities Press, 1969.

Jonas, Gilbert. *Freedom's Sword: The NAACP and the Struggle Against Racism in America, 1909–1969*. New York: Taylor & Francis, 2004.

E

East St. Louis (Illinois) Riot of 1917

Economic and political factors led the white population of East St. Louis, Illinois, to feel embittered toward the growing black population during 1916 and 1917. Specifically, the rapid influx of blacks from the South and labor strife led to growing tensions. Labor leaders incited a small riot in May 1917, resulting in several injuries but no deaths.

Tensions continued to rise afterward and reached a boiling point when blacks retaliated against whites by shooting at their homes and accidentally killing two police officers. One of worst race riots in the 20th century ensued with indiscriminate violence against the black population of the city, resulting in the deaths of at least 48 people.

East St. Louis is located on the shores of the Mississippi River across from St. Louis, Missouri. During World War I, many blacks from the South moved north in hopes of better economic conditions. East St. Louis saw a dramatic rise in the population of blacks in 1916 and 1917. Blacks poured into the city and found work, perceived by many whites as taking jobs away from the established white population. Whites also generally believed that violence and crime increased as the black population increased. The city had an established black middle class by 1916, and when some began to move into white neighborhoods, whites left the area, immediately selling their homes at reduced prices. Rising racial tensions over labor and housing in East St. Louis formed the backdrop for the riots of 1917.

The political culture of East St. Louis also contributed to the riots. The political system there was rife with corruption by 1916, contributing to a culture of lawlessness. Corruption became a racial issue during the 1916 election. Democratic leaders charged that Republicans had been bringing thousands of blacks from the South to vote Republican in the upcoming elections to ensure Republican control of the county. Democrats made similar colonization charges in other Northern states like Indiana and Ohio. Illinois went Republican in the 1916 presidential election, but in East St. Louis, whites who believed the colonization theory voted Democratic, increasing their antagonism against blacks.

Although migration and colonization were simmering issues, the problem of labor caused the most enmity toward blacks in East St. Louis. Two labor strikes in 1916 and 1917 created unrest among both white and black populations, and local newspapers predicted that a race riot could occur. The first strike occurred during the summer of 1916 when 4,000 meatpacking workers went on strike and practically shut down the plants. The meatpacking companies firmly stated that its workers could not unionize, and most of the workers returned under the promise that the companies would reinstate the organizers. The companies failed to hire any of them back. Throughout the conflict, the companies constantly threatened to use cheaper black labor if necessary. Union organizers frequently exaggerated the number of black workers and strikebreakers, and eventually the East St. Louis white population accepted the misleading statistics as fact.

The second labor strike originated in East St. Louis's aluminum factories. In early 1917, the Aluminum Ore Company employed nearly 2,000 workers, including approximately 500 blacks. The Aluminum Ore Employees Protective Association went on strike in response to phasing out association jobs but feared that the company would continue to hire more blacks. Instead, the company hired a professional strikebreaker, who obtained weapons, built a small army, and demolished the association. Workers blamed their failure squarely on the black population, claiming that their presence in the city gave companies the power to crush organized labor.

On May 10, 1917, a group of members from the Central Trades and Labor Union met with East St. Louis mayor Fred Mollman about their concerns regarding black workers. Mollman told them that he and the city council would address the problem and set a date for a public meeting with labor delegates. At the public meeting on May 28, union delegates and other white factory workers complained about the excessive number of blacks moving into the city, and the meeting quickly became heated. Shortly after the meeting, rumors circulated that blacks were attacking whites, and a mob formed to retaliate. On the streets, the mob attacked blacks who just happened to be in the way, and three blacks and three whites were shot. By the early morning hours, the mob had quieted down. There were a number of injuries, but no one was killed.

Following the riot of May 28, the East St. Louis police did nothing to prevent further incidents. The unions condoned the riot and placed blame on employers who had allegedly brought large numbers of blacks into the city. Only two weeks after the riot, Illinois governor Frank Lowden withdrew the Illinois National Guard who had earlier been called in to East St. Louis to prevent racial violence. Small mobs of whites beat blacks practically on a daily basis. Rumors began circulating that blacks had planned a major counterattack for July 4.

Late in the evening of July 1, 1917, whites in a Ford car fired shots at homes owned by blacks. When the car appeared a second time, a group of armed blacks fired back. The police received a report of blacks shooting at cars and dispatched an unmarked Ford police car to investigate. Thinking it was the car from which whites shot at black homes, blacks fired at the squad car. According to a reporter who was in the police car, 200 armed blacks immediately fired upon the car, killing one detective instantly and mortally wounding the other. The next morning, the car, with all of its bullet holes, was parked at the police station. The bullet-ridden car was all the proof that white residents needed to verify the rumors they had heard about black retaliation.

Labor leaders held a short meeting in the morning, and organizers told the crowd to return in the afternoon with guns. After the meeting, the group marched down one of the main thoroughfares and began to shoot at black passersby. By late morning, white East St. Louis residents joined with the laborers to form a mob and began to beat and club random blacks indiscriminately. Although the large majority of the rioters were white men, women and children also joined the mobs. Spectators lined the streets to watch, and after a beating or a shooting, bystanders would then participate by kicking wounded or dead victims. Several lynchings also took place during the riot. Rioters appeared to have no remorse for any of their actions either during or after the riot. Many of the rioters believed that victims deserved to suffer before dying. In some instances, medical personnel and sympathetic bystanders were unable to help victims as rioters threatened violence against them. Mobs also attacked homes where blacks lived, torching them to force out the occupants.

The Illinois National Guard slowly arrived in East St. Louis to restore order, but many guardsmen failed to protect victims, with some guardsmen actually participating in the riot. A minority of guardsmen actually prevented lynchings and were able to arrest rioters; however, large crowds easily overwhelmed the small number of guardsmen thinly dispersed throughout the city. East St. Louis police officers also provided little protection, often refusing to protect blacks and even participating in the violence in some cases.

Some blacks were able to mobilize and offer resistance, but this generally occurred in the fringe neighborhoods. In the riot area, approximately 100 blocks at and around downtown, blacks were generally helpless against the onslaught. The randomness of attacks and indiscriminate killings made it difficult for blacks to mobilize and retaliate. Many blacks did not have weapons because, prior to the riot, guardsmen confiscated guns in an effort to minimize their ability to retaliate.

By the time the riot was over well into the evening of July 2, the death toll was large. Official reports later noted that 39 blacks and nine whites were dead. The National Association for the Advancement of Colored People and the *Chicago Defender*, the nation's leading black newspaper, claimed that between 100 and 200 blacks lost their lives. Local white East St. Louis residents claimed that at least 400 were dead. Hospitals reported treating as many as 100 victims on that day, but many black victims probably refused treatment out of fear of being abused again. One newspaper suggested that 750 blacks received serious injuries. In terms of property, reports estimated about 300 buildings had been destroyed, totaling almost $400,000 in damages.

Shortly after the riots, the state's attorney failed to indict anyone because of his inability to locate witnesses and his belief that the riots constituted an appropriate response to the growing black population. However, more than a month later, a grand jury indicted 134 people, nearly one-third of whom were black. Only nine whites served time in the state penitentiary, and the court sentenced 12 blacks to the penitentiary. The harshest sentences were 14-year terms for two white defendants.

There was a large decrease in the black population of East St. Louis after the July 2, 1917, riot. Tensions between whites and blacks continued long after the race riot; schools remained segregated until the mid-20th century, and civic leaders often vetoed plans for the integration of clubs for fear of another race riot. The economic advantages of the city disintegrated during the Great Depression, and by the 1950s and 1960s, the white population abandoned the city. By 1970, East St. Louis was 97 percent black, becoming one of the largest nearly all-black cities in the country.

John A. Lupton

See also

Dyer, Leonidas C.; Race Riots in America; World War I. Documents: Report on the Memphis Riots of May 1866 (1866); Account of the Riots in East St. Louis, Illinois (1917); A Southern Black Woman's Letter Regarding the Recent Riots in Chicago and Washington (1919); The Cook County Coroner's Report Regarding the 1919 Chicago Race Riots (1920); The Final Report of the Grand Jury on the Tulsa Race Riot (June 25, 1921); Testimony from *Laney v. United States* (1923); The Governor's Commission Report on the Watts Riots (1965); Cyrus R. Vance's Report on the Riots in Detroit (1967); The Reports of the Oklahoma Commission to Study the Tulsa Race Riot of 1921 (2000–2001); Draft Report: 1898 Wilmington Race Riot Commission (2005)

Further Reading:

Asher, Robert. "Documents of the Race Riot at East St. Louis." *Journal of the Illinois State Historical Society* 65 (Autumn 1972): 327–36.

Johnson, Ben, et al. "Report on the Special Committee Authorized by Congress to Investigate the East St. Louis Riots." In *The Politics of Riot Commissions, 1917–1970: A Collection of Official Reports and Critical Essays*, edited by Anthony M. Platt. New York: Macmillan Publishing Company, 1971.

Rudwick, Elliott. *Race Riot at East St. Louis: July 2, 1917.* Reprint, Urbana: University of Illinois Press, 1982. Originally published Carbondale: Southern Illinois University Press, 1964.

Economic Opportunity Act of 1964

In August 1964, President Lyndon B. Johnson signed the Economic Opportunity Act, a piece of legislation that initiated the War on Poverty—the name given to the federal government's monumental effort to eradicate poverty in the United States. The act was the brainchild of Robert Sargent Shriver Jr., who became the director of the Office of Economic Opportunity (OEO). Some scholars believe that the Johnson administration assumed that poverty was, for the most part, not structural but instead a question of wasted human capital. As a result, the act was purportedly intended to encourage poor persons to organize themselves and to seek help from the federal government to raise their status. However, because high-ranking positions in the OEO were occupied primarily by whites and funding for the agency was insufficient, Rev. Martin Luther King, Jr. considered Johnson's benevolence to be a shrewd political move intended to stifle dissent and discontent. King believed that Johnson had no intention of attacking the underlying causes of poverty. Nevertheless, the act was meant to meet not only short-term economic needs, but also to seek remedies for long-range problems and thus result in permanent progress for the poor.

Under the direction of Shriver, the OEO established several programs that attempted to remedy the problem of the

President Johnson proudly holds out the Economic Opportunity Act, which he signed into law on August 20, 1964. (Bettmann/Corbis)

chronic unemployment of African Americans. The Concentrated Employment Program, the Manpower Development and Training Act, and the Work Incentive Program for Welfare Clients were supposed to be stopgap measures intended to provide job training and preparation for placement for the unemployable. Furthermore, OEO directed such programs as the Job Corps and Volunteers in Service to America—a sort of domestic peace corps—which were intended to enable African American youth to learn and acquire technical skills. Of the many programs, Head Start, an initiative that sought to train disadvantaged preschoolers, and Upward Bound, which strove to prepare the poor for higher education, were intended to bring about an end to poverty in the United States.

Perhaps the most controversial program created under the Economic Opportunity Act was the Community Action Program. This program, which was supposed to bring about the maximum participation of the poor in grassroots politics,

Equal Employment Opportunity Act of 1972

The Equal Employment Opportunity Act of 1972 amended the provisions of Title VII of the 1964 Civil Rights Act in several important ways to extend its jurisdiction and coverage, and to improve its effectiveness in ensuring equal job opportunities. Title VII prohibited employment discrimination based on race, color, sex, religion, or national origin. All areas of the employment process, including job advertisement, recruitment, testing, hiring and firing, compensation, assignment, and classification of employees, were covered by Title VII provisions. Title VII was enforced by the U.S. Equal Employment Opportunity Commission (EEOC), whose primary mission was to deal with complaints and obtain remedies for individuals and classes of individuals who had suffered discrimination.

The Equal Employment Opportunity Act of 1972 has extended the coverage of Title VII to educational institutions and all levels of governmental employees. In addition, the act has reduced the number of employees necessary for an employer to be covered by the provisions of the act, from 25 to 15, thereby increasing the number of employers that are subject to adhering to the act. The 1972 Equal Employment Opportunity Act has also extended the period of time that a party has to file a discrimination charge. Most importantly, the 1972 amendment has empowered the EEOC with litigation authority. If an acceptable conciliation agreement cannot be achieved, the EEOC now has the option to sue nongovernmental respondents such as employers, unions, and employment agencies. Finally, the act has amended the sex-discrimination provisions to prohibit employers from imposing mandatory leaves of absence or terminating pregnant women employees.

TARRY HUM

provided significant administrative training and experience for African Americans. It also enabled persons to network and interact with influential politicians who served as important connections. Yet, as a whole, the program did not have much long-range impact. The board meetings were often volatile. The politicians and middle-class professionals—not the poor people—took control of the significant policy issues. As a result of several outbursts between the poor and local political leaders, opposition by Democratic mayors and their city councils encouraged Congress to drastically cut the Community Action Program's federal and state funding, thereby eviscerating any political or economic power the poor could or would have.

Any assessment of the impact of the Economic Opportunity Act of 1964—both long range and short term—must be framed on two levels. First, it succeeded in enabling many persons who had long histories of unemployment to become members of the workforce. Second, it simultaneously nurtured rising expectations that were clearly unfounded. By giving the OEO a paltry budget—under $1 billion—Congress was providing the disadvantaged with a mere fraction of the funds necessary to fulfill its grandiose goals. In short, the act created an ambience in which African Americans rightly expected some viable remedy to their socioeconomic status. The frustration that resulted from the disparity of the exalted goals of the Johnson administration's rhetoric and the continuing realities of unemployment, poverty, and desperation that attended everyday life in African American ghettos in major urban areas turned those same residential areas of the disadvantaged into hotbeds of race riots and ghetto revolts.

VERNON J. WILLIAMS JR.

See also

War on Poverty and the Great Society

Further Reading:

Horton, Carol. *Race and the Making of American Liberalism.* New York: Oxford University Press, 2005.

Lemann, Nicholas. *The Promised Land: The Great Black Migration and How It Changed America.* New York: Random House, 1992.

Weisbrodt, Robert. *Freedom Bound: A History of America's Civil Rights Movement.* New York and London: W.W. Norton, 1990.

Education and African Americans

Throughout history, African Americans have struggled for equal rights and opportunities in America. One of the most visible and prominent entities that captures the essence of this struggle is the American education system. Segregation and inequality in the public school system dates back to the beginning of the country's history when states implemented policies that made it illegal for African Americans to learn to read or write. The punishment for disobeying the laws ranged from fines and imprisonment to death for both blacks and whites. After slavery ended, Jim Crow laws throughout the South continued to limit African American students' access to quality education. Several states, including Mississippi, Missouri, Florida, and Texas, had laws that prohibited black and white students from attending the same schools, thereby creating a system in which discrimination ran rampant and inequality was socially accepted. Over time, the education system has undergone many reforms that have attempted to limit discrimination and end segregation in public schools. These reforms were slowly implemented, often as a result of the U.S. court system compelling states to act.

One of the most noted court rulings that had a profound effect on legalizing segregated public schools was *Plessy v. Ferguson* (1896). In *Plessy,* the U.S. Supreme Court ruled that a Louisiana law that required the racial segregation of passengers in railway coaches was not racial discrimination on the condition that accommodations were equal in quality. In the same year that the *Plessy* verdict was handed down, the Georgia legislature reorganized its department of public education. It gave local school boards of education the authority and responsibility to make arrangements for segregated schools for blacks and whites. The schools were required to be equal, but efforts to ensure that equal and adequate educations were provided went largely unchecked. The states were left to police themselves. Although Jim Crow segregation in education ran rampant throughout the South, open segregation was practiced in other regions of the country.

Prior to the *Plessy* ruling, the Massachusetts Supreme Court had already begun to lay the foundation for segregated unequal school systems with its ruling in *Roberts v. the City of Boston* (1848). The Court unanimously agreed that the city of Boston did not have to allow five-year-old Sarah Roberts to attend an all-white school that was located in her neighborhood. Their ruling noted that segregated school systems existed for the good of all people and were allowed under the U.S. Constitution. This sentiment was further perpetuated in *Cumming v. Richmond County Board of Education* (1899). In *Cumming*, black taxpayers in Georgia unsuccessfully attempted to file a suit against the school board to stop operating a high school for white children until the board resumed the operation of the high school for black children.

The cornerstone of the segregated school argument was the belief that segregated schools would be equal. In fact, inequality was widespread. In most major cities, there was only one public school open for blacks compared with four public schools for whites. The lack of schools caused major overcrowding issues, especially in the South. Between 1939 and 1940, the average student-teacher ratio in black Southern schools was approximately 40 students to one teacher. The average student-teacher ratio for white students was about 29 students per teacher.

The salary range for black and white teachers was largely unequal. During the late 1930s, the average starting salary for white teachers ranged from $75 to $200 per month. Black teachers earned between $25 and $75 a month. Black schools also received considerably lower amounts in funding. States spent an average of $49.30 on a white student, while only $17.04 was spent on black students.

Although many African American activists had attempted to challenge segregated school systems legally, their efforts had been unsuccessful until the case of *Brown v. Board of Education* (1954). In the *Brown* case, third grader Linda Brown had to walk one mile through a railroad switchyard to get to her black elementary school, even though a white elementary school was only seven blocks away. Linda's father, Oliver Brown, tried to enroll his daughter in the white elementary school, but the principal refused. Oliver sued for his daughter's right to attend the school. The National Association for the Advancement of Colored People agreed to represent the family. Its team of lawyers, led by Thurgood Marshall, who would later become a U.S. Supreme Court justice, took the case all the way to the Supreme Court. Marshall argued that segregated school systems were grossly unequal and unconstitutional. In the end, the Court sided with Marshall's argument and denounced the doctrine of "separate but equal" facilities for education.

Chief Justice Earl Warren noted:

> Segregation of white and colored children in public schools has a detrimental effect upon the colored

> children. The impact is greater when it has the sanction of the law, for the policy of separating the races is usually interpreted as denoting the inferiority of the Negro group. . . . Any language in contrary to this finding is rejected. We conclude that in the field of public education the doctrine of "separate but equal" has no place. Separate educational facilities are inherently unequal.

After announcing the verdict in the *Brown* decision, the Court invited the counsel for both sides to reargue the case during the 1955 term so that Court could decide how to implement the decision. On May 31, 1955, the Court ordered that public schools be desegregated "with all deliberate speed." This order became known as *Brown* II.

Before the first *Brown* decision, segregation had been required in 17 states. After the second *Brown* decision in 1955, the border states of the Old South began to desegregate. In the Deep South states of Alabama, Mississippi, Louisiana, Arkansas, Florida, and Georgia, as well as in the Upper South states of North Carolina, Tennessee, and Virginia, the process was very slow. Five years after the verdict was rendered, only 19 school districts out of 1,581 in these states were integrated. Many of these states were using stall tactics to hinder integration.

Several states passed resolutions interposing their authority over the Court. Some state legislatures amended their constitutions to close public schools. Governors such as Thomas B. Stanley of Virginia announced that their states would resist integration of their public schools. When this method did not work, many of the citizens turned to violence in an attempt to keep black students from entering the doors of white public schools. In 1957, the violence reached a boiling point in Little Rock, Arkansas, when Gov. Orville Faubus called in the National Guard to prevent black students from gaining entrance into Central High School. After a second court order requiring that the students be admitted, Faubus withdrew the troops. The students were then attacked by a mob of angry white citizens. President Dwight D. Eisenhower was forced into action, sending in the U.S. Army's 101st Airborne Division to protect the students, while also federalizing 10,000 Arkansas National Guardsmen to keep beyond Faubus's control. One year later, in 1958, the Court was forced to reaffirm its authority in *Cooper v. Aaron*. The Court ruling highlighted the fact that the U.S. Supreme Court, not a state governor, served as the ultimate interpreter of the law. The governor of Arkansas had no authority to supersede a ruling that had been issued by the Court. The ruling further noted that violence or threats of violence could not be used as an excuse for denying black children their constitutional rights or to delay integration.

In *Griffin v. School Board of Prince Edward County, Virginia* (1964), the Court ruled that the Prince Edward County school district could not close its public school in an effort to prevent integration. The Court said that if the county closed its public schools, it would deny the black students the right to equal protection under the law. In *Green v. New Kent County Board of Education* (1968), the Supreme Court issued a ruling on the use by New Kent County, Virginia, schools of a freedom-of-choice plan to help promote integration. The Court found that the use of freedom-of-choice plans, as an integration technique, was not adequate to desegregate schools. In New Kent County after three years of operating under the freedom-of-choice plans no white students had attended a school that was previously black, and over 85 percent of the black students still attended the schools previously reserved for black students. Many of the black students were violently threatened and warned not to try to gain entrance into the all-white school.

In 1964 the court also struck down a statute that gave grants for tuition for white students to attend private schools. In the 1973 decision of *Keyes v. School District of Denver*, the Court expanded *Brown* to include de facto segregated public schools. In *Milliken v. Bradley* (1974), the Court ruled that schools were local for the purpose of *Brown*, and further decreed that the liberal judicial test of evidence usually granted in cases involving racial discrimination could not be evoked because suburban schools were involved. The test of evidence, strict scrutiny, required the defendant school district to carry the burden of proof of nonracial discrimination and not the plaintiff.

In the fall of 1970, the issue of busing as an integration tool took center stage as the Supreme Court heard a case concerning busing in North Carolina. The case arose over the constitutionality of a North Carolina statute, which had prohibited busing or the assigning of children to schools to achieve racial balance. A district court judge had asked the Charlotte–Mecklenburg County Board of Education three

"Education of the Negroes" (1899)

This New York Times *article by P. Butler Thomkins emphasized the importance of education and middle-class values in rescuing blacks from poverty in Mississippi at the turn of the century.*

Several years ago a young colored woman from Atlanta, a graduate of Spelman Seminary, went to teach school in a district where almost the entire population was black, and the story of the wonderful things which she accomplished was told last night at the Fifth Avenue Baptist Church by Mrs. William Scott, a lecturer for the American Baptist Home Missionary Society, who is also colored.

"The people were very poor," she said. "They live in wretched shanties, with not enough clothes to cover their nakedness. A man earned only $6 a month on the plantations, while those who rented land and worked it were sunk in debt. Their crops and their mules and even their shanties were mortgaged, and they paid 33 per cent interest."

The school that this poor girl went to teach was held in a log cabin, the floor was mud, and there wasn't a blackboard or a map or chart in it. Lots of the children walked eight miles to school, and they had no books or slates. The teacher had to hang a slate up for a blackboard.

After a while she called the people together and told them to take no more store orders for their pay. They obeyed, and within a year or two they were out of debt. Then the teacher called them again. "I'm going to have a tony society, like the while folks," she said. "It will be called the 'Hog Society,' and nobody can belong who doesn't own a hog."

There was great hustling among those negroes to get hogs. After a little they all had hogs, but the teacher gave most honor to the negroes who had the most hogs, and in this way she filled her people with ambition. To-day almost every negro family in that locality owns a three-room house and from twenty to sixty acres of land. They have a good school, and the community could not be recognized for what it once was.

The speaker drew a pitiable picture of the poverty of the Southern negroes in many districts, and told of the intense longing they had for education and religion. She quoted public officials of the South to the effect that it was the schools and missionaries alone which had kept the negroes patient, and had saved the country from a negro uprising.

Some men, she said, complained because so much had been spent and so little done in thirty-four years.

"Why?" she exclaimed. "What is thirty-four years in the development of a race? It is scarcely a beginning. It takes twenty-five years to bring up and educate a white man, and fifty years to being him to his best, and why should the negro be expected to do, in thirty-four years what it has taken the Anglo-Saxon people 1,000 years to accomplish?"

Mrs. Scott closed with an appeal to the Baptists to continue their work of education, declaring that there were no truer nor more loyal American citizens than properly educated negroes. (Education of the Negroes 1899)

times for a plan to achieve a comprehensive, integrated school system. After the third request, the judge developed a plan that included busing as a means to integrate the public school. The school board appealed to the Supreme Court. The Court upheld the ruling of the lower judge. This upset the fighters of integration.

Many white American citizens responded to the busing efforts in outrage. In South Carolina, a mob overturned two buses after first surrounding, screaming at, spitting at, and stoning its occupants. Also during the 1972 election year, Richard M. Nixon ran on an antibusing platform. He outlined a plan to eliminate the use of busing as a tool in the desegregation of school districts. He also asked the Congress to stop the ordering of new school buses until June 1973.

In 1972, Congress joined the president by providing funds to local schools districts through the Educational Amendments of 1972, which barred the use of federal funds for desegregation-related transportation; and the Equal Education Opportunity Act of 1974, which required the courts to exhaust all available means before approving busing to effect school desegregation. In 1980, Congress passed a bill that limited the Justice Department's authority to seek busing remedies through the courts, but the bill was vetoed by President Jimmy Carter.

Efforts to use busing as a tool for integration was not the only method that was applied. The Civil Rights Act of 1964 was another tool that played a very important part in the desegregation of public schools. The Act made the ending of segregated public education a statutory goal. Title II of the Act allowed lawyers seeking desegregation orders to skip the state courts and go directly to the federal courts. It also authorized the U.S. Department of Justice to bring desegregation lawsuits on its own initiative. This relieved black parents from some of the burden they had been forced to assume in previous years.

Title IV required the U.S. Commissioner of Education to conduct a survey of public education at all levels to determine the extent to which equal opportunity in education is denied to U.S. citizens because of race, color, religion, or national origin. Title VI provided for the termination of federal funds from any state or local program administered in a discriminatory manner. The Title states "that no person in the United States shall, on the grounds of race, color, or national origin, be excluded from participating in, or denied the benefits of, or be subjected to discrimination in any program or activity receiving Federal financial assistance." Federal agencies were directed to put the provision into effect—if necessary by discontinuing Federal assistance. Title VI of the Act provided the federal government with a powerful weapon by approving the withholding of tax money from school districts that persisted in disobeying the law.

Funds totaling some $867 million due to Southern and border state schools were threatened to be withheld. Few of these school districts would have been able to function without these funds. During the 1964–1965 school year, the proportion of black students who attended biracial classes was 10.9 percent. In 1965, the first year that Title VI became effective, the proportion rose to 15.9 percent. During the 1966–1967 school year, 24.4 percent of black children in the South as a whole were in desegregated schools. In border states, the percentage was 67.8 percent. In the Deep South, it was 16.9 percent.

Although these efforts made a major impact, segregation still existed. In the 1966–1967 school year, 65 percent of all first grade black students were in schools that were 90 percent or more black. Approximately 80 percent of white first graders were in schools that were 90 percent or more white.

The integration of public schools led to the demotion and displacement of many black educators. In the states of Texas, Arkansas, Kentucky, and West Virginia, between 55 and 60 percent of black principals were displaced. North Carolina, Virginia, Maryland, Georgia, and South Carolina experienced a smaller reduction, the proportion ranging between 35 and 37 percent. The reduction in black principals in Alabama, Mississippi, Louisiana, Oklahoma, Delaware, Florida, and Tennessee ranged from 40 to 45 percent. Approximately 5,000 teachers in 17 states were displaced. Many of the black teachers and administrators who maintained employment were placed in new positions without regard to their expertise, certification, or the personnel needs. They also faced discrimination in hiring, promotions, and retention polices. Several teachers filed lawsuits against the school district. In *Singleton v. Jackson Municipal Separate School Districts* (1970), the Fifth Circuit Court of Appeals rendered a decision forcing school boards to develop standards to ensure that all staff members be assessed according to competence rather than race. The court held that in the event of a personnel reduction, the more competent employee would be retained and no new personnel would be hired.

Barbara A. Patrick

See also

Affirmative Action; College Admission, Discrimination in; Educational Achievement Gap; Hypersegregation; *Savage Inequalities*

Further Reading:

Aldridge, Delores. "Litigation and Education of Blacks: A Look at the U.S. Supreme Court." *Journal of Black Studies* 8 (1978): 96–112.

Black, Merle, and John Shelton Reed. "Blacks and Southerners: A Research Note." *Journal of Politics* 44 (1982): 165–71.

Crain, Robert. "School Integration and Occupational Achievement of Negroes." *American Journal of Sociology* 75 (1970): 593–606.

Determan, Dean, and Gilbert Ware. "New Dimensions in Education: Title VI of the Civil Rights Act of 1964." *Journal of Negro Education* 35 (1966): 5–10.

"Education of the Negroes." *New York Times*, July 5, 1899.

Harris, John. "Education, Society, and the Brown Decision: Historical Principles Versus Legal Mandates." *Journal of Black Studies* 13 (1982): 141–54.

Morsell, John. "Racial Desegregation and Integration in Public Education." *Journal of Negro Education* 38 (1969): 276–84.

Reed, Rodney. "School Boards, the Community and School Desegregation." *Journal of Black Studies* 13 (1982): 189–206.
So, Alvin. "The Black Schools." *Journal of Black Studies* 22 (1992): 523–31.

Educational Achievement Gap

After the passage of *Brown v. Board of Education* in 1954, where the Supreme Court ruled that school segregation was inherently unequal and ordered the integration of schools, the educational achievement gap between blacks and whites became a dominant concern in U.S. society. Beginning in the 1960s, the federal government launched many programs and initiatives designed to narrow the black-white achievement gap. These federal initiatives included the Head Start Program, affirmative action, the desegregation of schools, and federal funding for poor families. Nevertheless, a significant gap still remains between black and white students, and a number of theories have been created to explain this educational achievement gap. The gap is significant because it points to structural and institutional inequalities in American society that have led to blacks having less educational opportunities than whites, indicating that the educational achievement gap will only be closed when corresponding institutional changes are made.

Many scholars, however, have attempted to look beyond institutional inequalities to explain the black-white educational achievement gap. One of the earliest of such theories, dominant in the early 20th century, concerns biological differences in intelligence. This theory argues that a difference in IQ among blacks and whites is responsible for unequal educational outcomes. In other words, this theory holds that blacks are biologically inferior to whites in terms of their brain development, which means they are less intelligent and thus less likely to succeed academically. While social scientists attacked this theory for its validity in the 1970s, it nevertheless reemerged in the 1990s. It was during this time that Richard Herrnstein and Charles Murray, authors of the 1994 book *The Bell Curve: Intelligence and Class Structure in American Life*, became leading proponents of biological determinism, arguing that racial differences in intelligence are genetic. This argument, however, has been heatedly debated, and numerous scholars have debunked the link between genetics and intelligence scores. It is generally accepted today that race is a determining factor neither in IQ levels nor academic achievement.

A second theory to explain the gap emerged in the 1960s when many claimed that blacks' failings could be explained by a culture of poverty, where academic achievement and hard work were frowned upon in favor of negative attitudes that constrained academic success. In the 1970s, anthropologist John Ogbu argued that the achievement gap was due to what he called a "culture of oppression" that existed among black students. According to Ogbu, after years of discrimination, exploitation, and segregation, blacks hold a deep-seated mistrust of the system. This in turn leads them to oppose the norms of mainstream society, which often inhibits educational mobility. Like biological determinism, this theory has been hotly debated and largely rejected, specifically because it blames the individual while ignoring structural inequalities that exist between blacks and whites.

A third theory aimed at explaining the black-white achievement gap concerns the influence of the family. In politician and sociologist Daniel Patrick Moynihan's 1965 report on the black family, he argues that the breakdown of the black family and the increasing number of single mothers caused poverty among black communities, which negatively affected the educational achievement of black students. While the Moynihan report stirred up much controversy as many on the left felt that Moynihan was vilifying the black family, one year later, the Coleman Report argued that family background was more important for academic achievement than the school one attends. Consequent research since the 1960s has also linked family background to educational achievement, as those from poorer backgrounds are more likely to have lower achievement scores than students from families with higher incomes. Since minority children are more likely to come from lower income families, the educational gap still persists.

While it is generally accepted that family background is one of the main factors explaining the achievement gap, sociologist James Samuel Coleman found in the late 1990s that the achievement of minority students was more dependent on the school they attended than it was for their white counterparts. Although the courts mandated school racial desegregation in 1954, desegregation was not swift, and many schools remained racially and economically segregated. While segregated minority schools can be successful, they are also more likely to be underfunded; therefore, there are less educational opportunities available at such schools than at white or integrated schools. Statistics show that students in racially isolated schools are more likely to experience higher teacher turnover, attend schools with more concentrated poverty, and experience other educational disadvantages compared to white students or students in integrated environments. Due to these institutional disadvantages, the test scores of students in segregated schools often lag behind those of students in schools with more economic resources.

The organization of the school has also been found to contribute to the black-white achievement gap. In the 1960s, American schools initiated a tracking system where students are placed in tracks depending on their academic abilities. It has been shown that black and minority students are often placed in nonacademic tracks, thereby limiting their opportunities to excel academically. Thus, track placement can be seen as an institutional factor contributing to the black-white achievement gap. High-track students are exposed to knowledge and behaviors such as critical thinking and independence that prepare them for higher education, while low-track students, who are disproportionately poor and minority children, are taught skills and behaviors that prepare them for lower-level jobs, limiting their abilities to excel in school.

While there have been many theories explaining the black-white educational achievement gap, there is disagreement in the field about which theory best explains the gap. However, most scholars cite institutional and social factors like family background and the educational environment as the main causes of disparate test scores. Although the achievement gap between whites and blacks has been a major concern in American society, there is also a significant achievement gap between whites and Latino students. Ultimately, it can be said that there is an educational achievement gap between white and minority students in general. Structural inequalities based on race have led to this achievement gap: inequalities that are not limited exclusively to black students.

Bobette Otto

See also

Education and African Americans

Further Reading:

Grissmer, David, Ann Flanagan, and Stephanie Williamson. "Why Did the Black-White Score Gap Narrow in the 1970s and 1980s?" In *The Black-White Test Score Gap*, edited by Christopher Jencks and Meredith Phillips, 182–226. Washington, DC: Brookings Institution Press, 1998.

Hallinan, Maureen T. "Sociological Perspectives on Black-White Inequalities in American Schooling." *Sociology of Education* 74 (2001): 50–70.

Hanushek, Eric A, John F. Kain, and Steven G. Rivkin. "New Evidence about *Brown v. Board of Education*: The Complex Effects of School Racial Composition on Achievement." *Journal of Labor Economics* 27 (2009): 349–83.

Kozol, Jonathan. *The Shame of the Nation: The Restoring of American Apartheid Schooling in America*. New York: Random House, 2005.

National Center for Education Statistics. "Achievement Gaps," http://nces.ed.gov/nationsreportcard/studies/gaps/.

Oakes, Jeannie. *Keeping Track: How Schools Structure Inequality*, 2nd ed. New Haven, CT: Yale University Press, [1985] 2005.

Orfield, Gary, Erica Frankenberg, and Lilliana M. Garces. "Statement of American Social Scientists of Research on School Desegregation to the U.S. Supreme Court in *Parents v. Seattle School District* and *Meredith v. Jefferson County*." *Urban Review* 40 (2008): 96–136.

Orfield, Gary, and Susan E. Eaton. *Dismantling Desegregation: The Quite Reversal of* Brown v. Board of Education. New York: New Press, 1996.

Orfield, Gary, and Lee Chungmei. "Why Segregation Matters: Poverty and Educational Inequality." Cambridge, MA: Civil Rights Project, 2005.

http://civilrightsproject.ucla.edu/research/k-12-education/integration-and-diversity/why-segregation-matters-poverty-and-educational-inequality/orfield-why-segregation-matters-2005.pdf.

El Teatro Campesino

In 1965, El Teatro Campesino (The Farmworkers' Theater) paved the way for a radical theater movement that continues to flourish in the United States today. A central force in the development of the Chicano movement, El Teatro

A performance of El Teatro Campesino, 1966. El Teatro Campesino is a theatrical troupe founded in 1965 as the cultural arm of the United Farm Workers. The original actors were all farmworkers, and El Teatro Campesino enacted events inspired by the lives of their audience. (Wayne State University)

Campesino was formed by Luis Valdez, a former farmworker and later member of the noted San Francisco Mime Troupe. The Teatro Campesino repertory company was founded to address sociopolitical issues affecting the Chicano community through the performances pieces they created, and Valdez worked closely with union organizer César Chávez to raise awareness about the farmworkers' plight and to attract funding for *la causa* (the cause of the Chicano Movement). Its celebrated synthesis of forceful politics with excellent dramatic writing and staging contributed to its singular effectiveness as protest and performance in the dynamic decades of the 1960s and 1970s. The first Chicano art to receive international acclaim, Teatro Campesino added performance tours in Germany, France, Italy, and other countries in the early 1970s to its growing college campus and protest rally venues, gaining widespread exposure and spin-off *teatros* along the way.

Using an improvisational style that recaptures the style of the *commedia dell'arte* troupes, which entertained audiences throughout Europe from the 16th to the 18th centuries, El Teatro Campesino developed a critical form of political theater in its use of *actos* (acts) that used simple props, satire, and audience participation to raise the consciousness of the farmworkers in their struggle to unionize on the back of flatbed trucks. By 1967, the theater troupe began more formal work and took their political agenda beyond the farmworkers' movement. The troupe began addressing issues like the struggle of Chicano soldiers during the Vietnam War in the play *Dark Root of a Scream*. This play, written by Valdez, departed from the style of the *acto* and took the form of the *mito* (myths). Through the *mitos* Valdez and the theater company continued to evolve as artists, exploring their art through the perspective of descendants of the great race that was the Mayan civilization. Their myths and heritage became an integral part of their theater.

In 1971 the company moved its operations from Delano, California, where Valdez had started the troupe, to San Juan Bautista, California. Ten years later, in 1981, with funding from the run of Valdez's musical *Zoot Suit*, the company renovated an old produce packing warehouse at 705 4th Street into a cultural space that hosts musical artists, comedians, dance troupes, and theater artists from all over the world. For over 25 years Teatro Campesino has been staging an evolving series of plays during the Christmas season titled *The Miracle, Mystery, and Historical Cycle of San Juan Bautista*. Every year the company presents either *La Virgen del Tepeyac*, in the style of the classical miracle play, or *La Pastorela*, a traditional shepherd's play, at the Mission San Juan Bautista. El Teatro Campesino has won numerous awards including an Obie Award and several Los Angeles Drama Critics Awards. Three plays written for El Teatro Campesino by Valdez (*Zoot Suit*, *Bandido*, and *I Don't Have to Show You No Stinking Badges!*) appear in the anthology titled *Zoot Suit and Other Plays* (1992).

The members of El Teatro Campesino have developed their work in the spirit of an ensemble style in which contributing artists play numerous roles and assume various responsibilities for each production. One artist may act, write, direct, stage manage, or produce the plays in a variety of productions. Through ritual, music, theater, and art, the company has built a foundation of important Chicano cultural expression.

Christina Marin

See also

Chicano Movement; Migrant Workers

Further Reading:

Elam, Harry. *Taking It to the Streets: The Social Protest Theater of Luis Valdez and Amiri Baraka (Theater: Theory/Text/Performance)*. Ann Arbor: University of Michigan Press, 2001.

Gonzalez-Broyles, Yolanda. *El Teatro Campesino: Theater in the Chicano Movement*. Austin: University of Texas Press, 1994.

Huerta, Jorge A. *Chicano Theater: Themes and Forms*. Ypsilanti, MI: Bilingual Press, 1982.

Valdez, Luis. *Luis Valdez—Early Works: Actos, Bernabé and Pensamiento Serpentino*. Houston: Arte Público, 1990.

Election Riots of the 1880s and 1890s

The Election Riots of the 1880s and 1890s resulted from the attempts by conservative whites to wipe out all residual opposition to their political takeover during the period known as Redemption. These riots constituted the second wave of violence inflicted upon blacks since Reconstruction. Also during this period, lynching emerged as one of the most commonly used tactics among whites to maintain their social, economic, and political power over blacks.

Redemption is the name given to the white conservative takeover of the Republican Southern state government that had been established during Reconstruction. Prior to Redemption, Democrats in one last attempt to salvage their political power engaged in riots in Memphis, Tennessee (1866), and New Orleans, Louisiana (1866). But those riots had disastrous repercussions, as the federal government sent in federal troops to maintain law and order in the South. Redemption, however, was more successful, as conservative white Democrats seized back control of their states one by one. For blacks and their white supporters, this was a terrifying period. Blacks and whites were mercilessly threatened, beaten, shot, and murdered. Whites devised new and elaborate tactics with masks and nightly visits to frighten their opposition. They unlawfully purchased and stole votes through trickery. The first wave of riots occurred throughout the Southern states but were most severe in New Orleans, Louisiana (1866; 1868; 1874); Memphis, Tennessee (1866); Meridian, Mississippi (1870); Vicksburg, Mississippi (1874); and Yazoo City, Mississippi (1975). By 1877, all Southern states belonged once again to the wealthy landowners and merchants of the Democratic Party.

Although Southern Democrats dared not reinstate the institution of slavery, they created a system that was analogous to it. They passed Jim Crow laws that mandated segregated facilities, such as schools, hospitals, asylums, cemeteries, and public transportation. Throughout the South, signs marked

White Only or Black Only were visible on fountains, in parks, and at restaurants. Segregation legitimated racism as well as the social, political, and economic existence of blacks. It also gave license to the maltreatment of blacks in social situations and encounters. Blacks, particularly in the rural South, were forced to work within the sharecropping system. Sharecropping prevented blacks from owning land and enslaved them to an interminable cycle of debt to the white landowner and merchant. Crucial measures such as the Civil Rights Act of 1866, the Fourteenth Amendment, and black male suffrage, which was sanctioned during Reconstruction, were ignored and blatantly violated at every turn.

In the 1880s and the 1890s, opposition to white Democratic political power still loomed in some parts of the South. Election violence was not new to Americans. Riotous behavior was a common means of political protest during the colonial era. In the early 1800s, election melees occurred between whites and ethnic groups such as the Irish and Germans in cities like New York (1834); St. Louis, Missouri (1854); Louisville, Kentucky (1855); and Baltimore, Maryland (1856; 1857; 1858).

Election violence in the American South was equally common. Lynching and riots were widely employed to establish and maintain political control. The "heaviest period of lynching" occurred between 1889 and 1919. Although whites were also victims, lynching mostly claimed black lives. Lynching did not only involve hanging but included death by shooting or burning. Black victims were frequently tortured prior to the lynching. Castration, mutilation, and whippings were common. Lynching was carried out for a number of reasons, including real or imagined crimes such as assault, rape, and murder, and offenses such as challenging white supremacy. Other reasons included white racism and resentment over black success.

In 1882, Choctaw whites of Alabama lynched Jack Turner, who was a major political impediment to the Democrats. He had run "the Republican political machine that had marshaled black voters in election" (Gilje, 1996: 104). White Democrats targeted black Republicans in Yazoo City, Mississippi. In 1898, several hundred whites in Lake City, South Carolina, participated in the house burning and shooting death of Frazier Baker. Baker had been appointed as the postmaster as a result of his support to the Republicans. When his wife, holding a baby, and three children ran out of the burning house, the mob shot at them. They wounded the mother and children and killed the baby.

In 1886, Democrats in Washington County, Texas, attempted to "seize ballot boxes in a Republican precinct." Armed black men confronted the white men. One black man shot and killed a white man. The authorities arrested eight blacks. In an act typical to the increasingly popular vigilantism, a masked white mob abducted three of the blacks from the jail and lynched them. White Republicans pressed authorities to investigate, but not only did the sheriff refuse to look into the lynching, the U.S. attorney failed twice to secure convictions.

A riot also broke out in Phoenix, South Carolina, in 1898. When a white Republican candidate for Congress called "for black men to fill out an affidavit if they were not permitted to vote," violence quickly ensued (Hine et al., 2000: 318). Democrats and Republicans engaged in a shoot-out. Although no one was killed at the shoot-out, angry whites invaded the nearby rural community of Greenwood County, where they ordered those men they did not kill to bow down and salute them.

The Wilmington, North Carolina, riot of the same year decimated the prosperous black community of Brooklyn. The origins of the riot can be traced back to white Democrats who were conspiring to remove the remaining black Republicans who held political offices and seats on the city council in Wilmington. Whites found their cause when Alex Manly, the editor of a local black newspaper, published an anti-lynching article that claimed that white men were as guilty of assaulting black women as the black men they accused of assaults against white women. This affront gave whites an opportunity to subdue their political adversaries, as well as to damage the well-to-do black community of Brooklyn. White mobs destroyed Manly's press and attacked blacks. Although "black officials resigned in a vain attempt to prevent further violence," at least 11 blacks were murdered and 1,500 Brooklyn blacks left their homes, which were then seized by whites at low cost. Only one black politician remained—George H. White, a congressman who represented Wilmington and North Carolina's second district. White "served out the remainder of his term and then moved north" (Hine et al., 2000: 318).

The violence did not cease with the election riots of the 1880s and 1890s. As white vigilante organizations and mobs terrorized blacks, particularly in the rural South, blacks fled, some migrating to Africa, some (known as the Exodusters) going westward. Others moved to urban centers in the South and the North, where they unfortunately met with more racial violence. Major race riots broke out in New Orleans, Louisiana (1900); New York City (1900); Springfield, Ohio (1904); Atlanta, Georgia (1906); Brownsville, Texas (1906); and Springfield, Illinois (1908).

Unlike the politically oriented riots of the 1880s and 1890s, the early-20th-century disturbances were brought on by other issues. In the New Orleans riot, a white mob hunted down Robert Charles after he shot and killed two police officers who had beaten him. Charles then killed two more officers. Afterward, a mob beat and murdered several blacks and destroyed a school. Charles killed another two officers as well as three other whites and wounded 20 more before being shot down by the mob. Competition for housing was the cause of the New York City riot. After Richard Dixon, a black man, was lynched for killing a police officer, a white mob ravaged a nearby black section of town.

The Atlanta riot was instigated by three Atlanta newspapers: the *Constitution*, the *Journal*, and the *Georgian*, which ran articles accusing black men of assaulting white women. The riot in Brownsville, Texas, was controversial. Evidence at the scene of a shoot-out pointed to black troops who had been harassed by locals. Without a hearing or trial, 167 soldiers were dismissed from the Army, barred from all military and government positions, and denied pensions or benefits. In the Springfield riot, whites rioted after George Richardson was accused of raping a white woman. It was later found that the accusation was false.

Out of this mayhem, the National Association for the Advancement of Colored People (NAACP) was forged. The NAACP was instrumental in attacking white violence against blacks and their communities. However, any black response to white crime was a precarious undertaking. When Ida B. Wells-Barnett voiced her outrage over lynching, her press was destroyed, her life was threatened, and she was forced to flee from Memphis, Tennessee, to Chicago (also the scene of numerous riots and attacks against blacks). NAACP participants were not immune to white hostility. Nevertheless, the NAACP, along with multiple anti-lynching societies and associations, waged a formidable battle through the press and with speeches and requests (although futile) to the federal government for protection. But their press coverage of white violence effectively kindled national sympathy and strengthened the growing opposition to violence within the South.

Black self-defense was a common reaction to the riots and lynching. However, the results were usually disastrous for blacks. In 1914, a 17-year-old was lynched because her brother murdered a white man who had raped her. A woman and her unborn child were violently killed when she vowed to bring to justice the men who had killed her husband. Numerous black men lost their lives as they tried to defend their homes and families from ravenous whites.

Federal, state, and local authorities did little to put a stop to the violence that engulfed the nation. After Redemption, the North lost interest in the problems of the South; it was preoccupied with other issues and felt that the conflict that had split the nation was over. Many Republican politicians were either murdered or bullied out of the South (*see* Randolph, Benjamin). The definitive end of federal intervention occurred as a result of the Compromise of 1877, which was made to settle the contentious election of Republican Rutherford B. Hayes. The most crucial result of this compromise was the promise to end Reconstruction as well as federal involvement in the affairs of the South. Thus, it was no surprise that the federal government was not responsive during the riots of the elections of the 1880s and 1890s.

Help from within the South had been generally nonexistent since Reconstruction. The authorities and prominent leaders who had the power to challenge the white mobs and vigilante organizations that were at fault were immobilized by threats to their lives and families. Whites were not exempt from the violence.

The culture of the South between the 1880s and 1890s was steeped in violence. Violence against blacks was encouraged in newspapers, children's stories and songs, and in the prevailing attitude that blacks were inferior, inhuman, and prone to crime. Although the incidences of lynching dwindled after the 1930s, the riots continued, with whites inciting riots throughout World War II. White mobs attacked the activists of the civil rights movement of the 1950s and 1960s. In the mid-1960s, the pattern shifted but the old problems remained; racism and police brutality were the main reasons young blacks rioted within their own communities.

GLADYS L. KNIGHT

See also

Black Self-Defense; Race Riots in America; Reconstruction Era; Vigilantism. Documents: Report on the Memphis Riots of May 1866 (1866); Account of the Riots in East St. Louis, Illinois (1917); A Southern Black Woman's Letter Regarding the Recent Riots in Chicago and Washington (1919); The Cook County Coroner's Report Regarding the 1919 Chicago Race Riots (1920); The Final Report of the Grand Jury on the Tulsa Race Riot (June 25, 1921); Testimony from *Laney v. United States* (1923); The Governor's Commission Report on the Watts Riots (1965); Cyrus R. Vance's Report on the Riots in Detroit (1967); The Reports of the Oklahoma Commission to Study the Tulsa Race Riot of 1921 (2000–2001); Draft Report: 1898 Wilmington Race Riot Commission (2005)

Further Reading:

Brundage, W. Fitzhugh, ed. *Under the Sentence of Death: Lynching in the South.* Chapel Hill: University of North Carolina Press, 1997.

Gilje, Paul A. *Rioting in America.* Bloomington: Indiana University Press, 1996.

Hine, Darlene Clark, William C. Hine, and Stanley Harrold. "White Supremacy Triumphant: African Americans in the South in the Late Nineteenth Century." Chap. 14 in *The African American Odyssey.* Englewood Cliffs, NJ: Prentice Hall, 2000, 306–31.

Olsen, Otto, ed. *Reconstruction and Redemption in the South.* Baton Rouge: Louisiana State University Press, 1980.

Ellison, Ralph (1914–1994)

African American fiction writer and cultural critic Ralph Waldo Ellison was born March 1, 1914, to Lewis and Ida Ellison in Oklahoma City, Oklahoma. Named after American philosopher and activist Ralph Waldo Emerson, Ellison was encouraged by his parents to pursue his creative talents. After graduating in 1932, Ellison left Oklahoma to pursue a degree in music at Tuskegee University. Discouraged by the academic atmosphere against the arts, Ellison dropped out of Tuskegee and moved to New York City. In a chance meeting, Ellison met poet Langston Hughes, who then introduced Ellison to writer Richard Wright. Introduced to the literary world by Wright and Hughes, Ellison joined the Federal Writers Project and began to write fiction and essays dealing with race, blackness, and identity in American society.

Invisible Man, Ellison's first novel, was released in 1952. The fictitious account, told by an anonymous African American man, traced his journey of identity in the rural South and urban North. Throughout the novel, the question of race is raised. Ellison's description of Southern blackness in relation to whites was most intense in the first chapter of the novel. The protagonist, under the impression he was to deliver his high school graduation speech to the prominent white men in the community, was instead forced to fight the "Battle Royal" against other local black boys. Blindfolded, the boys exchanged vicious blows. Ellison criticizes the incivility of Southern whites' convictions about African American masculinity. The brawl displayed the supposed primitivism black males possessed. After the match, the narrator takes part in the crazed scramble for crumpled bills and gold coins on an electrically charged rug. Electrocuted, bruised, and delirious, the protagonist then delivered his graduation speech, being largely ignored by his white audience. The narrator's heavy citation of Booker T. Washington's 1895 Atlanta Exposition Address softened the impact of the speech. Washington, a strong advocate of industrial education, was highly favored in the Southern white community. When the narrator mistakenly recited "social equality" instead of "responsibility," however, the mob reacts violently and demands an explanation. In fear of his life, the narrator stammered through an apology of his mistake and completed his speech. The smallest utterance of any individualized thought was rejected, as Ellison described with the hostility towards the narrator's mistaken reciting of the phrase "social equality." After completing the speech, he is given a thunderous applause and received a scholarship to the state's black college and a briefcase. That night, he dreamt of seeing his late grandfather at the circus. Ironically, the grandfather only laughs at the inscription "To Whom It May Concern: Keep This Nigger Boy Running." Ellison's underlying criticism of the South's racially abrasive social structure was enforced by the grandfather's amusement at the message. The social obedience displayed by the narrator only allowed him to remain in good graces because of his inability to create an identity of his own.

Ellison's other works, including the collections of critical essays *Shadow and Act* and short stories *Fly Home and*

Other Stories, also explore race and society. Ellison died in New York City in 1994 at the age of 80.

REGINA BARNETT

See also

American Literature and Racism; Baldwin, James; Toomer, Jean

Further Reading:

Ellison, Ralph Waldo. *Invisible Man*. New York: Random House, 1952.

Ellison, Ralph Waldo. *Shadow and Act*. New York: Random House, 1964.

Eminent Domain

Eminent domain is defined as government or government agencies—such as airports or highway commissions—using their power to take away private property in the name of remaking it for public use. The practice of eminent domain has also been used to demolish or seize public housing. Often, eminent domain is enforced in conjunction with urban renewal projects. Eminent domain is significant because historically, it has had a disproportionately higher negative impact on racial minorities than on whites in the United States. There are many examples in the United States of the power of eminent domain being abused or employed unfairly.

Early in the history of the United States, the Founding Fathers expressed concern about the possibility of government seizing private property without reason or compensation. The Fifth Amendment to the constitution addressed this fear, stating, "[N]or shall private property be taken for public use, without just compensation." While eminent domain was strongly resisted early in U.S. history, over time its use increased. According to the Castle Coalition, an organization dedicated to fighting the unjust use of eminent domain, the term has expanded significantly since it was linked with the concept of blight removal in the mid-20th century. *Blight removal* refers to government efforts to remove properties that are threats to public health and safety. While this practice initially used eminent domain to overtake and remove sites that were a real threat to public safety, over time it has become significantly abused. Since the 1980s in particular, eminent domain in the name of blight removal has expanded beyond purely public use projects, as tax-hungry governments have been known to take over safe and functional working-class neighborhoods and give them to private developers who promise increased tax revenues. Thus, eminent domain today has become a real threat to middle- and working-class neighborhoods, especially to those that are primarily home to minority citizens.

An important recent case that broadened the use of eminent domain was *Kelo v. the City of New London* in 2005.

Ten Worst Cases of Eminent Domain

This list includes a few of the top 10 worst cases of eminent domain in the United States according to the Castle. For more information, see the full report: http://castlecoalition.org/pdf/top_10_abuses/top_10_report.pdf

- Removing an entire neighborhood and the condemnation of homes for a privately owned and operated office park and other, unspecified uses to complement a nearby Pfizer facility in New London, Connecticut
- Approving the condemnation of more than 1,700 buildings and the dislocation of more than 5,000 residents for private commercial and industrial development in Riviera Beach, Florida
- A government agency collecting a $56,500 bounty for condemning land in East St. Louis, Illinois, to give to a neighboring racetrack for parking
- Seizing the homes of elderly homeowners in Mississippi and forcing them and their extended families to move in order to transfer the land to Nissan for a new, privately owned car manufacturing plant, despite the fact that the land is not even needed for the project
- Condemning 83 homes for a new Chrysler plant in Toledo, Ohio, that was supposed to bring jobs but ended up employing less than half the projected number because it is fully automated
- Forcing two families (along with their neighbors) to move for a private mall expansion in Hurst, Texas, while spouses were dying of cancer

The case began in 1998 when the pharmaceutical company Pfizer built a plant next to Fort Trumbull, a neighborhood in New London, Connecticut. In an effort to encourage further redevelopment, the city of New London handed over its power of eminent domain to the New London Development Corporation (NLDC), allowing this private body to take the entire neighborhood of Fort Trumbull over for private development. The lead plaintiff in the case, Susette Kelo, sued the city of New London, arguing that the city had misused its eminent domain power. The case eventually went to the Supreme Court, which ruled against Kelo, thereby allowing private entities to use eminent domain to seize property for economic development. The Court ruled in favor of New London because city officials argued the plan would benefit the city through higher taxes and more jobs, thereby justifying their decision to take possession of the Fort Trumbull homes and property. The Court's decision allows cities to use their power of eminent domain to transfer private property to developers if they think the developers will generate more economic growth. Essentially, the *Kelo v. New London* case identified private redevelopment plans as an acceptable public use project, thereby expanding the possible use of eminent domain.

Eminent domain has historically had a significantly more negative impact on people of color than on whites. Though the Fifth Amendment was intended to protect all citizens, this has not occurred in eminent domain practice. Those who are most vulnerable in our society often find they have limited protections against this practice. For example, scholars cite the Federal Housing Act of 1949 as an illustration of eminent domain affecting black neighborhoods disproportionately more than white neighborhoods. This Housing Act was in force until 1973 and provided federal funding for slum clearance and urban renewal projects, allowing cities to use the power of eminent domain to clear blighted neighborhoods for higher public uses. In the 24 years the program was in effect, over 1 million people were displaced, two-thirds of them African Americans. Blacks were five times more likely to be displaced than whites under the Federal Housing Act. Scholars have noted that because blacks were often confined to ghetto neighborhoods, more than two-thirds of the renewal projects were directed at black neighborhoods. Research psychologist Mindy Fullilove has pointed out that black citizens displaced by eminent domain do not just lose their home and all that is associated with it, but also their community and neighborhood—a loss which can have a lasting negative psychological impact. It is clear from the Federal Housing Act of 1949 that eminent domain can be misused to affect black citizens in disproportionately higher numbers than whites.

A more recent example of eminent domain being abused has been the rebuilding efforts in New Orleans following the devastation wrought by Hurricane Katrina. The circumstances surrounding the planned demolition and rebuilding of Charity Hospital in New Orleans illustrates this eminent domain abuse. Charity Hospital is the only public hospital in New Orleans, and it sustained only minimal damage during the hurricane and subsequent flooding. However, despite the efforts of the community and volunteers, Charity Hospital is slated for destruction. The State of Louisiana and Louisiana State University have both fought for this reconstruction project, working to clear the area surrounding the hospital for a new medical complex. In order to make space for the new medical buildings, the state has used its power of eminent domain to condemn and take possession of the neighboring buildings whose owners initially refused to sell. Over the course of this process, the racially diverse, working-class neighborhood of Lower Mid-City in New Orleans has been virtually obliterated. Not only will neighborhoods be destroyed because of these actions, but low-income New Orleans citizens—many of them black—will lose a vital source of health care. The example of Charity Hospital in New Orleans signifies that eminent domain can be seen as a racialized practice, as it has frequently been used to displace and disenfranchise black communities.

Kathrin A. Parks

See also

Fair Housing Act of 1968; Fair Housing Amendments Act of 1988; Fair Housing Audit; Housing Covenants; Housing Discrimination

Further Reading:

"50 State Report Card: Tracking Eminent Domain Since Kelo." The Castle Coalition. http://castlecoalition.org/index.php?option=com_content&task=view&id=2412&Itemid=129.

Berliner, Dana. "Government Theft: The Top 10 Abuses of Eminent Domain, 1998–2002." The Castle Coalition. http://castlecoalition.org/pdf/top_10_abuses/top_10_report.pdf.

Brandes Gratz, Roberta. "Why Was New Orleans' Charity Hospital Allowed to Die?" *The Nation*, May 16, 2011. http://www.thenation.com/article/160241/why-was-new-orleanss-charity-hospital-allowed-die?page=0,0#.
"Eminent Domain." U.S. Department of Housing and Urban Development. http://portal.hud.gov/hudportal/HUD?src=/program_offices/public_indian_housing/centers/sac/eminent.
Fullilove, Mindy T. "Eminent Domain and African Americans: What Is the Price of the Commons?" *Perspectives on Eminent Domain Abuse*. Institute for Justice. http://www.castlecoalition.org/pdf/publications/Perspectives-Fullilove.pdf (February 2007).
"*Kelo v. New London*: Lawsuit Challenging Eminent Domain Abuse in New London, Connecticut." Institute for Justice. http://www.ij.org/kelo.
"*Kelo v. City of New London*: What It Means and the Need for Real Eminent Domain Reform." Institute of Justice. http://castlecoalition.org/pdf/Kelo-White_Paper.pdf (September 2005).

Emmett Till Murder

In the summer of 1955, while visiting Money, Mississippi, 14-year-old Chicago native Emmett Till breached Jim Crow etiquette and spoke to a white woman. His punishment was murder. This horrific event revealed that Jim Crow laws and white supremacy were alive and well in the South. With great courage, Emmett's mother, Mamie Till Mobley, turned her personal tragedy into a catalyst for the civil rights movement. Emmett Till's death alerted the nation of the thriving persecution of African Americans under Jim Crow laws.

The son of Mamie and Louis Till, Emmett was born on the south side of Chicago in 1941. Although Till struggled with a bout of polio at age five, leaving him with a slight stutter, he became a confident child known for his pranks and outgoing personality. In the summer of 1955, Till went to Mississippi to visit relatives and stay with his uncle, Mose Wright. As a Mississippi native, Mobley warned her son of the ways of the South before he boarded the train. While Till had been exposed to segregation in the North, he was unaware of how far white supremacists would go to preserve their Southern way of life.

During his stay in Money, Till and his cousin, Curtis Jones, visited Bryant's Grocery and Meat Market on a Wednesday evening. While Jones started a checkers game with an older man outside the store, Till went inside and bought some gum. As Till left the store he said "Bye, baby" to white cashier Carolyn Bryant, the store owner's wife. The man playing checkers with Jones told the boys they should leave before Bryant got her pistol. The scared boys left quickly in Wright's 1941 Ford, and Till begged Jones not to mention the market incident to his uncle. Days passed without incident until Carolyn's husband Roy returned to Money after being away on a trucking job.

Late that Saturday night, Roy Bryant, along with his brother-in-law J. W. Milam, drove to Wright's cabin. Bryant and Milam greeted 64-year-old Wright with a flashlight and a gun. Bryant wanted the boy who talked to his wife. Wright pleaded with the two men asking them not to take the boy. He told them Till was just 14 and from the North; he did not know how to treat white folks. Bryant and Milam pulled Till out of his bed at gunpoint, dragged him into their car, and drove off. The men threatened Wright's life if he mentioned anything of the incident.

The next morning, Curtis Jones called the sheriff to report Till missing. Three days later, a boy fishing in the Tallahatchie River discovered Till's body. His body was so disfigured by the beating that Mose Wright could identify his nephew only by the initialed ring he wore; it was his father's. Before being shot in the head, Till was brutally beaten. His forehead was shattered on one side, an eye was gouged out, and a 75-pound cotton-gin fan was tied around Till's neck with barbed wire. After finding the body, Jones called Till's mother in Chicago.

After the casket arrived in Chicago, the mortician told Mamie Till Mobley that he signed an order for the sheriff of Money that promised Till's casket would not be opened. Mobley opened the casket herself. After seeing her only child's body mutilated beyond recognition, Mobley wanted everyone to see what happened to her 14-year-old son in the Jim Crow South. On September 3, thousands of people came to the open casket ceremony at Rainer Funeral Home. A picture of Till's lynched corpse also appeared in *Jet*, a weekly black magazine, for the whole nation to see.

Less than two weeks after Till's burial, Bryant and Milam were tried for the murder of Emmett Till in Sumner, Mississippi. Although four African Americans, including Mose Wright, were brave enough to testify against Bryant and

Milam in the segregated courthouse, the all-male, all-white jury deliberated a little over an hour before returning with not-guilty verdicts for both defendants. That same year, Bryant and Milam sold their confessional story of killing Emmett Till to white journalist William Bradford Huie, for $4,000. Their story appeared in *Look* magazine on January 24, 1956.

Emily Hess

See also
Lynching

Further Reading:

Hudson-Weems, Clenora. *Emmett Till: The Sacrificial Lamb of the Civil Rights Movement.* Troy, MI: Bedford Publishers, 1994.

Till-Mobley, Mamie, with Christopher Benson. *Death of Innocence: The Story of the Hate Crime That Changed America.* New York: Random House, 2003.

Whitfield, Stephen J. *A Death in the Delta: The Story of Emmett Till.* Baltimore: Johns Hopkins University Press, 1991.

End of Racism, The

The End of Racism is a study of contemporary racial disparities authored by Dinesh D'Souza and published in 1995 by the Free Press. D'Souza argues that any persisting racial inequalities are a consequence of people of color having a bad culture and the failing of society to follow color-blind principles. If, collectively, people studied the facts—as D'Souza outlines them—then race would eventually lose its power as a primary factor in society.

D'Souza begins the book by detailing four afflictions of society: black rage, white backlash, liberal despair, and multiculturalism. Black rage is the negative attitudes and actions that blacks wage against whites and are a consequence of past discrimination and a perception that unfair discrimination continues. An example of black rage is riots or the targeting of white people in criminal activity, such as theft. White backlash derives from the feeling that white culture is under assault by minorities and is characterized by nativist actions. Such actions include creating white-only groups or intentional white residential segregation. Liberal despair is rooted in the idea that racism continues to be a threat to society with no hope of change. Liberal despair includes a focus on racism and a belief that racism continues to be a dominant threat to the stability and equality of the United States. Finally, multiculturalism proposes that the United States is fundamentally racist; thus proportional representation and cultural relativism are needed to rectify racial inequities. Multiculturalism includes actively fighting for affirmative action and related policies as they believe all groups are of equal value and therefore should be equally represented in society's institutions. All four of these afflictions are part of a greater "race problem" in the United States, but D'Souza argues that racism is no longer a central problem in society and these four afflictions would essentially fade away if people would stop harping about racism. The problem that D'Souza does identify is the "black problem," the "destructive and pathological cultural patterns of behavior" of blacks, which can be solved only through a "program of cultural reconstruction" (1995: 24). Thus, racism is not a problem, and any racial discrimination that exists is actually "rational discrimination" based on people avoiding blacks' bad behavior. Moreover, among other strongly worded claims, D'Souza argues that plantation slavery was not a racist institution, that blacks wouldn't necessarily be better off had they not been enslaved, and that most, if not all, advanced knowledge on math, science, and language are a legacy of whites and white culture only. D'Souza's policy suggestion is that society needs to be color blind and race should be erased from government intervention, including repealing the Civil Rights Act of 1964 and permitting private corporations to discriminate in hiring when they feel necessary. Throughout the book, D'Souza makes many references to Martin Luther King, Jr.'s "I Have a Dream" speech where he advocates for a race-neutral society where people are not judged by the color of their skin. By invoking King's words, D'Souza aligns himself with well-known racial equality principles and strategically argues for a color-blind society.

Though D'Souza puts forth a well-written and well-researched book, he has come under assault for his cultural arguments and for denouncing the existence of institutionalized racism. After the book was published, two notable conservatives, Robert Woodson and Glenn C. Loury, resigned from the American Enterprise Institute where D'Souza was a research fellow (White 1995). Jack White (1995) wrote an editorial piece in *Time* magazine calling for a boycott of the book for its fallacies and inability to cultivate an honest conversation about race. *The Economist* (2005) magazine said the book is an overt defense of bigotry and prejudice and suggested D'Souza's lack of compassion for others. Similarly, Ellis Cose in *Newsweek* (1995) also said that D'Souza defends bigotry and that D'Souza speaks less about the end of racism and much more about the need to end civil rights programs intended to address racism. As can be gathered from these reviews, *The End of Racism* instigated conversation but also faced significant opposition.

Many conservative organizations and individuals hailed *The End of Racism* as a legitimate, well-argued book on the necessity to fix black culture and move past race. At the same time, it was widely criticized and is today seen as an example of how color-blind principles can be manipulated to advocate for racist beliefs and polices without sounding racist. Dinesh D'Souza is now the author of 12 books and has written a book with an accompanying documentary on the failures of an America headed by President Obama.

Hephzibah Strmic-Pawl

See also

Color-Blind Racism; Cultural Racism; Laissez-Faire Racism; Racism; Symbolic Racism; Systemic Racism

Further Reading:

Cose, Ellis. "Blinded by Color." *Newsweek*, September 25, 1995.

D'Souza, Dinesh. *The End of Racism: Principles for a Multiracial Society*. New York: Free Press, 1995.

"The End of Racism." *The Economist*, October 14, 1995.

White, Jack. "The Bigot's Handbook: Opinion." *Time*, October 2, 1995.

English-Only Movement

Although English is the language of the U.S. Constitution, government, and laws, the United States, like Great Britain, does not have an official language. English is the principal, or common, language rather than the official language. The framers of the Constitution were silent on this issue, and the question of the national language probably never came up at the Federal Convention.

Despite the existence of controversies over language issues at the local and state levels in early periods, English-only as a national movement did not surface until the early 1980s (Crawford 1991). In 1981, the late U.S. Senator S. I. Hayakawa introduced a bill calling for an amendment to the Constitution to declare English the official language of the nation. The bill was defeated. In 1983, Hayakawa and John Tanton, a Michigan ophthalmologist, environmentalist, and population-control activist, cofounded an organization called U.S. English, the principal force of the English-only movement, as an offshoot of the Federation for American Immigration Reform (FAIR), a Washington-based lobbying group. U.S English later outgrew its parent organization, and it now claims 1.7 million members. The goals of the group are to pass legislation at the national, state, and local levels to declare English the official language, to eliminate or reduce bilingual education, to abolish multilingual ballots, and to prevent translation of road signs and government documents into other languages. The growing use of the Spanish language by newcomers is of particular concern to U.S. English.

Largely as a result of the pushes of the group U.S. English and its allies, 27 states have designated English the official language of their states either constitutionally or by law, including Louisiana (1811), Nebraska (1920), Illinois (1969), Massachusetts (1975), Hawaii (1978), Virginia (1981 and 1996), Indiana (1984), Kentucky (1984), Tennessee (1984), California (1986), Georgia (1986), Arkansas (1987), Mississippi (1987), North Carolina (1987), North Dakota (1987), South Carolina (1987), Colorado (1988), Florida (1988), Alabama (1990), Montana (1995), New Hampshire (1995), South Dakota (1995), Wyoming (1996), Alaska (1998), Missouri (1998), Utah (2000), and Iowa (2002). Hawaii recognizes both English and native Hawaiian as the official languages. The effects of these laws are more symbolic than substantive. Bilingual education programs have remained intact in many states where official English-language legislation has been enacted.

Most new immigrants acknowledge the necessity for them to learn English as quickly as possible. The preeminence of English is not in danger. Second, such legislation has negative effects, including depriving Americans with limited English the ability of their essential rights to vote and of free speech, encouraging cutbacks in services for non-English–speaking newcomers, reducing resources for programs such as bilingual education, and destroying cultural heritage. Finally, English-only legislation is divisive and may stimulate

Senator Hayakawa arguing why English should be made the U.S. official language. (Bettmann/Corbis)

xenophobia and anti-immigrant sentiment and create a racially divided nation. It should be noted that English-plus, which champions the acquisition of strong English language proficiency plus the mastery of other languages, is the countermovement to English-only.

PHILIP YANG

See also

Alexander v. Sandoval (2001); Bilingual Education; Cultural Racism; Nativism and the Anti-immigrant Movements; White Nationalism; Xenophobia. Document: Proposition 227 (1998)

Further Reading:

Crawford, James. *Bilingual Education: History, Politics, Theory, and Practice*, 2nd ed. Los Angeles: Bilingual Education Services, 1991.

U.S. English. "Making English the Official Language." http://www.us-english.org.

Environmental Racism

Environmental racism refers to the deliberate placement of toxic and hazardous waste sites, incinerators, landfills, and polluting industries in communities populated mainly by minorities, including Latinos, African Americans, Asians, migrant farm workers, and the working poor. It also includes "any government, institutional, or industry action, or failure to act, that has a negative environmental impact which disproportionately harms—whether intentionally or unintentionally—individuals, groups, or communities based on race or color." As a consequence of these actions, the inhabitants in minority neighborhoods suffer from many health problems, including shorter life spans, higher rates of infant and adult mortality, cancer, and asthma. Communities populated predominantly by minority residents tend to have more commercial waste sites than do predominantly white communities. Fifty percent of the country's African American population and 60 percent of Latinos live in a community where levels of two or more toxins exceed government standards. Half of Asian/Pacific Islander Americans and American Indians live in areas with uncontrolled toxic waste sites. Areas with working incinerators hold 89 percent more minorities than the national average.

In 1987, the United Church of Christ Commission for Racial Justice conducted a study (*Toxic Wastes and Race in the United States*) on environmental racism and how it affects those in its polluted environments. The study found that (1) race was the most outstanding factor in the location of hazardous waste sites; (2) communities with a majority of minority residents housed the highest number of commercial hazardous facilities; (3) communities with one commercial hazardous waste facility had twice the national average minority population than those communities without said facilities; and (4) even though socioeconomic status played an important role in the location of these sites, the most outstanding factor was race, even after accounting for urban and regional differences.

Severe environmental racism is found in Emelle, Alabama, a poor, predominantly African American community. The community houses the largest hazardous waste landfill in the United States, receiving toxic materials from more than 40 states and many foreign countries. Another community victimized by environmental racism is the south side of Tucson, Arizona, where Hispanics are the majority of the population. An industrial toxic waste site there has caused high levels of cancers, birth defects, and genetic mutations among the residents. Also, Native Americans have often been approached by waste disposal companies in the hopes that they would allow dumping on their reservations in return for promises of improved economic conditions.

Why is environmental racism happening? There are several reasons. One reason is simply institutional racism; minorities pay a great price in terms of their health and overall quality of life in exchange for economic development, resources extraction, and industrialism. A second reason is for business purposes and profit. The industries that are polluting areas are attracted to poor neighborhoods because of the low land values and overall business costs associated with development in minority areas. Minority communities return the highest profits because of the low costs of development. Also, these areas are developed because of the low rate of opposition. Communities with higher incomes are more successful in controlling and staving off pollutant industries. A third and very important reason is the lack of power the residents of these neighborhoods have. These people lack information that should be given to them for informed consent, and they lack the political power necessary for fighting back against these polluting industries and companies.

How have minority communities fought environmental racism? Community activists have used strategies of the civil rights and antiwar movements of the 1960s and 1970s. The movement's goal is to fix the negative actions of the past and promote fairness in environmental decisions on a local, national, and international level. Many people have taken to protesting, marching, civil disobedience, and legal action. Community activists have tried to inform their residents on the issue with pamphlets, newsletters, classes, and other means in hopes of educating them so that they can help to fight environmental racism. They have begun using voter blocs as a way of forming the necessary clout to promote change. There is strength in numbers, and using these means will achieve the movement's specific goals.

TIFFANY VÉLEZ

See also

Academic Racism; Anti-racism; Biological Racism; Color-Blind Racism; Cultural Racism; Ideological Racism; Institutional Racism; Internalized Racism; Modern Racism; Racism

Further Reading:

Commission for Racial Justice, United Church of Christ. "Toxic Wastes and Race in the United States: A National Report on the Racial and Socio-Economic Characteristics of Communities with Hazardous Waste Sites." Public Data Access Inc. 1987.

Haltfield, Heather. *Toxic Communities: Environmental Racism.* 2003. http://cbcfhealth. org/content/contentID/1107.

Robinson, Deborah M. *Environmental Racism: Old Wine in a New Bottle.* 2000. http:// www.wcc-coe.org/wcc/what/jpc/echoes/echoes-17-02.html.

Weintraub, Irwin. *Fighting Environmental Racism: A Selected Annotated Bibliography.* http://egj.lib.uidaho.edu/egj01/weint01.html.

Wigley, Daniel C., and Kristin S. Shrader-Frechette. *Environmental Racism and Biased Methods of Risk Assessment.* http://www.piercelaw.edu/risk/vol7/winter/wigley.htm.

Equal Rights League

The Equal Rights League, also known as the National Equal Rights League (NERL), was an organization founded in 1908 by William Monroe Trotter to eliminate racial discrimination and segregation. It also engaged in the struggle against racial violence and advanced radical attitudes toward black self-defense. The Equal Rights League is often overshadowed by the more prominent National Association for the Advancement of Colored People (NAACP). Nonetheless, it made critical contributions for blacks during a very troubled period in American history by laying the groundwork for the imminent civil rights movement and was also, ironically, a harbinger for black militancy.

While many immigrant groups, white women, and the poor working class benefited from the reforms of the Progressive era of the 19th century, black life steadily worsened. Discriminatory Jim Crow laws (legalized segregation) stifled black progress, and rampant violence was at its peak. Leading the way for the black cause were the blacks themselves. Booker T. Washington, a prominent proponent of accommodationism, was at the forefront. W.E.B. Du Bois and William Monroe Trotter emerged as opponents to Washington's philosophy. They boldly called for integration and equal rights for blacks and spoke daringly against antiblack violence. In 1901, Trotter carried his arguments over into the *Boston Guardian*, a radical black newspaper. In 1905, Trotter and Du Bois organized the Niagara movement, which later became the NAACP.

Trotter was averse to the fact that the NAACP was run by whites, and he thought they were too moderate. The black-led NERL, with its philosophy of direct action, was Trotter's answer to what he saw as the question of what was needed to ensure black progress. Although NERL was predominantly black, there was at least one white leader and a few white members throughout the organization's existence. However, NERL never did achieve the success of the NAACP, as it did not have the monetary backing that came from affluent whites. Neither did it attain as much influence or acquire a large nationwide membership, since Trotter's radical views often isolated him from other blacks and the very people he sought for assistance.

In 1913, Trotter and other delegates from NERL met with President Woodrow Wilson to discuss discrimination in the government. Trotter customarily sent letters to, and met with, U.S. presidents, as did the leaders of the NAACP. This was a popular approach among conservative activists, whose objective was to collaborate with U.S. officials who had the power to affect legislation. Martin Luther King, Jr. and others would do the same in the 1960s. In 1914, the NERL delegates met again with Wilson. This meeting was disastrous for Trotter. He angered Wilson when he asserted the president's obligation to eliminate discrimination in the government.

In 1915, Trotter and various NERL members were among the more than 1,000 people who protested the showing of D.W. Griffith's *The Birth of a Nation*. This was a racist propaganda film that depicted blacks atrociously and glorified the Ku Klux Klan, a horrific organization that terrified and murdered blacks. There was a march, and everyone joined in the singing of "Nearer, My God, to Thee." (Several decades later, King would also lead several marches. The song of protest was "We Shall Overcome.") The group marched to the State House in Boston, Massachusetts. Gov. David Walsh agreed to enforce a 1910 censorship law and to prosecute the management of the Tremont Theatre, and requested that Trotter relay his message to the crowd. However, the movie, with various scenes censored, was still allowed in the theater. In 1920, Trotter was among the black leaders who spoke to Mayor Andrew Peters at City Hall in opposition of the return of the Griffith film to Boston. This time, the film was banned.

In 1917, the United States entered World War I. On the home front, newspapers reported rumors of black agitation and possible rebellion. NERL acknowledged how blacks were "bitter over discrimination" but stated, "We have no thought of taking up arms against our country. Ours has been to save the government from rebellion," and promised to "fight harder in war if they could expect better treatment in peace" (Fox 1970: 215). In 1919, President Wilson banned Trotter and other NERL delegates from taking a trip to France for the purpose of including racial equality in the peace treaty at Versailles.

Under the guise of a ship's cook, Trotter traveled to France anyway. He sent letters pleading with the principal negotiators to consider NERL's petition to end the "caste distinctions, proscriptions, and mob murder" against blacks (Fox 1970: 228). Trotter took advantage of every opportunity to expose the daily atrocities blacks experienced in the United States. The French were astonished, sympathetic, and receptive, but NERL's petition was not admitted into the peace treaty. Although the United States fought for peace abroad, it did nothing to stop the war against blacks at home and ignored the protests of its people.

Back in United States, Trotter was stunned and yet "grimly delighted" to hear that blacks were fighting back during the riots of the Red Summer of 1919 (Fox 1970: 232). He had warned in previous years that if the United States did not eradicate discrimination and put a stop to the senseless violence and lynching, blacks would eventually take matters into their own hands. Whites accused Trotter of inciting black violence. His views further ostracized him from his conservative black counterparts and made collaborative activism with NAACP troublesome.

Trotter and NERL's work did not stop there. Although they helped win pardons for black soldiers involved in the rioting in Houston, Texas, they failed to bring about the passing of the Dyer bill to illegalize lynching and the Madden bill to eliminate segregation on interstate railroad cars. The presidents of this era were not receptive to black issues, and NERL's radicalism was distasteful to many. Nevertheless, NERL made valiant and substantial efforts to challenge the pandemic violence and discrimination against blacks in the United States.

Gladys L. Knight

See also
Dyer, Leonidas C.; Jim Crow Laws; Trotter, William Monroe

Further Reading:

Fox, Stephen R. *The Guardian of Boston: William Monroe Trotter.* New York: Atheneum, 1970.

Ethnic Enclaves

An ethnic enclave is a social, economic, and cultural subsociety controlled by the ethnic group itself. It is a geographical area inhabited largely by members of the ethnic group that encompasses sufficient economic enterprises and social institutions to allow the group to function as a self-contained entity, largely independent of surrounding communities. Among the most famous ethnic enclaves are Cuban communities in Miami and Chinese communities in New York and San Francisco. Unlike a segregated, impoverished ghetto

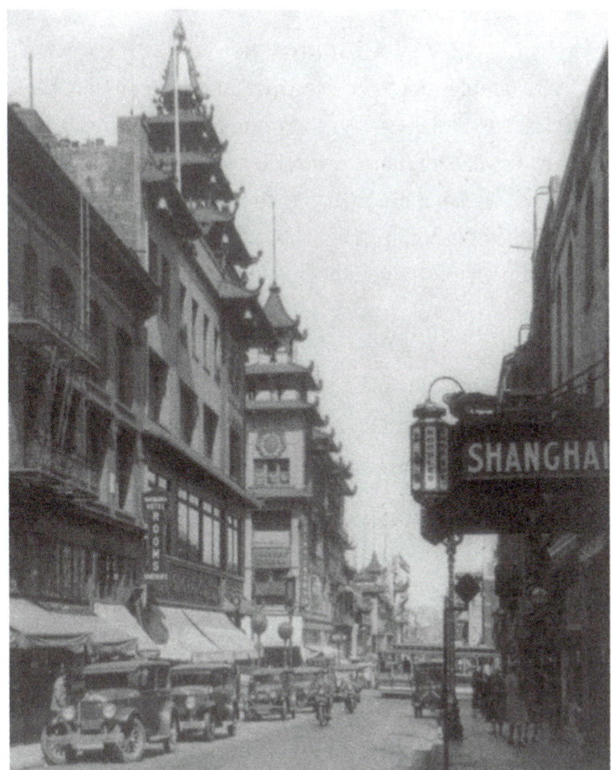

Cars line the streets in San Francisco's Chinatown, ca. 1929. (Library of Congress)

where members of outside groups typically control the local economy, the economy of the enclave is controlled by its members and profits are reinvested to the local economy, which leads to the economic success of the ethnic enclave. The enclave economy theory was developed by Alejandro Portes and his associates.

In an immigrant context, ethnic enclaves provide an avenue for upward economic mobility to immigrants who are disadvantaged in the labor market of the larger society by promoting positive returns on their human capital that may not otherwise be effectively used outside the enclave economy due to limitations imposed by the host society. Furthermore, ethnic enclaves often function as a cultural buffer for immigrants and protect them from language barriers and prejudice.

Ethnic enclaves are even more useful in aiding immigrants who have moved near their families. This tendency underscores the importance of relationships and networks provided by the enclaves. Likewise, immigrants who might wish to venture into business for themselves tend to thrive

Chinatowns

Clear examples of ethnic enclaves can still be observed in the various East Asian neighborhoods, such as the "Chinatown" areas of major urban centers across the United States like San Francisco, Boston, and Manhattan. In these neighborhoods, a network of businesses owned by members of the same ethnic community mutually support each other, allowing for the continuation of both the business subcommunity and also the ethnic community that the business owners represent. In areas like Vancouver's Koreatown, one can experience a cuisine and retail businesses unique to the Korean culture in a neighborhood markedly different from the rest of the city.

when they locate their business in regions where they have strong ties to an ethnic community. They can use networks of cooperation and mutual aid for advice, credit, and other forms of assistance. Thus, ethnic enclaves provide platforms from which Cuban Americans and Chinese Americans, for instance, can pursue economic success independent of their degree of acculturation or English language ability. The fact that certain immigrant groups that were less acculturated succeeded faster economically contradicts the prediction by the classic assimilation theory. This anomalous pattern of economic upward mobility has led to the development of an alternative theory called segmented assimilation proposed by Alejandro Portes and Min Zhou (*see* Segmented Assimilation).

The effectiveness of the ethnic enclave as a pathway toward successful economic adaptation has long been recognized by various scholars. However, ethnic enclaves cannot be a panacea for all immigrant groups, as they thrive only under certain conditions. An enclave requires a combination of business/financial expertise, reliable sources of capital, and a disciplined labor force willing to work for low wages in exchange for on-the-job training, future assistance and loans, or other delayed benefits such as rotating credit among coethnic members. In addition to this reciprocal relationship between employers and employees, bounded solidarity or social networks provided by the ethnic group is a key component of the ethnic enclave economy. Ties to the community create trust among the members that enhances market operations in the enclave that would be challenging in the economic market of the larger society. The tightness of the community can also serve as an enforcement mechanism with its ability to sanction those who violate the close bonds and trust among coethnic members. There exists a debate, however, as to whether enclaves are ultimately a positive or negative feature of ethnic communities. On the one hand, business owners can benefit from the built-in clientele that comes with ethnic solidarity. On the other hand, the same solidarity may generate expectations of special treatment by coethnics.

The ethnic enclave economy is related to but distinct from ethnic economies and middleman minorities. The ethnic enclave economy is a specific form of the ethnic economy: "the enclave economy concept should not be confused with the ethnic economy concept because the two are analytically distinguishable" (Zhou, 2011: 4). Ethnic economies per se do not need spatial concentration of ethnic firms, nor the servicing of their own ethnic groups. Neither do they necessitate that coethnics are buyers of their goods and services or suppliers to their firms. This is because the ethnic economy is comprised of the ethnic self-employed, their ethnic employees, unpaid family helpers, and ethnic employers. Those not working in the ethnic economy work

Cuban Exiles

The concept of ethnic enclaves developed out of studies of the Cuban exiles that arrived in Miami in the 1960s and 1970s. The immigrants assembled in neighborhoods that allowed for easy community interaction, which in turn led to businesses concentrated in a particular area. The network created by this community streamlined acquisition of knowledge about the U.S. economy and a supportive business training ground. Cubans who worked in banks would often arrange for "character loans," based on personal knowledge and reputation of a coethnic client, further increasing the opportunity to establish a foothold in the new markets. The network eventually expanded beyond the ethnic neighborhoods and found success in the general market as well. The benefits of this economic enclave manifested only for those immigrants who came in the early waves before the 1980 exodus.

in the general labor market. Ethnic economies need not possess an ethnic milieu within the firm. They are the context of ethnic entrepreneurs even if they employ nonethnic workers. In Portes's schema, ethnic enclave economies are firms that are clustered and whose owners and employees are coethnics. Middleman minorities typically serve ethnic groups different from their own; they do not serve coethnic customers. They still fall, however, under the umbrella of the ethnic economy because they are "ethnic-owned business firms, and they usually employ coethnics as workers (Light and Bonacich, 1988: xii). The enclave economy, thus, is a special case of ethnic economies. It exists in the context of coethnicity and a particular location. Economic activities that take place within them are ruled by bounded solidarity and enforceable trust.

Kazuko Suzuki

See also

Ethnicity; Ethnogenesis

Further Reading:

Kim, Sophia. "Is Living in an Ethnic Enclave Really So Bad?" *Canadian Immigrant.* April 11, 2012. http://canadianimmigrant.ca/community/is-living-in-an-ethnic-enclave-really-so-bad/.

Light, Ivan, and Edna Bonacich. *Immigrant Entrepreneurs: Koreans in Los Angeles 1965–1982.* Berkeley: University of California Press, 1988.

Portes, Alejandro, and Robert L. Bach. *Latin Journey: Cuban and Mexican Immigrants in the United States.* Berkeley: University of California Press, 1985.

Portes, Alejandro, and Lief Jansen. "The Enclave and the Entrants: Patterns of Ethnic Enterprise in Miami Before and After Mariel." *American Sociological Review* 54 (1989): 929–49.

Portes, Alejandro, and Robert Manning. "The Immigrant Enclave: Theory and Empirical Examples." In *Competitive Ethnic Relations*, edited by S. Olzak and J. Nagel. New York: Academic Press, 1986.

Portes, Alejandro, and Min Zhou. "Gaining the Upper Hand: Economic Mobility Among Immigrant and Domestic Minorities." *Ethnic and Racial Studies* 15 (1992): 491–518.

Portes, Alejandro, and Steven Shafer. "Revisiting the Enclave Hypothesis: Miami Twenty-Five Years Later." *Research in the Sociology of Organizations* 25 (The Sociology of Entrepreneurship) (2007): 157–90.

Roth, Wendy D., Marc-David L. Seidel, Dennis Ma, and Eiston Lo. "In and Out of the Ethnic Economy: A Longitudinal Analysis of Ethnic Networks and Pathways to Economic Success across Immigrant Categories." *International Migration Review* 46, no. 2 (2012): 310–61.

Sanders, Jimy M., and Victor Nee. "Limits of Ethnic Solidarity in the Enclave Economy." *American Sociological Review* 52 (1987): 745–73

Zhou, Min. *The Accidental Sociologist in Asian American Studies.* Los Angeles: UCLA Asian American Studies Center Press, 2011.

Zonta, Michela M. "The Continuing Significance of Ethnic Resources: Korean-Owned Banks in Los Angeles, New York and Washington DC." *Journal of Ethnic Migration Studies* 38, no. 3 (2012): 463–84.

Ethnic Options: Choosing Identities in America

In her book *Ethnic Options: Choosing Identities in America* (1990), Mary C. Waters first coined the term *ethnic option* to emphasize the tendency of many white Americans to choose their ethnic identity in the form of symbols. Ethnic options refer to people's voluntary choice of identification with one or more ethnic groups. The core element of ethnic options is this noncompulsory nature of white Americans' choice. A great majority of Americans are descendants of European immigrants. From this perspective, such a voluntary identification is generally possible from the third generation (grandchildren) of immigrants. But members of racial minorities do not have the choice, because ethnic and racial identities are imposed on them by U.S. society.

Immigrants tend to maintain their social ties with those who belong to the same ethnic group. They also practice the kind of lifestyle associated with their country of origin. Thus, the ethnic identity of immigrants and their spouses is generally determined by the country of their birth (national identity), hardly a voluntary choice of ethnic affiliation. The ethnic identification of the second generation is also heavily influenced, from the time of their birth throughout their childhood, by their parents' ethnic group. Although the children of immigrants have more freedom in selecting an ethnic group (to identify with) than their parents, they still identify with the ethnic group of their parents. They usually hold a hyphenated/combined American identity (Irish American, Italian American, etc.). For example, because of their intensive association with their parents and people of the same ethnic group, most children of German immigrants retained identification with German Americans, even when they were rapidly assimilated into American society as adults.

As demonstrated by the children of European immigrants, the second generation exhibits a high rate of interethnic marriage. By virtue of their parents' interethnic marriage, third-generation white Americans (the children of the second generation) are naturally exposed to multiple ethnic groups. As it is practically too cumbersome to identify with all of their parents' ethnic groups, they feel the need to choose one or two ethnic groups as their own. This is the idea of ethnic option, a voluntary choice of or identification with one or more ethnic groups. In reality, their voluntary choice of ethnic groups is somewhat diversified. While many third-generation white Americans simply think of themselves as Americans, a high proportion of them identify themselves with one or two ethnic groups, based on their parents' or grandparents' origins or heritage.

By the time they make a choice, however, the intensity of their identification with their chosen ethnic group tends to be considerably weakened. In fact, their ethnic identification resembles Herbert Gans's idea of symbolic ethnicity, meaning that they identify with symbols such as ethnic food and holidays, but little else. From the fourth generation on, their ethnic identification would be a result of ethnic options and selective identification with certain ethnic groups rather than acceptance of all the ascriptive ethnic groups. This option is available to whites only, so far. The basic condition for an ethnic option is the fact that members of white ethnic groups are not subject to discrimination. Thus, to a great majority of nonwhites in America, ethnic-group identification is not necessarily voluntary.

In a study published in 1990, Waters empirically examined the issue of ethnic options when she analyzed ethnic identification of multigeneration white Catholics using 1980 census data. She observed that many white Americans identify with several white ethnic groups, although they do not identify with all of the ethnic groups associated with their parents. She thus asked her informants about the meaning of their identification with multiple white ethnic groups. She further inquired about why and how many white Americans made their voluntary choice. These questions led Waters to interview white, middle-class Catholics in two communities, San Jose, California, and Philadelphia, Pennsylvania. She discovered that the respondents did not identify with all of their ancestors' ethnicities. They tended to simplify their ethnic identification. Second, their ethnic options varied with the respondents' age, social status, family structure, generation, and so on. Third, their ethnic identification was mostly that of symbolic ethnicity. Their choice of ethnic ties did not interfere with their daily activities. Still, most respondents identified with certain cultural traits of their chosen ethnic group(s) and felt they belonged to the chosen ethnic group(s).

Ethnic option is not always available to members of racial minority groups. Many white Americans assume members of racial minorities have the same option as whites. For example, blacks trace their origin to various ethnic groups in Africa and Caribbean countries. Nevertheless, U.S. society does not differentiate their various countries of origin. With their exposure to severe discrimination, moreover, blacks generally marry with each other. Consequently, their children are not exposed to multiple ethnic groups within the structure of the family. Even African Americans with multiple ethnic heritages do not have the option of making a voluntary choice.

Today, the children of Asian immigrants show a high rate of interethnic marriage among Asian Americans. Mia Tuan has shown that the children of such marriages have more experience of ethnic choice than do African Americans. However, what most of them experience is not an ethnic option but a shifting of their ethnic identity from a single Asian ethnic group (e.g., Chinese or Japanese Americans) to a broader Asian American ethnic group (e.g., Chinese-Japanese Americans) or to a pan-Asian identity. In these cases, as members of a racial group different from the whites, even the native-born Asian Americans are compelled to retain an Asian American identity and are more likely to be treated as foreigners in the United States. But interracial marriages (marriage of Asian children with non-Asians, especially whites) among Asian Americans are quite common as well, and studies on the ethnic identity among children of such interracial marriages exhibit a complicated picture. Often their ethnic identity ranges from an Asian ethnic group to white, but as long as some Asian features are visible they are also forced to retain their Asian American identity irrespective of their wishes.

Descendants of Latino immigrants are likely to face a situation similar to that of descendants of Asian Americans. Racial diversification among Hispanics is much more extensive than Asians. Thus, their experience of ethnic options is more complicated than white Americans' experience.

Shin Kim and Kwang Chung Kim

See also
Assimilation; Melting Pot Theory; Pluralism

Further Reading:

Alba, Richard D. *Ethnic Identity: The Transformation of White America*. New Haven, CT: Yale University Press, 1990.

Tuan, Mia. *Forever Foreigners or Honorary Whites? The Asian Ethnic Experience Today*. New Brunswick, NJ: Rutgers University Press, 1998.

Waters, Mary C. *Ethnic Options: Choosing Identities in America*. Berkeley: University of California Press, 1990.

Ethnic Retention and School Performance

Ethnic retention refers to immigrants or people of color embracing the characteristics of their culture, such as language, values and priorities, daily routines, social networks, and ethnic identity. Traditionally, educators and scholars believed that ethnic retention impedes the academic performances of students. This belief was based on the zero-sum assumption that, if a person is embracing "the other" culture, she/he could not be fluent in the skills that were valued in the United States. The assumption was also frequently made that children of color and immigrant children came from families and communities where the "American values" concerning academic and occupational success were not shared. In addition, they assumed that speaking languages other than English would slow the development of the English-language skills, in turn hindering students' overall academic achievement.

Interestingly, however, recent studies of children of immigrants have provided empirical evidence that disputes these assumptions. They have shown that retention of ethnic values, bilingualism, and ethnic identity is positively related to school performance. For example, Vietnamese high school students who were more closely tied to the Vietnamese communities and more fluent in the Vietnamese language were more successful in school performance and more college oriented than those who were less integrated into the ethnic community and less fluent in their mother tongue. Similarly, bilingual Latino and Asian American children tend to perform better in school than their counterparts who are English monolingual. These phenomena are counterintuitive, since higher degrees of ethnic retention are usually thought to hinder children's school performance.

Researchers have identified several factors that have contributed to this somewhat surprising trend. First, most Latino and Asian immigrants have come to the United States seeking better living conditions and expanded career opportunities. As such, adult immigrants tend to be heavily work-oriented and emphasize the value of a good education as the major channel for their children's social mobility. They have brought with them their work ethnic, frugality, punctuality, respect for adults, and value for education. Although these adults may not be able to directly assist children with schoolwork, they often attempt to enhance children's learning through other means. For example, they arrange for neighbors or relatives to supervise their children's homework study and/or enroll their children in after-school programs. In addition, immigrant parents instill in their children early on the importance of education and professional careers. It is further documented that Latinos and Asians who are new to the country are generally optimistic that success is the direct result of hard work. By contrast, African American children are often disillusioned by the realities of racism and think that their diligence frequently goes unrewarded.

Second, the children of immigrants who have retained their ethnic traditions are currently more successful in school than those who have not, partly because multicultural education in American schools makes their ethnic traditions valuable to their education. At the turn of the 20th century, when many Europeans were immigrating to the United States, the main goal of public education was to Americanize students. Thus, the children of immigrants at that time had to lose their cultural traditions and assimilate to American culture as soon as possible to succeed in school. However, the children of contemporary immigrants benefit from multicultural education in the form of bilingual education programs, bilingual counselors, and multiethnic curricula. Accordingly, the children of immigrants who are fluent in their mother tongue and familiar with the history and culture of their parents' homeland have opportunities to connect their ethnic backgrounds to schoolwork.

Research on African American students, however, has shown a different trend. Scholars have suggested that strong ethnic retention among African Americans may, in many cases, be predictive of poor school performance. It is argued that, as a reaction to the long history of racism and cultural devaluation, African American youths often express their ethnic retention by resisting the characteristics that are valued by their oppressors (e.g., excelling in school). This phenomenon is often called *cultural inversion*, and it is reflected in the concept of "acting White," which is a criticism frequently used in African American communities to discredit the authenticity of their peers who perform well in school. It should, however, be noted that ethnic retention among African Americans may take another form, one in which the retention is based primarily on their bond with African American culture and communities, rather than on rejection of the mainstream culture. When strong African American ethnic retention takes this particular form, there is no compelling reason to speculate that it would lead to poor school performance. The type of ethnic retention, rather than the degree of retention per se, thus appears to predict African American students' school performance. Therefore, while ethnic retention clearly has great implications for school performance, the relationship between the two is both complex and population specific.

DAISUKE AKIBA

See also

Oppositional Identity; School Segregation

Further Reading:

Akiba, Daisuke. "Effective Interventions with Children of Color: An Ecological Developmental Approach." In *Practicing Multiculturalism: Affirming Diversity in Counseling and Psychology*, edited by Timothy Smith. Boston: Allyn & Bacon, 2004.

Cross, William, Jr. *Shades of Black: Diversity in African American Identity*. Philadelphia: Temple University Press, 1991.

Rumbaut, Ruben. "The New Californians: Comparative Research Findings on the Educational Progress of Immigrant Children." In *California's Immigrant Children: Theory, Research, and Implications for Educational Policy*, edited by Ruben Rumbaut and Wayne Cornelius. San Diego: Center for U.S.-Mexican Studies, 1995.

Zhou, Min, and Carl Bankston. *Growing Up in America: How Vietnamese Children Adapt to Life in the United States*. New York: Russell Sage, 1998.

Ethnic Studies

As a discipline, ethnic studies is an interdisciplinary, multidisciplinary, and comparative study of racial and ethnic groups and their interrelations, with an emphasis on groups that have historically been neglected. The domain of ethnic studies includes all social aspects of racial and ethnic groups (e.g., their histories, cultures, institutions and organizations, identities, experiences, and contributions) and intergroup relations along social, economic, spatial, and political dimensions. Ethnic studies seeks to capture the social, economic, cultural, and historical forces that shape the development of diverse racial and ethnic groups and their interrelations.

Although scholars embarked on the study of racial and ethnic groups and their interrelations in prior periods in the United States, ethnic studies as a discipline did not emerge until the late 1960s. The civil rights movement, the women's movement, anti–Vietnam War demonstrations, and the emergence of Third World nationalist movements inspired student movements on university campuses.

In 1968, students at San Francisco State College (now San Francisco State University) and the University of California at Berkeley occupied the administrative offices at both campuses and demanded fundamental changes in higher education. The movement soon spread to many other campuses throughout the country. Students of color, as well as their white supporters, demanded better access to higher education, changes in curricula to reflect their ethnic cultures and perspectives, recruitment of minority faculty, and establishment of ethnic studies programs. As a result, ethnic studies programs were created in the late 1960s and the early 1970s as a means to assuage activist students. Among the initial programs were the School of Ethnic Studies at San Francisco State University and the Ethnic Studies Department at the University of California at Berkeley. Following their lead, African American, Asian American, Chicano/Chicana, and Native American studies programs emerged across the country. Ethnic studies as a discipline grew out of this historical context.

Ethnic studies adopts interdisciplinary, multidisciplinary, and comparative methodologies by combining and integrating approaches of various disciplines (e.g., anthropology, economics, history, political science, psychology, sociology, philosophy, literature, linguistics, and visual arts) and by comparing the histories, cultures, experiences, and social institutions of racial and ethnic groups. The emphasis of ethnic studies is on groups such as African Americans, Asian Americans, Latinos, and Native Americans. A primary reason is that traditional disciplines had largely omitted the history, culture, and experiences of minority groups and their contributions to the shaping of U.S. culture and society. Ethnic studies departments or programs are normally staffed with specialists in specific minority groups or in comparative studies of racial and ethnic groups. The discipline of ethnic studies seeks to recover and reconstruct the history of minority groups, to identify and credit their contribution to American culture and institutions, to chronicle their protests and resistance efforts, and to establish alternative values and visions, cultures and institutions.

In the United States, ethnic studies currently consists of several subfields: African American studies or Black studies, Asian American studies, Chicano studies, Puerto Rican studies, and Native American studies. All of these subfields share some common concerns, assumptions, and principles, but each subfield has its special interest in a particular minority group, is relatively autonomous, has its own constituency, and is represented by at least one national professional association, such as the American Indian Studies Association, the National Association of African American Studies, the National Council for Black Studies, the Association for Asian American Studies, the National Association for Chicana and Chicano Studies, and the Puerto Rican Studies Association. All organizations have their own publications. There are further divisions within some of these subfields. Chinese American studies, Japanese American studies, Filipino American studies, and Korean American studies are some examples of such divisions within Asian American studies.

Currently, there are more than 800 ethnic studies programs and departments in the country. The Comparative Ethnic Studies Department at the University of California at Berkeley and the Department of Ethnic Studies at the University of California at San Diego offer PhD degrees in ethnic studies. Scores of other universities offer master's degree and/or a bachelor's degree programs in ethnic studies or in one of its subfields.

The institutionalization of ethnic studies programs has been accompanied by a growing number of faculty engaged in ethnic studies teaching and research. The establishment of ethnic studies departments or programs and the recruitment of full-time faculty in ethnic studies have resulted in a prodigious amount of scholarship. Increasingly, ethnic studies courses have gained importance, becoming requirements for degree programs or a more prominent portion of curricula.

PHILIP YANG

See also

Ethnicity

Further Reading:

Bataille, Gretchen, Miguel Carranza, and Laurie Lisa. *Ethnic Studies in the United States: A Guide to Research*. New York: Garland Publishing, 1996.

Yang, Philip. *Ethnic Studies: Issues and Approaches*. Albany: State University of New York Press, 2000.

Ethnicity

Ethnicity is among the most highly contested and controversial concepts in the social sciences, along with race. Ethnicity is generally understood to be a combination of language, culture, shared history, religious beliefs, and other features that characterize a group of people. The issue of ethnic identity tends to be related to the group's understanding of itself and the relation of its individuals to each other.

To ordinary Americans, ethnicity often means where one came from. The colloquial American understanding may consider various ethnic groups culturally distinct to one degree or another, but they tend to view the origins of these groups as what sets them most clearly apart. To say that one

Ethnocentrism

Ethnocentrism is the tendency to evaluate other groups by the standards and values of one's own. It means that one's own group is the center of everything. Other groups, including their cultural practices, beliefs, lifestyles and even languages, are understood in reference to one's own. Such evaluation is usually negative. This produces a view of one's own group as being superior to others. Unlike racism, which is historically constructed, ethnocentrism is a universal belief and practice among people. Ethnocentric views have often been encouraged to help enhance group solidarity and cohesiveness. At the same time, this way of thinking has been the basis of separation, misunderstanding, misconception, hatred, and conflict between groups. Ethnocentrism encourages the creation of negative stereotypes, which lead to prejudice and discrimination and can escalate into xenophobia.

Throughout U.S. history, Americans have often demonstrated an ethnocentric view of the world. In the initial contact between European settlers and Native Americans, ethnocentrism was the dominant attitude of the settlers toward the "Indians" they encountered. The effort of Christianizing them was based on an ethnocentric assumption. White Americans' ethnocentric view of Chinese immigrants created the negative stereotype of the "yellow peril" that developed into the xenophobia of the 1870s and 1880s and culminated in the Chinese Exclusion Act of 1882. Nativism and anti-immigrant movements throughout U.S. history have been based on the ethnocentric view of white Anglo Protestantism as a superior culture into which all other groups should be assimilated. Movements against the Jewish immigrants and Catholics were also supported by white Protestants' ethnocentrism.

Heon Cheol Lee

is Irish or Italian in the United States is to say that one came originally from Ireland or Italy. The ultimate source of distinctiveness is that group members originally came from a particular place.

This everyday American concept of ethnicity is not far removed from Max Weber's classical understanding. Weber provided a classic definition of ethnicity, stating, "We shall call 'ethnic groups' those human groups that entertain a subjective belief in their common descent because of similarities of physical types of or customs or both, or because of memories of colonization and migration. . . . It does not matter whether or not an objective blood relation exists" (Weber 2010: 19). There are multiple grounds for ethnicity, whether a shared history, physical traits, or culture. For Weber, however, the most important defining characteristic of ethnicity is a shared ancestry among group members. To be more precise, it is important that group members share a common descent, or rather most importantly, a *belief* in a common descent. Ethnicity, then, is subjective.

Over time, ethnic studies moved away from focusing on shared origins. In its place, scholars began to focus more on the activity that characterizes a group in the present, rather than exclusively on how its members understood their past. By this account, current culture and practices matter more for defining ethnic groups than any vision of the past. An ethnic group under this definition, then, is defined by a common or shared culture, such as religion, shared values, language, and other behavioral patterns. This approach extends Weber's subjective perspective a step further by increasing the role that the individual actively plays in determining ethnic identity.

One challenge of a cultural definition of ethnicity appears in the case of acculturation, or the gradual blending of a minority culture into the dominant culture. Grandchildren of immigrants, for example, may have stronger cultural ties to the dominant culture of a host society in which they have been raised and immersed. Under the culture-centered definition of ethnicity, the descendants of immigrants may be in danger of losing their claims to "authentic" ethnicity. On the other hand, they could still very much feel connected to the story of origin shared by the ethnic group, even if their practices do not wholly reflect this. These weakened ties have been referred to as *symbolic ethnicity*, which does not affect everyday life like "authentic" ethnicity.

Schermerhorn's definition seems more useful in the current setting, adding contemporary insights on ethnicity to the Weberian tradition. He defines ethnicity as "a collectivity within a larger society having real or putative common ancestry, memories of a shared historical past, and a cultural focus on one or more symbolic elements defined as the epitome of their peoplehood" (Schermerhorn 1978: 12). Peoplehood, for Schermerhorn, can be constituted by a combination of kinship patterns, geographical concentration, religious affiliation, language, physical differences, and a shared story of origin. In this way, ethnic groups can be defined as self-conscious populations who see themselves as distinct.

Fredrik Barth's *Ethnic Groups and Boundaries* (1969) was influential in supporting the mutability of ethnic identity. It provided a novel, subjective account of ethnic identity, opposing the objective approach proposed by scholars such as Raoul Naroll in which shared common traits were seen as integral to an ethnic group. For Barth, members themselves, through social interactions, change the boundaries of ethnic groups. His notion of ethnic boundaries changed the focus of the study from the "static vs. dynamic" ethnicity to the source of subjective ethnic identities.

An important development in understandings of ethnicity that followed is the debate between perspectives that see it as fixed versus those that see it as fluid and flexible. The former is called the primordialist view and the latter the circumstantialist view. The debate emerged out of the challenges to the modernization thesis. As societies became more industrialized, scholars of modernization expected the decline of traditional ways of life. However, in the 1960s, ethnic revivals and assertion of distinctiveness actually persisted despite modernization. Primordialists claimed that this was owing to the immutable and essential nature of ethnic identity. On the other hand, circumstantialists (or instrumentalists) argued that, to the contrary, it was not the deep roots of ethnic identities that explained this phenomenon. Rather, it was an expression of individuals' and groups' assertion of particular identities when benefits were seen to accrue from holding them. Thus, they claimed that such ethnic identities were not immanent but rather fluid. Concrete social and historical situations determined ethnic choices. Circumstantialists consider ethnicity malleable and ethnic identities continuously negotiable within an individual and between groups. Therefore, in this view, ethnic groups could be treated as interest groups.

Ethnicity as a concept continues to evolve in response to new events and developments in society. It represents an attempt to capture both the immigrant experience and the dynamics at play in dominant majorities and the interactions between them. It is especially contentious owing to its linkage to race, nation, and nationalism. For instance, while race is closely associated with power differentials and political hierarchies, ethnicity tends to be associated with the idea of culture and distinctiveness. Disentangling the intricate connections between ethnicity, race, and nation is a central concern of contemporary social science.

Kazuko Suzuki

See also

Diversities, Ethnic and Racial; Ethnic Enclaves; Nativism; Stereotype; Xenophobia

Further Reading:

Barth, Fredrik. *Ethnic Groups and Boundaries: The Social Organization of Culture Difference.* Oslo: Universitetsforlaget, 1969.

Bernard, Frederick M. *Herder on Nationality, Humanity, and History.* Montreal: McGill-Queen's University Press, 2003.

Cornell, Stephen, and Douglas Hartmann. *Ethnicity and Race: Making Identities in a Changing World*, 2nd ed. Thousand Oaks, CA: Pine Forge Press, 2007.

Eller, Jack David. *From Culture to Ethnicity to Conflict: An Anthropological Perspective on International Ethnic Conflict.* Ann Arbor: University of Michigan Press, 1999.

Glazer, Nathan, and Daniel P. Moynihan. *Ethnicity: Theory and Experience.* Cambridge, MA: Harvard University Press, 1975.

Kelly, Joe. "Ethnic Identity: Yours, Mine and Ours." Newsletter, Fall 1999. New York: Families with Children from China, New York Chapter. http://nysccc.org/family-supports/transracial-transcultural/voices-of-parents/ethnic-identity-yours-mine-and-ours/.

Schermerhorn, Richard Alonzo. *Comparative Ethnic Relations: A Framework for Theory and Research.* Chicago: University of Chicago Press, 1978.

Swarns, Rachel L. "'African-American' Becomes a Term for Debate." *New York Times.* August 29, 2004.

Weber, Max. "What Is an Ethnic Group?" In *The Ethnicity Reader: Nationalism, Multiculturalism and Migration*, 2nd ed., edited by Montserrat Guibernau and John Rex, 17–26. Cambridge: Polity Press, 2010.

Ethnogenesis

The term *ethnogenesis* was coined by David Greenstone and made popular by Andrew Greeley in his 1974 book *Ethnicity in the United States: A Preliminary Reconnaissance*. Literally, ethnogenesis means "the creation of an ethnic group" or "ethnicization." In contrast to assimilationism, the aim of which is ethnic homogenization, Greeley proposed ethnogenesis as an alternative perspective for looking at ethnic differentiation in American society. The main argument of this perspective is that, over time, immigrant groups will share more common characteristics with the host group, but they still, to varying degrees, retain and modify some components of their ethnic culture, and they also create new cultural elements in response to the host social environment by incorporating their own culture and the host culture. This perspective emphasizes the importance of studying the genesis and history of ethnic groups.

Greeley developed the ethnogenesis perspective to explain the adaptation experience of European immigrants. According to Greeley, at the beginning the host group and the immigrant group may have some things in common. For instance, the Irish could speak English, and some groups were Protestants. As a result of adaptation over generations, the common culture enlarges. The immigrant group becomes similar to the host group, and the host group also becomes somewhat similar to the immigrant group. However, the immigrant group still keeps some elements of its culture and institutions, modifies some of its cultural and social structural characteristics, and creates some new cultural elements in response to the challenge of the host society. The result is a new ethnic group with a cultural system that is a combination of the common culture and its unique heritage mixed in the American crucible. The ethnogenesis perspective integrates assimilation theory and cultural pluralism theory by incorporating the ideas of partial assimilation, partial retention of ethnic culture, and the modification and creation of ethnic cultural elements in the same framework.

Philip Yang

See also

Assimilation

Further Reading:

Bernard, Frederick M. *Herder on Nationality, Humanity, and History*. Montreal: McGill-Queen's University Press, 2003.

Cornell, Stephen, and Douglas Hartmann. *Ethnicity and Race: Making Identities in a Changing World*, second edition. Thousand Oaks, CA: Pine Forge Press, 2007.

Weber, Max. "What Is an Ethnic Group?" In *The Ethnicity Reader: Nationalism, Multiculturalism & Migration*, second edition, edited by Montserrat Guibernau and John Rex, 17–26. Cambridge, UK: Polity Press, 2010.

Evers, Medgar (1925–1963)

Medgar Wiley Evers was the first National Association for the Advancement of Colored People (NAACP) field secretary in Mississippi. During the 1950s and early 1960s, Evers was one of the key activists in Mississippi, and was involved in many high-profile challenges to racial subjugation.

Born in Decatur, Mississippi, on July 2, 1925, Evers's early life was shaped by Jim Crow, and these experiences informed his later outlook and activities. The Evers family had a long history of standing up to racial oppression. Evers was named for his maternal great-grandfather, a half-Indian slave who had a reputation for being uncooperative with masters, while his maternal grandfather, the son of a white man, had reputedly shot two white men. Evers's father, James, instilled both racial and personal pride into Medgar and his older brother, Charles, who himself would become a civil rights activist in Mississippi. James Evers was a public worker and so less susceptible to the seasonal fluctuations of agricultural employment; he owned his own land and built the family home himself, and was therefore not at risk of eviction, as were so many black Mississippians who were tenants of whites. Throughout his childhood, Medgar witnessed his father's refusal to accede to many Jim Crow customs: he refused to step off sidewalks to allow whites to pass and, on one particular occasion, defended himself with a broken bottle against a white storekeeper who had tried to overcharge him. Several white men witnessed this incident, but no repercussions were directed at the Evers family.

Despite his father's defiance, Medgar was nonetheless exposed to the realities of Jim Crow in Mississippi. Friendships with several white children were abruptly severed as Medgar grew older, and while the Evers brothers had to walk to school, white children travelled by bus. In 1934, Medgar and his brother sneaked into a political rally given by Governor

Theodore Bilbo, who singled them out and warned the crowd that unless Jim Crow remained in place, such children would grow into adults who demanded the vote. From an early age, Evers developed an attitude to the racial norms of Mississippi that would shape the rest of his life. As children, he and Charles would fantasize about moving to South America, where they would buy land and refuse access to whites, while Medgar's response to the lack of respect shown to local blacks by white traveling salesmen was to let the air out of their car tires.

At the same time as indulging in such childish revenge fantasies, Evers developed an anger at black Mississippians' impotence in the face of Jim Crow. When a local black man was lynched and his clothes left as a reminder to the rest of the community, Evers struggled to understand how such atrocities could occur with no attempt by the black community to intervene or have the perpetrators brought to justice. Evers grew frustrated with black people who accepted the tenets of Jim Crow without challenge, in a way that his father never had. This frustration would stay with him as an adult.

In 1944, Medgar dropped out of the 11th grade to enlist in the army. He was posted to the 325th Port Company, where he served in England and France. As was true for many black Southerners who served in the armed forces, this was Evers's first visit out of his home state, and the contrast with Mississippi was stark. Although his unit was commanded by white officers, Evers found that the entrenched racial attitudes of Mississippi were absent, and his potential was recognized by at least one white lieutenant, who encouraged him to attend college when he returned home. The difference in racial attitudes was particularly noticeable when off duty, and in France, Evers befriended a white family and even dated their daughter. When he returned to Mississippi, however, Evers knew that he could not risk even writing to her, for fear that local whites would find out.

Spurred by their experiences in Europe, Medgar and a group of other black veterans, including his brother Charles, registered to vote, becoming the only blacks on the voters' roll in Decatur. As polling day approached, the Evers family home received both white and black visitors who urged Medgar and Charles not to vote for fear of reprisals. The Evers brothers took these warnings so seriously that on the night before the election, they armed themselves and waited for an expected attack, a familiar Mississippi tactic to dissuade blacks from voting. No attack came, but when the Evers attempted to vote, they were turned away from the polling station by a group of armed white men.

Medgar Evers was a civil rights leader who fought to improve the rights of African American citizens in Jackson, Mississippi, until he was murdered on June 11, 1963, the day after President John F. Kennedy's announcement that he was submitting the Civil Rights Bill to Congress. (Getty Images)

In 1946, Evers enrolled at Alcorn Agricultural and Mechanical College, the oldest state college for blacks in Mississippi. He featured strongly in campus life and participated in a wide range of extracurricular activities. He was a member of the debating team, the campus YMCA, the college choir, and the track and football teams as well as president of the junior class, editor of the 1951 yearbook, and editor of the college newspaper for two years. In his senior year, he achieved honor-roll grades. Evers's achievements saw him listed in the nationally published *Who's Who Among Students in American Colleges and Universities*. At Alcorn,

Evers met his future wife Myrlie Beasley, whom he married on Christmas Eve 1951.

While at college, Evers's racial attitude continued to harden, and he became increasingly antagonistic towards white people. Nonetheless, despite having spent time in Chicago during 1951, and in spite of his wife's desire to move away from Mississippi, Evers came to see what the state could be like without Jim Crow and became determined to stay and challenge racial subjugation. Evers's commitment to this ideal grew stronger when he and Myrlie moved to the all-black town of Mound Bayou, where he took a job with the Magnolia Life Insurance Company, operated by T.R.M. Howard, a wealthy black doctor and activist who had helped found the Regional Council of Negro Leadership. Evers's job exposed him for the first time to the entrenched poverty of black communities in the Mississippi Delta, and he soon joined the local NAACP branch, joining a statewide network of activists.

Embers of Evers's earlier radicalism still glowed and, inspired by Jomo Kenyatta's Mau Mau rebels in Kenya, he and his brother toyed with the idea of an armed black uprising in Mississippi. Evers ultimately dismissed this notion and instead became more deeply involved with the NAACP. In 1954, he volunteered as a test case to integrate the University of Mississippi and applied to its law school. The NAACP's Thurgood Marshall represented his case. After nine months, Evers's application was rejected on a technicality. This had brought him to the attention of the NAACP's national office, and in December 1954, he took up a post as the NAACP's first field secretary in Mississippi. His wife, Myrlie, acted as his secretary: in the office, Medgar insisted they refer to each other as "Mr." and "Mrs."

Evers's appointment coincided with the rise of massive white resistance to the *Brown v. Board of Education* (1954) ruling, and over the next few years, intimidation and violence disrupted the network of black activism that had developed in Mississippi. Undaunted, Evers travelled tirelessly throughout Mississippi, organizing NAACP chapters, collecting affidavits from blacks who had been intimidated by the White Citizens Council, urging people to sign petitions supporting school integration, and encouraging witnesses of crimes like the murder of George Lee in Belzoni to testify. Evers was involved in many high-profile incidents in Mississippi. During the trial of the alleged killers of Emmett Till, Evers scoured the delta looking for witnesses, and ferried reporters around so that they could see for themselves the reality of Jim Crow Mississippi.

By the early 1960s, Evers had become one of the most well-known civil rights activists in Mississippi, to both blacks and whites. This made him vulnerable to segregationists: his Mississippi State Sovereignty Commission file grew increasingly thick, and he was beaten while attending the trial of nine students who had tried to integrate a public library. However, his profile also gave him influence, and the Justice Department investigated the beating, signaling an increased federal interest in Mississippi. Evers's profile meant that he was involved in a wide range of civil rights episodes in the state, including James Meredith's attempt to integrate the University of Mississippi and a sustained boycott of downtown Jackson in 1962 and 1963. The boycott made him an even more visible target, and after his house was firebombed, he became increasingly concerned about his family's security. Despite initial wariness, Evers also tried to create links with other civil rights organizations like the Southern Christian Leadership Conference and Student Nonviolent Coordinating Committee during this period, often without the knowledge or approval of the NAACP's national office.

On June 11, 1963, the same evening that President John F. Kennedy gave a televised address in which he announced his attention to bring forward civil rights legislation, Evers was shot dead outside his home by Byron De La Beckwith, a White Citizens' Council member well known for his hatred of black people. He was shot while carrying T-shirts bearing the slogan "Jim Crow Must Go." Over 5,000 people attended Evers's funeral, and he was buried in Arlington National Cemetery. His brother Charles replaced him as NAACP field secretary. Beckwith was tried, although this twice resulted in hung juries and he was freed. In 1990, he was rearrested, and in February 1994, was found guilty of murdering Evers and sentenced to life imprisonment.

Simon T. Cuthbert-Kerr

See also

Civil Rights Movement; Jim Crow Laws

Further Reading:

Dittmer, John. *Local People: The Struggle for Civil Rights in Mississippi.* Urbana: University of Illinois Press, 1995.

Payne, Charles M. *I've Got the Light of Freedom: The Organizing Tradition and the Mississippi Freedom Struggle*. Berkeley: University of California Press, 1995.
Vollers, Maryanne. *Ghosts of Mississippi: The Murder of Medgar Evers, the Trials of Byron De La Beckwith, and the Haunting of the New South*. Boston: Little, Brown and Company, 1995.

Executive Order 9808

Executive Order 9808 (11FR 14153, December 7, 1946; 1946 WL 3907) was issued by President Harry S. Truman on December 5, 1946. Truman invoked Executive Order 9808 (EO 9808) in response to complaints of racial discrimination that surfaced during the administration of his predecessor, President Franklin D. Roosevelt. During World War II, Roosevelt received complaints from blacks that America's efforts to promote civil rights abroad were in conflict with the state of civil rights in America, particularly as it related to the extension of these rights to African Americans. Therefore, in June 1941, Roosevelt issued Executive Order 8802 to forbid government contractors from discriminating against blacks. This executive order also established a Fair Employment Practices Commission.

Truman's rationale for invoking Executive Order 9808 rested upon three basic premises:

1. The preservation of civil rights guaranteed by the Constitution is essential to domestic tranquility, national security, the general welfare, and the continued existence of our free institutions.
2. The action of individuals who take law into their own hands and inflict summary punishment and wreak personal vengeance is subversive to our democratic system of law enforcement and public criminal justice, and gravely threatens our form of government.
3. All possible steps must be taken to safeguard our civil rights.

In order to accomplish the goal of safeguarding civil rights under Executive Order 9808, Truman established the President's Committee on Civil Rights. This uncompensated, 16-member committee consisted of the following members: Sadie T. Alexander, James B. Carey, Robert K. Carr (executive secretary), John S. Dickey (first vice-chairman), Morris L. Ernst, Roland G. Gittelsohn, Frank P. Graham, Francis J. Haas, Charles Luckman, Francis P. Matthews, Franklin D. Roosevelt Jr. (second vice-chairman), Henry Knox Sherrill, Boris Shishkin, M. E. Tilley, Channing H. Tobias, and Charles E. Wilson (chair).

The committee was charged with the following tasks:

1. to inquire into and to determine whether and in what respect current law enforcement measures and the authority and means possessed by the federal, state, and local governments may be strengthened and improved to safeguard the civil rights of the people and
2. to make a report of its studies to the president in writing and . . . in particular make recommendations with respect to the adoption or establishment, by legislation or otherwise, of more adequate and effective means and procedures for the protection of the civil rights of the people of the United States.

In essence, Truman wanted the committee to investigate possible civil rights violations and recommend procedures to assist in the protection of civil rights for the American people.

Executive Order 9808 imposed an obligatory responsibility on "[a]ll executive departments and agencies of the Federal Government . . . to cooperate with the Committee in its work, and to furnish the Committee such information or the services of such persons as the Committee may require in the performance of its duties." Additionally, this order required "persons employed by any of the executive departments and agencies of the Federal Government . . . [to] testify before the Committee and [to] make available for the use of the Committee such documents and other information as the Committee may require." In October 1947, the committee submitted its final report, entitled *To Secure These Rights*. In December 1947, the committee was dismantled in accordance with the statutory language of EO 9808.

The committee's report was divided into four main sections—"The American Heritage: The Promise of Freedom and Equality," "The Record: Short of the Goal," "Government's Responsibility: Securing the Rights," and "A Program of Action: The Committee's Recommendations." Within its report, the committee emphasized that its investigation uncovered widespread acts—both individual and sanctioned by law—of civil rights violations. These violations existed in many forms (e.g., poll taxes and other unlawful voting restrictions, police brutality, lynching, employment discrimination, de jure segregation or Jim Crow laws). The committee concluded that such violations were at odds with the American heritage and the valued principles of liberty and equality. The committee wrote as follows: "Mr. President: Your Committee has reviewed the American heritage and we have found in it again the great goals of human freedom and equality under just laws. We have surveyed the flaws in the nation's record and have found them to be serious."

The committee suggested specific measures in order to safeguard the civil rights of Americans. Its recommendations spanned approximately 68 pages of the *To Secure These Rights* report. Recommendations such as the following were suggested by the committee:

1. reorganization of the Civil Rights Section of the Department of Justice (DOJ);
2. establishment of a special civil rights investigative unit within the Federal Bureau of Investigation;
3. establishment of state law enforcement agencies comparable to the Civil Rights Section of the DOJ;
4. establishment of a permanent Commission on Civil Rights in the Executive Office of the president;
5. establishment of permanent state civil rights commissions;
6. institution of state and local police training programs;
7. congressional enactment of laws to punish individual violators of civil rights; and
8. congressional enactment of laws imposing penalties against law enforcement personnel involved in police brutality and other forms of misconduct, anti-lynching laws, criminalizing law enforcement's employment of involuntary servitude, ending poll taxes and other voting restrictions, and abolishing discrimination in the armed forces.

The overall findings of the committee resulted in President Truman sending a special civil rights message to Congress urging the implementation of the committee's recommendations. In response to Truman's request, Southern members of Congress who adamantly opposed expansion of civil rights to African Americans threatened a filibuster. As a result, President Truman issued Executive Order 9981 (13 FR 4313, July 26, 1948) abolishing segregation in the armed forces and integration of all armed services.

Olethia Davis

See also

Desegregation; Executive Order 9981; Truman, Harry S.

Further Reading:

Executive Order 8802. June 24, 1941. http://www.eeoc.gov/abouteeoc/35th/thelaw/eo-8802.html (accessed June 12, 2008).

Executive Order 9808. 11 FR 14153, December 7, 1941. http://www.presidency.ucsb.edu/ws/index.php?pid=60711 (accessed June 12, 2008).

Executive Order 9981. 13 FR 4313, July 26, 1948. http://www.trumanlibrary.org/9981a.htm (accessed June 12, 2008).

MacGregor, Morris J., Jr. *Integration of the Armed Forces, 1940–1965.* Washington, DC: Center of Military History, 1989.

To Secure These Rights: The Report of the President's Committee on Civil Rights. Washington, DC: U.S. Government Printing Office, 1947.

Executive Order 9981

Beginning with the founding of the nation, the role of African Americans serving in their county's military has been hotly debated. At the opening of the American War for Independence, as some Northern colonies began enlisting free blacks into the ranks of their regiments, George Washington declared that no blacks, free or slave, would be permitted to serve in the Continental Army. However, when the Loyalist Virginia governor Lord Dunmore began enticing slaves with the promise of freedom if they left their masters and joined his "Ethiopian Regiment," at a time when the rebels were having difficulty recruiting men, Washington, though a slave owner, reconsidered his earlier prohibition on black troops, and, on January 17, 1776, the Continental Congress approved the enlistment of black troops into Washington's army. Over 5,000 black men fought for the American cause during the War for Independence, and they fought shoulder

Executive Order 9981, 1948

Establishing the President's Committee on Equality of Treatment and Opportunity in the Armed Forces.

WHEREAS it is essential that there be maintained in the armed services of the United States the highest standards of democracy, with equality of treatment and opportunity for all those who serve in our country's defense:

NOW THEREFORE, by virtue of the authority vested in me as President of the United States, by the Constitution and the statutes of the United States, and as Commander in Chief of the armed services, it is hereby ordered as follows:

1. It is hereby declared to be the policy of the President that there shall be equality of treatment and opportunity for all persons in the armed services without regard to race, color, religion or national origin. This policy shall be put into effect as rapidly as possible, having due regard to the time required to effectuate any necessary changes without impairing efficiency or morale.
2. There shall be created in the National Military Establishment an advisory committee to be known as the President's Committee on Equality of Treatment and Opportunity in the Armed Services, which shall be composed of seven members to be designated by the President.
3. The Committee is authorized on behalf of the President to examine into the rules, procedures and practices of the Armed Services in order to determine in what respect such rules, procedures and practices may be altered or improved with a view to carrying out the policy of this order. The Committee shall confer and advise the Secretary of Defense, the Secretary of the Army, the Secretary of the Navy, and the Secretary of the Air Force, and shall make such recommendations to the President and to said Secretaries as in the judgment of the Committee will effectuate the policy hereof.
4. All executive departments and agencies of the Federal Government are authorized and directed to cooperate with the Committee in its work, and to furnish the Committee such information or the services of such persons as the Committee may require in the performance of its duties.
5. When requested by the Committee to do so, persons in the armed services or in any of the executive departments and agencies of the Federal Government shall testify before the Committee and shall make available for use of the Committee such documents and other information as the Committee may require.
6. The Committee shall continue to exist until such time as the President shall terminate its existence by Executive order.

Harry Truman
The White House
July 26, 1948

to shoulder with white soldiers; there was no segregation in the Continental Army.

Black sailors and soldiers also fought for the United States against the British in the War of 1812. Some, like the New Orleans Free Black Militia who served with distinction under General Andrew Jackson, fought in all-black units, but the policy of segregating troops by race was not official. Indeed, the U.S. Navy, whose force was one-sixth African American during the War of 1812, found it almost impossible to segregate sailors on board ship. The aftermath of the War of 1812 saw a dramatic change in the U.S. government's policy regarding blacks in the military. In 1820, reacting in part to the fear of slave rebellion, the U.S. government announced that "No Negro or mulatto will be received as a recruit of the Army." As a result of the ban on black recruits, the 1846–1848 Mexican-American War was the only major U.S.

conflict in which no black soldiers participated, although some African Americans served in the navy during the war.

The policy of not accepting African Americans into the armed forces was still in place when the Civil War erupted in 1861. As George Washington had initially done in 1775, in 1861, Abraham Lincoln declared that the war would be a "white man's fight," and that no blacks, free or slave, would be accepted into the Union forces. Pressure from black leaders, most notably Frederick Douglass, combined with mounting losses, convinced Lincoln to accept black troops in 1862. Almost 180,000 African Americans served in the Union armed forces during the Civil War, in segregated units, as it was during the Civil War that the policy of creating separate units for black troops was made official policy. It was the creation of a Jim Crow army that would last until the 1950s.

Following the Civil War, black troops were organized into four units: the 9th and 10th Cavalry, and the 24th and 25th Infantry Regiments. Although often relegated to labor battalions, black troops fought with distinction in the West, in Cuba, in the Philippines, and in the World Wars in their segregated units. During World War II—a war fought against Nazi racism—the black press, led by the *Pittsburgh Courier*, launched the Double V Campaign: victory against racism and fascism abroad, and victory against segregation and discrimination at home. The National Association for the Advancement of Colored People (NAACP) also continued its campaign, begun during World War I, demanding the end to segregation in the armed forces, while black leaders repeatedly pointed out the inconsistencies of black troops fighting for freedom and democracy in a Jim Crow army.

Military leadership resisted desegregation, asserting that the army was not designed to be a social laboratory, and that the military would integrate when the rest of American society did. In 1946, the army reviewed its policy towards black soldiers in what became known as the Gillem Board. This committee acknowledged that the army had failed to make the best use of its black manpower during World War II, and recommended that African Americans should compose 10 percent of the postwar army (the policy actually included creating new all-black units, thereby increasing segregation), that blacks be given equal opportunity for advancement, and that the use of some base facilities (like recreation centers) be integrated. The board did not, however, challenge the army's traditional policy of segregating troops.

Black leaders such as the NAACP's Roy Wilkins were outraged by the recommendation of the Gillem Board, as it did not take any meaningful steps to end segregation in the army. Led by A. Philip Randolph, the labor leader whose 1941 March on Washington Movement had pressured President Franklin D. Roosevelt into signing Executive Order 8802, which created the Fair Employment Practices Commission, black leaders began demanding the end of the Jim Crow army. In November 1947, Randolph helped found the Committee Against Jim Crow in Military Service and Training to push for the desegregation of the military. Black leaders were encouraged when President Harry S. Truman issued his Civil Rights message to Congress in February 1948, which, among other things, called for the secretary of defense to end discrimination in the military as soon as possible. But both military leaders and Southern congressmen balked at the message, and it seemed that no progress on desegregation would come without pressure from black America.

Truman's call in March 1948 for the first peacetime draft in U.S. history provided Randolph with the opportunity he was looking for. Stating that "Prison is better than Army Jim Crow," Randolph pledged to lead black youths in a boycott of any universal military training program if the army was not fully desegregated. He kept the issue in the headlines by leading peaceful protests in major cities throughout the summer of 1948, urging young black men to refuse to register for the draft. While this tactic was not endorsed by all black leaders, some of whom thought that Randolph's threat would make black America look unpatriotic and therefore perhaps even harm the drive for civil rights, the president took Randolph seriously, especially as 1948 was an election year. On July 26, Truman issued Executive Order 9981, which stated that "there shall be equality of treatment and opportunity for all persons in the armed services without regard to race, color, religion or national origin," and "This policy shall be put into effect as rapidly as possible."

While some black leaders, including Randolph, criticized the executive order as weak in not openly ordering the immediate desegregation of the military, it did signal a drastic change by the U.S. government towards supporting integration instead of segregation. Resistance from both Congress and the military persisted, however. Both generals Eisenhower and Omar Bradley publicly criticized the president's order, going as far to say that it compromised national defense. Southern politicians also led the charge against desegregation, culminating in the Dixiecrat revolt at the 1948 Democratic National Convention. Most insidious were military officers who quietly and simply ignored the order, allowing the racial status quo to continue.

After initial resistance, both the navy and air force implemented desegregation rather quickly and easily in 1949. The army, much larger and more deeply entrenched in its traditions than the other two branches, proved to be much more intransigent. By 1950, army leaders still had made no plans for desegregating the units; instead, they had made only token changes regarding increased training and promotional opportunities for blacks. It took war in Korea to finally bring about the integration of the army. When the United States entered the Korean conflict in June 1950, the army was still rigidly segregated. Indeed, some of the first U.S. troops to reach the Korean Peninsula in the summer of 1950 were the all-black units of the 24th Infantry. While some army commanders attempted to maintain the segregated army, the demands of the war made continuing segregation both impractical and inefficient. Moreover, a number of officers came to believe that the all-black units were inferior to those of whites, and should therefore be eliminated and the white units integrated. While black soldiers condemned this assessment, during the Korean War, the all-black units were phased out as black troops were absorbed by the white units. By the end of the war in 1953, the integration of the U.S. military had finally come about, but the historic all-black units were a casualty of the process.

Thomas J. Ward, Jr.

See also

Civil Rights Movement

Further Reading:

Buckley, Gail. *American Patriots: The Story of Blacks in the Military from the Revolution to Desert Storm*. New York: Random House, 2001.

Dalfiume, Richard M. *Desegregation of the U.S. Armed Forces: Fighting on Two Fronts, 1939*. Columbia: University of Missouri Press, 1969.

Edgerton, Robert B. *Hidden Heroism: Black Soldiers in America's Wars*. Boulder, CO: Westview Press, 2001.